The
Institutionalist Tradition
in
Labor
Economics

The
Institutionalist Tradition
in
Labor
Economics

EDITED BY

DELL P. CHAMPLIN AND JANET T. KNOEDLER

M.E.Sharpe
Armonk, New York
London, England

Chapter 5 in this volume is reprinted from the *Journal of Economic Issues*
by special permission of the copyright holder, the Association for Evolutionary Economics.

Library of Congress Cataloging-in-Publication Data

The institutionalist tradition in labor economics / Dell P. Champlin and Janet T. Knoedler, eds.
   p. cm.
Includes bibliographical references and index.
ISBN 0-7656-1286-0 (alk. paper) — ISBN 0-7656-1287-9 (pbk.: alk. paper)
   1. Labor economics. I. Champlin, Dell P.   II. Knoedler, Janet T.

HD4901.I496 2004
331—dc22

2004040943

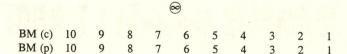

BM (c) 10   9   8   7   6   5   4   3   2   1
BM (p) 10   9   8   7   6   5   4   3   2   1

Contents

Figures and Tables

Introduction

1

The Institutionalist Tradition in Labor Economics

Dell P. Champlin and Janet T. Knoedler

Institutionalist labor economics was the dominant approach to labor in the United States until the 1960s, when mathematical and abstract approaches to economics became more influential.[1] Textbooks in labor economics that used to be written entirely in the institutionalist tradition began to include the institutionalist approach in one or two chapters, if at all. The shift in academic fashion did not eliminate the interest in or the need for the institutionalist approach. Indeed, a primary aim of this book is to demonstrate the continuing vibrancy and relevance of the institutionalist approach to labor economics. The contributors to this volume are leading practitioners of institutional economics and labor economics, and their essays portray the continued vitality of the institutionalist labor tradition, its long and interesting history, and the significance of its contribution to the field of labor economics.

Today the institutionalist tradition in labor economics exists in a wide variety of arenas. The current absorption of the economics profession in formalism and abstract theory has shifted attention away from those issues that most concern institutionalists, such as income distribution and inequality, the power of vested interests, and economic justice. As a consequence, labor specialists involved in these issues are now often found outside of eco-

nomics in related fields such as industrial relations, economic history, economic sociology, and public policy. Many of these labor specialists prefer to work outside of academia, in government, nonprofit organizations, and advocacy groups, where the primary focus is on current issues and policies—actual labor markets rather than theoretical ones. Many researchers are especially interested in issues of corporate power, income inequality, and labor market policy and are often active in pursuing reform of public policy in the best tradition of John R. Commons and his students. Not all of these specialists would use the label "institutionalist" to describe their work, nor necessarily do they have an appreciation for the legacy of early institutionalists such as John R. Commons, John Maurice Clark, or Thorstein Veblen. Yet these labor specialists today have many qualities in common with early institutionalists and represent a continuation of the institutionalist tradition. Thus, while institutionalist labor economists currently represent a minority of academic economists, the institutionalist approach to labor continues to attract a significant number of labor specialists.[2]

In the first section of this introduction, we briefly describe the distinctive characteristics that unify the institutionalist tradition in labor economics and provide the basis for its continuing appeal. As we discuss in the second section, these characteristics provide the organizing principle of the book. While each essay reflects the originality of our contributors, all exemplify the core themes that have characterized the institutionalist labor tradition from its beginnings over a century ago and that continue to energize researchers and labor specialists today.

The Institutionalist Tradition

We have chosen to use the term "institutionalist tradition" in this book because we want to emphasize common elements in a particular approach to labor economics. These common elements explain why this approach to economics has continued for over a century. While many in this tradition claim the title of institutionalist, belong to institutionalist organizations such as the Association for Evolutionary Economics (AFEE), the Association for Institutional Thought (AFIT), and the European Association for Evolutionary Political Economy (EAEPE), and publish in institutionalist journals, many do not. Yet there is sufficient commonality in this approach to justify our calling it a distinctive and continuing tradition. There are four key elements that characterize the institutionalist labor tradition:

- How any society provides for its economic needs is culturally and historically situated.
- The working rules of economic behavior are cultural, legal, and social rather than universal laws of nature.
- Markets are legal and cultural arrangements often characterized by relationships of conflict, power, and inequality.
- Government is an integral part of the economy, and appropriate economic policy is important

to ensure that the economy works in the interest of all members of society.

Culture and History

All economists recognize that history and culture play an important role in determining how any economy actually operates at any point in time. However, there are crucial differences in how institutionalists and neoclassical or deductive economists view this role. For institutionalists, economies do not exist in isolation but are embedded in cultures. Thus, history and culture are not just important, they must be an integral part of economic analysis. On the other hand, neoclassical or deductive economists view the economy as a separate and distinct system that has a logic of its own. Culture may affect the economic system—for example, social status and fashion affect spending habits, custom and gender roles influence occupational choices, and religious or ethical values determine attitudes toward inequality of income distribution—but customs, beliefs, and values are all external to "the economy." For neoclassical or deductive economists, culture essentially acts as a constraint on or a distortion of the economic system that may alter its proper functioning and reduce efficiency. In short, neoclassical economists view culture as an external force, while institutionalists maintain that culture and economies are inseparable—culture *is* the economy.

Because culture is so important, time and place matter for institutionalists. Thus, the economy of Japan in the twenty-first century is different from the economy of seventeenth-century France or nineteenth-century Brazil. U.S. labor markets in the twentieth-century steel and automobile industries function very differently from the textile industry of the mid-nineteenth century or the computer and software industry of today. In contrast, neoclassical economists believe that the same theory works for any economy in any historical time period. Differences in countries, industries, and historical time periods are important factors in specific outcomes, but underlying economic principles are the same. For neoclassical economists, institutionalists are overly concerned with historical detail. For institutionalists, neoclassical economists miss the point.

Working Rules

All economists use theories about economies and individuals engaged in economic behavior. Neoclassical economists place a great deal of emphasis on theory and have even accused institutional economists of having no theory.[3] That is, the criticism is not directed at what institutionalist theory says, but at the fact that the theory does not measure up in a methodological or scientific sense. The difference between the neoclassical view and the institutionalist view of a theory stems from the importance of culture and history discussed above. If all economic arrangements are cultural, then it is certainly possible to have theories. But it is not possible to have one grand theory that works for all economies in all time periods. In order to have a universal theory, one must believe that economies operate according to universal or natural laws that do not vary with time and place. Moreover, if such universality is the benchmark of a satisfactory economic theory, then the cultural approach of the institutionalists will not attain this standard. Neoclassical economics aspires to this "scientific" theoretical standard; institutionalists reject this standard in favor of a cultural approach.

The difference between the "universal" and the cultural economist is exemplified by the use of the word "law." Neoclassical economists begin with the idea of relative scarcity, a law of nature. Scar-

city requires choices, and individuals make these choices according to their own self-interest, a law of human nature. Markets operate according to the laws of supply and demand unless interfered with by ordinary human beings who may enact civil laws to alter economic outcomes. However, it is clear that the important laws are the natural laws, which are universal and unvarying, in contrast with civil laws or government policies, which are limited and temporary. For institutionalists, who do not believe that economies operate according to laws of nature, the word "law" is a cultural term. As John R. Commons pointed out in his well-known book, *Legal Foundations of Capitalism*, civil or common law determines the institutional arrangements of any economy. In addition, common law reflects the accumulated beliefs, attitudes, and customs of a culture. Rather than looking for the underlying natural laws of an economic system, institutionalists are interested in "working rules," a term also associated with Commons. In his classic *American Economic Review* article, Commons defines working rules as follows: "Working rules are continually changing in the history of an institution, and they differ for different institutions; but, whatever, their differences, they have this similarity that they indicate what individuals can, must, or may, do or not do, enforced by collective sanctions" (Commons 1931, 649).

Conflict, Power, and Inequality

Neoclassical economics is based on the notion of "harmony of interests." There is no conflict, except in cases of market failure or distortion. Marxists, on the other hand, see plenty of conflict and attribute it to capitalism. Common to both is the presumption that conflict can be eliminated by setting up the correct economic system. John R. Commons had a different view. In his autobiography, Commons states that he "made . . . Conflict of Interests, not the Harmony of Interests of the classical and hedonistic economists, the starting point of Institutional Economics" (quoted in Gruchy 1947). This basic vision sets Commons and other institutionalists apart from other economic paradigms. According to Commons, conflict cannot be eliminated; it can only be managed through institutional reform, especially reform of the legal system.

The power to attain one's goals and satisfy individual interests is not equally shared in any economy. Neoclassical economists recognize the pernicious influence of power to distort markets and reduce economic efficiency. The unequal distribution of power is a fundamental aspect of the Marxist critique of private property. Power is also a key theme of institutionalism's most famous intellectual, Thorstein Veblen. Max Lerner discusses the importance of power in his introduction to *The Portable Veblen*:

> America, which has produced the most finished and tenacious brand of business civilization, has also produced the most finished and tenacious criticism of it. That is the core meaning of Thorstein Veblen's work. It was a body of work bounded on both sides by the image of economic power. Veblen began his formative thinking in the 1880s, when trusts were emerging and the new "dynastic corporation" was planting itself squarely in the path of the traditional political ideals. His first published economic essay appeared in 1892, two years after the Sherman Anti-Trust Act. His last writing was done in the 1920s during the boom period of what was being called the "New Capitalism," when the monopolies came into their present power. (Lerner 1950, 1)

Inequality and income distribution are also subjects addressed by all economists, especially labor economists. As Allen Sievers notes, economists have long been concerned with poverty and inequality, although neoclassical economists, or what he calls the "central tradition," have reached very different conclusions:

> Inequality was condemned by the central tradition, but it was nevertheless an inescapable fact. Competition was extolled as a regulator even though there was some distress about its harmful effects. In the twentieth century theorists had to adjust their analysis to fit the widespread fact of non-competitive market behavior and its implications for inequality. The Great Depression was the most disquieting fact of all to the central tradition. Even so, it held that rhythmic movement implied recovery as well as a succession of depressions. The central tradition was growing uneasy, but it always had answers. (Sievers 1962, 61)

For institutionalists, egregious inequality and poverty are not inescapable but are the outcome of wealth and power. John Kenneth Galbraith analyzes the problem of social imbalance in his classic book, *The Affluent Society* (1958). Sievers summarizes the argument as follows:

> Our affluent nation devotes its wealth so preponderantly to the private sector that its standard of living is low in respect to the kind of community in which we live. We have neglected education, sanitation, public safety, transportation, recreation, housing, problems of air pollution, and the general cleanliness and beauty of our public surroundings. This imbalance has been created by the very growth and affluence of the private sector. (Sievers 1962, 66–67)

Institutionalism began in the last century with a tradition of reform, and this tradition continues today. Those working in the institutionalist tradition write on poverty, welfare, living wages, unemployment, corporate abuse of power, and other social issues.

Government and the Public Interest

The political philosophy of laissez-faire, which has long dominated conventional economics, holds that economic systems tend to work reasonably well in the long run and that consequently there are relatively few reasons for active government involvement in the economy. A more moderated view recognizes the existence of market "failures" such as externalized costs and benefits, so-called public goods, information problems, and transaction costs. In these circumstances, the private economy will not necessarily operate in the public interest. Thus, neoclassical economists tend to promote either no government intervention or limited, partial action under certain special circumstances.

Underlying the neoclassical view of the role of government is the notion that the private economy is "free," while government represents coercive force. In essence, for neoclassical economists the question of the role of government is the question of how much individual freedom must be relinquished to the state. Institutional economists have a radically different view of the economic functions of government and also of the source of coercion in the economy. Institutionalists, especially labor economists, begin with the premise that coercion or the lack of freedom for individuals can originate in the private economy as well as in the actions of government. When the coercion originates in the private economy, government can then serve to reduce coercion by intervening on behalf of individual citizens. The notion that coercion occurs in the private economy is discussed at great length by John Maurice Clark in his book, *Social Control of Business*:

> Suppose a laborer canvasses the field and finds no one offering a satisfactory living wage for his grade of work. He is "compelled" to accept less; but whence comes the compulsion? Does it come from the employer who last discharged him, or from an informal control of the market by the employers in general, or from the customs and habits of business, or from the "impersonal and immutable laws" of supply and demand? . . . But . . . society has some

responsibility for the compulsions of supply and demand, to the extent that it has power to alleviate them. And this impersonal machinery of private industry evidently has penalties at its disposal which often carry more material hardship than a jail sentence. Yet a jail sentence is coercion such as only the state can employ, while the loss of one's job is merely an incident of "free bargaining." The difference clearly lies, not in the weight of the penalty, but in the fact that putting a man in jail is a positive act, and leaving him to walk the streets looking for work is a negative act for which no one feels fully responsible. (Clark 1969, 6)

The Institutionalist Tradition in Labor Economics: Overview

The purpose of this necessarily brief excursion into institutional economics is to provide an introduction to the themes addressed by the essays in this book. This section presents the reader with a brief overview of the organization of the book and topics discussed in the remaining chapters.

Historical and Theoretical Perspectives

The first part of the book begins with Bruce Kaufman's comprehensive and useful comparison of the institutionalist and neoclassical schools of labor economics. For those unfamiliar with the institutionalist tradition, Kaufman's essay is invaluable. He not only reviews the origins of institutionalist labor economics but brings this tradition into the present by focusing on contemporary labor economics.

Chapters 3 and 4 discuss John R. Commons, probably the most famous institutionalist labor economist and certainly the most influential. Glen Atkinson's chapter on the expansion of markets and the competitive menace discusses a problem all too familiar in the age of globalization and demonstrates the applicability of Commons to the problems of today. The following chapter by J. Dennis

Chasse considers Commons and his role as reformer and asks what remains of the legacy of Commons and his students after nearly a century.

In Chapter 5, Dell P. Champlin and Janet T. Knoedler discuss the influence of two other prominent institutionalists, Thorstein Veblen and John Maurice Clark, on wages in the public interest. Rounding out the first section, Jon D. Wisman and Aaron Pacitti provide a historical overview of the U.S. labor market from an institutionalist point of view.

Institutionalist Thought on Labor Since World War II

Part II continues the theoretical survey of institutionalist thought in labor economics into the present. Chapters 7 and 8 explore in greater depth the postwar labor economists introduced in Bruce Kaufman's earlier essay. Douglas Kinnear discusses the well-known, post–World War II labor economists Lloyd Reynolds, John Dunlop, and Clark Kerr. Jerry Gray and Richard Chapman continue the survey into the 1970s and 1980s with a discussion of segmentation theory and dual labor markets.

This section of the book also contains theoretical critiques of the ubiquitous neoclassical labor market in which labor demand is derived from marginal productivity theory and labor supply is the outcome of an individual worker's utility choices on the allocation of time. It is commonly assumed that despite its lack of realism, neoclassical labor economics is undeniably theoretically coherent. The contributions of Ann Jennings, Robert E. Prasch, and Robert LaJeunesse challenge this assumption.

Institutionalist Analysis of Current Labor Issues

The third part of the book is designed to demonstrate the institutionalist approach in practice. That is, instead of talking about the institutionalist labor tradition, the chapters in this section show how it is done. Deborah Figart and Ellen Mutari, well-respected feminist economists, tackle the limitations of neoclassical theories of discrimination and offer an alternative vision. Barbara Wiens-Tuers explores one of the most troublesome aspects of contemporary labor markets, the rise of contingent work. Enrico Marcelli investigates the institution of unauthorized residency status and challenges the widespread belief that the low wages earned by immigrants are simply the predictable outcome of market forces. Janice Peterson takes on another important institution, retirement, noting that the prevailing view of retirement is likely to change as people work longer, live longer, and change their expectations for their lives after work. George DeMartino takes a new look at the concept of unionization and suggests that changes in our traditional understanding might revitalize the labor movement.

Social Justice

The fourth section of the book contains four contributions on the important, institutionalist theme of social justice. L. Randall Wray and Mathew Forstater argue that modern capitalist economies cannot achieve full employment without active government involvement and that governments should maintain full employment as a matter of social justice. Mayo Toruño discusses the importance of social norms in determining the kind of society we live in and, in particular, the status of labor. David Zalewski addresses the topical issue of executive compensation and the disconnect between pay and performance of the company. Finally, Richard McIntyre and Yngve Ramstad apply John R. Commons's concept of sweating to the current practice of subcontracting and, thus, link contemporary work with the theoretical discussions of the first part of the book.

The final chapter summarizes the institutionalist labor tradition as represented by the contributors to this book. One clear message of these chapters is a rejection of neoclassical labor theory as a useful or appropriate model. Instead of treating labor as a commodity like any other, institutionalists recognize "the worth of human labor and the dignity of the worker." (Champin and Knoedler, ed. 323) We close the book with comments on the prospects for workers in the twenty-first century.

Notes

1. In this book, we have chosen to use the following terminology: "Institutional economics" and "institutional economist" refer to economic writings and scholars who subscribe to the views described in this book. These terms are widely used and have become the standard terms used by institutionalists. In all other cases, we use the term, "institutionalist," rather than "institutional," because the latter term is used by all economists. Indeed, in recent years, some economists and political scientists have begun to use the term, "institutional approach" or "institutional analysis" to refer to any research involving institutions. For this reason, we believe that the terms, "institutionalist," "institutionalist labor economist," or "institutionalist labor economics" will provide more clarity when the intent is to refer to the school of thought in economics that is the subject of this book. Please note that Chapter 2 by Bruce Kaufman uses a slightly different convention.

2. For example, Paul Osterman, Clair Brown, Eileen Appelbaum, and Rosemary Batt continue the work begun by John Dunlop, Clark Kerr, and Michael Piore and Peter Doeringer in analyzing internal labor markets and have further developed and expanded on the concept of industry and job structures. In addition, their work is empirical in the institutionalist sense that they typically study specific industries or types of firms in order to understand how actual labor markets work.

3. Bruce Kaufman discusses this issue at length in Chapter 2.

References

Clark, John Maurice. *Social Control of Business*. 1926. Reprint, New York: Augustus M. Kelley, 1969.

Commons, John R. "Institutional Economics," *American Economic Review* 21, no. 4 (1931): 648–57.

Commons, John R. *Legal Foundations of Capitalism*. 1932. Reprint, Madison: University of Wisconsin Press, 1968.

Galbraith, John K. *The Affluent Society*. Boston: Houghton Mifflin, 1958.

Gruchy, Allen. *Modern Economic Thought: The American Contribution*. New York: Prentice-Hall, 1947.

Lerner, Max, ed. *The Portable Veblen*. New York: Viking Press, 1950.

Sievers, Allen. *Revolution, Evolution, and the Economic Order*. Englewood Cliffs, NJ: Prentice-Hall, 1962.

I

Historical and Theoretical Perspectives

2

The Institutional and Neoclassical Schools in Labor Economics

Bruce E. Kaufman

In this chapter I provide a description and review of the institutional and neoclassical schools in labor economics. By most accounts, the institutional tradition has declined markedly in intellectual vigor and number of adherents since its peak influence in the 1950s. Institutional labor economics today has practically disappeared from the mainstream part of the field and has only a small and declining presence in heterodox circles and allied subject areas, such as industrial relations. The neoclassical approach, on the other hand, has staged a remarkable resurgence. Up until the late 1950s in American labor economics, great skepticism and even hostility greeted attempts to apply neoclassical tools of microeconomics and price theory to labor markets; today, the neoclassical approach not only defines "best practice" but in the eyes of many participants is coterminous with economics itself.

How did labor economics get this way? Why did institutionalism and neoclassicism follow such divergent trajectories? Is there hope for an institutional revival in labor economics, or is institutionalism doomed to become a chapter in the history of economic thought? These are complex and important questions that, surprisingly, have received only modest attention to date. Provided below are

my answers, tendered only as one person's (possibly idiosyncratic) opinion. The conclusion I reach is that part of the decline of institutionalism is real, while another part is artificial and reflects changing conceptions of what defines the essence of "institutional" and "neoclassical." An alternative title for this chapter could be, Would the real institutional and neoclassical economics please stand up? To document this assertion, I proceed by first examining the central features of institutionalism in labor economics, followed by a similar analysis of neoclassicism.

Institutional Economics: The Conventional Wisdom

Although the details may differ, I suspect most mainstream labor economists hold fairly similar views about the essential features and principles of the institutional approach. This view, I conjecture, is reasonably well captured by the following quotations from these well-recognized and respected labor economists. Addison and Siebert, for example, describe the institutional approach in these words:

> Institutionalism in labor economics has come to mean an almost exclusively descriptive approach,

often reflecting the personal judgment that labor market facts are interesting in themselves. Sometimes included in the term is the antitheoretical view that facts speak for themselves. As a practical example, institutionalists assert that wages are not determined by supply and demand; rather, contemporary wage determination can only be understood as the product of social, political, and institutional forces. Institutionalists thus reject abstract general theories and advocate an inductive and interdisciplinary approach to research. (Addison and Siebert 1979, 4)

A similar depiction is given by Boyer and Smith:

Institutional labor economics emphasized the word *labor*. This approach was fact-based, its methodology largely was inductive, and it generally relied on a case study approach toward data-gathering. From the intensive, often historical, study of individual cases or events came detailed *descriptions* of various labor-market institutions or outcomes. Followers of this institutional approach differentiated "descriptive economics" from "economic theory," and saw their role as providing "data sufficiently concrete, definite, and convenient to form a basis for analysis, discussion, and criticism." (Boyer and Smith 2001, 201)

Thus, in the conventional view, institutionalism is heavily identified with criticism of orthodox theory; a fact-gathering, historical, and descriptive approach to research; and an aversion to formulating deductively derived theoretical generalizations and models. The decline of institutionalism, in turn, is a predictable consequence of two factors: first, in the words of Paul Samuelson (1951, 323), "In economics it takes a theory to beat a theory" and the institutionalists are widely perceived to have failed at this task, and, second, the proponents of orthodox economics succeeded in generalizing and extending their theory to account for or explain many of the seemingly aberrant or discrepant facts cited by the institutionalists.

Is the conventional wisdom on labor institutionalism a reasonably accurate portrayal? I shall argue that it captures a significant part of the truth and that in these respects institutionalism is "guilty as charged." But a closer examination of the record reveals, I believe, that the conventional wisdom also misses and misconstrues important aspects of institutionalism. When these are considered, a more positive and promising picture emerges. To make this case, however, I need to briefly step back and examine the corpus of institutional economics writ large.

Institutional Economics: Basic Principles

In looking for the basic principles of institutional economics, and given this volume's focus on labor, one can well argue that the appropriate place to start is with economist John R. Commons. Commons, after all, is widely considered one of the founding fathers of institutional economics and also played a leading role in the birth and development of the labor economics field in the early part of the twentieth century (Perlman and McCann 1998; Kaufman 1993). Rather than search for core principles of institutionalism in his labor writings, however, the better place is his theoretical magnum opus *Institutional Economics: Its Place in Political Economy* (1934a).

Contra conventional wisdom, one immediately notes that in the first paragraph of the book Commons uses the term "my theory" (or "theories") three times, suggesting that the book's purpose is not fact-gathering but theory-building. The nature of this theory, and its all-encompassing generality, are indicated in this statement: "The subject-matter of institutional economy . . . is not commodities, nor labor, nor any physical thing—it is collective action which sets the working rules for property rights, duties, liberties, and exposures" (523).

What Commons means by this is that all economic activity takes place within institutions, such as markets, firms, and families, and each institution uses "working rules" to regulate and structure production and exchange by defining property rights that, in turn, determine ownership of resources and the permissible and impermissible uses of these resources (Samuels 1995; Schmid 1987). In constructing his theory, Commons defines the basic unit of institutional economics as the "transaction," which represents a "legal transfer of ownership" or transfer of property rights (55). Commons distinguishes three kinds of transactions: *bargaining* (voluntary transfer of property rights to resources through market exchange), *rationing* (transfer of ownership rights to resources through the command of a superior), and *managerial* (transfer through management methods of the labor power purchased or owned by the firm but residing in the worker). In so doing, he defines the two principal methods for organizing production and exchange—markets coordinated by the price mechanism (the bargaining transaction) and formal organizations coordinated through command (a firm, a nonprofit or government agency, a socialist system of central planning using the rationing and managerial transactions). Today this distinction is often framed as the choice of "make versus buy."

Viewed from this perspective, institutional economics thus has a "macro" and "micro" research agenda. The macro agenda is to understand a society's choice of economic institutions, such as capitalism versus a socialist planned economy or markets versus firms; the micro is to understand the more detailed operation and outcomes of individual institutions, such as markets and their coordination through price and firms and their coordination through management command. In its macro version, institutional economics can thus be regarded as asking a deeper question than neoclassical economics, since the latter typically takes the institutional structure as a given (as in general equilibrium theory). More provocatively, institutional economics can also be seen as subsuming neoclassical economics as a special case, recognizing that the latter correctly models economic activity in that *subset* of situations where bargaining transactions occur in approximately competitive conditions (Kaufman 2003a). (Parenthetically, a corollary implication is that marginalism is compatible with an institutional approach, but only where underlying economic relations have the requisite degree of divisibility). One reason institutional economics is thus associated with the case study approach to research is that the researcher must first identify the relevant structural characteristics of the economic situation being studied before knowing which model or framework nested within institutional theory is best suited.

Commons initiated this line of theorizing in his *Institutional Economics,* but the impact on the economics profession remained quite modest given his obscure style of exposition and holistic approach to theory-building (Ramstad 1995). Several years later, however, Ronald Coase (1937) independently introduced some of the same issues and ideas in a way that economists could better understand, and several decades later Oliver Williamson (1985) took Coase's ideas, worked in some concepts from Commons, and developed a new body of theory commonly called "new institutional economics" (NIE).

Although the "old" institutional economics of Commons and cofounders Veblen and Mitchell and the new institutional economics of Coase and Williamson are not entirely commensurate (some would say not commensurate at all), in my view key points of linkage exist that provide the basis for synthesis. As Williamson (1985) acknowledges, for example, the fundamental unit of activity in NIE—the transaction comes from Commons—

while it has been elsewhere noted that another fundamental NIE concept—bounded rationality—was also anticipated by Commons and entered NIE through the work of Chester Barnard and Herbert Simon (Kaufman 1999a, 2003a). Also, it is worth noting that Williamson derives hypotheses and predictions about "make versus buy" by using a largely nonmarginal form of analysis he calls the "comparative institutional method," which is quite close to the "comparative method of reasoning" advanced by Commons (1950, 124), and like Commons he largely (but not completely) eschews equilibrium modeling.

Two points deserve highlight from this brief and very stylized overview of institutional economics. First, contrary to the conventional view, institutional economics is not just a set of research methods but also contains a core of theory, albeit one admittedly much more embryonic and less formalized than in neoclassical economics. Just as demand, supply, and price are at the core of neoclassical economics, "make versus buy" and transaction cost lie at the core of institutional economics (or the Commons/Coase version thereof, as I am interpreting and synthesizing it). The conventional wisdom is correct, on the other hand, that in theory construction institutionalism does emphasize to a much greater degree a grounded, inductive (or "adductive") methodology in which axioms and premises are adduced only after careful empirical investigation and fashioned with the express goal of being a good first approximation to reality.

The second point is that the existence of *positive* transaction costs provide the fundamental dividing line between institutional and neoclassical economics. As is widely recognized, the core version of neoclassical economics assumes a condition of zero transaction costs (Coase 1988; Dow 1997; Reder 1999), leading to a world of complete and costless contracting through markets. Institutional economics, on the other hand, rests on an assumption of positive transaction costs, leading to a world of incomplete contracts and the formation of a myriad of institutional entities to supplement and supplant market exchange. Positive transaction costs, in turn, arise from conditions of bounded rationality, imperfect information and fundamental uncertainty, poorly partitioned property rights, indivisibilities in production and utility functions, and imperfect legal enforcement of contracts by the political sovereign (Kaufman 2003a). These fundamental considerations play a key role, in turn, in institutionalist models and depictions of market economies. Central features, for example, are behavioral models of the human agent, imperfect market structures, information asymmetries and associated phenomena (e.g., moral hazard, principal/agent problems), resource and power inequalities, and the influence of social norms, cultural conventions, and ethical considerations.

The Institutional School in Labor Economics: The First Generation

With this background of basic principles, I now turn to a more detailed look at institutionalism in labor economics. Labor institutionalism spans four generations of contributors, beginning with Commons, his associates of the Wisconsin school, and many other well-known labor economists of the period (e.g., Robert Hoxie, Paul Brissenden). First considered is the first generation's methodological approach to labor research, followed by the substantive nature of its theory of economics and labor markets.

Research Methodology

The labor institutionalist's methodological approach to research is distinguished by four key features: the emphasis on fact-gathering, the importance of realism of assumptions, the virtues of a "go and see" participant/observer method of investigation, and the necessity of an interdisciplinary approach to theory-construction. These methodological predispositions arose, in turn, from the institutionalist's dual focus on reforming both orthodox theory and national labor policy and workplace employment practices. I start the story here.

The classical and neoclassical economics of the late nineteenth century and early twentieth century contained a heavy strain of laissez-faire philosophy. The reason is that the theory of humankind and the economy used by these economists rested on prototypical neoclassical theoretical assumptions, such as the "economic man" model of the human agent and a model of highly competitive markets, overlaid with normative assumptions about the sanctity of property rights and freedom of contract, the importance of individual initiative, and the social virtues of a Darwinian struggle for "survival of the fittest" (Fine 1956). Given this worldview, orthodox economists and their judicial and political compatriots tended to turn a blind eye toward labor problems on grounds that unemployment, poverty, and work accidents reflected personal choices, character defects, or the working out of natural law. They correlatively viewed trade unions and government regulation of employment conditions with considerable hostility, seeing the former as a form of monopoly and abridgement of freedom of contract and the latter as an unwelcome source of paternalism, corruption, interference with market forces, and facade for the enrichment of special interest groups.

A concrete example of the interplay of orthodox economic theory and conservative political and judicial opinion is workplace safety and health regulation and the "assumption of risk" doctrine (Moss 1996; Commons and Andrews 1936). Traditional economists and judges opposed govern-

ment intervention (such as a workers' compensation program) on the grounds that competitive markets provide workers, according to Adam Smith's theory of compensating wage differentials, a fully compensatory pay premium for greater risk. Thus, injured workers have no claim to state-provided accident benefits since they knowingly accepted the risk when they took the jobs and were compensated for doing so (implying that a workers' compensation payment would represent double payment). A second example concerns payment of workers with company-issued scrip. State laws requiring payment with cash wages were declared an unconstitutional abridgement of freedom of contract (Commons and Andrews 1936). One can easily imagine constructing a neoclassical model that explains the efficiency virtue of such a decision, given that unrestricted sorting in competitive labor markets allows all sides to gain from trade and that workers who do not want to be paid in scrip can easily quit such jobs and find a match with other firms willing to pay cash wages. This type of reasoning was, in fact, used by the courts of the late nineteenth century (Lehrer 1987).

We know that Commons and the other early institutional labor economists were self-professed social reformers and proponents (within bounds) of trade unions and government labor legislation. Kenneth Boulding (1957, 7) has stated, for example, that Commons was "the intellectual origin of the New Deal, of labor legislation, of social security, of the whole movement in the country toward a welfare state." In appreciating the institutional approach to labor economics, it is important to first understand *how* these economists became social reformers and, then, how this impacted their approach to research.

It is apparent from the autobiographies and biographies of the early institutionalist labor economists that their interest in labor and social reform in significant degree came from the transformative experience of coming into contact with real-life employment conditions and workplaces in America's mills, factories, and tenement lofts (Commons 1934b; Lescohier 1960; Eisner 1967; Douglas 1971). All of the leading institutionalists were schooled in orthodox theory, but they came to appreciate the huge gap between the theory and the reality of labor markets only when they experienced the work world firsthand. Commons (1934b) relates, for example, that his interest in labor and commitment to employment reform developed only after he lost his professorship at Syracuse University and began five years of personal investigation of employment conditions for, respectively, the U.S. Industrial Commission and Civic Federation (Gonce 2002). Later, he made a point of immersing his students in the real life of work, such as in the Pittsburgh Survey, where they lived for several months in steel towns and observed the life of steel workers, and in the investigative work for the U.S. Commission on Industrial Relations.

Out of the dual role of the early institutionalists as economists and reformers came the characteristic features of their research. Fact-gathering, for example, was crucial in order to present evidence refuting orthodox theory. According to orthodox theory, labor problems either do not exist (e.g., unemployment is a voluntary choice) or are best solved by individual initiative and market forces. Thus, the institutionalists had to demonstrate, in an early twentieth-century form of hypothesis-testing, the converse case—that, contrary to the orthodox null hypothesis, labor problems are serious and widespread and market forces do not solve them (indeed, in some cases they exacerbate labor problems). If the institutionalists were not successful in this effort, then obviously the next step—developing an alternative nonneoclassical theory—would have little purpose and would arouse scant

interest. In constructing an alternative theory, fact-gathering is again crucial in order to derive (or "adduce") more realistic assumptions and to identify the crucial forces and variables at work. Convinced that orthodox theory was in significant respects incorrect, the institutionalists took it as self-evident that the reason must be that its assumptions or structure are inaccurate. Thus, empirical investigation and fact-gathering, using a "go and see" approach where the researcher obtains personal, firsthand grounding in the subject through case study and participant/observer methods, has to precede theory development in order that its assumptions and structure are realistic, where "realistic" is used in the sense of being a good first approximation to reality. Finally, the "go and see" approach and commitment to realism of assumptions necessarily led the early institutionalists to take a holistic, interdisciplinary approach to research and theory-building, given that labor problems and the operation of labor markets and labor institutions are impacted not only by economic motives and forces but also by numerous psychological, social, legal, political, and historical forces. The early institutionalists were thus the academic founders of the field of industrial relations and treated labor economics and industrial relations as largely inseparable subjects (Kaufman 1993, 2004).

In sum, the institutionalists did indeed stress fact-gathering and a case-study, historically informed approach to research, and this approach was not a barren exercise in atheoretic descriptiveness but instead the handmaiden of theory development. Of course, this raises the next question—did the first generation of labor institutionalists develop theory?

Theory-Building

As with research methodology, consideration of the institutionalists' record in theory-building requires some attention to historical context. The institutionalist theory of labor markets had several roots, including German political economy, historical economics (English and German), the emergent field of sociology, the Social Gospel movement in America, and several late nineteenth-century American economists, such as Richard Ely, Henry Carter Adams, and Simon Patten (Jacoby 1990; Kaufman 1997, 2004; Perlman and McCann 1998). Ely, Adams, and Patten were among the young rebels in the American economics profession who rejected classical and early neoclassical theory as sterile exercises in deductive logic and scholarly apologias for laissez-faire. They sought to develop a new economics with a more psychologically informed, humanistic representation of the human agent, models of markets that recognized the growth of trusts and monopolies, and a view of the economic process that made it possible for institutions such as government and unions to promote social welfare. To promote their new paradigm, they organized the American Economic Association in 1885 (Fine 1956).

The most direct and immediate influence on the early labor institutionalists, however, came from Sidney and Beatrice Webb in England, and in particular their book *Industrial Democracy* (1897). In *Industrial Democracy* the Webbs endeavored to develop a new political economy that gave greater emphasis to the positive and normative consequences of collectivism, in opposition to what they regarded as the unduly individualistic tack of orthodox theory (Harrison 2000). Although the American first generation of labor institutionalists developed and extended their own brand of labor theory, in fundamental respects it was grounded on the ideas advanced by the Webbs.

The Webbs' first theoretical departure from orthodoxy was to analyze the determination of wages in terms of bargaining power rather than (or in addition to) supply and demand. Following Alfred Marshall, the Webbs note that in a perfect market wages are determined by supply and demand and workers receive a wage equal to the contribution to production of the last person hired (p. 646). But, they say, this conclusion has two problems. The first is that it masks the superior bargaining power capital exerts over labor in the wage determination process due to unequal endowments. Because the average worker needs the job far worse than the firm needs the worker, and because the worker's labor is perishable and has zero value if not sold today, the ordinary worker's reservation wage is typically quite low. As a result, the supply curve of labor to the market lies much further to the right than would be true if labor had a premarket endowment equal to capital. A similar outcome occurs in the labor market when government policy shifts factor endowments in favor of the interests of capital, such as in the early twentieth century when the U.S. government permitted unrestricted immigration.

From a Marshallian perspective, in a perfect market neither labor nor capital has market power, since both are wage and price takers, and thus an "equality of bargaining power" exists (Kaufman 1989). Further, the wage determined by supply and demand, although possibly quite low, is "optimal" in the sense that it reflects underlying opportunity costs and leads to an efficient allocation of resources. But, say the Webbs, when consideration is given to the unequal endowments capital and labor bring to the labor market, it is evident that firms in the aggregate are in a far superior position to workers in wage determination, leading to a marked *inequality* of bargaining power and a very low wage rate (656–57). This wage rate, in turn, may be nonoptimal in a larger social perspective, on grounds both of justice and of long-run economic growth and human well-being (e.g., less than a "living wage" will cause a reduction in future labor supply through ill-health, poor education, etc.).

Viewed broadly, labor may thus suffer from an inequality of bargaining power even in an erstwhile perfect labor market. But, say the Webbs, this raises the second problem with neoclassical theory. Orthodox theory presumes perfect markets, but they note that "competition between individual producers and consumers, laborers and capitalists, is, as the economist is now careful to explain, in actual life very far from perfect, and shows no tendency to become so" (648). They go on to note a number of imperfect aspects of labor markets, including asymmetric information, restrictions to mobility, barriers to entry in product markets, and involuntary unemployment. In each case, they claim, the net effect is to lead to a still greater inequality of bargaining power for labor (e.g., asymmetric information favors employers since they have superior information about market conditions; involuntary unemployment undercuts workers' bargaining power by making them compete with people desperate for work). The other consequence of these market imperfections is that they create an indeterminacy in wages in which demand and supply set only upper and lower limits to the wage rate. Within these limits, say the Webbs, the wage rate "can be decided only by higgling and bargaining" (649).

Another theoretical departure advanced by the Webbs is to argue that the human essence of labor fundamentally changes the operation of labor markets and makes their behavior and outcomes, particularly in the short run, incommensurate with other markets. The goal of neoclassical theory is to construct a general theoretical framework that explains in a unified manner all economic activity. In so doing, the penchant is to treat labor markets as similar to all other markets, to view labor as a commodity, and to model market outcomes as a determinant solution of the demand and supply functions. The Webbs, however, dispute these assertions. Because labor is not a commodity, the supply of labor is influenced by numerous psychological and sociological influences, such as the desire for fair dealing, security, and social status. As a result, wages are subject to considerable inertia, the amount of work effort (labor power) is a continuously bargained variable, and injustice leads to strikes and collective action not known in other markets.

Finally, the Webbs also put forward a different model for viewing the employer-employee relationship. In orthodox theory, the employment relationship is a species of market exchange, and the emphasis in theory is on the competitive structure of the market and the operation of supply and demand. Without denying this economic dimension, the Webbs point out that the employment relationship has an equally important political dimension (841–42). The very notion of an "employer" and "employee" presupposes an asymmetrical authority relation in which the former acts as the superior (or "master" in English common law) and order-giver while the latter is the subordinate (or "servant") and order-taker. While labor mobility and competitive pressure forces employers in a perfect market to treat workers equitably and with respect, in real-world markets (with positive transaction costs) mobility and competition are abridged and thus workers are exposed to varying degrees of arbitrary, unjust, and inhumane treatment. Both economic efficiency and social justice, therefore, are served by promoting democratic forms of workforce governance, such as through trade unions and protective labor legislation.

The conceptual framework and core theoretical ideas developed by the Webbs were adopted by the American institutionalists and then expanded and elaborated (a process described in detail in Kaufman 1997, 2000, 2003b, 2004). Looking at this work as a whole, seven principles emerge that represent, in my opinion, the core positive and normative components of the early institutionalists' "theory" of labor markets.

The first principle in their theory of labor markets concerns the end goal(s) that economic activity is meant to contribute toward. In neoclassical theory, maximum efficiency in the production and allocation of resources (Pareto optimality) is the end goal. The early institutionalists broadened the goals to three. Following the neoclassical economists, efficiency was one, but they added two others: economic outcomes must satisfy minimum standards of equity (justice) and must contribute toward human development and self-realization. A minimum standard of justice was incorporated into institutional theory by Commons's (1934a) concept of "reasonable value" (essentially the community's collective judgment on whether an economic outcome passes the test of reasonableness, as illustrated by the Supreme Court's frequent use of a "rule of reason"), while human development and self-realization were captured in Commons's contention that economic activity must contribute toward "expansion of the human will" and Richard Ely's statement (1886, 3) that an economy should promote "the full and harmonious development in each individual of all human faculties." This latter consideration is the foundational idea for what is now called "humanistic economics" (Lutz and Lux 1988).

A second principle that flows from the first is that economic theory should include in people's utility functions not only consumption goods but also variables representing the conditions and experience of work, and that where efficiency and the two other goals (justice, self-development) conflict a trade off should be made. Commons (1919, 33) states, that, from the orthodox point of view, "workers are treated as commodities to be bought and sold

according to supply and demand," but from the institutionalist perspective, "they are treated as citizens with rights against others on account of their value to the nation as a whole." Sumner Slichter (1931, 651–52) gets to the same idea when he says, "it is vitally important that the methods of production shall be planned not only to turn out goods at low costs but to provide the kind of jobs which develop the desirable capacities of the workers."

A third principle is that in economic theory the human agent should be modeled as purposive and self-interested, but with two significant amendments. The first is that human rationality is limited by what Commons (1934a, 874) referred to as "stupidity, ignorance, and passion." Decision-making thus has systematic biases and is sometimes illogical or irrational, while agents are prone to suboptimization and organizations are thus likely to have varying degrees of slack and above-minimum cost. The second amendment is recognition that many human emotions, such as feelings of injustice, hatred, love, and envy, arise from interactions or comparisons with other people, thus making behavior interdependent. For economic theory, this means that utility functions are interdependent and that decision-making is based in part on relative comparisons, making indifference curves, supply and demand curves, and other such constructs no longer stable functions (Slichter 1931, 625–27; Tversky and Kahneman 1991; Kaufman 1999b).

A fourth principle is that most labor markets contain significant imperfections, such as limited and asymmetric information, significant costs of mobility, limited numbers of buyers (firms), externalities and public goods at the workplace, and involuntary unemployment. In one group of labor markets, these factors give employers a monopoly-like market power over wages and working conditions, leading to noncompetitive and possibly exploitative outcomes for workers. In other labor markets, these imperfections create cutthroat competition in which wages and labor standards are depressed far below full employment standards, creating sweatshop conditions. In either case, labor markets will not give rise to fully compensatory wage differentials for hazards and other disagreeable factors, such as workplace accidents and long work hours, as predicted by neoclassical theory. For this reason, firms often do not bear the full social costs of production, leading to a misallocation of resources and shifting of costs to workers and communities (Stabile 1993).

Fifth, the market imperfections just cited create an inequality of bargaining power for many workers, particularly the less skilled and educated and in periods of less than full employment. One consequence is that wages for many workers are market-determined only within upper and lower bounds and within these limits they are determined by either administrative fiat or bargaining. Because wages are often administered prices, Commons (Commons and Andrews 1936, 372) notes that "today 'individual bargaining' in any real sense cannot exist" and that without union or government help "the inequality in withholding power between employer and employee is so great that the term bargaining is a misnomer." Reminiscent of the Webbs, he further states, "It is obvious that the individual laborer is at a great disadvantage in bargaining with the employer. . . . It is a case of the necessities of the laborer pitted against the resources of the employer" (373).

A sixth principle is that wage rates often are unable to equilibrate demand and supply and clear labor markets. One reason is that the wage rate performs a dual role in labor markets—it allocates labor, as in neoclassical theory, but also is used by firms to motivate labor (Slichter 1931, 592–650). The wage rate (or change in the wage) that meets

one objective often does not meet the other, leading to non-market-clearing outcomes. (In effect, there are more "targets" than "instruments" [Palley 1995].) A second reason is that wage cuts are often unable to eliminate involuntary unemployment due to insufficient aggregate demand. The early institutionalists were "proto-Keynesians" in that they believed the level of output and labor demand were primarily a function of the level of purchasing power, so they concluded that wage cuts often exacerbate the level of unemployment (Slichter 1931, 490–91).

Seventh, the early institutionalists believed that workers on net do not receive the full value of their marginal product (Slichter 1931, 616–39; Douglas 1934, 94). One reason is that firms often face a rising supply curve of labor even in relatively competitive labor markets (because inframarginal workers face positive costs of mobility and can be paid less than is necessary to attract new workers from the labor market), giving rise to an upward sloping marginal cost of labor schedule and an equilibrium wage that is less than the workers' marginal revenue product. A second is that specific on-the-job training and other sources of bilateral monopoly create an area of indeterminacy in wage rates and thus open the door to wage determination through bargaining. Given that workers on net suffer an inequality of bargaining power, they are likely to be underpaid relative to their productivity. A third reason is that involuntary unemployment in labor markets undercuts worker's bargaining power and also allows firms to pay a wage lower than the value of the marginal product.

Later Generations of Institutionalists in Labor Economics

It is generally agreed that Commons and his colleagues of the 1900–40 period constitute the first generation of institutional labor economists, but the existence and membership of successive generations of institutionalists are more controversial. Boyer and Smith (2001), for example, in their review of the history of labor economics, distinguish two other generations of institutionalists. The second generation is composed of "neoinstitutional" labor economists, such as John Dunlop, Clark Kerr, Richard Lester, Lloyd Reynolds, and Arthur Ross, who were dominant figures in the field between 1940 and 1960. Boyer and Smith also distinguish a third generation of institutionalists active in labor after 1960, but give this group no name. People they cite as third-generation institutionalists include Lester Thurow, Paul Osterman, Michael Piore, and Peter Doeringer. According to Boyer and Smith, the common denominator that puts these two groups of labor economists in the institutionalist camp is their adherence to a common research methodology—a descriptive, historical, and case-study approach, combined with rejection of price theory as a useful theoretical tool.

This account is not problem-free. For example, it has to be acknowledged that not all the labor economists included in these groups identify themselves as institutionalists and, indeed, some strongly deny the link (e.g., Dunlop 1988; Kerr 1988). Also problematic in this account is the future of institutionalism in labor economics, given that the institutionalist family tree is left truncated at the third generation of the 1970s and 1980s. And, as I shall argue below, making the unifying bond of institutionalism a commitment to a common research methodology is too narrow.

Taking a fresh look at the matter, I think a reasonable case can be made that in labor economics there have been four generations of institutional economists, at least if "institutional" is broadly defined. The first generation is centered on Commons and the Wisconsin school. The second generation of neoinstitutionalists comprises Dunlop, Kerr, and a number of "industrial relations" or "social" labor economists of that era, such as Lloyd Ulman and Neil Chamberlain. Although clearly distinct from the earlier Wisconsin school, these labor economists are, in my opinion, still reasonably included as neoinstitutionalists because of their rejection of standard microeconomic models of labor markets and concomitant emphasis on the role of the institutional "web of rules" in structuring labor market outcomes and relations (Dunlop 1958, 1984). The third generation of institutionalism in labor economics is more eclectic, spanning labor economists with a strong affiliation with industrial relations (e.g., Ray Marshall, Jack Barbash), structural unemployment (e.g., Charles Killingsworth), models of dual and segmented labor markets (e.g., Michael Piore, Peter Doeringer, Barry Bluestone), and post-Keynesian economics (Eileen Appelbaum).

The fourth generation of institutionalists in labor economics (1980 to the present) is the most diffuse and difficult to characterize. It all depends on how the term "institutional" is defined and where one looks. Starting most narrowly, if the marker of "institutionalist" is a person's self-identification with the "old" institutional tradition of Veblen, Commons, and Mitchell and publishing activity in a mainstream journal (e.g., *American Economic Review*, *Journal of Labor Economics*), institutionalism is near death. If the net is cast one step wider to include books on labor from an "old" institutional perspective, the vital signs start to show movement (e.g., Philips and Mangum 1988; Abraham and McKersie 1990; Galbraith 1998; Osterman, Kochan, Locke, and Piore 2001). Further improvement is registered by looking at labor-related journal publications in more heterodox areas of economics. The *Journal of Economic Issues* (sponsored by the Association for Evolutionary Economics), for example, features approximately a half-dozen papers each year by labor economists, and other heterodox-leaning journals (e.g., *Journal of Evolutionary Economics*, *Journal of Socio-Economics*, *Journal of Post-Keynesian Economics*, *Feminist Economics*) also contain a number of labor-related papers. If "institutionalism" is broadened further to include labor publications written from the "new" institutional perspective of Coase and Williamson and in journals catering to this approach (e.g., *Journal of Economic Behavior and Organization*, *Journal of Institutional and Theoretical Economics*), the body of labor institutional research expands considerably in size and activity. Broadening the search further to include contiguous fields, such as industrial relations and economic sociology, and scholars outside the United States, the state of health of labor institutionalism moves up yet another step (for example, Smelser and Swedberg 1994; Osterman 1999; Berg and Kalleberg 2001; Hyman 2001). Finally, if "institutionalist" is broadened still further to include people and studies that, although not explicitly identified as institutionalist, nonetheless develop their subjects using institutionalist or heterodox ideas and methods, then the fourth generation starts to have a real presence. Examples include Okun's *Prices and Quantities* (1981), Freeman and Medoff's *What Do Unions Do?* (1984), Solow's *The Labor Market as a Social Institution* (1990), Schor's *The Overworked American* (1991), Card and Krueger's *Myth and Measurement* (1995), Bewley's *Why Wages Don't Fall During a Recession* (1999), Marsden's *Theory of Employment Systems* (1999), and Boyer and Saillard's *Regulation Theory* (2002).

But, one has to ask, is it meaningful to include these four generations of economists in the institutional camp and, if so, what defines the common denominator that unites their work as institutional? At least with respect to the first three generations, Boyer and Smith provide an affirmative answer, based on their contention that the key characteristic of institutionalism is adherence to a common research method. While they argue, on one hand, that there has been and continues to be an institutional tradition in labor economics, at the same time they deny this tradition's status as a viable "school" or "paradigm"—at least if the sine qua non of these constructs is a core of theory.

The facts, I believe, support their conclusion but only about one-half of the reasoning to it. Any objective account of institutionalism in labor economics (e.g., Cain 1976, 1993; Sobel 1982) will agree that theory development has been spotty and of modest analytical breadth and depth, and that normative commitments have helped define the community of interest. But to dismiss institutionalism as neither interested in nor successful at theory-building is not an accurate generalization.

No matter what generation of institutionalists is examined, all are concerned with theory and theory development, albeit along heterodox lines. The case for the first generation has already been developed in this chapter, while the case for the second generation has been developed at length elsewhere (Kaufman 1988). Suffice it to note on this score that Dunlop and Ross spent considerable effort endeavoring to develop theories of union wage determination, Lester advanced a theory of wage differentials in labor markets, Reynolds published papers on the theory of the firm's labor supply curve and the theory of short-run wage determination, Dunlop advanced the idea of an internal labor market, and Kerr developed the idea of segmented ("balkanized") labor markets. The pinnacle of their theory-building efforts was the book *New Concepts in Wage Determination* (Taylor and Pierson 1957), described as a collective project to flesh out an alternative theory of wage determination.

Without going into great detail, an examination of the publications of people in generations three and four reveals that nearly all were (or are) actively engaged in theory development, at least if it is defined to extend beyond the use of standard microeconomics. Examples include Doeringer and Piore's (1971) theory of internal labor markets, Thurow's (1975) job competition model, Brown's (1985) institutional model of labor supply, Dickens and Lang's (1988) theory of segmented labor markets, Berger and Piore's (1990) theory of industrial dualism, Solow's (1990) social wage model, Palley's (1995) model of the minimum wage, Barker's (1997) transaction cost model of unions, Craypo and Cormier's (2000) depiction of low-wage labor markets, Hall and Soskice's (2001) institutionalist theory of "varieties of capitalism," and Altman's (2001) model of job satisfaction and economic performance. (Note that I am not claiming that all of these economists are self-described institutionalists, but only that these examples of their work are broadly institutional in method and/or theory.)

Moving to the next step, if these groups of labor economists had a common interest in theory development, is there a consistent intellectual thread in their work that qualifies it as institutionalist?

On the level of metatheory, the answer can only be no. I can find no evidence that the core organizing concepts of institutional economics (as I have defined them)—the transaction and transaction cost—as advanced by Commons and the NIE have informed or impacted research and model-building in the field of labor economics per se in any discernible way. Nor have institutional labor economists from generations two to four succeeded in articulating some other theoretical framework for the study of labor that even remotely challenges the generality and productivity of the neoclassical paradigm. Thus, I conclude that while these economists have contributed a diverse mix of heterodox-looking theories of a low to medium generality and abstraction, there is no larger, overarching ("paradigmatic") theoretical construct in labor economics of an institutionalist nature that unites them. Without such a core metatheoretical framework, in turn, it is difficult for institutionalism in labor economics to develop a clear identity as a viable research program, to attract a cadre of committed, self-identified participants, or to avoid being intellectually overrun by "economic imperialists" of the Chicago school.

Given this negative assessment, at a lower level of theorizing I think there are meaningful intellectual links that connect these four generations of labor economists and collectively make it possible to speak of them (or particular works) as members of a heterodox school broadly identified as institutionalist. These links are sevenfold:

1. Emphasis on the importance of long-lasting, substantively important deviant observations in labor markets, such as involuntary unemployment, large interindustry and interfirm wage differentials, and racial and gender patterns of employment and occupational attainment.

2. Belief that the traditional microeconomic model of demand and supply in competitive markets, while useful and insightful for certain purposes, is for many applications and situations seriously incomplete and thus misleading as an explanatory device for the determination of wages and other important labor outcomes.

3. Agreement with Keynes that labor markets are not self-equilibrating and that the process of adjustment to disequilibrium takes place primarily through changes in quantities (jobs) rather than prices (wages).

4. An attempt to construct an alternative theory of labor economics built on a behavioral model of the human agent, models of imperfect competition in labor markets, theories of organizational structure and behavior, and explicit incorporation of legal rules and social norms.

5. Emphasis on the importance of institutions in structuring labor markets and determining labor outcomes, along with a belief that institutions are, or can be, welfare-enhancing in labor markets rather than an anticompetitive source of inefficiency.

6. Belief that a satisfactory theory of labor markets and outcomes must be built on a multidisciplinary, social science foundation, and that "realism" in theory construction is a virtue.

7. Commitment on a normative level to a humanistic set of welfare criteria that includes efficiency but also other ethical goals, such as justice, opportunities for self-development, democratic procedures, and social order and integration.

The Neoclassical School in Labor Economics

I now move to an examination of the neoclassical school of labor economics and the reasons that the neoclassical approach has come to dominate labor economics research. The message of the preceding section is that getting the definition of "institutional" right makes a large difference in evaluating its prospects, adherents, and contributions. This same message applies to this section. But in describing the neoclassical approach, many contemporary economists err in the opposite direction. While "institutional" is treated too narrowly and as lacking theoretical content, "neoclas-

sical" is defined too broadly and its theoretical coherence accepted too uncritically.

To begin this discussion, some common agreement is needed on the features that constitute the core principles of neoclassical economics. Further, this benchmark needs to be widely accepted for otherwise defenders of neoclassical economics quickly accuse the critic of erecting a convenient straw man or failing to understand the subtleties and extensions of the theory. To avoid this problem, I look to the mainstream labor literature and see how other well-respected economists have characterized the key principles of the neoclassical paradigm.

The first example comes from Boyer and Smith. They provide this concise statement: "Neoclassical theory [is] a sparse model of maximizing behavior in the face of competition and constraints" (2001, 212). In a similar vein, Borjas provides this description: "In this [neoclassical] literature two unifying principles are used to interpret labor market behavior: (1) all agents in the economy (i.e., individuals, firms, unions, governments) maximize a well-defined objective function; and (2) there exists a market equilibrium which balances the conflicting goals of the various players in the labor market" (Borjas 1988, 21). Just to make sure that these quotations are representative and reasonably accurate, also consider the definition of "neoclassical" from the *MIT Dictionary of Modern Economic:*

A body of economic theory which uses the general approach, methods, and techniques of the original nineteenth-century marginalist economists. . . . In particular, they studied the possibility of a set of market prices which ensured the equality of supply and demand in all markets. The idea of a perfectly competitive economy in equilibrium, which may be attributed especially to Walras, is central to the neoclassical scheme. (Pearce 1999, 301)

These definitions highlight two common concepts that, I believe, are core principles of neoclassical economics: constrained maximization and market equilibrium. Constrained maximization does double duty. It is first the basis for the rational-actor model that provides the analytic description of the human agent in neoclassical economics. But constrained maximization also provides the fundamental *method* of model-building in neoclassical economics, together with the corollary concept of marginal analysis. The second core principle of neoclassical economics is market equilibrium. Neoclassical economics examines a variety of market structures, but it is uncontestable that the market structure at the core of the paradigm is a *competitive* market. This fact is indicated in the Boyer and Smith quote where they explicitly include the word "competition" and is explicitly stated in the definition from the *MIT Dictionary*. Also relevant is the statement of Kniesner and Goldsmith (1987, 1241): "The auction-market analysis of prices and quantities is the core of neoclassical economics."

Based on the evidence above, I postulate without further argument that the concepts of rational (maximizing) behavior and competitive markets are the theoretical foundation of neoclassical economics. These two concepts—and particularly the latter—seem to provide some basis for a falsification test of neoclassical theory and, further, provide intellectual space for other theories and paradigms. Illustratively, I argued in the last section that two of the core principles of institutional economics are bounded rationality and imperfect markets—the opposite side of the neoclassical coin. In actual fact, however, the intellectual reach of neoclassical economics—or what is widely perceived as neoclassical economics—has expanded far beyond the domain delimited by the standard definition of the paradigm, in the process "imperializing" nearly all the intellectual space in the discipline and crowding out other paradigms.

This imperializing and crowding-out phenomenon is vividly illustrated in Boyer and Smith's recent article, "The Development of the Neoclassical Tradition in Modern Labor Economics" (2001). In a number of places, for example, they equate "neoclassical" with "price theory" and "standard economic theory," which carry the connotation of the just-elaborated conventional conceptualization of the paradigm. But then, in numerous other places, they shift to a much more expansive notion of the domain and specification of neoclassical theory. With respect to subject area, for example, Boyer and Smith also describe the application of neoclassical theory to nonmarket topics, such as personnel economics and the economics of the family. Unlike markets, neither business firms nor families utilize competition and flexible prices as the mechanism for coordination, control, and allocation of resources.

Boyer and Smith also include within the corpus of neoclassical economics a surprisingly heterodox group of economists and a similarly heterodox set of theoretical revisions and additions to the basic price theory model. Examples are Akerlof and Yellen's "fair wage-effort" model (1990) and Solow's book *The Labor Market as a Social Institution* (1990), both of which modify the standard model by introducing norms of fairness into wage determination. (And Solow identifies the theoretical model as "institutional"!) These two models predict, in turn, that wages will exhibit considerable rigidity, will be set above the market-clearing level, and will lead to persistent involuntary unemployment. Boyer and Smith also claim as neoclassical works both Robert Frank's book *Choosing the Right Pond: Human Behavior and the Quest for Social Status* (1985), which argues that workers' desire for social status leads to within-firm individual wage differentials that are smaller than individual differences in marginal productivity, and a journal article by Jeremy Bulow and Lawrence Summers (1986) that uses the assumed link between wages and work effort to construct a model of dual labor markets that gives rise to noncompensating wage differentials and involuntary unemployment.

One is led to ask what distinguishes these diverse and fairly heterodox authors and models as "neoclassical," and correlatively why these people are neoclassical as opposed to the other labor economists who have also written on these issues but whom Boyer and Smith put into the neoinstitutionalist "fact-gathering" camp (e.g., Lester Thurow, Michael Piore, Paul Osterman). The answer Boyer and Smith give (in the context of discussing internal labor markets) is that, "Unlike the neoinstitutionalists, . . . neoclassical economists have built their studies of firm behavior upon models of *maximization in the face of constraints*" (215; emphasis added). I note that the word "competition" has fallen out of this definition, presumably reflecting the fact that demand/supply-type competition is not found within firms and other nonmarket institutions, and that "neoclassical" is in this version made synonymous with constrained optimization. This omission is not accidental or idiosyncratic, for Boyer and Smith elsewhere describe "maximizing behavior" as the distinctive feature of the neoclassical approach (e.g., 214).

The key point to make is that this heterogeneity of subjects and authors can be reconciled as "neoclassical" only by a dramatic broadening of what constitutes the essence of the paradigm. The way that this has been accomplished is to create two alternative versions of neoclassical theory: what I call *price theory* and *choice theory*.

Price theory is the conventional, core version of neoclassical economics. Price theory originated with Marshall and Walras and was pushed forward most aggressively and successfully by economists of the Chicago school, such as Stigler and Friedman. Their respective textbooks, *Theory of Competitive Price* (Stigler 1942) and *Price Theory: A Provisional Text* (Friedman 1962), are foundational treatments.

In his survey of the Chicago school, Reder (1982) provides a succinct statement of the core assumptions of the price theory version of neoclassical economics. The Chicago approach, he states, is built on one central premise and four auxiliary assumptions. The central premise (what he calls "Tight Prior Equilibrium") is "the hypothesis that decision makers so allocate the resources under their control that there is no alternative allocation such that any one decision maker could have his expected utility increased without a reduction occurring in the expected utility of at least one other decision maker" (11). The four assumptions (stated nearly verbatim are): most economic agents perceive prices of the goods or services they buy or sell to be independent of the quantities they transact (prices are parametric, as in perfect competition); prices people use to transact are market-clearing prices consistent with optimization by all decision makers; information is a scarce good that is available at an "optimal" level in the sense that the quantity produced equates marginal benefit and cost; and neither monopoly nor government intervention affects relative prices or quantities sufficiently to prevent either marginal products or compensation of identical resources from being approximately equal in all uses.

It is evident that if Reder's price theory definition of neoclassical economics is adopted, then many of the works that Boyer and Smith cite as neoclassical—e.g., those by Akerlof and Yellen, Bulow and Summers, Frank, Solow—do not come close to falling within this intellectual domain. The principal reason is that they all abandon the assumption of competitive markets and parametric price. Yet many economists will nonetheless claim that the work of people such as these is indeed neoclassical. How can this be?

The answer is that a second version of neoclassical economics has slowly developed in the guise of "choice theory." Price theory is about how an economy operates—it is a theory of how competitive prices coordinate economy activity. Choice theory switches the focus of economics to a verb—the study of economizing—and entails a theory of rational allocation of scarce goods to their most efficient use. In effect, neoclassical economics in its choice theory mode takes the first core component of the paradigm—the theory of rational (maximizing) behavior—and makes it the central driver of the theory and either extensively modifies the competitive hypothesis, holds it in "deep background" as a means to rationalize certain restrictions or relationships (e.g., the correspondence between the wage and marginal product of labor), or generalizes the equilibrium concept to extend beyond competitive markets. The end product is an elastic and all-encompassing theoretical tool that can be applied to practically all forms of human behavior.

The choice theory paradigm has its roots in the work of Jeremy Bentham and his postulate that all human behavior is guided by the desire to maximize pleasure and minimize pain. This idea now forms the core of choice theory—people exercise rational choice in pursuit of maximum utility, where utility is the difference between benefits (pleasure) and suitably specified costs (pain). The next major contributor was Lionel Robbins (1932), who defined economics as the study of how best to allocate scarce resources to alternative ends—that is, how to make the best choice. The real impetus to the "economics as a theory of choice" perspective has come, however, from the highly influential work of Gary Becker.

Becker (1976) does not define his approach to theorizing as "neoclassical," but rather in more general terms as the "economic" approach. Further, he explicitly states that it is better viewed as a *method* rather than a theory per se (5). He describes the economic approach in these words: "The combined assumptions of maximizing behavior, market equilibrium, and stable preferences, used relentlessly and unflinchingly, form the heart of the economic approach as I see it" (5). On the surface, this appears simply to be a restatement of the core features of neoclassical economics— maximizing behavior and stable preferences yield the rational-actor model, and market equilibrium suggests price determination in competitive markets. The difference is that Becker broadens the concept of "market" to include other forms of coordination, such as sorting in a marriage market, and broadens the price concept to include both money and shadow prices.

Becker's economic approach adroitly accomplishes several things: it significantly broadens the reach of economics, as in his claim that it "is applicable to all human behavior" (8); it also significantly generalizes economic theory by broadening the price construct to include all forms of opportunity cost; and Becker also reformulates consumption theory so "tastes" are effectively removed as an active determinant of behavior (neutralizing the disciplinary insurgency of behavioral economics). Equally significant, Becker's work further marginalizes heterodox economics and critics of mainstream theory by applying conventional economic tools and explanations to a host of nontraditional subjects and deviant observations. Likewise, by framing the economic approach as equivalent to the theory of rational choice, he perforce relegates alternative approaches to the very fringe of the discipline. If "orthodox" is rational choice, then "heterodox" must either be a theory of nonchoice or irrational choice. Finally, there seems to be no reason why the economic approach could not also incorporate transaction cost, thus co-opting the core of institutional economics.

It is the choice theory version of modern economics that allows Boyer and Smith to categorize the work of economists such as Akerlof and Yellen, Bulow and Summers, Frank, and Solow in the neoclassical camp in labor economics. But, returning to the original question, one has to ask: is their type of economics really neoclassical? Boyer and Smith answer with a straightforward yes. Others, such as Amable, Boyer, and Lordon (1997), argue that the paradigm has transitioned from one core version they call "fundamental neoclassicism" to another called "methodological neoclassicism," while Colander (2000) concludes that what now falls under the rubric of "neoclassical" is so expansive and heterogeneous that the term is hopelessly corrupted and should be abandoned. A better substitute term, argue both Colander and Solow (1997), would be "mainstream" economics. Both writers also agree that what distinguishes mainstream economics from neoclassical economics is that the former entails a more agnostic, applied approach to economic analysis built around the art of model-building. Mainstream economics thus subsumes neoclassical economics, much as choice theory subsumes price theory, with rather uncertain and not entirely consistent boundaries between the two approaches.

From Neoclassical to Modern Labor Economics

A similar evolution of thought and nomenclature has occurred in American labor economics since the 1950s. The term "neoclassical" first appeared in the mid-1950s in labor economics, gradually spread in usage and popularity, but then in the mid-

1980s began to be replaced by a new term: "modern" labor economics (e.g., Ehrenberg and Smith 2003). Modern economics is equivalent to mainstream economics in that both are built on a neoclassical foundation but are broader and more eclectic in their approach to theorizing.

In the discipline of economics, the term "neoclassical" gained widespread recognition and usage only after Samuelson, in the third edition (1953) of his best-selling principles text *Economics*, coined and made frequent reference to the concept of a "neoclassical synthesis." The synthesis was a marriage between the Walrasian/Marshallian microeconomic theory of price determination in competitive markets and the Keynesian theory of income determination at the macroeconomic level, with the idea that success at the macro level in maintaining full employment conditions through Keynesian demand management policies would provide the economic environment for demand and supply in individual markets to work out an efficient (competitive) allocation of resources.

Relatively quickly, the term "neoclassical" surfaced in labor economics. As then interpreted, "neoclassical" represented a market explanation for wage determination based on a theory of competitive labor markets. That is, neoclassical economics was synonymous with Walrasian and Marshallian–inspired price theory. Three pieces of evidence may be cited to illustrate this linkage. In the book *New Concepts in Wage Determination* (Taylor and Pierson 1957), the term "neoclassicism" appears in the index and the entry reads "see marginal productivity theory." Under "marginal productivity theory" are a number of page citations, and reading these passages reveals that the subject under discussion is the theory of competitive wage determination. The second piece of evidence comes from the textbook *Labor Econom-*

ics, published in 1957 by Paul Sultan. Chapter 21 is titled "Neoclassical Wage Theory." Again, most of the chapter is devoted to the marginal productivity theory of labor demand and the role of flexible prices in restoring market equilibrium. The third piece of evidence is this statement by Melvin Reder in his review of the wage literature: "There are two general approaches to the theory of wage structure. One is the market theory, or the competitive hypothesis, the other is what we might roughly term the institutional. Each has its place and, under pressure, most students of labor markets will concede this" (1958, 84). The important point to note is that Reder contrasts the competitive hypothesis to an institutional approach, suggesting that the distinction is not between theoretical and descriptive approaches but between two alternative theories—one that emphasizes competitive labor markets and another that emphasizes noncompetitive labor markets and institutional forces in wage determination.

In its price theory guise, neoclassical labor economics attracted considerable criticism. Pierson, for example, concludes, "When viewed against the complex and shifting network of relationships involved in the wage-determination process, discussed above, competitive price theory seems completely out of touch with the world of actuality. Except in a very loose or general sense, this hypothesis affords a poor basis for explaining wage relationships" (1957, 18). Despite this type of frequent dismissal, over the next two decades neoclassical-inspired labor economics decisively displaced its institutional rival, largely relegating the latter to the fringes of the field or to the adjoining field of industrial relations, while labor economics proper was methodically integrated into "the general framework of neoclassical theory" (Addison and Siebert 1979, 3). But, one must ask, what happened to all the deviant observations,

market imperfections, and complex social and institutional considerations in labor markets that institutional critics had thought were so damaging to the neoclassical project?

The answer involves two parts. The first I briefly mention, but the latter requires modestly more discussion because it was the key factor in the shift in neoclassical labor economics from a price theory to a choice theory mode.

The first weapon was largely defensive in nature and was intended to shield neoclassical theory from the critics who charged that it was hopelessly unrealistic. Most important in this effort was Friedman's essay: "The Methodology of Positive Economics" (1953). Friedman argued, convincingly to many economists, that a theory should be judged, not on its realism of assumptions, but on its predictive ability. His argument effectively silenced critics by ruling out arguments and evidence about the large gap between the theory's assumptions (perfect information, costless mobility, etc.) and conditions in the real world.

Even with this route foreclosed, institutionalist critics could still call into question the neoclassical paradigm by pointing out the numerous deviant observations in labor markets that seemed to contradict a competitive market model. Examples include nominal wage rigidity, substantial wage dispersion for similar types of workers, involuntary unemployment, the positive correlation between wage levels and firms' ability to pay, and substantial racial and gender differences in earnings and occupational attainment. But neoclassical labor economists also effectively neutralized this line of attack and, indeed, ingeniously turned the tables on their opponents. Their strategy was to demonstrate, using the tools of microeconomics, that the alleged deviant observations were themselves explicable as a product of rational, economizing behavior. Not only did this line of argument seem to square neoclassical theory with observed features of real-world labor markets, but it also appeared to demonstrate the remarkable explanatory power and reach of the theory. As a natural but seldom remarked-upon outgrowth of this theoretical extension, neoclassical labor economics also slowly morphed from an exercise in price theory to one of choice theory.

Arguably, the beginning point was 1957 with the publication of Becker's *The Economics of Discrimination,* which sought to reconcile discriminatory wage differentials and competitive markets by incorporating "tastes for discrimination." Several years later, Stigler (1962) demonstrated that an interfirm dispersion in wages and period of unemployment for job seekers is a rational and efficient product of imperfect information and job search, while Becker (1964) rationalized wages below marginal revenue product not as monopsonistic exploitation but a necessary payback on firms' investment in specific on-the-job training.

Rationalizing deviant observations with a choice theory model then picked up speed in the 1970s. One example is implicit contract theory and involuntary unemployment (e.g., Azariadis 1975). What appears to be a market failure (involuntary unemployment) may be an efficient outcome, according to implicit contract theory. The idea is that employees desire income security so they buy "income protection insurance" from the employer by agreeing to work for a lower but stable wage. If a negative demand shock hits the firm, the adjustment in employment is made by laying off low-seniority workers. Since both the firm and employed workers gain from this arrangement, the outcome (layoff unemployment) is efficiency-enhancing. In this spirit, Boyer and Smith remark, "In sum, it is the view of neoclassical labor economists that layoff unemployment is not inconsistent with economic theory" (2001, 211).

Other examples are readily available, for example, Polachek's (1981) argument that occupational segregation arises not from discrimination but differences among men and women in the amounts and types of on-the-job training. What these examples illustrate is the gradual but cumulatively significant abandonment or downgrading in labor economics of the competitive hypothesis and "tight prior equilibrium." Increasingly, unemployment, occupational segregation, and other deviant observations are shown to be consistent with rational choice and the logic of gains from trade, but it is no longer presumed that labor markets clear or workers of equal productivity are paid (approximately) equal wages.

Fast-forwarding to the present time, these trends have intensified and the examples multiplied. Model-building in labor economics has also exploded in terms of subjects and phenomena covered and technical sophistication. Not only has the competitive hypothesis increasingly become an adjunct of model-building, it has also increasingly moved to deep background while the rationality hypothesis does more of the heavy lifting. In the literature of the 1990s, this situation is well illustrated in the work of Lazear on personnel economics.

On one hand, Lazear affirms the fundamental importance of the competitive view of markets to modern economics, stating that "Adam Smith's concept of the invisible hand is a guiding principle in economics" (2000, 101). Yet his research in personnel economics in many cases examines subjects and builds models that are largely divorced from the competitive hypothesis and in some cases (e.g., tournament wage models) are arguably in direct contradiction of it. Indeed, the very concept of market equilibrium (one of the three fundamental components of Becker's economic approach) is quietly displaced in Lazear's version of modern labor economics by a more generalized quest on the part of economic agents for efficient outcomes (2001, 102–4).

Many other examples can be cited in which modern labor economists have generalized the conventional neoclassical price theory model. The same problem of consistency arises, however. A major area of model-building, for example, is incorporation of morale effects and social interactions ("relativities") into models of labor supply and wage determination, such as the efficiency wage literature (Weiss 1990). While the models are consistent with an augmented version of the rationality hypothesis, they generate rigid wages, involuntary unemployment, and other outcomes that are at odds with a competitive market economy.

In their account of neoclassical labor economics, Boyer and Smith (2001) conclude that all the models just reviewed—implicit contract theory, personnel economics, and social interaction and morale models—are neoclassical. The discussion of this section suggests, however, a more qualified assessment. Judged by the historical meaning of the term as defined by well-regarded economists, "neoclassical" means a model based on rational behavior and competitive equilibrium (market-clearing). Nearly all models in the mainstream labor literature maintain the rationality hypothesis, but a growing number relax the competitive hypothesis to the point where it does not hold in a substantive sense (as even close to a first approximation). The result is an intriguing, often insightful group of models that exhibit rational behavior, often generate efficient outcomes, yet lead to labor market institutions and outcomes that are a significant distance from those of the competitive economy envisioned in traditional neoclassical economics. How all of these models and theories add up to a working version of the invisible hand story—the bottom line of the neoclassical project—is not obvious nor explained in the literature. I conclude that

modern labor economics, like the larger body of mainstream economics, is sometimes neoclassical and sometimes not, with a tremendously gray and often inconsistent area in between.

Conclusion

I have endeavored to delineate the core features and intellectual boundaries of the principal competing schools of thought in labor economics: the institutional and the neoclassical.

The neoclassical approach starts with a perfect world and shows how the invisible hand of competition and self-interest coordinates economic activity, allocates resources, and determines prices, outputs, and the distribution of income. It takes as its model the discipline of physics. The core version of neoclassical theory rests on a model of the rational actor and competitive markets, with constrained optimization and equilibrium as the core tools for model-building. As neoclassical economics has extended its reach into nonmarket areas and sought to explain empirical puzzles and deviant observations, it has slowly metamorphosed into a more general and somewhat agnostic approach centered on model-building. In this guise, the old neoclassical economics of price theory shifts, at least in many applications, to a new version of neoclassical economics—often called mainstream or modern economics—centered on rational choice and constrained optimization (choice theory). The old neoclassical economics generally featured a strong normative commitment to competitive markets and minimal government intervention in private ordering; the new neoclassical economics— if it is indeed even reasonable to call it neoclassical any longer—recognizes that markets can in practice be inefficient for a variety of reasons, but as a general position still holds to a broadly competitive, invisible-hand view of the world.

The institutional approach tackles the paradigm issues of economics from the opposite end. It starts with an imperfect world with humans as they are, which is to say a model of an imperfect human agent living in a world of scarcity, uncertainty, and limited protections for life and property. Because all contracts are incomplete, people must solve the coordination, allocation, and pricing and output decisions through an evolutionary process of institution-building and a mix of markets, formal organizations, and social institutions (e.g., culture, norms of reciprocity, and justice). The institutional approach looks not to physics, but to biology, law, history, and the behavioral and organizational sciences, and it trades off formalism and analytical tractability for disciplinary holism and realism of assumptions. Since the world has significant imperfections, the invisible hand has equally significant shortcomings, so market outcomes are often inefficient and sometimes antisocial. In the old institutional economics, the perceived extent of imperfections (most centrally, unemployment), coupled with an ethical commitment to social justice and human self-development, led to a normative position that favored (within limits) greater institutional control and coordination of markets through government, trade unions, and other organizational entities. In recent years, the new institutional economics has taken a more neutral, middle ground, recognizing that institutional intervention carries its own costs and that government failure and union failure may entail worse outcomes than market failure.

The institutional and neoclassical schools vied for supremacy in economics into the 1940s (into the 1950s in labor economics), but since then the pendulum has swung sharply in favor of the latter (Yonay 1998; Rutherford 2001). Opinions will differ on the exact explanation, but I conjecture that most labor economists judge that the neoclassical

paradigm has been far more productive as a research tool and engine for discovery. The degree to which this outcome is due to the superiority of its *methods* or the superiority of its *theory*—or to some combination of both (or to a third factor, such as ideology)—is an interesting but as of yet unanswered question. Whatever the case, this superior productivity, coupled with factors having more to do with the sociology of science, has allowed the neoclassical school to also attract the bulk of the best intellectual capital in the field, in effect giving it a double advantage. Intellectual developments have then been reinforced by real-world developments that also favor the neoclassical side, including improved micro- and macroeconomic performance, the global shift toward free market economies, and the decline in the viability and perceived efficacy of market regulatory institutions (e.g., trade unions, protective labor law). Ironically, to the degree that market economies operate as if guided by an invisible hand, this improved performance tends to burnish the luster of neoclassical economics, yet it arises in part only because the visible hand of government—operating through Alan Greenspan, the Equal Opportunity Commission, the Securities and Exchange Commission, and other such institutions—has created the legal and macroeconomic environment in which self-interest and market supply and demand can effectively and fairly perform. But this institutional contribution is often taken for granted, if not viewed with skepticism.

The picture does not look entirely bleak for the institutional approach, however. There remain numerous deviant observations in labor markets that neoclassical (or mainstream) economics has difficulty explaining, and the trend toward free markets and deregulation brings with it a host of new problems that give institutionalists an opportunity to demonstrate the relevance of their craft. Further, institutional economists in recent years have succeeded in formalizing and developing a core theoretical model, built around the concept of transaction cost, that has demonstrated the ability to explain important economic phenomena, such as the boundary lines between "make versus buy," that neoclassical economics cannot. In this respect, institutional economics seeks to answer a different set of questions than neoclassical economics and thus has considerable room to grow and develop. Likewise, another as-of-yet largely unexploited set of ideas for a reinvigorated institutional labor economics comes from recent work of theorists, such as Arrow, Akerlof, and Stiglitz, on new, more realistic models of humans and markets. But for institutional economics in the labor field to make a significant comeback and contribution, potential has to be translated into action by a group of committed, talented people working on an agenda of heterodox theory-development built around the transaction concept.

Looking at the modern-day literature in labor economics, I am led to conclude that a portion of mainstream economics is "neoclassical" as that term has historically been understood, another portion falls outside the traditional definition, and a large part falls in an ill-defined middle area. Thus, the extent to which modern labor economics is neoclassical depends on how it is defined. If "neoclassical" is synonymous with choice theory, the rationality hypothesis and constrained maximization, then the vast proportion of labor economists are neoclassical and those claiming to be institutionalist —at least prior to the tenure decision—will asymptotically approach zero. If, however, neoclassical is defined as synonymous with price theory and a (largely) competitive, market-clearing model of markets, then a significant portion of practicing labor economists—and Nobel laureates—fall out-

side the neoclassical school and, in many cases, can be regarded as neoinstitutional (Schmid 2001; Phillips and Kinnear 2002). Although the "so what?" question can surely be asked about this conclusion, at the end of the day "neoclassical" and "institutional" are not just taxonomic labels empty of substance but represent quite different ways of conceptualizing and practicing economics.

References

Abraham, Katherine, and Robert McKersie. *New Developments in the Labor Market: Toward a New Institutional Paradigm.* Cambridge, MA: MIT Press, 1990.

Addison, John, and W. Stanley Siebert. *The Market for Labor: An Analytic Treatment.* Santa Monica, CA: Goodyear, 1979.

Akerlof, George, and Janet Yellen. "The Fair Wage-Effort Hypothesis and Unemployment." *Quarterly Journal of Economics* 105 (May 1990): 255–84.

Altman, Morris. *Worker Satisfaction and Economic Performance: Microfoundations of Success and Failure.* Armonk, NY: M.E. Sharpe, 2001.

Amable, Bruno, Robert Boyer, and Frederic Lordon. "The Ad Hoc in Economics: The Pot Calling the Kettle Black." In *Is Economics Becoming a Hard Science?*, ed. Antoine d'Autumne and Jean Cartelier. Brookfield, VT: Edward Elgar, 1997.

Azariadis, Costas. "Implicit Contracts and Underemployment Equilibria." *Journal of Political Economy* 83, no. 6 (1975): 1183–1202.

Barker, George. *An Economic Analysis of Trade Unions and Common Law.* Brookfield, VT: Aldershot, 1997.

Becker, Gary. *The Economics of Discrimination.* Chicago: University of Chicago Press, 1957.

———. *Human Capital.* New York: Columbia University Press, 1964.

———. *The Economic Approach to Human Behavior.* Chicago: University of Chicago Press, 1976.

Berg, Ivar, and Arne Kalleberg. *Sourcebook of Labor Markets. Evolving Structures and Processes.* New York: Kluwer, 2001.

Berger, Suzanne, and Michael Piore. *Dualism and Discontinuity in Industrial Societies.* New York: Cambridge University Press, 1980.

Bewley, Truman. *Why Wages Don't Fall During a Recession.* Cambridge, MA: Harvard University Press, 1999.

Borjas, George. "Earnings Distribution: A Survey of the Neoclassical Approach." In *Three Worlds of Labor Economics*, ed. Peter Philips and Garth Mangum. Armonk, NY: M.E. Sharpe, 1988.

Boulding, Kenneth. "A New Look at Institutionalism." *American Economic Review* 47 (May 1957): 1–12.

Boyer, George, and Robert Smith. "The Development of the Neoclassical Tradition in Modern Labor Economics." *Industrial and Labor Relations Review* 54 (January 2001): 199–223.

Boyer, Robert, and Yves Saillard. *Regulation Theory: The State of the Art*. London: Routledge, 2002.

Brown, Clair. "An Institutional Model of Wives' Work Decisions." *Industrial Relations* 24, no. 2 (1985): 182–204.

Bulow, Jeremy, and Lawrence Summers. "A Theory of Dual Labor Markets with Application to Industrial Policy, Discrimination, and Keynesian Unemployment." *Journal of Labor Economics* 4, no. 3, pt. 1 (1986): 376–414.

Cain, Glen. "The Challenge of Segmented Labor Market Theories to Orthodox Theory." *Journal of Economic Literature* 14, no. 4 (1976): 1215–57.

———. "Book Review." *Industrial and Labor Relations Review* 46, no. 3 (1993): 586–88.

Card, David, and Alan Krueger. *Myth and Measurement: The New Economics of the Minimum Wage*. Princeton, NJ: Princeton University Press, 1995.

Coase, Ronald. "The Nature of the Firm." *Economica* 4 (November 1937): 386–405.

———. *The Firm, the Market, and the Law*. Chicago: University of Chicago Press, 1988.

Colander, David. "The Death of Neoclassical Economics." *Journal of the History of Economic Thought* 22, no. 2 (2000): 127–43.

Commons, John R. *Industrial Goodwill*. New York: McGraw-Hill, 1919.

———. *Institutional Economics: Its Place in Political Economy*. New York: Macmillan, 1934a.

———. *Myself*. Madison: University of Wisconsin Press, 1934b.

———. *The Economics of Collective Action*. Madison: University of Wisconsin Press, 1950.

Commons, John R., and John Andrews. *Principles of Labor Legislation*. 4th ed. New York: Harper, 1936.

Craypo, Charles, and David Cormier. "The Working Poor and the Working of American Labor Markets." *Cambridge Journal of Economics* 24 (2000): 691–708.

Dickens, William, and Kevin Lang. "The Reemergence of Segmented Labor Market Theory." *American Economic Review* 78 (May 1988): 129–34.

Doeringer, Peter, and Michael Piore. *Internal Labor Markets and Manpower Analysis*. Lexington, MA: Lexington Books, 1971.

Douglas, Paul. *The Theory of Wages*. New York: Macmillan, 1934.

———. *In the Fullness of Time*. New York: Harcourt, Brace, Jovanovich, 1971.

Dow, Gregory. "The New Institutional Economics and Employment Regulation." In *Government Regulation of the Employment Relationship*, ed. Bruce Kaufman. Madison, WI: Industrial Relations Research Association, 1997.

Dunlop, John. *Industrial Relations Systems*. New York: Henry Holt, 1958.

———. "Industrial Relations and Economics: The Common Frontier of Wage Determination." In *Proceedings of the Thirty-Seventh Annual Meeting, Industrial Relations Research Association*. Madison, WI: Industrial Relations Research Association, 1984.

———. "Labor Markets and Wage Determination: Then and Now." In *How Labor Markets Work: Reflections on Theory and Practice by John Dunlop, Clark Kerr, Richard Lester, and Lloyd Reynolds*, ed. Bruce Kaufman. Lexington, MA: Lexington Books, 1988.

Ehrenberg, Ronald, and Robert Smith. *Modern Labor Economics: Theory and Public Policy*. 8th ed. New York: Addison Wesley, 2003.

Eisner, J. Michael. *William Morris Leiserson: A Biography*. Madison: University of Wisconsin Press, 1967.

Ely, Richard. *The Labor Movement in America*. New York: Thomas Crowell, 1886.

Fine, Sidney. *Laissez-faire and the General Welfare State: A Study of Conflict in American Thought, 1865–1901*. Ann Arbor: University of Michigan Press, 1956.

Frank, Robert. *Choosing the Right Pond: Human Behavior and the Quest for Social Status*. New York: Oxford University Press, 1985.

Freeman, Richard, and James Medoff. *What Do Unions Do?* New York: Basic Books, 1984.

Friedman, Milton. "The Methodology of Positive Economics." *Essays in Positive Economics*. Chicago: University of Chicago Press, 1953.

———. *Price Theory: A Provisional Text*. Chicago: Aldine, 1962.

Galbraith, James. *Created Unequal: The Crisis in American Pay*. New York: Free Press, 1998.

Gonce, Richard. "John R. Commons' 'Five Big Years': 1899–1904." *American Journal of Economics and Sociology* 61 (October 2002): 755–78.

Harrison, Royden. *The Life and Times of Sidney and*

Beatrice Webb: The Formative Years, 1858–1905. New York: St. Martin's Press, 2000.

Hyman, Richard. *Understanding European Trade Unionism: Between Market, Class and Society*. London: Sage, 2001.

Jacoby, Sanford. "The New Institutionalism: What Can It Learn from the Old?" *Industrial Relations* 29, no. 2 (1990): 316–40.

Kaufman, Bruce. "The Postwar View of Labor Markets and Wage Determination." In *How Labor Markets Work: Reflections on Theory and Practice by John Dunlop, Clark Kerr, Richard Lester, and Lloyd Reynolds*, ed. Bruce Kaufman. Lexington, MA: D.C. Heath, 1988.

———. "Labor's Inequality of Bargaining Power: Changes over Time and Implications for Public Policy." *Journal of Labor Research* 10 (Summer 1989): 285–98.

———. *The Origins and Evolution of the Field of Industrial Relations in the United States*. Ithaca, NY: ILR Press, 1993.

———. "Labor Markets and Employment Regulation: The View of the 'Old' Institutionalists." In *Government Regulation of the Employment Relationship*, ed. Bruce Kaufman. Madison: Industrial Relations Research Association, 1997.

———. "Emotional Arousal as a Source of Bounded Rationality." *Journal of Economic Behavior and Organization* 38 (February 1999a): 135–44.

———. "Expanding the Behavioral Foundations of Labor Economics." *Industrial and Labor Relations Review* 52 (April 1999b): 361–92.

———. "The Early Institutionalists on Industrial Democracy and Union Democracy." *Journal of Labor Research* 21, no. 2 (2000): 189–210.

———. "The Organization of Economic Activity: Insights from the Institutional Theory of John R. Commons." *Journal of Economic Behavior and Organization* 52, no. 1 (2003a): 71–96.

———. "John R. Commons and the Wisconsin School on Industrial Relations Strategy and Policy." *Industrial and Labor Relations Review* 57 (October 2003b): 3–30.

———. *The Global Evolution of Industrial Relations. Events, Ideas, and the IIRA*. Geneva: International Labour Organization, 2004.

Kerr, Clark. "The Neoclassical Revisionists in Labor Economics (1940–1960)—R.I.P." In *How Labor Markets Work: Reflections on Theory and Practice by John Dunlop, Clark Kerr, Richard Lester, and Lloyd Reynolds*, ed. Bruce Kaufman. Lexington, MA: D.C. Heath, 1988.

Kniesner, Thomas, and Arthur Goldsmith. "A Survey of Alternative Models of Aggregate U.S. Labor Market."

Journal of Economic Literature 25 (September 1987): 1241–80.

Kochan, Thomas, Harry Katz, and Robert McKersie. *The Transformation of American Industrial Relations*. New York: Basic Books, 1986.

Lazear, Edward. "Personnel Economics: Past Lessons and Future Directions." *Journal of Labor Economics* 17, no. 2 (1999): 199–236.

———. "Economic Imperialism." *Quarterly Journal of Economics* 115 (February 2000): 99–145.

Lehrer, Susan. *Origins of Protective Labor Legislation for Women, 1905–1925*. Albany: State University of New York Press, 1987.

Lescohier, Don. *My Story for the First Seventy-Three Years*. Madison, WI: Art Brush, 1960.

Lutz, Mark, and Kenneth Lux. *Humanistic Economics: The New Challenge*. New York: Bootstrap, 1988.

Marsden, David. *A Theory of Employment Systems: Micro-Foundations of Societal Diversity*. Oxford: Oxford University Press, 1999.

Moss, David. *Socializing Security: Progressive-Era Economists and the Origins of American Social Policy*. Cambridge, MA: Harvard University Press, 1996.

Okun, Arthur. *Prices and Quantities: A Macroeconomic Analysis*. Washington, DC: Brookings Institution, 1981.

Osterman, Paul. *Securing Prosperity: The American Labor Market: How It Has Changed and What to Do About It*. Princeton, NJ: Princeton University Press, 1999.

Osterman, Paul, Thomas Kochan, Richard Locke, and Michael Piore. *Working in America: Blueprint for a New America*. Cambridge, MA: MIT Press, 2001.

Palley, Thomas. "Labor Markets, Unemployment, and Minimum Wages: A New View." *Eastern Economic Journal* 21, no. 3 (1995): 319–26.

Pearce, David. *The MIT Dictionary of Modern Economics*. 4th ed. Cambridge, MA: MIT Press, 1999.

Perlman, Mark, and Charles McCann Jr. *The Pillars of Economic Understanding: Ideas and Traditions*. Ann Arbor: University of Michigan Press, 1998.

Philips, Peter, and Garth Mangum. *Three Worlds of Labor Economics*. Armonk, NY: M.E. Sharpe, 1988.

Phillips, Ronnie, and Douglas Kinnear. "Institutional Economics in Mainstream Journals: The 1950s versus the 1990s." Unpublished paper presented at the Conference on the History of Heterodox Economics, University of Missouri–Kansas City, Kansas, Missouri, 2002.

Pierson, Frank. "An Evaluation of Wage Theory." In *New Concepts in Wage Determination*, ed. George Taylor and Frank Pierson. New York: McGraw-Hill, 1957.

Polachek, Solomon. "Occupational Self-Selection: A Human Capital Approach to Sex Differences in Occupational Structure." *Review of Economics and Statistics* 63 (February 1981): 60–69.

Ramstad, Yngve. "John R. Commons' Puzzling Inconsequentiality as an Economic Theorist." *Journal of Economic Issues* 29 (December 1995): 991–1112.

Reder, Melvin. "Wage Determination in Theory and Practice." In *A Decade of Industrial Relations Research, 1946–1956*, ed. Neil Chamberlain, Frank Pierson, and Theresa Wolfson. Madison, WI: Industrial Relations Research Association, 1958.

———. "Chicago Economics: Permanence and Change." *Journal of Economic Literature* 20 (March 1982): 1–38.

———. *Economics: The Culture of a Controversial Science.* Chicago: University of Chicago Press, 1999.

Robbins, Lionel. *An Essay on the Nature and Significance of Economic Science.* London: Macmillan, 1932.

Rutherford, Malcolm. "Institutionalism Then and Now." *Journal of Economic Perspectives* 15 (Summer 2001): 173–94.

Samuels, Warren. "The Present State of Institutional Economics." *Cambridge Journal of Economics* 19, no. 4 (1995): 569–90.

Samuelson, Paul. "Economic Theory and Wages." In *The Impact of the Union*, ed. David McCord Wright. Freeport, NY: Books for Libraries Press, 1951.

———. *Economics.* 3rd ed. New York: McGraw-Hill, 1953.

Schmid, A. Allan. *Property, Power, and Public Choice.* 2nd ed. New York: Praeger, 1987.

———. "The Institutional Economics of the Nobel Prize Winners." In *Economics Broadly Considered*, ed. Jeff Biddle, John David, and Steven Medema. New York: Routledge, 2001.

Schor, Juliet. *The Overworked American: The Unexpected Decline of Leisure.* New York: Basic Books, 1991.

Simon, Herbert. *Models of Bounded Rationality.* Vol. 2. Cambridge, MA: MIT Press, 1982.

Slichter, Sumner. *Modern Economic Society.* 2nd ed. New York: Henry Holt, 1931.

Smelser, Neil, and Richard Swedberg. *Handbook of Economic Sociology.* Princeton, NJ: Princeton University Press, 1994.

Sobel, Irvin. "Human Capital and Institutional Theories of the Labor Market: Rivals or Complements?" *Journal of Economic Issues* 16, no. 1 (1982): 255–72.

Solow, Robert. *The Labor Market as a Social Institution.* New York: Blackwell, 1990.

———. "How Did Economics Get That Way and What Way Did It Get?" *Daedalus* 126, no. 1 (1997): 39–58.

Stabile, Donald. *Activist Unionism: The Institutional Economics of Solomon Barkin.* Armonk, NY: M.E. Sharpe, 1993.

Stigler, George. *The Theory of Competitive Price.* New York: Macmillan, 1942.

———. "Information in the Labor Market." *Journal of Political Economy* 70, pt. 2 (October 1962): 94–105.

Sultan, Paul. *Labor Economics.* New York: Henry Holt, 1957.

Taylor, George, and Frank Pierson. *New Concepts in Wage Determination.* New York: McGraw-Hill, 1957.

Thurow, Lester. *Generating Inequality.* New York: Basic Books, 1975.

Tversky, Amos, and Daniel Kahneman. "Loss Aversion in Riskless Choice: A Reference-Dependence Model." *Quarterly Journal of Economics* 106 (November 1991): 1038–61.

Webb, Sidney, and Beatrice Webb. *Industrial Democracy.* London: Longmans, Green, 1897.

Weiss, Andrew. *Efficiency Wages: Models of Unemployment, Lay-offs and Wage Dispersion.* Princeton, NJ: Princeton University Press, 1990.

Williamson, Oliver. *The Economic Institutions of Capitalism.* New York: The Free Press, 1985.

Yonay, Yuval. *The Struggle over the Soul of Economics: Institutional and Neoclassical Economics in America between the Wars.* Princeton, NJ: Princeton University Press, 1998.

3

Labor and the Menace of Competition

Glen Atkinson

The widening of markets across political jurisdictions raises concerns about the separation of political and economic institutions. Currently, the emergence of global markets has caused frequent speculation about the consequences of the widening of markets beyond effective political and legal authority. Many observers believe that without such authority shaping markets and influencing the behavior of participants in various markets, there will be a "race to the bottom" in terms of quality standards. One of the greatest concerns about the emergence of the global market is that firms will be forced by competition to pay the lowest wages and adopt the lowest working standards among all of the participants in the global market. Others believe that globalization and its effects on standards are inexorable and beyond the reach of public regulation. In this view, people will simply have to adjust to the vagaries of the evolution of free markets.

Fortunately, we do not have to simply speculate about the effects of this rapid widening of markets as if it were a unique phenomenon in history. One of many earlier examples is the effect of the rapid expansion of the railroads and the settlement of the West in the United States in the late nineteenth century. This was followed by extensive regulation of industry during the progressive period of the late nineteenth and early twentieth centuries. Another example, which will be explored at length in this chapter, is the effects on labor caused by the expansion of the market in the United States following the ratification of the Constitution. The reason this historical example is so illuminating is that John R. Commons and his associates documented the consequences of this market-widening process on labor. In my opinion, their work provides instruction on research methods to study probable effects caused by rapid geographic expansion of markets.

Labor and Markets

Before proceeding with the discussion of the specific effects of the market expansion on wages and working conditions, we need to explain that the expansion process examined by Commons transformed the organization of labor markets. After the first guild was incorporated in America in 1648, the shoemakers of Boston, there was a relatively harmonious relationship between labor and management. In fact, the master craftsman worked alongside journeymen and apprentices. As the market further expanded, working relations were transformed from guilds to factories. This harmony was ended in 1789 with "The Trial of the Boot and Shoemakers of Philadelphia, on an indictment for a combination and conspiracy to raise their wages" (Commons 1923, 226). We now tend to think of labor markets as factory owners and managers hiring workers on the open market. Because this chapter will trace out the evolution from guilds to factories, the reader will need to keep in mind that labor markets were being gradually transformed. Guilds were not free markets because they were controlled by custom and public regulation. One of the objectives of Commons and his associates was to develop theories to help us understand the consequences of the emergence of free markets for labor.

The concept of a free market for labor presumes that labor power is simply a tradable commodity that can be divorced from the other aspects of the human individual. According to John R. Commons (1919), this market view of labor is supported by two alternative theories. On the one hand, labor power is a commodity and would be compensated according to the scarcity of the particular skill. Employers studied labor market conditions and adjusted compensation according to the forecast of supply and demand of their particular market, and Commons learned from his investigations that these employers were proud of their ability to forecast the supply (1919, 1).

The alternative theory is to view labor power as a machine in factory production (Commons 1919, 7–16). According to this view, compensation of labor should not be an equal wage for all or even be adjusted for such characteristics as seniority. Instead, each worker would be compensated according to the value of his or her output. As owners will decide if a particular machine is worth purchasing by comparing its price to the value of its output, they compensate workers by a piece-rate rather than a wage.

Commons found neither of these theories to be untrue in their ability to explain behavior in labor markets, but they were both incomplete. Employers facing stiff competition will certainly strive to keep labor costs down, and they will say that they are forced to do this by the market. There are at least two problems with these free market theories for labor. First, a worker is more than a commodity or a machine. Workers are full-fledged citizens with family and community obligations. Second, and more important for the purpose of this chapter, allowing free competition to dictate treatment of workers can place both the firm and society on a path that will lead to an undesirable destination. The effects on firms of pursuing profits in highly competitive product markets are low wages and substandard working conditions. Commons called these effects the menace of competition. The menace of competition is a complete theory of free markets for labor because it explains the social effects as well as private gain.

Expansion of the Market and the Menace of Competition

Of course, factors other than the geographic expansion of markets affected the evolution of working conditions in the United States relative to other nations, and these factors need to be stated to appreciate the context in which market-widening occurred. Over the course of the eighteenth and nineteenth centuries, when the organization of production and work was being transferred from guilds to factories, labor markets in the United States had some features that distinguished them from markets in European countries. The early and peaceful adoption of universal manhood suffrage,[1] abundant land, and waves of immigration were important features that affected labor relations in the United States (Commons et al. 1918, 3–5).

Suffrage gave workers some political clout, and abundant land gave them hope that they could eventually escape the wage-earning class. However, immigration often led to clashes between groups of workers, which reduced their political clout and kept wages sufficiently low so that workers could not move out of the wage-earning class and into the landowning class. This interaction of hope and disappointment eventually led workers to realize that a permanent wage-earning class was being formed and spurred efforts to organize labor for protection of their class.

All of these features played an important role in determining labor conditions in the United States. However, for Commons, the greatest influence on labor conditions was simply the expansion of the market area: "The vast area of the United States, coupled with free trade within that area and a spreading network of transportation, has developed an unparalleled extension of the competitive area of markets, and thereby, has strikingly distinguished American movements from those of other countries" (Commons et al. 1918, 5–6).

The adoption of the federal Constitution in 1787 eliminated artificial barriers to trade among the states and laid the foundation for national markets in many industries. As local markets were expanded to a national dimension, personal contact between customers and producers was eliminated, craft skills became obsolete, and prices and quality of products were reduced. More intense price competition caused merchants and employers to press workers for reduced wages and eroded working conditions. This expansion of the market area and the resulting intensification of price competition occurred in most manufacturing industries, but it did not occur among such workers as musicians and longshoremen, where the market remained local. The case of the shoemakers provides the best documentation of the evolution of an industry and the consequences for the relations between producers and consumers on the one hand and employers and employees on the other because of the extension of the market. This case also shows how the affected workers attempted to organize to protect themselves from this competitive menace (Commons et al. 1918, 32–152; Commons 1923, 219–66).

In the beginning, many itinerant shoemakers would visit customers' homes to work up the raw material into finished shoes. Most of these shoemakers were not highly skilled and consequently the products were of low quality. These workers were dependent on the customer for food, lodging, work space, and raw materials. The workers provided only their labor and hand tools. These working conditions put the laborers at a serious disadvantage relative to the consumer.

The settled shoemakers, menaced by the low prices and bad ware of the itinerants, formed guilds to legally protect themselves from such competitive pressure. Local courts were given the authority to oversee the practices of the guilds and prevent abuse of this power. Still, the guild shoemakers gained some advantage relative to the customer because they were not dependent on the customer's provisions as the itinerant was. Also, a guild shoemaker was merchant, master, and journeyman, all in one person. All work was made to order as bespoke work.[2] The worker's success depended, in addition to workmanship and skill, on the ability to adjust price to quality. The guild shoemaker had to be both artisan and business owner.

The next step in the evolution of this industry was for the master to move from only custom or bespoke work for the neighborhood to shop work. In this step, the master would provide orders and raw materials for the journeymen to take home and work into finished products. These shoes would be stocked in the master's shop for display and sale. This was the beginning of the end for custom work, though it would take several decades for the end to come. This immense step from production as bespoke work to shop work was, arguably, the beginning of the path toward modern industrial capitalism and the beginning of adversarial labor management relations.

In the custom-order stage, the menace was bad ware. The guild prevented advertisement of bargain prices and sales in public markets that could lead to the erosion of quality. The producers were protecting themselves against consumers who could not judge quality. In the shop work stage, the master became employer as well as retail merchant, and the journeymen feared the merchant-employer was putting pressure on wages in order to move the inventory. The cleavage began to shift from between producer and consumer to between merchant-employer and employee, and the first strike in this industry over wages was filed in Philadelphia in 1805 (Commons 1923, 227).

The Rise of the Merchant Capitalist

Beginning in the early nineteenth century, highway, river, canal, and ocean transportation was improved so that markets could be further expanded, which revolutionized market practices (Commons et al. 1918, 88). Durable merchandise could be shipped economically from the manufacturing cities of the Northeast, such as Boston and Philadelphia, to the agricultural region of the South and West. However, two limiting factors had to be removed before domestic producers could successfully exploit these markets.

The first factor was what we now call logistics. Wholesale merchants traveled to the hinterland to secure orders from local retail merchants and then traveled back to the shops in the manufacturing cities to fill the orders. Since these shops were small-scale, staffed by a master who employed a few journeymen, the wholesale merchants had to visit many shops to find enough merchandise to fill their orders. This caused considerable extra expense and wasted time. It also put domestic manufacturers at a disadvantage relative to importers because the importers had warehouses that the wholesale merchants could visit to fill their orders. The foreign producers financed these facilities. For-profit commission warehouses and producer-organized cooperative warehouses were built to fill this vacuum for domestic manufacturers (Commons et al. 1918, 90).

The second factor that had to be dealt with was financing the more roundabout production that resulted because of the expanded markets. As production moved from custom work to shop work and then to market work, raw materials and finished products had to be financed until revenues from the sale were received.

Local shop owners purchased raw materials and provided them to the journeymen, who worked up the materials in their homes with their hand tools. Unlike custom work, however, this was speculative work. The master-merchant would not be remunerated until the products were sold in distant markets. But the raw material suppliers wanted to be paid at the time they delivered the materials, and workers needed to receive income at regular intervals. How were these expenses to be financed? As in the case of warehouses, the foreign manufacturers financed importers' goods during the entire marketing phase. This placed domestic manufacturers at a disadvantage in their ability to respond to the expanding markets.

Domestic financial institutions were seriously deficient to take on the task of financing production on such a large and expanding scale. In the political climate of the post–Revolutionary War years, some patriotic organizations rose to the occasion and provided initial capital and other assistance to help establish domestic industry so the new nation would not be dependent on foreign trade. However, these efforts did not satisfy the continuous need to finance the production and marketing of commodities.

Small manufacturers could only obtain operating loans that were secured by real, tangible property. Gradually this practice began to change.

> The earliest loans on evidences of intangible capital were made by merchants. A merchant would agree with a manufacturer, who had contracts or notes, to honour orders that he issued to his workmen in lieu of cash wages. He would then redeem the orders in merchandise. Such accounts would run until the manufacturer's customers made their remittances. . . .
>
> It will readily be seen that business was considerably hampered under a credit system that did not recognize intangible evidences of property. The small producer especially suffered under these conditions. (Commons et al. 1918, 89)

Intangible capital is based on *expectations* of the profitability of the firm, as a going concern, separate from the cost of the physical property. In boom periods, when expectations are high, the capitalized value of a firm will exceed the cost of the buildings, tools, and machinery.[3] This step to use intangible property to finance current production for future consumption was a giant step in the evolution of capitalism. It would have been impossible to finance a sufficient stock of inventory of shoes if the merchant capitalists could not have borrowed on expected sales, or their intangible capital, because they had no tangible capital.

Commons would argue that this institutional development preceded the technological change from hand tools to factory machinery. It can be argued that large-scale machinery will induce larger markets or that larger markets will induce improved technical apparatus. It was the position

of Commons that the constitutional elimination of trade barriers between the states led to an enlarged market. Financial innovations were needed, however, to reach the potential the expanded market offered. Why did merchants fill this void? Why did banks not supply the funding? There were only three banks in the system in 1791, with a capital value of $2 million. This increased to 246 banks in 1816, with nearly $90 million capital value, and then to a system value of nearly $204 million, including the Bank of the United States, in 1833 (Commons et al., 1918, 101). "The banking system expanded along with the activities of the merchant-capitalist, enabling him to convert the distant retailers' orders into bank credits and to stock up a surplus of goods in advance of actual orders" (Commons et al. 1918, 101).

Clearly, the financial system was responding to meet the needs of the expanded market. Perhaps it is worth repeating that the financial requirements were for working capital rather than machinery or other real property. Also, this is the step that allowed intangible capital to be used as security for business loans. Potential future sales were used to finance current production. This is the step that separates classical economic theory from the institutional economy. Money is not neutral and institutions do matter.

The most important point for the purpose of this chapter is that the emergence of merchant capitalism, and later employer capitalism, caused the shifting of relations and antagonisms between workers, employers, merchants, and financiers. It put additional downward pressure on wages and working conditions.

Labor and Merchant Capitalism

Neoclassical economic theory begins and ends with impersonal exchange between two individuals. No institutional context is provided to explain the structure of markets where these exchanges take place. In fact, the term "free" in "free markets" means free of institutional constraints. For Commons, in contrast, market exchange, or supply and demand, takes place within a structure of collective action. Exchange is organized by previous transactions that provide structure for markets.

> A transaction is two-sided: it is joint *action* [emphasis added]. In the transaction the terms of performance are agreed upon; or performance is executed according to working rules previously established or agreed upon. . . .
>
> In this way our theories of economics come to center on transactions and working rules, on the problems of organization, and on the way collective action becomes organized into going concerns. (Commons 1970, 21)

A transaction is the alienation and acquisition of property rights that are required before production and exchange can take place. These rights provide a security of expectations for all parties. It is difficult to imagine a supply or demand curve in the absence of enforceable property rights. Property rights are a means to bring mutuality and order out of conflict.

In addition to property rights, working rules that shape going concerns also provide some security of expectations. However, the term "working" means that these rules tend to be in transition in a dynamic economy. In the case of the evolution from guilds to merchant capitalism to factory production, the working rules, and the nature of the going concern, were radically transformed. It is the relative institutional power of various parties in negotiating these working rules that will determine the path of industrial evolution.

Because economic order emerges out of conflict, it is not a static state but evolves through a give-and-take process. Economics is not the science of choosing from a given set of alternatives as in neoclassical choice theory, and it cannot be developed from an individualistic, hedonic psychology. It is about negotiating a new order to fit a new set of conditions, and this is not always a pleasant process. Markets are evolving institutions embedded in other institutions. "The psychology of this give-and-take process of conciliation and agreement may be named negotiational psychology, to distinguish it from the pleasure-pain psychology of the individualistic economists since the eighteenth century" (Commons 1970, 29).

The rise of merchant capitalism with its expanded role of finance was just such a point when the economic order was renegotiated. However, we should not think of these negotiations as different parties sitting around a table considering offers and counteroffers. These negotiations were done with a great deal of ignorance and on the fly. "But these forms of collective action are not different from what people do. The organization of activity is simply the more stabilized aspects of activity. The form is part of the process" (Commons 1970, 21). In other words, transacting is not passive choosing from a menu but actions to shape the evolving institutional structure that will determine the distribution of the fruits of production.

Because the merchant capitalist was able to obtain credit on the value of intangible assets, the merchant capitalists were able to elevate their power relative to the workers and their employers. This is the point at which the merchant function was separated from the production and employer function. A new set of relationships was in the process of being created through transacting where the master craftsmen lost their merchant function to the merchant. In fact, a new merchant capitalist function was created separate from either the employer or retail merchant function. The master craftsman lost as much in this realignment as the journeyman.

Here occurs the separation of the merchant-function from the employer-function. The bargaining specialist, or the merchant capitalist, need no longer be one who has knowledge of the technical processes of the trade. These he turns over to a subordinate or to a master workman, who now merely becomes the labor contractor; while for himself the merchant capitalist retains those functions calling for his special skill in sizing up a market, driving a bargain, and commanding credit. (Commons et al. 1918, 101)

This is the step in the evolution of the industry at which the conditions captured by the Veblenian dichotomy were created.[4] This is the beginning of the dominance of the pecuniary role over the industrial. As we shall see, this is also the step at which price was elevated relative to quality of product. Also this is the step when the cleavage between producer and consumer was reduced and the relations between parties in the production process—capitalist, employer, and worker—were transformed. In short, this is when the economic order was renegotiated through new transactions, and there were winners and losers in this process.

In order to understand the new status of the worker, we must first explain the transactions between merchant capitalists and lenders. The merchant capitalist approached the banker with evidence of orders, which included prices and quantities. Without any real collateral to secure the loan, the merchant's only collateral was the reasonable expectation of receiving revenues from the orders that the retail merchants had placed with the merchant capitalist. Thus the banker, who had to believe that these market forecasts were reasonable, would feel more secure if the forecasts were low rather than high.

Retail merchants also squeezed the merchant capitalist from the other side of the transaction. Retailers knew their customers in their local markets and could play one merchant capitalist against another. Successful retailers had developed the goodwill of their customers, which they used against their suppliers.

> The only good will he [the merchant capitalist] could rely upon at the time was the good will of the retail merchant. Such devices as trade-names, trade marks, and advertised commodities, which now enable the manufacturer and wholesale merchant to reach the consumer over the head of the retail merchant, were still unknown. (Commons et al. 1918, 102)

The highest price forecast that a merchant capitalist could take to the bank were the prices established in the transactions between retail and wholesale merchants. Even then the bank would be cautious in accepting the sales forecast because the merchant had no other real or intangible capital to submit for security.

The merchant capitalist became increasingly dependent on bank finance during the first three decades of the nineteenth century. The merchant capitalists gained some advantage because they could obtain loans at a cheaper rate than a small operator and, because they bought in bulk, they could purchase raw materials at lower prices. However, the increase in the severity of price competition more than offset these lower costs. The producer could not reduce labor cost by installing machinery at this time, as mechanization was essentially limited to the textile industry (Commons et al. 1918, 102).

The only means of adjustment of labor costs were to decrease wages or to reorganize work, and, in fact, employers did both. The merchants set up small factories and hired skilled workers to cut patterns and work up the raw materials. These components were then distributed to less-skilled workers who assembled them in the home or smaller shops. Formerly skilled workers were paid skilled wages for all of the work, skilled and unskilled. Now their work was limited to the operations requiring skills. This separation of workers, particularly when the unskilled work was done at home, allowed women and children to be employed, and they were often paid by piece-rate. Later, convicts were also used for the unskilled tasks. The shift to home work and convict labor became commonplace during the first quarter of the nineteenth century. Often wage rates and hours of work were reduced for skilled work, but the family income remained the same by combining the income of the main wage earner with the rest of the family's earnings.

The masters were reduced to job contractors. Though they had come up through the trades, they owned no capital, as the merchant capitalist owned the raw materials and the journeymen owned their tools. The masters received the contract price from the merchant capitalist, and their income depended on how quickly and cheaply they could fill the order.

> They organized their workmen in teams, with the work subdivided in order to lessen dependence on skill and to increase speed of output. They played the less skilled against the more skilled, the speedy against the slow, and reduced wages while enhancing exertion. Their wages were "sweated" out of labour, their shop was a "sweatshop," and they the "sweaters." (Commons et al. 1918, 103)

This organization of work began in the shoe industry during the 1820s and spread to other handwork industries until the factory displaced it in the early twentieth century. The transition to the factory system ended merchant capitalism and created employer capitalism. Before taking up the discussion of the factory, however, we do not want to lose sight of the major point, which is that the extension of the market increased the level of the competitive menace. The drive to serve the expanding national market made production by custom work impossible. Products had to be turned out faster and without the aid of power machinery. Production for future sales in far-flung markets required financing, which the small shop owner

and master craftsman could not obtain. Only the merchant with substantial intangible property in the form of orders for commodities could secure a loan that would finance production and marketing costs. However, the lenders insisted that prices be held in check, and this requirement eventually meant that the major cost of production, labor, be reduced. This reduction was accomplished mainly by reorganizing work to speed up production, thereby sweating profits out of the workers.

Workers attempted to build protective organizations but this proved too difficult to accomplish because various classes of workers were pitted against each other. Also, workers did not understand the cause of the menace. The immediate culprit was the employer, but he was menaced by the merchant capitalist who provided the conditions of the orders for products. But the merchant capitalist could claim that the lenders dictated the situation. The real culprit was financial capitalism, which rested on the acceptance of capitalizing intangible property. Many skilled workers would probably have preferred to return to the good old days of the guild, but that system had been destroyed by the extension of the market and an increasing level of the menace of competition. This menace was caused by the marginal producer who can only survive in the highly competitive market by reducing costs. "Defining the 'marginal producer' as the one with the lowest standards of living and cost and quality of work, he is the producer whose competition tends to drag the level of others toward his own. . . . He is a menace rather than an actual competitor" (Commons 1923, 251).

The expansion of the market set loose severe price competition that required a response of drastic measures to cut costs. Among the measures to cut costs were reduced quality of products, lower wages, and, most important, the creation of sweatshop working conditions. This sequence of events defines the menace of competition. The menace set industry on a race to the bottom, and the path was blazed by ever more marginal producers.

Labor and Industrial Goodwill

The need to cut costs also provided the incentive to develop machinery that would make labor more productive. In order to use manufacturing equipment effectively, the workplace had to be reorganized into the factory. The seeds of the factory system can be seen in the reorganization of work in the waning days of merchant capitalism. It should be remembered, though, that the tools used in the sweatshops of merchant capitalism were hand tools owned by the workers themselves. The genesis of sweatshops was not the means of production but in the organization of the flow of work. Another seed of the factory system found in merchant capitalism was the development of banking institutions that were required to finance the production and purchase of the heavy, expensive factory equipment.

The merchant capitalist was eventually displaced by the employer capitalist who was the factory owner. This new capitalist class was able to deal directly with lending institutions because employer capitalists developed substantial intangible capital, or industrial goodwill. Goodwill is simply the difference between the value of the real assets of the factory and the market value of the going concern. There are several sources of goodwill, including patents, trademarks, monopoly power, and loyal customers. You can go to the bank with goodwill, and being able to go to the bank enhances your goodwill. The goodwill developed by the employer capitalists also allowed them to appeal to the consumer over the head of the merchant. Goodwill lifts the business above the daily menace of competition (Commons 1919, 25).

Another way for the capitalist to rise above the menace of competition is to produce more efficiently. When the need for skills was reduced during merchant capitalism and machines replaced hand tools in factory production, it was much easier to pursue higher profits by squeezing unskilled labor than by squeezing skilled handcraft workers. In the factory the boss is no longer a job contractor, but has the combined roles of employer and capitalist. In the role of employer the boss treated the worker as a commodity, subject to the laws of supply and demand, or as a machine. In the former case, compensation was in the form of wages, and in the latter case in the form of piece-rate payments. If the commodity theory was the company policy, it was almost certain that the company would have to follow the competition down to the lowest wages and working conditions. The more employers thought of production as a machine process, or as engineering design, the more likely they were to bring in scientific management consultants to design and measure work flows. Scientific managers considered workers to be a part of the machine process and paid according to output. Employers considered this policy consistent with the emerging industrial system, but workers believed it was one more dehumanizing scheme to speed up work—just a new form of the sweatshop.

Scientific management consultants thought like engineers, treating each separate individual as a component of the machine process. Each individual was given incentives to make more money, but this destroyed the solidarity of labor.

> But the goodwill of labor is a collective goodwill that does not play one laborer against another, or the unemployed against the employed, or take advantage of the needs of a class, but acknowledges labor's solidarity of interest as well as the individual laborer's self-interest. . . .

> Scientific management, since it begins and ends with individuals separated from their fellows, has the defects of autocracy. (Commons 1919, 19)

A preferred alternative, in the opinion of Commons, would be for firms to develop the collective goodwill of their labor force. Better working conditions would instill teamwork and worker loyalty, reduce turnover and training costs, and generally increase productivity. Any increase in a firm's productivity would be added to the total industrial goodwill of the firm and elevate it above the menace. Again, any action that would raise the firm above its competitors is a form of goodwill, showing up in its balance sheet and, in turn, allowing the firm to pay higher wages and provide better working conditions.[5]

Certain progressive employers recognized the value of labor's goodwill and enacted appropriate policies (Commons 1919, 17–18). Of course, most employers are not progressive, but leading firms can establish benchmarks for labor policies. Progressive firms establish reasonable standards such as reducing the length of the workday and workweek and refusing to use child labor. The government, then, has the responsibility of moving the most laggard firms up toward the benchmarks by regulation. The use of benchmarks bases regulatory policies not on idealism, but on a solid foundation that has already been achieved by best practices. Benchmarking could be a central feature in avoiding the competitive menace in a firm's relations with labor.

> Social coercion is necessary against private coercion, not because the state can elevate the people to a higher level than that attained by the free exercise of their own persuasive powers, but in order to prevent the lower and selfish elements from dragging the several institutions down. The state sets the minimum level below which the struggle for existence shall not be permitted to force an institution. (Commons 1967, 104)

This fundamental function of public authority requires the state to have as wide a scope as the private market. As national markets eroded local markets, national regulations began to usurp local customs and authority. This shift has been the source of continuous tension in American political economics. It remains to be seen if an effective political authority can be developed to govern the emerging global economy in order to avoid being driven to the bottom by the competitive menace.

Conclusions and Implications

Classical economists reasoned that the extension of the market through competitive free trade would maximize public welfare. Increasing division of labor and more capital to work with would increase labor productivity. They failed to foresee the downside caused by the menace of the marginal producer. Through his investigations, Commons found that unregulated competition would menace many workers and lead to low wages and sweatshop working conditions. His solution was to pursue appropriate institutional design to allow collective action by the working class, and to use the government to raise the standards of working conditions toward the best practices in the industry. He suggested that firms that enjoyed the benefits of intangible goodwill help their labor force create its own goodwill. In his opinion, this policy would not reduce the firm's goodwill but enhance it instead. His solution was not ideal, but reasonable given all of the conflicting interests. However, a party would not bargain in good faith with another party if the latter did not have the ability to act on its collective interests. For negotiations to work, all affected parties had to be in a position to be taken seriously.

It seems obvious that the work of Commons is directly applicable to the concerns raised currently by the globalization of production. The development of global production is an extension of the market, and the sequence of effects is creating a new competitive menace. We are creating new financial channels that place production facilities in locations around the world that pay the lowest wages and have deplorable working conditions. Unfortunately, as Richard McIntyre and Yngve Ramstad (2002) note, we do not have international institutions in place to control the menace unleashed by the effects of the expansion of the market. McIntyre and Ramstad recommend that the work of Commons be used to understand how to mitigate the effects of the competitive menace. In other words, not only is his work of historical interest, but it provides the best framework to deal constructively with a current process that is probably irreversible. If the expansion of the market through the globalization of production is going to continue, we need to find ways to see that workers will not be menaced by the marginal producer. Rather than being driven by the marginal producer, we need to find ways to promote and direct industrial goodwill.

Notes

1. Obviously, universal manhood suffrage is not the same as universal suffrage. Freed slaves did not win a constitutional guarantee for voting rights until 1870 and females had to wait until 1920 for this right. The point is that universal manhood suffrage was a radical step because it allowed nonpropertied workers to vote, which had significant effects on political power that affected labor. This measure has to be judged in the historical context.

2. Bespoke work means that the commodity is not produced until the order is placed and the price and quality of the product are agreed between producer and consumer.

3. Value based on expectations is a source of instability in modern economies. For example, many dot-com companies in the 1990s had no tangible capital though they had high capitalized values in reputable stock markets. The values of such properties evaporated when expectations changed.

4. Thorstein Veblen often made the distinction between industrial and pecuniary values. Industrial values encourage high quantity and quality of output. Pecuniary values encourage pursuit of money often at the sacrifice of quantity and quality of output (Champlin and Knoedler 2002, 878).

5. Any aspect of a firm that raises its financial value above the replacement cost less depreciation can be considered goodwill. A trademark, loyal customers, or loyal, efficient workers are just some of the factors that can create goodwill. Goodwill is measured as intangible value and raises the firm above the menacing competitors.

References

Champlin, Dell, and Janet Knoedler. "Wages in the Public Interest: Insights from Thorstein Veblen and J.M. Clark." *Journal of Economic Issues* 36, no. 4 (December 2002): 877–91.

Commons, John R. *Industrial Goodwill.* New York: McGraw-Hill, 1919.

———. "American Shoemakers, 1648–1895." In *Labor and Administration.* New York: Macmillan, 1923.

———. *A Sociological View of Sovereignty.* New York: Augustus M. Kelley, 1967.

———. *The Economics of Collective Action.* Madison: University of Wisconsin Press, 1970.

Commons, John R., David J. Saposs, Helen L. Sumner, E.B. Mittelman, H.E. Hoagland, John B. Andrews, and Selig Perlman. *History of Labor in the United States.* Vol. 1. New York: Macmillan, 1918.

McIntyre, Richard, and Yngve Ramstad. "John R. Commons and the Problem of International Labor Rights." *Journal of Economic Issues* 36, no. 2 (2002): 293–301.

4

John R. Commons and His Students

The View from the End of the Twentieth Century

J. Dennis Chasse

A hundred years ago, in the age of industrial violence (Adams 1966), John R. Commons told a group of exceptional graduate students that the labor problem was their problem (Raushenbush and Raushenbush 1979). Few economists would recognize their names now—William Leiserson, Elizabeth Brandeis, Paul Raushenbush, John B. Andrews, Edwin Witte, Arthur Altmeyer, Helen Sumner, Alvin Hansen, Selig Perlman, Harold Groves, and David Saposs. Call them the Commons gang. They played a larger role in national policy formation than Commons or than many more famous economists.

They did not receive rave reviews. Free market advocates attacked them for undermining market incentives; radicals for selling out the revolution; liberals for the inadequacies of unemployment compensation, for social insurance with regressive financing, for a degrading welfare system, and for a system of industrial relations that effectively deprives workers of any voice in their own working conditions.

This chapter asks what they thought, what they did, what their critics said, and what remains from a half century of criticism and history. First, it sketches the development of their thinking when they worked with Commons. Then it summarizes their role on the national stage. Next, it reviews the positions of their critics. It looks at how history has treated the positions of the critics, and it concludes by asking what remains after the criticism and the history. It answers that the Commons gang suffered from blind spots, but that they operated from a tenable model of economic evolution; that their vision was broader in some ways than that of their critics; and that policies derived from that vision remain effective in reducing poverty because they are geared toward shielding workers from the external costs of economic progress.

What Did They Think?

Commons, small, soft-spoken, disorganized, was not an impressive lecturer.[1] He taught mainly by engaging students in his projects and allowing them to interpret their experiences with him. At Friday night potluck suppers, Commons listened to them, encouraged them, and presented his own ideas. Students, therefore, did not imbibe Commons's ideas. Rather, their thinking developed in collaboration with his on his many projects.[2] The students differ in some ways from Commons and from one another,[3] but their writings reveal the shared conviction that a bargaining imbalance forced workers to bear the external costs of economic progress, that the American political system denied them adequate redress, and that the cure for this lay in a strategy of removing obstacles to collective bargaining and shifting external costs of economic growth from workers to firms.

They came to their conclusion during the course of many projects. The three major projects were: (1) a labor history study that produced an eleven-volume *Documentary History of American Industrial Society* and a four-volume interpretive *History of Labor in the United States*; (2) creation and operation of the Wisconsin Industrial Commission; and (3) staff investigations for the National Commission on Industrial Relations. The labor history study played the seminal role in the development of their thinking.

Labor History

Their interpretive history involved three tasks: first, choice of a framework within which to organize the data; second, identification of core reasons for worker discontent and labor organization; and third, specification of the kinds of organizations that could effectively improve the status of workers. David Saposs (1918, 25–30) addressed the framework. He contrasted two patterns for organizing data. One, following Karl Marx, selected stages related to production methods—hunter-gatherer, agriculture, handicraft, and industrial. The other pattern followed the German historical economists Gustav Schmöller and Carl Bücher. Schmöller related stages to the extension of markets—tribes, medieval fairs, towns, national economies. Bücher objected to Schmöller's emphasis on exchange relations, arguing that primitive societies emphasized sharing and considered trade immoral (Bücher 1902, 83–93). Bücher maintained that analysis should focus on the path between producers and the ultimate users. Saposs pointed out that these theories were not contradictory.

Marxist theory contains elements of market extension, and the Schmöller-Bücher theory contains elements of production methods (Saposs 1918, 27). But since the colonists were already in the handicraft and manufacturing stages, the extension of markets promised a better framework for investigating the genesis of labor problems in the United States (Saposs 1918, 28). Saposs added that both frameworks supported the same conclusion: that social relations really depend on the institution of private property and on the way it is defined by dominant classes (Saposs 1918, 28–29).

Commons and his gang used both Schmöller and Bücher for the second task—uncovering the roots of worker discontent. Following Schmöller, Commons and his gang looked at markets and bargains. All bargains resolve conflicts of interest. Power in bargaining depends on one party's ability to withhold what the other wants. In bargaining with a corporation, workers can withhold labor, but corporations can withhold from workers "the necessaries of life" (Commons and Andrews 1936, 509). The larger the corporation, the less the worker's bargaining power (Commons and Andrews 1936, 373–74, 509; Witte 1932, 291). Commons, following Bücher, noted that as markets expanded, an increasing complex of transactions separated the wage bargain from the price bargain. Specialized firms emerged to take over functions such as finance and shipping (Commons 1909, 59–67). Market power shifted back and forth within this complex of organizations. Those with market power forced upon others the "competitive menace" that reduces all to the level of the least ethical competitor. Consequently, many employers with whom workers bargained were themselves helpless. As a result, workers bore the external costs of economic progress—industrial accidents and diseases, unemployment, and poverty in old age.

Years later, William Leiserson summarized these conclusions with a question and an answer.

> Why should wage workers be paid by the piece, by the hour, by the day or by the month? We do not make payments to the investing and managing classes on this basis, and apparently the only reason wage-earners' incomes fluctuate with rainy and dry weather, with heat and cold, with buying seasons, with introduction of machinery and other improvements, with interruptions of work caused by miscalculations of management and with the alternations of busy and slack years is because they represent the weakest group in economic bargaining and cannot insist on steady payments. (Leiserson 1931, 622)

For their third task, asking which organizations were most effective at alleviating the plight of workers, Commons and his gang treated their history like one long experiment (Perlman and Taft 1935, 3–12). Utopian schemes—worker cooperatives, alliances with farmers or intellectuals, huge benevolent organizations—proved ephemeral (Saposs 1966, 73–76). Organizations such as the Industrial Workers of the World (IWW) sponsored successful strikes, but they had no lasting impact on working conditions because they left no permanent structure after the strike (Saposs 1966, 77–78). The success of the American Federation of Labor (AFL) rested on its ability to create a permanent structure by forcing employers to sign contracts, preferably enforcing a closed shop—and on its ability to enforce an almost military discipline on its members (Perlman and Taft 1935, 7–9). William Leiserson extended Commons's theory of industrial democracy, arguing for independent unions on "the principle that government derives its just powers from the consent of the governed working itself out in industry" (1920, 22). He compared industrial democracy to parliamentary governance with management representatives as one chamber, worker representatives as another, and the contract as a constitution (Leiserson 1920; 1922a).

Like Commons, Perlman and Taft accepted AFL "voluntarism" or dislike of any government intervention. They based this position, again, on experience. (Saposs and Leiserson later rejected this position.)

> Experience, notably in the Pullman strike case, taught American labor leaders that, whatever may have been the avowed purpose when powers were extended to the government, and whatever may have been the express assurances given to labor that such powers would never be used against labor, it is all in vain when the powers *that* be feel that with some stretching perhaps, the law might be applied to suppress labor's effort. The "voluntarism" of the Gompers group was not the result of an assiduous study of Herbert Spencer but of Attorney General Olney's invoking the Sherman Anti-Trust law and the Interstate Commerce Act against striking railway men. Throughout history every group with a "minority consciousness" feared strong government. (Perlman and Taft 1935, 6)

There was no positive experience with government to counterbalance this negative experience. Most efforts at passing labor laws proved futile (Perlman and Taft 1935, 6–7). This futility derived from unique aspects of American political culture. The American political system could not respond to labor problems in the way that European systems had responded (Commons 1918; Perlman 1928, 169–76). In Germany and Britain, workers united around the fight for universal male suffrage. In the United States, white male suffrage became universal during the 1830s before a large industrial class had developed, and American political parties coalesced around other issues. The spatial system of representation in the United States favored politicians who appealed to a cross-section of interest groups in a locality. This hindered the growth of the type of labor party that grew up in countries with proportional representation (Commons 1896). In addition, class restrictions that molded solidarity in European working classes were weaker in the United States, where upward mobility seemed less restricted (Perlman 1928, 162–64). Americans venerated property rights more than Europeans because agriculture had developed from small farms, not feudal estates (Perlman 1928, 155–60).

The American division of powers created other obstacles. The Constitution limited central government power over the states and gave courts the last word—unlike parliamentary systems in which legislatures can override courts.

> [T]he courts, blocking the way of a new aggressive class with precedents created to protect a dominant class, have had, in this country, a high authority unknown in other lands. By vetoing the laws which labour in its political struggles has been able to secure, the courts, joined to divergent state policies, have excluded or delayed labour from legislative influence. (Commons 1918, 9)

The term "dominant class" referred to a model of democracy Commons had developed in *A Sociological View of Sovereignty*. In that model, dominant groups impose their ideas of justice on everyone else (Commons 1899–1900; Chasse 1986). Notions of justice expand as formerly excluded groups force the ruling coalition to incorporate new rights into its concept of justice. In order to force their way in, however, they must organize outside the structure of the state.

That workers bore the costs of progress implied a general strategy of lifting those costs from them and encouraging the growth of organizations that improved their bargaining power. The major outlines of their strategy to achieve these objectives are most obvious in two of the practical projects in which Commons engaged his students: the creation and operation of the Wisconsin Industrial Commission, and staff work for the United States Commission on Industrial Relations (USCIR).

Two Commissions and a Strategy

Elizabeth Brandeis said that in 1910 Commons challenged his labor legislation class somewhat like this:

> The Legislature is coming in January of 1911, and I want to have a proposal on what to do about safety. What we've had is very inadequate. We've had laws on the books in Wisconsin, beginning in the '80s, and they don't do the job, and other states have equal difficulties. Who knows German to read what the Germans are doing? Who knows Swedish? (Raushenbush and Raushenbush 1979, 10)

Someone must have read Gustav Schmöller's 1874 article, "The Social Question and the Prussian State." Schmöller proposed social insurance administered by the monarchy because only the monarchy could be neutral (Haverkate 1985). On November 17, 1881, the German chancellor, Otto von Bismarck, adopting parts of Schmöller's solution, sent his famous message to the Reichstag—advocating sickness and accident insurance for German workers. But early twentieth-century American political culture could not accept a Prussian concept of the state (Commons 1913, 405). As an alternative, at this stage in his career, Commons advocated Charles S. Peirce's fallibilism and the solidarism of the sociologist Émile Durkheim, of economists such as Charles Gide and Charles Rist, and especially of the lawyer, politician, and peace activist, Léon Bourgeois. (Parsons 1963, 7; Altmeyer 1963, 124–25)

Peirce's definition of truth—"The opinion which is fated to be ultimately agreed to by all who investigate"—implied wide participation in investigations that affect public policy (Peirce 1992, 139; Parsons 1963, 7; Bourgeois 1931; Gide and Rist 1948, 545–70). Solidarists justified social insurance without losing the democratic concept of the state. They stressed that personal freedom depends on physical, intellectual, and moral bonds between all members of a given generation and between that generation and previous generations (Bourgeois 1931, 19–22). Unlike monarchists and socialists, solidarists did not identify society with the state. Bourgeois argued that states could not legitimately define rights and duties because states are merely "creations of men" (Bourgeois 1931, 39–40). Rather, legitimate rights and duties derive from contracts freely agreed to by parties of equal bargaining power. States then enforce these rights and duties (Bourgeois 1931, 60–62). Bourgeois claimed, however, that people agree to a "quasi-contract of association" when they choose to remain in a particular society. States must enforce that quasi-contract, and this implies the right to tax (Bourgeois 1931, 60–61, 65–66). People succeed or fail partly by their own efforts, but partly also because of luck and a social environment created not by individuals but by collective action (Gide and Rist 1948, 552–53). Consequently, the quasi-contract implies that success creates a debt to be repaid by supporting insurance that prevents in advance evils resulting from the roll of the industrial dice (Loubère 1986; Bourgeois 1931, 229–50). Mistrust of state power led solidarists to propose outside control by a "functional" legislature composed of representatives from occupational groups (Elbow 1966, 107–13; Zeldin 1973, 655–65). This philosophy informed the legislation proposed by Commons and passed by the Wisconsin legislature in 1911.

That legislation incorporated a four-part strategy: prevention, unified administration, defined reasonableness, and investigation. Commons applied the term *prevention* to merit-rated workers' compensation designed to shift costs from workers to firms and create an incentive to prevent accidents while supporting worker incomes. The

act unified responsibility for enforcement of all labor laws in the Wisconsin Industrial Commission, wiping out the fragmentation that had robbed previous labor laws of their effectiveness (Altmeyer 1932, 11–12). It defined reasonable safety as the best realistically attainable, removing a legal loophole created by the common law assumption of reasonable as average (Altmeyer 1932, 12; Brandeis 1935, 633, 640). It assigned investigation to a staff hired on the basis of merit and protected by civil service status but responsible to a functional advisory board composed of representatives appointed by labor and management organizations.

When Commons and Altmeyer insisted that the major role of the commission was investigation, not enforcement, they had a hidden agenda (Commons 1913, 396–97; Altmeyer 1932, 317). Obvious objectives included curtailment of bureaucratic domination, monitoring of effectiveness, and suggestions for corrective legislation. Altmeyer hinted at another objective when he decried the abandonment of general interest studies:

> The result has been that research which would develop facts of general interest is seldom undertaken. This tendency is to be deprecated because such research is most valuable in the development of intelligent public opinion and in the fashioning of appropriate methods of social control. (Altmeyer 1932, 317)

William Leiserson emphasized the value of combining research and administration in an institutionally neutral agency when he testified before the USCIR (U.S. Commission on Industrial Relations 1916, 344–57). Leiserson opined that anyone could describe a comprehensive unemployment program—unemployment compensation, public works, industrial training, and anticyclical monetary policy. Political opponents, however, would block such a program in any legislature in the country. But, added

Leiserson, a permanent neutral organization generating studies year after year in favor of such a program could break down political opposition.

Stunned by a wave of industrial violence, Congress created the U.S. Commission on Industrial Relations (USCIR) in August 1912. Short of funds and riven by internal conflict, the Commission disbanded and issued its final report in 1916. Commons served on the commission. Leiserson and Witte wrote major staff papers—on unemployment and injunctions respectively (USCIR 1916, 14).[4]

In his minority report to the commission, Commons summarized the policy positions he had developed with his students. At the center of those positions he placed what he called a national industrial commission entrusted with administering labor legislation and informing both administration and legislation by continuing research into the nation's labor problems. He proposed institutionalizing neutrality by protecting staff members with civil service status while making them accountable to an advisory board composed of representatives of management, organized labor, and advocates of unorganized workers. In addition, Commons recommended changes in the antitrust laws to permit centralized bargaining between labor and management and removal of legal restrictions on all nonviolent union tactics—including secondary boycotts, general strikes, and closed shops (Commons and Harriman 1916, 216–19; Witte 1932, 293–98). Commons opposed state certification of unions because he feared that it could become an instrument for government suppression of unions.

Commons advocated a comprehensive social security program financed by an inheritance tax (Commons and Harriman 1916, 222–23). His inheritance tax argument reflects solidarist influence:

> Inheritances are the principal means by which owners, without effort or thrift on their part, secure titles to wealth and its future continuous income. Consequently, for the Government to take a part of large inheritances which provide continuous income and to devote the proceeds to the purpose of making incomes more nearly continuous for those who are not able under existing conditions to do it for themselves appeals to the sense of justice. (Commons and Harriman 1916, 222–23)

This summarized their strategy. It was politically sophisticated and incremental, distinguished from most reformist programs by its close attention to the nitty-gritty of administration, its use of taxes to force internalization of costs, its use of administrative research to overcome political opposition, its support of union organization, and its use of advisory boards.

What Did They Do?

This section sketches some of the controversial ways in which the Commons gang influenced events on the national scene. First, they worked on campaigns of the American Association for Labor Legislation (AALL). Then, as the New Deal approached, Witte left his mark on the Norris-LaGuardia Act. Leiserson and Saposs helped save and protect the National Labor Relations Act. Witte and Altmeyer assisted at the birth and development of the Social Security system. Their contributions were real, but limited, beginning with the AALL.

A group of economists and social activists started the AALL in 1906 as a branch of the International Association for Labor Legislation (IALL). John Andrews soon became full-time secretary.[5] Andrews emerged into public view with the "phossy jaw" campaign (Lee 1966). Phosphorus eroded teeth and jawbones of workers in match factories, eventually eating away entire jawbones. The campaign against it, initiated by the IALL, succeeded in Europe, but not in the United States, where match manufacturers claimed that sanitary methods prevented the disease.

Andrews conducted a survey and discovered over 300 phossy jaw victims—many without jawbones (Andrews 1910). With advice from Miles Dawson, a lawyer and member of the AALL, Andrews wrote a bill using the federal government's taxing power to escape constitutional prohibitions. The bill imposed a tax equal to the difference in cost of production between phosphorus matches and safer matches. "Phossy jaw" disappeared.

As they moved to other issues, AALL members followed the phosphorous match pattern. They gathered information, wrote bills, sought allies, and mounted media and lobbying campaigns. The workers' compensation campaign moved successfully from state to state. The campaign for compulsory health insurance started well, but insurance companies mounted a deceptive and abusive publicity counteroperation. The publicity fanned anti-German and anticommunist passions, directing them against Andrews personally. The campaign collapsed in disaster (Numbers 1978; Starr 1982; Chasse 1994).

The AALL developed model programs for almost all problems—unemployment, occupational disease, excessive hours of work, old age poverty (Andrews 1915; Commons and Andrews 1936, 1–42). Progress was slow. But when the New Deal arrived, the AALL had a set of thoroughly researched proposals. Rarely, however, were these ideas implemented as desired. Ed Witte's labor proposal might constitute the only exception.

During his work on the USCIR, Witte, impressed by the British Trades Dispute Act of 1906, developed convictions about effectively removing such legal obstacles to labor organization as injunctions and yellow-dog contracts (Schlabach 1969, 61–63). Later, working as secretary to Congressman John Nelson of Wisconsin, Witte attacked the Clayton Anti-Trust Act, arguing that declaring that labor was an article of commerce was ineffectual window-dressing. In 1927, Witte got his chance to suggest an effective law. At the request of a subcommittee of the Senate Judiciary Committee, Witte joined Felix Frankfurter and Francis Sayre of Harvard, Herman Oliphant of Columbia University, and Donald E. Richberg, a labor lawyer. Together they hammered out the essential elements of what became, after four years of debate and modification, the Norris-LaGuardia Act, which effectively removed many obstacles to labor organization that Commons had listed in his minority report to the USCIR (Schlabach 1969, 69–71).

With the New Deal came the National Industrial Recovery Act (NIRA). The NIRA was designed by policy makers who wanted to hold income distributions constant and increase production (Dubofsky 1994, 109). Commons's students supported a weaker group—Senators George Norris and Robert Wagner, and Representatives Fiorello La Guardia and David Lewis. This group wanted to change the distribution of economic power. Senator Wagner managed to insert section 7a into the NIRA. Section 7a established workers' rights to unions and encouraged collective bargaining. Wagner chaired the National Labor Board empowered to enforce section 7a. William Leiserson served as the board's secretary. After the Supreme Court found the NIRA unconstitutional, Leiserson and Witte acted as consultants when Senator Wagner ordered his staff to write a bill protecting workers' right to organize. But the act that Wagner's staff wrote reflected his ideas, not those of the Commons gang. Wagner's staff, for example, made no provision for a permanent neutral industrial commission—a crucial component of any Commons type labor reform.

Congressional committees politicized the act when they rejected Wagner's tripartite governing committee and substituted a National Labor Relations Board (NLRB) appointed by the president with the approval by the Senate. President Roosevelt signed the National Labor Relations Act on July 5, 1935. Though the bill fell short of their ideals, Commons's students supported it and played crucial roles in assuring its survival, which appeared doubtful. The Supreme Court had vetoed five New Deal bills. Fifty corporate lawyers signed a pro bono brief calling the Wagner Act unconstitutional (Gross 1974, 172). For this reason, the NLRB gave priority to the act's constitutionality. J. Warren Madden, the board's first chairman, knew little about labor markets, but he was a competent lawyer. Madden placed lawyers in key positions and stressed the use of legal language (Gross 1974, 158).

The board hired David Saposs as director of economic research. Saposs organized a staff and developed evidence for court cases. Constitutionality revolved around the interstate commerce clause. Courts had ruled that this clause did not apply to manufacturing. Saposs and his staff focused on the interstate operations of the Jones and Laughlin Steel Corporation and on the social and economic effects of its unfair labor practices. The cases were argued before the Supreme Court on November 9, 10, and 11 of 1937. On April 12, 1937, the Court announced a series of decisions that by a 5 to 4 majority found the Wagner Act constitutional.

Commenting on David Saposs's contribution to the victory, James Gross wrote:

> Economic labor relations data helped build the case records on which the Supreme Court sustained the constitutionality of the Wagner Act in 1937. A few years later, J. Warren Madden would tell the Smith committee that the NLRB's development of the records in those cases was "a masterful job," "a perfectly splendid job," and that "a better piece of legal work has not been done." He might have added that there was no better illustration of the potency of a coordinated effort by the board's legal departments and the Division of Economic Research. (Gross 1974, 179)

Though the Wagner Act made it through the courts, it faced new dangers in Congress. Democrats held majorities in both houses, but southern Democrats allied with northern Republicans could kill or gut a law. Howard Smith of Virginia, chair of the House Rules Committee, wanted to gut the NLRA. The split between the AFL and the Congress of Industrial Organizations (CIO) put the board in a no-win situation. One board member, Edwin Smith, always sided with the CIO in disputed cases because he believed that workers had more power if they belonged to a large union. Consequently, the AFL joined employer groups and lobbied against the act.

Roosevelt appointed William Leiserson to the NLRB. Roosevelt hoped that Leiserson's reputation as a neutral mediator would mitigate criticism. Like Commons, Leiserson believed that government agencies should remain neutral in labor-management disputes. He objected to legal terminology that, in his view, confused workers and employers. He did not think that the government should impose laws, but rather that it should facilitate collective bargaining through which workers and employers would develop their own laws. Within the NLRB, Leiserson wanted to depend less on lawyers and more on economic research and mediation.

Lawyers dominated the NLRB. Consequently, sparks flew as soon as Leiserson arrived. He fired off many memos seeking to reduce centralization and give more authority to field offices. In questions of certifying the bargaining agent, Leiserson differed from other board members. J. Warren Madden, something of a civil libertarian, emphasized the right of individual workers to choose their own union. Edwin Smith wanted bargaining units to be as large as possible. Leiserson wanted to minimize government interference. This meant that, in industries where collective bargaining already existed, Madden would want a new election if some employees asked for it, Smith would favor a CIO-type organization, and Leiserson would favor existing arrangements.

When Madden's term expired, Roosevelt appointed Harry Millis. Millis, who, as an undergraduate, had studied under Commons at the University of Indiana, shared Leiserson's view. Roosevelt replaced Smith with Gerard Riley, who was pro-business. Leiserson could not save David Saposs, sacked in an anticommunist purge. In one sense, Leiserson failed. Economic analysis went out with David Saposs. Lawyer dominance increased over the years, and with it, the adversarial court model. The nation never got an industrial commission, and unions never achieved the status Leiserson wanted for them—publicly recognized representatives of all workers (Leiserson 1959, 8). In another sense, Leiserson succeeded. Representative Howard Smith's Rules Committee used his memos in ways that did some harm, but, by steering the NLRB toward the center, Leiserson saved it from the savage restructuring intended by Smith.

On June 29, 1934, with Executive Order No. 6757 President Roosevelt established the Committee on Economic Security (CES). He charged it with completing a comprehensive social security plan by December (Altmeyer 1966, 7). Edwin Witte was executive director, in charge of staff research. Arthur Altmeyer chaired the technical advisory committee. Since the staff was not assembled until August, the achievement of the CES was the creation of the entire social security structure in five months.[6]

Altmeyer headed the Social Security Administration from 1937 until 1953. He applied principles he had developed in his study of the Industrial Commission of Wisconsin (Altmeyer 1932, 308–24). In today's language, he established an "organizational culture" (Schein 1997). The Social Security Administration gained a reputation for efficiency and for a "client-serving ethic." This ethic earned a rebuke from the General Accounting Office, which accused Altmeyer of violating a law "prohibiting federal officials from encouraging claims against the government" (Derthick 1979, 30–31). Altmeyer held his ground. Of his first months, Arthur Schlesinger wrote:

> In the next months the Social Security Board swung into action with quiet efficiency. Facing an administrative challenge of staggering complexity, it operated with intelligence and competence. No New Deal agency solved such bewildering problems with such self-effacing smoothness. . . . For this prodigious achievement, founded on millions of records, clerks, and business machines, major credit went to Altmeyer. (Schlesinger 1959, 314–15)

Until 1973, praise continued for the agency's efficiency. It lasted past the retirements of Robert M. Ball, Social Security administrator, and Wilbur Cohen, secretary of health, education, and welfare at the end of the Johnson presidency (Derthick 1979, 18–19). Cohen, a Wisconsin graduate student, came to Washington with Witte and stayed on with Altmeyer. Ball, promoted from within, shared Altmeyer's views. They continued the tradition of incremental improvements through Medicaid, Medicare, and the beginning of Supplemental Security Income (Derthick 1979, 18–19). But the Social Security Administration was probably the only place in the national government where anything approached the ideals of the Commons gang—and here only in administration.

Generally, Commons's students could not push their own agendas. Witte's contribution to the Norris-LaGuardia Act was an exception. More often, the Commons gang supported policies they considered improvements, if less than ideal. And though praised at times, they did not escape criticism.

Why Were They Criticized?

Some critics name Commons or his students. Others attack the beliefs supporting their positions. This sketchy review starts with people who name names—policy and labor historians. It moves to those who do not—to economic historians, human resource managers, and economists of many stripes. Critics blamed Altmeyer and his successors for Social Security's real or imagined woes. Martha Derthick criticized them for encouraging a "myth" that gained political support for the expansion of benefits (Derthick 1979, 232). Derthick implied that they made the system too generous, and that this led to the financial woes of the seventies. But there is a substantial literature blaming them for being too stingy (Cates 1983; Skocpol and Ikenberry 1995). It starts with unemployment compensation.

In January 1932, Wisconsin passed the country's first constitutional unemployment compensation bill. The bill incorporated experience rating by requiring each firm to develop a compensation reserve financed by a payroll tax imposed on employers.[7] Experience rating was supposed to create an incentive for employers to reduce unemployment. Opponents of this "Wisconsin plan," Abraham Epstein, Isaac Rubinow, and Paul Douglas wanted compensation funded by employer, employee, and state contributions (Chasse 1991). Epstein and Rubinow, Eastern European immigrants, reasoned from convictions about state responsibility. They objected that experience rating would result in inadequate benefits. Douglas based his argument on the helplessness of individual firms during recessions. All three feared that a firm's workers would be abandoned once its reserves were exhausted. The final Social Security bill created a federal payroll tax that could be offset by state taxes financing unemployment compensation. The bill left states free to determine many details.

Jerry Cates, and later Theda Skocpol and John Ikenberry, repeated Epstein's objections, blaming current inadequacies in unemployment compensation on Witte, Altmeyer, and Commons (Cates 1983, 23–25; Skocpol and Ikenberry 1995, 148–60). They also blamed the "Wisconsin school" for weaknesses in other income maintenance programs. Depending largely on Cates's research, Skocpol and Ikenberry accused Altmeyer of keeping welfare payments demeaning and inadequate in order to protect the social insurance component of the system. Cates based his case on records of discussions and memos between Altmeyer and his staff in Washington. According to these records, Altmeyer insisted on strict accounting for assets of public assistance recipients and refused to enforce minimum benefit standards on states. In his left liberal critique and in his use of documents, Cates owes much to "new labor history."

New labor history started as a rebellion against the labor history of Commons and Perlman, who identified labor history with union history. Their methods appeared, from the standpoint of modern historiography, deficient (Brody 1980, 1983). Many new labor historians came from working-class backgrounds into a discipline long dominated by Anglo-Saxon Protestant elites. They wanted to study their own stories, stories of working people, not just stories of unions (Montgomery 1980). Next to the works of historians like Oscar Handlin, Richard Hofstadter, and C. Vann Woodward, Commons school products appeared unimaginative and boring. The British historian E.P. Thompson (1963) wrote a brilliant Marxist study of English working classes. Anxious to repeat his analysis for the United States, the new labor historians attacked Perlman's contention that workers were "job conscious," not class conscious, and they rejected Commons's position that expanding markets were the main cause of worker discontent and union organization in the United States (Commons 1909, 76). Alan Dawley, for example, demonstrated statistically that the Knights of St. Crispin in Lynn, Massachusetts, were wageworkers, not independent craftsmen, as Commons had claimed (Dawley 1976).[8]

Gabriel Kolko's *Triumph of Conservatism* exerted a strong influence on new labor historians. Kolko defined conservatism as "the attempt to preserve existing power and social relationships" (Kolko 1963, 2). He maintained that trust barons, threatened by competitive forces, promoted regulatory bodies to quiet discontent and squelch competition. Kolko claimed that progressive academics such as Richard T. Ely and John R. Commons were not interested in democratic control of the economy because "this would have meant the end of private property as then understood." Rather they tried to prevent socialism by "encouraging conservative unionism" (Kolko 1963, 214–15). James Weinstein (1968) applied Kolko's thinking to labor markets, proposing the thesis of "the liberal corporate state"—that the entire legal framework from the progressive era through the New Deal was the work of corporate leaders silencing dissent and maintaining control of the economy. Radical economists accepted the corporate liberal hypothesis (Edwards, Reich, and Weisskopf 1972; O'Connor 1973).

A related position in the legal literature argued that the NLRB and court decisions perverted Senator Wagner's original intent and made workers worse off than they had been before the Wagner Act's passage (Klare 1978; Tomlins 1985). Tomlins puts some of the blame on Leiserson. Wagner, he argued, wanted to change the legal conception of the union as a principal to that of an agent of the workers. But the concept of the union as principal was reinstated, robbing workers of their voice. Before Leiserson, the NLRB had defended the

agent conception, allowing workers to change unions after a contract had run one year. Leiserson at that time also seemed to support the agent concept (Tomlins 1985, 234). Once on the board, however, Leiserson's insistence on accepting existing contracts led him to defend entrenched unions with closed shop contracts (Tomlins 1985, 236–37). This meant that courts slighted member rights while protecting union rights to enforce contracts.

While labor historians moved left, economic historians moved right. Enthusiastic about applied microeconomics and about law and economics literature, they focused on market incentives and property rights. They questioned conventional wisdom about labor market discrimination (Higgs 1977) and the evils of the company store (Fishback 1986; Fishback and Lauzus 1989). They treated unions like antisocial rent-seeking monopolies (North, Anderson, and Hill 1983, 160, 167). They directly contradicted the Commons gang's belief in the social value of independent trade unions—and in this, they reflected a growing conventional wisdom that unions were, if not dangerous, irrelevant.

Within the corporate sector, opposition to Commons's defense of independent unions took the form of what Sanford Jacoby (1997) called modern manors—new feudalisms with managers as noble lords. When Commons outlined his position on centralized bargaining, William Mackenzie King, working for John D. Rockefeller Jr., proposed one type of modern manor—employee representation (Commons and Harriman 1916; Gitelman 1988). Elton Mayo, an Australian psychiatrist who studied group behavior, provided academic backing. Mayo, like Commons, wanted to render workplaces more humane. Unlike Commons, Mayo saw no conflict of interest in employment transactions. He opposed both unions and government intervention in the workplace (Schatz 1993, 91). Mayo's work grounded a Platonic theory of management.

Business schools would educate managerial philosopher kings who would rule with wisdom and prudence. Such a system left no room for participation by a rabble of uneducated workers.

Keynesian economists were equally Platonic. Keynes, a pure Platonist, disliked union leaders. He placed them together with business leaders in the warrior class, governed by animal spirits rather than by intellect (Keynes 1972, vol. 9, p. 319). For American Keynesians who melded neoclassical economics with Keynesian aggregate demand management, unemployment was mainly a macroeconomic issue. Unions can exacerbate the trade-off between unemployment and inflation by contributing to a wage-price spiral or, in later theory, by increasing the natural rate of unemployment (Layard, Nickell, and Jackman 1991, 83–149).

The rise of rational expectations and real business cycle theory increased the neoclassical twist of macroeconomics (Lucas and Sargent 1978). Neoclassical economics, with its deductions from rationally self-interested individuals, raised other questions about beliefs behind the Wisconsin agenda. Wage differentials compensate workers for accepting the risk of injury. Generous workers' compensation payments create a moral hazard. In the extreme case, workers are more willing to risk injury because they can expect compensation. A more credible case can be made for workers remaining out of the labor force longer because they are receiving payments. But the extreme case has been seriously advanced (Fishback and Kantor 2000). Generous unemployment compensation benefits create a similar moral hazard, creating an incentive for unemployed workers to remain outside the workforce.

The conventional wisdom rejecting the value of unions spread across the spectrum of economic opinion. H. Gregg Lewis's influential study of relative wages seemed to show that unions achieve benefits for their members at the expense of other work-ers (Lewis 1963). Within public choice theory, unions were viewed as "special interests" using their political power to exploit the average voter (Olson 1971). John Kenneth Galbraith, backing away from his theory of countervailing power, portrayed unions as organizations whose social usefulness had passed. Union membership began to decline in 1957, but Galbraith predicted that some unions would survive because of organizational inertia and because some unions support corporate planning structures (Galbraith 1967, 3, 262–81). Most economists simply ignored unions as irrelevant. In the United States, articles about unions in three major journals declined from 9 percent in 1940 to 0.5 percent in 1970, and of 350 articles in three major British journals, only 3 dealt with unions in 1970. (Hirsch and Addison 1986, 1)

What Is the Verdict of History?

The criticisms advanced by labor historians boil down to the corporate liberal hypothesis. The criticism implied by economic historians and economists of various stripes reduces to an assumption of the superiority of free, unfettered markets. Criticisms of the Wisconsin school's role in social insurance policy rest on assumptions about precisely what that role was and about such things as the effect of experience rating. The conventional wisdom about unions—now seriously questioned—undermines the Commons gang's model of the labor market. This section examines each of these criticisms in the light of history, concluding with the tenability of the historical model assumed by the Commons gang.

History and the Corporate Liberal Hypothesis

History weakens the corporate liberal hypothesis. Management fought every initiative advanced by

Commons and his students. Most managers and their "impartial" National Civic Federation even fought the AALL workers' compensation proposals (Moss 1996, 130–31). The Chamber of Commerce supported Social Security. There was a Business Advisory Group for the Committee on Economic Security, but the members were handpicked by Frances Perkins, the secretary of labor. The National Association of Manufacturers (NAM), the Illinois Manufacturers' Association, and the Ohio Manufacturers' Association violently opposed the Social Security Act (Witte 1962a, 89–90; Tynes 1996, 46, 57, 67–68). As for advocating "conservative unions," Melvyn Dubofsky cites continuous management attacks on unions, noting that not a single "corporate liberal" ever appeared to support the Wagner Act (Dubofsky 1994, 130). Sanford Jacoby cited the formation of management coalitions aimed at "tempering and taming" government (Jacoby 1997, 193). He also chronicled Fred Crawford's defiance of the NLRB. Crawford, the president of Thompson Products (now TRW), spearheaded the National Association of Manufacturers campaign that resulted in the passage of the Taft-Hartley Act (Jacoby 1997, 199–203). Ruthless management assaults on unions continue (Bronfenbrenner 1994; Lichtenstein 2002, 106–10). It is hard to portray the objects of such opposition as tools of "corporate liberals."

History and the Free Market Critique

There are two objections against studies purporting to show that the market economy worked well. First, such studies select data. Second, they do not touch the position that workers bore most of the costs of economic growth. To say markets worked well is to close out all sorts of information, some gathered by Commons and his students (Commons and Leiserson 1914), some by the United States

Industrial Commission (Manly 1916), much gathered by others (Patterson 2000, 3–18). John Andrews (1910) showed that, at least in the case of matches, firms were falsifying information. Statistical analysis of firm data in this case would definitely put the "con" into econometrics. But free market arguments, even if true, leave standing the position of Commons and his students that workers bore most costs of economic growth—unemployment, injury, occupational disease, early death, and poverty in old age.

History and Unemployment Compensation

The verdict on unemployment compensation is mixed. Critics make erroneous assumptions about the positions of Witte and Altmeyer and about experience rating. They may be correct about the theoretical superiority of a national versus a federal system, but they underweigh fears about political feasibility and constitutionality before 1936. Witte harbored doubts about experience rating (Schlabach 1969, 91). Altmeyer's views are hard to fathom, but he must not have felt strongly. Secretary Perkins and Altmeyer told Witte to avoid hiring staff members "strongly committed" to either side (Witte 1962a, 28). Epstein was not on the staff, but neither were Raushenbush, Groves, or other proponents of experience rating.

Commons's first bill created a statewide mutual insurance company. Common's bill was introduced into the Wisconsin State legislature every year from 1921 to 1930, but it never passed in that liberal state. William Leiserson, a Commons ally, wrote the Ohio plan, later proposed as a model by critics of the Wisconsin school. The Ohio legislature rejected that plan. In 1931, Paul Raushenbush and Harold Groves wrote a bill requiring firms to accumulate their own reserves. Groves cited as major inspirations for the bill Arthur Cecil Pigou's *Economics of Welfare* (1924), John Maurice Clark's *Economics of Overhead Costs* (1923), and Commons's merit-rated workers' compensation (Groves 1969, 147 addendum). The bill passed. In 1936, the legislature added partial pooling of reserves so that if a firm's reserves ran out, its employees would receive benefits from the pooled fund (Altmeyer 1963, 124).

Everyone feared Supreme Court rejection of a national plan (Perkins 1946, 291). Elizabeth Brandeis conveyed this fear to her father. The Supreme Court justice suggested the tax-offset provision not just to Elizabeth, but indirectly to Senator Wagner. Paul Raushenbush, at Wagner's request, wrote tax offsets into the first draft of the Wagner-Lewis unemployment compensation bill. Wagner withdrew the bill because President Roosevelt wanted to include unemployment compensation in a comprehensive Social Security bill (Raushenbush and Raushenbush 1979, 173–85). The Social Security bill kept the tax-offset provision and gave states considerable freedom in designing benefit levels and experience rating programs.

After the Supreme Court approved the National Labor Relations and Social Security Acts, fears about constitutionality abated. In 1938, Altmeyer complained that interaction between freedom to set benefit levels and to design experience rating permitted southern states to reduce taxes by reducing benefits. In 1941, he advocated a national system (Altmeyer 1966, 85, 133). The critics were right about the problems of a fiscal federal system. They were wrong about the motives of the Wisconsin school. They were wrong about experience rating.

The assumed conflict between adequacy and experience rating is spurious (Becker 1972, 29–42). Wisconsin never denied a claimant because a company's reserves were depleted (Becker 1972,

17). Experience rating creates an incentive for firms to reduce layoffs in downturns and to hire more slowly in recoveries. Empirical evidence consistently shows that experience rating reduces layoffs by between 20 and 50 percent, though the lower figure is probably more accurate (Card and Levine 1997; Anderson 1993; Anderson and Meyer 1993; Albrecht and Vroman 1999).[9] Evidence about the reduction in new hires is less abundant, but that reduction seems smaller than the one in layoffs.

History and Old Age Support

Critics blamed Witte and Altmeyer for inadequate benefits in old age assistance for its means test, for regressive payroll tax financing of old age insurance—and for a "mythic" justification that permitted a reckless expansion of benefits. Some of these criticisms reflect confusion about the autonomy of various actors in the creation of the Social Security program. Witte and Altmeyer were not members of the Committee on Economic Security.[10] They guided the staff, contributed to discussions, and drafted the proposal, but the proposal reflected committee consensus. President Roosevelt, the autonomous actor, rejected universal non–means-tested support programs (Martin 1976, 345). He also insisted on two separate systems because Congress could easily cut appropriations from general revenues (Perkins 1946, 284). With respect to old age insurance, the committee proposal called for general revenue supplements to payroll tax collections after 1965, the year in which actuaries projected that recipients of old age insurance would outnumber old age assistance recipients (Altmeyer 1966, 26). When Roosevelt saw the report, he insisted on a self-supporting system that did not depend on general tax revenues (Witte 1962a, 74; Altmeyer 1966, 29). Henry Morgenthau, Secretary of the Treasury, the last witness before the House Ways and Means Committee, presented Roosevelt's proposal. It doubled the payroll taxes in the original proposal. When Rexford Guy Tugwell, Undersecretary of Agriculture and a member of Roosevelt's braintrust complained to Roosevelt about the regressive nature of the payroll tax, the president replied:

> I guess you're right on the economics, but those taxes were never a problem of economics. They are politics all the way through. We put those payroll contributions there so as to give the contributors a legal, moral and political right to collect their pensions and their unemployment benefits. With those taxes in there, no damn politician can ever scrap my social security program. (Schlesinger 1959, 308–9)

In addition, critics blamed Altmeyer for the inadequacy of old age assistance benefits paid by many states (Cates 1983; Skocpol and Ikenberry 1995, 160–64). The language proposed by the committee required that states provide income "adequate to support a reasonable subsistence compatible with decency and health." The House Ways and Means Committee struck that phrase from the bill (Altmeyer 1966, 35). In the Senate, Senator Harry Byrd forced Witte to admit that someone in the federal government would decide the monetary value of a reasonable subsistence, and the Finance Committee removed the phrase (Altmeyer 1966, 39). Altmeyer later complained that the absence of a uniform need definition prevented the Social Security Administration from forcing states to provide adequate old age assistance (Altmeyer 1966, 80). The internal documents on which Cates based his argument simply reveal Altmeyer following congressional intent.

There are two responses to those who fault Altmeyer for the "myth" that contributions created a right. First, Altmeyer and Witte opposed the 1939 amendments that changed the system from reserve to pay-go financing. By ignoring accruing liabilities, Witte argued, the Vandenberg amendments would lead to future higher taxes and crises, and, more importantly, the pay-go debate distracted attention from the dire state of people not yet eligible for insurance benefits (Witte 1940, 119; 1962b, 10). Altmeyer fretted that the rate of return for contributions might fall below the rate of return on government bonds, robbing the program of popular support (Schieber and Shoven 1999, 87). Altmeyer envisioned investing some funds in private securities—somewhat along the lines of today's Calvert Fund or the TIAA-CREF Social Choice Account (Schieber and Shoven 1999, 70). The Supreme Court majority, in the case denying property rights to a Social Security pensioner, did so, in part, by rejecting the annuity analogy.[11] Had Witte and Altmeyer prevailed, the analogy would have been stronger.

Second, their alleged "myth" makes sense in the context of a Léon Bourgeois quasi-contract. The current generation raises the next generation and contributes to the support of older generations—gaining thereby the right to support by the generation it has raised. Finally, the term "myth" rests on a debatable concept of property, a concept reflecting the view of what Commons called the "dominant class."

History, Unions, and the Market Economy

History offers a test of the conventional wisdom that denies the relevance of unions and, by implication, the Commons gang's assumptions about the U.S. economy. Union membership climbed to 35 percent of the labor force just after World War II and then started falling. Many authors argue that the Taft-Hartley Act had little effect on unions or collective bargaining. Nelson Lichtenstein disagrees (2001, 117–22). By making supervisors ineligible for union membership, the act converted frontline union organizers into frontline management opposition. It permitted extensive management "communication" with employees. It outlawed closed shops and legalized so-called right-to-work laws. If the hypothesis on which Commons and his gang operated was incorrect, and the conventional wisdom was correct, the decline of unions would have no demonstrable negative effect, and there would be no evidence to support the position that weak bargaining power forces workers to bear the external costs of economic growth. Unfortunately, recent history has not refuted the assumptions under which the Commons gang operated.

In 1946, the CIO launched Operation Dixie, an aggressive organizing campaign south of the Mason-Dixon line (Griffith 1988; Lichtenstein 2002, 103–4). Unions wanted to prevent corporations from moving plants out of the unionized North to the low-wage South. The Taft-Hartley Act facilitated the counterattack of southern oligarchs who pioneered strategies still used by law firms specializing in union defeat. They try to subvert NLRB elections by confusing and frightening employees. Tactics include illegal firings, threats of plant shutdown, litigious delay, misinformation, and intimidation of workers (Lichtenstein 2002, 113; Bronfenbrenner 1994).

During the 1957–58 recession, a Senate committee dominated by antiunion southern Democrats and northern Republicans investigated union corruption. Lichtenstein notes that the committee's chief counsel, Robert Kennedy, typified late twentieth-century liberals in his "initial ignorance about all things working-class" (Lichtenstein 2002, 164). The committee's activities resulted in the Landrum Griffin Bill and declining union popularity. According to Gallup polls, public approval of unions dropped from 76 percent in 1957 to below 50 per-

cent in the 1960s (Lichtenstein 2002, 164). Union membership and influence declined steadily.

The growth of the civil rights movement combined with loose labor markets created problems that unions could not solve (Dubofsky 1994, 198). Though some AFL unions had racist backgrounds, the CIO had consistently supported civil rights. Dubofsky maintains that the Civil Rights Act of 1965 would not have passed without union support. Nevertheless, when firms began layoffs, minorities held the most vulnerable positions. By 1986 a book, influential in industrial relations circles, argued that the initiative in worker welfare lay no longer with unions but with human resource departments of large firms. Elton Mayo's philosopher kings had replaced the industrial democracy of John R. Commons (Kochan, Katz, and McKersie 1986).

A surge of takeovers by corporate raiders compelled managers to pay more attention to shareholder value (Osterman 1999, 33–67). The rising power of institutional investors forced a focus on short-term profits (Useem 1996, 25). As a result, firms shed workers even when profits were rising. The "high performance workplace" increased productivity and profits, but it did not benefit workers unless they were unionized (Osterman 1993, 107–13; Fairris 2002). The new power realities wreaked havoc with Elton Mayo's dream.

Boards of directors sacked CEOs at IBM, Kodak, and General Motors because their humane policies conflicted with the goal of "increasing shareholder value" (Osterman 1999, 66). In 1986 Kochan, Katz, and McKersie had cited IBM, Sears, Citicorp, Xerox, and Aetna as models of the new humane employer. David Brody pointed out that between 1986 and 1991 IBM eliminated 65,000 jobs. Sears, Citicorp, Xerox, and Aetna—all were forced into actions that conflicted with the interests of their employees. "Suddenly," Brody wrote, "instead of celebrating the new industrial relations, there are lamentations over the corrosive effects of job insecurity on employee motivation." Brody cited surveys of the Opinion Research Corporation. The percentage of white-collar employees who rated their firms favorably in terms of fairness fell between 1950 and 1980 from 80 percent to 40 percent. Among clerical workers, approval ratings for fairness fell from 70 to 20 percent. Brody added that the same sense of injustice prevailed before the rise of industrial unionism (Brody 1993, 259–61).

The decline of union power in the 1970s coincided with falling real wages, increasing poverty levels, and widening income distributions—even as GDP was rising (Danziger and Gottschalk 1993). Between 1979 and 1995, 40 percent of the workforce experienced an earnings decline of 10 percent or more (Osterman 1999, 77). The decline of manufacturing affected both earnings and union membership in all countries. But there was something unique about the United States. The bottom third of American workers earn less than the bottom third in Germany, Australia, or Sweden (Freeman 1999, 38–39). Homelessness, first noticed in 1981, became a chronic symptom of the declining middle class (O'Flaherty 1996). The reasons for increasing income disparity are many and disputed. Skill differentials have increased, but there are problems with conventional explanations—globalization and decline of manufacturing (Murphy and Welch 1993; Galbraith 1998). The globalization hypothesis resurrects the competitive menace with a new name: "the race to the bottom" (Palley 1998).

The decline of unions seems to explain 20 percent of the increasing dispersion of earnings (Card 1992; Freeman 1993). Using better data, Freeman questioned the conclusions of H. Gregg Lewis's 1963 study. Freeman found that unions reduce wage dispersion among both union and nonunion workers and lift blue-collar incomes closer to white-collar incomes (Freeman 1980; 1982). Then, Lewis reversed his earlier positions (1986). Case studies support this conclusion (Waddoups 2002). In addition, case studies of plant relocation and of deregulation support the suspicion that workers bear most costs of economic restructuring and growth (Rothstein 1986; Belman and Monaco 2001). History has not refuted the conceptualization of the labor market under which Commons and his gang operated.

That conceptualization can be partially translated into the language of monopsonistic and oligopsonistic markets. Such markets seem more pervasive than previously thought (Dickens, Machin, and Manning 1999; Bhaskar, Manning, and To 2002). James Galbraith disputes the skill explanation for growth at the high end of the wage scale (Galbraith 1998). Galbraith divides industries into three classes: capital or knowledge-good industries tend toward monopoly and can share rents with their workers. Service industries are the least concentrated and, though Galbraith does not use the term, most subject to the "competitive menace." Consumer-good industries lie in the middle. Galbraith makes the case that sharing of monopoly rents explains growing wage disparity better than skill differentials. Add Schumpeterian instability of monopoly, and a picture reappears similar to the one painted by Commons and his students in the *History of Labor*.

What Remains?

Critics correctly saw the narrowness of the labor market lens through which Commons and his students viewed the economy, but the critics themselves suffered from blind spots. They failed to separate what happened from what the Commons gang tried to do and why they tried to do it. What happened was a dual welfare system with all its problems (Tussing 1975). What they tried to do would still define a progressive agenda in the United States.

Suppose Altmeyer and Witte had succeeded in everything they tried to do. There would now be minimum standards for all social security and income maintenance programs—measured by an "income adequate to support a reasonable subsistence compatible with decency and health" (Altmeyer 1966, 35, 80). After fear of an adverse Supreme Court decision abated, Altmeyer advocated a national unemployment compensation system, or, failing that, strict standards for benefits, removal of the maximum on taxable wages, national eligibility standards, and actuarially sound experience rating. Altmeyer also supported national health insurance. And, of course, the AALL lobbied for other policies such as countercyclical fiscal policy.

Their position on unions is harder to assess. The NLRA reflects Senator Wagner's ideas and these only imperfectly. The United States never tried either Commons's centralized system or his neutral industrial commission. Moreover, economists of all stripes generally tend to mistrust union power. Even today, mainstream economics harbors foaming-mouthed union haters and advocates of individual bargaining who consider the decline of unions to be a good thing (Reynolds 1987; Troy 1999). The concomitants of union decline, cited above, weaken those positions.

Macroeconomists still find relations between union strength and the natural rate of unemployment (Layard et al. 1991, 83–143). But questions are increasingly raised about the natural rate of unemployment—and about the reliability and validity of unemployment rates themselves (Galbraith 1998; Wray and Pigeon 2000; Katz 2002). Even ignoring these qualifications, the relation

between unions and unemployment disappears for the centralized bargaining that Commons proposed (Layard et al. 1991, 129–35; European Commission 1999, 137).

Still some scholars worry about the decline of unions, and they have resurrected proposals that Commons advanced more than eighty years ago. Richard Block proposed creation of a tripartite national commission to investigate labor practices and suggest changes that would keep labor laws abreast of changing work environments. This normal maintenance, Block argued, would fill the role played by debate in parliamentary systems (Block 1994, 158–59). Commons made the same proposal in his minority report for the National Industrial Relations Commission. Dorothy Sue Cobble suggested removal of restrictions on all union tactics and removal of the need for union certification as a prerequisite to collective bargaining (Cobble 1994, 297–98). Commons suggested removal of all restrictions on union tactics and advised against government certification of unions, though he later offered qualified approval of the NLRB. Cobble also suggested centralized bargaining, which was the centerpiece of the system Commons proposed (Cobble 1994, 296; Commons and Harriman 1916, 214–15).

If all these changes were made, after-tax poverty levels would decline in the United States, but not to levels currently existing in the major European countries (Smeeding 1992). The Commons gang focused on poverty caused by labor market problems. Even as Commons wrote, Paul Douglas (1925) was arguing that no labor market reform could overcome the effect of family size on poverty. Later, Gunnar Myrdal (1944) highlighted perverse racial policies. When he proposed the Area Redevelopment Act, Senator Paul Douglas found another cause. But Congress later gutted the Area Redevelopment Act, and Gunnar Myrdal's book had little effect on racial inequities.

It took a black pastor, leading a formerly excluded group, to force ruling coalitions to add the concept of civil rights to their concepts of justice. This was how Commons envisioned social progress in his *A Sociological View of Sovereignty*. And it illustrates the sense in which Commons and his students differed from most other analysts. They were process-oriented rather than results-oriented. They incorporated freedom of assembly and specific policy proposals in one vision. The AALL started a process that produced a "seedtime" for the New Deal (Chambers 1963). Altmeyer, Cohen, and Ball—using solidarist logic that sounds like a shell game to individualist critics—justified another process in the Social Security Administration. And the process started by Dr. Martin Luther King may provide a justification for revising our labor laws.

Nelson Lichtenstein contrasts two cases (2002, 178–80). In one case, a group of African American employees sued Shoney's Corporation for discrimination. They were awarded $132 million. At about the same time, some Latin American women at California Sprint Corporation's *La Conexion Familiar* in San Francisco decided to form a union. Their pay was low; they were monitored on toilet and drinking water breaks; they faced demanding production quotas. Just before the NLRB election, Sprint closed the plant. The NLRB cited Sprint for fifty labor law violations, "including interrogation, bribes, threats, fabricating evidence," and firing workers for union activity. The NLRB ordered Sprint to reopen the plant. Sprint refused, appealed, and won. The women received no compensation. Could the process of civil rights expand beyond individual rights to collective rights?

Conclusion

The labor market lens through which Commons's students viewed poverty permitted them to define

rights above and beyond the charity given historically to the "undeserving poor." But that same lens closed out people condemned to poverty by other "social facts." In this sense, many critics had a point. But while their labor market lens narrowed their vision in one respect, it gave the students, in other respects, a broader perspective than that of many of their critics. For Commons's students, unions, freedom of assembly, and social security all comprised a single never-completed process of searching to remove unfairness from society. Ironically, in 1996, the Personal Responsibility and Work Opportunity Act ignored the labor market conditions that so occupied Commons and his students, and subsequent events underlined the importance of the process to which they tried to contribute (Northrop 1991; Kim and Mergoupis 1997; Peterson 2000; Ehrenreich 2001).[11]

Notes

This paper is a revision of one given at the annual meeting of the New York State Economics Association. A. Dale Tussing found real mistakes and made helpful comments on that paper. Dell Champlin and Janet Knoedler also suggested many improvements.

1. Harold Groves wrote of Commons that "He was under par in the powers of oral expression and seldom if ever eloquent. The secret of his success lay in his skillful use of the project method, his extraordinary dedication, his personal charm and his personal relations with his students" (Groves 1969, 117).

2. Articles summarizing their thinking are collected in *Labor and Administration* (Commons 1913), in introductory chapters to volumes of the history project (Commons and Andrews 1910; Commons 1918; Saposs 1918; Perlman and Taft 1935), and especially in (Commons 1909).

3. Harold Groves wrote of Perlman and Saposs: "I noted that Selig Perlman and David Saposs were both very Jewish, that they argued incessantly, and agreed on nothing" (Groves 1969, 119).

4. Adams (1966) wrote the definitive history of the commission. Commons's autobiography is not trustworthy here.

5. For more information about the AALL, see Chasse (1991).

6. Witte and Altmeyer must share credit with many others. Witte (1962a, 22–35) lists them all. Barbara Armstrong headed the social insurance group. Brilliant, dedicated, volatile, and acid, she called Witte "half-Witte" and Altmeyer "quarter-Witte" (Schlabach 1969, 109–12; Schieber and Shoven 1999, 31).

7. Joseph Becker (1972) provides the best historical and analytical treatment of experience rating.

8. Dawley missed the point of "American Shoemakers." He thought Commons was defending laissez-faire economics (Dawley 1976, 180–82).

9. Levine (1997) summarizes theory and evidence since 1970 with references to literature reviews.

10. The committee members were Frances Perkins, secretary of labor; Henry Morgenthau, secretary of the treasury; Henry Wallace, secretary of agriculture; Homer Cummings, attorney general; and Harry Hopkins, federal emergency relief administrator.

11. The case was *Flemming v. Nestor* 363 U.S. 603. Opinions of the majority and minority can be found at http://www.ssa.gov/history/nestor.html.

12. The program pushed "welfare mothers" into low-wage, dead-end jobs. Unable to afford child care, many had to leave their children to the streets, and when they lost those jobs, they were ineligible for unemployment compensation because of tightening requirements resulting from Reagan administration policies (Peterson 2000, 518).

References

Adams, Graham. *The Age of Industrial Violence 1910–1915: The Activities and Findings of the U.S. Commission on Industrial Relations*. New York: Columbia University Press, 1966.

Adams, Thomas S., and Helen L. Sumner. *Labor Problems: A Textbook*. New York: Macmillan, 1905.

Albrecht, James W., and Susan B. Vroman. "Unemployment Compensation Finance and Efficiency Wages." *Journal of Labor Economics* 17, no. 1 (January 1999): 141–67.

Altmeyer, Arthur. *The Industrial Commission of Wisconsin: A Case Study in Labor Law Administration*. Madison: University of Wisconsin Press, 1932.

———. "The Development of Social Security." In *Labor, Management and Social Policy: Essays in the John R. Commons Tradition*, ed. Gerald G. Somers. Madison: University of Wisconsin Press, 1963.

———. *The Formative Years of Social Security*. Madison: University of Wisconsin Press, 1966.

Anderson, Patricia M. "Linear Adjustment Costs and Seasonal Labor Demand: Evidence from Retail Trade Firms." *Quarterly Journal of Economics* 108 (November 1993): 1015–42.

Anderson, Patricia M., and Bruce D. Meyer. "Unemployment Insurance in the United States: Layoff Incentives and Cross Subsidies." *Journal of Labor Economics* 11 (January 1993): S70–S95.

Andrews, John B. *American Bureau of Industrial Research: Leaflet No. 3*. Mimeo. Madison, Wisconsin, 1907.

———. "Phosphorus Poisoning in the Match Industry." *United States Bureau of Labor Bulletin*, no. 86 (January 1910): 31–146.

———. "A Practical Program for the Prevention of Unemployment in America." *American Labor Legislation Review* 5, no. 2 (June 1915): 171–92.

———. *Administrative Labor Legislation: A Study of American Experience in the Delegation of Legislative Power*. New York and London: Harpers, 1936.

Becker, Joseph M. *Experience Rating in Unemployment Insurance: An Experiment in Competitive Socialism*. Baltimore: Johns Hopkins University Press, 1972.

Belman, Dale, and Kristen Monaco. "The Effects of Deregulation, Deunionization, Technology, and Human Capital on the Work and Work Lives of Truck Drivers." *Industrial and Labor Relations Review* 54, no. 2A (2001): 502–24.

Bhaskar, V., Alan Manning, and Ted To. "Oligopsony and Monopsonistic Competition in Labor Markets." *Journal of Economic Perspectives* 16, no. 2 (Spring 2002): 155–74.

Block, Richard, N. "Reforming U.S. Labor Law and Collective Bargaining: Some Proposals Based on the Canadian System." In *Restoring the Promise of American Labor Law*, ed. Sheldon Friedman, Richard Hurd, Rudolph Oswald, and Ronald Seeber. Ithaca, NY: ILR Press, 1994.

Bourgeois, Léon. "International Organization of Social Policies." *American Labor Legislation Review* 4, no. 1 (March 1914): 186–202.

———. *Solidarité*. Paris: Armand Colin, 1931.

Brandeis, Elizabeth. "Labor Legislation." In *History of Labor in the United States*, vol. 3, ed. John R. Commons, Don D. Lescohier, and Elizabeth Brandeis. 1935. Reprint, New York: Augustus M. Kelley, 1966.

Brittain, John A. *The Payroll Tax for Social Security*. Washington, DC: Brookings Institution Press, 1972.

Brody, David. "The Old Labor History and the New: In Search of the American Working Class." *Labor History* 20, no. 1 (Winter 1980): 111–26.

———. "Workers and Work in America: The New Labor

History." In *Ordinary People and Everyday Life: Perspectives on the New Labor History*, ed. James B. Gardner and Rollie Adams. Nashville, TN: American Association for State and Local History, 1983.

———. *Workers in Industrial America*. 2nd ed. New York: Oxford University Press, 1993.

Bronfenbrenner, Kate L. "Employer Behavior in Certification Elections and First-Contract Campaigns: Implications for Labor Law Reform." In *Restoring the Promise of American Labor Law*, ed. Sheldon Friedman, Richard Hurd, Rudolph Oswald, and Ronald Seeber. Ithaca, NY: ILR Press, 1994.

Bücher, Carl. *Carl Bücher's Industrial Evolution*. Trans. S. Morley Wickett. New York: Holt, 1902.

Card, David. "The Effect of Unions on the Distribution of Wages: Redistribution or Relabeling?" *NBER Working Paper* no. 4195, October 1992.

Card, David, and Philip Levine, "Unemployment Insurance, Taxes, and the Cyclical and Seasonal Properties of Unemployment." *Journal of Public Economics* 53 (January 1994): 1-29.

Cates, Jerry D. *Insuring Inequality: Administrative Leadership in Social Security*. Ann Arbor: University of Michigan Press, 1983.

Chambers, Clark. *Seedtime of Reform*. Minneapolis: University of Minnesota Press, 1963.

Chasse, J. Dennis. "John R. Commons and the Democratic State." *Journal of Economic Issues* 20, no. 2 (September 1986): 759–84.

———. "The American Association for Labor Legislation: An Episode in Institutionalist Policy Analysis." *Journal of Economic Issues* 24, no. 3 (September 1991): 799–827.

———. "The American Association for Labor Legislation and the Institutionalist Tradition in National Health Insurance." *Journal of Economic Issues* (December 1994): 1063–90.

Clark, John Maurice. *Studies in the Economics of Overhead Costs*. Chicago: University of Chicago Press, 1923.

Cobble, Dorothy Sue. "Making Postindustrial Unionism Possible." In *Restoring the Promise of American Labor Law*, ed. Sheldon Friedman, Richard Hurd, Rudolph Oswald, and Ronald Seeder. Ithaca, NY: ILR Press, 1994.

Commons, John R. *Proportional Representation*. Boston: Thomas Crowell, 1896.

———. *A Sociological View of Sovereignty*. 1899–1900. Reprint, New York: A.M. Kelley, 1967.

———. "American Shoemakers, 1648–1895: A Sketch of Industrial Evolution." *Quarterly Journal of Economics* 24 (November 1909): 39–83.

———. *Labor and Administration*. New York: Macmillan, 1913.

———. "Introduction." In *History of Labor in the United States*, Vol. 1, ed. John R. Commons, David J. Saposs, Helen L. Sumner, E.B. Mittelman, H.E. Hoagland, John B. Andrews, and Selig Perlman, 1918. Reprint, New York: Augustus M. Kelley, 1966.

———. *Industrial Goodwill*. 1919. Reprint, New York: Arno Press, 1969.

———. *Trade Unionism and Labor Problems*. 2nd series. New York: Ginn and Company, 1921.

———. *Myself*. New York: Macmillan, 1934.

———. *The Economics of Collective Action*. New York: Macmillan, 1950.

Commons, John R., and John B. Andrews. "Introduction to Volumes IX and X." In *The Documentary History of American Industrial Society*, ed. John R. Commons et al. Cleveland: Arthur H. Clark, 1910.

Commons John R., and John B. Andrews. *Principals of Labor Legislation*. 4th revised edition. 1936 reprint. New York: Augustus M. Kelley, 1967.

Commons, John R. and, Florence Harriman. "Report of Commissioners John R. Commons and Florence J. Harriman." In *Final Report of the Commission on Industrial Relations*. Senate Document No. 415. 64th Cong., 1st sess., 169–230. Washington, DC: Government Printing Office, 1916.

Commons John R., and William Leiserson. "Wage-Earners of Pittsburgh." In *Wage-Earning Pittsburgh*, ed. Paul Underwood Kellog, 1914. Reprint, New York: Arno Press, 1974.

Commons, John R., Ulrich B. Phillips, Eugene A. Gilmore, Helen L. Sumner, and John B. Andrews. *Documentary History of American Industrial Society*. 11 vols. Cleveland: Arthur H. Clark, 1910.

Commons, John R., David J. Saposs, Helen L. Sumner, E.B. Mittelman, H.E. Hoagland, John B. Andrews, and Selig Perlman. *History of Labor in the United States*. New York: Augustus M. Kelley, 1918–38.

Danziger, Sheldon, and Peter Gottschalk. *Uneven Tides: Rising Inequality in America*. New York: Russell Sage Foundation, 1993.

Dawley, Alan. *Class and Community: The Industrial Revolution in Lynn*. Cambridge, MA: Harvard University Press, 1976.

Derthick, Martha. *Policymaking for Social Security*. Washington, DC: Brookings Institution Press, 1979.

Dickens, Richard, Stephen Machin, and Alan Manning.

"The Effects of Minimum Wages on Employment: Theory and Evidence from Britain." *Journal of Labor Economics* 17, no. 1 (January 1999): 1–22.

Douglas, Paul H. *Wages and the Family*. Chicago: University of Chicago Press, 1925.

Dubofsky, Melvyn. *The State and Labor in Modern America*. Chapel Hill: University of North Carolina Press, 1994.

Durkheim, Émile. *The Division of Labor in Society*. 4th ed., Trans. George Simpson. New York: Macmillan, 1933.

Edwards, Richard L., Michael Reich, and Thomas Weisskopf. *The Capitalist System: A Radical Analysis of American Society*. Englewood Cliffs, NJ: Prentice Hall, 1972.

Ehrenreich, Barbara. *Nickel and Dimed: On (Not) Getting By in America*. New York: Henry Holt, 2001.

Elbow, Matthew H. *French Corporative Theory 1798–1948: A Chapter in the History of Ideas*. New York: Octagon Books, 1966.

European Commission: Directorate for Economic and Financial Affairs. *European Economy: The EU Economy 1999 Review*. No. 69. Luxembourg: Office for the Official Publications of the European Community, 1999.

Fairris, David. "Are Transformed Workplaces More Productively Efficient?" *Journal of Economic Issues* 36, no. 3 (September 2002): 659–70.

Fishback, Price V. "Did Miners 'Owe Their Souls to the Company Store'? Theory and Evidence from the Early 1900s." *Journal of Economic History* 46 (December 1986): 1011–29.

Fishback, Price V., and Shawn Everett Kantor. *A Prelude to the Welfare State: The Origins of Workers' Compensation*. Chicago: University of Chicago Press, 2000.

Fishback, Price V., and Dieter Lauzus. "The Quality of Services in Company Towns: Sanitation in Coal Towns During the 1920s." *Journal of Economic History* 49 (December 1989): 125–44.

Freeman, Richard. "Unionism and the Dispersion of Wages." *Industrial and Labor Relations Review* 34, no. 1 (October 1980): 3–23.

———. "Union Wage Practices and Dispersion within Establishments." *Industrial and Labor Relations Review* 36, no. 1 (October 1982): 3–21.

———. "How Much Has De-Unionization Contributed to the Rise in Male Earnings Inequality?" In *Uneven Tides: Rising Inequality in America*, ed. Sheldon Danziger and Peter Gottschalk, 133–63. New York: Russell Sage Foundation, 1993.

———. "The New Inequality in the United States." In *Growing Apart: The Causes and Consequences of Global Wage Inequality*, ed. Albert Fishlow and Karen Parker. New York: Council on Foreign Relations Press, 1999.

Freeman, Richard B., and Lawrence F. Katz. "Rising Inequality." In *Working under Different Rules*, ed. R.B. Freeman. New York: Russell Sage Foundation, 1994.

Freeman, Richard B., and James L. Medoff. *What Do Unions Do?* New York: Basic Books, 1984.

Galbraith, James. *Created Unequal: The Crisis in American Pay*. New York: Twentieth Century Fund, 1998.

Galbraith, John K. *The New Industrial State*. Boston: Houghton-Mifflin, 1963.

Gide, Charles, and Charles Rist. *A History of Economic Doctrines from the Time of the Physiocrats to the Present Day*. 2nd American ed. Trans. Robert Richards. Boston: D.C. Heath, 1948.

Gitelman, H.M. *The Legacy of the Ludlow Massacre: A Chapter in American Industrial Relations*. Philadelphia: University of Pennsylvania Press, 1988.

Griffith, Barbara S. *The Crisis of American Labor: Operation Dixie and the Defeat of the CIO*. Philadelphia: Temple University Press, 1988.

Gross, James A. *The Making of the National Labor Relations Board: A Study in the Economics and Politics of the Law*. Albany, NY: State University of New York, 1974.

Groves, Harold. *In and Out of the Ivory Tower*. Madison: Historical Society of Wisconsin, 1969.

Haverkate, Görg. "The State and the Social Insurance System after 100 Years of Statutory Accident Insurance." *International Social Security Review* 38, no. 4 (1985): 418–30.

Higgs, Robert. "Firm-specific Evidence on Racial Wage Differentials and Workforce Segregation." *American Economic Review* 67 (March 1977): 236–45.

Hirsch, Barry T., and John T. Addison, eds. *The Economic Analysis of Unions*. Boston: Allen & Unwin, 1986.

Jacoby, Sanford. *Modern Manors: Welfare Capitalism Since the New Deal*. Princeton, NJ: Princeton University Press, 1997.

Katz, Lawrence. "Comments on 'Current Unemployment Historically Contemplated' by Chinhui Juhn, Kevin M. Murphy, and Robert H. Topel." In *Brookings Papers on Economic Activity* 1, ed. William Brainard and George Perry. Washington, DC: Brookings Institution Press, 2002.

Kaufman, Bruce, E. "Models of Union Wage Determination: What Have We Learned Since Dunlop and Ross." *Industrial Relations: A Journal of Economy and Society* 41, no. 1 (January 2002): 110–58.

Keynes, John M. *The Collected Writings of John Maynard Keynes*. XXI vols. ed. Donald Moggridge. London: Macmillan for the Royal Economic Society, 1972.

Kim, Marlene, and Thanos Mergoupis. "The Working Poor and Welfare: Participation, Evidence, and Policy Directions." *Journal of Economic Issues* 31, no. 3 (September 1997): 707–28.

Klare, Karl. "Judicial Deradicalization of the Wagner Act and the Origins of Modern Legal Consciousness." *Minnesota Law Review* 62 (1978): 265–339.

Kochan, Thomas, Harry Katz, and Richard McKersie. *The Transformation of American Industrial Relations*. New York: Basic Books, 1986.

Kolko, Gabriel. *The Triumph of Conservatism: A Reinterpretation of American History, 1900–1916*. New York: Free Press, 1963.

Layard, Richard, Stephen Nickell, and Richard Jackman. *Unemployment: Macroeconomic Performance and the Labor Market*. New York: Oxford University Press, 1991.

Lee, W. Alton. "The Eradication of Phossy Jaw: A Unique Development of Federal Police Power." *The Historian* 29, no. 1 (November 1966): 1–21.

Leiserson, William M. "A Federal Reserve Board for the Unemployed." *The Annals* 69 (January 1917): 103–17.

———. "The Meaning of Labor Representation: The Agreement in the Clothing Industry." *The Annals* 90 (July 1920): 22–26.

———. "Constitutional Government in American Industries." *American Economic Review: Supplement* 12, no. 1 (March 1922a): 56–79.

———. "Collective Bargaining and its Effect on Production." *The Annals* 91 (September 1922b): 40–49.

———. "Who Bears the Business Risks?" *Survey Graphic* 65, no. 11 (March 1, 1931): 596–600, 622.

———. *American Trade Union Democracy*. New York: Columbia University Press, 1959.

Levine, Phillip B. "Financing Benefit Payments." In *Unemployment Insurance in the United States: Analysis of Policy Issues*, ed. Christopher J. O'Leary and Stephen A. Wandner. Kalamazoo, MI: Upjohn Institute, 1997.

Lewis, H. Gregg. *Unionism and Relative Wages in the United States*. Chicago: University of Chicago Press, 1963.

———. *Union Relative Wage Effects: A Survey*. Chicago: University of Chicago Press, 1986.

Lichtenstein, Nelson. *State of the Union: A Century of American Labor*. Princeton, NJ: Princeton University Press, 2002.

Loubère, L.A. "Bourgeois, Leon." In *Historical Dictionary of the Third French Republic 1870–1941*, ed. Patrick H. Hutton, Amanda S. Bourque, and Amy Staples. Westport, CT: Greenwood Press, 1986.

Lucas, Robert E., and Thomas J. Sargent. *After the Phillips Curve: Persistence of High Inflation and High Unemployment*. Boston: Federal Reserve Bank of Boston, 1978.

Manly, Basil. "Report of Basil Manly." In *Final Report and Testimony Submitted to Congress by the U.S. Commission on Industrial Relations*. 64th Cong., 1st sess. Vol. 1. Washington, DC: Government Printing Office, 1916.

Martin, George. *Madam Secretary: Frances Perkins*. Boston: Houghton-Mifflin, 1976.

Montgomery, David. "To Study the People: The American Working Class." *Labor History* 21, no. 4 (Fall 1980): 485–512.

Moss, David A. *Socializing Security: Progressive Era Economists and the Origins of American Social Policy*. Cambridge, MA: Harvard University Press, 1996.

Murphy, Kevin M., and Finis Welch. "Industrial Change and the Rising Importance of Skill." In *Uneven Tides: Rising Inequality in America*, ed. Sheldon Danziger and Peter Gottschalk. New York: Russell Sage Foundation, 1993.

Myrdal, Gunnar. *An American Dilemma: The Negro Problem and Modern Democracy*. New York: Harper Brothers, 1944.

North, Douglass C., Terry L. Anderson, and Peter J. Hill. *Growth and Welfare in the American Past*. Englewood Cliffs, NJ: Prentice-Hall, 1983.

Northrop, Emily. "Public Assistance and Antipoverty Programs." *Journal of Economic Issues* 25, no. 4 (December 1991): 1017–27.

Numbers, Ronald L. *Almost Persuaded: American Physicians and Compulsory Health Insurance 1912–1920*. Baltimore: Johns Hopkins University Press, 1978.

O'Connor, James R. *The Fiscal Crisis of the State*. New York: St. Martin's Press, 1973.

O'Flaherty, Brendan. *Making Room: The Economics of Homelessness*. Cambridge, MA: Harvard University Press, 1996.

Olson, Mancur. *The Logic of Collective Action, Public Goods, and the Theory of Groups*. Cambridge, MA: Harvard University Press, 1971.

Osterman, Paul. *Securing Prosperity: The American Labor Market: How It Has Changed and What to Do About It*. Princeton, NJ: Princeton University Press, 1992.

Palley, Thomas L. "The Child Labor Problem and the Need for International Labor Standards." *Journal of Economic Issues* 36 (September 2002): 601–615.

Parsons, Kenneth H. "The Basis of Commons' Progressive Approach to Public Policy." In *Labor, Management and*

Society: Essays in the John R. Commons Tradition, ed. Gerald G. Somers. Madison: University of Wisconsin Press, 1963.

Patterson, James T. *America's Struggle Against Poverty*. 3rd ed. Cambridge, MA: Harvard University Press, 2000.

Peirce, Charles S. "How to Make Our Ideas Clear." In *The Essential Peirce: Selected Philosophical Writings*, ed. Nathan Houser and Christian Kloesel. Bloomington: Indiana University Press, 1992.

Perkins, Frances. *The Roosevelt I Knew*. New York: Viking Press, 1946.

Perlman, Selig. *A Theory of the Labor Movement*. 1928. Reprint, New York: Augustus M. Kelley, 1968.

Perlman, Selig, and Philip Taft. *History of Labor in the United States, 1896–1932. Volume 4: Labor Movements*. 1935. Reprint, New York: Augustus M. Kelley, 1966.

Peterson, Janice. "Welfare Reform and Inequality: The TANF and the UI Program." *Journal of Economic Issues* 34, no. 2 (June 2000): 517–26.

Pigou, Arthur Cecil. *The Economics of Welfare*. 2nd ed. London: Macmillan, 1924.

Raushenbush, Paul, and Elizabeth Brandeis Raushenbush. *Our U.C. Story 1930–1967*. Madison, WI: Raushenbush and Raushenbush, 1979.

Reynolds, Morgan O. *Making America Poorer: The Cost of American Labor Law*. Washington, DC: Cato Institute, 1987.

Rothstein, Lawrence. *Plant Closings*. Dover, MA: Auburn House, 1986.

Saposs, David J. "Colonial and Federal Beginnings." In *History of Labour in the United States*, Vol. 1, ed. John R. Commons, David J. Saposs, Helen L. Sumner, E.B. Mittelman, H.E. Hoagland, John B. Andrews, and Selig Perlman. New York: Augustus M. Kelley, 1918. Reprint, New York: Augustus M. Kelley, 1966.

———. "The Labor Movement: A Look Forward and Backward." In *The Labor Movement: A Re-examination: A Conference in Honor of David Saposs*, ed. Jack Barbash. Madison: University of Wisconsin Press, 1966.

Schatz, Ronald. "From Commons to Dunlop: Rethinking the Field and Theory of Industrial Relations." In *Industrial Democracy in America: The Ambiguous Promise*, ed. Nelson Lichtenstein and Howell Harris. Washington, DC: Woodrow Wilson Center Press, 1993.

Schein, Edgar H. *Organizational Culture*. San Francisco: Jossey-Bass, 1997.

Schieber, Sylvester J., and John B. Shoven. *The Real Deal: The History and Future of Social Security*. New Haven: Yale University Press, 1999.

Schlabach, Theron. Edwin E. Witte: *Cautious Reformer*. Madison: Wisconsin Historical Society, 1969.

Schlesinger, Arthur M. *The Age of Roosevelt. Volume 1: The Coming of the New Deal*. Boston: Houghton-Mifflin, 1959.

Schwarz, John E. *America's Hidden Success*. New York: W.W. Norton, 1983.

Skocpol, Theda, and John Ikenberry. "The Road to Social Security." In *Social Policy in the United States*, ed. Theda Skocpol. Princeton, NJ: Princeton University Press, 1995.

Smeeding, Timothy. "Why the U.S. Antipoverty System Doesn't Work Very Well." *Challenge* 35 (January–February 1992): 30–35.

Starr, Paul. *The Social Transformation of American Medicine*. New York: Basic Books, 1982.

Thompson, Edward P. *The Making of the English Working Class*. New York: Vintage Books, 1963.

Tomlins, Christopher. *The State and the Unions: Labor Relations, the Law, and the Organized Labor Movement in America 1880–1960*. New York: Cambridge University Press, 1985.

Troy, Leo. *Beyond Unions and Collective Bargaining*. Armonk, NY: M.E. Sharpe, 1999.

Tussing, A. Dale. *Poverty in a Dual Economy*. New York: St. Martin's Press, 1975.

Tynes, Sheryl R. *Turning Points in Social Security: From "Cruel Hoax" to "Sacred Entitlement."* Stanford, CA: Stanford University Press, 1996.

United States Commission on Industrial Relations (USCIR). *Final Report and Testimony Submitted to Congress by the U.S. Commission on Industrial Relations*. 64th Cong. 1st sess. Document 415. Washington, DC: Government Printing Office, 1916.

Useem, Michael. *Investor Capitalism: How Money Managers Are Changing the Face of Corporate America*. New York: Basic Books, 1996.

Waddoups, C. Jeffrey. "Wage Inequality and Collective Bargaining: Hotels and Casinos in Nevada." *Journal of Economic Issues* 36, no. 3 (September 2002): 617–34.

Webb, Sidney, and Beatrice Webb. *Industrial Democracy*. London: Longmans, 1902.

Weinstein, James. *The Corporate Ideal in the Liberal State*. Boston: Beacon Press, 1968.

Wilcox, F.M., and A.J. Altmeyer. "The Wisconsin Idea of Safety." *The Annals* 123 (January 1926): 78–85.

Witte, Edwin. *The Government in Labor Disputes*. 1932. Reprint, New York: Arno Press, 1969.

———. "The Approaching Crisis in Old Age Security." *American Labor Legislation Review* 30 no. 3 (September 1940): 115–23.

———. *The Development of the Social Security Act*. Madison: University of Wisconsin Press, 1962a.

———. *Social Security Perspectives: Essays by Edwin E. Witte*, ed. Robert Lampman. Madison: University of Wisconsin Press, 1962b.

Wolff, Edward N. *Top Heavy: The Increasing Inequality of Wealth in America and What Can Be Done About It*. New York: New Press, 1996.

Wood, Adrian. *North-South Trade, Employment and Inequality*. Oxford: Clarendon Press of Oxford University Press, 1994.

Wray, L. Randall, and Marc-André Pigeon. "Can a Rising Tide Raise All Boats? Evidence from the Clinton Era Expansion." *Journal of Economic Issues* 34, no. 4 (December 2000): 811–45.

Zeldin, Theodore. *France: 1848–1945*. New York: Oxford University Press, 1973.

5

Wages in the Public Interest

Insights from Thorstein Veblen and J.M. Clark

Dell P. Champlin and Janet T. Knoedler

The issue of a living wage has generated considerable controversy since the first ordinance was passed in Baltimore in 1994 (ACORN 2001). The living wage controversy, like earlier disputes over a minimum wage and a family wage, is fundamentally a controversy over private and public interests. The dominant view in the economics profession ever since Adam Smith first made the case in the *Wealth of Nations* is that promotion of the private interests of business firms is the best means of ensuring the public interest.[1] According to this view, living wages raise the costs of firms, leading to distortions in prices and output levels. Indeed, opponents of living and minimum wages argue that raising wages above the "market" wage will end up hurting the intended beneficiaries of these ordinances by reducing employment and raising prices (Nordlund 1997; Murray 2001, 28). Hence living wages are deemed bad for business, bad for workers, and, ultimately, not in the public interest.

The purpose of this chapter is to make an argument for what we call wages in the public interest, relying on the important insights of Thorstein Veblen and John Maurice Clark. Both of these economists recognized that modern capitalist economies had enormous productive capacity that could eliminate all privation and want. The "public interest" view of an economy that can be drawn from Veblen and Clark, therefore, promotes the notion that in our highly productive, modern economic systems all individuals should have a right to an adequate share of the community's produce. Within this view, living wages should not be at all controversial. Indeed, the living wage becomes a useful and important barometer of economic welfare; it is simply a wage in the public interest.

In the first part of the chapter, we discuss Veblen's distinction between economic welfare and business prosperity and Clark's distinction between public and private interest. In the second part of the chapter, we examine the notion of business prosperity in the context of past doctrines for high and low wages. In the third part of the chapter, we put the current controversies over a living wage into perspective by recalling earlier views of subsistence wages, and we develop the concept of wages that provide adequate subsistence as being in the public interest. Finally, we conclude that ensuring subsistence or living wages to all members of society is a *minimum* standard of prosperity in any economy that would fulfill its basic task of provisioning all members of society.

Business Prosperity and Economic Welfare

Economic welfare, within a public interest context, places as its central concern and standard the welfare of all participants in an economy. In his *Theory of Business Enterprise*, Thorstein Veblen applied his dichotomy between industrial and pecuniary values to the question of economic welfare and made the following observation (1978, 177): A public interest definition of welfare would declare "times . . . good or bad according as the industrial processes yielded a *sufficient or an insufficient output of the means of life*" (178). In other words, according to Veblen, "before business principles came to dominate everyday life the common welfare, when it was not a question of peace and war, turned on the ease and certainty with which enough of the means of life could be supplied" (177). Therefore, for Veblen, the issue of economic welfare—in other words, economic welfare in the public interest—turns on the notion of sufficient output for the *entire* community and on an adequate portion of that output distributed to each member of the community.

But, according to Veblen, with the rise of modern corporate capitalism the concept of economic welfare came to be concerned exclusively with the private interests of firms. To quote Veblen on this point: "Since business has become the central and controlling interest, the question of welfare has become a question of price" (1978, 177). Elaborating, Veblen argued that modern corporate capitalism is an economic system governed by pecuniary interests, whereby "times are good or bad according as the process of business yields an adequate or inadequate rate of profits" (1978, 178). In other words, the concern, whether expressed by economists or by businesspersons, was no longer "whether the community's work was adequate to supply the community's needs" (177) but whether the business firms engaged in supplying that output could profit more by supplying less than sufficient output to the community. Here is the irony presented by modern corporate capitalism. The modern firm is able to produce substantial output in a highly efficient manner but does not always do so because the processes of modern industry are organized and managed by businesspersons with an eye toward making profits and not primarily toward meeting the community's needs. "Prosperity now means, primarily, business prosperity," Veblen wrote in 1904, "whereas it used to mean industrial sufficiency" (1978, 178). In contrast, a focus on the public interest, in a Veblenian context, examines the broader ability of a society to meet the material needs of all of its members (177).

Following Veblen, Clark described the conflict between public and private interest as being found in the "essential nature of private enterprise" (1923, 28–29). An elaboration on what is meant by the public interest, as opposed to the private interest, can be found in Clark's massive tome, *Social Control of Business*, written in 1928, where he tackled the question of the conflict between public and private interests in production head-on. Clark argued that "the central issue seems to be whether private industry can become an affair of 'production for use' and not (primarily or exclusively) for profit" (1969, 65). Later, Clark wrote in a report for his subcommittee for the Committee on Unemployment and Industrial Stabilization of the National Progressive Conference that "it is generally agreed that there is something seriously wrong with private enterprise as at present operating. It has succeeded in organizing the technique of production with marvelous efficiency, but it has failed miserably to utilize this technique to anything like its full capacity" (1932, 229). Full utilization of the industrial system could guarantee that all members of society would enjoy adequate sustenance. That is, industrial sufficiency would bring about an improvement in economic welfare as measured by the living standards of the lowest members of society. But Clark, as did Veblen, acknowledged that the tendency of business enterprise was to suppress the productivity of the industrial apparatus in service to greater profits and greater business prosperity. In short, Veblen and Clark recognized, early on, that in modern corporate capitalism the prosperity of firms has replaced the earlier notion of a broader, shared prosperity in the public interest. The economy is experiencing good times only if business is doing well.

Veblen's observation at the beginning of the twentieth century has become almost commonplace at the beginning of the twenty-first. High profits and a roaring stock market are now widely regarded as the key indicators of a prosperous economy. The concept of public interest and social prosperity being consistent with an economy that provides for all, as framed by Clark and Veblen,[2] has been replaced by a line of reasoning that begins with the conviction that all prosperity comes from business. Indeed, a better term for business prosperity might be that offered by Veblen: "business exaltation!"(1978, 183). Veblen's indictment of the dominance of pecuniary interests is a recurring theme among institutional economists. For example, in the following quote, David Hamilton called attention to the revered place of business in modern society:

> What does the businessman do? He works magic with money funds. He makes two shares of stock exist where but one existed before. He enhances pecuniary values. But what is of more import is the fact that in doing this he supposedly "creates" hotels, steamships, and railroads where none existed before. Thus, progress has been associated with his activities. (1970, 108)

The notion that economic welfare is the same as business prosperity is fully embedded in economic doctrine, and the very notion of a public interest has been completely swallowed up by self-interest as the governing principle for modern economics and modern economies. However, the point made by Veblen, Hamilton, and other institutional economists is that this leads to a peculiarly individualistic and one-sided view of social welfare. It is also a view of prosperity that disregards the welfare of many workers.

Business Prosperity and Wages

During the twentieth century, the belief that social prosperity is identical to business prosperity has dominated our understanding of wages. In the early part of the century, high wages were held to be in the public interest. However, support for high wages did not stem from the benefit accruing to workers but rather from the presumed benefits for business. As Henry Ford recognized, higher wages mean more demand for output (McCraw and Tedlow 1997). At the dawn of the twenty-first century, however, the high-wage doctrine has been set aside in favor of a low-wage doctrine (Taylor and Selgin 1999). Now economic prosperity is presumed to be best served by low wages that do not threaten inflation or squeeze profits. How do we reconcile these two conflicting conclusions? The common thread in both is that economic prosperity is conflated with business prosperity. These two incompatible views of wages stem from a shifting emphasis in economic theory, but no conflict exists in the underlying premise that economic prosperity and business prosperity are one and the same.

The high-wage doctrine can be traced to the recognition that raising workers' disposable income above a minimal subsistence level transforms workers into customers. Higher sales lead to higher output and, ultimately, to more jobs. Ford became one of the nation's most venerated persons—admired even by Vladimir Lenin—in the 1910s and 1920s for raising workers' wages so that they could buy the Model Ts that they were making (McCraw and Tedlow 1997, 275). As one French admirer of Ford put it, "in the last analysis, the customer controls the market and is therefore a free citizen of it. With Ford, the American worker became a customer" (quoted in McCraw and Tedlow 1997, 276). By the end of the 1930s, the high-wage doctrine had become an entrenched feature of U.S. macroeconomic policy (Taylor and Selgin 1999).[3]

Today, rising wages are socially constructed as an adverse trend that may be harmful to economic prosperity. This conclusion is implied in the policy actions of the Federal Reserve Board during the 1980s and 1990s, in the international trade and investment policy advice offered by mainstream economists, and in the incessant rhetoric over the new global economy (Altman 1998; Clark 1997; Thurow 1996). During the 1990s, rising wages were interpreted by the Federal Reserve Board as an early indicator of potential inflation that might threaten economic prosperity (Thurow 1996; Krugman 1999).[4] Veblen also pointed out that "[a]n era of prosperity does not commonly bring an increase in wages until the era is about to close" (1978, 212). Rising wages mean squeezed profits and a possible decline in investment. Moreover, the application of classical axiomatic microfoundations to the analysis of phenomena in a monetary economy means that demand for output is apparently no longer a worry for macroeconomists (Davidson 1999; Lindbeck 1998). The possibility of deficient aggregate demand has been shunted aside along with Keynes and memories of the Great Depression.[5]

Taylor and Selgin (1999) argued that the high-wage doctrine is an unfortunate "fallacy" that led many economists and policy makers to support passage of the Fair Labor Standards Act in 1937. The federal minimum wage law, which must be amended each time the wage is increased, has generated a vast literature. According to Jerold Waltman (2000), more has been written about the minimum wage than about any other economic policy. One consequence of the political wrangling that inevitably accompanies efforts to raise the minimum wage is that there is now a sizable literature supporting the low-wage doctrine. The conventional view of the minimum wage is that it is a market distortion that reduces economic welfare. A minimum wage set above the equilibrium market wage is a price floor that results in excess supply. The conclusion that the federal minimum wage causes unemployment has become so entrenched in economic literature that it is considered a textbook example of a price floor. The orthodox argument against the minimum wage is based on the notion that a market-clearing wage is *always* preferable. A market-clearing wage is, by definition, economically efficient compared to a wage floor above equilibrium. Whether this market-clearing wage is a low wage or a high wage has no bearing on this conclusion.

In the years since the passage of the Fair Labor Standards Act, empirical studies have challenged the belief that the minimum wage always causes unemployment. One of the more recent and well-known studies is that done by David Card and Alan Krueger (1995). Daniel Hamermesh (1995) argued that the effect of the minimum wage occurs with a substantial lag. Another study of the retail sector shows small employment effects on the sector overall and statistically insignificant employment effects on the low-wage restaurant sector (Partridge and Partridge 1999). The empirical debates notwithstanding, the relevant point for this chapter is the underlying standard of economic welfare. Opponents of the minimum wage as well as advocates are operating in the same theoretical framework. The conclusion of orthodox economic theory is that even if a significant number of workers receive less than a subsistence wage, any effort to correct the situation would actually be a decline in social welfare. In a tradeoff between one unemployed person and many people working for very low wages, the neoclassical economist would choose very low wages for the many. In a recent article, Martin Feldstein (1999) argued that one should apply the Pareto principle to raising the minimum wage. Starting from a state of full employment at less than a subsistence wage, the minimum wage should not be raised since it might make one person worse off—a worker who becomes unemployed as a result. Card and Krueger did not challenge this standard theoretical analysis. Indeed, by making unemployment the key question, they implicitly accepted the notion that the minimum wage is a price floor that has the potential to distort markets. In other words, as pointed out by Waltman (2000), proponents and opponents of the minimum wage are arguing within a very narrow range in which the route to economic prosperity remains business prosperity. Workers can participate in this prosperity only through the possession of a job—even a job that pays very poorly.

Under a high-wage doctrine, the conflation of business prosperity and economic prosperity still poses difficulties for workers. For example, while Ford is famous for his five dollars per day, a wage much higher than any offered by other employers of the time, he is equally famous for harsh working conditions and militant antiunionism (Bernstein 1966, 1970; Zieger 1986). Ford's aim was not economic prosperity but business prosperity—specifically that of his own business. The fact that

business prosperity also resulted in higher income for working families was merely a means to an end. Still, the notion that business interests are served by paying higher wages does clearly benefit workers. Less obvious is the more startling assertion that low wages are in the interests of workers. However, the reasoning is straightforward. Business provides jobs. Since the majority of income for society as a whole consists of wage income, society needs jobs. If high wages will lead to more jobs, then high wages are in the public interest. If low wages will lead to more jobs, then low wages are in the public interest.

What is remarkable about the low-wage doctrine, however, is the complete absence of a link between wages and living standards. *Any* minimum wage floor is considered a market distortion, inefficient, and a reduction of economic welfare. The federal minimum wage is currently 60 percent of the average poverty threshold for a family of four. In urban areas with high housing and transportation costs, the minimum wage is even more inadequate. For example, the living wage ordinance in Santa Cruz, California, is $11 an hour—more than double the current federal minimum wage of $5.15 (ACORN 2001). Despite the low level of the minimum wage, raising the wage is always politically difficult due to the now well-established low-wage doctrine (Levin-Waldman 1998). The living wage movement of the 1990s that began in Baltimore is an attempt to reestablish a link between wages and living standards. However, living wage advocates are also confronted with the dominance of the low-wage doctrine. For example, the Employment Policies Institute (EPI), an advocacy group opposed to wage mandates, argues that wages that enable a worker and dependents to live above the federal poverty level—living wages—are "too high" and potentially harmful to economic prosperity (Employment Policies Institute 1999).

Prosperity and the Quest for Livelihood

In this section, we discuss the concept of the subsistence wage. Our purpose is to contrast the present view of a minimum wage or living wage as a price floor that interferes with market equilibrium with the earlier view of a subsistence wage as a wage that is socially and economically sustainable.[6] The present concept is an abstract concept devoid of any social or cultural content. As such, it sustains the notion that business prosperity and social prosperity are one and the same. Allowing wages to fall—even to a very low level—is now constructed as a trend that will enhance the general social prosperity. In contrast, the concept of a subsistence wage as a wage that is socially and economically sustainable reflects a broader view of prosperity. Rather than depicting a well-functioning, prosperous economy as one in which business is doing well, a broader view requires that a prosperous economy be successful in its ultimate task of provisioning all members of society. In short, a society that provisions its members is a prosperous society. A society that does not accomplish the basic task of provisioning is not prosperous—no matter how prosperous a few individuals in that society may be.

Classical political economy is based on a static social system. In this system, as in modern society, the dominant class is the capitalist class. Classical theory, like the neoclassical theory that succeeded it, gave to the entrepreneur the key role in the economic system. All prosperity derived from the actions of the capitalist. Indeed, economic progress or prosperity is *defined* as capital accumulation in classical theory (Hamilton 1970). The increase in capital accumulation or economic growth provides the basis for a general improvement in living standards. Despite the fact that neo-

classical theory is a static theory rather than a dynamic one, the same doctrine is carried forward. An increase in business prosperity—today usually defined as an accumulation of *financial* capital—will lead to a general improvement in living standards. Thus, the current idolization of the entrepreneur has deep roots in economic doctrine. There is a fundamental difference, however. In classical political economy, business prosperity was the *source* of general prosperity. In modern economic thinking, business prosperity and general prosperity have become conflated. They are no longer separable notions. This difference, albeit a minor one, has important consequences for the wageworker.

In classical political economy, the capitalist may be the most significant player, but he or she is not the only player. The rentier class—so important in feudal society—is demoted to a socially useless and parasitic class that takes its cut of the economic pie without contributing to it. The laboring class is also transformed from feudal society in that it is now composed of free labor rather than serfs, indentured servants, or slaves.[7] This freedom means that workers are now "free" to work for a wage (Dobb 1946).[8] It also means that workers have no other source of livelihood except wage income. Polanyi (1957) believed this point to be so important that he dated the beginning of capitalism to the end of outdoor relief in England in 1834. It was work, starve, or go to the poorhouse.[9] If workers have no source of income other than wage income, then the lowest possible wage is the minimum amount necessary to sustain the worker. This notion, the so-called iron law of wages, is at the heart of Malthusian population theory. Any attempt to pay less than subsistence would ultimately result in fewer workers as they or their children died or as fewer children were born (Dobb 1946). The reduction in supply pushes wages up to subsistence again.

The Malthusian concept of subsistence was a physical one, since any fall in the subsistence wage led to a decline in the population. For David Ricardo, the goods necessary for physical subsistence were determined, in part, by social custom. Thus, a subsistence wage had to be sufficient to purchase not only those commodities necessary to sustain physical life but had to be enough to purchase a customary standard of living. As Maurice Dobb put it, "The worker, having grown accustomed to certain small comforts such as a glass of ale and a pipe of tobacco, would dispense with physical necessities rather than with these, if his wages were reduced. Habit, in other words, turned these comforts into 'conventional necessities'" (1946, 103). Admittedly, both Malthus and Ricardo were more concerned with explaining why wages could not rise above subsistence than they were with why wages would not fall. However, both writers followed Adam Smith in defining the subsistence wage as the lowest wage possible in a society in which workers had no other possible source of income.

With Marx, the subsistence wage continued to be the long-run tendency in the economic system. Like the classical economists discussed above, Marx's view of the subsistence wage is composed of two parts: an explanation of why wages will tend not to rise above subsistence and an explanation of why they could not fall below subsistence. In regard to the failure of wages to rise, Marx departed from the classical reliance on Malthusian population theory. In its place Marx used a concept of "relative" overpopulation—the industrial reserve army (Dobb 1946). Any tendency for wages to rise above subsistence is attributed to excess demand for labor. In Malthusian theory, this excess demand is counteracted by an increase in the labor supply. According to Marx, excess demand for labor will also be counteracted by an increase in labor supply. However, with Marx the increase in labor supply does not come from natural law, but from an inherent characteristic of capitalism. The capitalist keeps wages down by ensuring that labor will always be in a position of excess supply. This is accomplished by substituting "mechanical for human labour power" and through periodic economic crises that increase unemployment and push down wages (Dobb 1946, 107). In addition, the capitalist increases labor supply by bringing new groups of workers into the labor force. A recent example would be the requirement that poor women with children work for a wage contained in the welfare reform legislation of 1996. Whatever its stated purpose, the requirement has the effect of increasing the supply of low-wage workers. In addition, the capitalist may transport capital to other countries, thereby augmenting the domestic labor supply with the labor supply of another country—a familiar practice in leading industrial countries throughout the nineteenth and twentieth centuries.

The meaning of subsistence as used by Marx differs markedly from the meanings used by Smith and Ricardo. While Ricardo's use of Malthusian population theory ensured that the meaning of subsistence contained a physical or physiological element, the concept was primarily a cultural one. In classical theory, subsistence was composed of those commodities required to keep a human being in a particular culture alive and well. With Marx, subsistence is tied in with maintaining the working class. That is, subsistence meant not only keeping a human being alive and well but also keeping a *worker* alive and well. A human being requires food, shelter, clothing, and, according to Ricardo, a glass of ale. A worker, on the other hand, requires the additional commodities necessary to ensure viability as a wage laborer. Putting this distinction into a modern context, physical

subsistence might be satisfied by a wage sufficient to purchase physically necessary commodities. However, additional commodities are necessary to support a person who works. For example,
low wageworkers must pay for transportation to
their jobs. In some urban areas with extensive
public transportation, this cost may be nominal.
In other instances, the cost is not insignificant.
As jobs have moved from central cities to suburban locations, workers who continue to live in
central cities face major transportation problems.
Public transportation is often geared toward bringing suburban workers into the cities in the morn-
ing and taking them home in the evenings. In addition, suburban industrial districts are typically
designed for workers with automobiles, as are
many locations in the western part of the United
States. A wage insufficient to purchase transportation to a job in these locations could not be considered a subsistence wage.

Marx's concept of subsistence as the minimum
necessary to support a worker is also instructive
in light of recent welfare reform. Requiring women
who are single parents to work means that a subsistence wage must also include the cost of child
care.[10] Moreover, a subsistence wage must ensure
the perpetuation of the working class. That is, classical economists as well as Marx were concerned
with the behavior of the economic system over
time. A system that did not ensure the maintenance
of its resources would eventually decline. For
Marx, *reproduction* of the working class meant that
the subsistence wage must be sufficient to ensure
that children be nourished, educated, and social-
ized, because they are the future members of the
working class. Thus, the subsistence wage must
be sufficient to ensure that children of wageworkers
receive adequate child care and health care to meet
their physical needs. In addition, they must acquire
enough skills to take their place in the labor force

by completing formal education without pressures
to withdraw from school for economic reasons.

In essence, the notion that a minimum or subsistence level wage could be "too high" would have
been a nonsensical notion to classical economists
in the nineteenth century. According to Adam
Smith, the subsistence wage was the "natural"
wage (Smith 1909). Ricardo, relying on Malthus's
theory of population, also saw the subsistence wage
as a natural wage (Ricardo 1911). Ricardo and later
economists in the nineteenth century were interested in explaining why it was futile to attempt to
raise wages above subsistence. For example, the
wages fund doctrine was specifically developed
to explain why it was not possible to pay wages
above subsistence (Lapides 1998). However, if it
was futile for wages to rise above subsistence, it
was also inconceivable for wages to fall below
subsistence. Wages below subsistence were not
economically viable.

A century later, any meaningful notion of a subsistence wage has all but disappeared from neoclassical theory.[11] The classical "subsistence" wage
has become the neoclassical "minimum" wage.
There are several implications of this transformation. First, there is now no floor to wages that occurs as part of the theoretical economic system. In
standard *theory*, there is no level below which
wages cannot fall. In standard *policy*, the problem
of very low wages is acknowledged but not regarded as a serious *economic* problem. The concern for the physical deterioration of the worker
or for the deterioration of the work force as an
economic resource that preoccupied the classical
economists is now a question for the individual
rather than for society. In so doing, the question of
subsistence or provisioning is no longer a question that the economic system must address. Provisioning in neoclassical theory is a personal rather
than an economic problem.

Donald Stabile discussed the conversion of adequate wages into an individual problem in his insightful book, *Work and Welfare: The Social Costs of Labor in the History of Economic Thought* (1996). Stabile divided economic treatments of very low wages into two categories: the social obligations approach and the social insurance approach. The social obligations approach is analogous to the earlier classical approach and "represents an effort to gauge the impact of employment on the worker, the worker's family and other members of the community. It includes the costs of maintaining the economic system as an ongoing entity" (1996, 4). In contrast, the newer concept of social insurance is based on the notion that an individual's participation in a capitalistic economy is risky. The appropriate response to unavoidable risk is to obtain insurance. One should insure against the risk of failing to obtain the means of subsistence along with insuring against automobile accidents or damage to one's home. The insurance becomes "social" only when the risks are widespread enough that private insurers will not underwrite these risks. According to Stabile (1996), the key premise in the social insurance approach is that ultimately each individual worker is on his or her own in obtaining the means of livelihood, and failure to do so affects only the worker and his or her family. The policy implication of this viewpoint is that social safety-net programs constitute a social cost while providing a benefit enjoyed only by individual recipients. Minimum wage legislation and living wage ordinances would fall into the same category. Essentially, the government is seen as attempting to insure individuals against the risk of failure in a free labor market at the expense of private employers. Stabile attributed the assumption that a portion of the labor force living below subsistence has no impact on the economy as a whole to the development of what

he referred to as the "scientific treatment of labor" (1996, 165). In this approach, labor becomes a commodity with a market price, and the concept of subsistence—a cultural concept—disappears entirely. The notion that a viable economy requires adequate maintenance of all resources, including labor, is discarded in favor of the goal of individual utility maximization.[12]

The second implication of the shift from the classical "subsistence" wage to the neoclassical "minimum" wage is that the economic system is now dependent on government intervention. Clark argued in his *Economics of Overhead Costs* that business did not properly account for all costs of production, including labor.[13] "There is a minimum of maintenance of the laborer's health and working capacity which must be borne by someone, whether the laborer works or not" or else "the community suffers a loss through the deterioration of its working power" (quoted in Stabile 1996, 151). Clark's analysis is primarily focused on the problem of unemployment, but his arguments are equally relevant to inadequate wages. Society has an interest in the adequate sustenance of workers, including those who are currently unemployed as well as those who are working for a wage that could lead to the "depreciation" of labor as a resource. The situation was summarized succinctly by Stabile:

> Overhead costs are defined as those costs that exist no matter what level of production is chosen, even when the level chosen is zero. . . . Regarding workers, this means that they must feed, clothe and house themselves and their families, whether they are working or not. These costs will not go away, if workers cannot pay them, so someone else must, whether it be friends and relatives, eleemosynary institutions, or government. If these other agencies helped cover the social costs of labor, businesses were being subsidized by them. (1996, 151)

Thus, according to Clark's analysis of overhead costs, all employers of low-wage labor are engaging in cost shifting. In the case of a worker who receives less than subsistence, the overhead costs for this worker are being shifted to the worker's family or to society. However, overhead costs can be shifted to family members only to the extent that these family members are earning a sufficient income. For example, assume a worker in a family of four currently earns $5.15 per hour and, like many minimum wage workers, works less than forty hours per week and less than fifty weeks per year. If the worker works thirty hours per week for fifty weeks per year, he or she would earn $7,725 (ignoring payroll taxes or other deductions). A second worker in the household earning the same amount would still not raise the family above the poverty threshold of $17,463 (U.S. Census Bureau 2001).

Overhead costs can be shifted to society only to the extent that government programs are in place to cover some of these costs. Indeed, this is exactly what social programs do. Medical care, food stamps, child care, low-income housing, and other programs for the working poor are absorbing the unpaid overhead costs of labor. While the recipients of these programs benefit directly, business benefits indirectly from what amounts to a subsidy of labor costs. Clark concluded that the problem of overhead costs would not be rectified without government involvement: "the overhead cost of labor is a collective burden upon industry in general but the market does not allocate to each employer the share for which his own enterprise is responsible" (quoted in Shute 1997, 58). Two solutions to the problem are (1) social insurance programs that pay part of the subsistence of workers, either through cash payments or noncash transfers and (2) minimum wage legislation and living wage ordinances. Since the first solution is paid for by society through the tax system and the second falls directly on employers, it is not surprising which of these alternatives business prefers.[14]

Conclusion

The conflict between public and private interest is at the heart of most economic policy debates. This is particularly true of redistributive policies such as the federal minimum wage and local living wage laws. As Waltman pointed out, "Redistributive policies involve transfers of resources, with identifiable winners and losers" (2000, 2). What is particularly interesting about minimum and living wage laws, however, is the extent to which the debate has been dominated by the pecuniary notion of business prosperity. The winners and losers in the living wage debate are not on equal footing. Imposing a living wage benefits individual workers, but it does more than harm individual businesses. It threatens an economic prosperity that has come to be defined almost exclusively in terms of a rising stock market and the accumulation of financial wealth. The fact that this economic prosperity is not shared by a growing portion of society is an inconvenient detail that is best blamed on the individuals themselves. The point made by Veblen, Clark, and other institutional economists, however, is that the ultimate purpose of any economy is the provisioning of all members of society and not merely the enrichment of a few. Veblen's notion of economic welfare is a firmer foundation for true shared prosperity.

Notes

This chapter is reprinted from the *Journal of Economic Issues* by special permission of the copyright holder, the Association for Evolutionary Economics.

1. The concept of private interests as a governing principle for economic growth and welfare was most famously expressed by Adam Smith in the *Wealth of Nations*. To quote Smith, "[I]t is not from the benevolence of the butcher, the brewer, or the baker, that we expect our dinner, but from their regard to their self interest. We address ourselves, not to their humanity, but to their self-love, and never talk to them of our own necessities but of their advantages" (1909, 20).

2. Both Thorstein Veblen and J.M. Clark, at least in his early writings, used what has been termed, after Dudley Dillard, a monetary theory of production, or MTP (Dillard 1980). Veblen recognized that the goal of business firms was to transform money into more money, or M into M'. In this MTP context, firms are seen to employ a variety of strategies to transform the initial M into a larger M', with efficiency in production only one, and not necessarily the most useful, technique to increase their returns (Mayhew and Knoedler 1999). Clark (1923, 2), in particular, focused on the underutilized concept of overhead costs to argue that the archaic methods of calculating costs, both by modern firms and by economists, prevented private firms from recognizing the public interest in production.

3. More recently, William Greider (1997) and others have argued that the search for lower wages that is the basis of much foreign direct investment is on a collision course with increased output. In addition, the theory of efficiency wages provides another link between high wages and business interests (Altman 1998).

4. Thus, at the point in the business cycle when labor might finally begin to share in the general economic prosperity through rising wages, the prosperity must be curbed or brought back to the preferable state in which business gains but workers do not (see Thurow 1996). The participation of workers in the general prosperity generally takes the form of more work rather than higher wages (see Mishel, Bernstein, and Schmitt 2001). In typically prescient fashion, Veblen made the same observation: "To the workmen engaged in industry, particularly, substantial benefits accrue from an era of prosperity. These benefits come, not in the way of larger returns for a given amount of work, but more work, fuller employment, at about the earlier rate of pay" (1978, 211).

5. The declining importance of aggregate demand is found even among new Keynesians who claim to have rehabilitated Keynesian analysis (Lindbeck 1998). In a recent article, Paul Davidson stated:

> The New Keynesians have not contributed to the strengthening of Keynes' effective demand analytical system. Nor have they provided an analysis that is applicable to a money-contracting entrepreneurial system. Instead, New Keynesians have accepted classical axiomatic microfoundations, assuring an automatic mechanism to achieve full employment. Consequently, the contribution of the New Keynesians has been the invention of all sorts of short-run ad-hoc constraints (market failures) to the market mechanisms to prevent the nonmonetary classical system from achieving the short-run full employment equilibrium position assured by the very restrictive classical presumptions that both New Classical and New Keynesian theorists accept as universal truths. (1998, 581)

6. In a recent paper, Deborah Figart (2001) distinguished between the concept of a "living wage," which carries a strong ethical connotation, and the concept of a "subsistence wage," which does not. She went on to point out that a true living or "just wage" is far higher than a subsistence wage. These are valid comments. Lawrence Glickman (1997) made similar points in his discussion of the historical debates over the meaning of a "living wage." However, when translated into actual policy, the distinction between a living wage and a subsistence wage is less clear. For example, Waltman (2000) stated that one of the earliest state minimum wage laws was that passed by Massachusetts in 1912. The primary guideline for wage setting by Massachusetts labor boards was that "the wage should be adequate 'to supply the necessary cost of living and to maintain the worker in health'" (2000, 29). Similarly the living wage laws passed during the late twentieth century explicitly link the actual wage to federal poverty levels. Moreover, for purposes of our discussion, the concept of the subsistence wage is the more relevant concept. While one could certainly argue that an ideal society would provide all members of society with a "just" or living wage, the argument of our paper is that a subsistence wage is the minimum standard of a well-functioning economy.

7. The transformation of the laboring class into "free" labor was a long and difficult process. Indeed, one might argue that the process is not yet complete given the existence of labor conditions for immigrant labor that have many characteristics of indentured servitude and the continued persistence of slavery in many parts of the world (see ILO 2001).

8. The so-called freedom of the laboring class is an important institutional development. Later, this freedom of contract would be the basis of court challenges to state minimum wage laws, culminating in the *Adkins v. Children's Hospital* case in the early 1920s. This Supreme Court decision upheld the view that minimum wage laws were unconstitutional because they violated the freedom of contract between an employer and employee. This decision was reversed in 1936, opening the way for passage of the Fair Labor Standards Act in 1938 (Nordlund 1997).

9. One could also hope for private sources of support such as family members or charity, and many continue to do so in this century. For example, it is not uncommon for several families to live in one low-cost housing unit—the original tenant along with family members who would otherwise be homeless (see Jaworsky 1997).

10. Santa Clara County, California, the home of Silicon Valley, passed a living wage ordinance in 1995. The law mandates tax-abated firms to pay a minimum of ten dollars per hour and provide health benefits (ACORN 2001). However, the average hourly wage for a full-time, in-home child care worker (a nanny) on the San Francisco peninsula recently

25, 2000). While rates for child care outside of the home are lower, the cost is increasingly beyond the budget of even middle-class workers.

11. Modern wage theory includes a number of hypotheses regarding wage levels and differentials. For example, wages are determined by skill or human capital, by productivity, by industrial sector, by degree of responsibility, by the level of danger, by demographic characteristics of workers, and by supply and demand (see Ehrenberg and Smith 1999). Standard labor economics textbooks include a broad variety of concepts, hypotheses, and theories; however, there is no mention of a subsistence wage other than in a historical context.

12. Donald Stabile (1996) noted that modern economists' entirely individualistic treatment of labor ignores the fact that individual actions have impacts on third parties. The presence of externalities in any market means that there will be a difference between private costs and social costs. Thus, the "scientific approach to labor" did not, after all, entirely succeed in eliminating the concept of subsistence from modern economic theory. However, as Stabile pointed out, Arthur C. Pigou's concept of external costs is rarely applied to the labor market.

13. The contrast between Clark's approach and the modern "scientific" approach to labor reflects the contrast between social prosperity and business prosperity discussed in the previous section. From the point of view of the individual business firm, lower wages mean lower costs and higher profits. If workers receive less than subsistence wages, they are incurring hardships that affect only themselves and their families. Social costs may occur, but these are confined to the costs incurred by governments who choose to insure individuals against these hardships. That is, externalities may result when workers receive less than subsistence wages. However, the externalities are imposed by the workers who are unable to protect themselves against economic misfortune. On the other hand, in Clark's analysis, the social costs of paying less than a subsistence wage are imposed by employers who inaccurately limit their calculation of labor costs to actual wages paid rather than to the true cost of maintaining a labor force.

14. In their recent analysis of the net social wage, Anwar Shaikh and E. Ahmet Tonak (2000) found that the net social wage in the United States over the past fifty years is effectively equal to zero, indicating that business has effectively transferred no additional income to workers via the mechanism of a welfare state, thus exacerbating the falling real wage for most workers during that time.

References

Altman, Morris. "A High-Wage Path to Economic Growth and Development." *Challenge* 41 (January/February 1998): 91–104.

Association of Community Organizations for Reform Now (ACORN). "Living Wage Successes: A Compilation of Living Wage Policies on the Books," www.livingwagecampaign.org, March 2001.

Bernstein, Irving. *The Lean Years: A History of the American Worker, 1920–1933.* Baltimore: Penguin, 1966.

———. *Turbulent Years: A History of the American Worker, 1933–1941.* Boston: Houghton Mifflin, 1970.

Card, David, and Alan B. Krueger. *Myth and Measurement: The New Economics of the Minimum Wage.* Princeton, NJ: Princeton University Press, 1995.

Clark, John Maurice. *Studies in the Economics of Overhead Costs.* Chicago: University of Chicago Press, 1923.

———. *Long Range Planning for the Regularization of Industry.* New York: New Republic, 1932.

———. *Social Control of Business.* 1928. Reprint, New York: Augustus M. Kelley, 1969.

Clark, Kim. "Reasons to Worry about Rising Wages." *Fortune,* July 7, 1997, 26–27.

Davidson, Paul. "Keynes' Principle of Effective Demand versus the Bedlam of the New Keynesians." *Journal of Post-Keynesian Economics* 21, no. 4 (Summer 1999): 571–88.

Dillard, Dudley. "A Monetary Theory of Production." *Journal of Economic Issues* 14, no. 2 (June 1980): 255–73.

Dobb, Maurice. *Wages.* 3rd ed. London: Nixbet, 1946.

Ehrenberg, Ronald G., and Robert S. Smith. *Modern Labor Economics: Theory and Public Policy.* Baltimore: Addison Wesley Longman, 1999.

Employment Policies Institute. "The Employment Impact of a Comprehensive Living Wage Law: Evidence from California," www.epionline.org, July 1999.

Feldstein, Martin. "Reducing Poverty, Not Inequality." *Public Interest* 137 (Fall 1999): 33–41.

Figart, Deborah M. "Ethical Foundations of the Contemporary Living Wage Movement." *International Journal of Social Economics* 28, no. 10–12 (2001): 800–14.

Glickman, Lawrence B. *A Living Wage: American Workers and the Making of Consumer Society.* Ithaca, NY: Cornell University Press, 1997.

Grieder, William. *One World, Ready or Not.* New York: Touchstone, 1997.

Hamermesh, Daniel S. "Review Symposium: Myth and Measurement: The New Economics of the Minimum Wage." *Industrial and Labor Relations Review* 48 (July 1995): 835–38.

Hamilton, David. *Evolutionary Economics.* Albuquerque: University of New Mexico Press, 1970.

International Labor Office (ILO). "Forced Labour, Human

Trafficking, Slavery Still Haunt Us." *World of Work* 39 (June 2001): 4–5.

Jaworsky, Paul. *Poverty and Place: Ghettos, Barrios, and the American City*. New York: Russell Sage Foundation, 1997.

Krugman, Paul. "Greenspan's Candor." *New York Times Magazine*, May 23, 1999, 24.

Lapides, Kenneth. *Marx's Wage Theory in Historical Perspective: Its Origins, Development, and Interpretation*. Westport, CT: Praeger, 1998.

Levin-Waldman, Oren M. "Exploring the Politics of the Minimum Wage." *Journal of Economic Issues* 32, no. 3 (September 1998): 773–802.

Lindbeck, A. "New Keynesianism and Aggregate Economic Activity." *Economic Journal* 108 (1998): 167–80.

Mayhew, Anne, and Janet Knoedler. "The Firm in Interwar Institutionalist Thought." Paper presented at the History of Economics Society meeting, Greensboro, SC, USA, 1999.

McCraw, Thomas K., and Richard S. Tedlow. "Henry Ford, Alfred Sloan, and the Three Phases of Marketing." In *Creating Modern Capitalism*, ed. Thomas K. McCraw. Cambridge, MA: Harvard University Press, 1997.

Mishel, Lawrence, Jared Bernstein, and John Schmitt. *The State of Working America, 2000–2001*. Ithaca, NY: ILR Press, 2001.

Murray, Bobbi. "Living Wage Comes of Age." *Nation*, July 23–30, 2001, 24–28.

Nordlund, Willis J. *The Quest for a Living Wage*. Westport, CT: Greenwood Press, 1997.

Partridge, Mark D., and Jamie S. Partridge. "Do Minimum Wage Hikes Reduce Employment? State-Level Evidence from the Low-Wage Retail Sector." *Journal of Labor Research* 20, no. 3 (Summer 1999): 393–415.

Polanyi, Karl. *The Great Transformation*. Boston: Beacon Press, 1957.

Ricardo, David. *The Principles of Political Economy and Taxation*. New York: Dutton, 1911.

Shaikh, Anwar, and E. Ahmet Tonak. "The Rise and Fall of the U.S Welfare State." In *Political Economy and Contemporary Capitalism*, ed. Ron Baiman, Heather Boushey, and Dawn Saunders. Armonk, NY: M.E. Sharpe, 2000.

Shute, Lawrence. *John Maurice Clark: A Social Economics for the Twenty-First Century*. New York: St. Martin's Press, 1997.

Smith, Adam. *An Inquiry into the Nature and Causes of the Wealth of Nations*. New York: P.F. Collier, 1909.

Stabile, Donald R. *Work and Welfare: The Social Costs of Labor in the History of Economic Thought*. Westport, CT: Greenwood Press, 1996.

Taylor, Jason, and George A. Selgin. "By Our Bootstraps: Origins and Effects of the High-Wage Doctrine and the Minimum Wage." *Journal of Labor Research* 20, no. 4 (Fall 1999): 447–62.

Thurow, Lester. "The Crusade That's Killing Prosperity." *American Prospect* (March–April 1996): 54–60.

U.S. Census Bureau. "Poverty 2000," www.census.gov/hhes/poverty/threshld/thresh00.html, January 26, 2001.

Veblen, Thorstein B. *Theory of Business Enterprise*. New Brunswick, NJ: Transaction Publishers, 1978.

Waltman, Jerold. *The Politics of the Minimum Wage*. Urbana: University of Illinois Press, 2000.

Zieger, Robert H. *American Workers, American Unions, 1920–1985*. Baltimore: Johns Hopkins University Press, 1986.

6

U.S. Labor Reexamined, 1880–1930

Success, Ideology, and Reversal

Jon D. Wisman and Aaron Pacitti

The modern character of the struggle between the interests of labor and capital took form between 1880 and 1930. It was a period in which ascendant industrial capital brutalized American labor. Capital became increasingly concentrated and engaged in anticompetitive practices, while labor was increasingly proletarianized—from self-employed to wageworkers. Workers lost control over the work process as orders increasingly came from above. Jobs were deskilled. Workers faced the competition of wave after wave of immigrants. And strikes were repressed with extreme prejudice.

Yet within this hostile environment, labor managed to make considerable progress. Although there were clear losses in control over the work process, workers' real wages increased and popular support for labor led to substantial prolabor social legislation. Indeed, during the first two decades of the twentieth century, labor increased its relative power vis-à-vis capital.

Labor's successes, however, were to be partially reversed during the 1920s. These reversals followed upon heightened public antipathy toward labor that translated into a significant political swing in favor of the interests of capital and initiated a decline in labor's relative power. The principal weapon deployed to rally the public against labor was ideological: the charge that labor had become unpatriotic, embracing un-American attitudes, even the tenets of socialism and communism. This charge was made palpable by labor's increasing militancy, especially its strikes and work stoppages during World War I.

This chapter surveys the struggles of labor against capital during this formative period between 1880 and 1930. It focuses upon the manner and extent to which labor's increasing successes, and especially its increasing militancy, set in motion forces that enabled the interests of capital to delegitimate labor's cause ideologically and partially reverse its gains. This reversal was especially pronounced in the 1920s.

The Divided Interests of Capital and Labor

Within the history of modern economics beginning with Adam Smith, there have been two divergent and generally contradictory interpretations of the character of capitalist society. Major classical economists such as Adam Smith, David Ricardo, and John Stuart Mill typically embraced both, without fully grasping the contradiction. When they focused principally on markets, they saw capitalist society as fundamentally harmonious: buyers and sellers conclude their contracts freely. However, when they broadened their focus beyond the market nexus, they saw society divided into classes with often divergent interests.

Since its beginning in the late nineteenth century, modern mainstream economics has generally restricted its focus to markets and consequently viewed economic relationships as harmonious.[1] Heterodox economists, by contrast, have insisted that this narrow focus ignores the fact that broad economic phenomena cannot be adequately grasped if the larger institutional matrix within which markets are embedded is not drawn explicitly into the analysis.

Karl Marx broke with the ambivalent stance of the classical school by exposing harmony as an ideological consequence of a narrow market focus. Markets constituted a "surface reality" of harmony, beneath which the principal conflictual causal forces could be found. These forces emanated out of the "social relations of production"—especially property rights—that under capitalism pitted the interests of capital against those of labor. Indeed, Marx defined the *differentia specifica* of capitalism as a social system in which workers are separated from ownership and control of the means of production. The rise of capitalism was the traumatic social transformation during which this separation of workers from tools and resources occurred. Once workers were forced to search out employment from those who owned or controlled the means of production, a fundamental struggle ensued: forced by competition to seek the highest profits possible, capitalists would strive to squeeze the greatest amount of work from labor for the least pay, whereas workers would struggle for higher pay, greater economic security, better working conditions, and more control over their own lives.[2] To achieve their goals, the interests of both capital and labor would attempt to draw upon social, political, and ideological structures.

Although this study draws upon Marx's characterization of capital-labor strife as a defining characteristic of capitalism, it does not embrace the specific lawlike theoretical formulations he built upon it. Instead, the approach taken here is closer to that of American institutionalism. The manner in which the tensions between capital and labor play out in a given historical period is dependent upon the cultural conditions of the time.

The conflict of interests between capital and labor marked the character of American industrial society. As will be seen below, the interests of labor were pitted against those of capital both within the firm and in the political arena over such issues as the length of the working day, the intensity of the work pace, the introduction of new technology, the right to organize into unions, health and safety within firms, child labor, and the desirable rate of immigration. But most importantly, this framework clarifies the manner in which even labor's successes created antagonisms that empowered the interests of capital. From the early 1880s to 1920, labor made considerable progress. But it was during the last fifteen years of this period that labor experienced its greatest advances—a sort of crescendo of its power. However, this very success emboldened labor to set into motion forces that allowed the interests of capital to reduce those successes significantly during the 1920s.

This study suggests that labor's successes in the early twentieth century set in motion a number of processes that became antithetical to labor's long-term relative power. Indeed, the history of labor's struggles between 1880 and 1930 suggests that so long as capital is controlled by interests divergent from those of labor, labor's relative gains appear to set in motion forces that promise at least a partial reversal.[3] Indeed, the fate of American labor since World War II supports such a hypothesis (Wisman 2002).

From Self-Employment to Wage Labor

Industrialization came in earnest to the United States only after 1865. Earlier, most of the workforce (excepting slaves in the South) retained substantial control over the workplace. At least half of all adults were self-employed, either in agriculture, crafts, or small proprietorships as owner-workers. And even those who became wage-workers retained substantial control over the workplace as late as the 1880s. Production was relatively small-scale and technology relatively uncomplicated. Indeed, it was not uncommon for the "boss" to simply purchase the equipment and allow the workers to determine how to produce a given amount of output and how to divide among themselves the payment received (Montgomery 1987, 13; 1983, 111).

But the increasing maturity of industrialization radically changed the labor process. The number of Americans employed in manufacturing as wageworkers increased from 2.5 million in 1870 to 11.2 million in 1920 (Dubofsky 1996, 3). And increasingly, production decision-making became the prerogative of management. An ideological defense of a separation between mental and manual labor evolved, especially in the work of Frederick Winslow Taylor, founder of "scientific management." The goal, according to Taylor, was "to take all the important decisions and planning which vitally affect the output of the shop out of the hands of the workmen, and centralize them in a few men, each of whom is especially trained in the art of making those decisions and in seeing that they are carried out" (cited in Sohn-Rethel 1978, 151). In fact, any creative participation by the worker was to be forbidden: "Under our system the workman is told minutely just what he is to do and how he is to do it; and any improvement which he makes upon the orders is fatal to success" (cited in Sohn-Rethel 1978, 152). Taylor clearly understood that what was at stake was the divided interests of capital and labor. The greatest problem facing management, he argued, "lay in the ignorance of the management as to what really constitutes a proper day's work for a workman" (Taylor 1947, 53). Much of scientific management consisted of strategies for getting workers to reveal their full potential. It was a conscious and deliberate endeavor, as Montgomery has put it, to "uproot those work practices which had been the taproot of whatever strength organized labor enjoyed in the late nineteenth century" (1979, 27).

The consequence was that wageworkers became progressively deskilled and the tacit knowledge owned by skilled craftsmen became increasingly devalued in the face of management attitudes and changing technology (Braverman 1974). Moreover, as Hoxie has put it, "any craft would be thrown open to the competition of an almost unlimited labor supply" (1920, 132). Further, by 1920, only about 20 percent of workers would remain self-employed.

Unlike their counterparts in Europe, American workers did not have to fight for the franchise as well as higher wages and better working conditions.[4] The interests of capital were outnumbered at the ballot box. To succeed in the political realm, capital had to count on success in the realm of ideology. It would have to capture the allegiance of the self-employed, as well as some portion of the working class itself.[5] For much of this period, popular disgruntlement with rising industrial concentration made capital's ideological challenge daunting.

The Juggernaut of Industrial Power

The thirty-five-year period between the end of the Civil War and the end of the century witnessed the maturation of industrialization in the United States. Labor faced a dramatic increase in the economic power of capital as firms merged into ever-larger entities and businesses joined together in trade associations. As they gobbled up their competitors, their industries became less competitive and their monopoly profits enabled them to fend off labor strikes. Labor, by contrast, was highly divided by crafts, ethnicity, and race. Further, because the character of much technological change was labor-displacing or skill-reducing, it worked against the interests of labor. Nevertheless, by the end of the century, labor had managed to achieve considerable organizational and political success.

In face of increasing industrial concentration and coordination, labor struggled to organize, to become, in Galbraithian terms, a countervailing power. And labor's successes at doing so after 1869 were accompanied by ever-greater militancy. A notable example is the massive strike by railroad workers in 1877 initiated in response to a series of reductions in wages. It unfolded, in Dubofsky's words, into "the most massive and destructive industrial conflict in the late nineteenth-century industrial world" (1996, 44).

However, the zeal and violent rhetoric of workers gave capital the ideological weapon it needed to check labor's popularity and political power. Defenders of the interests of capital alleged that workers had become dangers to law and order, that they advocated anarchy and the overthrow of American institutions. A huge antilabor propaganda campaign followed the 1886 Haymarket Square bombing and the subsequent repression of labor in Chicago. It was to be the nation's first red scare. The interests of capital had landed upon a patriotic mode of propaganda to incite public opinion against worker interests.

The success of this propaganda initiative is evident in court verdicts. Where workers mustered solidarity for higher wages or better working conditions, or to oppose wage reductions, the verdicts handed down by local judges increasingly blocked their efforts. Underlying these judicial decisions was the constitutional doctrine of "freedom of contract." Collective labor actions were deemed in violation of this doctrine. More ominously for labor, in 1886, the U.S. Supreme Court decreed in *Santa Clara County v. Southern Pacific Railroad* that a corporation is a person for the purposes of the Fourteenth Amendment to the Constitution (Ross 1994, 25 fn6). Essentially, human rights were extended to the corporation. No such status was granted to labor unions.

The Supreme Court also upheld *(In re Debs)*, in 1895, local judge-issued injunctions that banned strikers from picketing, holding meetings, conferring with union officers, publishing articles, or seeking the support of the public. The famed leader of the National Railway Union, Eugene Debs, and three other leaders were sent to jail for violating such an injunction (Ernst 1995, 76–77).

Yet capital did not manage to turn public sentiments entirely against labor. The public was becoming incensed at the anticompetitive behavior of the trusts. Outrage led Democratic president Grover Cleveland to declare in 1888 that the people were being "trampled to death beneath an iron heel" of the trusts that were rapidly "becoming people's masters" (cited in Welch 1988, 17). By 1890, twenty-one states had attempted to curb monopoly power with antitrust statutes. In response, trusts frequently changed the states in which they were incorporated. Congress, facing public insistence that the problem could not be solved at the state level, passed the Sherman Antitrust Act in 1890 (unanimous in the House, 52 to 1 in the Senate), its principal clause stating that "every contract, combination in form of trust or otherwise, or conspiracy in restraint of trade among the several states . . . is hereby declared illegal" (cited in Letwin 1965, 94–95).[6]

However, the industrial merger movement gained its greatest impetus in the decade following passage of the antitrust act.[7] Not only did the Supreme Court interpret the law conservatively, but the act was more frequently used against labor than against its purported target. Labor was alleged to be using its solidarity to obstruct or limit commerce. And, in 1908, the Supreme Court ruled in the Danbury Hatters case *(Loewe v. Lawlor)* that trade unions were subject to the Sherman Act (Ernst 1995, 151–52). Moreover, union members could be held individually liable for damages to the company.

But support for labor was evident in other domains and some of the reforms proposed by labor organizations "nominally succeeded" (Robertson 2000, 37). In 1883 Congress created the Senate Committee on Relations between Labor and Capital to investigate labor issues and disputes. In its investigations of strikes, the committee "showed considerable sympathy to the strikers' point of view." By 1898, the United States Industrial Commission was formed and its findings "anticipated much of the Progressive Era labor reform agenda" (Robertson 2000, 77). Labor's political fortunes were improving.[8]

Indeed, the political spectrum was swaying leftward. Behind the argument of protecting American wage earners from low-wage foreign competition, Republican president Benjamin Harrison sought tariff protection in 1888. Arguing for the equivalent of a "living wage," he proclaimed that "we should have in America a class of workingmen earning adequate wages that would bring comfort into their homes and hope in their hearts" (cited in Hedges 1971, 186). Nor was Harrison shy in associating with radical and militant labor leaders.

And in spite of repression, especially in the courts, labor managed to create unions that would eventually nearly match the national reach of corporations.[9] During the last two decades of the nineteenth century, labor's militancy continued to increase: the number of work stoppages nearly quadrupled and the number of workers belonging to unions tripled.

Labor's Halcyon Period

It might have been expected that labor's increased militancy would sour public support. But business behavior got yet worse press. Muckraking journalists began to "expose the corruption of business and the squalor and poverty of the city" (Wynn 1986, 9).[10] They revealed the sordid, dangerous conditions confronting workers, while the increasingly open display of the excesses of wealth by the captains of industry during the Gilded Age of the Gay Nineties met the ire of a population still largely embracing the tenets of Protestantism.[11] Reform-minded journalists revealed the need for change and delivered news of progress made on behalf of labor in Europe. England had embarked on a "New Liberalism" that established welfare measures, while Bismarck's Imperial Germany did the same. Moreover, the worker hardships attendant on the severe depression of the early 1890s "softened the public attitude towards organized labor" (Taft 1983, 115). Large corporations were increasingly viewed with distrust. The seamy side of capitalism was widely exposed.

The broad popularity of books by social critics such as Henry George (*Wealth and Poverty*), Edward Bellamy (*Looking Backward*), Upton Sinclair (especially *The Jungle*) and Thorstein Veblen (*Theory of the Leisure Class*) also revealed a public sympathetic to labor. For the first two decades of the new century, during the Progressive Era and

World War I, labor substantially increased its power vis-à-vis capital.

There was a significant "change in attitudes toward labor, particularly in government circles" (Wynn 1986, 87), exemplified by enactment of Progressive Era policies. President Theodore Roosevelt, while not explicitly favoring labor over capital, was staunchly antitrust. Most notably, he took the railroads to court for violations of the Sherman Act and won the suit in 1904 (Gould 1996, 35).

Prolabor aspects of Roosevelt's administration included the advocacy of employer liability laws, regulation of the use of injunctions in labor disputes and urging arbitration rather than military force to resolve strikes (Wynn 1986, 87), income taxes to mitigate income inequality, and "greater supervision of large corporations" (Gould 1996, 89). A workmen's compensation system for certain federal employees was established in 1908 (Robertson 2000, 233).[12]

By 1908, public outrage at the level of collusion between politicians and corporations led twenty-two states to enact laws prohibiting corporations from making political campaign contributions. Twelve states enacted measures requiring supervision of lobbyists. This new "system of governance" had the intention of regulating the behavior of capital and wealthy elites and, thereby, implicitly promoting the general interest of labor (Gould 1996, 76).

Although the Sherman Antitrust Act had been used against labor in the courts, there was strong popular sentiment that workers should have the legal right to organize and that employers should have to bargain honestly with them (Cox and Bok 1965, 78–79). Passage of the Clayton Act in 1914 represented the consummation of twenty years of public demand for favorable labor legislation.[13] Because it partially exempted unions from the antitrust laws, Samuel Gompers proclaimed it to

be "labor's charter of freedom" (Cox and Bok 1965, 78).[14]

The enhanced relative power of workers was evident in other domains. During the first decade of the twentieth century, union membership increased by nearly 60 percent. Unemployment rarely exceeded five percent (U.S. Bureau of the Census). The average workweek declined from 57.3 hours to 54.9 hours.[15] And for the period of 1890 to 1914, real wages for factory workers increased by 37 percent (Rees 1961).

Broad social pressures prompted the creation of the National Child Labor Committee in 1904 to investigate the status and condition of working children and to propose needed legislation (U.S. Department of Labor 1962, 13). By 1909, all but six states had established a minimum age for factory work, and by 1913, nineteen had eight-hour-day laws for children under sixteen. Public sentiment was also forcing Congress to take action. The Federal Children's Bureau was established in 1912 and the Keating-Owen Bill of 1916 forbade interstate or foreign commerce if the production involved the use of children under fourteen years of age (U.S. Department of Labor Standards 1962, 38).

Industrial technology brought with it industrial accidents. Preventable tragedies in mines, steel mills, and factories in general "raised public indignation to a high pitch" (U.S. Department of Labor 1962, 147). Outrage was fueled by popular works such as Upton Sinclair's *The Jungle*. State laws began to mandate safety inspections. By 1900, sixteen states provided for factory inspections. By 1908, a compensation program was established for certain injured federal employees. By 1916, forty states had compensation programs, most of which survived constitutionality challenges (Robertson 2000, 48, 233).

In the late nineteenth century, labor had pressured states to establish labor departments and data collection bureaus to inform the worker of "how much of that which he produces belongs to him as a reward for labor done" (Powderly 1890, 168). In 1913 labor succeeded at the national level with the establishment of the Department of Labor. The "Secretary of Labor [was to] have power to act as mediator and to appoint commissioners of conciliation in labor disputes whenever in his judgment the interests of industrial peace may require it to be done" (cited in Bernstein 1966, 220). These "commissioners of conciliation" were former trade union officials[16] with extensive knowledge of the American workers' conditions, hardships, and concerns. By law, the Labor Department was required to promote the interests and welfare of workers. Labor now had a legal voice in the federal government.

Immigrant labor posed a continual threat to labor's interests. Immigrants put downward pressure on wage rates and were frequently brought in to replace strikers.[17] Labor's successes in this domain were not always attractive.[18] Playing upon racist sentiments, with labor's strong support, the Chinese Exclusion Act of 1882 prohibited entrance of Chinese "coolie" immigrants into the United States. Passage of the Alien Contract Labor Law of 1885 and the Immigration Act of 1891 placed certain restrictions on the intentional importation of unskilled workers (Lane 1987, 85). But major curbs on unskilled immigrant labor came only in the 1917 Immigration Act, which required a literacy test for all immigrants. Finally, with the assistance of nationalistic sentiments, the Johnson Act of 1921 put a three percent quota (based on the number of that nationality resident in the United States at the time of the 1910 census) on new immigrants from any nation (Lane 1987, 190).

With the election of Woodrow Wilson and the widespread electoral success of the Democratic Party, the "progressive platform" advanced at both the state and federal levels. Democrats were delivering on their promises to labor (Gould 1996, 131). Wilson had strongly emphasized in his campaign speeches that the nation's well-being depended upon labor's well-being. It should be noted that he was being pulled left of center by the rising popularity of the Socialist Party.[19] Wilson claimed that "genuine spokesmen of the whole country," must look after and improve the situation of labor (Wilson cited in Davidson 1956, 30–31). He strongly advocated a legal framework within which labor could organize, a federally established and enforced minimum wage, and a strong, trusting bond between labor and the Democratic Party (Davidson 1956, 76, 280, 339, 359). In 1917, he became the first president to deliver an address at an American Federation of Labor (AFL) convention. He proclaimed that labor's condition was not to be "rendered more onerous by the war" and that, in most disputes, "[labor is] reasonable in a larger number of cases than the capitalists" (cited in Wynn 1986, 96).[20] With the creation of the National War Labor Board (NWLB), Wilson announced a "new deal for American labor," wherein workers would have an equal role with capital in determining federal labor policy (Wynn 1986, 101).

During World War I, maintaining a high level of output was imperative. And as Mary van Kleeck, coauthor of a policy statement issued by the Office of the Chief of Ordnance, put it, "industrial history proves reasonable housing, fair working conditions, and a proper wage scale are essential to high production" (cited in Wynn 1986, 105). In return, labor would work diligently and not strike. Labor's ever-improving welfare seemed guaranteed. A General Order issued in 1918 by the Office of the Chief of Ordnance insisted that "during the war every attempt should be made to conserve in every possible way all our achievements in the way of social betterment" (cited in Wynn 1986, 105). Labor's position was fortified to the extent that "an aggressively anti-union policy" became "impossible" (Nelson 1997, 94). During the 1910s, union membership rose 47.7 percent.

Yet foretelling a disastrous turn for labor, real wages began a slight downward trend during the war (Douglas 1966, 210). This was the result not of lower nominal wages, but rather of higher than normal levels of war-induced price inflation. Although real wages held up for most of organized labor, they fell for unorganized workers. In response to this decline and rising wartime profits, labor became increasingly militant and broke its promises.[21] Labor "began to use the strike weapon as never before." Between 1915 and 1918, the number of work stoppages tripled and strikes "raged with singular intensity" in the munitions and armaments industry (Dubofsky 1996, 129), resulting in a 10 percent fall in labor productivity (Brody 1993, 12). Labor had been accepted as a partner in determining federal policy and it was not holding up its end of the bargain. As the war ended, labor's failure to fulfill its informal no-strike pledge caused it to lose credibility, not only with government officials, but with the public as well.[22] Labor could no longer be trusted and capital could finally "end . . . two decades of retreat before hostile public opinion, legal harassment . . . and the growing strength of organized labor" (Carey 1995, 62).

Capital's Response to Labor's Newfound Prominence

Although slow to do so, the American public eventually rallied behind its government in support of World War I. A foreign enemy unified the American people. And as frequently is the case when a war ends, for unity to hold, a new enemy must be identified. The Bolshevik Revolution in Russia made this possible. For the interests of capital, the revolution was an ideological windfall. Labor's emboldened stance would be interpreted as alliance with an extreme foreign doctrine.

Already, as the war drew to a close, labor was being depicted as "unpatriotic," putting its own material interests above that of the nation in a time of war.[23] Between April 6 and October 5, 1917, over 6 million workdays were lost to strikes (Montgomery 1987, 370). By 1918, unemployment fell to a mere 1.4 percent, further emboldening labor. As unions pursued their goals with increasing inflexibility, employers fought back (Robertson 2000, 258). Business interests embarked on a campaign to demonstrate the patriotism of business and the dangers inherent in labor's intransigence.[24]

The socialist wing of the labor movement was especially persecuted. It was denied the use of the mails to distribute literature. Eugene Debs and a socialist congressman from Milwaukee were imprisoned on charges of sedition. So too were over 200 Wobblies. Purged of its active left, the labor movement would become "American," with its leadership ever more dominated by an increasingly tame AFL, and "demands for nationalization of industries, a six-hour day, government guarantees of union rights, a labor party, and strikes to demand freedom for political prisoners . . . disappeared from [its] proceedings altogether" (Montgomery 1987, 7).[25]

Before the 1920s, it was not uncommon for strikes to "enlist influential outsiders prominent social workers, [and] philanthropists" (Nelson 1997, 89). But in the 1920s, under assault from business interests that depicted labor as ignorant, disruptive, and socially dangerous, external support for labor waned. Increasingly, labor's struggles were portrayed as part of a communist conspiracy to turn the United States into the Western version of the Soviet Union.[26]

In 1920, the Democratic Party—the major party most sympathetic to labor's interests—lost the White House. The Republican Party would hold onto the White House until 1932 when the social cataclysm of the Great Depression returned public sympathy to labor.

Ushering in the new decade of the 1920s and spearheading capital's rapid increase in economic, political, and ideological power, Presidential candidate Warren Harding was viewed as "the businessman's darling." Capital "universally applauded him" for his dedication and commitment to restore normalcy by checking the power of labor (Downes 1970, 599). *The Wall Street Journal* (June 16, 1920) noted that Harding would create a "common sense constructive administration" and that his nomination was received "with universal favor by investors" (cited in Downes 1970, 623). Building upon this sentiment, a Pacific coast business journal, *The Argonaut* (June 19, 1920), depicted him as a man who "possesses in a large endowment the pure gold of common sense" (cited in Downes 1970, 623). Such a constitution led B.C. Forbes (*Forbes*, August 21, 1920) to opine that Harding's policies would be "more conducive to business confidence" (cited in Downes, 1970, 623).

Harding continually made reference to labor's failure to uphold its end of the wartime bargain. He claimed, as quoted in the AFL's newsletter, *The Federationist* (September 1920), that labor had "intimidated" Congress into passing the wartime prolabor legislation (cited in Downes 1970, 621). Perhaps best demonstrating Harding's desire to restore the nation to a state of normalcy was his creation of something resembling a new holiday, Businessman's Day.[27] It was to be held one week after Labor Day. He encouraged the nation's business leaders on the first Businessman's Day, September 10, 1920, to offer their "expert counsel" in upcoming political affairs (Downes 1970, 626, 628).

Calvin Coolidge is well known for his frank admission that "the business of America is business." Herbert Hoover, while not as forward with his language, clearly opposed the collective action of labor and spoke often and firmly regarding the virtues of economic individualism and liberty (Singer 1976, 21–34).

This onslaught of antilabor, procapital rhetoric reinforced the increasingly held view that untrustworthy labor was the enemy of harmony and normality. As Cox and Bok put it, this ideology appealed to the "psychological desire for a return to normalcy, post war reaction, and anti-Red hysteria" (1965, 83). Strikes and boycotts were depicted as counter to the American notion of individualism. Labor came to be increasingly "harried in the courts, libeled as a Communist conspiracy in the press, [and] knocked about by company thugs" (Perrett 1982, 34).[28]

Driven by robust growth in productivity, the U.S. economy in the 1920s prospered. Although real wages generally increased (Douglas 1966),[29] the increase in inequality was far more striking. For instance, the share of total income received by the richest 5 percent of the population increased from 24.3 percent in 1919 to 33.5 percent in 1929. The real prosperity of the 1920s was reserved for those residing at the top of the income scale (Bernstein 1966; Stricker 1985). The number of millionaires rose from 7,000 in 1914 to 35,000 by 1928. Contributing to this heightened inequality were tax "reforms" that reduced corporate taxes and lowered the maximum personal income tax rate from 65 to 32 percent (Sobel 1968, 52–53).

In spite of robust economic growth, much of the working class suffered chronic job and financial insecurity. An undertow of technological unemployment continually threatened industrial workers. The unemployed had difficulty locating full-time positions, and between 35 and 40 percent of nonfarm families lived below the poverty line (Stricker 1985).

Labor's loss of power was nowhere more evident than in its declining ability to act collectively. The depression of 1921–22 crushed many unions and demoralized workers. Their generally weakened state enabled employers to force yellow-dog contracts upon them. Work stoppages in the 1920s decreased by 57 percent and the number of workers participating in organized strikes fell by 69 percent. The interests of capital launched an "open shop" drive that, playing on patriotic sentiments, was termed the "American Plan." Collective action was presented as not only ineffective, but also unpatriotic. As Irving Bernstein put it, "In the mansion of the dominant business philosophy, there was no room for trade unionism. Those shrewd managers who conceived the 'American Plan' sold the idea that collective action was worse than bad, it was un-American" (1966, 88). Capital celebrated the traditional American value of rugged, self-reliant individualism as opposed to the subversive foreign values of collectivism.

The American free enterprise system, by contrast, promoted the value of "social harmony, freedom, democracy, the family, the church, and patriotism." Advocates of "government regulation of the affairs of business" were also characterized as subversive (Carey 1995, 27). As a member of the National Association of Manufacturers remarked, "you can hardly conceive of a more un-American, a more anti-American institution than the closed shop. It is really very remarkable that it is allowed to exist under the American flag" (cited in Bernstein 1966, 147). The association created an Open Shop Department in 1920 to collect and disseminate antiunion and antilabor information.

Understandably, within this ideological climate, labor's interests fared poorly in judicial decisions. Between 1921 and 1930, William Howard Taft

served as chief justice of the Supreme Court. In both voice and action, he served to keep labor subservient to the needs of capital. Early in his career, when informed that federal troops had killed thirty striking Pullman employees, he responded, "Everybody hopes that is true" (cited in Bernstein 1966, 190). He held that "corporate wrong is almost wholly beyond the reach of the courts" (cited in Duffy 1930, 47). He even went so far as to refer to the Senate in 1922 as a "Bolshevik body," and, six years later, to labor as a "class distinctly arrayed against the Court" (cited in Mason 1964, 93). Although trade unions were lawful associations, the Taft Court ruled that striking to aid workers in another striking craft—a sympathy strike—was unlawful. The extreme form of a sympathy strike—the general strike—suffered the same fate. Even boycotts were ruled illegal.

Further revealing its procapital bias, the Court ruled that unincorporated labor organizations were to be held financially liable for their actions. Previously, unincorporated associations were not deemed to be legal entities and therefore capable of neither suing nor being sued. Picketing did not fare any better. Chief Justice Taft alleged that such methods "however lawful in their announced purpose inevitably lead to intimidation and violence"; the word "picket" is itself "sinister" and suggests "a militant purpose" and as such is "unlawful and can not be peaceful" (cited in Bernstein 1966, 194). Workers could no longer legally form picket lines. The courts issued as many antilabor injunctions during the 1920s as during the entire period from 1880 to 1920 (Bernstein 1966, 200).

Other gains by labor were reversed. Although the U.S. Supreme Court had upheld the constitutionality of minimum wage legislation in Oregon in 1917 (U.S. Department of Labor Standards 1962, 114), the Court deemed similar legislation in the District of Columbia unconstitutional in 1923.[30]

State courts swiftly arrived at similar rulings in Kansas, Arkansas, and Utah. The few state statutes establishing minimum wages that remained on the books were "dead letters" (Bernstein 1966, 232). Child labor legislation, which had earlier won broad support, was struck down by the Supreme Court shortly after the end of the war (Perrett 1982, 33).

Although workers retained the legal right to organize, the court system made attempts to do so as difficult and legally hazardous as possible. And, if workers succeeded in organizing all the same, they found it nearly impossible to participate in any meaningful or symbolic activity, since participating, or even advocating such activities was deemed criminal.

Undergirding these court decisions was the doctrine of "freedom of contract" that had been continually utilized against the interests of labor since the mid-1880s. Indeed, adherence to this doctrine gave to judicial decisions a conservative slant that often ran counter to more liberal legislative intentions. The notion of liberty of contract was ensconced in the U.S. Constitution and thus overrode conflicting state laws (Champlin and Knoedler 2003, 310). This doctrine held that all contracts are consequent of the free decisions of the contracting parties. Thus any legislation that sought to protect one of the parties, such as labor in its contracting with the owners of capital, was found to violate freedom of contract.[31] What labor came to suffer in the 1920s was an ever more virulent interpretation of this doctrine such as to nullify many of the gains labor had earlier acquired through the political process.

Even the voice labor had achieved in the national government through the Department of Labor was largely silenced. The Department's budgets were slashed. Between 1919 and 1930, the number of cases brought before the conciliation service decreased by approximately 70 percent, as the group had only thirty-eight commissioners to deal with labor disputes (Bernstein 1966, 221). The department had no legal authority to enforce, let alone produce a settlement. Understandably, employers typically refused to participate in the department's initiatives.

The Anatomy of Reversal

That labor's fortunes turned so abruptly is striking. But World War I, early on, had partially deflected attention from labor's increasingly intransigent stance. Throughout the decade between 1910 and 1920, labor's successes had made it ever more optimistic and emboldened. All of this created a sense that labor would become ever more powerful and American society would become ever more equal and just.[32] The rhetoric and behavior of labor leaders and reformers became more strident, less compromising. Labor had created the conditions for its fall. All that was needed was a triggering event.

That event was the war and its immediate aftermath. As Neil Wynn put it, the war "created a greater and wider sense of instability than was normally the case. The combination of international chaos with political division, riots and labor troubles at home, created an enormous sense of unease" (1986, 201). Labor's breaking of the informal no-strike pledge was the pivotal sin.

As heterodox economics has long maintained, the division of interests between capital and labor is ever-present within capitalism. Once workers gained the franchise, the site of conflict was shifted substantially to the political sphere. And here, in terms of numbers, labor had the clear advantage. This advantage could be effectively countered by capital only in the ideological sphere. Capital's attempt to crush labor's power in the economic sphere through collusion both within capital and with government threatened to enhance labor's position ideologically. Circumstances fortuitous to the interests of capital created an ideological windfall in the form of patriotism. Labor's increasing relative power could be presented as against the national interest, as unpatriotic. The reversal of the 1920s was based upon capital's ability to play the patriotism card well enough to ideologically capture part of the working class itself, which would, as Veblen speculated pessimistically concerning Marx's hope for class solidarity, "sink their force in the broad sands of patriotism" (1919, 442).

Patriotism is not, of course, the only ideological weapon capital might wield to check or reverse labor's power. This is seen in a more contemporary instance of labor's reversal of fortunes following an extended period of successes. For approximately a quarter century after World War II, labor significantly increased its relative power. Workers shared the benefits of robust productivity gains. Major welfare programs were established. The distribution of income became slightly less unequal. Poverty decreased substantially. And government instituted broad measures that would establish a far better safety net and safer working conditions. Yet this halcyon period for labor was followed by a quarter century during which labor's relative status and power declined. Although in this instance patriotism was not absent from capital's ideological arsenal (with regard to the loss of Vietnam, dollar devaluation, and the supposed "end" of the "American century"), capital's use of ideology became far more subtle and sophisticated. It nurtured and drew upon a virulent strain of neoclassical economics in the form of supply-side economics. The fruit of labor's successes would be discredited on grounds that it thwarted incentives to work hard, to save, to invest, and to be entrepreneurial.[33]

Perhaps the greatest ideological accomplishment of the interests of capital since the late nineteenth century is that workers are no longer likely to seriously ponder the prospect of owning or controlling the tools and resources with which they work—even though workplace democracy has been a social ideal for well over 150 years.[34] The prevailing "habit of thought" is that workers would not be capable of responsibly controlling the firms in which they work. But it may be that labor's escape from the apparent contradiction that its successes establish the conditions for its failures lies in workers increasingly taking control and ownership of capital.

Notes

1. Ironically, the most prominent bastion of "scientific" economics today, the American Economic Association, took note of the central importance of tensions between the interests of capital and labor. Its initial 1886 constitution stated that "the conflict of labor and capital has brought into prominence a vast number of social problems, whose solution requires the united efforts, each in its own sphere, of the church, of the state, and of science" (cited in McNulty 1980, 143). It was, of course, far more oriented toward an institutionalist approach at the time.

2. Thorstein Veblen redefined this conflict of interests as between the habits of thought of business people with pecuniary interests and the industrial habits of thought of engineers and workers. John R. Commons also viewed the focus upon conflict as a defining characteristic of institutional economics: "I made . . . Conflict of Interests, not the Harmony of Interests of the classical and hedonistic economists, the starting point of Institutional Economics" (1934, 97).

3. This hypothesis is merely speculative at this juncture. Whether it might be broadly true of American capitalism, or modern capitalism generally, will require further study. The authors plan to examine whether other instances of substantial worker success set in motion forces that led to reversal in other modern capitalist economies.

4. American capital, however, had two advantages not possessed by its European counterparts. In the United States, workers were far more divided by ethnicity and race (see Commons 1904), thereby impeding the formation of the same degree of "craft and class loyalties [that] supported an interlocking structure of labor unions and working class political parties [in Europe]" (Jacoby 1997, 12–13). And unlike in Europe, there was no aristocracy to side with labor to check the power of the bourgeoisie.

5. The interests of capital had to develop support for bourgeois values, to enlist, as Sellers has put it, "conservative clerics and the emerging professional/intellectual elites of lawyers, doctors, professors, writers and artists to school all classes in a pansectarian middle-class culture of effortful 'character' and self-improvement" (1991, 364).

6. The intensity of public outrage at anticompetitive business practices had also led to the creation of the Interstate Commerce Act of 1887, laying the legal framework for the nation's first agency regulating business.

7. Indeed, "one third of US manufacturing assets were subject to merger in the years 1898–1902 alone" (Harvey 1990, 125). This "wave of mergers and consolidations . . . would be unrivaled for nearly a century until the 1980s" (Wachtel 2003, 164).

8. In fact, in terms of income, workers were doing well. Real wages between 1860 and 1890 increased by 50 percent (Long 1960).

9. The extended reach of the interests of capital was being fueled by new technologies: in the financial domain by the telegraph, the stock ticker, and the telephone; in the geographic domain by railroads (Wachtel 2003, 160).

10. Articles by muckrakers regularly appeared in periodicals such as *The Nation*, *McClure's*, *Harper's*, and *Collier's*, all with significant national circulation.

11. Louis Galambos has convincingly argued that the greatest decade of antibusiness sentiments in U.S. history was the Populist period of the 1890s (1975, 275).

12. Understandably, Roosevelt's actions reaped hostile responses from capital. Capital portrayed his "popular clamor" and political thought not as the result of educated observation, but rather as the result of a lack of economic erudition. As an Ohio banker put it, "the great trouble with [Roosevelt] is that he is not a business man and does not understand commercial affairs" (cited in Gould 1996, 93).

13. The Clayton Act had "two sections inserted at the request of organized labor." The "celebrated" section six declared:

> That the labor of a human being is not a commodity or article of commerce. Nothing contained in the anti-trust laws shall be construed to forbid the existence and operation of labor . . . organizations, instituted for the purpose of mutual help, and not having capital stock or conducted for profit, or to forbid or restrain individual members of such organizations, from lawfully carrying out the legitimate objects thereof; nor shall such organizations, or the members thereof, be held or construed to be illegal combinations or conspiracies in restraint of trade, under the anti-trust laws. (cited in Taylor and Witney 1992, 45)

14. Yet once labor's fortunes were checked in the 1920s, the Clayton Act "subsequently . . . proved to be less supportive of labor than he [Gompers] had imagined" (Wynn 1986, 89).

15. An eight-hour day had been mandated in 1892 for workers under the employ of firms with federal or state government contracts (U.S. Department of Labor Standards 1962, 83).

16. The first secretary of labor had been a leader of the United Mine Workers Association.

17. Hatton and Williamson (1995) estimate that competition from new immigrants retarded real wage growth by about 6 to 9 percent from 1890 to 1914.

18. American blacks were typically treated even worse than immigrants. Few unions permitted them membership.

19. The strength of the Socialist Party of the United States from 1901 to 1917 made it the only sustained third party of any significance in the twentieth century (Weinstein 1967).

20. It was common for companies to reject mediation in labor disputes and to "flatly refuse" to cooperate with suggested proposals (Montgomery 1987, 348).

21. Samuel Gompers, for instance, had vowed to the Council of National Defense that labor would not use the war to "change existing standards" (Montgomery 1987, 375).

22. Radical labor leaders were frequently imprisoned, harassed, or beaten for speaking out against the war, which was interpreted as a form of sedition. The clearest example is Eugene Debs's infamous speech and subsequent arrest in Canton, Ohio, in 1918.

23. Efforts to associate business interests with values held by American patriots were being developed and implemented during World War I. The Americanization campaign portrayed both domestic and foreign radicals as a threat to the free enterprise system and, hence, the United States. Commercial groups tried to Americanize immigrant workers by offering educational materials on cultural and industrial issues, thus orienting the individual's conception of freedom and harmony to that of a smoothly functioning market-based economy. The Council of National Defense officially endorsed federal funding of the campaign, which the government made part of its war program (Carey 1995, 37–58).

24. A leader of the National Association of Manufacturers proclaimed, "Business and patriotism go hand in hand. Industrialism is beneficent, civilizing and uplifting. It is the enemy of war, of despotism, of ignorance and poverty. In truth, its foes are the foes of mankind" (cited in Watts 1991, 28–29).

25. An indication of the AFL's conservatism is that it strongly opposed unemployment insurance until 1932. It remained neutral in the presidential election between Hoover and Roosevelt.

26. When the Great Steel Strike ended in 1920, labor "had been predictably represented by government and business interests as a Bolshevist revolutionary challenge to American society" (Carey 1995, 63).

27. Unfortunately for the owners of capital, this holiday did not catch on.

28. Within this antilabor environment, the Socialist Party of America began a decline from which it would never fully recover (Weinstein 1967).

29. In manufacturing, wages increased less than did productivity, and between 1923 and 1929 weekly earnings declined about 20 percent, and about 8 percent in steel production (Bernstein 1966, 66–67). Charles Holt argues that per capita income for the lowest 93 percent of the nonfarm working class actually decreased by 4 percent from 1923 to 1929 (Holt 1977).

30. The original impetus for creating a wage floor stemmed from women's organizations. They viewed a minimum wage as "an expression of the public interest in protecting the health of the mothers and future citizens of this country" because "a large proportion of families studied could not earn enough for the absolute necessities of living" (U.S. Department of Labor 1962, 108–9). Massachusetts was the first state to enact minimum wage legislation in 1912.

31. As Champlin and Knoedler point out, "Protective labor legislation was justified on the basis of public health. [Thus, for example] it was deemed to be in the public interest to protect women not because they were workers but because they represented motherhood. . . . It was clear that the 'public' in public health did not include workers themselves" (2003, 310).

32. Thus the *New Republic* could state: "We have already passed to a new era, the transition to a state in which labor will be the predominating element" (cited in Dubofsky 1996, 133).

33. This reversal of labor's fortunes has been examined by Wisman 2002.

34. For example, one of the most widely read of nineteenth-century mainstream economists, John Stuart Mill, wrote:

> The form of association . . . which, if mankind continues to improve, must be expected in the end to predominate, is not that which can exist between a capitalist as a chief, and work people without a voice in the management, but the association of the labourers themselves in terms of equality, collectively owning the capital by which they carry on their operations, and working under managers elected and removable by themselves. (1871, 772)

References

Bernstein, Irving. *The Lean Years: A History of the American Worker, 1920–1933*. Boston: Penguin Books, 1966.

Braverman, Harry. *Labor and Monopoly Capital: The Degradation of Work in the Twentieth Century*. New York: Monthly Review Press, 1974.

Brody, David. *Workers in Industrial America*. New York: Oxford University Press, 1993.

Carey, Alex. *Taking the Risk Out of Democracy*. Chicago: University of Illinois Press, 1995.

Champlin, Dell P., and Janet T. Knoedler. "Corporations, Workers, and the Public Interest." *Journal of Economic Issues* 37, no. 2 (June 2003): 305–13.

Commons, John R. "Labor Conditions in Meat Packing and the Recent Strike." *Quarterly Journal of Economics* 19 (November 1904): 1–32.

———. *Myself*. New York: Macmillan, 1934.

Cox, Archibald, and Derek Curtis Bok. *Cases and Materials on Labor Law*. Brooklyn, NY: Foundation Press, 1965.

Davidson, John Wells, ed. *A Crossroads of Freedom: The 1912 Campaign Speeches of Woodrow Wilson*. New Haven, CT: Yale University Press, 1956.

Douglas, Paul Howard. *Real Wages in the United States, 1890–1926*. New York: Houghton-Mifflin, 1966.

Downes, Randolf, C. *The Rise of Warren Gamaliel Harding 1865–1920*. Columbus: Ohio University State Press, 1970.

Dubofsky, Melvyn. *Industrialism and the American Worker, 1865–1920*. Wheeling, IL: Harlan Davidson, 1996.

Duffy, Herbert S. *William Howard Taft*. New York: Milton, Balch, 1930.

Ernst, Daniel R. *Lawyers Against Labor: From Individual Rights to Corporate Liberalism*. Chicago: University of Illinois Press, 1995.

Galambos, Louis. *The Public Image of Big Business in America, 1880–1940*. Baltimore: Johns Hopkins University Press, 1975.

Gould, Lewis L. *Reform and Regulation: American Politics from Roosevelt to Wilson*. Prospect Heights, IL: Waveland Press, 1996.

Harvey, David. *The Conditions of Postmodernity*. Oxford: Blackwell Publishers, 1990.

Hatton, Timothy, and Jeffrey Williamson. "The Impact of Immigration on American Labor Markets Prior to the Quotas." Working Paper No. 5185, National Bureau of Economic Research, 1995.

Hedges, Charles. *Speeches of Benjamin Harrison*. Port Washington, NY: Kennikat Press, 1971.

Holt, Charles F. "Who Benefited from the Prosperity of the Twenties?" *Explorations in Economic History* 14 (1977): 277–89.

Hoover, Herbert. "Campaign Speech, October 22." In *Campaign Speeches of American Presidential Candidates 1928–1972*, ed. Aaron Singer. New York: Frederick Ungar, 1982.

Hoxie, Robert Franklin. *Scientific Management and Labor.* New York: D. Appleton, 1920.

Jacoby, Sanford M. *Modern Manors: Welfare Capitalism Since the New Deal.* Princeton, NJ: Princeton University Press, 1997.

Lane, A.T. *Solidarity of Survival: American Labor and European Immigrants, 1830–1924.* New York: Greenwood Press, 1987.

Letwin, William. *Law and Economic Policy in America: The Evolution of the Sherman Antitrust Act.* New York: Random House, 1965.

Long, Clarence. *Wages and Earnings in the United States, 1860–1890.* Princeton, NJ: Princeton University Press, 1960.

Mason, Alpheus Thomas. *William Howard Taft: Chief Justice.* New York: Simon and Schuster, 1964.

McNulty, Paul J. *The Origins and Development of Labor Economics.* Cambridge, MA: MIT Press, 1980.

Mill, John Stuart. *Principles of Political Economy, 1871,* Reprint, Clifton, NJ: Augustus M. Kelley, 1973.

Montgomery, David. *Workers' Control in America.* Cambridge: Cambridge University Press, 1979.

———. "Workers' Control of Machine Production in the Nineteenth Century." In *The Labor History Reader,* ed. Daniel J. Leab. Urbana: University of Illinois Press, 1985.

———. The *Fall of the House of Labor.* Cambridge: Cambridge University Press, 1987.

Nelson, Daniel. *Shifting Fortunes: The Rise and Decline of American Labor, from the 1820s to the Present.* Chicago: Ivan R. Dee, 1997.

Perrett, Geoffrey. *America in the Twenties: A History.* New York: Simon and Schuster, 1982.

Powderly, Terence V. *Thirty Years of Labor, 1859–1889.* New York: Augustus M. Kelly, 1890.

Rees, Albert. *Real Wages in Manufacturing, 1890–1914.* Princeton, NJ: Princeton University Press, 1961.

Robertson, David Brian. *Capital, Labor, and State.* Lanham, MD: Rowman and Littlefield, 2000.

Ross, William G. *A Muted Fury: Populists, Progressives, and Labor Unions Confront the Courts, 1890–1937.* Princeton, NJ: Princeton University Press, 1994.

Sellers, Charles. *The Market Revolution.* New York: Oxford University Press, 1991.

Smith, Adam. *The Wealth of Nations.* Chicago: University of Chicago Press, 1976.

Sobel, Robert. *The Great Bull Market: Wall Street in the 1920s.* New York: W.W. Norton, 1968.

Sohn-Rethel, Alfred. *Intellectual and Manual Labour.* Atlantic Highlands, NJ: Humanities Press, 1978.

Stricker, Frank. "Affluence for Whom—Another Look at Prosperity and the Working Classes in the 1920s." In *The Labor History Reader,* ed. Daniel J. Leab. Urbana: University of Illinois Press, 1985.

Taft, Philip. "Workers of a New Century." In *A History of the American Worker,* ed. Richard B. Morris. Princeton, NJ: Princeton University Press, 1983.

Taylor, Benjamin, and Fred Witney. *U.S. Labor Relations Law: Historical Development.* Englewood Cliffs, NJ: Prentice Hall, 1992.

Taylor, Frederick Winslow. *Scientific Management.* New York: Harper and Row, 1947.

United States Bureau of the Census. *Historical Statistics of the United States, Colonial Times to 1957.* Washington, DC: Government Printing Office, 1960.

United States Bureau of Labor Standards. *Growth of Labor Law in the United States.* Washington, DC: Government Printing Office, 1962.

Veblen, Thorstein. "The Socialist Economics of Karl Marx and His Followers." In *The Place of Science in Modern Civilization.* New York: Russell and Russell, 1919, 431–56.

Wachtel, Howard. *Street of Dreams—Boulevard of Broken Hearts: Wall Street's First Century.* London: Pluto Press, 2003.

Watts, Sarah Lyons. *Order Against Chaos: Business Culture and Labor Ideology in America 1880–1915.* New York: Greenwood Press, 1991.

Weinstein, James. *The Decline of Socialism in America, 1912–1925.* New York: Monthly Review Press, 1967.

Welch, Richard E. *The Presidencies of Grover Cleveland.* Lawrence: University Press of Kansas, 1988.

Wisman, Jon D. "Did U.S. Labor's Post–World War II Successes Lead to Its Subsequent Woes?" Paper presented at the annual meeting of the Association for Institutionalist Thought, Albuquerque, New Mexico, April 13, 2002.

Wynn, Neil A. *From Progressivism to Prosperity: World War I and American Society.* New York: Holmes and Meier, 1986.

II

Institutionalist Thought on Labor
Since World War II

7

Two Sides of the Same Coin

Institutionalist Theories of Wage Rates and Wage Differentials

Douglas Kinnear

The methods and foci of labor economists of the post–World War II era are aptly illustrated by the work of several major labor economists, particularly Lloyd Reynolds, John Dunlop, and Clark Kerr. These three, without embracing the moniker "institutionalist," were nonetheless practicing economics of the type that most institutionalists would appreciate, and were tackling questions of interest to institutionalists. As Kerr wrote in 1988, "The group of labor economists who gave dominant leadership to the field in the United States from 1940 to 1960 chose, in the phrasing of Lionel Robbins, 'the interpretation of reality—the low road—over the building of theoretical *a priori* models'" (Kerr in Kaufman 1988, 4; italics in original). Much of their most influential work examined the wage determination process and the nature and causes of wage differentials. Focusing on the demand side of labor markets (rather than on labor supply and labor mobility as determinants of market outcomes), which implicitly assumes employer power over the employment relation, further demonstrated their heterodox viewpoint.

This chapter will examine the theories that were developed to explain wage determination and wage differentials; in the process, it will illustrate the new path that was being forged for labor economics by institutionalist practitioners. Concepts such as segmented labor market theory, internal labor market theory, and theories of unions' effects on wage rates were developed in this era, and these theories continue to be mined today by analysts seeking to explain wage rate determination and differentials.

Wage Differentials: An Emerging Topic

> Within the last decade, however, there has been a heartening renaissance of interest in the determination of relative wage rates. A substantial body of articles has accumulated in the United States, concerned mainly with interindustry differentials but with some attention to other aspects of wage structure. . . . The importance of the theoretical and practical problems in this area surely requires little demonstration. (Reynolds and Taft 1956, 2)

These words, written by Lloyd Reynolds and Cynthia Taft in 1956, noted a shift in labor economists' attention that had been occurring, as they pointed out, for the previous decade. Labor economists had found a renewed interest in wage rate determination, previously thought to be a settled subject. That interest was fueled, in part, by the abundant evidence of wage rate differentials that had compelled labor analysts to reexamine their conceptions about labor markets. The existence of wage differentials, not wage equality, was often the norm for similar types of labor, even in the same geographic area; in this sense, the study of wage determination and the study of wage differentials were two sides of the same coin.

The problem with the mainstream model of labor markets was explained by Kerr as follows:

> Abundant evidence now testifies that it would, in the absence of collusion, be almost more correct to say that wages tend to be unequal rather than the other way around. The avalanche of wage data by occupations and by localities during World War II at first bewildered and later convinced War Labor Board economists. Occupational wage rates, locality by locality, in the absence of collective bargaining displayed no single "going rate" but a wide dispersion. Absence of a single price was found to be the general rule. A sure sign of collusion, not of the working of market forces came to be the existence of a uniform rate. The market, it seemed, set rather wide limits and within these limits employers could develop policies as high-, medium-, or low-paid firms, and workers could accept high, medium, or low rates. Nonwage conditions of employment, such as welfare provisions, sick leave with pay, and so forth, were found to reinforce rather than offset the rate inequalities. (Kerr 1950, 71)

Dunlop put it even more tersely in 1944 when he wrote, "The automatic pricing mechanism as model or institution in the labor market is dead" (Dunlop 1944, 228). Thus, these economists considered the competitive market model to have little explanatory power when applied to labor markets. These were not mere impressions: substantial empirical evidence supported these assertions. For example, Richard Lester's 1945 *Southern Economic Journal* article, "Diversity in North-South Wage Differentials and in Wage Rates Within the South," demonstrated that wage differentials for some occupations were actually greater within the same southern labor market area than they were between the North and the South (Lester 1945, 258). As Lester concluded, "The above facts point to the need for a reformulation of wage theory in terms of a range of rates within limits that change with conditions, in place of the conceptions of a single rate that equates demand and supply" (Lester 1945, 260–61).

Origins of Segmented Labor Market Theory and Internal Labor Market Theory

Segmented labor market theory treats "the" labor market as actually many labor markets delineated by various barriers to entry. *Internal labor markets* are composed of personnel policies that define conditions of job tenure, promotion, and rewards for workers already employed in a market and which effectively limit their competition with outsiders. Both of these theories help explain lack of labor mobility, reduced competition for certain jobs, and thus some portion of the wage differentials observed by the aforementioned economists. This section will explore the institutionalist origins of these theories in the writings of Clark Kerr and John Dunlop.

A seminal work on the noncompetitive aspects of labor markets was Clark Kerr's 1954 article, "The Balkanization of Labor Markets." In this article, Kerr envisioned a continuum of labor markets ranging from the very long-run, multigenerational market in which a person's descendants may compete for jobs with anyone else's descendants, to the extremely short-run market in which most jobs are not even open and hence there is very little competition. Kerr was concerned with the middle ground, a time period in which "several men and several jobs, rather than all men and all jobs or one man and one job, may face each other" (1954, 94). While acknowledging that there still were very competitive markets for particular skills, Kerr developed a theory of an "enclosure movement" that was arising in much of the labor market as the result of government actions and great changes in the economy, including the growing size of employing firms, the rise of "bureaucratic rules," and increasing union membership and power (1954, 96). These phenomena were creating "institutional markets" for labor defined by formal and informal rules that

> state which workers are preferred in the market or even which ones may operate in it at all, and which employers may or must buy in this market if they are to buy at all. . . . Such institutional rules are established by employers' associations, by the informal understandings of employers among each other (the "gentlemen's agreement"), by companies when they set up their personnel policies, by trade unions, by collective agreements, and by actions of government. (1954, 93)

These institutional rules divide *the* labor market into *several* labor markets, each with its own set of procedures for admission and hiring. Kerr was building on the work of J.E. Cairnes, who recognized the existence of noncompeting groups in the labor market in the form of socioeconomic classes such as white-collar workers and manual laborers.[1] Other precursors included Bloom and Northrup (1950) and Lloyd Reynolds, who observed, "The firm is the hiring unit and . . . each company employment office is really a distinct market for labor" (1951, 42).

Kerr did not go so far as to suggest that there are as many labor markets as there are employment offices, but he did postulate that within each of Cairnes's groups are many other noncompeting groups separated by this increasingly larger set of barriers; thus he rejected the idea of a single labor market. What form did these institutional rules take? Kerr stated that they are "enormously varied," but divided them into "two general systems of rules, each with important subtypes" (Kerr 1954,

97). The two general systems are the "communal ownership approach" characteristic of craft unions and the "private property method" characteristic of industrial unions.

In the former case, the craft union maintains a monopoly over all employment within a certain geographic and skill nexus, creating and enforcing its own preferences and rules regarding union membership and thus labor supply, and beyond that it applies rules that differentiate the relative rights and entitlements of the various categories of union members—apprentices, members who transfer from other locals, and local members of various levels of seniority, for example. Workers are tied not to specific employers, but rather to their craft or profession, and once they have gained admittance to the union—and hence the profession, most workers move horizontally from one position to another, in the manner prescribed by the union's rules. In this system, then, the craft union establishes the entry criteria and the rules directing movement among positions.

In the latter case—the "private property method"—the "plant or company or industry is the market" but "the union may impose its scale of preferences on the employer" (Kerr 1954, 99). Seniority rules govern hiring and advancement in this system: each employee is, assuming adequate performance, the only person with a claim on the position, and if the worker leaves, the next person on the seniority list is the only person with a claim on the opening. The union establishes a set of rules governing hiring and advancement that serves to wed individual workers to individual employers, with job change and professional advancement almost a certainty in the long run. Movement between employers is an option, but an unattractive one that would often put the worker back to the bottom of the new firm's seniority list. The resulting high mobility costs in the "private property" case potentially expand the firm's discretion over wage rates and other conditions of employment, further demonstrating the power that emanates from the demand side of labor markets.

Kerr's knowledge and descriptions of labor markets were based on empirical analysis as well as on his firsthand experience with the institutions of these markets, experience that included service with the War Labor Board during World War II. As he wrote in 1988, he learned through this experience that real labor markets did not necessarily conform to the textbook descriptions:

> The board's basic wage policy was to stabilize wages at the "going rate," which we set out eagerly to find with the help of the Bureau of Labor Statistics (BLS). We actually found it only where there was no competition—where union rates universally applied. Otherwise, wage rates for the same occupation varied greatly within the same labor market areas. . . . We tried mostly to find a modal spread of rates, but often found two or three, and turned that (or them) into the official going rate. (Kerr in Kaufman 1988, 7)

Thus, early in his career, Kerr realized that the textbook description of competitive labor markets that he had learned in graduate school was not always an accurate depiction of the real world.[2] His replacement for this standard description was a theoretical explanation based on his observations of actual labor markets in which barriers to entry led to unequal wage rates even for workers with identical skills. Both the communal property system and the private property system illustrate the closed nature of certain labor markets. As Kerr wrote in "The Balkanization of Labor Markets:"

> The important market for the worker is the internal plant market with its many submarkets spelled out in great detail. Movement is vertical in the plant instead of horizontal as in the craft market; and workers fight over seniority rights instead of unions over craft jurisdictions. (Kerr 1954, 100)

Thus Kerr recognized the "internal labor market," a set of rules and procedures that delineate rights to job tenure, promotion, and other rewards for those workers already *in* the market, as well as the "external market," comprising the portion of the labor force outside of a particular internal market (1954, 102). In the communal property case of the craft union, "the internal market is the area covered by the jurisdiction of the local union, and in the industrial case it is the individual plant" (1954, 102). In either case, the internal market is off-limits to outsiders—"The 'haves' are separated from the 'have-nots' not by a union card, but by a place on the seniority roster" (1954, 100). Kerr further recognized that there are institutionally established "ports of entry" through which outsiders may enter an internal labor market (1954, 101). These ports allow outsiders entrance to the internal market; outside of these ports, the outsiders are not directly competing for jobs with the insiders. Thus, competition is diminished, and there is a credible explanation for wage rate differentials.

Kerr was not alone in theorizing about the restrictions on competition in the labor market. His contemporary John Dunlop was also instrumental in the development of internal labor market theory. In the process, Dunlop posited that labor markets are not just riven with barriers, but that they are fundamentally different from other markets. A relatively comprehensive statement of the work that was being done by Dunlop and his peers is contained in the 1957 book *The Theory of Wage Determination*.[3] Although Dunlop contributed only one chapter to this work, it is a fairly broad, comprehensive chapter entitled "The Task of Contemporary Wage Theory." The task, as Dunlop laid it out over forty years ago, was to discover "what determines the general level of real wage rates? The money level? What determines the structure of wage rates among firms, industries, and occupations?" (Dunlop 1957, 13). These are the main questions, he feels, that a modern theory of wages must answer.

In this work, Dunlop extended internal labor market theory by making a distinction between what he referred to as the "political" and the "economic" theories of wages, with the former meaning the internal labor market and the latter referring to the external labor market. Both, according to Dunlop, must be studied: "The decisional process internal to a management organization or a union is an appropriate area of research, but this subject does not pre-empt the theory of wages. Moreover, a large part of the institutional study of decisions should seek to show the impact of external, including market developments, on internal decisions" (Dunlop 1957, 14). Twenty-seven years later, Dunlop was still echoing his theme that an analyst must not focus exclusively on either the internal or external labor markets, but his emphasis had shifted: he argued that the researcher must acknowledge "the limitations of competitive models as applied to labor markets and wage determination, the special features of pricing labor services," and he then went on to approvingly cite J.R. Hicks's statement that there are "important social elements even in the free market part of wage determination" and that "wages are not simply determined by supply and demand" (Dunlop 1984, 12). As Dunlop wrote in 1988, "An understanding of labor markets and compensation requires a recognition that the workplace is a social organization at least informally, and that labor markets take on significant social characteristics that do not characterize commodity and financial markets and that are not readily encapsuled in ordinary demand and supply analysis" (Dunlop 1988, 50).

Dunlop's suggestion that "a large part of the institutional study of decisions should seek to show

the impact of external, including market developments, on internal decisions" was heeded by, among others, Harry Katz. In the early pages of his comprehensive study of evolving labor relations in the U.S. auto industry, Katz writes: "Like the seminal work of John Dunlop (1957), my theoretical framework recognizes the central role that economic pressures exert as an environmental factor shaping the design of industrial relations systems" (Katz 1985, 5). While Katz goes on to explain that his view differs from Dunlop's in important respects—primarily in his emphasis on the role of "historical factors" shaping unique labor relations systems—his study follows Dunlop's methodological advice in analyzing external forces on the internal processes determining labor outcomes (Katz 1985, 5).

For Dunlop, the bottom line is not to be found in any simple typology, nor in a simple cause-effect relationship: he clearly indicates that the key to understanding labor markets lies in looking at them as organic wholes, considering *both* the internal and the external forces:

> In the absence of unions, firms or groups of managements make wage decisions, and under conditions of collective bargaining the parties reach agreement on wage scales. It is indeed appropriate to study the processes, procedures, and influences which determine decisions in these organizations and their agreement making processes. But it does not advance understanding of decision-making in organizations to label the process as either "political" [internal] or "economic" [external]. (Dunlop 1957, 14)

Dunlop drew out many of the implications of the external/internal labor market distinction, such as the concepts of "job clusters" and "wage contours."[4] A job cluster is

> a stable group of job classifications or work assignments within a firm (wage determining unit) which are so linked together by (a) technology, (b) by the

administrative organization of the production process, including policies of transfer and promotion,
or (c) by social custom that they have common wage-
making characteristics. (Dunlop 1957, 16)

A wage contour is

a stable group of firms (wage determining units)
which are so linked together by (a) similarity of product markets, (b) by resort to similar sources for a
labour force, or (c) by common labour market organization (custom) that they have common wage-
making characteristics. (Dunlop 1957, 17)

The wage pattern of a job cluster is centered
around what Dunlop called "key rates," which are
essentially the rates that serve as the benchmarks
from which the others are derived; a key rate arises
from a "key job" which "may simply be a 'good'
cross-comparison job, because of similarity of job
content, but usually a key job has significance because of its importance as to number of employees or key skill" (Livernash 1957, 152). An example of a key rate would be the highest wage in a
cluster, as this may be the one that is first negotiated by a union and then serves as the basis for the
derivation of what Dunlop calls the "associated
rates." The wage contours are groupings of firms
around a set of jobs, and in this grouping there are
leaders and followers. Thus, the cause-effect chain
can be imagined as running from a dominant firm
or firms to the follower firms, with the influence
being in the key rates; then, in each firm in the
wage contour, the key rates establish the pattern
of associated rates. Yet there is no *single* wage rate
for any of the occupations; rather, there are just
these channels that *influence* the rates, in direct
proportion to the tightness of a firm's relationship
to the leader(s) in a wage contour. As Dunlop
writes, "The key rates in the job clusters constitute the channels of impact between the exterior
developments in the contour and the interior rate

structure of the firm" (Dunlop 1957, 19). Thus, it
is through the key rates that the external labor
market, reflecting conditions of supply and demand in the wage contours, impacts the internal
labor market. Yet the external market is only one
of the forces on a firm's internal wage structure,
and the strength of the influence will depend on
numerous factors, as explained by a contemporary
of Dunlop, E. Robert Livernash:

Internal relationships are strongest within narrow
functional groups. . . . Among clusters, the internal
ties are stronger: (1) in relating a narrow group to a
larger group of which it is a distinct part; (2) within
roughly comparable skill bands; and (3) where
closely comparable or identical jobs are found in
several functional groups. As concerns comparisons
and ties between broader clusters, the internal forces
grow weaker and the market ties, including historically established relationships, become stronger.
(Livernash 1957, 157–58)

The concepts of job clusters and wage contours
helped to explain wage differences among firms
even in the same locality for seemingly identical
(in terms of quality) labor. As opposed to modern
theorists who look to the supply side of a labor
market for explanations of such wage variations,
Dunlop found an explanation on the demand side.
Specifically, he felt that the level of competition in
the product markets tended to filter through to affect the relative wages in the labor markets (Dunlop
in Kaufman 1988, 57; Dunlop 1957, 22), and further that the employers—who are demanding labor—and their institutional rules had an important
effect on wage rates and levels of employment. Thus,
within a wage contour, the product market in which
a firm operates will have an impact on the key rates
that establish the structure of wage rates within the
firm, with less competitive product markets yielding higher revenues and hence higher wage rates
(Dunlop 1957, 21–22). This explanation was sup-

ported by Lloyd Reynolds, who wrote that "the main reason why the wage levels of different plants tend to move together is . . . the fact that the wage-paying ability of most firms is moving in the same direction at the same time," and that "the size of the wage increases given by different firms tends to be uniform within clusters of firms whose limits are defined by (1) interplant rivalry for markets, and (2) interunion rivalry for members" (Reynolds 1951, 230–31).

It is ironic that Dunlop, who is credited with being one of the first economists to differentiate between internal and external labor markets,[5] would caution against placing too much emphasis on the distinction. This seeming ambivalence is in line, however, with his approach, which is to analyze each market according to its own characteristics, rather than according to any completely predetermined model. Indeed, acknowledging the importance of "social elements" in wage determination virtually necessitates this approach, which is substantively similar to the emphasis that John R. Commons placed on field work in learning how labor markets actually operated.

Later influential work on labor market segmentation came from Doeringer and Piore (1971) and still reflected traditional institutionalist themes, including the role of power in resource allocation and income determination and the consequences of immobilities for labor allocation. (It is worth noting that Doeringer and Piore wrote PhD dissertations under John T. Dunlop in the mid-1960s.)

Efficiency Wage Theory

As Dunlop noted, his explanation begs the question "But why do the firms pay more, simply because they can afford to do so?" (Dunlop 1957, 22). He felt that the explanation is not to be found in union power, since the phenomenon is so general; rather,

In periods of tightness in the labour market the various contours are able to bid for labour, and a differentiated structure of rates reflecting the product market contours and competitive conditions tends to be established. For a variety of reasons these differentials are not readily altered in a looser labor market. There are costs involved in making a wage change or changing a differential among sectors. Newer and expanding employers using the same type of labour have to pay more to attract a labour force, and a differential once established by a contour is not easily abolished. (Dunlop 1957, 22)

While this explanation is credible, there is an alternative interpretation that Dunlop apparently did not consider. The fact that firms in newer product markets pay higher wages than other firms employing similar labor may be explained by the workers' perceived stability of employment. A new product market may present, to the worker, a less secure job, and hence the firm may have to pay a higher wage rate in order to attract labor. Additionally, a newer firm may be more likely to be reaping high profits in a newer industry, with the higher profits translating into higher wage rates. Of course, this interpretation puts the cause of wage differentials squarely on the supply side of the market, which Dunlop was wont to do.

Lloyd Reynolds in 1951 also wondered why some firms will pay higher wages than they need to in order to attract labor; in this inquiry he was joined by Lester, who also recognized that some firms pay more than necessary in order to maintain a decent work force.[6] Reynolds offered several explanations, including the possibility that a high wage "simplifies the recruitment problem" by allowing the firm to more easily attract and hire better-than-average workers, and also to expect from them greater-than-average efficiency, since they are being paid a wage premium (Reynolds 1951, 232). By considering the relationship between wage rates and workers' productivity or efficiency, Reynolds placed himself in a long and distinguished line of economists who have contemplated the same question,[7] a question that eventually gave rise to efficiency wage theory. Reynolds's assertion regarding the effect of higher-than-market wage rates on workers' efficiency, along with the empirical work that helped establish the frequency of wage inequalities and the theories to explain these inequalities, undoubtedly fueled the later development of efficiency wage theory. Efficiency wage theory is an attempt to explain the existence of involuntary unemployment in a competitive labor market peopled with rational employers and workers.[8] As this theory has developed, it has explained the efficiency of higher-than-necessary wage rates (i.e., higher than would be implied by a strict equilibrium of supply and demand) with several hypotheses; these include the "shirking model," which hypothesizes that above-market wage rates will raise the cost to the worker of being terminated and hence will reduce shirking (i.e., enhance work effort), and the (logically similar) "labor turnover model," which hypothesizes that firms will offer a wage premium in order to reduce labor turnover. Efficiency wage theory can also help explain the segmentation of labor markets: in the primary sector, where there may be a strong relationship between wage rates and productivity, above-market wage rates may be paid, while in the secondary sector, where the relationship between wage rates and productivity is more tenuous, the labor market may clear at an equilibrium wage rate.

While efficiency wage theory is institutionalist in origin (and heterodox in its conclusion that equilibrium may not determine wage rates and employment levels), it has obviously inspired thinkers in different directions. More broadly, it is interesting to note that these institutionalist approaches to labor market analysis have likewise motivated later labor economists in varied directions. For example,

while institutionalist labor analysts developed the reasoning that gave rise to efficiency wage theory, the hypothesis that some firms pay above-equilibrium wage rates has been firmly lodged within the mainstream.[9] At the same time, the essential idea of segmented labor market theory—that barriers break *the* labor market into *many* labor markets— is still closely associated with institutionalism rather than the mainstream.[10]

Dunlop on Wage Levels

The above discussion illuminates Dunlop's analysis of the *structure* of wage rates; regarding the *level* of wages, Dunlop states, "I have always preferred to begin the discussion of the general level of wages with the recognition that the concept is a substantial abstraction, and a vast complex of wage, salary, and benefit structures is the reality." A few pages later he writes, "The single, macro wage standard is a conceptual and practical mistake" (Dunlop in Kaufman 1988, 64, 67). Thus, there is no illusion here that there is any sort of general wage rate, or even that particular skills in the same market will generate equal wage rates. This much can, in fact, be gathered from the above discussion on the structure of wage rates, and indeed represents the fundamental view of wages held by these theorists—that understanding wage determination and understanding wage differentials are essentially the same process. Even among various sectors, Dunlop sees little possibility of what he refers to as "general wage changes," since the ties that bind the sectors together are so contorted and characterized by labor contracts of various lengths. But Dunlop does see some factors that will influence general wage levels throughout the economy. He claims that he does *not* believe that levels of employment are the cause of changes in wage rates; instead, he argues that a depression, with its consequent negative effects on final goods prices and on profit margins, is the only event that will bring a reduction in nominal wage rates, while increases in general price levels and any other factors that increase profit margins, such as rising labor productivity, will drag money wage rates up (Dunlop in Kaufman 1988, 65; 1944, chs. 6 and 7). Of course, this is essentially the theory behind the Phillips curve, which is itself just an empirical regularity (although some would argue that it is not even *that* anymore).

Dunlop's above beliefs on wage determination, elucidated in 1988, are confusing in light of his more comprehensive, but much earlier, writings on the subject. In 1954 he put forth a model purporting to explain the "general level of wages" as a function of the level of employment and profits, thus seemingly taking him back to the Phillips curve explanation that he explicitly later disavowed (Dunlop 1957, 23). How to reconcile these two positions? Dunlop may have been trying to emphasize a theoretical explanation instead of the empirical regularity expressed by the Phillips curve—but this does not really make sense in light of his partiality toward empirical study. He does, however, subject this relationship to statistical testing and estimates the coefficients of the function.

Generally, however, Dunlop felt that in the long run the rate of increase of wage rates will be most closely tied to the rate of inflation, while increasing labor productivity and profits will have a much less direct effect. Incidentally, he also believes that even "massive unemployment" is unlikely to drive wage rates down (Dunlop in Kaufman 1988, 71).

Effect of Unions and Collective Bargaining on Wage Rates

These labor economists, as explained, placed little faith in the marginal productivity theory of wage rate determination. This belief, coupled with their focus on the economic outcomes of the labor market, made them ideally suited to analyze the impact of labor unions on wage rates. As Lloyd Reynolds noted in 1988,

> what were labor economists working on and writing about in the forties and fifties? Without having counted books and articles, I feel safe in saying that the greatest volume of work was on trade unionism and collective bargaining. . . . The focus was on union and management decision making, collective bargaining processes, and their economic impact. (Reynolds in Kaufman 1988, 125)

"Economic impact" of course includes the effects of unions and collective bargaining on wage rates. The influence of labor market trends, especially the rapid rise in union membership from the 1930s through the 1950s, on the research programs of this era is obvious. These labor economists generally looked to the demand side of the labor market as the chief determinant of wage rates and other conditions of employment; their evidence diminished the impact of competition on the supply side, particularly through the channel of labor mobility, on wage rates and wage differentials. Labor mobility is further diminished as a determinant of market wages by the power of labor unions, which as the post–World War II institutionalists found, tended to erode the power of competitive market forces in wage determination: as Reynolds pointed out, "It is still true that potential mobility determines the lowest wage which an employer can pay and retain his labor force. The *effective* lower limit to wages, however, is the rate which the union can be persuaded to accept. This will normally be higher, and often very much higher, than the limit set by mobility alone."[11] Thus mobility, already suspected of having little influence on wage rates, is further diminished.

As Kaufman (1994, 162–69) has noted, the institutionally minded labor economists of this era were concerned with several aspects of unionized labor markets, including the determinants and goals of union wage policies. On this topic, Dunlop offered his *Wage Determination Under Trade Unions* in 1944. In this work, Dunlop took a rather mainstream approach to the question by arguing that "an economic theory of a trade union requires that the organization be assumed to maximize (or minimize) something" (Dunlop 1944, 4). Dunlop proceeded to argue that, for theoretical purposes, the best maximum is the wage bill for the total union membership—in other words, he proposed a model that treated the union as analogous to the business firm (Dunlop 1944, 44). Thus, given a couple of economic constraints, one could calculate the union's optimal wage rate.

Although this model of union behavior was not universally accepted (Kaufman 1988, 165–67), Dunlop did initiate an active dialogue on the issue, with others arguing that unions' wage goals were motivated more by comparative and political factors, such as the wage rates earned by members of other unions and the union leaders' desires to maintain their positions.[12] Dunlop countered this argument in the 1950 edition of *Wage Determination Under Trade Unions*:

> In recent years it has become popular, almost a fad, to declare that wage determination under collective bargaining is essentially a political process. . . . But the thesis must be rejected that wage determination under collective bargaining is to be explained most fundamentally or fruitfully in terms of a political process. (Dunlop 1950, iii)

He went on to offer many arguments to support his contention, including much that obviously came from his firsthand contacts with union leaders, such as his statement that "the view that wage fixing under collective bargaining is fundamentally to be examined in a political context reveals considerable ignorance of the habits of mind of labor leaders and the intimacy of their knowledge of the technology and economic facts of an industry" (Dunlop 1950, iv). While acknowledging that labor unions, in part depending on their age, the time span examined, and the "nonincome objectives of wage policy" (1950, 46), among other considerations, may not always simply attempt to maximize a dollar value, he nonetheless thought that for analytical purposes—for analyzing a union's response to changing economic variables such as the prices of the goods produced and technical considerations—it is best to assume that a labor union attempts to maximize the group's earnings.

Conclusion

The postwar labor economists recognized the contradiction that was posed to mainstream theory by the empirical evidence of substantial wage differentials. These theorists developed convincing explanations of these phenomena—including some, such as efficiency wage theory, that have entered the mainstream body of labor economics. The combination of empirically driven inquiry, recognition of the role of demand-side power in employment relations, and an emphasis on labor immobilities makes these theories uniquely institutionalist in both method and substance. The view of collective bargaining as another extramarket determinant of wage rates pushed the theory of wage determination even further away from the realm of simple supply-demand analysis. In sum, the work discussed in this chapter represents a classic application of institutionalist methods and constitutes a lasting contribution to the understanding of modern labor markets.

Notes

1. J.E. Cairnes, (1874, 67–68), as cited by Kerr (1954), p. 93, note 3.

2. Kerr (1954, 6) recounts that his "first contact with academic labor economics," at Stanford in 1932–33, included Hicks's *The Theory of Wages*, "a well-argued description of a rational world of nearly perfect competition."

3. John T. Dunlop (1957). This book contains the proceedings of the 1954 Round Table Conference of the International Economic Association. See in particular Dunlop's Introduction and Chapter 1.

4. See, for example, Osterman in *Internal Labor Markets*, ed. Paul Osterman (1984), p. 2.

5. See Dunlop (1957, 16–20), for his work on these topics.

6. Reynolds, (1951, 232). Richard Lester (1948) also recognized the connection between wage rates and workers' productivity and the problems it creates for marginal productivity theory. On p. 200 he observed: "A number of firms believe that to obtain and maintain employee morale, good labor relations, and a high-quality labor force, the company should aim to lead competitors in wage increases and to pay wages somewhat above competitors in each locality."

7. John Dunlop (1957), gave a brief inventory of some of the thinkers to have considered this issue. He traces it back through Sumner Slichter, J.W.F. Rowe, H.L. Moore, Alfred Marshall, and Francis A. Walker.

8. For an overview of efficiency wage theory, see Janet L. Yellen, (1984, 200–5); and George Akerlof and Janet L. Yellen (1986).

9. See, for example, N. Gregory Mankiw (2003, 166–67).

10. Kaufman and Hotchkiss refer to the development of segmented labor market theory as part of a "third phase of institutionalism." See Kaufman and Hotchkiss (2003, 31).

11. Lloyd Reynolds, (1948, 274) (emphasis in original). Reynolds offers many citations to bolster his claims about labor mobility. Clark Kerr also offers a description of this type of labor market, which he calls the "The Natural Market," and cites it as "the most ordinary occurrence" of the five different types of labor markets that he describes. See Kerr (1986, 199–200).

12. Observed by Kaufman, in *How Labor Markets Work*, pp. 166–67. Most notably, Arthur Ross argued that "a trade union is a political agency operating in an economic environment." See Ross (1948, 12).

References

Akerlof, George, and Janet Yellen, eds. *Efficiency Wage Models of the Labor Market*. Cambridge: Cambridge University Press, 1986.

Bloom, Gordon F., and Herbert R. Northrup. *Economics of Labor and Industrial Relations*. Philadelphia: Blakiston, 1950.

Cairnes, J.E. *Political Economy*. New York: Harper, 1874.

Doeringer, Peter B., and Michael J. Piore. *Internal Labor Markets and Manpower Analysis*. Lexington, MA: D.C. Heath, Lexington Books, 1971.

Dunlop, John T. *Wage Determination Under Trade Unions*. New York: Macmillan, 1944.

———. *Wage Determination Under Trade Unions*. New York: Macmillan, 1950.

———. ed., *The Theory of Wage Determination: Proceedings of a Conference Held By the International Economic Association*. London: Macmillan, 1957.

———. "Industrial Relations and Economics: The Common Frontier of Wage Determination." In Proceedings of the Thirty-Seventh Annual Meeting, Industrial Relations Research Association. Madison, WI: Industrial Relations Research Association.

Dunlop, John. *Industrial Relations Systems*. New York: Henry Holt, 1958.

Hicks, John R. *The Theory of Wages*. New York: Peter Smith, 1948.

Katz, Harry. *Shifting Gears: Changing Labor Relations in the U.S. Automobile Industry.*" Cambridge, MA: MIT Press, 1985.

Kaufman, Bruce E., ed. *How Labor Markets Work: Reflections on Theory and Practice by John Dunlop, Clark Kerr, Richard Lester, and Lloyd Reynolds*. Lexington, MA: D.C. Heath, 1988.

———. "The Evolution of Thought on the Competitive Nature of Labor Markets." In *Labor Economics and Industrial Relations*, ed. Clark Kerr and Paul D. Staudohar. Cambridge, MA: Harvard University Press, 1994.

Kaufman, Bruce E., and Julie L. Hotchkiss. *Labor Economics*. 6th ed. Mason, OH: South-Western Publishing, 2003.

Kerr, Clark. "Labor Markets: Their Character and Consequences." In *Proceedings of the Second Annual Meeting*: Madison Industrial Relations Research Association, 1950.

———. "The Balkanization of Labor Markets." In *Labor Mobility and Economic Opportunity*. New York: John Wiley, 1954.

———. *Economics of Labor in Industrial Society*. San Francisco: Jossey-Bass, 1986.

Kinnear, Douglas. "The 'Compulsive Shift' to Institutional Concerns in Recent Labor Economics." *Journal of Economic Issues* 33, no. 1 (March 1999): 169–81.

Lester, Richard. "Diversity in North-South Wage Differentials and in Wage Rates Within the South." *Southern Economic Journal* 12 (July 1945): 238–62.

————. *Insights into Labor Issues*. New York: Macmillan, 1948.

Livernash, E. Robert. "The Internal Wage Structure." In *New Concepts in Wage Determination*, ed. George W. Taylor and Frank C. Pierson. New York: McGraw-Hill, 1957.

Mankiw, N. Gregory. *Macroeconomics*. 5th ed. New York: Worth Publishers, 2003.

Osterman, Paul, ed. *Internal Labor Markets*. Cambridge, MA: MIT Press, 1984.

Reynolds, Lloyd. *A Survey of Contemporary Economics*. Vol. 1. Homewood, IL: Richard D. Irwin, 1948.

————. *The Structure of Labor Markets*. New York: Harper, 1951.

Reynolds, Lloyd G., and Cynthia Taft. *The Evolution of Wage Structure*. New Haven, CT: Yale University Press, 1956.

Ross, Arthur. *Trade Union Wage Policy*. Berkeley: University of California Press, 1948.

Yellen, Janet. "Efficiency Wage Models of Unemployment." *American Economic Review* 74, no. 2 (May 1984): 200–5.

8

The Significance of Segmentation for Institutionalist Theory and Public Policy

Jerry Gray and Richard Chapman

Our goal is to recall the major contributions of a group of theorists whose influence should not be allowed to wane in modern institutionalist labor market theory. Clark Kerr (1988, 34) identified this group as the "new generation of labor economists arising since about 1975," and we will refer to them as "segmentation theorists." Kerr, one of the leading figures in postwar labor economics, asserted that this new generation of theorists was on its way to "being the best ever as they seek a judicious blending of econometrics with realistic observation" (1988, 34). Our brief review of segmentation theory is intended to highlight major elements that should be retained in the institutionalist tradition and to indicate the usefulness of these elements for addressing contemporary labor market problems.

Four studies of poverty and underemployment in ghetto labor markets of the late 1960s were the original seeds of segmentation theory (Gordon 1972, 43), but the fact that these conditions persisted in spite of general economic prosperity was the more crucial motivating factor.[1] The persistence of poverty and underemployment in times of general prosperity challenged orthodox principles of compensating wage differentials and traditional Keynesian explanations of poverty and underemployment. This tension, and the case study methodologies of early researchers, gave rise to

the fundamental tenet of segmentation theory: labor markets were divided into essentially distinct segments (Piore 1975; Bluestone 1970; Doeringer and Piore 1971).[2] These segments were characterized not only by earnings differentials, but also by qualitative differences in working conditions, methods of skill acquisition, job mobility patterns, and work norms or rules (Piore 1975, 126).

A rich form of segmentation theory dominated institutionalist labor analysis from the late 1960s to the late 1970s, but began to fade just as the labor market realities of the 1980s and 1990s seemed to require explanations of stubbornly persistent segmentation amid indicators of general prosperity. What are the more important explanations of the increasing inequality in the distribution of income; of the increasing use of part-time, contingent, and temporary work arrangements; of the increasing proportion of college graduates working in high-school jobs; of the increasing within-group inequality? Most importantly, why would all these trends emerge during such an unusual and generally sustained period of expansion? We believe that key elements of segmentation theory should inform the study of these and other similarly pressing questions.

Any attempt to identify key elements of segmentation theory is destined to spur debate. Hoping for renewed discussion and debate of segmentation approaches, we boldly list five key elements and later elaborate on each in turn. First, rejecting the logical implications of neoclassical production theory and marginal productivity theory of factor payments may be the most important legacy of segmentation theory. Second, research was also significantly advanced by the hypothesis that a simple dichotomy between the primary and secondary sectors omitted critical distinctions *within* the primary sector. A third key element of segmentation theory was the effort to describe the essential features of actual training and production processes. Fourth, theorists also linked segmentation to the nature of demand for products rather than to competitive differences between industries and firms. Fifth, richer understandings of training and production processes focused attention on work histories, behavioral traits, subcultures, and "mobility chains" (Piore 1975, 125–28). These complex and interrelated elements gave rise to a new understanding of segmentation as the *expected* outcome of labor market processes, rather than the result of premarket effects or competitive imperfections that caused deviation from some hypothetical optimum.

Our primary goals are to offer a succinct review of segmentation theory and to indicate its usefulness in explaining contemporary labor market problems. A suitable review requires a brief explanation of two distinct hypotheses in the segmentation literature. A short review of the dual hypothesis will be followed by a more thorough review of these five key elements of segmentation theory. A subsidiary goal in this review is to indicate some of the many linkages between segmentation theory and institutionalist analysis. The second, briefer section of the chapter will indicate some of the ways that segmentation theory is useful in comprehending labor market problems and designing ameliorative policy.

Distinguishing Dual and Segmentation Approaches

Before taking up each of these five key elements, we must discuss the two generally discernible hypotheses in the institutionalist tradition so that our identification of segmentation theorists will not be misunderstood. We label these hypotheses the "dual" approach and the "segmentation" approach. Dual and segmentation approaches overlap in ways, but the dual hypothesis posits rather direct parallels between labor market segments and "core" and "periphery" industrial structures, while the segmentation hypothesis is more complex. We first discuss some commonalities and then elaborate the distinctive elements in the dual and segmentation approaches.

Dual and segmented approaches share common heritage, time frame, and set of concerns, but differ in underlying causal arguments. Both approaches emerged from an earlier generation of work that focused attention on the "balkanization" of labor markets and elevated skepticism about compensating wage differentials from an intriguing aside to the very focus of attention. The work of this earlier generation remained largely descriptive (Kerr 1950, 1954; Dunlop 1957; Fisher 1951), but the next generation of institutionalist theorists began to develop discernible causal arguments about the origin and maintenance of segmentation.[3] The dual approach posited parallels between industrial structure and labor market structure. Qualitative differences between dual labor market structures reflected the dichotomy between the highly competitive but low-productivity, low-profitability "periphery" and the highly monopolistic, productive, and profitable "core" (Bluestone 1970, 2). "Thus, those in the periphery (competitive) sector will receive lower incomes and lower returns to education, and do so in more dangerous, less pleasant, and more precarious jobs than those employed in the core (monopoly) sector" (Friedman 1984, 185). Accordingly, the "superprofits" earned in the core could be used to fund discrimination on the basis of race and gender or to elicit optimal job performance (Hodson and Kaufman 1982, 731). The dual approach anticipated elements of "efficiency wage" arguments in viewing higher wages and better working conditions of core employment as mechanisms for controlling work activity.

While the simple dual approach constituted an important beginning, it was analytically conventional and founded on forms of evidence that were losing currency in the profession as the Chicago school gave rise to an emphasis on supply-side considerations through abstract modeling and econometric tests based on large survey data sets (Kaufman 1988, 181–87).[4] The dual hypothesis resulted in a "theory" of segmentation founded on competitive difference, which viewed segmentation as an arguably aberrant deviation from some optimum and offered limited guidance for public policy. More satisfying theory would render segmentation a generally expected outcome of modern labor market processes, even within individual firms. Researchers also found little evidence in conventional empirical results to support an underlying core-periphery distinction that captured important elements of industrial structure. If the dual hypothesis were correct, one would expect to find homogeneous labor market characteristics within sectors. Empirical evidence "strongly suggests that core and periphery sectors are anything but homogeneous in labor market characteristics" (Hodson and Kaufman 1982, 734). Industries with high market concentration were not particularly likely to be capital intensive or unionized, and there was little support for differential distributions of minorities and women between core and periphery sectors. The dual approach ultimately proved

to be less convincing and compelling than the segmentation approach.

Segmentation Approach

Having listed five key elements of segmentation theory, we now group these elements into characteristics of segmentation, causal arguments, and the linkages between activities in firms and the society in which they are located. Rejecting neoclassical production theory and identifying distinctions within the primary sector are central characteristics. Causal arguments emerged in the analysis of actual training and production processes and in the nature of demand for product. Attention to work histories, behavioral traits, subcultures, and institutions linked activities in firms to the social context in which they occur.

Rejection of Production Functions and Marginal Productivity Theory

Rejection of orthodox conceptions of production functions and marginal productivity theory was one of the more important and recurring themes in segmentation approaches. Segmentation theorists consistently argued that labor market analyses should focus more systematic and rigorous attention on the nature of jobs rather than on the nature of people in those jobs. Viewing this argument as a simple difference in emphasis on the demand side or supply side risks losing one of the essential elements of segmentation theory. Instead, institutionalist theory, following Richard Lester's (1946) critical, early insight, should remain unequivocal about *explicitly* rejecting marginal analysis for wage and employment problems. This fundamental point of departure frees segmentation theory from being marginalized to a "special case" of neoclassical analysis and opens avenues of inquiry that will more usefully inform public policy.

Following Lester, Vietorisz and Harrison (1973) mounted one of the few *direct* challenges to production functions and marginal productivity theory. "There can be no theory of labor market segmentation as an endogenous phenomenon within the economic system as long as the theory remains committed to the neoclassical paradigm, because labor market segmentation is an instance of divergent development rather than convergence to equilibrium." They argued for an "alternative set of conceptions" in place of the "long list of qualifications and special assumptions" required to explain segmentation in orthodox theory. One alternative conception was that "mechanization and automation are instances of irreversible change in the social organization of the process of production, rather than marginal adjustments along the capital-labor isoquants of a changeless production function" (Vietorisz and Harrison 1973, 367). For example, sharply declining relative wages of those without postsecondary education is not expected to halt or reverse paths of technological innovation.

While this chapter represents the most explicit rejection of neoclassical production theory, the segmentation literature was replete with observations that segmentation is the *expected* outcome of occupational structures that are relatively unresponsive to changes in the supply or wages of various skills. Observations that labor was the last factor taken into account, and that managers were often unaware of local wage information when adopting productive technologies strained orthodox conceptions (Doeringer and Piore 1971; Berger and Piore 1982). Harrison (1972, 23) argued that "it is important to note that programs designed merely to increase the mobility of the labor force will not be successful in the elimination of poverty. While particular individuals now denied access to high-wage jobs may benefit from removal of market barriers,

low-wage jobs will still exist." Segmentation was not reducible to issues of restricted mobility because a constant theme was that increasing education and training or eliminating discrimination would only reallocate people among existing jobs (Thurow 1972; Bluestone 1970).

Thurow captured important features of the power of this alternative analysis by usefully contrasting the conceptions of a neoclassical "wage-competition model" with conceptions of an institutionalist "job-competition model." He argued that labor markets did not function to equilibrate supply and demand of existing job skills through wage fluctuations but instead served to match trainable individuals with training ladders (Thurow 1972, 72). Clearly focusing attention on the demand side and structure of occupational opportunities, Thurow asserted that an individual's wage was determined by the distribution of job opportunities in the economy and an individual's *relative* position in the labor queue (Thurow 1972, 71).[5] He stressed segmentation arguments in his observation that many job skills could be acquired only by participating in work activity and that employees do the great majority of this largely informal training. Labor market institutions evolved to facilitate effective training, and one of these institutional arrangements was that wages were more attached to the characteristics of jobs than to the supply and demand of job seekers.[6] Without such arrangements, workers would have incentives to prevent the transmission of useful knowledge of job performance because each "trainee" would be a potential competitor.

Critical Distinctions Within the Primary Sector

Another important advancement of segmentation theory was the division of the primary sector into an upper tier and a lower tier. Piore (1975, 126) argued that concern for disadvantaged workers might have focused attention too narrowly on distinctions between primary and secondary sectors and overlooked important distinctions *within* the primary sector. The unrelenting decline in manufacturing employment over the last twenty-five years makes this division in the primary sector indispensable to analysis of contemporary U.S. labor markets.

Descriptions of employees and employment characteristics in the dual approach captured only a certain segment of the preferred jobs in the economy, so Piore divided the primary sector into an upper and lower tier. Lower-tier occupations were characterized by employment stability, well-defined patterns of advancement, and formal administrative work rules to organize production. In contrast, professional and managerial jobs in the upper tier had higher pay and status and more promotional opportunities. Employees in these jobs had mobility and turnover patterns reminiscent of the secondary sector, with the critical difference that wide variations in employment histories were generally associated with advancement. Internalized codes of behavior tend to organize production in the upper tier of the primary sector, while idiosyncratic personal relationships between workers and supervisors perform this role in the secondary sector. Formal educational attainment is generally required for employment in the upper tier, where work provides economic security, but more variety and room for individual creativity and initiative. Robert Reich (1991) fails to credit segmentation theory in his analysis, but one cannot reread Piore's descriptions of labor market segments without immediately recognizing important parallels to Reich's categories of symbolic-analytic services, routine-production services, and routine-personal services. Reich's useful analysis of increasing inequality by way of these categories

tends to support the view that segmentation theory should influence modern institutionalist labor theory.

Actual Processes of Production and Training

Segmentation theorists also advanced labor analysis by focusing attention on *actual processes* of production, and of learning and training on the job (Doeringer and Piore 1966; Doeringer and Piore 1971; Piore 1968, 1975). This key element is a characteristic of the segmentation literature that developed into a causal argument. In keeping with the institutionalist tradition, their methodologies included observing productive activities and interviewing participants. One of the seminal pieces emerged "from a series of interviews of management and union officials in more than 75 companies during the period 1964 to 1969" (Doeringer and Piore 1971, 8). Descriptions of "automatic and incidental learning" and production and training as joint products of a single process belied the usefulness of conceptualizing labor market activities as exchanges of income for control over given quantities of human capital (Piore 1975).

These descriptions not only challenged orthodox theories that generally incorporate training as a "shift in the focus of the educational process and distribution of training costs" (Doeringer and Piore 1971, 17), but also prompted the view that actual training processes were a cause of persistent segmentation. Internal labor markets evolved to facilitate effective training when job skills are best acquired in actual work activity and taught or modeled by coworkers.[7] That is, without "chances of advancement, equity and due process in the administration of work rules, and, above all, employment security" (Piore 1975, 126), workers would have incentives to prevent skill acquisition by potential competitors. Descriptions of actual processes of skill acquisition highlighted the critical role of internal labor market characteristics in facilitating effective training and production.

What most markedly distinguished segmentation analyses of training from mainstream treatments was the emphasis on informality. The process was variously described as osmosis, exposure, experience, or working one's way up through promotion (Doeringer and Piore 1971, 18). Workers depended on one another and on supervisors for training and, therefore, the distinction between jobs tended to blur as the process of production and training occurred as a "rolling readjustment of tasks between experienced and inexperienced workmen" (Piore 1968, 441–45). Piore was the most consistent proponent of the significance of the training process in generating and maintaining segmentation (Doeringer and Piore 1971; Piore 1968, 1973, 1975; Berger and Piore, 1981). He claimed that the persistence of distinct segments in labor markets was "generated by a single difference—the way in which people learn and subsequently understand the work they perform" (Berger and Piore 1981, 17). In the earliest studies of persistent segmentation, "fundamental questions arose about the functions and importance of job stability" (Gordon 1972, 8). Internal labor markets arise in settings where, through exposure, experience, and osmosis, employees engaged in normal productive activities would acquire many of the skills required at a higher level *prior* to promotion. The significance of this argument is heightened in a context we have outlined, where many job skills can be acquired only by performing work activity and where the overall structure of occupational opportunities is not a function of wages.

Nature of Demand for Products

A more fundamental causal argument was that segmentation reflected demand in product markets through the choice of technology. In this view, technological choices were dominated by the standardization, stability, and certainty of product demand. Standardization and predictability are more fundamental because these characteristics of product demand are necessary to support the detailed division of labor and integrated production processes that facilitate informal training through osmosis in relatively stable work environments. Highly integrated, often capital-intensive technologies were utilized in production for stable and predictable product demand. Less capital-intensive, more batch-oriented technologies were utilized in production for markets characterized by more "flux and uncertainty" in product demand.[8] Requirements for effective training and job performance in these different settings contributed to segmentation. Special features of production and training in primary occupations created more stable, high-paying employment and discernible career paths. Work and training activities that did not require stable, reliable work forces created unstable, low-paying employment in the secondary sector. In this way, labor market segmentation was linked to the uneven impact that product market fluctuations exerted on certain groups of workers (Berger and Piore 1981, 15).[9]

The segmentation approach did not rely on assumptions of *direct* parallelism between dual economic sectors and dual labor markets, assumptions that had found little empirical support in econometric tests of survey data. The advantage of segmentation formulations is that, while stability and predictability of product demand may be correlated with competitive conditions, they are distinct concepts that imply different modes of thought. For example, segmentation theory offered a more robust framework for comprehending the increasing use of contingent and subcontracted employment arrangements, even *within* core firms and industries. In this view, primary characteristics emerge for employees hired onto firm payrolls to satisfy a predictable level of product demand. Secondary characteristics persist for subcontracted workers, who are more readily activated and released to satisfy fluctuating components of product demand.[10] However, arguments concerning the persistence of segmentation on racial and gender bases were not as simple and direct as they were in the dual approach. The "competitive imperfections" that made overt discrimination a possibility was not a fundamental assumption, and this brings us to the final element of segmentation theory, which reveals the most obvious links to the institutionalist tradition.[11]

Mobility Chains and Automatic and Incidental Learning

Notions that variations in job stability impact not only skill acquisition, but also subcultures appear in early segmentation writings.[12] But Piore's "Notes" (1975) most clearly linked actual training and production processes to work histories, behavioral traits, subcultures, and mobility chains through the mechanism of "automatic and incidental learning" (AIL). This analysis promulgated institutionalist traditions of drawing from other disciplines by linking labor market outcomes to the larger society in which they are maintained and reinforced (Hodgson 2000; Rutherford 2001).

Doeringer and Piore (1971, 33) noted early in the literature that one of the characteristics of primary employment is that "interaction among workers is an important part of the production process." They claimed that one of the important "skills" necessary for acceptable performance in the primary sector was smooth interaction with other workers, and that homogeneity in any work group facilitated norms and customs that were instrumental to efficient production. Piore argued that the orthodox model is ill suited for understanding the causes of segmentation because it fails to adequately incorporate the processes through which behavioral traits are developed and maintained. In his own arguments, he emphasized learning that occurs through a sort of osmosis, wherein the individual is automatically assimilated into the new environment through exposure. Identifying this process as AIL, Piore used this concept to capture the processes that form and maintain subcultures. In fact, Piore developed the useful concept of "mobility chains" and explained these discernible patterns of occupational mobility by appealing to processes of AIL. His analysis ultimately linked labor market divisions to "the sociological distinctions between middle-class, working-class, and lower-class subcultures" (Piore 1975, 130–34). These linkages followed from his view that AIL shaped environmental traits and role patterns in the family, among peers, at school, and on the job.

An important corollary of this analysis was that segmentation theorists believed that training costs and work performance would be correlated with behavioral attributes such as reliability, attendance, promptness, absenteeism, and predictability. This belief followed from observations concerning the highly informal nature of much job training, the significance of interaction among workers, and the view that output, innovation, and training were joint products of a single process (Piore 1968). Doeringer (1969, 249) claimed that unreliability on the job rather than lack of skill seemed to be a more serious cause of ghetto unemployment. This early intuition was supported by work showing that employers' requirements were unrealistically stringent for the actual levels of skill required in occupations (Berg 1970; Hamilton and Roessner 1972; Hecker 1992, 7). Berger and Piore (1981, 11) were "impressed with how easily the skills required for moving from one segment to another are acquired by most people." Thus, behavioral attributes such as reliability were viewed to be important variables in the primary sector. The significance of formal education in the upper tier of the primary sector mitigated, but did not eliminate, the significance of behavioral traits in employment decisions.

Consequently, a significant element of segmentation research focused attention on a wider range of "survival strategies" within the secondary sector that impacted behavioral traits in fundamental ways. The secondary sector was understood to be composed of a number of subsectors characterized by low incomes and high turnover, which served to reinforce instability (Bluestone 1970; Bluestone, Murphy, and Stevenson 1973; Harrison 1972, 1977, 1978; Fusfeld 1973). These subsectors included training programs, antipoverty programs, irregular activities, and work activities. None of these activities alone was sufficiently stable or high-paying to provide for an individual, or perhaps more importantly, for a secure family environment. Rational survival in the secondary sector required movement in and out of each of these subsectors, which were used singly or in combination to generate income. Life in the secondary sector, then, was composed of circulation among an interrelated web of activities that were all characterized by instability, unpredictability, and low pay. In this way, low wages and high turnover associated with production for unstable and unpredictable product markets were reflected and reinforced in many aspects of life in the secondary sector, and *rational* survival strategies served to preclude primary employment over time.[13]

Summary of the Five Key Elements of Segmentation

Briefly summarizing these five key elements will facilitate our policy discussion. Segmentation is ultimately linked to characteristics of product de-

mand that give rise to differences in production technologies and acquisition of job skills. More stable demand for standardized products supports more capital-intensive, highly integrated technologies that require the relative security of primary markets to facilitate systems in which production and training are joint products of a single process. AIL imparts critical job skills and facilitates the smooth interaction among workers that is "an important part of the production process" in internal labor markets (Doeringer and Piore 1971, 33). However, AIL also tends to reinforce behavioral patterns that are rational survival strategies in the secondary sector, but obstacles to employment in the primary sector. Identifying critical distinctions within the primary labor market is another key element that has been reaffirmed in Reich's more recent taxonomy of jobs (1991). However, Reich's emphasis on educating citizens to be symbolic analysts highlights the most essential element of segmentation theory, which explicitly rejects conceptions of technological choices as "marginal adjustments along a capital-labor isoquant." This essential element is an unfailing emphasis on occupational structures and the nature of jobs, rather than the nature of people in those jobs. Educating more people for symbolic-analytic work may alter the identity of people in those jobs and will almost certainly raise the credentials necessary to secure such jobs, but will do little to increase the number of jobs that require sophisticated problem solving and analytic reasoning skills.[14]

Policy

The ultimate motivation for reviewing these key elements is our view that important segmentation insights began to fade even as labor market issues of the 1980s and 1990s seemed to require explanations of stubbornly persistent segmentation amid general economic prosperity. For example, inequality and employment stability were always central features of segmentation analysis. Efforts to reverse disturbing trends in employment stability and inequality of the last two decades should be informed by segmentation theory.[15] Another advantage of segmentation analysis is that several prominent findings that prove troubling for standard labor theory are the expected outcome in a segmentation framework. The "striking and important puzzle" of increasing within-group inequality (Levy and Murnane 1992, 1364), the rising proportion of college graduates in noncollege jobs (Hecker 1992; Pryor and Schaffer 1997; Gray and Chapman 1999), and the failure to find disemployment effects associated with increases in the minimum wage (Card and Krueger 1995) are not at all anomalous in segmentation approaches. Policy derived from core analyses to ameliorate *expected* outcomes should inspire more confidence than policy derived from analyses based on a "long list of qualifications and special assumptions" (Vietorisz and Harrison 1973, 367).

The fundamental policy implication of segmentation approaches could not be clearer. If employment conditions and income distribution are determined by product market demand and the nature of occupational opportunities, then efforts to ameliorate poverty, underemployment, and inequality must target the demand side of labor markets. Targeting human capital characteristics through education and training programs may alter who works in any particular job, may raise the qualifications necessary to attain a job, and will almost certainly improve the bargaining power of employers, but will not alter the overall distribution of income or prevalence of poverty and underemployment (Thurow 1972; Gray and Chapman 1999). Even cursory review of employment projections should make this fundamental policy implication immediately apparent (Hecker 2001).[16] Advocacy of demand-side policy should continue to be the most important element of institutionalist theory, along with renewed efforts to understand the underlying determinants of occupational structures. Our necessarily brief discussion of particular policy approaches will focus on aggregate-demand policy and minimum wages.

Aggregate Demand Policy

Truly full employment is by far the most important element in reducing poverty, underemployment, and inequality. We need not belabor arguments capably made by others (Vickrey 1992, 1994; Eisner 1999), but do want to link the significance of aggregate demand policy to the insights of segmentation theory. Foremost among these linkages is the hypothesis that segmentation reflects the flux and uncertainty in product markets. While the business cycle cannot be eliminated, a target of 4 percent *under*employment would expose a smaller proportion of the labor force to this flux and uncertainty than the 5.2 percent unemployment figure currently used by the Congressional Budget Office as the official estimate of full employment.[17] Institutionalist theorists should continue to make the case for fiscal stimulus and the important role of governments as employers of last resort. Furthermore, segmentation theorists view employment histories as a more important determinant of access to primary employment than human capital characteristics.[18] More aggressive aggregate demand management would create more stable employment histories for more people and may even spur technological adaptations conducive to stability. Finally, if employment patterns reflect and reinforce subcultures, then more stable employment for more people may alter subcultures within schools, families, and at work.

Significantly, lower average underemployment

increases the costs of discriminating on the basis of race and gender. In segmentation analysis, wages and working conditions reflect the nature of jobs more than the nature of individuals. As a result, discrimination may not impose any cost on employers if there are sufficient numbers of the underemployed in "preferred" categories. At lower levels of underemployment, it may ultimately impose costs on employers to bid more fully employed categories of workers away from other employment. This point also goes to issues of statistical discrimination, which may be a profit-maximizing strategy when there is significant underemployment and when behavioral traits are important to training and job performance. The observation that employers simply do not hire the poor for primary employment no matter what quality of training they acquire (Harrison, 1972) does not have to be understood as discriminatory if it is coupled with the insight that "workers are not usually barred because of lack of work skills but because they work unreliably and intermittently" (Gordon 1972, 76). The lower the level of underemployment, the more costly it would be to use gender and race as rough indicators of expected job stability.

Minimum Wages

Increasing the minimum wage or introducing livable wage ordinances are other demand policies that flow from segmentation theory (Spriggs and Klein 1994; Pollin, Brenner, and Luce 2002; Martin and Giannaros 1990; Sklar 2002). Rejecting traditional, marginal productivity analysis of labor demand requires a reinterpretation of the effects of increasing the minimum wage. Segmentation theory implies that given technologies require relatively fixed numbers of workers. Therefore, raising the minimum wage is not expected to result in layoffs to the point where the marginal revenue product is equal to the higher wage. The far more significant effect of raising wages would be to redistribute income from owners to workers. This redistribution is mitigated if competitive conditions are so feeble that major portions of the increase can be passed along to consumers, but this does not temper our support. Given a long history of employment projections that strongly confirm Harrison's (1972) assertion that low-wage jobs will always exist, we simply advocate for higher wages in these jobs. In the long run, raising minimum wages may induce technological change, but such changes are more likely to create employment characteristics associated with the primary, rather than the secondary, sector. It is interesting to note that the expectations of segmentation theory are perfectly consistent with the findings of Card and Krueger (1995) that so alarmed orthodox labor theorists.

Conclusion

This review of decades-old research with indications of current policy significance is intended to motivate future research in the institutionalist tradition. Some of the more obvious applications would be to study Temporary Assistance to Needy Families reforms and effects on historical patterns of mixing work and welfare, to study living wage ordinances and their effects on job stability and "mobility chains," and to study the increasing instability among white-collar workers and the implications of these trends for segmentation hypotheses. We also hope that this review of key elements of segmentation theory will prompt institutionalist researchers to revisit this important literature and undertake new studies of the elements we have reviewed. Conceivably, dissertation committees tolerant of case studies, documentary evidence, and "closer touch with facts and broader ranges of data" (Rutherford 2001, 178) can be formed in modern graduate programs to nurture updates of these elements.

For example, researchers could study managers' and production engineers' awareness of local wage information when designing production technologies. Historical occupational projections could be scrutinized to study the responsiveness of occupational structures to human capital investments. Reich's (1991) tripartite categories could be critically assessed in light of the long-standing literature he does not credit, while his observations may be explored for the ways they advance segmentation analysis. Careful case studies of actual processes of skill acquisition and skill requirements for particular occupational classifications would usefully update work of the early 1970s and yield evidence on the efficacy of emphasizing formal education policies to reduce inequality. Early segmentation analyses predate thoroughgoing globalization considerations, and contemporary research may fruitfully explore the effects of globalization on the flux and uncertainty of product demand at all levels in the firm, again extending Reich's more recent analysis. Finally, orthodox economics has broadened its own notoriously narrow horizons to include important findings in psychology (Dubner 2003). This should embolden institutionalist researchers to return to the tradition of incorporating insights from other disciplines, such as sociology and learning theory, to better comprehend the maintenance and reinforcement of labor market and social institutions that buttress persistent segmentation. Twenty years ago, Lester Thurow (1983) titled his critical chapter on standard labor market theory "The Sargasso Sea of Economic Shipwrecks." It is time for institutionalist theorists to update useful old charts provided by segmentation theorists to navigate new research that will avoid the horse latitudes and huge mats of orthodox sargasso seaweed that hinder useful progress in labor market research.

Notes

1. These studies took place in Boston, Chicago, Detroit, and Harlem. The intellectual, and even student-teacher, relationships between leading labor economists and this "new generation" of labor economists is reflected in these very early works. Peter Doeringer, David Gordon, Michael Piore, and Michael Reich authored the Boston study and did their PhD work at Harvard, where John Dunlop taught. Barry Bluestone did his PhD work at Michigan, where Daniel Fusfeld taught, and both were involved with the study of Detroit labor markets. Other important contributors to segmentation theory, Thomas Vietorisz and Bennett Harrison, did some of their early work in Harlem's labor markets. Significantly, all four of these "realistic studies" yielded similar findings, despite the lack of "much contact among them" (Gordon 1972, 43).

2. This fundamental tenet received three distinct articulations. We discuss dual and segmentation hypotheses later in the paper. The dual articulation is well represented by Barry Bluestone, while the segmentation articulation is well represented by Michael Piore. The third articulation is not discussed in this paper, but has been called the "radical" articulation. David Gordon, Michael Reich, and Richard Edwards began to develop this articulation as graduate students at Harvard, where Dunlop taught.

3. Whether leading postwar labor economists such as Kerr, Dunlop, Lloyd Reynolds, and Richard Lester are properly classified as institutionalist theorists has been widely discussed (Kaufman 1988, 187–90). For ease of expression in this section, we label this older generation as institutionalist, along with their "students" who developed both the dual and segmentation approaches in the late 1960s and early 1970s. See notes 1 and 2.

4. Malcolm Rutherford (2001, 177–78) is quite good on the point of what is taken as "empirical evidence" in the institutionalist tradition. He asserts, "In the institutionalist vision, empirical evidence was not limited to quantitative and statistical methods, but could include case studies [and] documentary evidence." He quotes J.M. Clark's argument that "Economics must come into closer touch with facts and embrace broader ranges of data than 'orthodox' economics has hitherto done" (1927, 221).

5. Emphasis on *relative* productivities anticipates arguments made by Robert H. Frank and Philip J. Cook (1995).

6. Concepts of internal labor markets are discussed in the section of this chapter headed *Actual Processes of Production and Training.*

7. The concept of internal labor markets appears in Kerr's treatment of the "balkanization" of labor markets (1954), but was featured by Doeringer and Piore (1971), who cited specificity of job skills, significance of on-the-job training, and workplace custom as important factors in shaping job ladders and wage structures. The concept stands for a complex set of practices that tends to protect workers from raw market forces and determines typical promotional patterns and wage structures within firms.

8. Leading postwar labor theorists generally implicated product demand as a source of segmentation, and this line of reasoning was further developed in the segmentation literature. Kaufman (1988, 70) credits postwar theorists with arguments that "the job structure of a firm is heavily influenced by the nature of the product produced, and particularly the technology of production."

9. Though it was not linked to increases in part-time, contingent, and temporary employment in Berger and Piore's (1981) analysis, this observation seems especially pertinent to these increasingly important labor market phenomena.

10. Mangum, Mayall, and Nelson (1985) is a good early work linking contingent work to basic segmentation arguments. Kinnear (1999, 175) argues, "The mainstream approach to labor economics, with its emphasis on workers' rational decision making, is unsuited for analyzing the rise of contingent labor and the problems it creates."

11. The emphasis on institutions integral to the maintenance and reinforcement of segmentation reestablished early institutionalist appeals to other disciplines, and disciplines such as sociology and learning theory are examples of similar appeals by this "new generation of labor economists."

12. For example, Piore (1973) is an earlier formulation of similar ideas, but these notions characterize many early studies of "ghetto labor market problems" (Gordon 1972).

13. This element of segmentation theory has important applications to Temporary Assistance to Needy Families reforms, but the potentially devastating consequences of legislative prohibitions on mixing work and welfare beyond sixty months of welfare support have not been in place long enough to study adequately. We believe institutionalist theorists should use segmentation theory as a foundation for assessing welfare reforms and contributing to policy discussions. Harrison (1978) is especially important in this regard.

14. Even if the United States were able to secure a larger share of worldwide symbolic-analytic jobs, this would do little to reduce the number of low-paying jobs in the economy. Of the roughly 22.2 million jobs projected to be added to the economy between 2000 and 2010, more than half (12.8 million) are expected to require no education beyond high school and only some form of work-related training. One-third of all new jobs created in the decade (7.6 million) are expected to require only short-term on-the-job training, which is defined

as a short demonstration of job duties or one month or less of on-the-job experience or instruction. The Office of Occupational Statistics and Employment Projections seems to expect this characteristic of the occupational structure to occur regardless of the education and training provided to potential employees (Hecker 2001).

15. It is significant and striking that segmentation theory originally focused on "ghetto employment problems." A number of themes emerged early in studying these problems. (1) "Low income or 'poverty' in the United States in the 1960s is largely a matter of economic *distance*" (Gordon 1972, 4, emphasis in the original). (2) Unemployment was viewed as a "small component of a much broader syndrome of labor market difficulties" that included low wages, job instability, menial work, low skills, poor job information, and inadequate job access (Gordon 1972, 6). (3) "Increasingly, a concept of underemployment replaced unemployment as the core manpower policy formulation, encompassing most of these new symptoms" (Gordon 1972, 6). As a result, "fundamental questions arose about the functions and importance of job stability," and interest moved away from simple unemployment to a concept of underemployment. Researchers "began to suspect that one could easily mistake the disadvantages of the 'underclass' by speaking simplistically of their 'low skills' or 'productivities'" and "it became apparent that researchers should investigate the structure of demand more thoroughly" (Gordon 1972, 8–10). Nearly all of these insights about "ghetto labor market" problems seem clearly to apply to a much broader spectrum of the work force in the 1980s and 1990s.

16. See note 14.

17. Measures of *under*employment first came into use under pressure of the early insights from segmentation theorists (Gordon 1972; also see notes 1 and 15). Underemployment measures were recently updated by the Bureau of Labor Statistics. The new U-6 measure, for example, is defined as total unemployed, plus all marginally attached workers plus total employed part-time for economic reasons, as a percent of the civilian labor force plus all marginally attached workers. Marginally attached workers are available for a job and have looked for a job in the recent past. Since the new measures were implemented in 1994, the annual U-6 measure averages to 8.8 percent while the traditionally reported U-3 averages to 5.0 percent. Given the insights of segmentation analysis, the U-6 measure would be a more useful indicator of the "slack" in national labor markets and of the attendant human and economic costs.

18. This is especially important to racial differences in earnings. As a rough indicator, the average annual unemployment rate for whites was 5 percent over the last ten years, while it was very nearly 10 percent for blacks (9.87 percent). This simple difference in employment histories and *statistical* indicators of stability may well affect access to primary employment.

References

Berg, Ivar. *Education and Jobs: The Great Training Robbery*. New York: Praeger Books, 1970.

Berger, Suzanne, and Michael J. Piore. *Dualism and Discontinuity in Industrial Societies*. New York: Cambridge University Press, 1980.

Bewley, Truman F. *Why Wages Don't Fall During a Recession*. Cambridge, MA: Harvard University Press, 1999.

Bluestone, Barry. "The Tripartite Economy: Labor Markets and the Working Poor." *Poverty and Human Resources* 5 (1970): 15–35.

Bluestone, Barry, William M. Murphy, and Mary Stevenson. *Low Wages and the Working Poor*. Ann Arbor, MI: Institute of Labor and Industrial Relations, 1973.

Bradsher, Keith. "A Split Over Fed's Role: Clashes Seen After Vice Chairman Says Job Creation Should Be a Policy Goal." *New York Times*, August 29, 2001, D1.

Cain, Glen G. "The Challenge of Segmented Labor Market Theories to Orthodox Theory: A Survey." *Journal of Economic Literature* 14, no. 4 (1976): 1215–57.

Card, David, and Alan B. Krueger. *Myth and Measurement: The New Economics of the Minimum Wage*. Princeton, NJ: Princeton University Press, 1995.

Clark, John M. "Recent Development in Economics." In *Recent Developments in the Social Sciences*, ed. Edward C. Hayes. Philadelphia: Lippencott, 1927.

Doeringer, Peter B., and Michael J. Piore. "Labor Market Adjustments and Internal Training." Proceedings, Industrial Relations Research Association, 21st Annual Meetings, 1966.

———. *Internal Labor Markets and Manpower Analysis*. Lexington, MA: D.C. Heath, 1971.

Doeringer, Peter B. *Programs to Employ the Disadvantaged*. Englewood Cliffs, NJ: Prentice-Hall, 1969.

Dubner, Stephen J. "Calculating the Irrational in Economics." *New York Times*, June 28, 2003, D1.

Dunlop, John T. "The Task of Contemporary Wage Theory." In *The Theory of Wage Determination*, ed. John T. Dunlop. London: Macmillan, 1957.

Eisner, Robert. *The Selected Essays of Robert Eisner. 1, The Keynesian Revolution: Then and Now; 2, Investment, National Income and Economic Policy*. Cheltenham, UK: Edward Elgar, 1999.

Frank, Robert H., and Philip J. Cook. *The Winner-Take-All Society*. New York: Martin Kessler Books, 1995.

Ferman, Louis A., Joyce Kornblush, and Alan Haber. *Poverty in America*. Ann Arbor: University of Michigan Press, 1965.

Fisher, Lloyd. "The Harvest Labor Market in California." *Quarterly Journal of Economics* 65, no. 4 (1951): 463–91.

Friedman, Samuel. "Structure, Process and the Labor Market." In *Labor Economics: Modern Views*, ed. William Darity Jr. Hingam, MA: Kluwer-Myhoff, 1984.

Fusfeld, Daniel. *The Basic Economics of the Urban Racial Crisis*. New York: Holt Rinehart and Winston, 1973.

Gordon, David. *Theories of Poverty and Underemployment*. Lexington, MA: Heath, Lexington Books, 1972.

Gray, Jerry, and Richard Chapman. "Conflicting Signals: The Labor Market for College-Educated Workers." *Journal of Economic Issues* 33, no. 3 (1999): 661–75.

Hamilton, Gloria Shaw, and J.D. Roessner. "How Employers Screen Disadvantaged Workers." *Monthly Labor Review* 95, no. 4 (1972): 14–21.

Harrison, Bennett. *Education Training and the Urban Ghetto*. Baltimore: Johns Hopkins University Press, 1972.

———. "Institutions on the Periphery." In *Problems in Political Economy: An Urban Perspective*, ed. David M. Gordon. Lexington, MA: D.C. Heath, 1977.

———. "How American Households Mix Work and Welfare." *Challenge* 21 (1978): 49–54.

Hecker, Daniel. "Reconciling Conflicting Data on Jobs for College Graduates." *Monthly Labor Review* 115, no. 7 (1992): 3–12.

———. "Occupational Employment Projections to 2010." *Monthly Labor Review* 124, no. 11 (2001): 57–84.

Hodgson, Geoffrey M. "What Is the Essence of Institutional Economics?" *Journal of Economic Issues* 34, no. 2 (2000): 317–29.

Hodson, Randy, and Robert L. Kaufman. "Economic Dualism: A Critical Review." *American Sociological Review* 47, no. 6 (1982): 727–39.

———. "Federal Reserve's Chief Suggests New Rate Rise May Be Needed." *New York Times* July 21, 1994, A1.

Kaufman, Bruce. "The Postwar View of Labor Markets and Wage Determination." In *How Labor Markets Work*, ed. Bruce Kaufman. Lexington, MA: Lexington Books, 1988.

Kerr, Clark. "Labor Markets: Their Character and Consequences." *American Economic Review* 40, no. 2 (1950): 278–91.

———. "The Balkanization of Labor Markets." In *Social Science Research Council, Labor Mobility and Economic Opportunity*, 92–110. New York: John Wiley, 1954.

————. "The Neoclassical Revisionists in Labor Economics (1940–1960) R.I.P." In *How Labor Markets Work*, ed. Bruce Kaufman. Lexington, MA: Lexington Books, 1988.

Kinnear, Douglas. "The 'Compulsive Shift' to Institutional Concerns in Recent Labor Economics." *Journal of Economic Issues* 33, no. 1 (1999): 169–81.

Lester, Richard. "Shortcomings of Marginal Analysis for Wage-Employment Problems." *American Economic Review* 36 (March 1946): 63–77.

Levy, Frank, and Richard Murnane. "U.S. Earnings Levels and Earnings Inequality: A Review of Recent Trends and Proposed Explanations." *Journal of Economic Literature* 30, no. 3: (1992): 1333–81.

Mangum, Garth, Donald Mayall, and Kristin Nelson. "The Temporary Help Industry: A Response to the Dual Internal Labor Market." *Industrial and Labor Relations Review* 38, no. 4: (1985): 599–611.

Martin, Linda R., and Demetrios Giannaros. "Would a Higher Minimum Wage Help Poor Families Headed by Women?" *Monthly Labor Review* 114, no. 8 (1990): 33–37.

Peterson, Janice. "Welfare Reform and Inequality: The TANF and UI Programs." *Journal of Economic Issues* 36, no. 2 (2000): 517–27.

Piore, Michael J. "On-the-Job Training and Adjustment to Technological Change." *Journal of Human Resources* 82, no. 4 (1968): 435–49.

————. "Fragments of a Sociological Theory of Wages." *American Economic Review* 63, no. 2 (1973): 377–84.

————. "Notes for a Theory of Labor Market Stratification." In *Labor Market Segmentation*, ed. Richard C. Edwards, Michael Reich, and David Gordon. Lexington, MA: D.C. Heath, 1975.

Pollin, Robert, Mark Brenner, and Stephanie Luce. "Intended versus Unintended Consequences: Evaluating the New Orleans Living Wage Ordinance." *Journal of Economic Issues* 36, no. 4 (2002): 843–75.

Pryor, Frederic, and David Schaffler. "Wages and the University Educated: A Paradox Resolved." *Monthly Labor Review* 120, no. 7 (July 1997), 3–14.

Reich, Robert B. *The Work of Nations: Preparing Ourselves for 21st Century Capitalism*. New York: Knopf, 1991.

Rosen, Sherwin. Review of David M. Gordon's *Theories of Poverty and Underemployment*. *Journal of Political Economy* 82, no. 2 (1974): 437–39.

Rutherford, Malcolm. "Institutional Economics: Then and Now." *Journal of Economic Perspectives* 15, no. 3 (2001): 173–94.

Sklar, Holly. *Raise the Floor: Wages and Policies That Work For All of Us*. Boston: South End Press, 2002.

Spriggs, William E., and Bruce W. Klein. *Raising the Floor: The Effects of the Minimum Wage on Low-Wage Workers*. Washington, DC: Economic Policy Institute, 1994.

Thurow, Lester. "Education and Economic Inequality." *Public Interest* 28 (1972): 66–81.

————. *Dangerous Currents: The State of Economics*. New York: Random House, 1983.

Tolbert, Charles, Patrick M. Horan, and E.M. Beck. "The Structure of Segmentation: A Dual Economy Approach." *American Journal of Sociology* 85, no. 5 (1980): 1095–116.

Vickrey, William. "Chock-Full Employment Without Increased Inflation: A Proposal for Marketable Markup Warrants." *American Economic Review* 82, no. 2 (1992): 341–45.

————. Public Economics: *Selected Papers by William Vickrey*, ed. Richard Arnott, Kenneth Arrow, Anthony B. Atkinson, and Jacques Dreze. Cambridge, UK: Cambridge University Press, 1994.

Vietorisz, Thomas, and Bennett Harrison. "Labor Market Segmentation: Positive Feedback and Divergent Development." *American Economic Review* 63, no. 2 (1973): 366–76.

9

Dead Metaphors and Living Wages

On the Role of Measurement and Logic in Economic Debates

Ann Jennings

The first economic theory that came under my eyes was not calculated to make me think highly of economists. My mind intuitively rejected the iron law of wages, the immutable law of supply and demand, and similar so-called natural laws.

—Samuel Gompers

In the decades following the Civil War, when the U.S. labor movement gradually shifted from a wholesale denunciation of "wage slavery" toward acceptance of wage labor on the basis of "living wages" (Glickman 1997), standard economic theories of the day were not its ally. A century later, despite shifts in both the strategies of living wage advocates and the theoretical foundations of economics,[1] labor activists and mainstream economists remain largely opposed. The "immutable laws of supply and demand" (Gompers, quoted in Mussey 1927, 235) are still widely supposed to contradict the possibility of a net benefit to workers from any method of setting wages "above market level"—whether by collective bargaining, national minimum wage statutes, comparable worth policies, or today's local living wage ordinances.

This position is maintained even in the face of contrary empirical findings. Daniel Hamermesh, in a critique of Card and Krueger's (1995) comprehensive and well-publicized study that failed to find much of the expected disemployment effect from minimum wages, stated:

> [Card and Krueger's] arguments on the employment effects of the minimum wage are in the same vein as those on the losing side in the old antimarginalist controversy. The authors challenge economic notions that make logical sense with new evidence; but they never offer any convincing theoretical explanation for why the old logic fails. (Hamermesh 1995, 838)

Hamermesh's statement reflects mainstream economists' long-standing faith in the reliability of deductive theoretical logic. Institutionalists, like the earlier antimarginalists,[2] have focused instead on more realistic and historically complex explanations and cultural interpretations of evolving wage setting processes.

But are neoclassical models of the labor market really so logically compelling? Or do they, instead, rest on unexamined assumptions and accumulated historical commitments that undermine their apparent logical rigor and reliability? Neoclassical economics is itself a set of evolving social practices structured, in part, by a heritage of cultural beliefs and favored metaphorical precepts (including mathematics). In this analysis, I will focus particularly on several "dead metaphors," or figures of speech in such common usage that their content has been taken for granted and passes unexamined. Dead metaphors are particularly vulnerable to historical "slippage" that can lead to misperceptions of the actual content of theoretical arguments, to the loss of any specifiable links with actual social processes and, further, to theoretical incoherence. A lack of concern for historical, cultural, and rhetorical processes may cause blindness to the ways in which the "old logic fails." (Hamermesh, 1995, 238)

In what follows, I will first describe the supply and demand frameworks that have grounded economists' opposition to higher wage policies, such as current living wage campaigns, and note some startling logical discontinuities. Next, I will discuss how neoclassical uses of metaphor have resulted in an analysis with no connection to actual processes in labor markets; the analysis serves, instead, to naturalize and depoliticize the market arguments of standard theory. As I will show, the process by which real-world referents for favored metaphors were lost, and logical problems crept in, is clearly visible within the work of such major figures as J.B. Clark, Alfred Marshall, and Paul Douglas. Finally, I will reconsider the debates over living wages today in the context of these findings.

Theories of Supply and Demand in Labor Markets

Despite differences in orthodox economic theories in the two periods, living wage arguments from both the nineteenth and the late twentieth centuries represent challenges to the theoretical framework of standard supply and demand. Neoclassical formulations of labor markets began in the 1880s and 1890s, with the work of William Stanley Jevons,

Marshall, and Clark, although nineteenth-century opponents like Samuel Gompers were responding to still prevalent classical wage theories. Classical theory's "iron law of wages" constructed long-run "natural wages"—a wage just sufficient to reproduce the working class at a socially defined standard—on the basis of the wage fund doctrine, on the demand side, and Malthusian population theory, on the supply side. Short-run "market wages" might deviate from the natural wage rates referred to by the iron law, but wages either above or below the natural rate could not persist indefinitely.

The wage fund doctrine stated that employers had a fixed pool of liquid capital from which to pay workers' wages. Consequently, if individual wage rates were higher, clearly fewer workers could be employed. The wage gains of some individual workers would then come entirely at the expense of others, unless the supply of workers could somehow be restricted. In 1848, John Stuart Mill summarized the classical view of the matter as follows:

> Wages, then, depend mainly on the demand and supply of labour, or as it is often expressed, on the proportion between the population and capital [*read: the wage fund*]. . . . Wages (meaning, of course, the general rate) cannot rise, but by an increase in the aggregate funds employed in hiring labourers, or by a diminution in the number of competitors for hire; nor fall, except either by a diminution of the funds devoted to paying labour, or by an increase in the number of labourers to be paid. (quoted in McNulty 1980, 76–77)

Mill abandoned the wage fund doctrine twenty years later, in 1869. It was another twenty or thirty years, however, before the work of Marshall and Clark, in particular, produced the new accounts of labor markets that eventually, though only after another extended period of decline, supplanted the classical theories (McNulty 1980).

Despite the shift from classical to neoclassical

Figure 9.1   **The Labor Market**

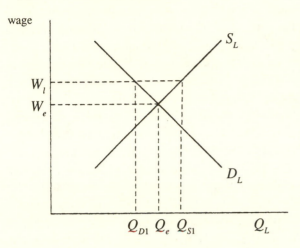

foundations, the orthodox view of labor supply and demand still warns of the futility of attempting to raise wages above (presumably competitive) market rates. The graphical representation in Figure 9.1 of short-run neoclassical supply and demand, known simply as "the labor market," seems quite straightforward.

Where the downward-sloping labor demand (D_L) curve crosses the upward-sloping labor supply (S_L) curve, a market-clearing wage (w_e) should result, implying sufficient employment for all workers willing and able to work at w_e. Higher wages—including all cases where the wage is "administered," whether by unions or government—such as w_1—should cause employers to move back up the labor demand curve and hire less labor. The amount of unemployment that results (Q_{S1}—Q_{D1} at w_1) should exceed the disemployment effect (Q_e—Q_{D1}), however, because more workers seek employment at w_1 than at w_e.

The quantitative magnitude of disemployment effects along D_L is more apparent than real, however; as McCloskey (2002) has recently argued, only *qualitative* magnitudes are actually depicted.

What she means is that Q_L reflects a series of logical deductions—a qualitative argument based, she says, on purely mathematical reasoning, with no specific quantitative measures (or, as we shall see, actual measurability) involved. Deducing a downward-sloping D_L curve suggests *why* disemployment should occur with higher wages, and that *some* should occur, but not *how much*.

Even this qualitative mathematical logic turns out to be quite slippery, though, and not as rigorous as we might imagine. The logical basis for D_L is quite different from that for S_L. There is a problem, it seems, with the qualitative units for Q_L that a simple classroom example can illuminate.

Conventional undergraduate accounts of labor demand rest on the theory of marginal productivity. In the short run, when capital is fixed in quantity, the marginal productivity of labor declines as additional workers are employed, leading to a downward-sloping marginal revenue product (MRP) curve. MRP is then shown to be the firm's D_L curve, and students are taught that profit-maximizing firms should hire labor up to the point where the last worker's MRP equals the (given) market wage (assuming perfect competition in the labor market). At this point, students habitually object. They argue that, in that case, the last worker hired will add nothing to profits! Implicitly, the students are suggesting that the firm's D_L curve is a step function, rather than a smoothly downward-sloping curve. They reject the notion that workers can be subdivided into smaller and smaller units—arms and legs, perhaps? They suppose that labor is measured in physical units, as the number of workers, which is indeed what most textbook examples encourage.

It is quite tempting to "help" students past their disinclination to hire the last worker by suddenly switching the denomination of labor from physical to time units. Suppose, for example, that it is only the last hour or minute of the last worker's day that adds nothing to profits. Students are usually satisfied with this bit of prestidigitation, but we should not be so hasty. The use of time units, it seems, threatens the theoretical existence of short-run diminishing returns, which are based solely on the use of more labor with a fixed quantity of capital. The capital-labor ratio, Q_K/Q_L, should fall as Q_L is increased. But does it, when we adjust *hours of labor*?

Suppose that, using time units in short-run production, we extend a worker's day by hours or minutes at the margin. Are the hours of capital also extended? If so, Q_K is not fixed, Q_K/Q_L does not fall, and there are no diminishing returns to labor—the sole reason for the downward slope of MRP and the firm's short-run labor demand under competitive conditions. If the hours of capital are not extended, then Q_K falls to zero for the marginal time units. In neither case can we define an acceptable short-run demand for labor curve at all. For the desired result, *both labor and capital must be denominated in physical units*, so that the physical number of workers is expanded while the physical quantity of capital is held constant.[3] In that case, the students' implied step function for D_L is entirely correct.

The lack of a smoothly downward-sloping labor demand curve is not especially troubling; Hicks (1932, 25–26; see below) noted and accepted this result. The more serious problem comes with attempting to match the physical units of D_L with the units of S_L. In undergraduate textbooks, theoretical accounts of short-run labor supply are based on analyses of labor-leisure tradeoffs. Individual workers (and/or households) must allocate their scarce time to either nonmarket uses (leisure) or market uses (paid labor). This is carried out within a fairly standard utility-maximization framework and leads to a market S_L curve derived from the summation of optimal individual hours of labor supply at various wage rates. Q_L must be denominated in time units (hours of labor), since that is

what individuals are allocating. If so, however, D_L and S_L cannot be drawn on the same graph, since the horizontal axis would require different units—physical units versus time units—for Q_L.

If short-run diminishing returns and the downward slope of labor demand require physical units of labor (the number of workers), it follows that market representations of the short-run labor supply curve cannot be derived solely from aggregations of individual workers' labor-leisure tradeoffs: the units for Q_L along S_L are wrong. Nor can the time units along S_L be readily converted to physical units. It is logically insufficient, for example, to try to determine the physical number of workers by dividing aggregate hours of labor supplied by the length of a standard workday. Not all workers work the same hours (the use of labor-leisure tradeoffs must, specifically, permit this), and, if we cannot be certain how many workers work at the same time (as Q_L along D_L requires; see note 3), the coherence of D_L is threatened, as well.[4]

It is also more common today for labor economists to discuss the wages of particular occupations, rather than an abstract, aggregate wage, as was once the case. Now, however, we must consider workers' occupational choices, which are not explained by labor-leisure tradeoffs. While most undergraduate labor textbooks simply skip any derivation of labor supply in this context, Filer, Hamermesh, and Rees (hereafter FHR) offer one, albeit brief, exception, saying:

> With respect to . . . labor markets . . . for particular occupations, relative labor supply schedules . . . typically slope upward throughout. Income effects of rising wages may dominate substitution effects for those currently employed in a specific market, thus reducing their labor supply. If wages in one market rise relative to those in other markets, however, the overall change in labor supply will come largely through the attraction of workers from [other labor markets]. (FHR 1996, 130)

The authors pass smoothly from hours of labor supply (the income and substitution effects of labor-leisure tradeoffs) to the number of workers (who are attracted by the relative wage of the occupation). A labor supply curve is then drawn (FHR 1996, 131), with no discussion of how to derive a labor supply curve from the theory of occupational choice, nor of how qualitatively different units can be added, nor of the fit between the new S_L curve and the requirements of D_L. The new S_L curve looks identical to one derived from labor-leisure tradeoffs, and we are left with the impression that sufficient logical assurances for it exist.

It may seem questionable to rely on undergraduate labor economics courses and textbooks to argue that mismatched quantitative units for labor supply and demand reflect incoherence in the qualitative logic of standard labor market theories. Surely, we might suppose, these lapses are corrected in more advanced treatments. But they never are. Advanced work is too specialized to discuss labor demand (see Hamermesh 1993) and labor supply (see Killingsworth 1983) together, while questions of qualitative units in theory come up only occasionally, in fairly narrow theoretical contexts.

Undergraduate textbooks then reflect such gaps and disparities. One popular current text (Ehrenberg and Smith 1997) gives examples of short-run labor demand in either the number of workers or in "employment" (units unspecified; 69–75); in the mathematical appendix, however, short-run labor demand is derived from long-run isoquant analysis, where capital is denoted in physical units while labor is measured in hours (94ff.). The FHR text consistently specifies time units for both short-run labor supply and demand. This appears to make Q_L for labor demand consistent with the standard time units for labor supply—but consistency with labor supply is not the reason that time units were

selected[5] nor, as already argued, can a proper case of short-run diminishing returns result.

Hamermesh has acknowledged that significant logical difficulties exist within short-run theories of labor market demand (1993), but he does not mention the "units" problem. He objects, instead, to the supposed divisibility of short-run fixed capital and argues that long-run theories, with variable capital, are stronger. So, although standard economic representations of "the labor market" are for the short run, consider FHR's treatment of long-run labor demand and supply. Time units are used for Q_L (as in FHR's short-run analysis) and for Q_K (see note 5). While there are no diminishing returns to worry about, it is still impossible to deduce how much capital and labor are used at the same time, since workers' shifts could vary or overlap. The productivity of labor—and hence, D_L—is then not logically determinate (see note 4), even in McCloskey's qualitative terms. Nor do these units for D_L match FHR's units for long-run supply; the latter are now in physical units, based on human capital and occupational choice theories (where hours are irrelevant). Thus, for the long run, FHR's units for D_L are time units, while S_L is denominated in the number of workers.

Now that economists usually consider particular, occupational labor markets (not an aggregate one), the problem of mismatched units for Q_L might be reduced somewhat if labor-leisure tradeoff analyses were simply discarded, as unnecessarily problematic. FHR, for example, could use physical units for Q_L on D_L, for both the short and long run, and base S_L on the physical units of labor market entrance decisions (when the wage exceeds the opportunity cost of working), occupational choices linked to relative wages, and human capital theory. Some problems would still remain, but the largest one might be that neoclassicals would be deprived of the opportunity to convince undergraduates that the existence of the labor supply curve is based on logical deduction—since no careful derivation of labor supply from occupational choice or human capital theory has been developed.

The most plausible explanation for these logical disjunctures, and the utter lack of notice they have attracted, comes from the history of labor supply and demand theories. Neoclassical labor demand theories are much older than neoclassical labor supply theories, which appeared only in the 1950s, with the work of Lewis (1957), on labor-leisure tradeoffs, and Mincer (1958), which launched the modern development of human capital theory. By then, units questions for labor demand had already been thoroughly obscured (see below). Lewis's and Mincer's work restated, in acceptable neoclassical terms, the basis for labor supply relationships that had already been accepted for generations, long before their neoclassical theoretical reformulations.

The early neoclassicals changed many of the terms of economic explanation, introducing new, especially mathematical, tools and metaphors. But they also recycled many classical understandings and metaphors, among them diminishing returns and the existence (in some form) of labor supply and demand relationships. In what follows, I focus on the history of these metaphors, to analyze the slippages, loss of linkages, and logical disjunctures that evidently can result when metaphorical meanings are transported to new contexts, without adequate recognition of their content and/or logical connections.

Empty Metaphors in Standard Theory

If your only tool is a hammer, everything else in the world tends to look like a nail.

— Pat Choate

In standard labor economics, the diagrammatic representation of supply and demand relies on a Cartesian coordinate system, in which quantities of labor and levels of wages are represented as horizontal and vertical distances. This spatial metaphor requires, however, that imaginary, standard units of labor be established before the diagram can be drawn. All qualitative differences among actual labor must be reduced somehow to their *quantitative essences*, known among economists as "efficiency units" (Stigler 1941).

The practice of representing heterogeneous labor in homogeneous efficiency units began quite early in the neoclassical tradition of labor economics.[6] J.B. Clark defined his homogeneous units of labor as follows:

> [W]e may use the familiar term, unskilled labor, and treat the work performed by a man with no exceptional skill or endowment as constituting the unit of which we are speaking. A superior artisan, however, represents many of them. (Clark 1899, 63)

Thus, if some (skilled) workers receive higher actual wages than others (with fewer skills), this need not imply that they are paid more *per unit of labor*. Rather, the wage paid is spread over a larger number of efficiency units of labor, so that the "efficiency wage" paid may be equalized across all workers (see also Marshall 1953, 549). Cartter (1959, 15) comments that "[t]his simplification allows us to speak generally about *the wage rate*, rather than a whole structure of wage rates for various degrees of skill" (emphasis in original). Although it is a convenient method for theorizing wages in an *aggregate* labor market, as Clark, Marshall, and most other neoclassical economists did before World War II, this also means that neither the wages nor the quantities of labor represented in standard supply and demand diagrams are, even in principle, observable.

Institutionalist labor economists, such as Reynolds (1948), have complained about this fundamental unobservability of efficiency labor units and wages. One can never know, empirically, whether wages are actually paid in accordance with their theoretical correlates. This raises considerable difficulties for any empirical test of standard theories, as Reynolds noted, and potentially larger concerns about the content of the Cartesian metaphors involved in standard theory. Descartes himself saw the main virtue of his system in the prospect of discovering the (supposed) uniformities of nature through actual measurement (Hadden 1994). There is little dispute that all quantification and measurement are metaphorical, in the sense that standard units for counting must first be defined. But do the counting metaphors that Descartes imagined have any content, if the units specified cannot be used to count anything? What, then, is the connection between McCloskey's abstract, "qualitative" mathematical reasoning and the world we wish to understand?

Metaphors are involved in virtually all human thought (Lakoff and Johnson 1980) and are both necessary and unavoidable in economics. They provide concepts and categories for day-to-day understandings and, by transferring and redeploying meanings from one context to another, they facilitate the growth of new understandings. But they also tend to impose borrowed structures on the new understandings that may obscure important features of the phenomena under study. This can, in turn, undermine the content of the metaphors themselves.

Metaphors that have been widely accepted may no longer be perceived as metaphors at all. Having lost their original startling impact, they are sometimes referred to as "dead metaphors."[7] But dead metaphors are not inoperant; their meaning is accepted without further thought and the question of their aptness simply passes below the radar screen. Though "the power of metaphors resides in their linkages to other discourses and texts" (Kay 2000, 296), the nature of the linkages and key elements of the original meanings—the various dimensions and context—of the borrowed terms may fade as well. Kay refers to this as "catachresis," by which a metaphor *for* a metaphor is constructed, with attendant slippages and omissions. Catachresis, Kay says, results in "a signifier without a referent" (24).[8] Thus measurement requires a metaphor, but unmeasurable efficiency units of labor are a metaphor for a metaphor.

Barthes (1972, 114), meanwhile, described a similar logical case as a "second-order semiological system," which he then identified with the foundation of mythologies. Mythologies falsely universalize by removing the historical referents of signifiers; they naturalize meanings by emptying them of specific content. They are especially useful, he argued (142–45), as a mode of "depoliticized speech"—which is to say, speech that is deeply political, but not represented that way. The supply and demand metaphors that neoclassical labor economists borrowed from their classical predecessors are a good example of this.

John Lie has provided perhaps the broadest commentary on the troubling metaphors of economics by questioning neoclassical theory's universalized conception of commodities and markets in general:

> What is the market in orthodox economics? Most economists follow Cournot in suggesting that price uniformity within a particular area signifies the existence of a market. The market clears—supplies are exhausted, while demands are satisfied at a given price. But what is the sociological description of the market? Milton Friedman, for example, writes: "the central characteristic of the market technique of achieving coordination is fully displayed in the simple exchange economy that contains neither en-

terprises nor money." This accords with the dictionary definition: "Generally any context in which the sale and purchase of goods and services takes place. There need not be any physical entity corresponding to a market." . . . The very abstraction of the market—its ontological indeterminacy—allows for its universal applicability. (Lie 1997, 342)

Shorn of any historical or social specificity and equally applicable to all "cases," the market model is an abstraction built on an abstraction, a catachresis, "a signifier without a referent"—and proves an ideal vehicle for "depoliticized" social speech.

Pure markets exist both everywhere and nowhere. But if neoclassical economics has no other conception of markets *except* its models of supply and demand and "schedules of bids and offers" (Galbraith 1997, 11–12), we are left with the insight of Pat Choate that began this section: when there is only one, universal conception of the market, all exchanges look like supply and demand, and all wages look like market-clearing wages reflecting marginal productivities. With no accepted neoclassical method for measuring productivity, the nature of wages becomes a matter of faith. The logically incoherent presentations of labor supply and demand in undergraduate textbooks become the means for perpetuating the neoclassical mythology; *pace* Keynes, they are truly a subject for undergraduates and are rarely revisited by scholars, except to impart them anew.

Metaphorical Slippage in Q_L

The strange state of metaphorical units for Q_L in theories of labor supply and demand has a fairly clear historical origin. Here, I will address the matter rather briefly, through metaphors that neoclassicals borrowed from classical economics—diminishing returns and supply and demand itself—and the later introduction of dimensionless

mathematical terms in neoclassical production functions.

J.B. Clark's *Distribution of Wealth* (1899) is widely credited as "the first full and comprehensive statement of the theory of marginal productivity" (McNulty 1980, 120).[9] His neoclassical account relied on a fairly direct borrowing from Ricardian diminishing returns in agriculture. Ricardo had focused mainly on diminishing returns at the extensive margin of cultivation of land, but also made note of the intensive margin. Clark discussed both, as well, but emphasized the intensive margin and, more importantly, generalized the result to any case in which a variable factor of production (e.g., labor) is applied in increasing amounts to a fixed factor (e.g., land or capital). Clearly this is a case of metaphorical borrowing and extension, by analogy, of an earlier set of understandings. Although he offered nothing resembling the isoquant-isocost approach now in standard use, and he had no theory of the firm, Clark's diminishing returns metaphor remains the basic means of teaching downward-sloping, short-run labor demand curves to budding undergraduate economists.

In *The Distribution of Wealth*, Clark's first case was indeed agricultural:

> We shall introduce the men into the field one at a time, and see what product is virtually created by each of them. With one man in a field of a given size, a certain crop will, on the average, be secured. With two men, the crop will not be doubled; for the second worker will create less than the first one. This reduction in the productivity of successive units of labor, as they are set tilling a field of a certain extent, furnishes the basis for a general law. (1899, 163)

But soon: "Instead of the plantation in our late illustration, we will think at once of the world, with its innumerable industries and its complete outfit of agents and appliances" (173). Clark continued:

> Give, now, to this isolated community a hundred million dollars' worth of capital, and introduce gradually a corresponding force of workers. Put a thousand workers in to the rich environment that these conditions afford, and their product *per capita* will be enormous. Their work will be aided by capital to the extent of a hundred thousand dollars per man.... Add, now, a second thousand workers to the force; and, with the appliances at their service *changed in form—as they must be*—to adapt them to the uses of the larger number of men, the output per man will be smaller than before.... Where one of the original workers had an elaborate machine, he now has a cheaper and less efficient one. (174–75; emphasis in original)

Clark, then, saw no difference between the agricultural and manufacturing cases, but the classroom example given above suggests otherwise. It may not matter, in agriculture, whether the "additional units" of labor applied to a fixed amount of land are physical units (the number of workers) or time units (hours of labor), but proper diminishing returns in manufacturing will result only if physical units are considered. Clark's only discussion of units concerned the "efficiency units" cited earlier; his own descriptions consistently involved physical units of labor (and land; the capital units were also, in some sense, physical[10]). Used metaphorically, the new context should have imposed specific new requirements on diminishing returns but, perhaps because the account was already so fanciful, neither Clark, nor any subsequent theorist, seems to have noticed. The diminishing returns metaphor silently slipped its mooring, to drift on the currents of other unexamined metaphors.

Marshall's work demonstrates the slippage of quantitative metaphors associated with agricultural diminishing returns even more clearly. He begins: "We may suppose a farmer to be thinking of send-

ing the horses over a field once more; and after a little hesitation he decides that it is worth his while, but only just worth his while to do it" (1953, 154). Clearly there are no additional farmers or horses, but there is an extension of their use in time units. Then, in manufacturing:

> If a manufacturer has, say, three planing machines there is a certain amount of work he can get out of them easily. If he wants to get more work from them he must laboriously economize every minute of their time *during the ordinary hours, and perhaps work them overtime*. Thus after they are once well employed, every successive application of effort to them brings him a diminishing return. At last the net return is so small that he finds it cheaper to buy a fourth machine than to force so much work out of his old machines: just as a farmer who has already cultivated his land highly finds it cheaper to take in more land than to force more produce from his present land. (168–69; emphasis added)

Here, economizing "every minute of their [the planing machines'] time during the ordinary hours" evidently refers to the effect on the intensive margin of adding additional efficiency units of labor—through greater skill or work intensity or, perhaps, adding further workers, but the machines are also made to work harder ("get more work from them"); has Marshall added efficiency units of capital, as well? The machines are not improved, but clearly their intensity of "work" (imagine, perhaps, a speedup of power machines) has increased. Marshall also allows the time use of the machines to vary ("and perhaps work them overtime"), with no identifiable basis for change in Q_K/Q_L. Offered as an example of short-run diminishing returns, however, only labor is seen to vary. The original agricultural case, in which the units for labor (or capital) seem not to matter—and the land is seen, perhaps, as implacably fixed in physical quantity—is so compelling that the quantitative units of the manufacturing case are obscured. The confounding influence of efficiency units passes without any comment whatever.

Clark claimed to have produced a theory of wages (as well as rent and interest) by means of diminishing returns. Marshall disagreed, however: diminishing returns gave only a theory of labor demand, which was but "one of the causes that governs wages" (Marshall 1953, 518; and see McNulty 1980, 123). The oversight suggests that Clark's analysis was undertaken within a framework that simply presumed older supply concepts inherited from classical economics. Thus, on the matter of labor supply, Clark said only, in passing, that the "mere growth of population . . . is an impoverishing influence" (1899, 167).

Marshall is perhaps best known for framing the theory of supply and demand—the central metaphorical structure of all of neoclassical economics —in "modern" terms. He was far more explicit on labor supply than Clark, though he again focused on classical population issues (and the number of workers). He also added consideration of how (higher) wages might affect the lifespans and productivity of workers, however, as well as some discussions of the likelihood that workers had unequal bargaining power with their employers. In other words, like many of his early neoclassical contemporaries (including Clark), Marshall thought that "market" wages might well be too low. Today's neoclassical opponents of living wage policies have paid little attention to his views, perhaps because the supply and demand concepts he borrowed, and only partially reconstructed, from classical economics provided too compelling a template. Marshall reestablished the market's universal presence for all of his successors with the market diagrams now described as the "Marshallian scissors," without any of the reconstructed choice-theoretic arguments now usually given for labor supply.[11] The market diagram's metaphorical complexity,

and the slippages and peculiar disjunctures it relies on, have gone unexamined, while questions of its empirical referentiality (such as Reynolds's) are simply dismissed.

In subsequent work, when quantitative units were described—most often without the efficiency units necessary for consistent graphical representations—they remained quite slippery. Thus Hicks, considering the divisibility of labor (the students' implicit step functions noted earlier), remarked,

> Labour . . . is not indefinitely divisible. In a very large number of cases it is practically impossible to engage anything less than a whole man [!]; even if we mean by a fraction of a man, a man for less than the whole of the time which is conventionally devoted to wage earning employment [!]. . . . we cannot suppose that he remains unemployed for the rest of his time. He will want to find another employer for that [time]. (Hicks 1932, 25–26)

Underemployment was too unrealistic to consider, evidently, but the realism and/or consistency of quantitative metaphors utterly escaped Hicks's field of vision.

Two years later, Paul Douglas provided one more crucial element in the obfuscation of quantitative issues in labor economics. The expression of production functions such as $Q = AK^a L^b$ in pure, dimensionless algebra implied no particular units for K and L at all, and seemed to sanction whatever units were most convenient. The advantages of algebraic tools to economic theorists seem evident. The Cobb-Douglas function is smoothly differentiable (Hicks's—albeit confused—concern with the divisibility of labor has been forgotten) and is often used to produce the isoquants that commonly represent the firm's production options. But algebraic systems have no necessary external referents at all; devices and relationships appear to originate entirely from their internal logic. While this abets their supposed universal applicability, it can also strip analyses of any test of correspondence to real-world concerns or requirements—such as quantitative units or measurement. This is evident in Douglas's own work. Though he began his *Theory of Wages* (1951a [1934]) by saying that "we shall have to assume as our unit an hour of work" (16), he then proceeded, throughout the rest of the book, to provide all of his theoretical examples in the number of workers (cf. 37–44) and his empirical studies in "man-years" (i.e., physical units) rather than "man-hours" (125).

While McCloskey (2002, 9–16) holds that the beauty and virtue of qualitative mathematical reasoning is its assistance to valid deductions, requiring only valid premises, we see here that mathematical metaphors also mislead, by obscuring important elements of the premises in question. Thus, by the time that H. Gregg Lewis (1957) introduced the logic of labor-leisure tradeoffs for labor supply theories, the implications for quantitative units of labor were simply not discussed. Q_L had already long since lost any real-world content, and the existence of both supply and demand was long since a compulsory article of faith.[12] The strange usages in labor economics textbooks today fit comfortably into this story.

Dead Metaphors and Living Wages

The standard market view of wages, dominant among economists at least since Ricardo, has never been in doubt among orthodox practitioners; theory may express and transmit neoclassical beliefs, but their foundations lie in unstated political commitments to classical liberal principles of laissez-faire. The naturalization of the market is a means of representing the things we cannot change. Wages cannot be raised without reducing employment and hurting workers, unless labor supply or demand has shifted appropriately. Thus neoclassicals hold

that, even though the demand for low-wage labor is thought inelastic, so that higher wages would result in higher total wage bills for remaining workers, living wage ordinances that set price floors for wages paid by contractors to state or local government will still result in pareto-losses.[13] And, since higher wages can be profit-maximizing for employers only if the MRP of the last worker is also higher, the least able and productive workers (those with the fewest skills) are most likely to be let go. Most of the burden of "above market" wages should then fall on the most disadvantaged groups (Neumark 2002), who are likely to either be unemployed altogether or swell the ranks of "noncovered" workers and reduce wages somewhere else.

The logic for such pronouncements is far more elusive than is generally supposed, but even within a neoclassical framework, the result is not actually assured. Consider, for example, the possibility that low-wage workers and/or households are target earners. This would be the case if some minimum level of cash income is necessary to maintain a household so that, below that level, market and nonmarket uses of time cease to be readily substitutable (see Brown 1982). Potential workers with no nonwage, alternative sources of cash income could then be forced to offer more labor at lower wages than at higher wages. Higher wages could allow such workers to quit second jobs, or allow low-income households to send fewer workers into the labor market, and might be necessary to afford low-wage workers the sorts of realistic choices (and "substitutability") that neoclassical theory takes for granted.

The question of necessary income thresholds can readily be linked to more institutionalist analyses, such as Piore's (1979) argument that low-wage firms in marginal and/or highly competitive markets may wish to raise wages, but be unable to do so unless all their competitors do. The argument could also apply to many firms competing for public service contracts. Without living wage ordinances, low-wage, "beggar-thy-neighbor" strategies may become a primary means of winning public contracts. Low-income households struggling to meet basic needs may then face continuing downward pressure on their wages.

Such logic may well be playing out today, in the context of recent political moves to impose the "discipline of the market" on several fronts, including reduced public support for unions and collective bargaining, declines in the real value of the minimum wage, efforts to shrink the size and cost of government, and new work requirements and time limits in recent welfare reform legislation. The aggregate effect of all of these is to redistribute income upward, through lower prices for goods and/or services and reduced tax burdens on incomes and property, thereby increasing the often invidious income differentials associated with social class and related distinctions by race/ethnicity, gender, and nontraditional family formations. In this political context, living wage ordinances and campaigns may be seen as an explicit policy to alter, at the state and local level, the maldistributive effects of increasingly neoliberal federal policies on low-income groups.

Living wage campaigns are rooted in several kinds of arguments, both old and new (for more detailed discussions, see Pollin and Luce 1998; Glickman 1997). Among the older arguments is the view that firms who pay poverty- or subpoverty-level wages do not bear the full social cost of maintaining and reproducing the labor they employ; they are, in that sense, both parasitic and exploitive (see Figart, Mutari, and Power 2002). A second strand, dating to J.R. Commons but more recently expressed by Piore (1979; see above), is that some forms of business competition, such as by low

wages, are socially destructive, leaving firms unable to raise wages to desirable levels unless their competitors are forced to, as well. A third strand flows out of increasing awareness and theoretical discussions of structural discrimination; these often suggest that market-oriented societies produce social (and job) structures that distribute and reproduce social positions of relative privilege and disadvantage (Brown 1988). In some versions, discrimination is seen as a tool for determining assignments to less privileged positions, while, in others, existing social images of the relative value and appropriate roles of various groups will themselves help to define and structure jobs and opportunities (see Figart, Mutari, and Power 2002). Another recent strand has been the recognition of the enormous scale and scope of "corporate welfare" policies and tax breaks that benefit wealthy and socially powerful groups; living wages help to ensure that public expenditures also benefit less advantaged groups (Pollin and Luce 1998).

Taken together, these various strands imply several things. First, individual choices, abilities, and resourcefulness are not the only, or even the main, determinants of the distribution of social benefits from market processes. Second, markets do not faithfully reflect impersonal productivities or efficiency-maximizing methods of achieving profits, and competition may be perverse and welfare-reducing. Finally, social policies are important elements in the social construction of "fairness" and tend to worsen invidious distinctions in some periods, while challenging or reducing them in others. Public discourse is thus an important element of the nature and configuration of social inequalities (see Kessler-Harris 2002); widely held misconceptions and myths can help to prescriptively generate objective conditions that mimic the fictional causal process they espouse.

The neoliberal rhetoric of "free markets" is a

mask for market power and wealth at the expense of more democratic and egalitarian values. Myths that markets are inevitably efficient, reflect the "objective" value of labor and other productive social contributions, and are unbiased arbiters of maximum economic well-being are rationalized by the sorts of naturalized, nonreferential, and logically incoherent metaphorical structures already examined here. In that context, conventional arguments against living wages have little demonstrable basis in what is, or is not, socially possible—except their own prescriptive political force in framing social values. Like Card and Krueger's careful (1995) study of the actual effects of minimum wage legislation, unfairly dismissed by neoclassicals because it did not adequately operationalize or replace their obscure (and incoherent) theoretical terms, the merits of living wage campaigns should not be judged by their conformity to neoclassical theoretical and political commitments.

The notion that firms that contract to provide public services cannot afford to pay living wages, or that the public cannot afford to pay them, or that low-income groups do not deserve them, reflects mainly the values of dominant social groups who do not wish to bear the full social costs of their own standard of living. Market mythologies, based on universalized, nonreferential, incoherent, and unexamined metaphors only serve to conceal the broader political agenda of those who benefit from maldistributed incomes and the struggles of low-income workers and households. From an institutionalist standpoint, the depoliticized speech of nonreferential market metaphors is but another of the myths that Veblen (1899) identified long ago as social foundations and rationalizations for invidious distinctions. He argued then that the most conservative social groups are those who benefit most from existing arrangements, because they have no need for reasonable policies for social

improvement and no desire to pay for them, and those who benefit least, because their existence is too precarious to afford the necessary adjustments in their lives. We should add, today, that when most Americans consider themselves middle-class and comfortably immune from the likelihood of outright want, a complacent sense of entitlement, and an accompanying devaluation of those whom market forces have benefited little, may extend well down the scale of status and income rankings (Galbraith 1992). Market mythologies, abetting our dominant social prejudices, serve, like all myths, to depoliticize the things we do not wish to change. Living wage campaigns seek to make actual changes, but also to repoliticize and challenge such preconceptions and the dead metaphors on which they are based.

Notes

1. Glickman (1997, 62) says that the term "living wages" probably first appeared in 1874, in an article by British labor radical Hugh Lloyd Jones. Whereas nineteenth-century labor leaders sought living wages based on "self-help" among independent (white, male) trade unionists, today's living wage advocates focus on state and local ordinances imposing wage floors for the employees of public contractors. Economists, meanwhile, have replaced classical with neoclassical tools and theories.

2. The antimarginalist controversy was a debate begun by Lester (1946) and Machlup (1946). Lester, a leading figure among the institutionalists who then dominated labor economics, presented survey evidence that employers did not know their marginal cost and, therefore, could not optimize in a neoclassical manner. Machlup, a neoclassical marginalist, responded that drivers did not know the speed of oncoming cars, yet still managed to pass other cars without collisions. The marginalist victory in labor economics was not clear until the late 1960s, however, when textbooks began to emphasize the labor supply innovations of Lewis (1957) and Mincer (1958).

3. The upshot of concerns with physical versus time units for capital and labor use is that diminishing returns require a falling ratio of physical capital to physical workers, simultaneously applied over a specified (fixed) time period. We cannot switch to time units for labor without confronting prob-

lems with capital's time use and the resulting K/L ratio. Outside of agriculture, time units are never the relevant quantitative dimension of either variable labor or fixed capital in proper cases of diminishing returns. For another example, suppose that we fix the hours of capital, while varying the number of physical workers; consider, say, two or three workers employed over a single hour, in combination with two hours of machine time. We will still have to determine the physical number of machines to which the two or three workers have access during their hour. If the two hours of machine time refer to one machine over two successive hours, only the first hour of the machine's time matters. *One machine* is relevant; the *second hour* is not.

4. Suppose, for example, that we counted eight hours of work per day as "one worker" along S_L. If the eight hours came from two workers working four hours each, this would be two workers along D_L if they work at the same time, but only one worker along D_L if they work at different times. This possibility cannot be excluded, since the derivation of S_L is specifically based on variations in individuals' hours of labor.

5. The reason for using time units is given by Rees (1973, 59–60) in the first edition of *The Economics of Work and Play*. It concerns the units for *capital* (!), which are measured in hours "to allow for differences in the life of capital equipment."

6. Similar concepts, such as Marx's "abstract labor time," already existed, however.

7. The term "dead metaphor" is in such common use in discussions of metaphor and rhetoric that it has, itself, been seen as a dead metaphor (see Richards 1936, 102).

8. Unlike older theories of metaphors, which viewed their use as a process of "likening" one context to another, more current theories suggest that the transferred meanings are changed by their new context, but this may mean that they are stripped of original connotations and connections. Kay (2000), for example, describes the use of information metaphors in the human genome project, in which DNA becomes "communication" with neither a speaker nor a listener.

9. As Douglas (1957b [1947]) notes, Clark first presented his argument to the American Economic Association in 1888. See also Clark (1889).

10. Although Clark allowed the number and quality of machines to change, this was mainly a method of imagining capital's physical divisibility across workers. If effect, he was attempting to hold the number of physical efficiency units of capital constant; today's theorists would probably reject his method as too unrealistic (see Hamermesh 1993), but his units were less confused than those of many subsequent accounts.

11. "We might as well reasonably dispute whether it is the upper or the under blade of a pair of scissors that cuts a piece of paper, as whether value is governed by utility [demand] or cost of production [supply]" (Marshall 1953, 348). Marshall himself drew no labor supply and demand diagrams in his *Principles of Economics* text, but Pigou (1905, 228 ff.), for example, was drawing them by 1905, without any intervening development of labor supply theories—and with no discussion of units for Q_L.

12. But consider Samuelson's remarks of 1951:

> I fear that when the economic theorist turns to the general problem of wage determination and labor economics, his voice becomes muted and his speech halting. If he is honest with himself, he must confess to a tremendous amount of uncertainty and self-doubt concerning even the most basic and elementary parts of the subject. (Samuelson 1951, 312)

Coming at a time when neoclassical labor economists were struggling to regain dominance from the institutionalists and most discussions of labor supply focused on the behavior of labor unions, the arrival of a theory of labor supply based on individual utility maximization must have been seen as a major advance. Eventually, as the influence of the Chicago labor economists grew, interest in any of the institutional details of labor relations all but vanished from labor economics. Institutionalists were slowly banished, to separate industrial relations programs or to schools of management (see Kaufman 1993).

13. Under less-than-competitive conditions (especially monopsony), it is recognized that higher "administered" wages could be consistent with higher levels of employment, but monopsony is thought rare in the specific types of employment situations most likely to be affected by either higher legislated minimum wages or higher mandated living wages for the employees of county or municipal contractors.

References

Barthes, Roland. *Mythologies*. New York: Hill and Wang, 1972.

Brown, Clair. "Home Production for Use in a Market Economy." In *Rethinking the Family*, ed. Barrie Thorne and Marilyn Yalom, 151–67. New York: Longman, 1982.

———. "Income Distribution in an Institutional World." In *Three Worlds of Labor Economics*, ed. Garth Mangum and Peter Phillips, 51–63. Armonk, NY: M.E. Sharpe, 1988.

Card, David, and Alan Krueger. *Myth and Measurement*. Princeton: Princeton University Press, 1995.

Cartter, Allen. *Theory of Wages and Employment*. Homewood, IL: Richard D. Irwin, 1959.

Choate, Pat. *The High-Flex Society.* New York: Alfred Knopf, 1986.

Clark, J.B. "The Possibility of a Scientific Law of Wages." *Publications of the American Economics Association* 4, (1889): 39–63.

The Distribution of Wealth. New York: Macmillan, 1899.

Douglas, Paul. *The Theory of Wages.* 1934. Reprint, New York: Kelley and Millman, 1957a.

———. "Remarks to AEA." 1947. In Douglas, *The Theory of Wages,* 1957b.

Ehrenberg, Ronald, and Robert Smith. *Modern Labor Economics.* 6th ed. Reading, MA: Addison-Wesley, 1997.

Figart, Deborah, Ellen Mutari, and Marilyn Power. *Living Wages, Equal Wages.* New York: Routledge, 2002.

Filer, Randall, Daniel Hamermesh, and Albert Rees. *The Economics of Work and Pay.* 6th ed. New York: Harper Collins, 1996.

Galbraith, James. "Dangerous Metaphor: The Fiction of the Labor Market." Public Policy Brief no. 36. Annandale-on-Hudson, NY: Jerome Levy Economics Institute, 1997.

Galbraith, John Kenneth. *The Culture of Contentment.* New York: Houghton Mifflin, 1992.

Glickman, Lawrence. *A Living Wage.* Ithaca, NY: Cornell University Press, 1997.

Hadden, Richard. *On the Shoulders of Merchants.* Albany: SUNY Press, 1994.

Hamermesh, Daniel. *Labor Demand.* Princeton, NJ: Princeton University Press, 1993.

———. "Comments." *Industrial and Labor Relations Review* 48 (July 1995): 835–38.

Hicks, John R. *Theory of Wages.* New York: Macmillan, 1932.

Kaufman, Bruce. *The Origins and Evolution of the Field of Industrial Relations.* Ithaca, NY: Cornell University Press, 1993.

Kay, Lily. *Who Wrote the Book of Life?* Stanford, CA: Stanford University Press, 2000.

Kessler-Harris, Alice. *In Pursuit of Equity.* New York: Oxford University Press, 2002.

Killingsworth, Mark. *Labor Supply.* Cambridge, UK: Cambridge University Press, 1983.

Lakoff, George, and Mark Johnson. *Metaphors We Live By.* Chicago: University of Chicago Press, 1980.

Lester, Richard. "Shortcomings of Marginal Analysis for Wage-Employment Problems." *American Economic Review* 36 (March 1946): 71–75.

Lewis, H. Gregg. "Hours of Work and Hours of Leisure." *Proceedings of the Ninth Annual Meeting,* Industrial Relations Research Association, 196–206. Madison, WI: IRRA, 1957.

Lie, John. "Sociology of Markets." *Annual Review of Sociology* 23 (1997): 341–61.

Machlup, Fritz. "Marginal Analysis and Empirical Research." *American Economic Review* 36 (September 1946): 515–54.

Marshall, Alfred. *Principles of Economics.* 8th ed. (1st ed. 1890). New York: Macmillan, 1953.

McCloskey, Dierdre. *The Secret Sins of Economics.* Chicago: Prickly Paradigm Press, 2002.

McNulty, Paul. *The Origins and Development of Labor Economics.* Cambridge, MA: MIT Press, 1980.

Mincer, Jacob. "Investment in Human Capital and Personal Income Distribution." *Journal of Political Economy* 56 (August 1958): 281–302.

Mussey, Henry. "Eight-Hour Theory in the American Federation of Labor." In *Economic Essays: Contributed in Honor of John Bates Clark,* ed. Jacob Hollander. New York: Macmillan, 1927.

Neumark, David. *How Living Wage Laws Affect Low-Wage Workers and Low-Wage Families.* San Francisco: Public Policy Institute of California, 2002.

Pigou, A.C. *Principles and Methods of Industrial Peace.* London: Macmillan, 1905.

Piore, Michael. "Wage Determination in Low-Wage Labor Markets and the Role of Minimum Wage Legislation." In *Unemployment and Inflation,* 197–206. White Plains, NY: M.E. Sharpe, 1979.

Pollin, Robert, and Stephanie Luce. *The Living Wage.* New York: New Press, 1998.

Rees, Albert. *The Economics of Work and Pay.* New York: Harper and Row, 1973.

Reynolds, Lloyd. "Toward a Short-Run Theory of Wages." *American Economic Review* 38 (June 1948): 289–308.

Richards, I.A. *The Philosophy of Rhetoric.* Oxford: Oxford University Press, 1936.

Samuelson, Paul. "Economic Theory and Wages." In *The Impact of the Union,* ed. David Wright. New York: Harcourt, Brace, 1951.

Stigler, George. *Production and Distribution Theories.* New York: Macmillan, 1941.

Veblen, Thorstein. *Theory of the Leisure Class.* New York: Macmillan, 1899.

10

How Is Labor Distinct from Broccoli?

Some Unique Characteristics of Labor and Their Importance for Economic Analysis and Policy

Robert E. Prasch

A core proposition of mainstream economic theory is that labor is a commodity whose properties are not essentially different from any other. From this formative premise, the labor market is represented as just another market, from which it follows that it can be analyzed in the same manner as any other salable commodity—with a straightforward application of the theory of supply and demand.[1] To the extent that other considerations matter, they are thought to be in the domain of "normative economics," which most practicing economists take to be a preanalytic set of attitudes, prejudices, or agendas that are to be excluded from theoretical and scientific analysis.

This state of affairs is somewhat anomalous since labor economics has long held an independent status as a distinct field of scholarship (Kaufman 1993; McNulty 1980). Even today the economics profession features a large contingent of scholars who identify themselves as "labor economists." Annually, numerous books, academic journals, and conferences are devoted to the study of the labor market. Only agricultural and financial markets have consistently drawn comparable interest from the economics profession over the years.

The following chapter will inquire into some of the unique aspects of labor that generate these conundrums, despite implicit or explicit denials that

the labor market has idiosyncratic qualities that can be traced to the specific attributes of the commodity exchanged there. Stated simply, this chapter will examine a few of the qualities that make labor inherently different from other marketable commodities such as broccoli, fresh fruit, or bags of concrete. Everyone recognizes that there is a difference in substance—labor is human and for this reason different in form and ethical status from a bag of concrete. What is at issue is the proposition that labor, considered as a salable commodity, embodies some qualities or features that fundamentally modify the market process.[2] The specific qualities of labor to be covered include the following: (1) Labor cannot be separated from its providers. (2) Labor cannot be stored. (3) Labor embodies the quality of self-consciousness. This last observation has several implications that will be discussed. The chapter will close with the observation that labor is the one "factor of production" that most of us wish, in the end, to see well compensated. A few concluding remarks will end this chapter.

Labor Cannot Be Separated from Its Provider

Physically, legally, ethically, and economically, labor is a commodity that, by its nature, cannot be readily separated from its provider. In almost every instance, the employee must be present to deliver the contracted-for labor services. This fact alone makes labor unique, and even more so in countries that value human rights. Stated simply, when buying labor the purchaser enters, at least in part, into a caretaker relationship with the purveyor of that labor—the worker's person. Decisions that a firm may, or may not, make with regard to the health and safety of its workforce necessarily have lasting implications for the workers it hires during and well after the conclusion of a particular task or employment contract (Commons and Andrews 1916, 1–34; Commons 1924, 283–312).

It follows from this that individual laborers and, in the event of widespread suffrage, the state each and severally have a direct and ongoing interest in the conditions under which labor is employed. One can reasonably conclude, as did John Commons, that the state, through contract and labor law, is effectively a third party to every labor contract (Chasse 1986, 767–69). Enlightened employers, who are inclined to view a healthy, educated, and largely content labor force as a source of enhanced productivity, also have an interest in the protection of this resource. Not surprisingly, regulation of the workplace and the labor contract represents some of the first, and most important, examples of state intervention in the market economy (Commons and Andrews 1916; Millis and Montgomery 1938; Seager 1907, 412–33).

By contrast with labor, consider the circumstances of the vast majority of commodities that are traded in markets. Broccoli, to take one example, can be exchanged between persons with few legal encumbrances pertaining to it. The purchaser of a quantity of broccoli, by establishing a legal claim over it, has what in law is termed a "right of exclusive disposal." She might eat it, let it mold in the refrigerator, or present it as a gift to someone else, without violating the rights of the broccoli in question or those of its original or previous owners.

Thankfully, modern statutes no longer allow such "freedom" when labor is purchased. Labor, but not the laborer, can be purchased for a short period only. The options open to the purchaser of labor are much narrower than in the case of broccoli. The extent of the purchasers' rights over the use to which this labor is put is constrained by moral sanction, the Occupational Health and Safety Administration (OSHA), tort law, numerous state and federal regulations, and even criminal statutes. While the past twenty-five years have seen some erosion in the extent to which employers feel constrained with regard to their treatment of their employees, the legal system, and most thinking people, still maintain that a profound difference exists between labor and other marketable commodities.

Labor Cannot Be Stored

A second assumption underlying the received theory of the labor market is the idea that all workers will be able to enter into a successful exchange of their labor for some price, however low. Moreover, mainstream theory implicitly posits that the "penalty" exacted for a failure to consummate an exchange is that one is left in the economic condition and circumstance that existed prior to one's decision to accept or reject a particular contract. Drawing upon this crucial if rarely articulated assumption, economists typically, almost instinctively, conclude that a "free exchange" between consenting adults "must" make everyone better off. From this premise it follows that if market participants decide that they do not wish to accept the current market price for their goods, they have the option to either consume their own goods or "store" them at a very low cost. This option is implicit behind the "free entry and exit" assumption that is the cornerstone of the theory of competitive markets promulgated in mainstream economic theory (Prasch 1995).

For labor, the situation is not so straightforward. To begin with, labor cannot be stored by the employee. A day of work missed cannot be readily recovered since the temporal dimension of life means that our past is—well, in the past. By contrast, broccoli, while perishable, can be stored for a period of time. The owner even has the option to refrigerate or freeze it, thereby greatly extending its useful qualities as a marketable commodity.

In addition, people have needs that must be met. To grasp the importance of this observation, "needs" must be distinguished from "wants" or "desires." In conventional usage, wants have a whimsical quality to them: I may want an ice cream cone or a pink Cadillac. Needs, on the other hand, suggest a sense of urgency. At the most basic level, I need food, water, clothing, and shelter if I am to survive. Moreover, in a complex social system such as the United States, needs are more extensive than merely food, water, clothing, and shelter. If I am to participate in such a society, my needs will, in all likelihood, include a minimal level of personal grooming, clothing consistent with the norms of my workplace, and access to certain modes of communication, including literacy, a telephone, and, in an increasing number of workplaces, the Internet.

Crucially, if the needs specific to retaining my social status and relationships are not met, the penalty is greater than a simple failure to achieve a desired level of happiness or personal fulfillment. There is a good chance that I will be unable to maintain my current capacity for social and economic interaction. Various penalties, including the loss of my job, can be expected to occur if I cannot meet the cultural and consumption norms and standards of a given work or social environment. In short, our needs place us, as social and physical beings, under constraints that are more pressing than is suggested by the term "wants." Economists are simply in error when they insist that virtually all needs can be reduced to the category "wants" and that satisfying our needs necessarily serves to increase "utility."[3] Needs must be met if we are to remain at our previous level of satisfaction since a failure to do so may lead to a deterioration in our health, well-being, and economic capacity. By contrast, unless we are children, a failure to fulfill our wants leaves us where we were before we considered acquiring the good in question (Frankfurt 1984; Levine 1988, 1–33; Lutz and Lux 1979, 3–75; Prasch 1999b, 2003; Sen 1999, 87–110).

While it is true that employers and owners of companies are also people who have needs, in a world without full employment they have the option of withdrawing from any given labor contract and hiring someone else. Even in the event of a tight labor market, employers have more options. Depending on the specifics of their business, they could relocate their firms or move into a different market. If all else fails, employers always have the option of dissolving their businesses and becoming laborers themselves. It follows that employers are at least three transactions—first selling their wares, then selling their businesses, and then selling their labor—away from experiencing unmet needs. It follows that needy persons without assets will generally do worse when they are bargaining with persons or entities who are trying to satisfy their wants (Pound 1909; Prasch 1995; Hale 1923, 1943).

The necessity for workers to exchange their labor for wages in order to meet their needs, and the potential for physical and mental deterioration in the event that such an exchange does not occur, have long been understood by economists. The difference between then and now is that this phenomenon was once considered an important element of labor economics. In the words of Sidney and Beatrice Webb, "The mere fact that the man is without occupation, and without income, even if he is not yet actually in want, means in the great majority of cases, that he is suffering degeneration in skill, in health and in character, and that he is running grave risk of demoralisation" (Webb and Webb 1911, 139).[4] This idea also played a fundamental role in Karl Marx's understanding of the labor market as a locus of exploitation:

> For the transformation of money into capital, therefore, the owner of money must find the free worker available on the commodity-market; and this worker must be free in the double-sense that as a free individual he can dispose of his labour-power as his own commodity, and that, on the other hand, he has no other commodity for sale, i.e., he is rid of them, he is free of all the objects needed for the realization of his labour-power. (Marx 1977, 272–73)

Karl Polanyi also stressed the institutional and sociological framework behind the establishment of the "modern" labor market:

> This effect of the establishment of a labor market is conspicuously apparent in colonial regions today. The natives are to be forced to make a living by selling their labor. To this end their traditional institutions must be destroyed, and prevented from reforming, since, as a rule, the individual in primitive society is not threatened by starvation unless the community as a whole is in a like predicament. . . . It is the absence of the threat of individual starvation which makes primitive society, in a sense, more human than market economy, and at the same time less economic. (Polanyi 1944, 163–64)

Prior to the "analytic revolution" that swept through the economics profession of postwar America, these issues were more widely understood in this country too. For example, John Bates Clark observed, "Hunger-discipline disqualifies the worker for [sic] making a successful bargain, and if the employer were everywhere at liberty to take men for what, under such pressure, they might individually offer to work for, he might get them for very little" (Clark 1913, 292).

If employees could store their labor at zero cost or, in what comes analytically to the same thing, if labor simply had no unmet needs, its bargaining power would be substantially enhanced. The ability to withdraw, if only for a short period, from the market enables employees to refuse an offer that is on the table while negotiating or searching for a better one. Being forced, through unmet needs, to accept a take-it-or-leave-it offer implies that workers have little bargaining power and therefore a reduced chance of being paid the full value of their labor. As Clark observed long ago, "Workers have something to sell, and they must be able to withhold it if they are to have an effective voice in fixing the price that they will get" (Clark 1902, 553).[5] Liberals, particularly those whose ideas once influenced the Democratic Party, understood Clark's point. Take, as an example, the following passage from President Franklin Delano Roosevelt's 1944 State of the Union address:

> We have come to a clearer realization of the fact, however, that true individual freedom cannot exist without economic security and independence. "Necessitous men are not free men." People who are hungry, people who are out of a job are the stuff of which dictatorships are made. (Roosevelt 1995, 87)

As it is unlikely that labor will ever experience zero storage costs, a reasonable alternative in a market-oriented society is a policy of full employment. Workers will still require a job paying a living wage to ensure that their needs are met, but with full employment the threat to quit a position becomes more credible, thereby increasing the bargaining power of actual and potential employees.[6]

Once the role of the "free entry and exit" assumption so characteristic of orthodox labor economics is understood, it becomes apparent that it is anything but an innocent "simplifying assumption." Rather it is a substantive assumption, in the sense that much of what passes for knowledge about the operation, efficiency, and fairness of contemporary labor markets is based upon it. Without full employment, relative bargaining power becomes a crucial determinant of the market process. It follows that policies derived from an ill-considered presumption of full employment must be reconsidered if the facts do not support that assumption. At the most abstract level, there is a simple and direct lesson in all of the above. In an economy without full employment, it is relative bargaining power, not "skills" or "productivity," that determines the wage structure. Moreover, supply and demand models that implicitly assume full employment necessarily obscure this fundamental reality and for that reason can lead us to erroneous conclusions and flawed policies.

Labor Embodies the Quality of Self-Consciousness

A third characteristic specific to labor that is often ignored is its capacity for reflection or self-consciousness (Frankfurt 1971). This capacity, when considered at all by mainstream economists, is subsumed in a narrow and highly constrained manner under the "labor-leisure tradeoff" that is thought to determine the labor supply decision. This approach posits that people hold fixed attitudes regarding the relative merits of leisure versus additional income. Moreover, these views are thought to be determined prior to an employee's

entry into the labor market and to be limited to a determination of the willingness of each laborer to supply a given quantity of labor at any given real wage. Whatever the merits of this approach when economists are formulating a theory of consumption, when it comes to labor markets, this perspective necessarily sets aside the importance of people's capacity for independent assessment and reflection on their experiences in the labor market or at their place of work. This is a crucial, if conventional, oversight.

Despite the wishful and misguided hopes of generations of Taylorist employers, labor is distinctly not a "tool" in the sense of a passive implement that can be utilized or not at the discretion of its purchaser. Experience and introspection suggest that perceived fairness and quality of treatment on the job can be as important as monetary compensation in eliciting employee loyalty and effort. The human capacity for reflection enables people to consider, and make judgments, concerning the qualities of a given place of employment. Such judgments have implications for how, and even if, people will continue to work at a particular job or location. By contrast, a capacity for reflection is not commonly associated with broccoli, fruit, bags of concrete, or other marketable commodities. While it would be unwise to suppose that people's capacity for reflection is regularly or routinely exercised, we should nevertheless be wary of economic theories that altogether ignore it, especially in the event that widely held norms of fair play are being openly flouted.[7]

In general, when mainstream economists assume that individuals maximize across a fixed utility map, they also assume away the more complex but crucial, idea of reflection. We know that people do act, even when the facts of a given situation make action costly, dangerous, irresponsible, or unwise. Labor history, to say nothing of military or entrepreneurial history, presents numerous instances of people making expensive or risky choices simply because it was the right thing to do.[8]

Reflection or self-consciousness is unique to the productive input called labor.[9] It is clear that broccoli or a bag of concrete cannot have an aesthetic, moral, or any other attitude or response to how it is treated or thinks it is being treated. A bag of concrete will not think it is being treated unfairly if it is fully used up before another bag is even opened. Broccoli will not feel violated or cheapened if it is given away to someone else. As the late economist Alfred Eichner so wonderfully stated, "It is a matter of indifference to the barrel of oil that is sold whether it is used to heat a house of God or a house of prostitution" (Eichner 1985, 79; see also Marshall 1920, 471). People, on the other hand, do show up to work with a developed sense of right and wrong in conjunction with a set of experiences, ideas, and expectations concerning the job they have been asked to do. Management must either modify, work with, or confront these norms and expectations. It rarely has the option of ignoring them altogether, as these attitudes will directly affect the quality and quantity of work that managers can get from a given labor force. Collectively, the factors considered in this paragraph suggest a partial answer to why management is, and should be, taught in a different department from operations research.

Now, we know that horses, mules, and camels also have the quality of consciousness. They even exhibit learned behavior. But it would be a stretch to argue that they reflect on their surroundings or draw larger meanings from what they have been asked to do. While I am not prepared to present a treatise on the origin and meaning of reflection in juxtaposition to consciousness, I am confident that most understandings of these terms would acknowledge that the idea of reflection, drawing as

it does on the ideas of learning, context, and time to make judgments, is unique to adult human beings (Frankfurt 1971).[10]

In labor markets, and labor relations within a firm, the fact of reflection makes an enormous difference. For example, in the contemporary United States, the cultural understanding that we label common sense supports the norm of equal pay for equal work for all of the employees of any given establishment. A machine or a mule, by contrast, would not object if you paid less for its services than you did for another, identical, machine or mule. However, people will object to such treatment unless a compelling reason is offered that satisfies their sense of justice. For example, seniority is widely considered a valid reason to pay one person more than another for the same work.[11]

Drawing upon such considerations, John Maynard Keynes and neoinstitutionalists such as Frank Pierson, Clark Kerr, and John Dunlop, among others, observed that some of the value that workers place on their wage is its level relative to others in the same workplace or industry (Keynes 1936, 4–22; Taylor and Pierson 1957, 3–31; Kaufman 1993, 75–102). These theorists built upon the simple observation that a person's compensation is often deemed satisfactory or unsatisfactory depending upon the structure of the wage bargain and how much comparable workers are paid. Professional arbitrators and other labor relations experts know that within every firm and even industry there is not simply a wage, but a wage hierarchy that guides and reinforces expectations concerning relative wages. John Dunlop developed his idea of "job clusters" and "wage contours" to illustrate some of these dynamics (Dunlop 1957). Smart managers know that they should avoid disturbing these hierarchies without a compelling reason. This is because arbitrary wage adjustments that ignore the social and firm-level values implicit in an established wage structure can lead to a significant drop in morale, a strike, or other disruption in the smooth operation of the production process.

Indeed, the idea that people are beings with a capacity for reflection and, consequently, a concern for their treatment and status at their place of work points to the role that effective organization can play as a factor in economic production. These ideas, combined with some frustration with mainstream labor economics as a field of research, contributed to the development of industrial relations as an independent field of scholarship and professional activity (Kaufman 1993, 75–102). Collectively, these insights have been the basis for several important studies of the role of organization in the development of modern economies (Lazonick 1991; Chandler 1977, 1962).

The Relationship of High Productivity to High Wages

One reason for the popularity and widespread acceptance of the supply and demand theory of price and wage determination is its simplicity. Certainly it has the rhetorical advantage of a one-size-fits-all quality to it. This venerable theory features only two equations, the supply and demand schedules respectively, and two unknowns, the equilibrium real wage and the quantity of labor bought. In this theory, labor supply is determined by the income-leisure tradeoff implicit in the decision-making of every potential laborer, and is derived from the marginal disutility of labor. Demand is derived from the marginal product of labor.[12]

A fundamental problem with the supply and demand theory, as it is conventionally applied to the labor market, is somewhat elementary. If the marginal product of labor schedule is *at least partially determined by the wage level,* then the model may no longer be said to feature a unique

equilibrium solution. As it happens, there are several good reasons to believe that labor's productivity, and hence marginal productivity, is related to the level of wages. As previously mentioned, the capacity for self-consciousness suggests that people can work at several different levels of effort while on the same job. Couching their statements in the anthropologists' language of "gift exchange," economists such as George Akerlof have argued that improved wages and workplace conditions can enhance workers' morale, thereby improving performance and lowering the costs associated with turnover (Akerlof 1982). Alternatively, with a higher wage a firm's workforce may enjoy "employment rents" that, in turn, generate an incentive to provide a greater effort while on the job (Bowles 1985; Shapiro and Stiglitz 1984). Finally, higher wages may contribute to greater workplace performance through improved health and physical well-being (Leibenstein 1963).

Despite the important and widely known literature surveyed in the previous paragraph, mainstream economists retain their commitment to the marginal product theory of distribution, with its corollary that a high level of marginal productivity is the fundamental cause of high wages. Yet, and in part because of the research described above, it is not too difficult to argue that the direction of causation runs both ways.

The causal argument that attributes high wages to high marginal productivity will not be reviewed here as it is familiar to us all—basically, highly skilled labor earns a scarcity premium. As to the argument being developed here, that high wages contribute to high productivity, there are two basic points to be made. First, as economists as diverse as Adam Smith (1776, 72–97), Harvey Leibenstein (1963), David Gordon (1996), and the several "efficiency-wage" theorists referred to above have argued, there is a causal link that runs from high wages to high productivity. The reasons, again, are that high wages lead to greater effort, greater willingness to learn, improved morale, and lower turnover. Additionally, they can induce greater productivity within the firm by forcing firms to reduce inefficiency within management and the process of production (Altman 2001). I should add that these several arguments were widely understood and accepted by the mainstream of American economists during the Progressive Era (Prasch 1998, 1999a).

Second, goods can be more readily sold in a high-wage economy, and, of course, high-wage jobs with substantial benefits can be offered when a firm operates in a prosperous and growing economy. If the market is large and, as a consequence, the division of labor can be greatly advanced, we can expect the high productivity that facilitates the payment of high wages. But notice the caveat. This can only be the case if the market is large and already features high incomes. A poor country does not have a large market, even if there are a lot of hardworking and resourceful people in residence. The fact is that goods must be in demand if the market is to be large, and demand is a function of both the desire for goods and the incomes of potential consumers. For this reason we find ourselves in a theoretical dilemma resembling that of the proverbial chicken and egg. High wages lead to the possibility of a high-productivity economy, and high productivity results in high wages.

American trade policy is therefore a legitimate public concern since an important consequence of losing well-paid manufacturing and technology jobs is the erosion of our high-wage economy and, with it, the erosion of our large internal market for consumer products. Now these causal relationships are not immediately apparent to the individuals or firms making everyday decisions in the market-

place. Any given firm's contribution to the purchasing power of the American labor force is rather limited. It follows that firms have an ever-present incentive to reduce their own wage bill, while continuing to sell their goods in the high-wage American market. Clearly, if all firms simultaneously pursue this strategy, and the aggregate market shrinks, every firm will experience a decline in revenues. As revenues fall off, the measured rate of productivity growth will also decline or stagnate, independently of the level of skills or work ethic that we may wish to ascribe to our nation's workforce (Prasch 1999c, 1996).

When the events described in the previous paragraph transpire, we are typically treated to the sight of orthodox economists with lifetime job security proclaiming that since productivity growth is declining, labor market "flexibility" is needed to restore the "competitiveness" of the economy. As these economists tell us, such policies are just "common sense."[13] The problem with this "common-sense" vision is that it examines the magnitude of the wage bill from the perspective of the isolated employer—who views wages exclusively as an element of the firm's costs. Their common sense forgets that as income, wages are the most important component of the expenditure stream. Put simply, each firm's wages, when spent by employees, represent the revenue of some other firms. Low or falling wages are a threat to these revenues and the high-wage economy that a substantial revenue stream can support.

High Wages Are not a Problem—
They Are the Objective

One might have hoped that the idea expressed in this heading would not require an extended argument. Regrettably, contemporary discussions of economic theory and policy, imbued as they are with a "business" or "common-sense" perspective, tend to overlook this idea. To some extent, this oversight occurs because discussions in the business-oriented media are generally, if subconsciously, permeated with a perspective that largely reflects rentier interests. As a result, rising wages and levels of employment are often viewed as an inflationary threat to the economy, to be resisted by restrictive monetary policy (Thurow 1996). Before he embraced the rhetoric of the so-called New Economy, Federal Reserve chair Alan Greenspan shared this same bias. To combat the supposed evils associated with a nonzero rate of inflation, Greenspan, to the applause of mainstream economists and financiers, adjusted the short-term rate of interest in an effort to trim increases in employee compensation in addition to keeping the overall level of employment close to a mythical "natural rate" (Galbraith 1998, 171–82). Unfortunately, the business press, the Fed, and too many economists have forgotten the simple point enunciated so long ago by Adam Smith:

> No society can surely be flourishing and happy, of which the far greater part of the members are poor and miserable. It is but equity, besides, that they who feed, clothe and lodge the whole body of the people, should have such a share of the produce of their own labour as to be themselves tolerably well fed, clothed and lodged. (Smith 1776, 88)

Such sentiments have important implications. Clearly, it is a sign of progress in economic affairs if the prices of commodities fall over time. Machinery, better management, innovation, and improved techniques are all ostensibly aimed at improving our quality of life through the successive cheapening of commodities. Equally clearly, lower labor costs per unit of output over time are a sign of progress in commercial affairs. But it should matter to us if this latter result occurs through innovation or from a general reduction in wages,

although from the perspective of the firms involved this distinction may appear to be of no importance.

Conclusion

In light of the above argument, it is reasonable to conclude that labor markets are different from other markets in tangible ways that matter to the social scientific project we call economics. That this proposition and its implications have long been understood is evident in the response of Barbara Grimes, a law professor at the University of California, to a United States Supreme Court decision overturning minimum wage legislation in 1923:

> Human labor is not a mere commodity to be bartered and sold. It is the essence of human life itself. And because the conditions relating to the sale of labor, the performance of labor and the mode of payment of labor, have important social results expressed in terms of social well being or ill being, the liberty of contract in regard to the sale of labor has been repeatedly interfered with by legislative enactment in the valid exercise of the police power and as such sustained by the highest courts of the land. (Grimes 1925, 117–18)

Despite the theoretical currents of much of the past fifty years, differences between labor and commodities such as broccoli, fruit, or bags of concrete should not be dismissed by economists as "normative" and for that reason irrelevant to economic theorists. Because labor cannot be separated from its providers, cannot be stored by its providers, and embodies the capacity for reflection, it is evident that labor markets are prone to their own unique dynamics. These realities, individually and collectively, provide an important economic explanation for the often contentious evolution of labor law over the past several centuries (Steinfeld 2001). Additionally, we must recall that labor is the one factor of production that most of us wish, in the end, to see well compensated.

Finally, economists risk a great deal of error when they suppose, in the name of "simplicity" or "mathematical elegance," that labor should be theorized along the lines of an abstract, inanimate commodity. That labor is neither inanimate nor just another commodity was once well understood by economists. It follows that what is needed is not a project of discovery so much as one of recovery. Once this recovery is accomplished, we will find out what we once knew—that labor has unique features that are of great consequence to the project of theory construction, policy formulation, and the revival of economics as a thoughtful and meaningful social science.

Notes

The author would like to thank Janet Knoedler, Dell Champlin, Falguni Sheth, and Laurel Houghton for their assistance on various drafts of this paper.

1. While a few economists, such as James K. Galbraith (1997) and Robert Kuttner (1997, 68–109) have presented contrary views, the treatment of labor as "just another commodity" is simply taken for granted by the mainstream of contemporary economists. However, the historical record indicates that the commodification of labor was actually the result of a specific historical process. As Karl Polanyi pointed out, "To separate labor from other activities of life and to subject it to the laws of the market was to annihilate all organic forms of existence and to replace them by a different type of organization, an atomistic and individualistic one" (Polanyi 1944, 163). For this reason, he considered labor one of several "fictitious" commodities that were necessary for capitalism to emerge as a social system (Polanyi 1944, 68–76). For a recent, compelling presentation of the development and economic importance of the fictitious commodities traded in commodities markets, see William Cronon, "Pricing the Future: Grain" (Cronon 1991, 97–147). On the historical evolution of the labor contract in England and the United States, see Robert Steinfeld (2001).

2. Along with most thinking people, I understand that any theory must abstract from the particulars of the existent situation if it is to be of value. The trouble is that this point is often presented as a blanket defense of a specific set of abstractions—those of the neoclassical school of economics.

What is neglected is that there is an art behind the formulation of abstractions. Specifically, to construct a plausible theory, we must not abstract from the essential characteristics of a particular problem or situation and thereby distort, rather than simplify, the phenomena we are investigating.

3. Arguing that the category of "needs" was economically meaningless used to be a cornerstone of economics instruction in the early 1980s (cf. Heyne 1983, 16–32). It is evocative, given the World Bank's recent, aggressive initiative to privatize the provision of water in third world countries, that Paul Heyne used the example of water to illustrate his point. Today's textbooks strongly imply or suggest that needs do not exist, but the language employed is not as confrontational as it was twenty years ago.

4. A detailed, disturbing survey of academic studies of the causal relationship between downward mobility and various social problems such as alcoholism, teen pregnancy, and divorce is presented in David Gordon (1996, ch. 5).

5. Some readers have remarked on the apparent irony of these several quotations from John Bates Clark in light of his being the first to articulate the marginal product theory of distribution. However, reading Clark's theory of distribution in the context of his more policy-oriented essays confirms that he clearly thought that the specific structure of any particular market could modify the generalizability of his theory of distribution (Prasch 2000a, 2002; Clark 1902, 2002). To Clark, unlike the positivists who later adopted and deployed his theory of distribution, the realism of one's initial assumptions mattered on both ethical and policy grounds.

6. For a bold suggestion as to how full employment could be achieved without causing undue government expenditure or inflationary pressures, see Philip Harvey (1989) or L. Randall Wray (1998, 122–54). Despite the revenues that business can be assured of when workers are flush with good wages, we can expect well-organized and well-financed objections to such a policy. The reason is that management prerogatives are difficult to impose when employees can plausibly threaten to quit (Kalecki 1971, 138–45). Moreover, high levels of employment provide the material foundation for cultural changes that social conservatives object to. For example, sustained periods of high employment and rising wages, such as occurred in the 1940s and 1960s, provided more independence for women, minorities, and teenage children. What followed was an erosion of what are called "traditional" morals. Briefly, in market societies, people are as free as they can afford to be. Rising employment rates increase people's sense of freedom, but they also reduce the prerogatives of those at the top of the social and economic hierarchy. Thus the genuine and heartfelt sense of alarm evinced by cultural conservatives and plutocrats during sustained periods of prosperity.

7. The recent rise of "agency theory" is an effort to retrieve an aspect of this issue. Limited as it is by its "economistic"

preconceptions, it nevertheless is an important attempt by mainstream economic theorists to recover some of the understanding that was lost during the drive to transform economic theory into a purely atomistic, analytic field of study after the war.

8. Besides history, psychology, and literature, recent work in evolutionary and experimental economics affirms that people will sacrifice earnings to enforce norms of fairness (cf. Carpenter 2002; Carpenter, Matthews, and Ong'ong'a 2003).

9. Given my seemingly chronic mishaps, I do sometimes harbor a suspicion that computers also have a capacity for independent reflection and decision-making.

10. Indeed, it is precisely because children are thought to be lacking a sense of context and a developed capacity for reflection that we do not grant them the legal rights and responsibilities that we conventionally extend to adults.

11. As is well known, for much of American labor history gender and race were widely taken to be valid reasons for discrepancies in opportunity or pay within the same workplace. Happily, these flawed conventions have become less legitimate over the past century (Figart, Mutari, and Power 2002, 16–33).

12. John Maynard Keynes severely, and properly, criticized the proposition that the marginal disutility of labor determined the aggregate labor supply schedule (1936, 4–22). Additionally, this proposition can be challenged on both theoretical and empirical grounds even if we disregard macro considerations (Derobert 2001; Prasch 2000b; Sharif 2003). The second assumption, that the demand for labor is dependent upon the marginal product of labor, was undermined by the capital controversies of the 1950s and 1960s (Hunt and Schwartz 1972; Harcourt 1972). While each of these several critiques is interesting, reviewing them here would take us too far afield from the topic of this essay.

13. I will note, since I have checked, that the economists making such pronouncements generally perceive calls for "flexibility" in their own compensation or terms of tenure to be rather vulgar.

References

Akerlof, George. "Labor Contracts as Partial Gift Exchange." *Quarterly Journal of Economics* 97 (1982): 543–69.

Altman, Morris. *Worker Satisfaction and Economic Performance: Microfoundations of Success and Failure.* Armonk, NY: M.E. Sharpe, 2001.

Bowles, Samuel. "The Production Process in a Competitive Economy: Walrasian, Neo-Hobbesian, and Marxian Models." *American Economic Review* 75, no. 1 (March 1985): 16–36.

Carpenter, Jeffrey P. "Punishing Free-Riders: How Group Size Affects Mutual Monitoring and the Provision of Public Goods." *Middlebury College Economics Discussion Paper,* No. 02–06, 2002.

Carpenter, Jeffrey P., Peter Hans Matthews, and Okomboli Ong'ong'a. "Why Punish? Social Reciprocity and the Enforcement of Prosocial Norms." *Middlebury College Economics Discussion Paper,* No. 02–13R, 2003.

Chandler, Alfred D. *Strategy and Structure: Chapters in the History of the Industrial Enterprise.* Cambridge, MA: MIT Press, 1962.

———. *The Visible Hand: The Managerial Revolution in American Business.* Cambridge, MA: Harvard University Press, 1977.

Chasse, John D. "John R. Commons and the Democratic State." *Journal of Economic Issues* 20, no. 3 (September 1986): 759–84.

Clark, John Bates. "Is Authoritative Arbitration Inevitable?" *Political Science Quarterly* 17, no. 4 (December 1902): 553–67.

———. "The Minimum Wage." *Atlantic Monthly,* September 1913, 289–97.

———. "Anarchism, Socialism and Social Reform." *Journal of the History of Economic Thought* 24, no. 4 (December 2002): 451–62.

Commons, John R. *The Legal Foundations of Capitalism.* 1924. Reprint, New Brunswick, NJ: Transaction Publishers, 1995.

Commons, John R., and John B. Andrews. *Principles of Labor Legislation.* New York: Harper & Brothers, 1916.

Cronon, William. *Nature's Metropolis: Chicago and the Great West.* New York: Norton, 1991.

Derobert, Laurent. "On the Genesis of the Canonical Labor Supply Model." *Journal of the History of Economic Thought* 23, no. 2 (June 2001): 197–215.

Dunlop, John T., ed. *The Theory of Wage Determination.* New York: St. Martin's Press, 1957.

Eichner, Alfred S. *Toward a New Economics: Essays in Post-Keynesian and Institutionalist Theory.* Armonk, NY: M.E. Sharpe, 1985.

Figart, Deborah M., Ellen Mutari, and Marilyn Power. *Living Wages, Equal Wages: Gender and Labor Market Policies in the United States.* New York: Routledge, 2002.

Frankfurt, Harry G. "Freedom of the Will and the Concept of a Person." *Journal of Philosophy* 68, no. 1 (January 1971): 5–20.

———. "Necessity and Desire." *Philosophy and Phenomenological Research* 45, no. 1 (September 1984): 1–13.

Galbraith, James K. "Dangerous Metaphor: The Fiction of

the Labor Market." *Policy Brief.* Annandale-on-Hudson, NY: Jerome Levy Economics Institute, 1997.

———. *Created Unequal: The Crisis in American Pay.* New York: Free Press, 1998.

Gordon, David. *Fat and Mean: The Corporate Squeeze of Working Americans and the Myth of Managerial "Downsizing."* New York: Free Press, 1996.

Grimes, Barbara. "Constitutional Law: Police Power: Minimum Wage for Women." *California Law Review*, reprinted in *The Supreme Court and Minimum Wage Legislation*, ed. National Consumer's League. New York: New Republic, 1925.

Hale, Robert. "Coercion and Distribution in a Supposedly Non-Coercive State." *Political Science Quarterly* 38 (1923): 470–94.

———. "Bargaining, Duress, and Economic Liberty." *Columbia Law Review* 43, no. 5 (July 1943): 603–28.

Harcourt, Geoffrey C. *Some Cambridge Controversies in the Theory of Capital.* Cambridge: Cambridge University Press, 1972.

Harvey, Philip. *Securing the Right to Employment: Social Welfare Policy and the Unemployed in the United States.* Princeton, NJ: Princeton University Press, 1989.

Heyne, Paul. *The Economic Way of Thinking.* 4th ed. Chicago: Science Research Associates, 1983.

Hunt, E.K., and Jesse G. Schwartz, eds. *A Critique of Economic Theory: Selected Readings.* Harmondsworth, UK: Penguin, 1972.

Kalecki, Michal. *Selected Essays on the Dynamics of the Capitalist Economy.* New York: Cambridge University Press, 1971.

Kaufman, Bruce E. *The Origins and Evolution of the Field of Industrial Organization.* Ithaca, NY: Cornell University Press, 1993.

Keynes, John Maynard. *The General Theory of Employment, Interest and Money.* New York: Harcourt Brace, 1936.

Kuttner, Robert. *Everything for Sale.* New York: Knopf, 1997.

Lazonick, William. *Business Organization and the Myth of the Market Economy.* New York: Cambridge University Press, 1991.

Leibenstein, Harvey. *Economic Backwardness and Economic Growth: Studies in the Theory of Economic Development.* New York: Wiley, 1963.

Levine, David P. *Needs, Rights, and the Market.* Boulder, CO: Lynne Rienner, 1988.

Lutz, Mark, and Kenneth Lux. *The Challenge of Humanistic Economics.* Reading, MA: Benjamin Cummings, 1979.

Marshall, Alfred. *Principles of Economics.* 1920. Philadelphia: Porcupine Press, 1949.

Marx, Karl. *Capital.* Vol. 1. Trans. Ben Fowkes. New York: Vintage, 1977.

McNulty, Paul J. *The Origins and Development of Labor Economics: A Chapter in the History of Social Thought.* Cambridge, MA: MIT Press, 1980.

Millis, Harry A., and Royal E. Montgomery. *Labor's Progress and Some Basic Labor Problems.* New York: McGraw-Hill, 1938.

Polanyi, Karl. *The Great Transformation: The Political and Economic Origins of Our Time.* 1944 Reprint, Boston: Beacon Press, 1957.

Pound, Roscoe. "Liberty of Contract." *Yale Law Journal* 17, no. 7 (May 1909): 454–87.

Prasch, Robert E. "Toward a 'General Theory' of Market Exchange." *Journal of Economic Issues* 29, no. 3 (September 1995): 807–28.

———. "Free Trade and the Future of the Welfare State." *Global Justice* 2, no. 2 (Spring/Summer 1996): 42–58.

———. "American Economists and Minimum Wage Legislation During the Progressive Era: 1912–1923." *Journal of the History of Economic Thought* 20, no. 2 (1998): 161–75.

———. "American Economists in the Progressive Era on the Minimum Wage." *Journal of Economic Perspectives* 13, no. 2 (Spring 1999a): 221–30.

———. "Needs." In *Encyclopedia of Political Economy*, ed. Phillip A. O'Hara. New York: Routledge, 1999b.

———. "Developing the Principles of a Managed Trade System." *Journal of Economic Issues* 23, no. 2 (June 1999c): 411–17.

———. "John Bates Clark's Defense of Mandatory Arbitration and Minimum Wage Legislation." *Journal of the History of Economic Thought* 22, no. 2 (June 2000a): 251–63.

———. "Revising the Labor Supply Schedule: Implications for Work Time and Minimum Wage Legislation." In *Working Time: International Trends, Theory, and Policy Perspectives,* ed. Lonnie Golden and Deborah Figart, chapter 10. New York: Routledge, 2000b.

———. "An Introduction to 'Anarchism, Socialism and Social Reform' by John Bates Clark." *Journal of the History of Economic Thought* 24, no. 4 (December 2002): 443–49.

———. "Technical Change, Competition, and the Poor." *Journal of Economic Issues* 37, no. 2 (June 2003): 479–85.

Roosevelt, Franklin Delano. "State of the Union: 1944." *Franklin Delano Roosevelt: Fireside Chats.* New York: Penguin, 1995.

Seager, Henry Rogers. *Introduction to Economics.* New York: Henry Holt, 1907.

Sen, Amartya. *Development as Freedom.* New York: Knopf, 1999.

Shapiro, Carl, and Joseph Stiglitz. "Equilibrium Unemployment as a Worker Discipline Device." *American Economic Review* 74 (June 1984): 433–44.

Sharif, Mohammed. "A Behavioral Analysis of the Subsistence Standard of Living." *Cambridge Journal of Economics* 27 (March 2003): 191–207.

Smith, Adam. *An Inquiry into the Nature and Causes of the Wealth of Nations.* 1776. Chicago: University of Chicago Press, 1976.

Steinfeld, Robert J. *Coercion, Contract, and Free Labor in the Nineteenth Century.* New York: Cambridge University Press, 2001.

Taylor, George W., and Frank C. Pierson, eds. *New Concepts in Wage Determination.* New York: McGraw-Hill, 1957.

Thurow, Lester. "The Crusade That's Killing Prosperity." *American Prospect* no. 23 (March-April 1996): 54–59.

Webb, Sidney, and Beatrice Webb. *Industrial Democracy.* London: Longmans, Green, 1911.

Wray, L. Randall. *Understanding Modern Money: The Key to Full Employment and Price Stability.* Northampton, MA: Edward Elgar, 1998.

11

An Institutionalist Approach to Work Time

Is Labor Truly Irksome?

Robert M. LaJeunesse

"Work is so much more fun than fun."

—Noel Coward

One of the most pregnant questions to be harvested from Thorstein Veblen's (1954, 78) fertile field of inquiry was whether "man instinctively revolts at effort that goes to supply the means of life?" The question has engendered a great deal of research among institutionalist economists. The theme of the instinctual commitment to the furtherance of the life process is featured prominently in the works of noteworthy institutionalists such as Clarence Ayres, Marc Tool, John Kenneth Galbraith, James R. Stanfield, and others. Challenging the irksomeness of labor not only strikes at the very foundation of neoclassical economics, but also provides insight into the behavioral psyche of economic agents, which in turn fosters alternative visions of the societal division of labor.

If individuals were truly free to make personal decisions regarding work time, work durations could serve as a touchstone for the veracity of the neoclassical paradigm. Yet, because human beings are social animals—subject to the influences of tradition, emulation, religion, government, and other institutions—the choices made with respect to work time may tell us little about their inveter-ate proclivities. Do individuals avoid labor out of a natural indolence? Do others work long hours simply for the promise of more material possessions? And would they make these same choices if the labor market were less predacious? Institutionalism, founded in the works of Veblen, posits that people do not possess a natural aversion to work, but rather, like all other animal species, manifest an "instinct for workmanship." If freed from the hierarchical labor market that is built upon the neoclassical tenets of self-interest, utility maximization, and scarcity, most individuals would display enough effort and industry to afford society a material abundance. Thus, the current division of labor may be more reflective of the effects of Veblen's predatory/pecuniary power than a manifestation of free will.

The purpose of this chapter is to investigate how the institutionalist view of human behavior and the related critique of the neoclassical labor market elucidate our understanding of the societal division of labor. After reviewing the behavioral assumptions of neoclassical theory, the institutionalist view of human behavior is presented. This view focuses on Veblen's contention that labor is not irksome and that neoclassical theory is subverted by the realization that humankind possesses an instinct for workmanship. The institutionalist method is then used to comment on the inability of both workers and employers to obtain optimal work hours. In an effort to anticipate the future of work time, the analysis concludes with an examination of the history of work hours and current work time trends.

The issue of work time is particularly suited to institutionalism because its holistic, systemic, and evolutionary method of inquiry fosters a deep understanding of the issue.[1] For example, the work time issue requires a holistic approach in order to achieve a true understanding of the relations between employers, workers, families, government, and others involved in the allocation process. Moreover, the work time issue cannot be fully understood without at least a modicum of evolutionary background to be used, if nothing else, for comparative purposes. Knowledge of the historic struggle to reduce work time and the evolution of economic thought on the subject affords a better understanding of the present pressures toward work time reduction. The institutionalist approach carefully considers historical and evolutionary circumstances and contends that they play an important role in the development of any economic theory.

Theoretical Approaches to Behavior and Work

Conventional Canons of Behavior and Work

In the neoclassical constructs of economic behavior, the aversion to work is a central characteristic of "economic man." As a shrewd calculator of pleasure and pain, economic man maximizes his utility through the acquisition of more and more goods, and minimizes his pain by avoiding toil. Since the hedonistic behavioral assumptions surrounding economic man pervade every corner of neoclassi-

cal theory, a great deal of received economic thought has been predicated on the axiomatic acceptance that work is irksome. The tradeoff between consumption and leisure, a cornerstone of the neoclassical notion of factor and product scarcity, depends upon the belief that an individual's chief desire is to obtain the goods produced by labor while avoiding the effort by which the goods are produced. The neoclassical analysis of scarcity, diminishing marginal utility, and voluntary unemployment all follow from the crucial assumption that market work is loathsome. The notion of scarcity, for instance, is largely dependent upon the fact that work time is limited by the hours in the day. Veblen (1954, 78) summarizes the reliance of neoclassical microeconomic theory on the aversion to labor when he writes, "the economic beatitude lies in an unrestrained consumption of goods, without work; whereas the perfect economic affliction is unremunerated labor." There are few realms in which the neoclassical reliance on the behavioral traits of economic man are more pronounced than in the labor market. It is therefore instructive to review the neoclassical approach to determining individual work hours as well as the mainstream explanation of trends in average work hours.

In the neoclassical labor market, firms hire (demand) labor up to the point at which wages equal marginal products. Stiff competition in product markets ensures that all firms pay workers of homogeneous quality an equivalent wage. It follows immediately that the marginal product of like workers in all industries is equalized. It is worthy of mention that workers in this textbook model are numerous and uncombined so that it would not be plausible for them to withhold their labor and alter employment levels. The multitude of homogeneous workers also allows the firm to realize various output levels at relatively stable labor costs.

The allocation of work hours is then a result of

Figure 11.1 **The Traditional Labor Supply Curve**

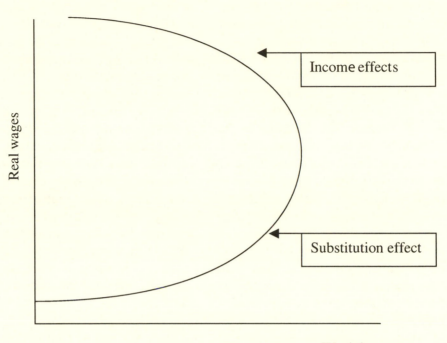

sovereign workers striking agreements with competitive firms based on worker preferences of income and leisure time. The intersection of the labor supply and labor demand curve determines the real wage and the aggregate level of employment. Firms, hiring workers in competitive factor markets, are subject to the prevailing wage and work time preferences of workers. Just as employers would be hard-pressed to find any workers when offering abysmally low wages, competitive factor markets also restrain them from demanding excessively long work hours from their employees. The orthodox assumption of perfect competition consequently results in work hours being determined primarily by the labor supply phenomenon, representing the will of workers rather than the might of employers.

Mainstream labor market analysis holds that the supply curve for labor is upward sloping—as if labor were any other factor of production. However, the labor supply curve is typically afforded a special status. Based on the assumption of an aversion to labor, most labor market theorists accept that the curve can bend backward as the income effects of higher wages dominate the substitution effects. As income rises, an additional hour of leisure has a higher opportunity cost, inducing workers into longer hours. This is the substitution effect. Normally, economists envision substitution effects dominating decision-making at lower wage rates. Under the income effect, increases in income induce workers to work less, or, in effect, consume more leisure. As seen in Figure 11.1, the substitution effects are reflected in the upward-sloping section of the labor supply curve, while the income effects are shown on the backward-bending portion.

Neoclassical economists routinely appeal to free will as an argument against work time regulations. A legislated reduction of hours, it is argued, would be an infringement upon the liberties of those who wished to work longer. In the neoclassical mindset, work time decisions should be the prerogative of the sovereign worker. This sovereign worker mentality also imbues the neoclassical interpretation of the historical record surrounding work hours. The marginalists, for example, chose to explain the late nineteenth-century movement for shorter hours as the propensity of workers to seek free time as real incomes rose. The movement toward shorter hours was thereby trivialized in mainstream economics as a simple consumer choice calculus between goods and leisure, rather than a bona fide means of bringing about improvements in labor productivity and societal welfare. Thus, although a minority of economists questioned the social justice of industrial economies and the ability of workers to make truly sovereign decisions, concern over the length of work time was lost as economic growth and deregulated labor markets persisted as lodestars of economic policy.

Behavior and Work in the Institutionalist Paradigm

The institutionalist critique of the neoclassical behavioral assumptions has its genesis in the works of Thorstein Veblen. Although Veblen devotes prodigious energy to the systematic pillorying of "economic man," his focus on the aversion to work is particularly useful in understanding work time allocation. Veblen notes that "economic man" is an anomaly in the natural world, since an aversion to work would be a unique distinction of human beings compared to other species: "A consistent aver-

sion to whatever activity goes to maintain the life of the species is assuredly found in no other species of animal" (1954, 80). Therefore, this foreign characteristic must have been introduced to the human race by some institutional, social, or otherwise external influence.

Veblen claims that this conflict with nature not only is unexplained by neoclassical theorists, but is also backward. As a species with higher mental and social capacities than other animals have, humans are "endowed with a proclivity for purposeful action" and a distaste of futility of action (80). Although the impulse manifests itself in a variety of ways, the instinct itself is a universal feature of humanity. Seeing others spending their life to some purpose and reflecting on one's own life as having economic or industrial merit engenders a universal sense of satisfaction. Veblen also points out that the avowed aversion to work is not a revulsion against effort in and of itself. Prodigious energy is expended in activities such as sports, politics, war, and other employments that yield no product that is of primal human use. Yet such effort is often viewed as less repugnant than market work under the prevailing paradigm of economic behavior.

Although Veblen did not comment on work time at any great length, his essay titled "The Instinct of Workmanship and the Irksomeness of Labor" is particularly insightful when examining how individuals view the work process in a capitalistic setting. For Veblen, the aversion to labor, seemingly ubiquitous in industrial democracies, is merely a habit of thought created by invidious displays of predatory power. In Veblenian terms, "sportsmanship" behavior may appear to dominate the instinct of workmanship if those with a proclivity to fight or pillage rather than work unduly influence cultural customs and norms. In explaining why labor is often viewed as irksome, Veblen writes:

> If mankind is by derivation a race not of workmen but of sportsmen, then there is no need of explaining the conventional aversion to work. . . . Work is unsportsmanlike therefore distasteful, and perplexity then arises in explaining how men have in any degree become reconciled to any but predacious life. (83)

Since the spoils of workmanship result from a dominance over oneself, there is little room for exploitation and hence little to attract the predacious individual. It was only with the establishment of hierarchical market-based work, and the concomitant predation that followed, that an aversion to paid work developed. Only domineering souls will try to rid themselves of the "need" to work in order to devote more time to exploitative pursuits. Society has thus come to think of leisure time as synonymous with superiority, wealth, and power. Leisure time becomes an invidious display of wealth and is, therefore, neurotically coveted by individuals from nearly every station of society.

The "neurosis" stems from the fact that the cultural mores compelling us toward the pursuit of leisure time are in discord with what our natural instincts are telling us. Veblen offers convincing evidence that humanity has historically been driven by workmanship rather than sportsmanship:

> Throughout the history of human culture, the great body of people have almost everywhere, in their everyday life, been at work to turn things to human use. The proximate aim of all industrial improvement has been the better performance of some workmanlike task. . . . It will not do to say that the work accomplished is entirely due to compulsion under a predatory regime, for the most striking advances in this respect have been wrought where the coercive force of a sportsmanlike exploitation has been least. . . . Whenever they dispassionately take thought and pass a judgment on the value of human conduct, the common run of mature men approve workmanship rather than sportsmanship. (84)

The lesson in Veblen's analysis is that purposeful activity is not in and of itself irksome, but laboring under a predatory or "sportsmanlike" system may create the confusion that it is the labor rather than the work environment that is resented. The irksomeness of labor is not a physical reaction but a learned response that has been engrained through a long process of predatory behavior. Veblen refers to this confusion, or workplace disharmony, as a sort of spiritual disincentive:

> The irksomeness of labor is a spiritual fact; it lies in the indignity of the thing. The fact of its irksomeness is, of course, none the less real and cogent for its being of a spiritual kind. Indeed, it is all the more substantial and irremediable on that account. Physical irksomeness and distastefulness can be borne, if only the spiritual incentive is present. (95)

In his advocacy of a guaranteed annual income, Clarence Ayres (1944, 310) has suggested that higher passive income could go a long way in reversing the spiritual influence and allow workers to "do more things better."

Culturally instilled values of competition and acquisitiveness create a demand for leisure as a display of conspicuous wealth, not as a means of escaping social involvement or useful effort. The fact that those in the lower stations of the labor market typically show a greater aversion to work speaks to the fact that the revulsion does not necessarily stem from the work itself, but from the pernicious influences systemic to a market-based division of labor. Likewise, those in the higher echelons of the income stratification often display inordinately sedulous work habits even though their personal wealth has long afforded them a material surfeit. Institutionalists have endeavored to show that a restructuring of economic activity— perhaps by supplanting market production with household production or volunteerism—may well lead to a more enjoyable way of obtaining material sufficiency.

Barriers to Achieving Optimal Work Hours

This section applies the institutionalist critiques and techniques to comment on the ability of employees and employers to choose a work hours allocation that is efficient from both an industrial and societal perspective. The simple model of a choice between income and leisure has proven ineffectual in explaining the stability of the average American workweek and other labor market trends. Stephen Hill (1994, 129) writes that "economic theory has failed in the task of yielding unambiguous conclusions about the effect on working-time of changes in parameters such as real wages, and the productivity of labor and capital." The basis of the neoclassical approach is that individual employees freely choose their work hours.[2] Yet, as individual bargaining over work time is rare, institutional forces (such as unions, laws, tradition, culture, and power) generally decide basic hours. Given these influences and the myriad information asymmetries that exist between workers and employers, there may be only a narrow range of hours from which workers are able to choose.

Limits to Individual Work Time Optimization

Assuming temporarily that workers are not browbeaten into long hours, there is still nothing in the conventional labor market model that ensures that workers will discount future labor in a manner that is optimal for themselves or society. A plethora of institutional forces weighs upon the individual worker, frustrating progress toward an optimal work time allocation. Even within the neoclassical parlance, the worker's choice between consumption and labor cannot be generalized because it depends on whether income or substitution effects dominate. As either productivity or income rises, for example, the worker can afford the same amount of consumption goods with less labor or more goods with constant labor. The orthodox explanation contends that when productivity or income rises to some psychological threshold, income effects will begin to dominate substitution effects and work time will be reduced.

The question then to be addressed is whether the level of this psychological threshold is conducive to the welfare of society. If individuals are disproportionately governed by acquisitive behavior, they may make work time decisions that inflict substantial costs on third parties. In practice, workers may fail to internalize the true costs of longer work hours. With the existence of an externality abating the income effect, the labor substitution effect will tend to be the predominant force in the utility function, compelling workers to choose more work over free time. Workers may therefore be making labor supply decisions that are not optimal from a sociological viewpoint because their utility calculations do not accurately reflect the social costs of additional work hours.[3]

If the social cost of work time is not given adequate consideration under current labor arrangements, negative externalities will result. Governed by avarice in their work time decision-making, workers can create a burden to society in the form of low future productivity, high health care costs, a lack of skills transfer to younger workers, and lower fertility rates, to name a few. Modern market economies have displayed a bias toward producing tangible goods over leisure. Accumulation of material wealth has reduced time to money. The resultant dearth of leisure time for those enamored of large stocks of material possessions may have profound sociological consequences that are not entirely obvious. Consequently, the benevolent aspects of less market work are often sacrificed during the accretion of still more material goods.

If workers are not cognizant of many of the negative aspects of longer hours, their utility maximization is not likely to result in socially favorable outcomes. Thus, the failure of the income/leisure utility model to incorporate substantial negative externalities limits its relevancy and usefulness in explaining worker behavior. The backward-bending portion of the labor supply curve is brought into question by the existence of work time externalities as well as by recent survey data that tend to refute the notion that workers decrease their work time as incomes rise. The recent recalcitrance of work time in the face of rising productivity and income suggests that workers tend instead to increase the level of income and consumption they feel they need to achieve in order to be satisfied. Likely unaware of the social costs of discounting future work, workers often display a high rate of time preference when choosing current hours over future work time. Therefore, the notion of a "target income" or "target consumption" level is useful in illustrating why the income effect may be largely impotent.

Higher wages might induce workers to cut back on hours once a target consumption level is achieved, but there is nothing that ensures that the target level of income is an absolute measure. The backward-bending assumption of the labor supply curve is therefore not a foregone conclusion. Although some labor economists believe that unions, younger workers, and married couples will inevitably make their preferences for shorter work hours felt in the labor market, desire alone may not succeed. A variety of institutions, ceremonies, traditions, and influences may keep workers from opting for reduced work time. J.S. Duesenberry (1949) was one of the first economists to point out how rising *average* incomes could confound the income effect of higher wages. His relative income hypothesis—commonly used as a sociological theory explaining the rising secular average propensity to consume—argued that satisfaction does not increase with rising income, because as everyone receives more income, relative incomes remain more or less unchanged. Rising average incomes deny an individual the higher status attendant to higher wages and create added pressure for longer hours and still more income.

John Kenneth Galbraith (1984) has also illustrated that a target level of income may indeed be a creeping minimum, constantly redefined by the capitalists' efforts to fabricate new wants and desires. Given the impressionable nature of consumer demands in a capitalist society, workers may never attain their target incomes. In other words, there is nothing to ensure that target incomes are based on *absolute* needs as opposed to the *relative* needs that serve merely to differentiate us from our neighbors. As a result of ever-rising target incomes, the backward-bending portion of the labor supply curve may be better represented by a vertical schedule as shown in Figure 11.2.

A long-run vertical supply curve would predict rather stable workweeks over time. Indeed the *average* workweek in America has remained relatively constant over the last three or four decades—hovering between thirty-three and thirty-eight hours per week (excluding overtime). Considering the income and productivity advances achieved during this period, recalcitrant workweek statistics question the efficacy of the income effect to bring about a reduction in the average workweek. The stability of the average workweek lends credence to the notion of a partially vertical supply curve.

The fallacy of composition creates an additional barrier for any fledgling worker movement intent on altering the work time distribution. Standards that are good for society at large are not immediately beneficial to the pioneers that often suffer while goading society toward those higher standards. Al-

Figure 11.2   **Labor Supply Under Constrained Income Effects**

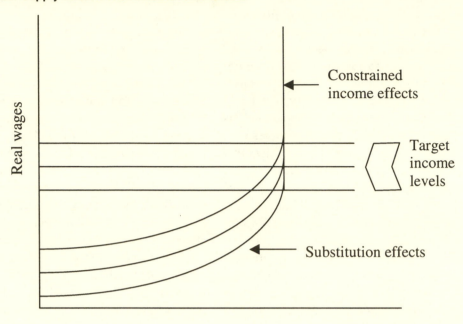

Work hours

though the majority workers may covet and endorse shorter hours, being the first to voluntarily reduce work hours may be detrimental, if not disastrous, to an individual's career. The fear of appearing indolent or being passed over for promotion will tend to limit any one worker's alacrity for reduced hours. Widespread cultivation of the virtue of long working hours makes it difficult for any one individual to break from tradition. Refusing to work overtime, for example, will often raise the ire of colleagues who regularly volunteer to work extra hours for the firm. Any effort to reduce hours on behalf of the workers must then be achieved collectively.

Limits to Work Time Optimization at the Firm Level

The orthodox model purports that competition forces firms to passively accept the wages and work hours fleshed out by the market. Relaxation of the competitive assumption, however, creates the possibility that the employer actually takes an active role in the determination of work hours. Indeed, most orthodox labor economists admit that competition is imperfect and that the firm has a modest amount of influence in the determination of work hours. Yet the recalcitrance of high unemployment in industrialized economies coupled with prodigious labor surpluses in developing nations suggests that employers possess substantial power in determining work hours. In the absence of unions, the balance is tilted further in the favor of employers, giving them greater bargaining power over the actual terms of the employment contract. Moreover, the bargaining power of the employee is thought to be weaker for hours than for wages, since wages can often be negotiated individually, but standard hours schedules are typically offered on a take-it-or-leave-it basis.[4]

Even America's most prominent pioneer in reducing workweeks was under no illusion that the move toward short work time was a manifestation of workers individually registering their desire for more leisure over greater income. Henry Ford (1926, 45) opined that:

> The hours of labor are regulated by the organization of work and by nothing else. It is the rise of the great corporation with its ability to use power, to use accurately designed machinery, and generally to lessen the wastes in time, material, and human energy that made it possible to bring in the 8-hour day.

Ford viewed the process of determining work time as a power struggle between management and labor, in which labor was greatly disadvantaged. On this score, Ford may have had a much better understanding of economics than many of the contemporary labor economists who afford the worker far greater influence in the determination of work hours. Thus, the determination of work hours may be skewed in the employer's favor far more than orthodoxy admits. These bargaining inequities then beg the question, how well-equipped is the firm in determining *optimal* work hours?

Like individuals, firms may be acting in a rational manner even though negative externalities may result from the work schedules they demand from their employees. Orthodox value theory typically regards the losses suffered in the course of the planned market as accidental and exceptional. Self-interested beings will behave in a manner that signals their choices and most external costs will eventually be reflected in market prices. Mainstream economics has come to purport that labor market intervention should be tolerated only in those few cases in which the direct or indirect losses suffered by third persons cannot be resolved by private market solutions.

One problem with this approach is that there may

be a variety of externalities that are not recognized as such. William Kapp was one of the more influential scholars to delineate the social costs of business activity. While orthodox theory has continued to regard the losses suffered at the hand of the market as minuscule and exceptional, Kapp believed that social losses or "external" costs should not fall outside the scope of economics proper. Kapp (1950, 9) noted that "to measure development in terms of a single monetary indicator . . . is a selection of one goal and hence an exclusion of other goals." Valuing labor inputs by the narrow measure of profits produced, for instance, may be highly problematic if doing so ignores the other important social functions performed by workers.

Kapp outlined two reasons why the unregulated market economy failed to achieve "the maximization of the want-satisfying power of scarce resources" (11). The first is the presence of obstacles to the rational behavior of consumers and entrepreneurs as well as outright nonrational behavior patterns in modern industrial society. The second obstacle is that social returns and costs diffuse themselves throughout society and, since they cannot be sold in markets or adequately appraised in terms of dollars, are largely neglected by private enterprise. Kapp also pointed out that while the social costs of production are sometimes felt immediately, in many instances the ill effects of unfettered market activity remain hidden for considerable periods of time. This seems to be particularly true of excessive work hours. Whereas extremely long work hours may come to bear immediately on the health or morale of the worker, a nagging or gradual increase in work time or work intensity might only manifest itself in larger societal problems. Market failure in the determination of work hours often results in harmful consequences and damages inflicted upon third persons for whom private entrepreneurs are seldom held accountable. Moreover, negative externalities may only be observed with a time lag. Thus, subaltern labor productivity or increasingly deviant behavior of successive generations may be the only indication of whether or not erstwhile work schedules were onerous.

Not only is the human factor in the *current* production process subject to deterioration, but the production and upkeep of the long-term workforce is also at issue. Monetary outlays are required to raise a new generation of workers and provide them with some kind of training, varying from the elementary erudition of the unskilled worker to the highly specialized training of professional workers. Such costs are relatively constant in that a certain minimum must be provided under all circumstances whether the worker is employed or not. As John Maurice Clark (1923, 11) has commented, "if it is not borne, if the maintenance is not forthcoming, the community suffers a loss through the deterioration of its working power." In this sense, the costs of labor, or at least a substantial part of them, constitute a kind of overhead cost not solely for the individual worker but for the society as a whole.

Under current labor market conditions, the fixed costs of labor are translated into variable costs. This translation results from the fact that the laborer is a free person who sells his services by means of a free wage contract. Under such a system, the burden of all overhead costs of labor falls upon the individual worker. "He is under our social system, a free being, responsible for his own continuous support and that of his family; hence his maintenance is his own burden and not an obligation of industry, except so far as he can exact wages that will cover it" (Clark 1923, 17). Clark's analysis has been antiquated somewhat by the establishment of social security systems, but in large measure industry still escapes much of the fixed cost of maintaining the labor force.

Although Clark and Kapp related the fixed cost of labor to the social costs of unemployment, the concept also lends itself to the distribution of work time. Indeed, the underemployment of a segment of workers is a direct corollary of unemployment, and the overwork of other segments may dramatically increase the fixed costs of labor by hindering the maintenance of both the current and future workforce. Thus, although the firm's work time optimization process may appear to be "rational," the diverse, hidden, and lagged nature of the negative externalities of work time may result in significant social costs.

In addition to the aforementioned difficulties that may keep a firm from internalizing the external costs of excessive work time, the firm may also face substantial barriers to rational behavior. Many economists have followed the institutionalists' lead in questioning the firm's ability to act in a perfectly rational manner and yield an optimal allocation of goods and resources. Barriers to the allocation process such as bounded rationality, myopia, and habituation may result in a work time regime that is far from optimal for the worker, society, or the firm itself.[5]

Beginning with the assumption that firms act rationally in order to maximize profits and minimize costs, it has been shown that the rationality of economic actors may be both costly and bounded (Wall 1993).[6] At times, truly rational behavior imposes substantial observation, communication, and calculation costs upon the agent. A firm may indeed incur substantial costs attempting to estimate the costs that long work hours might inflict upon society or the productivity implications of a work time reduction. Capturing the social costs of health problems associated with workplace stress, for instance, is not only time-consuming but also expensive. The logical assumption, therefore, is that most firms would devote few, if any, resources to the endeavor of sorting out the social costs related to its labor schedule.

In addition to presuming that agents have the volition to engage in such analysis, advocates of rational behavior often overlook the cognitive limits of individuals. If firms find it daunting to calculate all of the costs that are external to their labor process, it seems nearly impossible for them to internalize those costs and implement a socially optimal workweek. The rationality assumption supposes that decision makers understand all the consequences of their actions and are able to assign a probability to each state of nature. In the "large world," considering all of the events that are relevant to a decision may be an awesome undertaking. Considering again the issue of work-related stress caused by long hours, it may require the knowledge of both a medical doctor and a social scientist to properly measure all of the costs associated with various work time regimes. Thus, completely rational behavior may be not only a costly task but a Herculean one. As a result, Kent Wall (1993, 331) claims that "information processing tends to be parsimonious, and solutions tend to be simple-minded."

Even if firms possess the resources and ability to calculate the rationality of the workweek, behavioral models predict that a deviation from the status quo is more often the exception than the rule. Max Weber (1922) suggested that *traditional* behavior, which composes the bulk of everyday actions, is a pattern of response determined by ingrained habituation. In terms of exchange relations, such as those in the labor market, well-practiced or institutionalized routines can be thought of as traditional behavior. Such behavior may become part of the firm's corporate culture. Thus, a firm may obstinately adhere to a pattern of transacting for no other reason than "this is the way it has always been done."

Mere myopia might also militate against firms implementing shorter work hours. If the produc-tivity benefits are felt with a lag or dispersed among the whole of society, the payout to the firm may be too distant for a near sighted employer to grasp. K.W. Rothschild (1960, 89) was groping toward this notion in the 1960s:

> The beneficial effects of more leisure and "better nerves" will need some time to make themselves felt. In so far, then, as employers tend to take a rather short view of their actions, they will quite logically resist any reduction of working hours unless it is accompanied by a corresponding reduction in total wages.

Rothschild's central argument was that due to a high level of risk aversion generally displayed by employers, competition alone could not ensure that optimal time schedules would be established. He suggested that employers would normally need to experience an external shock before changing standard times, even when the new schedule could prove more productive than the old one. Chris Nyland (1989, 172) offers a similar observation: "If so innovative an entrepreneur as Ford needed to be pressured by an acute shortage of labour power or fear of unionism before he would introduce rationalized worktimes, the overwhelming majority of capitalists would require a good deal more pressure."

Although orthodoxy has traditionally dismissed these market imperfections as inconsequential, the growth of new institutional economics is causing many economists to place more emphasis on the magnitude and pervasiveness of shortcomings within the standard competitive model. Meanwhile, the work of original institutional economists has long suggested that a reliance on a market determination of work time is rife with imperfections from both the labor demand and labor supply perspectives. Externalities, insatiable target incomes, and ingrained ceremonies are all reasons why workers may fail to chose an optimal mix of labor and leisure. Firms, possessing the bargaining power to disproportionately influence the scheduling of work time, may be equally impaired in demanding an optimal number of hours from their employees because their decisions are often hampered by an inability to measure external costs, bounded rationality, cognitive limits, myopia, ingrained habituation, and other limitations.

The diversity and significance of market imperfections in the labor market shed a penumbra of suspicion on the notion that sovereign workers and competitive firms can arrive at a socially optimal workweek if left to their own devices. The path toward an optimal workweek may not be determined by timeless, immutable natural laws, as was the path of the planets under Newton's classical mechanics. The search for a superior path is often complicated by the fact that the search is usually localized and sequential. An improved procedure or standard may only be implemented when it is deemed necessary by the unmet goals of those possessing the authority to bring about changes. Meanwhile, society is saddled with practices that were deemed "good enough" by powerful vested interests but may still be inadequate from a broader sociological perspective.

Although society might be gradually progressing toward a socially optimal workweek, we could be temporarily stuck in a "good enough" stage. Modern work times could simply be an artifact of a time when workers' bargaining power was minimal or when Calvinist work ethics held greater sway. The survival of the customary workweek has contributed to the illusion that it was objectively determined, but the reality is starkly different from the perception. Institutionalists aver that institutions sometimes cause established behaviors and social structures to seem "natural" and therefore warranted when little could be farther

from the truth. Institutions also confer power on groups of people whom Veblen referred to as "vested interests," placing them in a predatory position. In the case of work hours, the modern division of labor (the forty-hour week in the United States) may appear to be in some sort of natural equilibrium, when in fact it is a result of manifold influences conferring substantial power on certain actors. As Gary Cross (1989, 234) points out, "The contemporary distribution of time and money is not a natural allocation of work, rest, and material need: there is no physiological or psychological optimal workday and workyear, which once reduced, need not be further reduced." Indeed, the institutionalist approach to work time suggests that a Panglossian acceptance of a market-determined, forty-hour workweek should be seriously reconsidered in light of our rapidly changing economic and social system.

Historical Work Time Lessons

Work Time in Precapitalist Societies

Myopic historical accounts of work time often give the impression that contemporary workweeks are relatively humane. Comparing a forty-five-hour workweek with the excruciatingly long weeks that were common during the Industrial Revolution paints a favorable picture of modern working conditions. Delving deeper into the history of work time, however, provides a starkly different perspective. Within feudal societies, for instance, many more holidays were afforded the working class—in some years almost 150 annually. The work of the feudal serf was seasonal, which resulted in substantial leisure time for workers during the fallow season. Moreover, many experts argue that even during the harvest the work was conducted at a rather leisurely pace by today's standards.[6]

Searching further into our ethnographical past provides even greater evidence that the grueling work durations of the nineteenth century were a historical aberration. Marshall Sahlins (1972) argues that what we often refer to as primitive societies should be more appropriately termed "original affluent societies." Since hunters and gatherers are less subject to the narrow calculus of "Homo economicus," they tend to enjoy greater amounts of leisure time than their industrialized counterparts. According to Sahlins, "a good case can be made that hunters and gatherers work less than we do." Rather than a continuous travail, "their quest for food is intermittent, leisure abundant, and there is a greater amount of sleep in the daytime per capita per year than in any other condition of society" (14, 16).

The leisurely work habits and casual attitudes toward time that were common among our progenitors ended with the mechanization introduced during the Industrial Revolution. The transformation from a tradition and command economy to a market society was not smooth and gradual but long, tortuous, and sometimes bloody. In England, the bonds and customs of the medieval world were broken as peasants were expelled from their lands and forced to migrate to production centers. The British enclosure laws, the state fixation of wages, and the self-interested manipulation of the food supply effectively enslaved the peasant to the factory owner.[7]

Expensive investments in machinery during the Industrial Revolution caused the need for longer production runs. In order to economize on the costs of training and downtime, nineteenth-century employers regularly subjected workers to long work durations. Mechanization was unfettered by natural limits to the workday since gas lamps surmounted the daylight issue. The longer runs led to a greater demand for factory labor, which was effectively satisfied by the colonization of the agrarian household.

As workers became reliant on increasingly sophisticated machines to perform their tasks, lower training costs associated with long work hours accrued to the capitalist. The fewer workers to mix their labor with a particular machine, the lower the training costs associated with a particular level of production. Employers also came to believe that the more workers utilizing a specific machine, the greater the potential for productivity loss involved with transition time and reduced experience. As a result, standardized work intervals became much longer in industrialized economies than in less automated countries.

The long workweeks brought about by the Industrial Revolution were, fortunately, a historical anomaly. It was generally agreed that the expensive equipment used during the Industrial Revolution should not be left idle, but surely more than one worker should be responsible for its efficient utilization. Class conflict and growing labor unrest (often manifest in high absenteeism and employee turnover) eventually forced employers to abandon long work times. Although the shortened day arguably became more intense, workweeks did eventually decline somewhat.

The historical investigation of work time illustrates how focusing our frame of reference on the era of the Industrial Revolution can lead to erroneous conclusions about trends in work time. Political economist John Rae (1894, 217) offered insightful commentary on the topic:

> It would appear then, from many different sources of evidence, that in the old England before the industrial revolution, people everywhere accustomed to season their toil with a due admixture of repose. It is the short day, after all, like liberty, that is ancient; long hours, at least in this country, are but a modern and happily transitory innovation.

Rae also took exception to the notion that the short hours movement grew out of a penchant among the skilled workers for shorter hours as a result of greater real incomes. "This theory of the origin of the short hour movement, while containing elements of theoretical plausibility, is not in accordance with the historical facts" (218). It was not the high-paid workers that were demanding shorter hours with their newfound, greater disposable income, but just the opposite. Rae believed that relatively low-paid workers had been the true gadflies in demanding shorter hours, often sacrificing out of their abject penury to obtain them. History therefore suggests that a modern movement toward shorter hours would have to transcend multiple income stratifications to have lasting and widespread effects on our societal division of labor.[8]

Contemporary Work Time Trends

In the last three decades, the typical U.S. worker has rarely chosen (or been given the choice) to exercise productivity dividends in the form of reduced work times. Instead, spending trends (between World War II and the mid-1970s) show that 75 to 80 percent of the productivity dividend has been used to finance greater consumption and production, with the remaining portion used to increase leisure.[9] Since the 1970s, modest gains in leisure time have nearly been erased by the sedulous work habits shown by Americans—particularly in the late 1990s. Examining a longer period, Stephen Hill (1994, 69) concludes, "since 1950 it appears that most of the benefits from rising real wage rates have been taken in the form of extra income." In a 1980 United Nations study, Shipley (1980, 50) states that, "left to themselves, workers will continue to barter leisure and rest time and possibly some of their health for more money."

These observations lend credence to admonitions that Americans are stuck in an insidious work-and-spend cycle—a Faustian bargain of work for money.

There is growing evidence, however, that workers want out of the "capitalistic squirrel cage" and would like to be freed of the "gospel of consumption."[10] In the late 1990s, a growing number of labor strikes in the United States centered on overtime or excessive work hours.[11] The greater visibility of work time conflict in the 1990s was likely a result of two related developments: society's increased resistance to arduous work schedules, and labor's greater bargaining power in a time of relatively tight labor markets.

Work time anxieties are not only manifest in the spate of recent labor strikes, but also articulated by workers in surveys and grassroots political organizations. The *1997 National Study of the Changing Workforce* reports that 63 percent of workers would prefer to work less. Male and female workers are equally eager to reduce their market work hours and would trim their workweek by approximately eleven hours on average if given the opportunity. Additionally, the proportion that would like to work fewer hours has increased by 17 percentage points since 1992. Multiple surveys of the U.S. workforce even show a growing willingness on the part of workers to forfeit a portion of their pay for more leisure time. According to a poll conducted by KRC Research, 49 percent of Americans say society puts too much emphasis on paid work and not enough on leisure (Saltzman 1997, 78). That is a monumental shift in thinking from just eleven years ago, when the Opinion Research Corporation found that only 28 percent of workers felt that way (ibid).

Institutional economists have long been concerned about the societal implications of the habituation of material acquisitiveness. Galbraith

(1984, 288) posed an incisive work time question when he asked, "Why should life be made intolerable for so many [workers] to make things of small urgency?" The tendency in democratic industrial societies to identify commodities with human needs can be viewed as an affront to societal welfare. What Marx referred to as commodity fetishism is seen as pernicious to human progress because it obfuscates the true social relations within industrial economies. According to Stanfield and Stanfield (1980, 210), the capitalistic structure is made to "appear as relations among things or commodities, rather than among people." This ethos of avarice causes individuals to seek fulfillment and solutions to their problems through the accumulation of commodities. Acquisitive behavior clouds the true rewards of work, trivializing the act of labor as merely a means to obtain more possessions. Americans have come to identify the "good life with the goods life," living by the maxim that "if you are unhappy, you should buy something" (Brown 1985).

Evidence suggests that the American workforce is increasingly demanding fewer paid work hours—even at the sacrifice of higher income. Labor market fluctuations aside, the stage may be set for a greater resistance to long work hours than in the recent past. If an effective resistance were to render market work less irksome, a "workweek revolution" could foster increased labor productivity and societal improvements, providing benefits to both present and future generations of American workers.

The Future of Work Time and Society

Social change and the altered composition of the paid labor force have placed work time back in the political and economic limelight. The last few decades have witnessed a sea change in who works and how they work. The feminization of the workforce and the growth of part-time labor contracts have drastically altered the labor market, yet labor policies governing work schedules and employment in the United States are mired in a pre–World War II mentality. The disconnect between what we expect from market employment and what we are held accountable for has led to an erosion of our social fabric. Workers, families, and even employers routinely experience anxieties in balancing work schedules and the social and personal needs of individuals and their families.

In a postmodern world of material abundance, society's central objective should be to answer Socrates' time-honored question, what is the good life? Growing numbers of people will face a dilemma that was previously only a concern for the landed rich—how to achieve personal growth and self-realization. John Maynard Keynes (1978, 46) anticipated that workers in the twenty-first century would be nearing the day when "three-hour shifts or a fifteen-hour week would be quite enough to satisfy the old Adam in most of us," leaving the American worker to face the real problem of how to use his freedom from pressing economic cares, how to occupy the leisure, which science and compound interest will have won for him, to live wisely and agreeably well."

Freed of the pressing need to work, the wealthy Athenians of ancient Greece sought self-realization in public service, military adventures, philanthropy, the arts, theology, ethics, and moral philosophy. Today, many would categorize these "active" endeavors as work rather than leisure activities, and indeed some people have managed to derive their incomes from like activities. Yet it remains an open question whether Americans will seek self-realization through greater earning and spending or through these other pursuits, which are less dependent on paid work.

Notes

1. For more on the "storytelling approach," see Wilbur and Harrison (1978).

2. For a defense of preference-driven work time, see Rubin and Richardson (1997).

3. Over five decades ago, Wesley Mitchell observed individual consumption patterns that would bankrupt many enterprises and concluded that "the vast majority [of households] would gain as much from wiser spending as increased income." As this description is perhaps more accurate today, more leisure time among contemporary workers might provide the time and energy needed for improved household consumption, partially obviating the need for more income. See Mitchell (1937).

4. See Owen (1989).

5. Leibenstein's X-efficiency analysis also provides important criticisms of the firm's ability to optimize its input use. It is omitted here only because it does not fit into the traditional institutionalist vein. See Leibenstein (1980).

6. For pre-industrial histories of work time, see Schor (1991), Hunt (1995), and Hunnicutt (1988).

7. See Nyland (1989).

8. Juliet Schor (1991) and others have argued that the quickest way to reduce work hours would be through income redistribution from the wealthy to the poor. Another expedient would be to redistribute wealth from capital to labor. Low-paid workers may currently find it difficult to afford shorter hours, but given the productivity gains experienced over the last fifty years, *corporations* can certainly afford shorter hours. The experience in Scandinavian countries and the more socialistic European countries lends credence to the effectiveness of income redistribution reducing work hours. The focus on redistributing income is important because the institutionalist notion of emulation challenges the ability of rising aggregate income levels to generate shorter hours.

9. See Levitan and Belous (1977).

10. The terminology is from Galbraith (1984) and Hunnicutt (1988). Stanfield refers to the cycle as a "treadmill syndrome." See Stanfield and Stanfield (1980, 439).

11. Both the Bell Atlantic and U.S. West strikes of 1998 were instigated by mandatory overtime (*AP* Aug. 1998). Additionally, on April 24, 1997, General Motors workers walked off the job to register their demand that GM hire more employees in order to curtail overtime hours (*USA Today*, April 24, 1997). In another case, 183 Food Lion employees filed a class-action suit claiming that the company pressured them to work extra hours "off the clock." In a 1993 capitulation, Food Lion settled with the U.S. Labor Department, agreeing to pay $16.2 million in back wages to 30,000 to 40,000 employees.

References

Ayres, Clarence. *The Theory of Economic Progress*. Chapel Hill: University of North Carolina Press, 1944.

James T. Bond, Ellen Galinsky, and Jennifer E. Swanberg. *The 1997 National Study of the Changing Workforce*. New York: Families and Work Institute, 1998, www.familiesandwork.org/nationalstudy.html.

Brown, Douglas. "The Budapest School: A Post-Marxian Defense of the Mixed Economy." PhD Dissertation, Colorado State University, 1985.

Clark, J.M., "Some Social Aspects of Overhead Costs." *American Economic Review* 13, no. 1 (March 1923): 50–59.

Cross, Gary. *A Quest for Time*. Berkeley: University of California Press, 1989.

Duesenberry, James S. *Income, Saving, and the Theory of Consumer Behavior*. Cambridge, MA: Harvard University Press, 1949.

Ford, Henry. *The World's Work*. New York: Doubleday, 1926.

Galbraith, John Kenneth. *The Affluent Society*, 4th ed. Boston, MA: Houghton Mifflin, 1984.

Heilbroner, Robert, and Lester Thurow. *Economics Explained*. New York: Touchstone Books, 1998.

Hill, Stephen. "Time at Work: An Economic Analysis." In *Working Time and Employment: A Review of International Evidence*, ed. Roche, William K., Brian Fynes and Terri Morrissey. Dublin: University of Dublin, 1994.

Hunnicutt, Benjamin. *Work Without End*. Philadelphia, PA: Temple University Press, 1988.

Hunt, E.K. *Property and Prophets*. New York: HarperCollins, 1995.

Kapp, William K. *The Social Costs of Private Enterprise*. Cambridge, MA: Harvard University Press, 1950.

Keynes, John Maynard. *Collected Writings of John Maynard Keynes*. Vol. 9. Cambridge, UK: Cambridge University Press, 1978.

Leibenstein, Harvey. *Inflation, Income Distribution and X-Efficiency Theory*. London: Croom Helm, 1980.

Levitan, Sar, and Richard S. Belous. *Shorter Hours, Shorter Weeks: Spreading the Work to Reduce Unemployment*. Baltimore: Johns Hopkins University Press, 1977.

Mitchell, Wesley C. *The Backward Art of Spending Money, and Other Essays*. New York: Augustus M. Kelley, 1937.

Nyland, Chris. *Reduced Work Time and the Management of Production*. Cambridge, UK: Cambridge University Press, 1989.

Owen, John D. *Reduced Working Hours: Cure for Unemployment or Economic Burden?* Baltimore, MD: Johns Hopkins University Press, 1989.

Rae, John. *Eight Hours for Work.* London: Macmillan, 1894.

Rothschild, K.W. *The Theory of Wages.* Oxford, UK: Blackwell, 1960.

Rubin, Marcus, and Ray Richardson. *The Microeconomics of the Shorter Working Week.* Aldershot, UK: Avebury, 1997.

Sahlins, Marshall. *Stone Age Economics.* Chicago: Publishing, 1972.

Saltzman, Amy. "When Less Is More." *U.S. News and World Report,* October 27, 1997: 78.

Schor, Juliet. *The Overworked America: The Unexpected Decline of Leisure.* New York: Basic Books, 1991.

Shipley, P. In *Changes in Working Life: Proceedings of an International Conference on Changes in the Nature and Quality of Working Life,* ed. Duncan, K.D., and Michael M. Gruneberg. Chicester, UK: John Wiley and Sons, 1980.

Simon, Herbert A. *Rationality in Decision Making.* Cambridge, UK: Cambridge University Press, 1997.

Stanfield, James R., and Jacqueline B. Stanfield, "Consumption in Contemporary Capitalism: The Backward Art of Living." *Journal of Economic Issues.* 14, no. 2 (June 1980): 437–51.

U.S. News/Bozell worldwide poll, conducted by KRC Research and Consulting. New York: 1997.

Veblen, Thorstein. *Essays in our Changing Order.* New York: Viking Press, 1954.

Wall, Kent. "A Model of Decision Making under Bounded Rationality." *Journal of Economic Behavior and Organization* 20, no. 3 (April 1993): 331–52.

Weber, Max. *Wirtschaft und Gesellschaft, bearbeitet von Max Weber.* Tubingen: J.C.B. Mohr, 1922.

Wilbur, Charles K., and Robert S. Harrison, "The Methodological Basis of Institutional Economics: Pattern Model, Storytelling and Holism." *Journal of Economic Issues* 12, no.1 (March 1978): 61–89.

III

Institutionalist Analysis of Current Labor Issues

12

Wage Discrimination in Context

Enlarging the Field of View

Deborah M. Figart and Ellen Mutari

A theory of discrimination is inseparable from a theory of wage setting. In contrast with neoclassical and neoinstitutionalist models that isolate the price dimension of wages, our framework for understanding wage setting places labor markets within a larger context. Our multidimensional approach not only allows us to tell a richer and less deterministic story, it also highlights the differing experiences of wage earners by gender, race and ethnicity, and other salient characteristics. We treat wages, in the words of John Commons, as "a *process* and not an *attribute*" (1923, 111; italics in original). As we will see, a feminist institutionalist analysis of wage setting has methodological implications for how we measure and study discrimination.

Discrimination as a Distortion of Price Mechanisms

The economics literature on discrimination can be seen as constructing an argument that the wages of certain groups are not set at the appropriate price. Rational employers will hire workers when the value of their contribution to the firm's productivity is greater than (or at least equal to) their wages. According to mainstream economists, discrimination interferes with fair wage setting by violating the equivalency of productivity and remuneration. Other considerations besides a rational economic calculus of costs and benefits enter into the process.

The most influential work on discrimination is based on Gary Becker's pioneering dissertation, published by the University of Chicago Press (1957). Becker proposed that individuals (either employers, coworkers, or customers) may have a "taste for discrimination" developed outside the labor market. A taste for discrimination is based on a combination of prejudice and ignorance. Employers who have or who cater to such tastes pay a wage premium for desirable workers (pure nepotism). The strength of this preference can be measured by the amount of income an employer is willing to sacrifice, which Becker refers to as a "discrimination coefficient." Alternatively, undesirable workers will obtain employment only at wages that are lowered by the amount of the discrimination coefficient (pure discrimination). In either scenario, the discriminating employer pays relatively higher wages, raising the costs of production. Uninhibited market forces should punish discriminators, according to Becker, since nondiscriminating firms with lower costs would be more competitive. If the industry is not competitive, however, discrimination may persist for a long time.

The theory of statistical discrimination, first attributed to economists Edmund Phelps (1972) and Kenneth Arrow (1973), suggests that discrimination may, in fact, be rational and therefore profitable. Because employers have imperfect information about potential employees, it may be cost-effective to judge individuals using generalizations about groups of employees. In some cases, the generalization may be based in ignorance or in outdated information. Even if the generalization is statistically true about the group average, it may not be true about individual job applicants. For instance, if employers *believe* that most women quit when they get pregnant, follow their husbands when transferred, call in sick more frequently than men, and/or are not candidates for promotions, this belief will influence hiring and wage decisions about individuals who may not engage in any of these behaviors. In fact, employers who testified against the proposed Equal Pay Act while alternative versions were debated between 1945 and eventual passage in 1963 made such generalizations about working women (Figart, Mutari, and Power 2002, ch. 8).

Both of these mainstream stories about discrimination locate discrimination in market failure. Factors exogenous to the dynamics of the market create discriminatory tastes and distort the flow of information. By implication, a perfectly competitive capitalist economy with perfect information should erode discrimination. This assumes that basic wage determination models remain unchanged by the fact of discrimination.

What about structural theories of discrimination? What unites neoinstitutionalist and structural theories of discrimination and differentiates them from mainstream perspectives is their focus on institutional, rather than individual, discrimination. Institutional discrimination has less to do with short sighted or ignorant employers adhering to stereotypes and assumptions and more to do with structural features of labor markets and employment practices. Structural theories of discrimination, both within neoinstitutional economics and within radical political economy, also focus on the interaction between market forces and the factors that determine bargaining power. Therefore, we turn to a brief summary of neoinstitutionalist and radical theories as they developed out of institutional economics.

Founders of American institutionalism or institutionalist political economy following World War I tried to bring more realism to economic theory. The work in this tradition, now called "old" or "original" institutionalism, rejected the individualism within neoclassical economic theory. Habits, customs, norms, internal relativities, inertia, and other factors such as technological change and productivity were crucial in explaining the actual practice of wage setting inside firms and the functioning of labor markets. Institutionalists "argued that both the allocation and pricing of labor were increasingly effected through a complex web of institutional forces in lieu of market forces. In contrast to neoclassical theory, therefore, explaining the existence, stability and evolution of particular job/wage structures became the focal point underlying their analysis of labor markets" (Gimble 1991, 626).

A second generation of scholars who contributed to wage theory in the 1940s and 1950s are sometimes called "neoinstitutionalists" because their theories combined marginal analysis and supply and demand with nonmarket factors to explain wages, and thereby wage differentials or wage discrimination (Gimble 1991). This research on wage setting was accomplished through extensive case studies of how labor markets work, often studies inside the "black box" of the firm. What distinguished the group of postwar institutionalists from their neoclassical contemporaries was their work on structured (later segmented) labor markets and the importance of job clusters and wage contours, concepts initially developed by John T. Dunlop in *Wage Determination Under Trade Unions* (1966 [1944]). Neoinstitutional economists, in their work on wage contours, dual labor markets, and internal labor markets, emphasize the multiplicity of labor markets and wage rates defined in relation to each other within firms.

The work of these pioneers was not primarily concerned with wage differentials (or occupational segregation) by gender or race-ethnicity. Instead, this work focused on the social construction of class-based status hierarchies. The application of structural wage theory to wage differentials by gender and by race-ethnicity can be found in two theoretical streams. First, the "crowding hypothesis," adapted by Barbara Bergmann (1974), observes that blacks and women in the labor force, by virtue of their limited bargaining power, are concentrated in a relatively small subset of occupations. An oversupply of workers in the labor markets for these jobs drives down their wage rates. If the markets for different occupations and different groups within the labor force are institutionally separated, the forces of supply and demand will not correct wage imbalances. In fact, Bergmann argues that discrimination in the form of occupational segregation may be profitable for employers if it is a generalized practice.

The second stream, segmentation theory within radical political economy, also evokes the concept of separable (or segmented) labor markets, in this case characterized by firm size and structure as well as the gender and race-ethnicity of the labor supply (Reich, Gordon, and Edwards 1973). Wage differentials are partly explained by men's concentration in unionized jobs in oligopolistic firms where wage increases can be passed on to consumers; women, in contrast, work in industries such as textiles, apparel, and services where, for much of the postwar period, domestic and then global competition maintained downward pressure on wages. However, as Rhonda Williams (1995) has noted, wage differentials are also explained by employers' and white male workers' interest in maintaining divisions among workers. Such divisions may reduce workers' bargaining power and therefore their ability to raise their socially defined living standard.

As indicated above, these structural theories have many advantages over mainstream approaches. However, neoinstitutionalists and radical segmentation theories tend to presume that the basic occupational structure of the economy and the relative quality of jobs are determined without considering the gender or racial-ethnic assignment of workers. In other words, gender and race-ethnicity do not factor into the construction of the "places" in an occupational structure, they merely determine the places to which a particular worker has access. Gender theory, on the other hand, argues that socially constructed notions of gender (and race-ethnicity, class, age, and so on) actually shape the available places. Gender is not only crucial in assigning people to places in the gendered division of labor, but in the very definition of labor as a whole. Gender is used when defining or redefining occupational classifications and setting their relative pay scales. Acknowledging that cultural, institutional, and psychological forces play such roles calls into question the extent to which labor market decisions are made by rational individuals. Further, both mainstream and heterodox economics accounts of discrimination tend to treat wage differentials as distortions of market wages. Structural barriers and customs preventing the flow of labor between dual or segmented labor markets are obstacles to the equalization of wage rates for

Figure 12.1 **A Framework for Understanding Wage Setting**

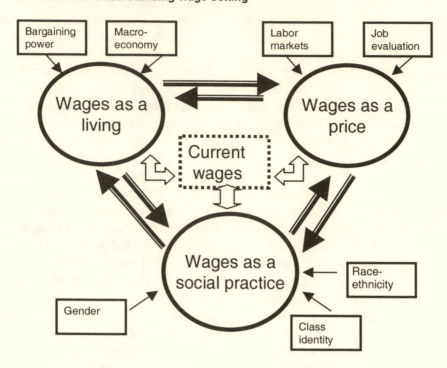

workers with equal potential productivity. Wages determined as a type of price remains the primary focus. Instead, our framework, outlined in the subsequent section, treats the organization of gender, race-ethnicity, and class segments as well as structural features of labor markets as integral to the development of wages as a price. By going beyond markets and treating culture as internal rather than external to the economy, as developments in gender theory and feminist work on organizations have done, our framework represents a return to the type of analysis developed by Original Institutional Economics (OIE).

Enlarging the Field of View

In a survey of twentieth-century wage policies and practices, Figart, Mutari, and Power (2002) iden-
tify three implicit wage theories invoked by economic actors and policy makers. In our view, each of these dimensions—wages as a living, wages as a price, and wages as a social practice—captures important elements of the wage setting process that interact with each other in a given place and time. They are not intended as necessarily competing frameworks, but as different dimensions of the wage setting process that economic actors have chosen to underscore to greater or lesser degrees. Figure 12.1 illustrates these interactions, providing a framework for understanding wage setting.

Wages as a living refers to the concept of setting wages according to socially defined appropriate living standards in order to maintain the reproduction of the labor force and macroeconomic growth. Classical political economists such as Marx emphasized that the relative bargaining power of capitalists and workers at the level of the economy as a whole determined how these living standards were defined. Systemic needs, for social reproduction and sustainable growth, also influence living standards. Dell Champlin and Janet Knoedler (2002) argue that this conception of wages is also compatible with an institutionalist analysis of "the public interest." Therefore, in our diagram, bargaining power and macroeconomic dynamics are depicted as external factors determining the level of appropriate living standards. Bargaining power itself is influenced by many factors, including the level of employment, the degree of unionization, and technology—factors frequently emphasized by post–World War II neoinstitutionalist scholars.

As the price of an input to the production process, wages are a cost that must be offset by an at least equal benefit to the individual employer purchasing labor services, the equality of exchange. This benefit is the revenue gained by selling labor's product. Market mechanisms, specifically adjustments in the quantity of labor supplied and demanded, are hypothesized to regulate wages until costs and benefits are equalized. Labor markets are therefore depicted in the figure as external factors determining *wages as a price*. Demand for labor, in neoclassical analysis, is based primarily upon the marginal productivity of workers and the structure of product markets that influences the revenue earned by selling labor's product. Job evaluation systems can also be used to set relative wages within firms, however, these are often designed in a way that replicates market wages outside the firm.

We also have identified *wages as a social practice* because they are a means of reinforcing or redefining how women and men of different classes, races, and ethnicities should live. External factors influencing social practice therefore include gender, race-ethnicity, and class identity. During most of the twentieth century, the male breadwinner family was a hegemonic archetype and institution for situating not only one's gender, but also one's race-ethnicity and class identity as well (see Figart, Mutari, and Power 2002 for a further elaboration). Social practices are organized by gender, class, and race-ethnicity in the workplace, the union hall, the welfare office, and other locations in addition to the family. The analysis of wages as a social practice goes beyond simply saying that culture and social norms are external factors affecting economic behavior. Reflecting the OIE perspective, we treat wages as part of culture, thus asserting the unity of economic and cultural processes (Austen 2000).

All three dimensions of wages—living, price, and social practice—influence the level of workers' current wages (the center of the diagram). Since there are feedback effects between current wage levels and the three dimensions, the arrows are bidirectional.

We refer to this framework as enlarging the field of vision because, according to our analysis in the previous section, mainstream and neoinstitutionalist economic theories have tended to focus on the top-right portion of Figure 12.1. External labor markets and internal wage practices such as job evaluation systems influence wages set as remuneration for an input to production. Becker's tastes and statistical discrimination theories treat gendered and racialized social practices as exogenous factors intruding on this process. Dual labor market and segmentation theories focus on the interaction between market forces and the structural factors that determine the relative bargaining power of groups of workers. Which workers occupy these places are determined through noneconomic processes. Our framework treats these other dimensions of wages—wages as a living and a social practice—as *endogenous* to wage setting processes.

This framework provides a dynamic analysis of wages, including relative wages, that focuses on both rigidity and change. This is not an equilibrium-based framework. The wage setting process depicted in Figure 12.1 is an outgrowth of the cumulative causation among the three faces of wages. This cumulative causation leads to a certain rigidity in relative wages, especially given the feedback effects between current wage levels and the three faces.[1] However, there have been major transformations in women's and men's economic lives and the meaning of this economic activity in their lives. A disruption in any of the underlying factors in wage setting processes—bargaining power, labor markets, job evaluation, or the organization of gender, race-ethnicity, and class identity —interrupts the cycle, facilitating social change. As noted by J.R. Stanfield, changes in social systems are not random, nor do they occur "by virtue of some natural law working without human agency" (1999, 234).

This analysis of wage setting has implications for how we understand discrimination. Associating gender and race-ethnicity solely with discriminatory processes assumes that basic wage determination models remain unchanged. In this sense, discrimination becomes a special case of market failure. Our framework seeks to develop a methodology in which gender relations, class identity, and race-ethnicity are incorporated into the analysis from the very beginning. That is, discrimination theory is not separable from wage theory.

Detecting and Quantifying Discrimination: Methodological Issues

Our approach to discrimination as endogenous to wage setting processes has methodological impli-

cations as well. Conventional economic methods for documenting the existence and extent of wage discrimination utilize regression analysis. Two methodological approaches are common: the dummy variable method and the residual method, also known as the Oaxaca method. In this section, we explain and critique both methods. Specifically, these two mainstream quantitative methods tend to neglect the processes by which gender, race-ethnicity, class identity, and sexuality interact with and shape social practices and institutions (see Figart 1997). As noted by sociologist Joan Acker, "Variables interacting with other variables are only constructs with no agency to do anything. Although most theories assume some sort of process lying behind the relations between variables, those processes are rarely directly studied" (1991, 391). Dunlop himself warned of the limits of mainstream methodology:

> One of the more dangerous habits of mind that economic theory may create is an imperialism that insists that all aspects of economic behavior, particularly any activity related to markets, can be explained by models with the usual economic variables. . . . A fundamental tenet of the following pages is that modes of behavior that are broader than economic theory contribute materially to the understanding of wage behavior. (1966, 5)

The vast majority of empirical work on discrimination has focused on gender and/or race-ethnicity so the following discussion concentrates on these two forms of discrimination, though the empirical techniques have been applied to other forms of discrimination, including sexual orientation (see Badgett 1995).

In the first methodological approach, the dummy variable method, the race and/or gender characteristics of interest to the researcher are incorporated as a series of dichotomous variables in a regression of pooled data (that is, data on different demographic groups are combined). Wage rates, more specifically the natural log of wages, is the dependent variable. In these models, white or male is generally the omitted variable, treating whiteness and maleness as a benchmark or norm to which other groups are compared. For example, a dummy variable for "Sex" will be coded "1 if female, 0 if not." A negative slope coefficient for a race or gender dummy variable indicates that one is paid less simply by virtue of identity, ceteris paribus. In the example above, a male is coded as "0" for the "Sex" variable and the sex term essentially drops out of the wage equation (since any coefficient multiplied by 0 equals 0). Being male, thus, has no effect on wages. The key to this method, as in all wage regressions, is to incorporate independent variables for as many wage determinants as possible, including measures of human capital and structural variables such as industry, occupation, and union status.

It is interesting to compare this empirical methodology with the analysis originally suggested by Becker (1957). His "tastes and preferences" theory asserts that either employer, employee, or customer discrimination causes employers to give hiring preferences to whites and/or males. The result, based on traditional supply-and-demand analysis, is that whites and/or males receive higher wages compared with other employees. Becker is agnostic on the choice between nepotism models (preferences for whites/males) versus discrimination models (bias against minorities/women); both lead to the same result. Empirically, however, it matters. To model the nepotism scenario, wage premiums for males, the dummy variable should equal "1 if male, 0 if not," with female wages being the omitted variable and thus the norm. The expected coefficient on white and/or male earnings would be positive. But we have not seen empirical studies where women's wages were the norm and males received a premium.

In any case, the interpretation of the slope coefficient in the dummy variable method is problematic. On the one hand, it is a direct measure of some forms of wage discrimination and therefore useful as a tool for feminist advocacy. On the other hand, it is not the full measure of discrimination. The mean values of other variables specified in the models may be affected by the feedback effects of discriminatory processes. For example, workers' investments in education and years of experience on the job may be influenced by their perception of the returns to such investments. Wage discrimination may encourage married couples to adopt a traditional division of labor between paid and unpaid work. While traditional models present us with two options—either women choose certain jobs (supply side) or employers discriminate (demand side)—in reality, these dynamics of choice and constraint cannot be isolated from each other. A related problem is that the use of dummy variables implicitly conceives of race and gender as independent of other specified wage determinants. Although such multicollinearity is not technically fatal to wage regressions, the correlation among variables becomes more important if we are interested in the relative size of coefficients rather than simply their statistical significance.[2]

The assumption that the right-hand-side variables in a wage regression are independent is slippery for structural as well as human capital variables. The history of unionization, for example, shows that union status is profoundly bound up with the race and gender of an industry's work force. Racial-ethnic diversity was used by employers to inhibit unionization, while many unions historically neglected women and African Americans as organizing targets. When organized, union membership in a historically female-dominated textile or service sector union might not be comparable with membership in a manufacturing-based industrial union—even as unions increasingly cross boundaries in recruiting new members.[3] Similar problems occur with variables such as industry and occupation. Research on pay equity and wage discrimination against female-dominated occupations, for instance, has indicated that occupations are themselves frequently gendered male or female. Feminist researchers have therefore incorporated a separate measure of discrimination into their models by estimating the negative impact of percent female (or percent minority) in an occupation on the wage (Treiman and Hartmann 1981; Sorensen 1994; Figart and Lapidus 1995). Yet this research did not stop with simply quantifying the problem. Feminist researchers have also focused on the process of occupational segregation and the devaluation of women's work (see Figart 1997 for a summary).

A third weakness of the dummy variable method is that the dummy variables themselves are not truly independent. Discrimination experienced by women of color is not simply additive of race and gender discrimination as separate processes. In her qualitative research on statistical discrimination, Ivy Kennelly (1999) uncovered employer stereotypes of black women as single mothers that were distinct from assumptions made about either white women or black men. As noted by Joyce Jacobsen and Andrew Newman (1995) in a survey of labor economics articles published from 1947 to 1995, the increased use of dummy variables to model gender differences attempts to "control for" the use of gender without examining the interaction of gender with other variables including race. Interaction variables (such as those used by Lapidus and Figart 1998) are one way of improving model specifications.

Further, the image of race and gender as things to be "controlled" is illuminating. It implies that gender and race are marginal to the analysis of wages, that is, descriptive characteristics of individual labor market participants that do not fundamentally challenge the basic theoretical constructs of wage determination models. The omitted variables (generally white, male) are set as norms; whiteness and maleness are not subjected to scrutiny. As recent work in gender theory has argued, however, one cannot comprehend the social construction of femininity without examining masculinity as well (Connell 1995; Hoffert 2003). In the specific case of wages, it is implausible to view white male wages as unaffected by the discriminatory processes in society. Whether they are lower or higher than some mythical norm is difficult to determine because of the existence of both "class struggle effects" and "job competition effects" (Shulman 1996). Class struggle effects, grounded in radical segmentation theory, imply that white male wages are lower than they would be in the absence of discrimination because employers are able to "divide and conquer" the labor force. Job competition effects imply that white male workers themselves benefit from excluding other groups from higher-status jobs (see Williams 1995).

The second mainstream methodology for estimating discrimination was developed by Ronald Oaxaca (1973).[4] This method is very widely used because of its decomposition properties. Oaxaca defines discrimination as the "unexplained" portion of the wage differential between two groups. Based on the assumption that human capital and other productivity-related variables are legitimate bases for wage differentials, Oaxaca's method seeks to "explain" as much of the differentials as possible with these explanatory variables. Separate wage regressions are run for groups of interest, such as men versus women. Each regression equation contains the same human capital and structural variables. To decompose the explained and unexplained parts of wage differentials, the method then proposes a hypothetical: what would the ratio of women's wages to men's wages be if women were more like men? This can be achieved statistically in two ways, using the male mean values or the female mean values.[5] The more common approach is to use the men's mean values of the independent variables as the norm, and match them with the female coefficients to ascertain what women would earn if they had men's levels of education, experience, and so on. If the legitimate reasons for the wage differential were eliminated (captured by the difference in the original and newly estimated equations), would women still earn less, on average, than men? In essence, this technique separates differential means or characteristics of women and men (such as differences in years of experience and education) from differential slope coefficients that represent the returns to those characteristics. Oaxaca argues that the latter, the differential returns by gender, constitutes discrimination.

The Oaxaca method shares many of the same problems as the dummy variable method. Feedback effects and other "illegitimate" reasons for differences in means are ignored (see Grimshaw and Rubery 2002). By focusing on differential outcomes, the method cannot illuminate how and why discrimination occurs or elucidate the agency of economic actors in discriminatory processes. Conceptually, the Oaxaca method poses unique problems. It has come to be called the "residual method" because it defines discrimination as the portion of wage differentials that is "left over" after the best possible specification of wage determinants. Some mainstream economists continue to argue that the residual, and thus discrimination, would be small or zero if wage regression models could only be correctly specified. Escalating both the number of variables and the complexity of regression techniques, these researchers seek to minimize the unexplained residual in order to buttress theories that discount the existence of discrimination. In this battle over the correct specification of the directly measurable variables, discrimination itself is rendered as something amorphous. Invoking the language of Simone de Beauvoir, discrimination becomes "other"; we know discrimination only by what it is not.

Implications for Research

Mainstream statistical techniques "may obscure more than they reveal because they are unable to incorporate the complexity of institutional and other societal-specific factors in the shaping of the wage structure" (Grimshaw and Rubery 2002, 2). Because of the limitations discussed above, research on discrimination needs to draw from the roots of OIE and embrace inductive case study methodologies and other pluralistic research methods used in the social sciences and, yes, even in the humanities. Borrowing from their predecessors, institutionalist studies of discrimination would engage in methodological pluralism, adding qualitative research to quantitative research. Unlike the flurry of research by institutionalist labor economists during and after World War II, little contemporary representations of research in the institutionalist tradition attempts to "go inside" the black box and discern how employers structure both jobs and wages, and the role of those behaviors in wage discrimination.

However, we have learned a tremendous amount about how discrimination becomes embedded in wage setting from organizational sociologists studying gender and racial-ethnic hierarchies; these studies have the potential to broaden our understanding of class as well (Acker 2000). These mesolevel studies avoid the mechanistic analysis associated with multiple regression. According to Joan Acker, organizational studies have demonstrated that "class, race, and gender patterns are not just the shards of history, but are continually created and recreated in today's organizations, as people are hired, promoted or fired, as wages are set, and as managers, supervisors, and workers organize and execute their daily tasks" (2000, 198). Organizational studies can also illuminate the conditions under which discriminatory processes are likely to be stronger or weaker, reinforced, or eroded (see, for example, Bridges and Nelson 1989; Anderson and Tomaskovic-Devey 1995).

Organizations, nevertheless, are not the only relevant sites for discussions of discriminatory wage setting processes. Households and the state must factor into a holistic approach. Households are crucial locations for the development of provisioning strategies (Wheelock and Oughton 1996). Therefore, to truly overcome the false dichotomy of supply-side versus demand-side explanations of relative wages, households must be reintroduced into institutionalist economic analysis. Finally, the state is not an external corrective to market failures but an important site for establishing social norms and customs. Political movements for different forms of wage regulations and policies affect wage setting processes (Figart, Mutari, and Power 2002). These political movements are guided by implicit theories regarding the functions of and standards for wage setting. They influence the state, which, through its actions and inactions, can readjust bargaining power (influencing wages as a living), modify the structure of product and labor markets and the relative supply of and demand for labor (influencing wages as a price), and sanction particular models of gender and racial-ethnic relations (influencing wages as a social practice). The issue is not whether or not the state will intervene in wage setting, but how.

In conclusion, wage setting (and thereby discrimination) occurs in multiple sites. A feminist institutionalist theory of discrimination will be complex and nondeterministic. Methodological pluralism is crucial to the study of discriminatory wage setting processes.

Notes

1. Shulman (1992) finds a similar metaphor of a vicious circle in the work of Gunnar Myrdal.

2. For a discussion of size versus statistical significance, see McCloskey and Ziliak (1996).

3. For example, since 1985, the largest United Auto Workers local in the state of Michigan is composed of clerical and administrative support employees who are state civil servants (Figart and Kahn 1997).

4. Although Oaxaca's name has become associated with this technique, a similar method was developed contemporaneously by Alan Blinder (1973). A modification that incorporates overall wage distributions in a country, used in cross-national studies of the gender-based wage gap, was introduced by Juhn, Murphy, and Pierce (1991).

5. Neumark (1988) proposes an alternative, using a weighted average, that bypasses the choice between men's means and women's means. This assumes a middle ground between pure nepotism and pure discrimination.

References

Acker, Joan. "Thinking About Wages: The Gendered Wage Gap in Swedish Banks." *Gender and Society* 5, no. 3 (1991): 390–407.

———. "Revisiting Class: Thinking from Gender, Race, and Organizations." *Social Politics* 7, no. 2 (2000): 192–214.

Anderson, Cynthia D., and Donald Tomaskovic-Devey. "Patriarchal Pressures: An Exploration of Organizational Processes That Exacerbate and Erode Gender Earnings Inequality." *Work and Occupations* 22, no. 3 (1995): 328–56.

Arrow, Kenneth. "The Theory of Discrimination." In *Discrimination in Labor Markets*, ed. Orley Ashenfelter and Albert Rees. Princeton, NJ: Princeton University Press, 1973.

Austen, Siobhan. "Culture and the Labor Market." *Review of Social Economy* 58, no. 4 (2000): 505–21.

Badgett, M.V. Lee. "The Wage Effects of Sexual Orientation Discrimination." *Industrial and Labor Relations Review* 49, no. 4 (1995): 726–38.

Becker, Gary S. *The Economics of Discrimination*. Chicago: University of Chicago Press, 1957.

Bergmann, Barbara R. "Occupational Segregation, Wages and Profits When Employers Discriminate by Race or Sex." *Eastern Economic Journal* 1, nos. 2–3 (1974): 103–10.

Blinder, Alan S. "Wage Discrimination: Reduced Form and Structural Estimates." *Journal of Human Resources* 8, no. 4 (1973): 436–55.

Bridges, William P., and Robert L. Nelson. "Markets in Hierarchies: Organizational and Market Influences on Gender Inequality in a State Pay System." *American Journal of Sociology* 95, no. 3 (1989): 616–58.

Champlin, Dell P., and Janet T. Knoedler. "Wages in the Public Interest: Insights from Thorstein Veblen and J.M. Clark." *Journal of Economic Issues* 36, no. 4 (2002): 877–91.

Commons, John R. "Wage Theories and Wage Policies." *American Economic Review* 13, no. 1, supplement (1923): 110–17.

Connell, R.W. *Masculinities*. Berkeley: University of California Press, 1995.

Dunlop, John T. *Wage Determination Under Trade Unions*. New York: Augustus M. Kelley, 1966 [1944].

Figart, Deborah M. "Gender as More than a Dummy Variable: Feminist Approaches to Discrimination." *Review of Social Economy* 55, no. 1 (1997): 1–32.

Figart, Deborah M., and Peggy Kahn. *Contesting the Market: Pay Equity and the Politics of Economic Restructuring*. Detroit: Wayne State University Press, 1997.

Figart, Deborah M., and June Lapidus. "A Gender Analysis of U.S. Labor Market Policies for the Working Poor." *Feminist Economics* 1, no. 3 (1995): 60–81.

Figart, Deborah M., Ellen Mutari, and Marilyn Power. *Living Wages, Equal Wages: Gender and Labor Market Policies in the United States*. London: Routledge, 2002.

Gimble, Daniel. "Institutionalist Labor Market Theory and the Veblenian Dichotomy." *Journal of Economic Issues* 25, no. 3 (1991): 625–48.

Grimshaw, Damian, and Jill Rubery. "The Adjusted Gender Pay Gap: A Critical Appraisal of Standard Decomposition Techniques." Unpublished paper for Equal Opportunities Unit in the European Commission, 2002.

Hoffert, Sylvia D. *A History of Gender in America*. Englewood Cliffs, NJ: Prentice Hall, 2003.

Jacobsen, Joyce P., and Andrew E. Newman. "Cherchez les Femmes? How Labor Economists Study Women." Presented at International Association for Feminist Economics Conference, Tours, France, 1995.

Juhn, Chinhui, Kevin M. Murphy, and Brooks Pierce. "Accounting for the Slowdown in the Black-White Wage Convergence." In *Workers and Their Wages: Changing Patterns in the United States*, ed. Marvin H. Kosters. Washington, DC: American Enterprise Institute Press, 1991.

Kennelly, Ivy. "'That Single-Mother Element': How White Employers Typify Black Women." *Gender and Society* 13, no. 2 (1999): 168–92.

Lapidus, June, and Deborah M. Figart. "Remedying 'Unfair Acts': U.S. Pay Equity by Race and Gender." *Feminist Economics* 4, no. 3 (1998): 7–28.

McCloskey, Deirdre, and Stephen T. Ziliak. "The Standard Error of Regressions." *Journal of Economic Literature* 34, no. 1 (1996): 97–114.

Neumark, David. "Employers' Discriminatory Behavior and the Estimation of Wage Discrimination." *Journal of Human Resources* 23, no. 3 (1988): 279–95.

Oaxaca, Ronald. "Male Female Wage Differentials in Urban Labor Markets." *International Economic Review* 14, no. 3 (1973): 693–709.

Phelps, Edmund S. "The Statistical Theory of Racism and Sexism." *American Economic Review* 62, no. 4 (1972): 659–61.

Reich, Michael, David M. Gordon, and Richard C. Edwards. "A Theory of Labor Market Segmentation." *American Economic Review* 63, no. 2 (1973): 359–65.

Shulman, Steven. "Metaphors of Discrimination: A Comparison of Gunnar Myrdal and Gary Becker." *Review of Social Economy* 50, no. 4 (1992): 432–52.

———. "The Political Economy of Labor Market Discrimination: A Classroom-Friendly Presentation of Theory." *Review of Black Political Economy* 24, no. 4 (1996): 47–64.

Sorensen, Elaine. *Comparable Worth: Is It a Worthy Policy?* Princeton, NJ: Princeton University Press, 1994.

Stanfield, James Ronald. "The Scope, Method, and Significance of Original Institutional Economics." *Journal of Economic Issues* 33, no. 2 (1999): 231–55.

Treiman, Donald J., and Heidi I. Hartmann. *Women, Work and Wages: Equal Pay for Jobs of Equal Value*. Washington, DC: National Academy Press, 1981.

Wheelock, Jane, and Elizabeth Oughton. "The Household as a Focus for Research." *Journal of Economic Issues* 30, no. 1 (1996): 143–59.

Williams, Rhonda M. "Consenting to Whiteness: Reflections on Race and Marxian Theories of Discrimination." In *Marxism in the Postmodern Age: Confronting the New World Order*, ed. Antonio Callari, Stephen Cullenberg, and Carole Biewener. New York: Guilford Press, 1995.

13

Nonstandard Labor Through an Institutionalist Lens

The More Things Change, the More They Stay the Same

Barbara A. Wiens-Tuers

Contingent and nonstandard labor represent but one change in the relationship between employer and employee and the U.S. economy over the last twenty years. And yet contingent and nonstandard labor are nothing new to the U.S. labor scene. A closer examination of nonstandard and contingent labor highlights the ebb and flow of institutional structures and norms that constitute the labor market and the broader economy. Using an institutionalist approach to analysis yields interesting insights into nonstandard and contingent labor, the foremost being that, often times, the more things change, the more they stay the same.

Institutions affect individual decisions because individuals operate within a larger social, cultural, and legal context. Yet the institutions themselves are created and altered by human beings, in other words, individuals, or groups of individuals. One of the defining debates among scholars who are interested in institutional analysis is the appropriate unit of analysis and direction of causation, what Hodgson (1998) calls the "chicken and egg debate." Should the focus be on the individuals who create the institutions (a micro or reductionist approach) or on the institutions that shape individual decisions (a macro or holistic approach)?

The bottom line for researchers in the institu-tionalist tradition is that institutions matter in economic analysis. The economy is viewed as an open and evolving system affected by technological change and embedded in a broader set of social, cultural, political, and power relationships where there may be no long-run equilibrium (Hodgson 2000). The evolution of institutions and changes in the larger environment, the importance of history and context, are critical to understanding current economic relationships. According to Kerr (1988), a labor economist out of context deserves the same fate as a fish out of water because an event cannot be understood without reference to its context. And just as nothing in nature is static, neither is the environment or institutional context in which businesses and households make their decisions.

The institutionalist approach to analysis relies heavily on empirical observations and data collection as well as use of historical material to create stylized facts and to uncover underlying structural features that explain those facts or observations. Following in this tradition, the first section of this chapter looks at data to examine trends and patterns in the use of contingent and nonstandard labor. The first section also sets out definitions of contingent and nonstandard labor. This task is important because in the literature the terms are used in a broad and inconsistent way that can lead to confusion when measuring and discussing the impact of nonstandard and contingent work on employees and employers. The second section of this chapter discusses nonstandard labor in the larger context of the changing macroeconomy and changing demographics in order to understand the shift away from the employment model that described labor relations in the 1950s and 1960s. The third section briefly highlights the debates about outcomes for the economy and for workers employed in nonstandard jobs. The concluding section comments on changes in the workplace and workplace institutions and suggests issues to be considered as policy makers, households, and businesses face the dynamics of evolving economic institutions.

What Is Nonstandard Employment and What Do the Data Say About It?

What Is It?

Clearly defining what contingent labor and nonstandard labor are as well as what they are not is critical to understanding what has and has not changed. The terms are used to describe a wide range of employment structures and are used differently by different researchers. The first step is to separate the notion of contingency in employment from the institutional structure of the employment relationship. The term "contingent" was first used by Audrey Freedman in 1985 (Freedman 1996) to describe a working relationship that was to exist only when needed by an employer. In the broadest sense, all employment is contingent. Employer exposure to structural change, shocks in product demand, and changes in input or output prices generate the possibility of labor force adjustments.

The Current Population Survey (CPS) provides the most commonly used operational definitions

of contingent work (see Appendix for a full description of the definitions of contingent employment used by the CPS). In discussing contingent employment, this chapter uses the CPS "Estimate 3" definition of contingent work, the broadest measure of contingency, which refers to workers who do not expect their job to last. A key point is that a worker may be in both a contingent job and an alternative work arrangement, but one is not a necessary condition for the other. However, some types of employment arrangements are much more likely to be contingent than others. For example, agency temporaries are likely to be in contingent jobs while contract or leased employees are more likely to be in long-term jobs.

Turning next to how people are employed, direct employment arrangements involve employees who perform work for the firm or the employer that hired them; in other words, they are employees of the recipient of their services. Direct employment implies that by common law the employer is entitled to specify the tasks to be accomplished and to control virtually every aspect of the workplace (Nye 1988; Hylton 1996). Direct employees are covered by various laws that do not cover other types of employees. For example, independent contractors and temporary employees do not have the same rights under the National Labor Relations Act to be included in a bargaining unit with the direct employees of a firm. Title VII of the Civil Rights Act of 1964 may be enforced only against "employers." Workers' compensation premiums are the responsibility of the direct employer. An employer trying to reduce mandated benefit costs and the cost of their administration may do so in two ways: reclassify an employee as an independent contractor or use indirect, intermediated employment arrangements (Hylton 1996). The Occupational Health and Safety Acts applies to all employers, and liability in the case of leased

Figure 13.1 **Employment Categories**

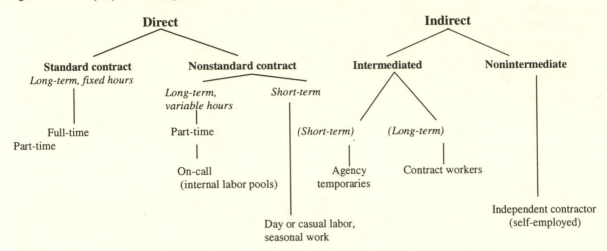

Standard or traditional employment   Nonstandard or nontraditional employment

employees may lie with both the direct employer and the firm for which the work is actually performed (Dennard 1996). All employees (direct or not) are covered by the Fair Labor Standards Act.

Indirect employment arrangements are defined as jobs where employees are not employed by the recipients of their services. Within indirect employment arrangements there may be third-party or intermediated employment arrangements or nonintermediated arrangements. Third-party or intermediated employment arrangements include employees of temporary help services or leasing companies who perform their services for a third party or business. These workers are the direct employees of the temporary or leasing agency. Indirect employment arrangements without intermediaries include independent contractors and consultants who are hired for a specific job or project on a nonpermanent basis. While independent contractors may have contracts for the delivery of specific services, they are

not considered direct employees of the firm. The defining characteristics and distinctions of indirect and direct employees are often controversial, especially in the case of independent contractors.

The basis for defining standard and nonstandard contracts is based on Sloane and Gaston (1991). They describe standard employment contracts as implicit or explicit contracts that imply full-time permanent jobs. For the purposes of this chapter, a standard contract is extended to include part-time workers with regular or predictable hours of work. In nonstandard employment contracts, flexibility in the number of hours and/or in employment (contingency) is built into the job contract. Expanding on Sloane and Gaston's (1991) basic idea, this chapter will refer to jobs in which a worker has a standard contract and is in a direct employment relationship as a standard job or standard employment. Everything else will fall under the heading of nonstandard employment (see Figure 13.1). The standard employment relationship, the one that typifies how most people think about post–World War II jobs, may be specified by either an implicit or explicit agreement or contract, and it may be union or nonunion.

What is interesting to note about what is referred to in much of the literature as standard or traditional employment—full-time, full-year work with a single employer—is that it is a relatively recent phenomenon of the post-Depression and post–World War II period. Employment throughout the history of the United States has generally been tenuous at best with few institutionalized protections for workers. Most jobs before the New Deal had many of the same characteristics that are now associated with contingent and nonstandard labor. Women and nonwhite men have always faced a labor market dominated by contingent jobs (Morse 1998).

What Do the Data Say?

In the United States, the total number of people employed increased 15.2 percent from January 1992 to January 2001, while the number of people employed in the personnel supply industry (SIC 736) increased by 149 percent over the same period (Bureau of Labor Statistics 1992, 2001). Personnel supply includes both traditional employment agencies and help supply firms, mainly temporary help agencies. The Organization for Economic Cooperation and Development (OECD) reported that contingent jobs are a significant feature of employment in all OECD countries, but the incidence varies. One of every three jobs is contingent in Spain, and one in twenty jobs in Luxembourg, the Slovak Republic, and the United States is considered contingent (*OECD Employment Outlook* 2002).

In order to provide a reference point for thinking about what happened to contingent and non-

standard labor over the recent boom, this section of the chapter starts by using data from "Contingent and Alternative Employment Arrangements" (BLS 1995, 1997, 1999, and 2001) which is a supplement to the Current Population Survey (CPS). The CPS, the source of official government statistics on employment and unemployment, has been conducted for over fifty years. The CPS obtains monthly interviews from 56,000 households scientifically selected on the basis of area of residence to represent the nation as a whole. The data are weighted to represent the proportion of actual persons in the population that the sample person represents. While the definitions and measures provided by the CPS may not capture all the nonstandard employment arrangements used in the workplace, they do provide a starting point for discussing the most prevalent types of alternative and contingent work (see Appendix for complete definitions of alternative and contingent work used by BLS in the CPS).

In Table 13.1, data show that, overall, contingent employment dropped from 4.9 percent of total employment in February 1995 to 4.0 percent of total employment in February 2001. This is not an unexpected result given the tight labor markets of the late 1990s, where employers might have sought to reduce turnover and increase attachment of employees with skills in high demand. The percentage of workers in contingent jobs decreased over the same period for all employment arrangements except independent contractors. Workers in traditional (standard) arrangements had the lowest percentage of contingent jobs, going from 3.6 percent in 1995 to 2.9 percent in 2001. Agency temporaries had the highest percentage of contingent jobs: 66.5 percent of jobs in 1995 and 55.4 percent in 2001.

In nonstandard employment arrangements, the big story here is the lack of a big story here (see

Table 13.1

Contingent Workers as a Percentage of Total Number of People Employed: 1995–2001

	1995	1997	1999	2001	Percent change
Contingent employment arrangements: total	4.9	4.4	4.3	4.0	−18.4
Independent contractor	3.8	3.5	2.9	4.1	7.9
On-call	35.2	26.7	28.0	24.6	−30.1
Agency temporary	66.5	56.8	55.9	55.4	−16.7
Contract	19.8	16.7	20.2	17.1	−13.6
Traditional	3.6	3.4	3.2	2.9	−19.4

Source: Bureau of Labor Statistics, "Contingent and Alternative Employment Arrangements" (1995, 1997, 1999, and 2001), a supplement to the Current Population Survey (CPS), and author's calculations using Estimate 3 of contingent employment.

Table 13.2

Nonstandard (Alternative) Employment: 1995–2001 (as percent of total employed)

	1995	1997	1999	2001
Alternative employment arrangements: total	9.7	9.9	9.3	9.4
On-call	1.7	1.6	1.5	1.6
Temporaries	1.0	1.0	0.9	0.9
Contract	0.5	0.6	0.6	0.5
Independent contractors	6.7	6.7	6.3	6.4
Prefer traditional employment				
On-call	56.7	50.1	46.7	43.4
Temporaries	63.6	59.2	57.0	44.4
Independent contractors	9.8	9.3	8.5	8.8

Source: Bureau of Labor Statistics, "Contingent and Alternative Employment Arrangements" (1995, 1997, 1999, and 2001), a supplement to the Current Population Survey (CPS), and author's calculations using Estimate 3 of contingent employment.

Table 13.2). The CPS identifies four main alternative (or nonstandard) forms of employment: independent contractors, agency temporaries, contract workers, and on-call workers. Overall, alternative employment as a percentage of total employment changed little, going from 9.7 percent in 1995 to 9.4 percent in 2001. Most of the decline is accounted for by the drop in the number of independent contractors, while the proportion of agency temporaries, contract, and on-call workers remained essentially unchanged. For employees in alternative employment arrangements, the prefer-

ence for traditional employment declined over the period. Relative to standard employment, most independent contractors strongly prefer their arrangements and, accordingly, the decline in the preference for a traditional job is small. The preference for traditional work by agency temporaries and on-call workers, while still high, fell during the expansion of the late 1990s. By 2001, 44.4 percent of agency temporary workers and 43.4 percent of on-call employees said they would prefer a standard job.

The statistics reported by the CPS are the re-

Table 13.3

Alternative Employment: Employer/Establishment Survey Data
(percentage of establishments using alternative employment)

National Employment Survey	1992	1997	National Employer Survey	1994	1997
Any agency temps or contract workers	38.3	50.3	Any temporary agency workers	14.8	39.4
Any direct-hire temporaries	25.0	18.2			
Ratio of intermediated to standard workers	0.088	0.067			
Ratio of direct nonstandard to standard workers	0.083	0.161			

Sources: "Organization of Work in American Business." Paul Osterman (1992 and 1997) and author's calculations. Data is weighted. Kruse and Blasi (2000) using National Employer Survey from 1994 and 1997.

sults of interviews with individuals who are self-reporting information. Surveys of employers also ask about establishment use of alternative work arrangements, primarily agency temporaries, contract workers, and on-call or direct-hire temporaries. The first employer survey presented here is Paul Osterman's national establishment surveys for 1992 and 1997, which are telephone surveys of a representative sample of American establishments with fifty or more employees. Appropriately weighted, the surveys are representative of the entire economy (Osterman 1999). Osterman identifies two types of nonstandard work arrangements for his survey. The first is temporary or contract workers who work at the establishment but are on the payroll of another organization (indirect, intermediated employment). The second group is on-payroll contingent workers who are workers on the establishment payroll but who do not have the same protection as regular employees (direct employees but not a standard "contract"). The first group is identified in this chapter as intermediated temporaries and the second group as direct-hire temporaries. Table 13.3 shows the percentage of establishments that used intermediated and/or direct-hire temporaries in 1992 and 1997. In 1992, 38.3 percent of establishments used inter-

mediated temporaries, and in 1997 the number increased to 50.3 percent of establishments. In contrast, in 1992, 25.0 percent of establishments used direct-hire temporaries, and the number decreased by 1997 to 18.2 percent of establishments. It is interesting to note that although fewer establishments used direct-hire temps, the establishments who did use them did so in larger numbers. At the same time, although more establishments used intermediated workers, on average the workers tended to constitute a smaller proportion of the firms' workers.

Kruse and Blasi (2000) use the National Employer Surveys, administered by the U.S. Census Bureau in 1994 and 1997 to managers in private, for-profit establishments with twenty or more employees, to look at changes in the use of temporary agency workers. Based on this establishment-level data weighted to reflect the larger population, they find that in 1994, 14.8 percent of establishments used agency temps and in 1997, 39.4 percent were using agency temporaries (see Table 13.3).

What are some demographics of workers in contingent and nonstandard jobs? In 2001, the CPS reported that the characteristics of contingent and nonstandard workers had changed little from prior surveys. Table 13.4 lists selected characteristics of contingent and nonstandard workers. In 2001, con-

Table 13.4

Selected Characteristics of Contingent and Nonstandard Workers 2001 (in percent)

	Female	Nonwhite	Less than a high school diploma*	Part-time	Health insurance (provided by employer)
Standard employment	47.8	16.2	8.8	16.8	83.1 (58.3)
On-call	46.9	16.4	8.2	47.4	70.0 (29.8)
Temporaries	58.9	31.6	14.7	20.8	48.1 (10.7)
Contract	29.4	23.2	9.0	10.3	80.1 (52.1)
Independent contractors	35.5	11.7	8.5	24.8	72.5 (n/a)
Noncontingent	50.0	16.0	8.8	16.9	82.5 (55.0)
Contingent	46.8	18.4	13.4	41.8	63.6 (20.4)

Source: Bureau of Labor Statistics, "Contingent and Alternative Employment Arrangements," (2001), USDL 01–153,
  *Ages 25–64.

tingent workers tended to be younger than noncontingent workers, were slightly more likely to be black or Hispanic, less likely to have health insurance, and much more likely to be doing part-time work than noncontingent workers. Characteristics of workers in standard and nonstandard jobs and characteristics of workers in the different types of nonstandard jobs vary widely. Temporary agency workers are more likely to be female, black or Hispanic, and between the ages of twenty and thirty-four, and not to have a high school diploma than workers in any other type of employment. On the other hand, independent contractors are more likely to be white, male, and over thirty-five years of age.

The Context

Employment flexibility that is embodied in nonstandard and contingent employment arrangements flows from the common law policy of employment-at-will. Employment-at-will means that an employee is free to leave a job when he or she wishes and that the employer may release or fire an employee as he or she wishes. In the United States, employment-at-will expresses the social attitude as well as the common law that the employment relation creates no continuing or permanent ties between the employer and the employee. While employment-at-will was designed to prevent "owner-slave" conditions, the other extreme is the creation of a disposable labor force.

On the employer side, employment-at-will is tempered, in part, by adjustment costs. Factors that alter the cost of employment adjustments through layoffs and firing include explicit and implicit costs such as search, hiring and training cost, severance pay, and contributions to private and public health and retirement programs (Oi 1962, Golden 1990; Hamermesh and Pfann 1996). Until the 1970s, employment-at-will for workers was mitigated by expanding product markets and the relative stability of the post–World War II economy. This allowed a certain degree of job security and attachment in part through the creation of internal labor markets and unions that enforced employment security and layoffs based on seniority (Osterman 1993).

Unions sought to transform as many jobs as possible into full-time, year-round, long-term employment with a single employer. The unions' effect on nonunion firms was for nonunion firms to follow suit (Osterman 1999). Muhl (2001) writes that the federal legislation of the 1960s protecting workers reflected the changing view of the relationship between workers and employers. The courts and the legislature in this period began to recognize that employment is central to a person's livelihood and well-being and that employers frequently have structural and economic advantages when negotiating with employees. This era was characterized by the industrial relations/union model and was dependent on forces specific to that time: explicit federal support of unionization, weakened employer resistance to unionization, and rapid economic growth (Carré, duRivage, and Tilly 1995).

Alongside the events described above, temporary help firms emerged in the late 1940s with what was referred to as "triangular employment rela-tionships," which means that a temporary help firm assigned workers to its clients while placing the workers on its own payroll so the temporary help firm became their employer (Gonos 1998). According to George Gonos (1998), this arrangement allowed the temporary help firm's clients to utilize labor without taking on the specific social, legal, and contractual obligations that had been attached to employer status since the New Deal and World War II. Dean Morse (1998) maintains that as early as the late nineteenth century, American society had developed a negative attitude about the kinds of people who did irregular, intermittent, or part-time work (peripheral jobs). They were seen as outsiders and inferior to those who worked in the "central core" of the economy in full-time, full-year jobs (standard employment). Peripheral work was done by subordinate demographic groups, such as new immigrants, people of color, and women, because core full-time, full-year jobs were controlled by white, Protestant males. These attitudes made it possible for the government to neglect to give workers that do irregular, intermittent, or part-time work the same protections as standard workers.

Labor market demographics started to change during World War II when women started entering the labor force in larger numbers. One view of the growth of nonstandard jobs, such as agency temporaries, is that they fulfilled workers' evolving need for flexibility in employment. From the "supply side" or households, the rise in flexible employment and nonstandard jobs coincided with the increased participation of married women in the labor force. Assuming that married women desire less rigid working hours, employers responded to changing preferences and choices of workers by providing more nonstandard and flexible employment. Nonstandard jobs are beneficial for some workers in that they cannot always work a regular forty-hour-a-week job due to family obligations or because they are attending school. Temporary work also provides a way for workers to sample several jobs and several employers. Temporary jobs give the "gregarious grandma" a way to work, not for economic reasons, but for diversion and recreation (Henson 1996). Evidence indicates that many non-standard workers are in that situation voluntarily, especially those in categories that enjoy labor market advantages (Cohany 1996).

However, some literature on movement into nonstandard employment (the supply side) develops a "push/pull" framework (Wiens-Tuers and Hill 2002). For example, Cohen and Bianchi (1999) discuss workers' response to constraints (pushed into a type of employment), often due to economic need, and response to opportunities (pull). Perhaps not surprisingly, they find the income push factor is strong, especially for those in households with low educational levels. Golden and Applebaum (1992) and Golden (1996) analyzed assertions that movement into the temporary help sector was due in part to demographic changes. While they found pull factors in that more married women and older workers in the labor force desired flexibility in scheduling, most factors associated with the movement into temp work were push factors. They saw the diminished bargaining power of labor as important in shifting the balance of power from labor to management. A drop in the demand for regular or core workers creates a surplus of permanent workers who go into temp work. The temp sector is therefore composed not only of those with preference for temporary work, but also of people who are overflow from permanent employment (Golden 1996).

An interesting push factor discussed in the literature is character. For example, workers who can not pass the rigorous screening of regular employment take temporary jobs. Other people respond-

ing to push factors include workers in transition, such as new graduates, retirees, women reentering the labor force after raising children, the newly divorced, and workers who lost jobs, not because of poor performance, but rather because of personnel policy changes on the part of employers (Farber 1999). Rothstein (1996) points to such push factors as marital status changes and the birth of a child. Zeytinoglu (2000) combines the push and pull factors by suggesting that employers take advantage of the life situations of women with family obligations, while push factors predominate for nonwhite men, who are pressured into temporary work as a form of occupational discrimination.

Some scholars feel that the growth of nonstandard and contingent jobs is driven by employers or the "demand side." Starting in the late 1960s and early 1970s, the U.S. economy faced growing competition within global product markets as Japan and Europe rebuilt their economies after World War II. Computer technology was evolving rapidly and trade increased, causing structural changes in the U.S. economy. Merger and acquisition activity blossomed in the wake of financial market deregulation as firms, seeking to compensate for falling levels of profit, reorganized into more efficient units. Mergers and acquisitions were used as a way to solve the principal/agent problems of corporations, return control to shareholders, and induce management to maximize shareholder value (Jensen 1988). The perception held by many corporate managers was that the solution to profit squeeze was to be a "lean, mean machine" able to respond quickly to changes in product markets and to shareholder pressure. Rigid labor markets and implicit job security deriving in part from nonmarket institutions broke down as market forces drove the move to a more flexible labor market (Abraham 1990; Golden and Applebaum 1992; Gordon 1996; Kinnear 1999). Much of this flexibility was achieved through the use of contingent and nonstandard labor.

The industrial and financial restructuring of the 1980s had its dark side, with rampant job losses leaving American workers feeling insecure and powerless (Blinder and Yellin 2001). In the wake of falling profits coupled with growing shareholder pressure, many firms responded to the risks associated with uncertain input costs and production for volatile product markets by shifting employment risk to employees (Belous 1989; Duca 1998). Firms increasingly turned to nonstandard work arrangements, in part, as an unintended consequence of laws that had eroded the employment-at-will doctrine, making it harder to adjust levels of employment (Houseman 1998). Autor (2000) also suggests that union presence and, more importantly, the efforts of the courts to protect workers against unjust dismissal fostered the growth of temporary help employment. There was an increase in the number of firms that began to outsource employment as well as production. This created economies of scale for temporary services, increased the acceptability of these practices, and increased competitive pressures on those firms that had not adopted flexible employment practices (Cohen, Dickens, and Posen 2001). The growth of the temporary industry and temporary work has had more of an impact on employment and uncertainty and changing norms than the actual numbers show in the same way that the impact of unions was felt on nonunion firms during the 1950s and 1960s (Osterman 1999).

Why did economic restructuring come early (relative to what was going on in Europe) and go so far in America? The country's legal and social institutions come into play as reflected in the more hard-edged brand of capitalism practiced in the United States, where legal barriers to layoffs are negligible (Blinder and Yellin 2001). Arthur and Rousseau (1996) note that American society provides a strong cultural tradition of individualism and do-it-yourself reliance; the American emphasis on the payoffs for self-reliance and hard work in this world of new opportunities minimizes discontent for those who feel disenfranchised. It is of great importance for the United States that a characteristic of American labor is the lack of class consciousness and the chance for upward social and economic mobility, or at least the perception of upward mobility (Pelling 1960).

Outcomes

It must be kept in mind that the norms and institutions that constitute the labor market have no value in their own right—they are a means to an end. The end is the welfare of people whose lives are shaped by the labor market (Osterman, Kochan, Locke, and Piore 2001). Nonstandard and contingent employment arrangements are heralded by some researchers as the key to flexible business strategies and success in the competitive, international business arena. There is evidence that , over the 1990s, both low unemployment and low wage growth were due, at least in part, to the presence of temporary employment. Katz and Krueger (1999) present evidence that states with a greater presence of temporary agency employment experienced lower wage growth in the 1990s and that the growth in temporary employment may have accounted for a 0.4 percentage point reduction in the unemployment rates. Using case studies from selected industries, Houseman, Kalleberg, and Erickcek (2001) find that temporary help agencies expanded the supply of labor and mitigated the need for companies to raise wages for new or existing workers. In addition, they find that firms may use temporary agencies as a way to screen workers so that workers who are considered "risky" have a chance to prove themselves. Nayar and Willinger (2001) find that using temporary and part-time workers (they use the term "contingent" in their paper) may be risky for the firm in that temporaries may not have the same commitment to the company, but the risk is offset by the ability of the firm to easily adjust the amount of labor it uses in times of slow demand. This keeps costs down. Nayar and Willinger conclude that using contingent workers improves gross profit margins and creates higher stock returns.

Even among workers in alternative employment who claim that they preferred traditional work and that their nonstandard job was the only one they could find, DiNatale (2001) reasons that a significant portion of temps and on-call workers might be unemployed if these employment arrangements did not exist. Freedman (1996) writes that contingent work is preferable to unemployment in that it provides an income and a way to network and that the least costly way to find such work is through labor market intermediaries such as temporary agencies. Temporary agencies may even increase the amount of security an individual worker can achieve since they recycle people into other assignments that provide income, exposure, and additional skills and experience.

However, there is another view about the outcomes of many nonstandard jobs. Many scholars view nonstandard and contingent employment as the new embodiment of dual labor markets, where there is a core of full-time, full-year standard jobs alongside peripheral or nonstandard jobs that do not have the same protections as core jobs (Mangum, Mayall, and Nelson 1985; Herzenberg, Alic, and Wial 2000). Dual labor market models express discontinuities perceived to distinguish labor markets segments that are qualitatively different. The focus is on the differences among jobs and not the differences among individuals. Dual-

ism has its roots in the flux and uncertainty that are part of the economic system and in the uneven impact of the parameters of the system upon various factors of production and different groups of workers (Piore 1980). Dual labor market analysis is a particularly useful framework to understand nonstandard jobs as it focuses on the structural differences between types of employment arrangements and the impact of those structures on economic and social outcomes for workers.

The increased ability of managers to use nonstandard employment arrangements is not necessarily a reflection of a corresponding employee preference for nonstandard employment. A substantial percentage of agency temporaries and on-call workers would prefer traditional or standard employment. Burtless (1999) argues that people in temporary jobs involuntarily (nonstandard workers who would prefer standard employment) may not necessarily have been unemployed otherwise. They could have instead been directly employed by companies that now contract out for their labor force. Some nonstandard jobs, particularly agency temporaries, are associated with low pay, few benefits, and little employment security. Most temporary help services workers make less than workers in standard employment arrangements for a similar job; the exception is high-skill and white-collar workers (Segal and Sullivan 1995). Temporaries tend to be young, nonwhite, female, less educated, and less skilled (Cohany 1996; Hipple and Stewart 1996). Tenure as a temporary worker may carry not only short-term consequences such as low pay, few benefits, and variable working hours (Belman and Golden 2000; Polivka, Cohany, and Hipple 2000; Wiens-Tuers 1998), but also long-term consequences in the form of lower wages, less benefits, and lower rates of homeownership, as well (Ferber and Waldfogel 1998; Wiens-Tuers, 2002).

Conclusion

Although the growth of nonstandard and contingent labor is but one change in a host of changes in the labor market, its impact goes beyond absolute numbers because regular employees are well aware of nonstandard and contingent employees and their implicit threat (Osterman 1999). The pendulum is swinging back in the direction of the loosening of ties between employer and employee. Even standard employment today is portrayed as more tenuous, and entailing fewer reciprocal obligations between employers and workers, with workers building their careers by moving between organizations instead of within them (Bernhardt and Marcotte 2000). Some researchers predict that if current trends continue, a large portion of the workforce will move from job site to job site and derive compensation and security from their access to multiple employment opportunities rather than from long-term employment with a single firm (Cobble and Vosko 2000). Arthur and Rousseau (1996) call this the "boundaryless career," which is the opposite of an "organizational career." A boundaryless career includes a range of possible forms of work that defy traditional employment assumptions. While a boundaryless career may be heralded as increasing flexibility and creating more upward mobility for workers in an economy where unemployment is low and markets are booming, it becomes extremely problematic for workers in a recessionary economic climate.

According to Osterman (1999), a political and intellectual struggle, sometimes overt and sometimes hidden, is taking place over the shape of the American labor market and the rules that will frame it for the future. There is concern that in unregulated form, nonstandard, "flexible" work, even if it is on a continuous basis, cannot provide a satisfactory level of economic independence, or provide adequate job security, and gives limited protection against arbitrary unemployment (Walsh 1990). But there is nothing inevitable or preordained about the course of social and economic change; it does not follow a "natural law." Institutions are not necessarily socially efficient, and formal and informal rules are often created to serve the interests of those with the power to devise the new rules or maintain the old ones. The norms and values that shaped the labor market of the last twenty years were often those of the shareholders and not the stakeholders, of global corporations and financial markets and not employees. As employers shift more responsibility for adequate income, health insurance, and pension plans onto workers, flexibility may turn from a positive into a negative, with the resulting catalog of problems representing a mandate for intervention in the public policy and collective bargaining arenas (Carré, duRivage and Tilly 1995).

Appendix

The following definitions are those used by the Bureau of Labor Statistics in the "Contingent and Alternative Employment Arrangements, February 2001" Survey (USDL 01–153) and in the Current Population Survey. The CAEAS was conducted along with the CPS in 1995, 1997, 1999, and 2001. Contingent workers are those who do not have an implicit or explicit contract for ongoing employment. Persons who do not expect to continue in their jobs for personal reasons, such as retirement or returning to school, are not considered contingent workers, provided that they would have the option of continuing in the job were it not for these personal events.

Estimate 1

Wage and salary workers who expect their job will last for an additional year or less and who had worked at their jobs for one year or less. Self-employed workers and independent contractors are excluded from this estimate. For temporary help and contract workers, contingency is based on the expected duration and tenure of their employment with the temporary help or contract firm, *not* with the specific client to whom they are assigned.

Estimate 2

Workers, including the self-employed and independent contractors, who expect their employment to last for an additional year or less and who had worked at their jobs (or been self-employed) for one year or less. For temporary help and contract workers, contingency is determined on the basis of their tenure with the client to whom they are assigned, instead of their tenure with the temporary help or contract firm.

Estimate 3

Workers who do not expect their job to last. Wage and salary workers are included even if they already have held the job for more than one year and expect to hold the job for at least an additional year. The self-employed and independent contractors are included if they expect their employment to last for an additional year or less and they had been self-employed or independent contractors for one year or less.

Types of Alternative Arrangements

Independent contractors: Workers who are identified as independent contractors, independent con-

sultants, or freelance workers, whether they are self-employed or wage and salary workers.

On-call workers: Workers who are called to work only as needed, although they can be scheduled to work for several days or weeks in a row.

Agency temporaries: Workers who are paid by a temporary help agency, whether or not their job is temporary.

Contract workers: Workers who are employed by a company that provides them or their services to others under contract and who are usually assigned to only one customer and usually work at the customer's worksite.

References

Abraham, Katharine G. "Restructuring the Employee Relationship." In *New Developments in the Labor Market: Toward a New Institutional Paradigm*, ed. Katharine G. Abraham and Robert McKersie. Cambridge, MA: MIT Press, 1990.

Arthur, Michael B., and Denise Rousseau. "Introduction." In *The Boundaryless Career*, ed. Michael B. Arthur and Denise Rousseau. New York: Oxford University Press, 1996.

Autor, David H. *Outsourcing at Will: Unjust Dismissal Doctrine and the Growth of Temporary Help Employment.* Working Paper 7557. Cambridge, MA: National Bureau of Economic Research, February 2000.

Barker, Kathleen, and Kathleen Christensen. "Controversy and Challenges Raised by Contingent Work Arrangements." In *Contingent Work*, ed. Kathleen Barker and Kathleen Christensen. Ithaca, NY: Cornell University Press, 1998.

Belman, Dale, and Lonnie Golden. "Nonstandard and Contingent Employment: Contrasts by Job Type, Industry, and Occupation." In *Nonstandard Work: The Nature and Challenges of Changing Employment Arrangements*, ed. Françoise Carré, Marianne Ferber, Lonnie Golden, and Stephen A. Herzenberg. Champaign, IL: Industrial Relations Research Association, 2000.

Belous, Richard. *The Contingent Economy: The Growth of Temporary, Part-Time and Subcontracted Work.* Washington, DC: National Planning Institute, 1989.

Bernhardt, Annette, and Dave E. Marcotte. "Is 'Standard Employment' Still What It Used to Be?" In *Nonstandard Work: The Nature and Challenges of Changing Employment Arrangements*, ed. Françoise Carré, Marianne Ferber, Lonnie Golden, and Stephen A. Herzenberg. Champaign, IL: Industrial Relations Research Association, 2000.

Blinder, Alan S., and Janet L. Yellin. *The Fabulous Decade: Macroeconomic Lessons from the 1990s.* New York: Century Foundation Press, 2001.

Bureau of Labor Statistics, U.S. Department of Labor. "New Data on Contingent and Alternative Employment Examined by BLS." USDL 95–318. August 1995.

———. "Contingent and Alternative Employment Arrangements, February 1997." USDL 97–422. December 1997.

———. "Contingent and Alternative Employment Arrangements, February 1999." USDL 99–362. December 1999.

———. "Contingent and Alternative Employment Arrangements, February 2001." USDL 01–153. May 2001.

Burtless, Gary. "Comments and Discussion" on Lawrence F. Katz and Alan B. Krueger, "The High-Pressure U.S. Labor Market of the 1990s." *Brookings Papers on Economic Activity* 1 (1999):66–72.

Carré Françoise J., Virginia L. duRivage, and Chris Tilly. "Piecing Together the Fragmented Workplace." In *Unions and Public Policy*, ed. L. Flood. Westport, CT: Greenwood Press, 1995.

Cobble, Dorothy Sue, and Leah F. Vosko. "Historical Perspectives on Representing Nonstandard Workers." In *Nonstandard Work: The Nature and Challenges of Changing Employment Arrangements*, ed. Françoise Carré, Marianne Ferber, Lonnie Golden, and Steven A. Herzenberg. Champaign, IL: Industrial Relations Research Association, 2000.

Cohany, Sharon R. "Workers in Alternative Employment Arrangements." *Monthly Labor Review* 119, no. 10 (October 1996): 31–45.

Cohen, Jessica, William T. Dickens, and Adam Posen. "Have New Human-Resource Management Practices Lowered the Sustainable Unemployment Rate?" In *The Roaring Nineties*, ed. Alan Krueger and Robert Solow. New York: Russell Sage Foundation and Century Foundation Press, 2001.

Cohen, Philip N., and Suzanne M. Bianchi. "Marriage, Children, and Women's Employment: What Do We Know?" *Monthly Labor Review* 122, no. 12 (December 1999): 22–30.

Dennard, H. Lane Jr. "Governmental Impediments to Employment of Contingent Workers." *Journal of Labor Relations* 27, no. 4 (Fall 1996): 595–612.

DiNatale, Marisa. "Characteristics of and Preference for Alternative Work Arrangements, 1999." *Monthly Labor Review* 124, no. 3 (March 2001): 28–49.

Duca, John V. "How Increased Product Market Competition May Be Reshaping America's Labor Markets." *Economic Review.* Federal Reserve Bank of Dallas (fourth quarter, 1998): 2–16.

Farber, Henry S. "Alternative and Part-Time Employment Arrangements as a Response to Job Loss." *Journal of Labor Economics* 17, no. 4(2) (1999): S142–S169.

Ferber, Marianne A., and Jane Waldfogel. "The Long-term Consequences of Nontraditional Employment." *Monthly Labor Review* 121, no. 5 (May 1998): 3–12.

Freedman, Audrey. "Contingent Work and the Role of Labor Market Intermediaries." In *Of Heart and Mind: Social Policy Essays in Honor of Sar A. Levitan*, ed. Garth Mangum and Steven Mangum. Kalamazoo, MI: W.E. Upjohn Institute, 1996.

Golden, Lonnie. "The Expansion of Temporary Help Employment in the U.S., 1982–1992: A Test of Alternative Economic Explanations." *Applied Economics* 51, no. 9 (September 1996): 1127–41.

Golden, Lonnie. "The Insensitive Workweek: Trends and Determinants of Adjustment in Average Hours." *Journal of Post Keynesian Economic* 13, no. 1 (Fall 1990): 79–110.

Golden, Lonnie, and Eileen Appelbaum. "What Was Driving the 1982–1988 Boom in Temporary Employment? Preferences of Workers or Decisions and Power of Employers." *Journal of Economics and Sociology* 51, no. 4 (October 1992): 473–93.

Gonos, George. "The Interaction between Market Incentives and Government Actions." In *Contingent Work*, ed. Kathleen Barker and Kathleen Christensen. Ithaca, NY: Cornell University Press, 1998.

Gordon, David. *Fat and Mean: The Corporate Squeeze of Working Americans and the Myth of Managerial "Downsizing."* New York: Free Press, 1996.

Hamermesh, Daniel S., and Gerard Pfann. "Adjustment Costs in Factor Demand." *Journal of Economic Literature* 32, no. 3 (September 1996): 1264–92.

Hensen, Kevin D. *Just a Temp.* Philadelphia: Temple University Press, 1996.

Herzenberg, Stephen A., John A. Alic, and Howard Wial. "Nonstandard Employment and the Structure of Postindustrial Labor Market." In *Nonstandard Work:*

The Nature and Challenges of Changing Employment Arrangements, ed. Françoise Carré, Marianne Ferber, Lonnie Golden, and Stephen A. Herzenberg. Champaign, IL: Industrial Relations Research Association, 2000.

Hipple, Steven, and Jay Stewart. "Earnings and Benefits of Contingent and Noncontingent Workers." *Monthly Labor Review* 119, no. 10 (October 1996): 22–30.

Hodgson, Geoffrey M. "The Approach of Institutional Economics." *Journal of Economic Literature* 36 (March 1998): 166–92.

———. "What Is the Essence of Institutional Economics?" *Journal of Economic Issues* 34, no. 2 (June 2000): 317–29.

Houseman, Susan N. *Why Employers Use Flexible Staffing Arrangements: Evidence from an Establishment Survey.* Working Paper 01–67. Kalamazoo, MI: W.E. Upjohn Institute for Employment Research, June 1998.

Houseman, Susan N., Arne L. Kalleberg, and George A. Erickcek. *The Role of Temporary Help Employment in Tight Labor Markets.* Working Paper 01–73. Kalamazoo, MI: W.E. Upjohn Institute, July 2001.

Hylton, Maria O'Brien. "Legal and Policy Implications of the Flexible Employment Relationship." *Journal of Labor Research* 27, no. 4 (Fall 1996): 583–93.

Jensen, Michael C. "Takeovers: Their Causes and Consequences." *Journal of Economic Perspectives* 2, no. 1 (1988): 41–48.

Katz, Lawrence F., and Alan B. Krueger. "The High Pressure U.S. Labor Market of the 1990s." *Brookings Papers on Economic Activity* 1 (1999): 1–87.

Kerr, Clark. "The Neoclassical Revisionists in Labor Economics (1940–1960)—R.I.P." In *How Labor Makets Work: Reflections on Theory and Practice*, ed. Bruce Kaufman. Lexington, MA: D.C. Heath, 1988.

Kinnear, Douglas. "The 'Compulsive Shift' to Institutional Concerns in Recent Labor Economics." *Journal of Economic Issues* 33, no. 1 (March 1999): 169–81.

Kruse, Douglas, and Joseph Blasi. "The New Employee-Employer Relationship." In *A Working Nation*, ed. David T. Ellwood. New York: Russell Sage Foundation, 2000.

Mangum, Garth, Donald Mayall, and Kristin Nelson. "The Temporary Help Supply: A Response to the Dual Internal Labor Market." *Industrial and Labor Relations Review* 38, no. 4 (July 1985): 599–611.

Morse, Dean. "Historical Perspective: The Peripheral Worker (1969)." In *Contingent Work*, ed. Kathleen Barker and Kathleen Christensen. Ithaca, NY: Cornell University Press, 1998.

Muhl, Charles J. "The Employment-at-Will Doctrine: Three Major Exceptions."*Monthly Labor Review* 24, no. 1 (January 2001): 3–11.

Nayar, Nandkumar, and F. Lee Willinger. "Financial Implications of the Decision to Increase Reliance on Contingent Labor." *Decision Sciences* 32, no. 4 (Fall 2001): 661–81.

North, Douglass C. *Institutions, Institutional Change and Economic Performance.* New York: Cambridge University Press, 1990.

Nye, David. *Alternative Staffing Strategies.* Washington, DC: Bureau of National Affairs, 1988.

Oi, Walter. "Labor As a Quasi-Fixed Factor." *Journal of Political Economy* 70, no. 6 (December 1962): 538–55.

Organization for Economic Cooperation and Development. "Taking the Measure of Temporary Employment." In *The Organization for Economic Cooperation and Development OECD Employment Outlook.* Paris: OECD Publications Service (July 2002).

Osterman, Paul. Survey: "Organization of Work in American Business." Corporate Human Resource Development, 1992 and 1997.

———. "Pressure and Prospects for Employment Security in the US." In *Employment Security and Labor Market Behavior*, ed. Christoph Buechtemann. Ithaca, NY: ILR Press, 1993.

———. *Securing Prosperity.* Princeton, NJ: Princeton University Press, 1999.

Osterman, Paul, Thomas A. Kochan, Richard M. Locke, and Michael J. Piore. *Working in America! Blueprint for the New Labor Market.* Cambridge, MA: MIT Press, 2001.

Pelling, Henry. *American Labor.* Chicago: University of Chicago Press, 1960.

Piore, Michael J. "Dualism as a Response to Flux and Uncertainty." In *Dualism and Discontinuity in Industrial Societies*, ed. Suzanne Berger and Michael J. Piore. New York: Cambridge University Press, 1980.

Polivka, Anne E., Sharon R. Cohany, and Steven Hipple. "Definition, Composition, and Economic Consequences of the Nonstandard Workforce." In *Nonstandard Work: The Nature and Challenges of Changing Employment Arrangements*, ed. Françoise Carré, Marianne Ferber, Lonnie Golden, and Stephen A. Herzenberg. Champaign, IL: Industrial Relations Research Association, 2000.

Rothstein, Donna S. "Entry into and Consequences of Nonstandard Work Arrangements." *Monthly Labor Review* 119, no. 10 (October 1996): 75–82.

Segal, Lewis M., and Daniel G. Sullivan. "The Temporary

Labor Force." *Economic Perspectives* 19, no. 2 (March/April 1995): 2–19.

Sloane, Peter J., and Anne Gaston. "The Flexible Firm and Its Determinants." In *A Flexible Future*, ed. Paul Blyton and Jonathan Morris. New York: Walter deGruyter, 1991.

Walsh, Tim. Flexible Labour Utilization in the Private Sector." *Work, Employment and Society* 4, no. 4 (1990): 517–530.

Wiens-Tuers, Barbara A. "The Relationship of Race and Outcomes of Non-Standard Labor." *Journal of Economic Issues* 32, no. 2 (June 1998): 575–85.

———. "There's No Place Like Home: The Relationship of Nonstandard Employment and Home Ownership over the 1990s." *Journal of Economics and Sociology.* Forthcoming 2005.

Wiens-Tuers, Barbara A., and Elizabeth Hill. "How Did We Get Here from There: Movement into Temporary Employment." *Journal of Economic Issues* 36, no. 2 (June 2002): 303–11.

Zeytinoglu, Isik U. "Gender, Race, and Class Dimensions of Nonstandard Work." *Industrial Relations* 55, no. 1 (Winter 2000): 133–67.

14

The Institution of Unauthorized Residency Status, Neighborhood Context, and Mexican Immigrant Earnings in Los Angeles County

Enrico A. Marcelli

Unauthorized Immigration as Economically Desirable and Politically Problematic

The rising number of unauthorized Mexican immigrants residing in the United States—estimated to be up from approximately 2 million in 1990 to almost 5 million as of 2000—is partly the consequence of an increasingly selective U.S. immigration policy toward Mexico since the mid-1960s that generated the institution of unauthorized residency. Unauthorized residency status in the United States is an institution because it is a historically generated set of context- and location-specific constraints on and opportunities for employment in particular occupations and socioeconomic integration among certain foreign-born residents which achieves order and predictability. In other words, institutions may be identified by observing human behavior that is habituated or stabilized by rules that have some underlying cultural or intellectual justification, "constitute the arenas in which people try to accomplish their aims," and "imply 'you may' as well as 'thou shalt not,' thus creating as well as limiting choices" (Neale 1987, 1179–82).

There are at least three ways of framing how authorized residents of the United States tend to view unauthorized immigration. First, unauthorized immigration is *desirable*—especially in an increasingly internationalized economy—for U.S. employers needing easy access to an industrious workforce willing to work for relatively low wages (a politically conservative or liberal view). Second, the presence of a disenfranchised, nonintegrated, unauthorized immigrant constituency requires group representation, and thus unauthorized immigration is politically *problematic* (a politically radical view). And third, because the lower-priced goods and services that unauthorized workers provide are desirable but various associated negative social consequences of a concentrated lower-wage population are not, unauthorized immigration is both economically *desirable* and politically *problematic* (the conflicted middling view).

This chapter focuses only on one economic aspect of unauthorized residency status among Mexican-born workers while controlling for other individual- and neighborhood-level characteristics —whether and how that status impacted the workers' hourly earnings relative to authorized resident workers in 2001 in Los Angeles County. It is important to understand whether unauthorized residency status impacts earnings for at least two reasons. First, the presence of immigrants who are unauthorized to reside in the United States may place greater downward pressure on earnings in lower-skilled labor markets than their presence alone suggests because some may "accept jobs at lower wages than they would if they had a legal right to work, or they may be subject to threats and intimidation by employers" (Bailey 1985, 221). Second, unauthorized residency status may dissuade efforts to advance socioeconomically, or what Arsène Dumont termed "social capillarity" more than a century ago (Lorimer 1959, 144), due to fears of detection and deportation. In short, unauthorized residency may harm those in the United States with such a status and others with whom they compete in the labor market.

I focus simply on the first issue—how unauthorized residency status influences earnings among Mexican immigrants (e.g., socioeconomic capillarity)—in an effort to anchor attention on how one historically created institution affects one labor market outcome in one metropolitan area. Other important questions associated with unauthorized residency status, but not addressed here, include how an influx of unauthorized immigrant workers influences authorized residents' labor force outcomes (Bailey 1985; Bean, Lowell, and Taylor 1988; Marcelli, Pastor, and Joassart 1999; Massey 1987; Winegarden and Khor 1991), and unauthorized Mexican residents' local fiscal impact on publicly subsidized education, health, and welfare services (Marcelli and Heer 1998).

Investigating whether unauthorized residency status negatively impacts Mexican immigrants' earnings is consistent with what Joseph Dorfman (Dorfman et al. 1964, 8) terms "the historico-legal approach" and with Vernon Briggs's claim—essentially echoing John R. Commons (1907)—that U.S. immigration "is a subject that is especially amenable to study and interpretation by institutional economists" because it is a "policy-driven phenomenon" and as such is temporal and contextual (Briggs 1996, 371). In the present context, unauthorized Mexican immigration may be viewed as historical, location-specific, and determined in large measure by government regulation rather than competitive labor markets alone.

The next section of this chapter lays out the historical context in which the institution of unauthorized residency status emerged, essentially arguing that beginning with the acquisition of California and other states from Mexico in the mid-nineteenth century, the migration and integration of Mexican immigrants has been governed and regularized by U.S. immigration and labor policies. A third section argues that Los Angeles is a particularly good place to study the labor market effects of unauthorized residency status among Mexican immigrants because of their high concentration in this location and the region's historic dependence on Mexican labor in several key industries. In the fourth section, I discuss how labor market segmentation theory provides a useful conceptual framework for understanding the labor market outcomes resulting from the presence of unauthorized immigrant workers. In short, it is the nature of the jobs (labor demand) rather than the characteristics of the workers (labor supply) that is pertinent for understanding labor market outcomes. Section five outlines how past research has addressed the main methodological obstacles that need to be overcome when attempting to determine what factors explain wage disparities between any two groups of workers, and a sixth section explains the data and methodology I employ in this chapter. Finally, a seventh section presents the results of this analysis and a concluding section argues that these suggest the need for enforcing existing labor, health, safety, and environmental laws in the United States, for raising the minimum wage despite the employer resistance these measures are likely to spark, and for treating Mexico differently and separately in U.S. immigration policy given its proximity and importance to the U.S. economy.

Historical and Legal Foundations of the Institution of Unauthorized Residency Status

Although the institution of unauthorized residency status was created in 1875 to discourage Asian immigration to the United States, it was only gradually extended to Mexican immigrants with the termination of the Mexico–U.S. labor program in 1964 and as Mexico was placed under the national quota system, which disallowed more than 20,000 immigrants per annum from any one nation, 1972. In short, to ensure a steady supply of workers to the United States, the institution of unauthorized residency status did not apply to Mexican immigrants from 1875 to 1972.

The discovery of gold in Coloma, California, in January 1848 and the forced sale of one-third of Mexico to the United States less than two weeks later, for instance, led promptly to the successful solicitation of capital-poor Mexican immigrant workers (*gambusinos*) from the Mexican state of Sonora by U.S. mining firms at a time when many such workers were experiencing harsh treatment from native Californians (Standart 1996) and no federal or state laws governing mining existed. As the number of relatively successful Mexican migrant miners rose to a level generating envy among some native miners, however, the latter developed their own self-serving mining laws that were premised on the long-standing Spanish-American codes wherein property rights depended on resource discovery and development (McWilliams 1968, 141–42).[1] Under these circumstances, many Mexican immigrant miners found it in their interest to return to Mexico or to move south to the Los

Angeles area (Standart 1996), but they and all other foreign-born residents remained legally authorized to reside and work in the United States.

Not until 1875, when the first federal legislative limitation on specific groups of immigrants— e.g., convicts and prostitutes but targeting Chinese immigrants who had gradually replaced Mexican migrant laborers in the mines—was passed were some immigrants from certain nations prohibited to reside legally in the United States (Heer 1996). And although subsequent restrictions on immigration were adopted through 1941, a system of administrative exemptions and extended periods of informal nonenforcement of immigration and labor statutes between the 1875 law and the onset of the Great Depression ensured American employers in specific industries an ongoing flow of Mexican immigrant workers (Stoddard 1976). In other words, although the institution of unauthorized residency status existed, it did not apply to Mexicans.

Even after the Depression and the onset of World War II, the United States implemented what was initially promoted by government officials as a temporary, emergency Mexican labor program to satisfy perceived labor shortages. This "bracero" program evolved into "an institutionalized feature of U.S. and Mexican agriculture" and remained in place until 1964 (García y Griego 1996, 45). More than exempting Mexican immigrants from immigration restrictions established for other groups before the Depression, this program invited them to the United States to work and encouraged their residency.

Although this program ended in 1964 and on the surface appeared to bend toward the same cultural forces that produced the Economic Opportunity and the Civil Rights Acts of 1964 (i.e., protection of native-born minority workers' economic opportunities), passage of the 1965 Immigration Act yet again left Mexican immigrants virtually free to enter and reside in the United States. Both the termination of the Mexican worker program and the 1965 Immigration Act were given political impetus by the publication in 1964 of John F. Kennedy's *Nation of Immigrants*, which called for primary changes. First, annual immigration quotas based on estimated national distributions of foreign-born residents according to the 1890–1920 Censuses for Eastern Hemispheric nations—quotas that had been in place since the 1920s—were to be replaced by a common national quota of 20,000 per year and a preference system based more on family reunification than nationality or skills. And second, Western Hemispheric nations were to remain exempt from any quota limits on entry. In short, Mexico remained exempt from the new restrictions.

All of this changed in 1972 when the 20,000 annual national quotas and the preference system to which Eastern Hemispheric nations had been subjected were extended to Mexico and other Western Hemispheric countries, and a labor-certification exemption for the parents of U.S.-born residents (e.g., foreign-born Mexican parents) was repealed. Despite the historic cultural, economic, and political relationship with Mexico, its geographic proximity to the United States, and the support of presidents Ford and Carter for higher quotas for Mexico, the termination of the bracero program in 1964 and the 1972 legislation combined to create the residential category of unauthorized Mexican immigrant. There were no legal limitations to U.S. entry for Mexican immigrants—even nonbracero migrant workers until 1972. It is only during the past 32 of 156 years of Mexican immigration that a Mexican immigrant could be an unauthorized resident of the United States.

In contrast to increased U.S. efforts to facilitate the cross-border movement of capital, commodities, goods, and information culminating in the passage of the North American Free Trade Agreement (NAFTA) in 1994, U.S. immigration legislation passed in 1986, 1990, and 1996 further reduced Mexican access to legal visas, militarized key portions of the Mexico–U.S. border, and penalized legal but noncitizen immigrants (Massey, Durand, and Malone 2002). Such institutional impediments to legal immigration—running against the historic and contemporary demographic and economic relationship between Mexico and the United States—have increased incentives to enter illegally and to settle long-term in the United States (Marcelli and Cornelius 2001).

Why Study Unauthorized Mexican Immigrants in Los Angeles County?

There are two good reasons to study how unauthorized residency status impacts Mexican immigrants' earnings in Los Angeles County. First, the county represents the single largest concentration of unauthorized Mexican immigrants in the United States. Approximately 73 percent of all unauthorized immigrants in California in 2000 were Mexican-born (1.6 of 2.2 million) and almost 17 percent of all unauthorized Mexican immigrants residing in the United States were in Los Angeles County (814,000 of 4.8 million).[2] Because one is likely to, and may efficiently, observe unauthorized Mexicans working in Los Angeles County, it represents an ideal social laboratory for investigating the economic effects of unauthorized residency status. Second, Los Angeles County represents a distinct economic domain that has become dependent upon a steady flow of unauthorized Mexican immigrants (Marcelli 1999). This dependence is sustained not only by employers' desire for relatively industrious workers who will accept lower wages, will tolerate unhealthy work conditions, and are located efficiently through migrant job networks, but also by unauthorized immigrants whose initial instrumental aspirations (to make money rather than gain social status) enable employers to meet variable and uncertain demand in industries such as textiles, agriculture, and construction (Piore 1979, 50–85). The geographic concentration of, and socioeconomic dependence upon, this population in Los Angeles County makes the region a particularly attractive place for studying Mexican immigrant earnings by residency status.

Our findings may be summarized as follows. Unauthorized residency status is estimated to exact a considerable wage penalty on adult Mexican immigrant male workers, but not on Mexican immigrant female workers. Unauthorized Mexican immigrant female workers are estimated to have earned only 4.6 percent less than their authorized female compatriots, but unauthorized Mexican immigrant males earned fully 33.7 percent less than their male compatriots in Los Angeles County. Furthermore, only 26.1 percent of the male wage gap is found to be attributable to traditional individual characteristics, 4.2 percent was influenced by one's neighborhood environment, and 3.6 percent was the result of whether one was affiliated with a labor union. Interestingly, −1.1 percent is "explained by" what job a Mexican immigrant male had, implying that according to the occupational distribution of authorized and unauthorized Mexican immigrant males the wage gap ought to have been smaller than was observed.

Overall, fully 67.2 percent of the male wage gap is not explained by conventional individual, neighborhood, and institutional factors. Some of this unexplained gap may be attributable to the unobserved individual characteristics of Mexican immigrant workers, such as the quality of one's education. However, recent research that has been statistically able to identify this part of the unexplained component of the Mexican immigrant male

wage gap by performing longitudinal analyses in which unobserved characteristics are unlikely to change (Kossoudji and Cobb-Clark 2002; Rivera-Batiz 1999) reports similar levels of remaining unexplained wage variance (e.g., discrimination).

The main contribution of this chapter is that it offers the first empirical evidence from the 2000s that unauthorized Mexican immigrant males continued to experience policy-enabled (institutionalized) wage discrimination initially detected in the early 1980s and rediscovered using data from the early 1990s. Results also support the hypothesis that residing in a densely Latino-populated neighborhood where homeownership is higher than in other neighborhoods positively affects Mexican immigrant workers' hourly earnings. Thus, in addition to individual characteristics, geography and policy may influence Mexican immigrants' earnings.

Theoretical Framework

The analysis below is informed by ideas introduced by labor market segmentation theorists in the 1970s who emphasized that distinct labor market segments are characterized not only or even primarily by earnings differentials resulting from competitive forces, but more fundamentally by different context-specific and historically specific working conditions and associated norms and rules, occupational mobility patterns, and methods of skills acquisition. This perspective (usefully reviewed and distinguished from "dual" labor market theory by Gray and Chapman in this volume) starkly contrasts with marginal productivity theory by highlighting the social determinants of occupational characteristics and structures and providing an analytic framework in which occupational segmentation is an expected outcome that varies with the flux and uncertainty in product markets. Consequently, lower-strata jobs and workers are not relegated to specific (e.g., garment, textile, construction, restaurant) industries that are traditionally associated with informality and uncertainty, but are likely to exist in any industry experiencing some variability in product demand. In short, rather than characterizing segmentation narrowly within particular industries and focusing on factors that dissuade or impede socioeconomic capillarity, we may see segmentation as the result of irreversible historic migrations, technological innovations, and investments generating occupational segments that absorb product demand fluctuations and are generally unresponsive to changes in labor supply or wages. Wages, in this conceptualization, are socially attached to the characteristics of jobs rather than antiseptically or abstractly influenced by the supply of and demand for potential workers.

Piore (1979, 15–49) suggests that many native-born residents understand this—that most of the jobs filled by contemporary unauthorized immigrants have been and are characteristically different than those desired and occupied by natives. The jobs tend to require few skills (as traditionally defined by education rather than attitude, dispositions, or ability to work with others), be low-paying, connote inferior social status, involve unpleasant working conditions, carry considerable insecurity, offer few advancement opportunities, occur in unstructured work environments, and have highly informal, personal or paternalistic supervisor-subordinate relations. Such work has included job slots as diverse as janitor, gardener, construction worker, seamstress, retail clerk, restaurant worker, paint crew supervisor, and child care provider. Although unauthorized Mexican immigrants fill many of these lower-rung jobs in Los Angeles County today, historically such work was performed by American Indians and Asian immigrants, or by South and East European immigrants and black migrants in other parts of the country. In short, "it is the employers, not the workers, and the jobs, not the incomes, that are strategic" for understanding the nature of employment in lower-rung strata of contemporary labor markets (Piore 1979, 19).[3]

Still, it remains possible to observe who fills which jobs at a particular point in time and compare the workers' occupational distributions, earnings, and other conditions of employment with those of workers in other ethnic and racial groups by gender and nativity to estimate the character and structure of labor demand. Marcelli and Heer (1997), for example, without denying that employers, employees, and government programs may channel workers into specific jobs and industries by race, ethnicity, and gender, also find that unauthorized residency status among Mexican immigrants is highly correlated with their relative concentrations in food service, construction laborer and trades, machine operator, material handler, and agricultural jobs. The only other occupational distribution that resembles that of unauthorized Mexican immigrants is that of legal male Mexican immigrants. Among authorized female Mexican immigrants, as well as authorized male and female Latino immigrants from other countries, occupational distributions differ considerably from that of unauthorized Mexican workers, and the distributions of all other ethnic and racial groups are even more disparate. All of this intimates, when viewed in the historic context of Mexico–U.S. immigration and U.S. immigration policy as described in the second section of this chapter, that the jobs unauthorized Mexican immigrants do and the consequences of this work are understandable only in light of evolving labor and migration policies, native-born aspirations, and employer hiring decisions that have socially linked certain unstable and relatively low-paying, low-status jobs with this population over time.

It is the nature of these jobs (labor demand) rather than the characteristics of the workers (labor supply), then, that is pertinent for understanding labor market outcomes in the perspective of labor market segmentation theory. And if unauthorized residency status confers inferior social status or workplace treatment, then comparing these workers' earnings to others'—while controlling for individual characteristics—may serve as a proxy for job insecurity, opportunities for upward mobility, subordinate-supervisor relations, and working conditions in general. Indeed, Marcelli, Pastor, and Joassart (1999) report that unauthorized Mexican and other Latino immigrant workers in Los Angeles County in 1990 experienced wage penalties resulting from their residency status whether employed in occupational segments having low, intermediate, or high proportions of informal workers from multiple ethnic and racial groups. The effect was pervasive across industries even after controlling for their human capital characteristics.

What follows builds on the segmented labor market theory offered by Piore (1979) and recent developments in multilevel econometrics or "ecometrics" (Hox 2002; Raudenbush and Sampson 1999) that permit us to estimate the impact of one's neighborhood and social networks on crime and health (Sampson, Morenoff, and Gannon-Rowley 2002), education (Mayer and Jencks 1989), labor market outcomes (Aguilera 2003, 2002; Pastor and Marcelli 2000) and migration decisions (Palloni et al. 2001) in addition to the effects of individual-level factors.[4]

Disentangling the Effect of Unauthorized Residency Status on Immigrant Earnings

Separating the influence of unauthorized residency status from other individual-, geographic-, and institutional-level determinants of earnings requires careful attention to various potential data and econometric problems. Below, I first discuss how viewing the impact of individual-level determinants in a tripartite conceptual framework permits one to understand several potential selectivity biases that may hinder econometric analyses of earnings disparities due to the existence of unobservable or "omitted" variables. I then review findings from studies during the past two decades that have tried to "handle" these potential problems as a precursor to discussing the data and model I employ in the subsequent section.

Econometrically, individual-level factors influencing differences in hourly earnings between authorized and unauthorized immigrants may be usefully separated into three broad categories: (1) differences in the productivity-related characteristics of the two types of workers, (2) differential returns to these characteristics, and (3) unobservable characteristics. The first category typically consists of human capital characteristics such as schooling, language ability, and work experience—which may also indirectly influence wages through occupational status (Powers and Seltzer 1998a, b), as well as various demographic controls for gender, marital status, and years residing in the United States. The second category is influenced by employer discrimination (Portes and Bach 1985), occupational segmentation (Piore 1979) due to job search and social network constraints, and unauthorized Mexican immigrants' desire to minimize the risk of detection and deportation rather than maximizing earnings per se (Borjas and Tienda 1993). The third category may include the quality of one's education or duration of residency in the country of origin before migration (Rivera-Batiz 1999), lower reservation wages among unauthorized immigrants resulting from the clandestine nature of their residency status (Kossoudji and Cobb-Clark 2002), or one's more compliant "attitude" and ability to work well with others (Waldinger and Lichter 2003).

The existence of these third-category individual-level factors implies that a sample is nonrandom and thus is associated with selection bias. If respondents in a sample being analyzed systematically differ from those who are excluded by some unseen characteristic that is correlated with one of the measured explanatory variables, then estimates of how individual and institutional factors influence wage outcomes are likely to be inaccurate. In the present analysis, there are two types of selection bias that need to be addressed.

The first is selection into the international Mexican migrant worker population and the second is selection into the U.S. labor market. Samples of migrant workers collected in Mexico are likely to overstate the wage gap between unauthorized and authorized migrant workers because they are likely to contain a disproportionate number of relatively unsuccessful migrants. Conversely, samples collected in the United States are likely to underestimate the wage gap because they exclude such unsuccessful migrant workers. Regardless of where the data are collected, however, another possible source of bias emerges when international migrant workers in the sample are systematically different from those who are not in the sample—if respondents are only from manufacturing firms or densely populated neighborhoods, for instance.

There are two main reasons why I do not attempt to correct for these possible selectivity biases. First, the most sophisticated studies that have attempted to do so have uncovered little or no bias (Massey 1987) or have not controlled for it because the econometric techniques for adjusting for such bias are not considered robust (Blau and Kahn 1997; Rivera-Batiz 1999; Trejo 1997). Second, and more importantly, I am concerned only about wage differences between unauthorized and authorized Mexican immigrants who currently reside in the United States in a specific urban location, so any

selectivity due to return migration will be absent. But even if bias did exist, the estimated disparity in earnings would be conservative.[5] Assuming one can control for productivity-related characteristics and employing U.S. data, it is therefore possible to test for labor market discrimination unauthorized Mexican immigrants may experience because they work in a lower-strata labor market segment characterized by low pay, poor working conditions, and low social status (Rivera-Batiz 1999).

Despite these methodological hurdles, during the past two decades the quality of data and research on how unauthorized residency status affects Mexican immigrants' earnings has improved considerably (Table 14.1). The earliest studies employed random data from Los Angeles County and found that unauthorized residency status was negatively associated with hourly wages. Heer and Falasco (1983) report that unauthorized Mexican migrants earned wages that were 14 percent lower than authorized Mexican migrants after controlling for other individual characteristics using the 1980–1981 Los Angeles County Parents Survey (Heer 1990). Morales (1983) reports that unauthorized migrants from twenty-one automobile manufacturing companies earned $1.79 less per hour than their authorized compatriots. And although Kossoudji and Ranney (1986) report similar findings using data on returned migrant workers collected in Mexico, Chiswick (1984), employing North and Houstoun's (1976) unauthorized immigrant apprehension data, suggests that unauthorized status per se has no effect on unauthorized Mexican wages but that other measured individual characteristics do. Bailey (1985) subsequently used Chiswick's (1984) results to develop a conceptual analysis and concludes that 80 percent of the unauthorized-authorized migrant wage gap is explained by observed characteristics and the remaining portion by lower reservation wages.

Table 14.1

Studies of How Unauthorized Residency Status Among Mexican Immigrants Impacts Earnings
(1983–2003)

Authors	Results	Data
Heer and Falasco (1983)	Wage rates rose with educational attainment and duration in the United States, but undocumented workers earned 14 percent less than legal Mexican immigrants, other things equal.	323 undocumented Mexican migrants in the 1980–81 Los Angeles Parents Survey (Heer 1990).
Morales (1983)	Controlling for other characteristics, undocumented migrants earned $1.79 less than their legal compatriots. Wages, however, also rose with job experience for both populations.	3,231 workers—undocumented, legal permanent residents, naturalized citizens from twenty-one firms in Los Angeles County, 1980–82.
Chiswick (1984)	Although illegal Mexican aliens earned 30 percent less than other illegal aliens in the United States, observed characteristics rather than legal statusper se explains the illegal-legal Mexican worker wage gap.	292 illegal male aliens apprehended in the United States in 1975 who were at least 16 years old and reported an occupation in the United States (North and Houstoun 1976), and the 5 percent 1970 PUMS.
Bailey (1985)	Observed characteristics other than illegal residency status explain approximately 80 percent of the illegal-legal wage gap, and the lower reservation wages of undocumented immigrants help explain the remaining portion of the wage gap.	Chiswick (1984)
Kossoudji and Ranney (1986)	Controlling for both observable (e.g., education, work experience) and unobservable characteristics (e.g., risk aversion, motivation), undocumented status is found to have negatively influenced wages.	541 returned male migrants who had worked in the United States during 1978.
Massey (1987)	Undocumented legal status among Mexican male immigrants had no direct effect on wages, but may have reduced wages indirectly by lowering job tenure.	232 males ages 15 to 65 in 885 households from one community in Michiocan and three communities in Jalisco were followed to their California destination between November 1982 and September 1983.
Gill and Long (1989)	Controlling for human capital, personal, and job characteristics, findings provide no evidence of a wage differential based on immigration status. However, when the model is respecified to exclude job characteristics, evidence is found that an immigration status wage differential may exist.	499 Hispanic garment workers in Los Angeles.
Borjas and Tienda (1993)	Undocumented immigrants earn about 30 percent less than documented immigrants, and about half of this wage gap is attributable to regional origin (a proxy for skill level). Surprisingly, the illegal-legal immigrant wage gap widens with age.	15 percent sample ($N = 3,427$) of the Legalization Application Processing System (LAPS) data and a pooled extract ($N = 86,189$) of the 1983, 1986, and 1988 Current Population Survey (CPS) data.

Cobb-Clark and Kossoudji (2000)	Legalization did not augment the wage outcomes of unauthorized Latina workers, and returns to human capital remained relatively low compared to legalized Mexican and Central American men. It is speculated that these differences are due to women being more likely to be isolated and to work alone, thus being disconnected to important social networks. Traditional gender roles in the home may also contribute to this outcome.	987 legalized Mexican and Central American women from the 1989/1992 Legalized Population Survey (LPS) who worked prior tolegalization, entered the United States after 1975, and were born between 1944 and 1967. A comparison sample of 778 Latina women (immigrants and U.S.-born) from the National Longitudinal Survey of Youth (NLSY) is used as a control for macroeconomic changes.
Rivera-Batiz (1999)	Observed characteristics of legal and illegal immigrants other than residency status explain only 48 percent (43 percent) of the male (female) wage gap, and wage gains of recently amnestied immigrants are mostly due to changed legal status rather than changes in observed or unobserved characteristics.	2,035 legalized Mexican immigrants from the 1989/1992 LPS, and 2,163 from a 10 percent sample of the 5 percent 1990 PUMS.
Kossoudji and Cobb-Clark (2002)	The wage penalty for having been unauthorized prior to IRCA implementation is estimated to range from 14 percent to 24 percent between the time of entry into the United States and 1992. The wage benefit of legalization under IRCA was about 6 percent (net of investments in human capital).	689 legalized Mexican and Central American men from the 1989/1992 LPS who worked prior to legalization entered the United States after 1975, and were born between 1944 and 1967. A comparison sample of 578 Latino (immigrants and U.S.-born) from the NLSY is used as a control for macroeconomic changes.

Demographer Douglas Massey (1987) significantly advanced this early literature by employing data collected on both sides of the Mexico–U.S. border and correcting for possible selectivity bias. Unauthorized residency status is estimated to have negatively affected Mexican immigrant wages not directly, but indirectly by lowering job tenure. Gill and Long (1989) provide some supporting evidence for this occupational segmentation hypothesis.

Research results produced during the 1990s are also conflicted. Borjas and Tienda (1993), employing immigrant legalization application data and Current Population Survey data, argue that wage differences between unauthorized and authorized immigrants are explained almost entirely by national origin skill differences. Similarly, Cobb-Clark and Kossoudji (2000) fail to detect any residency status effect when analyzing Mexican and Central American female wages, but offer one of the two first longitudinal studies. Rivera-Batiz (1999) offers the other, and both his cross-sectional and longitudinal analyses reveal strikingly consistent results that contradict those finding no residency status effect. Whereas an estimated 51 percent of the unauthorized-authorized male wage gap, and 57 percent of the female wage gap, are unexplained by observed individual characteristics using cross-sectional data, 56 percent of male gap and 62 percent of female gap are not explained when using longitudinal data. The putative advantage of using longitudinal data is that one can isolate the portion of unexplained wage variance that is attributable to unobserved factors so that what remains can be attributed to resi-

dency status discrimination or social status differ-
entiation resulting in differential employment outcomes more generally. For instance, if one were to
find that 45 percent of a wage gap between two
populations is explained by traditional demographic
and human capital variables, the remaining unexplained variance (55 percent) can only be attributable to unobserved factors or differential returns
(one of which is employer discrimination) to observable factors. To tease out what part of these two
effects may be attributable to discrimination, one
can estimate the returns to observed characteristics
over a relatively short period of time (say four or
five years) during which unobservable individual
characteristics are unlikely to have changed. This
is exactly what Rivera-Batiz (1999) does, and the
fact that most of the wage gap remains unexplained
strongly suggests that unauthorized Mexican immigrant status itself negatively impacted hourly
earnings in the early 1990s.

Kossoudji and Cobb-Clark (2002) build on
Rivera-Batiz (1999) by comparing the estimated
determinants of wages over time for legalized (formerly unauthorized) Mexican and Central American men and a comparison group of authorized
Latino immigrants. This permits them to control
for economy-wide effects that may have impacted
other workers equally. Contrary to their earlier
work that focused on Latina workers (Cobb-Clark
and Kossoudji 2000)—but consistent with Rivera-
Batiz (1999), Kossoudji and Ranney (1986), Heer
and Falasco (1983), and Morales (1983)—
Kossoudji and Cobb-Clark (2002) estimate a 14
to 24 percent unauthorized residency wage penalty between date of entry into the United States
and 1992 (postlegalization) and that legalization
itself independently boosted the wages of the legalized population by about 6 percent.

In sum, econometric research over the past two
decades has reported conflicting results. With the
collection of better data on unauthorized immigrants
and the use of more sophisticated econometric
methods, however, it appears that unauthorized residency status exerted—at least in the early 1990s—
an independent negative effect on the hourly earnings of Mexican immigrant males residing in the
United States that likely reflects the character of
the jobs they do and their lower social status. Still,
the question of how the institution of unauthorized
residency status influences earnings remains an
empirical one because the relatively undesirable
work conditions experienced by many unauthorized
immigrants is a positive function of the extent to
which illegality (1) restricts their access to particular employers and (2) makes job searching risky or
difficult; and a negative function of (3) unauthorized immigrants' ability to obtain credible fake
documents and (4) the quality of their social networks. In other words, there are theoretical reasons
why unauthorized residency status may or may not
adversely impact immigrant earnings.

Data and the Empirical Model

Below, I analyze recent individual-level data randomly collected from households in Los Angeles
County to test for the effect of residency status on
Mexican immigrant workers' wage outcomes. Although these data have the disadvantage of being
cross-sectional, they are almost a decade newer
than those employed in all previous studies, were
randomly collected, and thus are generally representative of more recent Mexican immigrants in
Los Angeles County.

The 2001 Los Angeles County Mexican Immigrant Residency Status Survey (LAC-MIRSS)

The 2001 Los Angeles County Mexican Immigrant
Residency Status Survey (LAC-MIRSS) is a ran-

dom sample of 456 households in which at least one person was born in Mexico and 829 foreign-born Mexicans who resided in Los Angeles County in July 2001. Specifically, 125 census blocks were randomly selected from 12,476 in which there were at least twenty residents and in which at least 75 percent of the population were of Hispanic (or Latino) origin according to the 2000 Census PL-94–171 data. These 125 blocks were located within 108 census tracts.[6] LAC-MIRSS interviewers were predominantly Mexican-born adult females who were provided with picture identification cards showing their affiliation with University of California at Los Angeles, neighborhood maps, address lists identifying which households to approach, and questionnaires in English and Spanish that had been developed and piloted by researchers from UCLA, El Colegio de la Frontera Norte (COLEF), and the Coalition for Humane Immigrants Rights in Los Angeles (CHIRLA). Previous fieldwork in 1994 and in 2001 LAC-MIRSS pretesting revealed that the combination of a local reputable university, a Mexican university, a local immigrant rights organization, and Mexican-born female interviewers boosted response rates—especially for sensitive questions regarding residency status and economic issues. The overall household response rate of the LAC-MIRSS is 62 percent, and although slightly lower than average for household surveys, the rate is encouraging given that we were surveying in relatively dense, impoverished neighborhoods likely to have high proportions of unauthorized Mexican immigrants and consisting of a disproportionate number of informal housing units. Census block sample weights were computed and corrected for both block and household level nonresponse rates.

Finally, that we were able to obtain residency status data for 98 percent of our sample suggests that respondents were comfortable answering these relatively sensitive questions of LAC-MIRSS interviewers. Slightly less than half (46 percent) of adult respondents admitted to residing in the United States without being a naturalized citizen, a legal permanent resident, or a temporary visitor. For purposes of this paper, only adults who worked at least two weeks, earned between \$1.00 and \$25.00 per hour in 2000, and had values for all explanatory variables are included in the analysis.

Modeling the Determinants of Hourly Earnings

Because research has shown that unauthorized Mexican male and female workers' labor market experiences diverge considerably, I estimate equation [1] using the entire LAC-MIRSS sample, as well as separately by gender and residency status, where the natural logarithm of hourly earnings of person i of sex j in neighborhood k is given by

$$\log W_{ijk} = \beta_0 + \beta_1 UMI_{ij} + \beta_2 MALE_{ij} + \beta_3 MIDDLE_{ij}$$
$$+ \beta_4 HIGHSCH_{ij} + \beta_5 EXP_{ij} + \beta_6 EXPSQ_{ij}$$
$$+ \beta_7 NOENGLSH_{ij} + \beta_{8ij} + PROFTECH_{ij}$$
$$+ \beta_9 FARMING_{ij} + \beta_{10} OPERAT_{ij}$$
$$+ \beta_{11} PRODUCT_{ij} + \beta_{12} SINGLE_{ij}$$
$$+ \beta_{13} UNION_{ij} + \beta_{14} PCTMIN_{ijk}$$
$$+ \beta_{15} PCTOWN_{ijk} + \beta_{16} POPDENSE_{ijk} + U_{ijk},$$
$$[1]$$

and W_{ijk} is the hourly wage rate reported by the individual. U_{ijk} represents an error term that is usually (and here) assumed to be randomly distributed among the population. All remaining variables (followed by their expected directional impact on hourly earnings in parentheses) are defined in Table 14.2. The control group in the regression analyses

Table 14.2

Definitions of Variables Used in Regression Analyses of Hourly Wages of Foreign-Born Mexican Adults, Ages 18–64, Los Angeles County, 2001

Dependent variable	Gross earnings divided by weeks and hours worked in 2000
W	
Individual characteristics	
UMI (–)	Dummy variable = 1 if person assigned unauthorized residency status
MALE (+)	Dummy variable = 1 if person is male
ELEMENT (control group)	Dummy variable = 1 if person completed less than five years of schooling
MIDDLE (+)	Dummy variable = 1 if person completed five to nine years of schooling
HIGHSC (+)	Dummy variable = 1 if person completed high school or higher
EXP (?)	Time or experience in Mexico = age minus years residing in the United States
EXPSQ (?)	Square of EXP
NOENGLSH (–)	Dummy variable = 1 if person claimed not to be able to speak English at all
PROFTECH (+)	Dummy variable = 1 if person was employed in managerial, professional, technical, sales, or administrative occupation
FARMING (?)	Dummy variable = 1 if person was employed in an agricultural occupation
OPERAT (+)	Dummy variable = 1 if person was employed as an operator, fabricator, or laborer
PRODUCT (+)	Dummy variable = 1 if person was employed in a precision, craft, or repair occupation
SERVICE (control group)	Dummy variable = 1 if person was employed in a service occupation
SINGLE (–)	Dummy variable = 1 if person is not currently married
UNION (+)	Dummy variable = 1 if person is a member or affiliated with a labor union
Neighborhood context	
PCTMIN (?)	Percent nonwhite residents in person's census block
PCTOWN (+)	Percent owning their home in person's census block
POPDENSE (?)	Number of persons per square mile in person's census block

Source: 2001 Los Angeles County Mexican Immigrant Residency Status Survey (LAC-MIRSS) and 2000 U.S. Census Summary File 3.

are those who completed less than five years of schooling (ELEMENT) and those who worked in a SERVICE occupation.

Because of the multilevel nature of the data and model employed here, I attempt to adjust for the effects of population clustering at the census block level—that is, the level at which the LAC-MIRSS data were collected and at which our three neighborhood variables are defined. Again, this is important because if respondents in our sample are not completely independent—as is likely to be the case when taken from the same neighborhood or household—then the assumption of low levels of interrespondent correlation assumed by most statistical tests will be violated (Hox 2002). Use of

STATA's cluster function produces robust standard errors on all regression coefficients, thus generating more conservative estimates of statistical significance than would be obtained by using ordinary least squares regression techniques that do not control for geographical clustering of observations and a higher level of confidence in our estimated effects.

As a final stage of the analysis and following Rivera-Batiz (1999), I use the coefficients generated when estimating the coefficients for Mexican male immigrant workers separately to examine how human capital, occupation, labor union membership, and neighborhood context help explain the unauthorized-authorized wage gap. This so-called Blinder-

Table 14.3

Sample Means and Proportions by Residency Status and Sex, Foreign-Born Mexicans, Ages 18–64, Los Angeles County, 2001

	Unauthorized				Authorized			
	Male	(s.d.)	Female	(s.d.)	Male	(s.d.)	Female	(s.d.)
Dependent variable								
W (dollars)	7.240	(3.589)	6.881	(3.460)	10.928	(5.106)	7.214	(2.789)
Natural log of W	1.876	(0.454)	1.850	(0.369)	2.276	(0.506)	1.896	(0.425)
Individual characteristics								
ELEMENT	0.180	(0.386)	0.090	(0.288)	0.123	(0.329)	0.214	(0.413)
MIDDLE	0.483	(0.052)	0.477	(0.503)	0.358	(0.481)	0.467	(0.502)
HIGHSC	0.337	(0.475)	0.433	(0.499)	0.520	(0.501)	0.319	(0.469)
EXP	22.2	(8.5)	22.6	(8.6)	16.9	(8.3)	19.5	(8.3)
EXPSQ	566.2	(458.8)	584.3	(426.5)	354.6	(302.3)	447.4	(386.9)
NOENGLSH	0.279	(0.451)	0.350	(0.480)	0.145	(0.354)	0.289	(0.456)
PROFTECH	0.055	(0.230)	0.277	(0.451)	0.216	(0.413)	0.271	(0.447)
FARMING	0.055	(0.230)	0.014	(0.119)	0.047	(0.212)	0.008	(0.087)
OPERAT	0.440	(0.499)	0.273	(0.449)	0.370	(0.484)	0.396	(0.492)
PRODUCT	0.320	(0.469)	0.135	(0.344)	0.229	(0.421)	0.082	(0.276)
SERVICE	0.129	(0.336)	0.280	(0.452)	0.134	(0.342)	0.234	(0.426)
SINGLE	0.514	(0.502)	0.410	(0.495)	0.265	(0.443)	0.433	(0.498)
UNION	0.098	(0.298)	0.070	(0.257)	0.187	(0.391)	0.117	(0.323)
Neighborhood context								
PCTMIN	0.949	(0.046)	0.951	(0.050)	0.948	(0.043)	0.946	(0.045)
PCTOWN	0.240	(0.249)	0.182	(0.209)	0.417	(0.294)	0.372	(0.248)
POPDENSE	34,368	(21,069)	41,228	(20,849)	25,772	(15,693)	26,777	(15,837)
N	113		70		149		87	
N (weighted)	246,875		126,374		358,745		212,221	

Source: 2001 Los Angeles County Mexican Immigrant Residency Status Survey (LAC-MIRSS) and 2000 U.S. Census Summary File 3.

Oaxaca wage decomposition procedure, which is well-known to labor economists who study employer discrimination, is used to estimate what components of the wage gap are explained by unobserved characteristics or employer discrimination (Blinder 1973; Oaxaca 1973; Oaxaca and Ransom 1994).

Results: Estimated Effect of Unauthorized Residency Status on Hourly Earnings

Table 14.3 reports the means and standard deviations for each variable. Unsurprisingly, authorized Mexican males and females earned more than their unauthorized compatriots, and unauthorized males earned approximately 34 percent less than authorized males. The male wage gap is consistent with previous research (Chiswick 1984; Massey 1987; Rivera-Batiz 1999), but the slight (5 percent) wage gap between unauthorized and authorized women diverges from that reported elsewhere (Cobb-Clark and Kossoudji 2000). Part of this unexpected, small female wage gap may be due to unauthorized Mexican women in our sample having acquired slightly more schooling than authorized Mexican women: 43 versus 31 percent, for instance, completed high school. But it may also be attributable to unauthorized Mexican women having been older at the time

Table 14.4

Multilevel Regression Estimates of Hourly Earnings Among Foreign-Born Mexicans by Gender, Ages 18–64, Los Angeles County, 2001

	All	Men	Women
Individual characteristics			
UMI	−0.223***	−0.226***	−0.106*
	(0.050)	(0.079)	(0.063)
MALE	0.206***		
	(0.052)		
MIDDLE	0.123	0.065	0.133
	(0.077)	(0.092)	(0.098)
HIGHSC	0.276***	0.177*	0.360***
	(0.098)	(0.101)	(0.129)
EXP	−0.007	0.004	−0.027*
	(0.014)	(0.015)	(0.014)
EXPSQ	0.000	0.000	0.001**
	(0.000)	(0.000)	(0.000)
NOENGLSH	0.045	0.018	0.088
	(0.070)	(0.107)	(0.061)
PROFTECH	0.050	0.011	0.091
	(0.081)	(0.121)	(0.103)
FARMING	−0.166***	−0.267***	0.007
	(0.064)	(0.084)	(0.107)
OPERAT	0.003	−0.086	0.184*
	(0.060)	(0.097)	(0.106)
PRODUCT	0.183**	0.128	0.282**
	(0.077)	(0.110)	(0.118)
SINGLE	−0.144**	−0.250***	0.068
	(0.058)	(0.079)	(0.076)
UNION	0.266***	0.302***	0.104
	(0.095)	(0.109)	(0.144)
Neighborhood context			
PCTMIN	0.132	0.056	−0.086
	(0.387)	(0.512)	(0.630)
PCTOWN	0.178	0.233	0.125
	(0.202)	(0.186)	(0.264)
POPDENSE	0.000	0.000	0.000
	(0.000)	(0.000)	(0.000)
INTERCEPT	1.722***	2.102***	1.812***
	(0.352)	(0.476)	(0.665)
R-squared	31.0%	35.3%	24.9%
N	399	249	150

Source: 2001 Los Angeles County Mexican Immigrant Residency Status Survey (LAC-MIRSS) and 2000 U.S. Census Summary File 3.
Note: Statistically significant at the 99 percent (***), 95percent (**), and 90 percent (*) confidence level.

of entry into the United States and consequently having had more time to acquire work experience in Mexico. Alternatively, it does not appear to be due to their relatively advanced English ability, to having secured jobs that traditionally pay more, to being married, to being in a union, or to residing in neighborhoods likely to offer access to beneficial social capital.

The larger observed wage penalty of unauthorized Mexican males, on the other hand, appears to correlate with all explanatory variables as expected. Unauthorized Mexican male workers had fewer years of schooling and poorer English ability, filled lower-status jobs, were more likely to be single, and were less likely to be in a union than authorized Mexican immigrant male workers. It is necessary, however, to consider these factors simultaneously by gender in order to discern which, if any, of the explanatory variables independently influenced wage outcomes among Mexican immigrant workers residing in Los Angeles County in July 2001.

Table 14.4 intimates that unauthorized residency status is likely to have negatively impacted hourly earnings among female and male foreign-born Mexican workers in Los Angeles County. The residency effect, however, appears to have been stronger among men than women. Conversely, having completed some high school had a stronger positive influence among women, and their experiences in Mexico had a relatively small negative effect. Whereas women working as operators, fabricators, and laborers or in precision, craft, and repair occupations earned higher wages than those employed in service jobs, the only independent occupational effect on men's hourly earnings was negative—those working in farming jobs fared worse than those with service jobs. Finally, being affiliated with a union had a positive impact on male wages and neighborhood context apparently had no influence.

These differential results by gender lend some support to the notion that men and women face different labor market opportunities, and in Table 14.5 I further investigate the determinants of hourly earnings among men and women separately but also by residency status. Several results warrant some discussion. First, traditional demographic and human capital characteristics are estimated to have been important determinants of unauthorized Mexican men and authorized Mexican women's wages only.[7] For authorized men and unauthorized women, none were statistically significant. Second, occupational segregation is estimated to have been more important for the same two groups for whom human capital seems to have mattered—unauthorized men and authorized women. Third, we saw in Table 14.3 that a much larger percent of authorized compared to unauthorized Mexican males were affiliated with a labor union (18.7 versus 9.8 percent), and the regression results reported here confirm that legalization conferred greater opportunity to join a union among Mexican immigrant males. This was not the case for Mexican immigrant women, for whom neighborhood context seems to have been substantially more important. While authorized Mexican males also experienced a wage boost emanating from characteristics of their neighborhoods (e.g., from higher home-ownership rates and population density), residing in neighborhoods with higher proportions of other Latinos had a much stronger positive effect on the hourly earnings of unauthorized Mexican women. This suggests that place-based social networks may be more important for female than male Mexican immigrants.

Employing these estimated coefficients and the Blinder-Oaxaca wage determinant decomposition technique allows us to see what proportions of a wage gap are attributable to individual characteristics, occupational segregation, labor union affiliation, and neighborhood characteristics. Because the female Mexican immigrant wage gap is relatively tiny (4.6 percent), I do this only for male workers. Figure 14.1 shows that most of the wage gap (67 percent) is unexplained by traditional individual characteristics (26.1 percent), occupational segregation (−1.1 percent), union member-

Table 14.5

Multilevel Regression Estimates of Hourly Wages Among Foreign-Born Mexicans by Gender and Residency Status, Ages 18–64, Los Angeles County, 2001

	Men		Women	
	Unauthorized	Authorized	Unauthorized	Authorized
Individual characteristics				
MIDDLE	0.212**	−0.065	0.247	0.076
	(0.082)	(0.151)	(0.169)	(0.115)
HIGHSC	0.350**	0.010	0.242	0.414***
	(0.140)	(0.179)	(0.200)	(0.135)
EXP	0.017	−0.005	−0.020	−0.028
	(0.032)	(0.014)	(0.018)	(0.018)
EXPSQ	−0.001	0.000	0.000	0.001*
	(0.001)	(0.000)	(0.000)	(0.000)
NOENGLSH	0.153*	0.004	−0.073	0.167*
	(0.083)	(0.128)	(0.067)	(0.090)
PROFTECH	−0.265	0.128	0.133	0.101
	(0.166)	(0.140)	(0.121)	(0.137)
FARMING	−0.649***	−0.058	0.158*	0.112
	(0.198)	(0.135)	(0.085)	(0.191)
OPERAT	−0.322**	0.069	−0.102	0.412***
	(0.156)	(0.119)	(0.098)	(0.140)
PRODUCT	−0.185	0.292	0.064	0.410**
	(0.189)	(0.185)	(0.109)	(0.192)
SINGLE	−0.261***	−0.216	−0.153	0.220**
	(0.078)	(0.140)	(0.092)	(0.089)
UNION	−0.028	0.351***	0.161	0.084
	(0.089)	(0.118)	(0.098)	(0.177)
Neighborhood context				
PCTMIN	−0.252	0.740	2.480***	−0.584
	(0.774)	(0.917)	(0.632)	(0.898)
PCTOWN	0.052	0.530**	−0.291	0.281
	(0.229)	(0.253)	(0.184)	(0.352)
POPDENSE	−0.000002	0.00001*	−0.000002	0.000001
	(0.000002)	(0.000005)	(0.000002)	(0.000004)
INTERCEPT	2.377***	1.193	−0.356	2.009**
	(0.940)	(0.996)	(0.648)	(0.996)
R-squared	39.4%	24.5%	44.5%	37.9%
N	106	143	64	86

Source: 2001 Los Angeles County Mexican Immigrant Residency Status Survey (LAC-MIRSS) and 2000 U.S. Census Summary File 3.

Note: Statistically significant at the 99 percent (***), 95 percent (**), and 90 percent (*) confidence level.

ship (3.6 percent), and neighborhood context (4.2 percent). This sizable unexplained component of the male wage gap is larger than the 52 percent obtained from Rivera-Batiz's (1999) cross-sectional analysis of unauthorized Mexican workers in the late 1980s and the 56 percent obtained

after controlling for possible unobserved individual characteristics, such as quality of education and attitude, using 1987 data.

In sum, the first empirical evidence available from the twenty-first century using random data and ecometric methods suggests that unauthorized

Mexican males (at least in Los Angeles County) continued to experience the employer-based wage discrimination detected when applying econometric methods to data collected in the late 1980s and early 1990s (Kossoudji and Cobb-Clark 2002; Rivera-Batiz 1999) and originally hinted at by social scientists employing data from the late 1970s and early 1980s (Gill and Long 1989; Heer and Falasco 1983; Morales 1983; Kossoudji and Ranney 1986; Massey 1987). Conversely, although results reported here also confirm Cobb-Clark and Kossoudji's (2000) finding that unauthorized Mexican women did not experience wage discrimination, they refute the argument made by Bailey (1985), Borjas and Tienda (1993), and Chiswick (1984) that unauthorized residency status does not have an independent and sizable depressive impact on Mexican male hourly earnings.

Conclusion

Research on labor markets by institutional economists may be distinguished by (1) its perception of a labor problem that is social in nature and may be usefully addressed with public policy, (2) its familiarity with the history of the problem in order to understand its legal, social, and political aspects, and (3) its recognition of the existence of power in labor markets (Woodbury 1988).

The perceived problem addressed here is the deleterious wage impact of the institution of unauthorized immigrant residency status among foreign-born Mexicans in Los Angeles County at the beginning of the twenty-first century. I have argued that termination of the Mexico–U.S. bracero program in 1964 and the extension of the 20,000 country-specific annual immigration quota to Mexico and other Western Hemispheric nations in 1972 essentially created the possibility that Mexican immigrants could be "unauthorized" to reside and work in the United States, whereas this had been the case only for convicts, prostitutes, Asian immigrants, and other select groups until that time. But others have written much more thoroughly on the historic political generation of unauthorized residency status among Mexicans residing in the United States (Heer 1996; Massey, Durand, and Malone 2002), and my purpose has mainly been to test only one potential socially detrimental aspect of this institution—the effect of unauthorized residency status on Mexican immigrant earnings and by extension, employment conditions—by applying multilevel econometric techniques to data collected by faculty, students, and one community-based organization. The founding fathers of American institutionalism—Veblen, Commons, and especially Mitchell—would likely have viewed such a systematic, hands-on approach as a continuation of the historic integration of demography, economics, and sociology (Grossbard-Shechtman 2002) that R.A. Gordon and certain other early institutional economists desired (Dorfman et al. 1964, 123–47; Elliott 1984, 89).

There are two main policy implications that flow (one explicitly and one implicitly) from the estimated 34 percent unauthorized-authorized Mexican male wage gap and the likelihood that most (67 percent) of this gap emanates from social forces (such as employer discrimination, public attitudes toward unauthorized immigrants and the work they do, and migrant job networks) rather than unobserved individual characteristics (such as the quality of one's education or attitudinal constitution). First, the ongoing employer discrimination against unauthorized Mexican workers first detected in the early 1980s by Heer and Falasco (1983) and Morales (1983) directly implies that more resources need to be devoted to enforcing labor, health, safety, and environmental laws in the

Figure 14.1 **Components of Wage Gap Among Foreign-Born Mexican Males by Residency Status, Percent, Los Angeles County, 2001** (in percent)

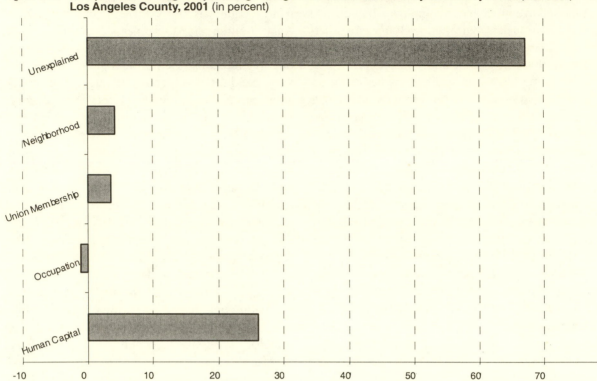

Source: 2001 Los Angeles County Mexican Immigrant Residency Status Survey (LAC-MIRSS) and 2000 U.S. Census Summary File 3.

United States and to raising the minimum wage despite the employer resistance these measures are likely to spark.

Second, the United States, like the European Union, should admit its dependence on immigrant labor. The U.S. government should at least triple the number of legal permanent resident visas available to Mexico from the absurdly low quota of 20,000 (the Dominican Republic, for instance, shares no border with the United States, is much farther away, has 10 percent of Mexico's population, but has the same quota). The United States should also create a new temporary migrant work program permitting 300,000 two-year visas annu-

ally and a new legalization program for those migrant workers who can provide credible evidence that they have resided and worked continuously in the United States for some number of years (Massey, Durand, and Malone 2002). This second category of policy recommendations does not, of course, derive explicitly from the ecometric results reported above, but is supported by much related research (Cornelius 1998; Harris 2002; Heer 1996; Marcelli 2004; Marcelli, Pastor, and Joassart 1999; Piore 1979; Schmidt and Salt 2001; Simon 1999). While their implementation is likely to reduce the differential treatment of unauthorized and authorized workers, these immigration policies alone will not eliminate the need for continued enforcement of demand-side regulations. Lower-wage U.S.-born and foreign-born workers both experience labor market constraints and opportunities based on age, gender, ethnicity, and race (Ehrenreich 2001; Hondagneu-Sotelo 2001).

Ultimately, of course, each of us must decide for ourselves the value of social science research findings and defend the policy recommendations attached to them. Because it is cross-sectional, the sample of foreign-born unauthorized and authorized Mexican immigrants employed here unfortunately does not permit a decisive separation of the unexplained component of the observed Mexican male unauthorized-authorized immigrant wage gap into unobserved individual characteristics and broader social forces. And it is a sample that is biased toward those Mexican immigrants residing in relatively densely populated areas within Los Angeles County. Nonetheless, Kossoudji and Cobb-Clark (2002) and Rivera-Batiz (1999) report similar differential employment conditions among unauthorized Mexican males as are reported here even after controlling for unobserved characteristics that may change over time. The modest contribution of this chapter, then, has been to provide an overview of the historic political generation of the institution of unauthorized residency status in the United States and the first empirical estimates of socially generated wage and employment discrimination toward unauthorized Mexican immigrant workers in the twenty-first century using random data. One promising direction for future research is suggested by our finding that unauthorized female Mexican immigrant workers' wages were higher among those who resided in neighborhoods with higher proportions of Latino-residents—subsequent labor market outcome studies should attempt to incorporate better measures of neighborhood context and social capital,

as well as native-born employee and employer attitudes toward the work unauthorized Mexican immigrants currently perform.

Notes

A grant from the University of California's Institute for Labor and Employment and support from the University of California at Los Angeles, Lewis Center for Regional Policy Studies made this research possible. I would also like to thank David Heer of the University of California at San Diego, Jorge Santibañez and Jesus Montenegro of El Colegio de la Frontera Norte (COLEF), and Susan Alva of the Coalition for Humane Immigrant Rights of Los Angeles (CHIRLA) for their assistance with designing and implementing the 2001 Los Angeles County Mexican Immigrant Residency Status Survey (LAC-MIRSS). Tony Roman of the University of Massachusetts Boston assisted me with the computation of sample weights, and I have benefited greatly from discussions with and suggestions from Paul Ong, Dell Champlin, Jan Knoedler, and Sherrie Kossoudji.

1. These particular mining laws remained in effect until 1866. Furthermore, similar northern labor migrations occurred inside what is today Mexico following the discovery of silver in Zacatecas in 1546 and from Sinaloa to Sonora to California with the spread of the Spanish presidios and missions (Lorey 1999, 17–23). The missions, in fact, are the institutional precursor of contemporary day labor hiring sites in California.

2. These estimates were computed using the 2001 Los Angeles County Mexican Immigrant Residency Status Survey (LAC-MIRSS) and the Census Bureau's 1 percent Public Use Microdata Samples (PUMS), and then compared to those provided by the U.S. Immigration and Naturalization Service (United States INS 2001).

3. Waldinger and Lichter (2003) provide a more recent and sophisticated analysis of how both immigrant networks and employer preferences in Los Angeles County influence the ethnic and racial distribution of hiring queues across industries.

4. Hierarchical or multilevel factors are said to exist when individuals are *nested* within larger geographic social units that may impact a variable under investigation. One's neighborhood, for example, may provide access to social capital or prevent social entry that is beneficial to finding higher-paying jobs (Waldinger and Lichter 2003). The term "ecometrics" (compared to "econometrics") captures the notion that factors throughout an ecosystem and across various levels (e.g., individual, neighborhood, school, workplace) may influence individual or aggregate outcomes.

5. *Period* (e.g., economic conditions in the host nation upon entry), *cohort* (e.g., mean educational attainment of one's entry group), and *duration* (or experience) effects are other factors that may also influence immigrant wage gaps, but the first two are relevant only in longitudinal analyses (Kossoudji and Cobb-Clark 2002).

6. There were a total of 2,054 census tracts and 89,614 census blocks in Los Angeles County in 2000 (our sampling frame). As a proportion of this sampling frame, therefore, the 12,476 blocks with at least 20 residents and 75 percent of their populations being Latino represented approximately 14 percent of the all blocks in the county, and our sample of 125 blocks represented 1 percent of our 20-resident, 75 percent Latino universe. The associated 108 census tracts represented 5.3 percent of all tracts defining Los Angeles County. Our original plan to sample from census blocks with at least 50 percent of their populations being Latino was changed in light of the relationship between percent foreign-born Mexican and percent Latino observed at the Public Use Microdata Area level when analyzing 1990 Public Use Microdata Sample data. We also decided to sample at the census block rather than the census tract level because our imposed sample selection criterion of 75 percent Latino was unlikely to be as efficient at locating foreign-born Mexicans as was the 25 percent foreign-born Mexican criterion applied in our 1994 LAC-MIRSS.

7. The positive coefficient on NOENGLSH is surprising but understandable if unauthorized Mexican males are more likely to fill manual labor jobs for which no or very little English language ability is required. This is indeed the case for many in Los Angeles County.

References

Aguilera, Michael Bernabé. "The Impact of Social Capital on Labor Force Participation: Evidence from the 2000 Social Capital Benchmark Survey." *Social Science Quarterly* 83, no. 3 (September 2002): 853–74.
———. "The Impact of the Worker: How Social Capital and Human Capital Influence Job Tenure of Formerly Undocumented Mexican Immigrants." *Sociological Inquiry* 73, no. 1 (February 2003): 52–83.
Bailey, Thomas. "The Influence of Legal Status on the Labor Market Impact of Immigration." *International Migration Review* 19 (1985): 220–38.
Bean, Frank D., B. Lindsay Lowell, and Lowell J. Taylor. "Undocumented Mexican Immigrants and the Earnings of Other Workers in the United States." *Demography* 25, no. 1 (1988): 35–49.
Blau, Francine and Lawrence Kahn. "Swimming Upstream: Trends in Gender Wage Differential in the 1980s." *Journal of Labor Economics* 15 (1997): 1–42.

Blinder, Alan S. "Wage Discrimination: Reduced Form and Structural Estimates." *Journal of Human Resources* 8 (1973): 436–55.
Borjas, George J., and Marta Tienda. "The Employment and Wages of Legalized Immigrants." *International Migration Review* 27, no. 4 (1993): 712–47.
Briggs, Vernon, Jr. "Immigration Policy and the U.S. Economy: An Institutional Perspective." *Journal of Economic Issues* 30, no. 2 (June 1996): 371–89.
Chiswick, Barry R. "Illegal Aliens in the United States Labor Market: Analysis of Occupational Attainment and Earnings." *International Migration Review* 18, no. 3 (1984): 714–32.
Cobb-Clark, Deborah A., and Sherrie A. Kossoudji. "Mobility in El Norte: The Employment and Occupational Changes of Unauthorized Latin American Women." *Social Science Quarterly* 81, no. 1 (March 2000): 311–24.
Commons, John R. *Races and Immigrants in America.* New York: Augustus M. Kelley, 1967 [1907].
Cornelius, Wayne A. "The Structural Embeddedness of Demand for Mexican Immigrant Labor: New Evidence from California." In *Crossings: Mexican Immigration in Interdisciplinary Perspectives*, ed. Marcelo M. Suárez-Orozco. Cambridge, MA: Harvard University Press, 1998.
Dorfman, Joseph, Clarence E. Ayres, Neil W. Chamberlain, Simon Kuznets, and Robert A. Gordon. *Institutional Economics: Veblen, Commons, and Mitchell Reconsidered.* Berkeley: University of California Press, 1964.
Ehrenreich, Barbara. *Nickel and Dimed: On (Not) Getting By in America.* New York: Metropolitan Books, 2001.
Elliott, John E. "The Institutionalist School of Political Economy." In *What Is Political Economy?* ed. David Whynes. New York: Basil Blackwell, 1984.
García y Griego, Manuel. "The Importation of Mexican Contract Laborers to the United States." In *Between Two Worlds: Mexican Immigrants in the United States*, ed. David G. Gutiérrez. Wilmington, DE: Scholarly Resources, 1996.
Gill, Andrew, and Stewart Long. "Is There an Immigration Status Wage Differential Between Legal and Undocumented Workers? Evidence from the Los Angeles Garment Industry." *Social Science Quarterly* 70, no. 1 (1989): 164–73.
Grossbard-Shechtman, Shoshana. "A Demographer on the Cusp Between Economics and Sociology: An Interview with David Heer." In *The Expansion of Economics: Toward a More Inclusive Social Science*, ed. Shoshana Grossbard-Schectman and Christopher Clague. Armonk, NY: M.E. Sharpe, 2002.

Harris, Nigel. *Thinking the Unthinkable: The Immigration Myth Exposed*. New York: I.B. Tauris, 2002.

Heer, David M. *Undocumented Mexicans in the United States*. New York: Cambridge University Press, 1990.

———. *Immigration in America's Future: Social Science Findings and the Policy Debate*. Boulder, CO: Westview Press, 1996.

Heer, David M., and Dee Falasco. "Determinants of Earnings Among Three Groups of Mexican Americans: Undocumented Immigrants, Legal Immigrants, and the Native Born." Paper presented at the annual meetings of the Population Association of America, Minneapolis, Minnesota, 1983.

Hondagneu-Sotelo, Pierrette. *Doméstica: Immigrant Workers Cleaning and Caring in the Shadows of Affluence*. Berkeley: University of California Press, 2001.

Hox, Joseph. *Multilevel Analysis: Techniques and Applications*. Mahwah, NJ: Lawrence Erlbaum Associates, 2002.

Kennedy, John F. *A Nation of Immigrants*. New York: Harper and Row, 1964.

Kossoudji, Sherrie A., and Deborah A. Cobb-Clark. "Coming Out of the Shadows: Learning About Legal Status and Wages from the Legalized Population." *Journal of Labor Economics* 20, no. 3 (2002): 598–628.

Kossoudji, Sherrie A., and Susan I. Ranney. "Wage Rates of Temporary Mexican Migrants to the U.S.: The Role of Legal Status." Discussion paper. Ann Arbor: University of Michigan, Population Studies Center, 1986.

Lorey, David E. *The U.S.–Mexican Border in the Twentieth Century*. Wilmington, DE: Scholarly Resources, 1999.

Lorimer, Frank. "The Development of Demography." In *The Study of Population: An Inventory and Appraisal*, ed. Philip M. Hauser and Otis Dudley Duncan. Chicago: University of Chicago Press, 1959.

Marcelli, Enrico A. "Undocumented Latino Immigrant Workers: The L.A. Experience." In *Illegal Immigration in America*, ed. David W. Haines and Karen E. Rosenblum. Westport, CT: Greenwood Press, 1999.

———. "Unauthorized Mexican Immigration, Day Labour, and Other Lower-wage Informal Employment in California." *Regional Studies* 38, no. 1 (2004): 1–13.

Marcelli, Enrico A., and Wayne A. Cornelius. "The Changing Profile of Mexican Migrants to the United States: New Evidence from California and Mexico." *Latin American Research Review* 36, no. 3 (2001): 105–31.

Marcelli, Enrico A., and David M. Heer. "Unauthorized Mexican Workers in the 1990 Los Angeles County

Labour Force." *International Migration* 35, no. 1 (1997): 59–83.

———. "The Unauthorized Mexican Immigrant Population and Welfare in Los Angeles County: A Comparative Statistical Analysis." *Sociological Perspectives* 41, no. 2 (1998): 279–302.

Marcelli, Enrico A., Manuel Pastor Jr., and Pascale M. Joassart. "Estimating the Effects of Informal Economic Activity: Evidence from Los Angeles County." *Journal of Economic Issues* 33, no. 3 (1999): 579–607.

Massey, Douglas S. "Do Undocumented Migrants Earn Lower Wages than Legal Immigrants? New Evidence from Mexico." *International Migration Review* 21, no. 2 (1987): 236–74.

Massey, Douglas S., Jorge Durand, and Nolan J. Malone. *Beyond Smoke and Mirrors: Mexican Immigration in an Era of Economic Integration*. New York: Russell Sage Foundation, 2002.

Mayer, Susan E., and Christopher Jencks. "Growing Up in Poor Neighborhoods: How Much Does It Matter?" *Science* 243 (1989): 1441–45.

McWilliams, Carey. *North from Mexico: The Spanish-Speaking People of the United States*. New York: Greenwood Press, 1968.

Morales, Rebecca. "Transitional Labor: Undocumented Workers in the Los Angeles Automobile Industry." *International Migration Review* 17, no. 4 (1983): 570–94.

Neale, Walter C. "Institutions." *Journal of Economic Issues* 21, no. 3 (1987): 1177–1206.

North, David S., and Marion F. Houstoun. *The Characteristics and Role of Illegal Aliens in the United States Labor Market: An Exploratory Study*. Washington, DC: Linton, 1976.

Oaxaca, Ronald. "Male-Female Wage Differentials in Urban Labor Markets." *International Economic Review* 14 (1973): 693–709.

Oaxaca, Ronald, and Michael Ransom. "On Discrimination and the Decomposition of Wage Differentials." *Journal of Econometrics* 61 (1994): 5–21.

Palloni, Alberto, Douglas S. Massey, Miguel Ceballos, Kristin Espinosa, and Michael Spittel. "Social Capital and International Migration: A Test Using Information on Family Networks." *American Journal of Sociology* 106, no. 5 (March 2001): 1262–98.

Pastor, Manuel, Jr., and Enrico A. Marcelli. "Men N the Hood: Skill, Spatial, and Social Mismatches Among Male Workers in Los Angeles County." *Urban Geography* 21, no. 6 (2000): 474–96.

Piore, Michael J. *Birds of Passage: Migrant Labor and*

Industrial Societies. New York: Cambridge University Press, 1979.

Portes, Alejandro, and Robert Bach. *Latin Journey: Cuban and Mexican Immigrants in the United States*. Berkeley: University of California Press, 1985.

Powers, Mary G., and William Seltzer. "Occupational Status and Mobility Among Undocumented Immigrants by Gender." *International Migration Review* 32, no. 1 (Spring 1998a): 21–55.

———. "Gender Differences in the Occupational Status of Undocumented Immigrants in the United States: Experience Before and After Legalization." *International Migration Review* 32, no. 4 (Winter 1998b): 1015–46.

Raudenbush, Stephen W., and Robert J. Sampson. "Econometrics: Toward a Science of Assessing Ecological Settings, with Application to Systematic Social Observation of Neighborhoods." *Sociological Methodology* 29, no. 1 (1999): 1–41.

Rivera-Batiz, Francisco L. "Undocumented Workers in the Labor Market: An Analysis of the Earnings of Legal and Illegal Mexican Immigrants in the United States." *Journal of Population Studies* 12 (1999): 91–116.

Sampson, Robert J., Jeffrey D. Morenoff, and Thomas Gannon-Rowley. "Assessing 'Neighborhood Effects': Social Processes and New Directions in Research." *Annual Review of Sociology* 28 (2002): 443–78.

Schmidt, Sandra, and John Salt. "The Development of Free Movement in the European Union." In *Caught in the Middle: Border Communities in an Era of Globalization*, ed. Demetrios G. Papademetriou and Deborah Waller Meyers. Washington, DC: Carnegie Endowment for International Peace, 2001.

Simon, Julian L. *The Economic Consequences of Immigration*. 2nd ed. Ann Arbor: University of Michigan Press, 1999.

Standart, Sister Mary Colette. "The Sonoran Migration to California, 1848–1856." In *Between Two Worlds: Mexican Immigrants in the United States*, ed. David G. Gutiérrez. Wilmington, DE: Scholarly Resources, 1996.

Stoddard, Ellwyn R. "A Conceptual Analysis of the 'Alien Invasion': Institutionalized Support of Illegal Mexican Aliens in the U.S." *International Migration Review* 10 (1976): 157–89.

Trejo, Stephen J. "Why Do Mexican Americans Earn Low Wages?" *Journal of Political Economy* 105 (1997): 1235–68.

U.S. Immigration and Naturalization Service. *Estimates of the Unauthorized Immigrant Population Residing in the United States: 1990 to 2000*. Washington, DC, 2001. http://uscis.gov/graphics/shared/aboutus/statistics/Ill_Report_1211.pdf.

Waldinger, Roger, and Michael I. Lichter. *How the Other Half Works: Immigration and the Social Organization of Labor*. Berkeley and Los Angeles: University of California Press, 2003.

Winegarden, C.R., and Lay Boon Khor. "Undocumented Immigration and Unemployment of U.S. Youth and Minority Workers: Econometric Evidence." *Review of Economics and Statistics* 73, no. 1 (1991): 105–12.

Woodbury, Stephen A. "Power in the Labor Market: Institutionalist Approaches to Labor Problems." In *Evolutionary Economics: Institutional Theory and Policy*, Vol. 2, ed. Marc R. Tool. Armonk, NY: M.E. Sharpe, 1988.

15

Retirement

Evolving Concepts and Institutions

Janice Peterson

Global population aging promises to be one of the major social issues of the twenty-first century and has important implications for the way societies define retirement.[1] In the industrialized nations of the world, people are "living longer, having fewer children and retiring sooner" (Taqi 2002, 107). These trends are raising concerns among prominent researchers and policy makers about pension financing and future labor supply. A widely advocated policy response is to increase the labor force participation and extend the working lives of older people by increasing eligibility ages for public pension benefits and restricting early retirement options. In this context, the concept of retirement is moving away from one of no work after a particular age (Taqi 2002, 107; Schulz 2002, 96).

As the concept of retirement changes to include increasing amounts of work, many aging and retirement policy researchers, as well as advocates for older people, argue that workplace institutions and the nature of work itself must also change. Increases in the flexibility of working time and in opportunities for retraining, as well as an expansion of what society considers work, are examples of the institutional and attitudinal changes that are seen to be necessary components of any effort to lengthen the working lives of older people.

Institutionalist labor economics has the potential to contribute a great deal to the policy discussion concerning older workers and the changing meaning of retirement. Traditional discussions of aging and retirement trends often miss the broader social and economic context of these changes and may limit the scope of policy discussions. Taking a broader perspective can contribute to the development of comprehensive policies to address the needs and challenges of aging populations. This chapter argues that institutionalist labor economics is consistent with broader, more comprehensive approaches to aging policy (such as those associated with the concept of active aging) and provides a useful framework for developing progressive policies for older workers.

This chapter begins with a brief overview of the key trends in population aging and retirement practices, and the concerns surrounding these trends, which lie behind the growing research and policy interest in increasing work among older people in industrialized nations. The next section presents the concept of active aging as an alternative to traditional economic approaches to older worker policies, highlighting active aging discussions of pensions, employment, citizenship, and health. The final section seeks to identify key insights from institutionalist labor economics that are particularly relevant to current policy discussions concerning older workers and changing conceptions of retirement. This section highlights similarities between institutionalist and active aging approaches, identifies core values in institutionalist labor economics, and discusses the relevance of these institutionalist core values for the development of older worker policies.

Population Aging and Retirement: Trends and Concerns

Population aging is commonly defined as an increase in the number or percentage of people who have lived to or beyond a certain age, typically age sixty-five (National Research Council 2001, 30–31). Long-term trends toward lower fertility and lower mortality have generated growing numbers and proportions of older populations throughout the world. In addition, the age structure of the populations in many industrialized nations also reflects the significant but transitory fertility increase of the post–World War II baby boom (National Research Council 2001, 1). The population aged sixty-five and older increased by 289 million globally over the second half of the twentieth century and by 99 million over the last decade (National Research Council 2001, 31). The share of the population aged sixty-five and older in the industrialized nations is predicted to increase modestly between 2000 and 2010; after 2010, however, the numbers and proportions of elderly persons are projected to increase rapidly as large postwar birth cohorts in many nations begin to reach age sixty-five (National Research Council 2001, 31–32).

While their populations have been aging, many industrialized nations have also experienced a trend toward earlier retirement over the last half-century.

Retirement—defined as an age-related withdrawal from the workforce—is a historically recent phenomenon.[2] Prior to the Industrial Revolution, older people were not "retired"; the emergence of retirement as a phase of life is generally linked to the growth in economic productivity and increase in leisure accompanying industrialization (Schulz 2002, 85). In the United States, for example, two out of three American men over the age of sixty-five were employed at the beginning of the twentieth century. In 1950, less than half of men age sixty-five and older held a job, and by 1985, just 16 percent of men over the age sixty-five were employed or actively seeking work (Burtless and Quinn 2002, 3).

The declining labor force participation of older people—particularly older males—has been a dramatic economic trend in many parts of the world.[3] While this decline appears to have leveled off in many industrialized nations in the last decade, it has typically done so at historically low rates (National Research Council 2001, 8). This trend toward earlier retirement in many industrialized nations has been widely studied and is seen to reflect a number of factors, including increasing affluence, changing social norms, the structure of social insurance programs and private pensions, and the use in many nations of early retirement as a way to reduce the number of employees during periods of downsizing and restructuring (Burtless and Quinn 2002, 3–5; National Research Council 2001, 66–68, 78–85; Jepsen 2002, 34–35).

Population aging in many ways represents a human success story: "For the first time in history, many societies have the opportunity to age" (National Research Council 2001, 30). But it also poses important challenges for the researchers and policy makers of the twenty-first century. The projected aging trends, particularly in combination with the shift toward earlier retirement that has taken place in many nations, are raising concerns—and, in some circles, extreme alarm—about future pension financing (particularly public pensions) and future labor supply. While there is general agreement that these aging and retirement trends are significant, there is very little agreement on the extent to which they constitute a "crisis" or on how to redefine retirement in aging societies.

Population aging and trends toward earlier retirement raise concerns about public pension financing because, taken together, they mean that there is a decline in the ratio of those who are engaged in economic activity to those who have withdrawn from economic activity. This implies that the ratio of those who contribute to public pension systems to those who draw benefits from them is also declining. Many authorities argue that if these trends persist, they will pose a threat to the financial viability of public pension systems (Taqi 2002, 107).

Some analysts argue that public social insurance schemes are already in a state of crisis and will not survive the impact of demographic aging. The World Bank, for example, in its influential volume *Averting the Old Age Crisis*, writes that in the face of population aging and the decline of informal support systems for the aged (such as extended families), "formal systems, such as government backed pensions, have proved both unsustainable and very difficult to reform. . . . The result is a looming old age crisis that threatens not only the old but their children and grandchildren, who must shoulder, directly or indirectly, much of the increasingly heavy burden of providing for the aged" (World Bank 1994, xiii).

Population aging and retirement trends also raise concerns that the future supply of labor will be inadequate to meet the needs of key economic sectors and to sustain economic growth (Taqi 2002, 108). Some analysts see contracting workforces

leading to global macroeconomic crises. Paul Hewitt of the Center for Strategic and International Studies (CSIS), for example, writes that rapidly depopulating nations face the threat of "aging recessions," whose negative consequences may infect other nations through global economic relations. In addition, he argues that the "social crisis of labor shortages" will replace the problems of unemployment and thus undermine the rationale for the welfare states established in the industrialized world after World War II (Hewitt 2002).

From the perspective of aging-induced pension and workforce crises, current retirement practices and institutions in the industrialized world are seen to be unsustainable and a source of large intergenerational inequities. Hewitt, for example, argues:

> Today, throughout the industrial world, retirement has become a lengthy period of state-supported leisure for surging populations of retirees, a high percentage of whom, thanks to modern medicine and less disabling forms of work, remain able-bodied well into their seventies. Until now, this state of affairs has been a tolerable form of excess only because enough young people were willing to bear the increasing economic burden. (Hewitt 2002, 14)

Drawing on this perspective, proposals to scale back traditional pay-as-you-go public pension and other social insurance programs, and to restructure such programs to promote (and in some cases require) the increased labor force participation of older people, dominate many policy discussions on the future of retirement in the industrialized world.[4]

Although aging crisis arguments are influential, many scholars challenge the crisis interpretation and examine aging and retirement issues from alternative perspectives. James Schulz of Brandeis University, for example, argues, "One of the biggest hoaxes perpetuated in the industrialized world today is the promulgation of the notion that the ageing of the population around the world has created a 'crisis'" (Schulz 2002, 86). Schultz argues that aging crisis interpretations are "almost always supported solely by demographic projections of rising 'dependency ratios' and projections of sharply increasing social security tax rates based on controversial assumptions" (87). Dalmer Hoskins of the International Social Security Association echoes this argument, calling on the research and policy community to bring "some balance to the discussion of demographic ageing and its implications for social security" (Hoskins 2002, 15).

Research on aging from this alternative perspective recognizes that the meaning of old age is socially constructed—it varies across less and more affluent nations and has evolved within industrialized societies over time—and that policy responses to population aging are malleable. Until recently, in the industrialized world, "the stereotypical view of individual aging was one of overall decline and certain inevitable outcomes: cessation of work, increasing disability, deteriorating social networks, and often a descent into poverty" (National Research Council 2001, 17). Today, however, we know that the experiences and characteristics of older people are as varied as those of younger ones in many ways. Resistance to change in the attitudes and practices regarding older persons, however, can pose challenges to the development of progressive aging policies.

One promising approach to these challenges is to recast the discussion of aging and retirement policies into an active aging context.[5] The concept of active aging, which emerged in the 1990s, is closely associated with the work of the World Health Organization (WHO), which has called for a new paradigm of aging: "one that views older people as active participants in an age integrated society and as active contributors" (Schulz 2002, 96). Active aging proponent Alan Walker of Sheffield University defines active aging as an intergenerational strategy, seeking to involve "all age groups in the process of ageing actively across the whole of the life course" (Walker 2002, 124). The maintenance of intergenerational solidarity is an important feature of active aging approaches. Walker argues that active aging "is about all of our futures and not just about older people. We are all stakeholders in this endeavor" (Walker 2002, 124–25).

From an active aging perspective, changing retirement practices and institutions are viewed not in the context of rolling back years of state-sponsored leisure that are burdening society, but as part of a larger vision of a "society for all ages" in which "everyone has a place and to which all have a chance to contribute without distinction of age or any other personal characteristics" (Sigg 2002, 8). Promoting employment is an important part of an active aging strategy, but it is approached quite differently than it is in more traditional approaches to increasing the labor force participation of older people. Active aging suggests a "general lifestyle strategy for the preservation of physical and mental health as people age, rather than simply trying to make them work longer" (Walker 2002, 124).

Older Worker Policies: Active Aging Approaches

To date, policy discussions of older workers have typically focused on ways to increase their labor force participation.[6] Discussions of increasing the labor force participation of older people have, in turn, focused largely on changing the work incentives in public and private pension systems. This emphasis reflects traditional economic analyses of retirement decision-making, which model the retirement decision as a rational, individual choice based on a tradeoff between income and leisure.

Public and private pension systems are seen to include features that have distorted this decision-making process, including incentives that have led to the increase in early retirement. In order to correct these distortions, it is recommended that governments restructure pensions to change these incentives by, for example, increasing statutory retirement ages and restricting provisions for early retirement.[7]

Active aging approaches are based on a very different understanding of retirement decision-making. While the structure of pension systems is viewed as one potentially important factor, retirement decision-making is seen to be the complex result of interaction between many actors in the economy. From this perspective, the increase in early retirement reflects more than individual choices between work and leisure; it also reflects public policy choices, the practices of trade unions and governments, as well as societal and employer attitudes toward older workers. Consequently, active aging approaches call for an integrated and comprehensive policy strategy for older workers, not one exclusively targeting pensions and other social insurance programs (Jepsen 2002, 25–26, 43–46).

Active aging approaches recognize the interconnected nature of pensions, employment, citizenship, and health, and attempt to join them in a new vision of aging and retirement (Walker 2002, 121). Active aging approaches to public pension reform, for example, focus on the need to increase the flexibility of retirement options, as opposed to simply increasing statutory retirement ages. Most pension systems in the industrialized nations were established when lifetime (male) employment was common and full retirement at a specified age provided "a clearly defined end to working life" (Walker 2002, 126). Today, however, fewer and fewer workers move directly from full-time employment into full-time retirement, and a significant proportion of older people want to continue working full- or part-time and retire more gradually, rather than retire at a fixed age. Active aging approaches call for making pension systems more "employment friendly" and responsive to the diversity among older people by instituting flexible retirement ages and partial pension options (Walker 2002, 126–27).

Active aging proponents argue, however, that while pension issues are important, the debate over pension reform should not be allowed to obscure other relevant and complex issues, such as the labor market prospects of older workers (Sigg 2002, 6). Traditional approaches to older worker policies that focus on increasing pension ages without addressing ageism and the labor market barriers faced by older workers threaten to "consign older workers to exclusion, low income and, eventually, inadequate pensions" (Walker 2002, 18). Further, without efforts to encourage employers to recruit and retain older workers, making pensions more "employment friendly" is not very meaningful.[8]

Ali Taqi of the International Labor Office (ILO) calls for addressing the issue of older people and work with the objective of "promoting greater equality of opportunity" (Taqi 2002, 112). This, he argues, will require progress in three areas of labor market policy: strengthening the position of older people in the labor market by promoting training and workplace flexibility; changing attitudes toward older workers; and prohibiting age discrimination in employment (107, 113). While the active labor market strategies for older workers discussed in different national contexts vary in detail, these three areas of labor market policy reform are core components to this approach to developing older worker policies (see, for example, Jepsen, Foden, and Hutsebaut 2002).

Lifelong learning is one of the cornerstones of active labor market strategies for older workers.

While having opportunities to improve and update knowledge and skills is important for all workers, it may be especially critical for people whose education and occupational training were acquired years ago (Taqi 2002, 113). Further, lifelong learning in an active aging context means not just updating the skills and training required to stay in the workforce longer, but acquiring the skills and knowledge necessary to engage in new types of work and pursue second careers for workers who desire or need to do something different as they age.

Another important aspect of improving access to labor markets is "making work and the working environment friendlier to older people"—a matter both of "attracting older people to employment and of offering realistic possibilities for them to seek jobs" (Taqi 2002, 114). Polices directed toward this end include the promotion of opportunities for part-time work and other forms of workplace flexibility, such as adapting work organization and job content to the needs of older people and allowing people to shift into different types of jobs as they age (Taqi 2002, 114). Thus, active aging calls for increased flexibility in working time, work practices, and the type of work available, recognizing that people may need not only to work less but to work differently in different phases of their working lives.

Negative attitudes toward older workers are found to be one of the principle obstacles to increasing employment opportunities for older people (Taqi 2002, 114). Commonly accepted stereotypes and preconceptions about older workers include beliefs that older workers are less productive, that their mental, physical, and creative capabilities decline with age, and that they are unable or unwilling to undergo training and learn new things. Research has found many of these beliefs to be untrue and/or irrelevant to job requirements. Educational initiatives to counter negative stereo-

types and foster more positive attitudes toward older workers are a critical component of an active aging approach (Taqi 2002, 115). Further, active strategies for older workers call for the prohibition of age discrimination in employment. While most industrialized countries have enacted legislation prohibiting employment discrimination on the basis of race, sex, religion, and various other grounds, very few have laws banning age discrimination (Taqi 2002, 116).

Employment remains the primary mechanism for social inclusion in industrialized economies, so promoting employment opportunities for older people is an important part of active aging strategies. One thing that distinguishes active aging from traditional approaches, however, is that remaining active in paid employment is viewed as only one response to the challenges of aging.[9] Active aging approaches focus on a broader range of activities than those normally associated with paid work, such as volunteer work in the community, and emphasize the "inclusion of older people as full citizens" (Walker 2002, 124). Activity is defined to include "all meaningful pursuits which contribute to the well-being of the individual concerned, his or her family, the local community or society at large" (Walker 2002, 124) and is conceptualized in terms of new forms of "citizen participation" (Schulz 2002, 99). Recognizing the value of and encouraging activities not currently counted as employment are seen to have the potential both to enrich the lives of older individuals and to provide social support to aging populations (Walker 2002, 132–33).

Active aging approaches also emphasize the central importance of health, and the connections between health and activity. An individual's health can determine both level and type of activity (ill health, for example, is an important factor in early retirement), but activity can also be an important contributor to good health. Thus, active aging proponents emphasize that strategies must "be sensitive to this relationship and aim to recognize and prevent ill-health and disability rather than assuming that everyone can be equally active" (Walker 2002, 131). Traditional approaches to increasing the labor force participation of older people by increasing pension ages without addressing possible negative impacts of employment on health run the risk of both reducing the quality of life of older people and increasing disability and health costs (Walker 2002, 130–32).

Active aging proponents also emphasize the necessity of recognizing and addressing the diversity that exists among older people in any policy strategy aimed at extending working lives. Working later in life can have very different implications for the "large numbers of workers . . . engaged in arduous and uninteresting work" than for those in less physically difficult and/or more fulfilling jobs (Hoskins 2002, 14). Poor health is more likely to be an issue for older workers in physically demanding jobs, who are also likely to have lower incomes and fewer alternative employment options. In addition, women's retirement decisions and situations often differ from men's for a number of reasons, including care-taking responsibilities throughout their life course, different labor market earnings while employed, and, in many cases, different provisions in public pension policies (Hoskins 2002, 14; Jepsen 2002, 36–38).

In summary, traditional approaches to rethinking the meaning of retirement in aging societies typically focus on reducing the amount of leisure enjoyed in retirement by raising the age at which individuals withdraw from the labor market and recasting the definition of retirement to include increasing amounts of paid employment. Active aging strategies also envision retirement as more than "stopping paid employment and engaging in more leisure activities" (Schulz 2002, 96). Active aging strategies, however, define work and activity more broadly to include pursuits that do not involve wage labor or production for profit. Retirement is viewed as, ideally, a "period of life where a variety of special activities compete with the traditional activities of work and leisure for the attention and time of older people" (Schulz 2002, 96).

Insights from Institutional Economics

As an approach to social inquiry and policy analysis, institutional economics has much in common with the concept of active aging and active aging strategies. The institutionalist social value criterion of instrumental efficiency—the conviction that "the direction is forward which provides for the continuity of human life and the noninvidious recreation of community through the instrumental use of knowledge" (Tool 1979, 293)—is consistent with the guiding vision of active aging approaches—the "society for all ages" where "everyone has a place and to which all have a chance to contribute without distinction of age or any other personal characteristics" (Sigg 2002, 8). Like active aging approaches, institutionalist analysis is holistic, viewing the "fabric of society as a woven pattern that must be appraised and adjusted in as integrative a manner as possible" (Petr 1984, 8). Institutional economics is also fundamentally activist in nature (Petr 1984, 7), grounded in the belief that economic analysis should be directed toward "the resolution of real problems facing real people in real political economies" (Tool 1979, 293).

The institutionalist tradition in labor economics embodies this instrumental, holistic, activist approach and is deeply rooted in the conviction that "labor economics is inextricably linked to practice" and dedicated to "identifying actual labor problems and implementing various solutions to mitigate them" (Gimble 1991, 628). Several key themes—or core values—that emerge in the works of institutionalist labor economists are particularly relevant to the discussion of older workers. Perhaps most fundamentally, institutionalist labor economics has, since its inception, rejected market-oriented theories that treat labor as simply another factor input to be used in a production process (Gimble 1991, 628). Institutionalist labor economics has instead focused on the institutions and practices that make labor and the work process a complex, cultural phenomenon (Gimble 1991, 637). Thus, institutionalist labor economics embodies the core values that labor is not a mere commodity and that labor markets cannot be disembedded from their broader institutional and cultural settings.

Institutionalist labor economics also embodies the core value that work should be a source of dignity and self-fulfillment. For institutionalist labor economists, the crucial question has always been: "what types of job structures or organizations of work foster individual creativity, self-motivation, human development, self-fulfillment, noninvidiousness and nonalienation in the work process" (Gimble 1991, 637–38). That is, the focus of institutionalist labor analysis and policy is on how employment can be structured to "foster the 'instinct of workmanship' serving as both a means and an end for human development" (Figart 2003a, 322).

Building on these core values, contemporary institutionalist labor economists have focused attention on the structures of invidious employment and on policies to eliminate invidious distinctions in employment processes and workplace practices. Institutionalist economist Deborah M. Figart defines invidious employment as that which "stigmatizes categories of work and workers, creating status-based hierarchies in labor markets. Distinctions between high- and low-wage jobs, long hours and short hours, men and women, whites and people of color, and paid and unpaid labor create value judgments about the relative worth of economic contributions" (Figart 2003b, 403). Thus, she argues that progressive labor policy should have as its goal the promotion of noninvidious employment. Noninvidious employment means that workers should not be excluded from full and equal participation in the workplace, nor should the value of their contributions be distorted, on the basis of irrelevant personal characteristics. Further, noninvidious employment recognizes that "the work of society is more than paid work" and that "life's work, in its many forms, creates value and should be rewarded accordingly" (Figart 2003b, 380).

The core values of institutionalist labor economics provide important insights for the development of active labor market strategies for older workers, and for appropriately embedding these strategies in a broader active aging approach. Institutionalist labor economics provides a rich understanding of changing retirement practices, based on the fundamental premise that labor markets, workplace and work practices are culturally embedded institutions. This approach provides the necessary context for understanding both the decisions to leave the workforce at different ages and the barriers older people may face in trying to remain in the workplace. A detailed analysis of the financial incentives of pension systems is of little value in understanding retirement behavior without taking into account the broader legal and economic institutions, social attitudes, and norms that shape this behavior.

Further, if policies to encourage longer working lives are to be noncoercive and life-enhancing, they must be designed and implemented with an understanding and conviction that workers are not mere commodities to be exchanged in markets and used as inputs in a production process. Older people are diverse in their personal characteristics, desires, and work histories. Class and gender differences can make the prospect of extending working lives an unbearable burden for some, while it can be the source of new opportunities and enrichment for others.

The core institutionalist value that work can and should embody the "instinct of workmanship" must be central to the development of older worker policies. The belief that job structures and work practices should foster individual creativity and human development raises quality-of-work and working-life issues that are fundamental to the well-being of all workers, but are perhaps brought into a particularly sharp focus in the discussion of extending working lives. Studies find that many older people want to work later in life if they can do work that is meaningful in an environment that is welcoming and flexible. Policies that seek to extend the working lives of older people are more likely to be successful, and more likely to be progressive, in the context of a policy agenda to promote good jobs and improve the quality of working life for all workers.

Institutionalist definitions of "good jobs" include job structures and work practices that "enable workers to participate in family, community, and political life" (Figart 2003b, 380). The arguments that "the work of society is more than paid work" and that "life's work, in its many forms, creates value and should be rewarded accordingly"(Figart 2003b, 380) are relevant to discussions of increasing work among older people and are consistent with active aging arguments for defining the activities and contributions of older people more broadly than paid employment. Attributing value to the unpaid work of women and men in families, communities, and other spheres throughout the life course is critically important to efforts to broaden the discussion of changing retirement practices.

And finally, the goal of striving for noninvidious employment speaks directly to the necessity of fighting age discrimination in employment. Many active aging proponents see fighting ageism and prohibiting age discrimination in employment as the necessary conditions that must be met before other active strategies for older workers can be considered. Although, to date, institutionalist labor economists have focused more attention on other forms of invidious distinction and discrimination in the labor market, fighting age discrimination is consistent with the goals of institutionalist scholarship and activism and should receive more attention.

Conclusion

While there is room to debate the specifics of population aging, it is a phenomenon that is placing various types of pressures on existing institutions and fostering institutional change. Of particular importance are the policy proposals by many researchers and policy makers in the industrialized nations to extend the working lives of older people. These proposals commonly focus on increasing the eligibility ages of public pension systems and restricting early retirement options. In this context, the concept of retirement is evolving to include increasing amounts of paid employment among older people.

Policy proposals to increase retirement ages and the labor force participation of older people in many cases reflect the view that population aging constitutes a crisis that, in conjunction with contemporary retirement practices, is threatening the solvency of public pension systems and economic growth, as well as causing severe intergenerational inequities. The concept of active aging provides an alternative approach to addressing the challenges of population aging and rethinking the meaning of retirement—an approach that strives to strengthen intergenerational solidarity and to promote the full participation of older people in society in a variety of ways.

Active aging proponents emphasize that older worker policy discussions should not focus solely on restructuring pension systems, but should also take into account the labor market opportunities of older people, the value of their nonmarket work, and their health. Active aging approaches to pension reform focus on making pension systems more flexible, allowing those who wish to remain employed and retire gradually the opportunity to do so, rather than increasing eligibility ages. In addition to gradual or phased retirement options, older people may need or desire the option to work shorter hours or in different types of jobs over an extended period of time. Active aging proponents call for increasing the availability of various forms of workplace flexibility, strengthening the position of older people in the labor market through lifelong learning, and fighting negative attitudes toward older workers and age discrimination in employment.

Institutionalist labor economics is consistent with active aging approaches and provides insights for active labor market policies for older workers. Core values drawn from institutionalist labor economics—for example, that labor is not a commodity; that labor markets cannot be disembedded from their cultural setting; that work should foster human dignity and self-fulfillment; and that labor policies should promote noninvidious employment—can support and guide the development of specific active labor market policies. The institutionalist commitment to the full participation and noninvidious inclusion of all people in society can contribute to the establishment of a realistic and

humane discussion of older workers and the changing meaning of retirement in aging societies.

Notes

The views expressed in this chapter are those of the author and do not necessarily reflect the views of the U.S. General Accounting Office.

1. Although population aging is most often associated with industrialized nations, older populations in developing countries "typically are growing more rapidly than those in the industrialized world" (National Research Council 2001, 35). This has important consequence for economic development in these nations (see, for example, Apt 2002).

2. The definition of retirement is a topic of debate and raises a number of important questions: Should retirement refer to withdrawal from paid employment only? Should leaving the workforce to care for a sick family member or because of a disability constitute retirement? At what age does leaving the workforce constitute retirement? (Shaw and Hill, 2002). Typically, researchers identify those who are retired based on two characteristics: nonparticipation in the paid labor force and the receipt of retirement income. However, not everyone who receives some form of retirement income is considered to be retired (e.g., someone who has retired from the military after twenty years of service and is pursuing a second career), and some people who receive most of their income from retirement programs, and are considered to be retired, continue to work for pay (Purcell 2002, 1).

3. It is important to note that declining older male labor force participation has not been experienced in many developing countries, and even among the industrialized nations there are important differences (National Research Council 2001, 69).

4. Concerns about an aging crisis, for example, inform the World Bank's approach to social security reform—a "three-pillar approach" including "a publicly managed system with mandatory participation and the limited goal of reducing poverty among the old; a privately managed, mandatory savings system; and voluntary savings" (World Bank 1994, xiv). The 2002 Commission on Global Aging of the Center for Strategic and International Studies also draws on aging crisis arguments to support a variety of aging policy recommendations, such as scaling back pay-as-you-go pension and other social insurance programs and instituting pension system changes to increase the labor force participation of older people (Center for Strategic and International Studies 2002).

5. The definition of active aging discussed here draws on the work of Alan Walker and other contributors to a spe-

cial edition of the *International Social Security Review* (2002), the journal of the International Social Security Association.

6. The definition of "older worker" varies widely and can refer to workers as young as forty years of age. In the international literature, older workers are generally defined as those fifty years of age and older. Consequently, discussions of older workers may address either the issue of reducing early retirement—that is, leaving the workforce before the statutory retirement age (typically sixty-five years of age)—or the issue of encouraging work after the statutory retirement age (see, for example, United States General Accounting Office 2003).

7. See National Research Council (2001, chapter 3), and Jepsen (2002) for an overview of this literature.

8. There is a growing literature on active labor market strategies for older workers that reflects these concerns (see, for example, Jepsen, Foden, and Hutsebaut 2002).

9. The concept of active aging was preceded by the concept of productive aging, developed during the 1980s. Productive aging was defined as "any activity by an older individual that produced goods and services, or developed the capacity to produce goods and services, or develops the capacity to produce them, whether they are paid for or not" (Walker 2002, 123). Critics of the productive aging concept argued that even though productivity was being defined more broadly then in traditional economics, it still presented an overly economistic vision of late-life activity. Active aging approaches seek to define activity more broadly and to place more emphasis on quality of life and mental and physical well-being (Schulz 2002, 95; Walker 2002, 124).

References

Apt, Nana Araba. "Ageing and the Changing Role of the Family and Community: An African Perspective." *International Social Security Review* 55, no. 1 (January–March 2002): 39–47.

Burtless, Gary, and Joseph F. Quinn. "Is Working Longer the Answer for an Aging Workforce?" Issue Brief, Center for Retirement Research, Boston College, December 2002.

Center for Strategic and International Studies. *Meeting the Challenge of Global Aging*. Washington, DC: Center for Strategic and International Studies, 2002.

Figart, Deborah M. "Labor Market Policy: One Institutionalist's Agenda." *Journal of Economic Issues* 37, no. 2 (June 2003a): 315–22.

———. "Policies to Provide Non-Invidious Employment." In *Institutionalist Analysis of Economic Policy*, ed. Marc R. Tool and Paul D. Bush. Boston: Kluwer Academic Publishers, 2003b.

Gimble, Daniel. "Institutional Labor Market Theory and the Veblenian Dichotomy." *Journal of Economic Issues* 25, no. 3 (September 1991): 625–48.

Hewitt, Paul. "The End of the Postwar Welfare State." *Washington Quarterly* 25 (Spring 2002): 7–16.

Hoskins, Dalmer. "Thinking About Ageing Issues." *International Social Security Review* 55, no. 1 (January–March 2002): 13–20.

Jepsen, Maria. "The Scientific Debate on Older Workers." In *Active Strategies for Older Workers in the European Union*, ed. Maria Jepsen, David Foden, and Martin Hutsebaut. Brussels: European Trade Union Institute, 2002.

Jepsen, Maria, David Foden, and Martin Hutsebaut, eds. *Active Strategies for Older Workers in the European Union*. Brussels: European Trade Union Institute, 2002.

National Research Council. *Preparing for an Aging World*. Washington, DC: National Academy Press, 2001.

Petr, Jerry L. "Fundamentals of an Institutionalist Perspective on Economic Policy." *Journal of Economic Issues* 18, no. 1 (March 1984): 1–17.

Purcell, Patrick J. "Older Workers: Employment and Retirement Trends." *CRS Report to Congress*, October 18, 2002.

Schulz, James. "The Evolving Concept of 'Retirement': Looking Forward to the Year 2050." *International Social Security Review* 55, no. 1 (January–March 2002): 85–105.

Shaw, Lois, and Catherine Hill. "Retirement Decision-Making and Economic Outcomes for Men and Women." In *Macmillan Encyclopedia of Aging*, ed. David Ekerdt. New York: Macmillan, 2002.

Sigg, Roland. "Introduction: The Challenge of Ageing for Social Security." *International Social Security Review* 55, no. 1 (January–March 2002): 3–12.

Taqi, Ali. "Older People, Work and Equal Opportunity." *International Social Security Review* 55, no. 1 (January–March 2002): 107–20.

Tool, Marc R. *The Discretionary Economy*. Santa Monica, CA: Goodyear, 1979.

United States General Accounting Office. *Older Workers: Policies in Other Nations to Increase Labor Force Participation*. GAO-03–307, February 2003.

Walker, Alan. "A Strategy for Active Ageing." *International Social Security Review* 55, no. 1 (January–March 2002): 121–37.

World Bank. *Averting the Old Age Crisis*. New York: Oxford University Press, 1994.

16

Organizing the Service Sector

From "Labor" to "Stakeholder" Unionism

George DeMartino

The labor movement in the United States is by now well into its fifth consecutive decade of decline. Having reached its apex in the mid-1950s, the movement has suffered a loss of union density across the private sector and a corresponding erosion in moral legitimacy and political leverage. By all accounts, the past fifty years have been devastating for America's unions and its workers.

The demise of unionism has generated great concern among labor leaders, activists, and supporters beyond labor's ranks. There now exists a massive literature that examines the causes of labor's crisis and offers diverse strategies for labor renewal. In this chapter, I will pass over this literature in order to reserve space to advance an alternative account of labor's difficulties and an alternative suggestion for labor reform. Unlike much of the existing literature, and in keeping with the institutionalist tradition, I want to turn our attention to what I call "union identity." I will suggest that reorienting our attention to union identity opens up all sorts of strategies for reform. Indeed, I will present one possible new union identity, which I call "stakeholder unionism." This kind of unionism would welcome as full union members diverse constituencies who share the labor movement's commitment to justice for the marginalized, but

who are now excluded from the movement by restrictive notions of just who can be a union member. To make this case, I will provide a case study of a recent health care strike in Denver, Colorado, where I live. I will provide an account of this strike as it actually occurred and then present an alternative, fictitious account of how a reinvented labor movement might have waged this struggle. The goal of this exercise is to suggest that achievable avenues for union reinvention are available—avenues that might begin to reverse labor's fortunes in a way that meets the needs of not just waged workers but other marginalized groups in society as well.

Exploring Union Identity

For the sake of brevity, let me dispense quickly with the contemporary debate about the causes of the contemporary union crisis (DeMartino 1997a).[1] On one side stand those who emphasize factors and forces external to the union movement—factors such as globalization, industrial restructuring, and adverse ideological changes in the Democratic Party and in society. Each of these factors is taken to have produced an environment that is hostile to the interests of labor. This kind of explanation predominates among union officials and other insiders. On the other side of the debate are those who emphasize factors internal to the union movement itself. These analysts typically cite the conservatism of union leaders and autocratic union governance as the primary causes of union decline. In this account, unions are seen to have forfeited their legitimacy by adopting a "pure-and-simple" or "business" orientation that accepts the broad contours of capitalist society and which merely seeks a better deal for the employed workers that unions represent. Notably absent from business unionism is fervor for broad social justice and the courage to pursue it even when the odds are long. This view predominates among left-leaning observers and many progressive union activists. Advocates of this view want to hold labor accountable for its own demise and to inaugurate internal reforms that can reinvigorate labor from the inside.

Both positions in this debate identify important factors that must be included in any comprehensive account of labor's difficulties. But both accounts suffer from a failure to pursue sufficiently the question of union identity. By union identity I refer to these questions: what is a union, and consequently, who is a legitimate union member? By virtue of what set of practices or circumstances should a person be considered a potential constituent of the union movement? To date, most union leaders and their progressive critics have focused exclusively on a person's employment status. It is a commonplace that unions are first and foremost organizations of and for waged workers—they are *labor* unions, after all, not student unions, or environmental associations, or consumer organizations. This is what they have been, what they are, and what they should be. Though unions form all sorts of coalitions with these other groups, these are to be external linkages between what are and should be distinct organizations. The two camps in the debate over labor's decline therefore share an important commitment to employment-based collective bargaining as *a*, if not *the* chief union strategy. Taking this commitment as a given, the debate over the union crisis contests matters such as how unions might restore their ability to organize workers and bargain effectively with employers.

Breaking with this consensus, I would suggest that the contemporary crisis requires a deeper analysis, one that reexamines the matter of union identity. This analysis serves to remind us that the contemporary union crisis is a crisis of one particular union model, and it suggests that the project to restore the union movement might therefore be as simple (or as difficult) as envisioning and enacting an alternative union identity.

Enterprise Unionism and Contested Commodities

Let us begin, then, by posing and answering a question: what is the economic identity of contemporary unionism? How should we theorize unions from an economic perspective? Most institutionalist and other work on this question focuses on their effects in labor markets, but I want to turn the focus back on unions as institutions themselves, internally. Following the work of Frank Annunziato (1990), I suggest that U.S. unions today might fruitfully be theorized as capitalist business enterprises.[2] This form of unionism emerged early in the twentieth century during a period of labor foment and experimentation, and has been consolidated especially since the purge of Communists from the movement in the 1950s. It bears emphasis that to theorize unions as enterprises is not to say they are just that—they are many other things besides (but so is General Motors, for that matter). Nor is it to say that they are literally capitalist enterprises—in many respects, they are clearly not that. The exercise is predicated on the belief that theorizing them in this way might yield critical insights about the causes of the union movement's demise and, equally important, point to new, viable strategies for revitalization.

Just like other service sector enterprises, unions today sell a service commodity for a fee to their customers. Following Annunziato, let us call this commodity "union representation." It is secured through the principal union practice of employment-based collective bargaining. The terms of the labor contract secured through bargaining provide due process in cases of discipline, wage increases, a degree of job security, and so forth. Unlike the terms and conditions of employment offered by employers in nonunion environments, the terms of the labor contract may not be revoked or altered unilaterally at the employer's whim. Hence, the commodity union representation transforms "benefits" into "rights," at least for the duration of the contract. Unions attempt to market this service commodity through organizing drives, during which the union must convince potential customers of their need for the service. Payment for this service takes the form of union dues.

This claim may seem absurd to those who have participated in or are knowledgeable about labor affairs. Union representation has several attributes that certainly seem to disqualify it as a commodity. Let me try to anticipate and respond to one likely objection in this regard. The production of the service union representation and its appearance on the market generally require extraordinary sacrifice and effort from the unions's potential and current customers. Union members must sometimes be enlisted in protracted struggles to secure this commodity. And these struggles often draw in many other people in the community whose activism is required to secure union rights. Securing and sustaining union representation is therefore a continuous campaign, a struggle, a mission —it is something far different from a trip to Wal-Mart to buy a pair of jeans.

Most commodities, of course, entail no such struggle. But this feature of the union's commodity is hardly unprecedented. Consider, for instance, handguns, explosives, abortions, pornography, marijuana and other narcotics, fee-based sexual services, genetic materials, and cigarettes. Today, all of these are commodities in the United States. Yet all share a critical feature: they are what I will call "contested commodities." That is, they are produced and marketed under siege—against the opposition of well-mobilized groups with a strong interest in preventing their presence in the marketplace. The viability of all these contested commodities therefore entails economic, political, and ideological struggle. In the case of union representation, corporations (and others) undertake tremendous expense and effort to disrupt the production and sale of this commodity. As a consequence, the production of this commodity often requires a broad campaign to secure support from people in the community beyond those who will receive the direct benefits of union representation—again, just like the production and sale of handguns, abortions, and other contested commodities.

The struggle over contested commodities does not end with their appearance on the market, however. The contest comprises not just whether an entity can be commodified, but also what will be its properties, and how it may be used. How much nicotine can be loaded into a cigarette, and where can it be consumed? How powerful and lethal can a handgun be, and where can it be carried and discharged? This is true of the union's commodity as well. What "use value" can it convey? What is subject to mandatory bargaining, and what is excluded? What means may members and the union employ to enhance workers' bargaining position during contract negotiations and to ensure that the benefits defined by the resulting contract are honored? All of this is contested by those who stand to lose most from a vibrant labor movement—and from the widespread production and sale of the commodity union representation.

Contradictory Conditions of Existence of Commodity Unionism

Emphasis on the need for mobilization to secure and sustain the conditions of existence for this commodity production and sale sheds light upon the contemporary union crisis. At a minimum, the success of this transaction requires the provision of uncompensated labor and the acceptance of substantial risk by union members; mobilization of support from outsiders; the acquiescence if not outright support of political leaders; and a combination of legal and extralegal strategies by the union to win corporate acquiescence.

But this aspect of union representation rests on a fundamental contradiction that must be continually managed by the union movement. One necessary condition for the sale of any commodity is that the use value it provides not be generally available outside of the market for it. After all, people will hardly buy a commodity when it (or some close substitute) is available for free. Like other commodity providers, then, the union must market something that customers cannot otherwise obtain. Let us call this the "union differential": it refers to those benefits derived from the commodity union representation that are not available to nonmembers. But this means that unions must be wary of government initiatives to generalize the benefits of union representation to nonunion members. And indeed, U.S. unions have historically displayed an ambivalent attitude toward universal employment protections. They have concentrated their legislative efforts instead on labor law reform that will facilitate union representation, such as strengthening sanctions against employers that violate the National Labor Relations Act (NLRA) (Brody 1967; Aronowitz 1983).[3]

But the need to secure the union differential confronts a second, equally important condition of existence that is largely hostile to it. As I emphasized above, the fact that this service is produced and marketed under siege requires that union members and others outside the union bear risk and provide uncompensated labor (among other things) to ensure its production and sustenance. But why would they do this? Those who buy Ford automobiles do not regularly mobilize to secure access to this commodity, and would no doubt find laughable a request from the Ford Motor Company that they do so. Historically, workers have undertaken such efforts precisely because and to the degree that union representation is seen to be not a commodity, but instead a social movement defending a valuable right. People generally do not put their incomes, careers, family relationships, and even lives on the line to ensure the production and sale of a commodity—but they do, sometimes, when some higher (nonpecuniary) value is at stake. Some people campaign for the right to buy and possess handguns because they see gun ownership as a constitutional right; others risk their lives to ensure legal and safe abortions because they view abortion as an expression of a woman's fundamental right to exert control over her own body. Similarly, workers sometimes engage in struggles to secure and sustain union representation in the belief that so doing defends a fundamental right. Union organizing and bargaining campaigns reflect the aspiration for human dignity and justice. On these grounds, workers have historically fought against the state, police, corporate power, and sometimes the clergy, community leaders, and even family members to secure union representation. And indeed, they are warranted in doing so—union organization *is* a fundamental right, and union struggles *are* potentially struggles for higher human and social values. Moreover, the fight to secure union representation can be and often is an extraordinarily ennobling experience.

But here lies the contradiction: securing the first condition of existence, the union differential, may undermine the second, the willingness of people to struggle in defense of unionism. This is especially true if and when eligibility for union representation depends on restrictive employment criteria that exclude many who need collective organization and protection. Under this circumstance, the commodity nature of union representation may be revealed, jeopardizing the union's purchase as a social movement worthy of broad support and sacrifice. In this case, unions may come to be branded as a special interest whose claim to social movement status is self-serving and disingenuous. When this happens, for instance, the broader community may not be so willing to endorse union strikes, while even union members might chafe at the idea of letting union leaders dictate how they should vote or whether they should strike. They certainly would not let insurance industry executives tell them how to vote; why, then, should they let union industry executives? Nor are they apt to be moved by union appeals regarding what they should be prepared to sacrifice for the "good of the union."

I offer the above account as an encapsulation of much of what has gone wrong in the U.S. labor movement over the past five decades. By the 1970s, unions had come to be viewed broadly as special interests that placed the needs of their "privileged" members above those of other citizens. Union strikes were seen as acts of extortion that harmed the public. Union leaders were seen as corrupt, out of touch, and lacking in moral authority. In this context, erstwhile allies in the Democratic Party found it expeditious to abandon the labor movement when it came under attack by corporations and Republicans.

A second contradiction of enterprise unionism is that many workers have come to take an *instrumental* as opposed to *expressive* view of union membership, as many observers have by now argued. Having been trained by unions themselves to view them as providers of the union differential, many workers have come to evaluate union membership against just this criterion. Rather than ask how union membership contributes to a campaign for social justice, many merely ask whether they are getting good value for their dues payments. They ask whether the union is in a position to deliver the goods. Will the cost of striking be offset by the direct financial benefits that the strike might induce? Just as consumers of other goods might perform a cost/benefit analysis in contemplation of a purchase, so do many workers today assess their union membership in precisely these terms. To conclude this point, if the union movement today confronts in U.S. workers educated consumers rather than social campaigners, I would suggest that it has little right to lament their pecuniary bent.[4]

Reinventing Unionism

The foregoing analysis begs an important question: what might unionism look like were it not centered on commodity sale, or on the union differential?

In the first instance, reinventing unionism would require raising anew and without restrictive preconceptions the question of who can and should be a union member. As I have mentioned, labor's predominant answer for the past seventy years or so has been waged workers. Reinventing unionism would require revising this answer. Why restrict membership to this group? Why not invite at least some of the self- or independently employed (e.g., house cleaners and nannies) into the ranks of labor? And what of casual and part-time laborers who find intermittent work through temporary employment agencies? Or nonwaged workers, such as those who labor for their own families in the household?

But in answering this question, we should go further to ask, why restrict unionism just to those who labor—and why restrict the focus of union practice to people's employment situation? It is certainly not always the case that workers are most oppressed, most vulnerable, and most needful of representation and protection. Workers may indeed be exploited or otherwise aggrieved by the treatment they receive from the institutions they serve. But these institutions have other identifiable "stakeholders," and some of these might have equally strong claims, needs, grievances, and interests in organizing to secure basic fairness. To take just one example, consider those who struggle in and with America's woefully deficient public school system. The teachers who work in these schools need union representation, and they generally have access to membership in *teachers'* unions. But consider now the students who suffer the far more debilitating lifelong effects of inadequate school funding and overcrowding. Might not they, their families, and communities also find in a reconstituted, expansive *education* union a voice for their grievances and a vehicle for campaigning for progressive school reform? In short, reinvention might lead to the transformation of labor unions into what I will call stakeholder unionism, a unionism that joins waged workers with other constituencies who need union representation.

Reconceptualizing union membership opens up the possibility for a reconceptualization of union structure and governance, agenda and strategy. How might other stakeholders be integrated into organizations that have historically counted only waged workers among their membership? Would the union have distinct departments focusing on its now distinct constituencies? Or would the divide between waged workers and other stakeholders be institutionally effaced, in order to ensure that the union speaks to the broad needs and aspirations of all its members? What would be the agenda of this new, expansive union, and how would this agenda be achieved? Certainly, it would continue to defend the work-related interests of waged workers, and it would also likely continue to engage in collective bargaining with their employers. But now, possibly, employment-based collective bargaining would take its place as just one among equals in a wide range of new union practices. Perhaps this union would also negotiate with government agencies, financial institutions, developers, universities, churches, perhaps even wealthy owners of sports franchises when these actors are in a position to advance the interests of its broad membership. On the other hand, this kind of union might find that collective bargaining and industrial action are not always the most effective way to promote the diverse aspirations of its membership. In this case, the union might engineer some combination of consumer boycotts, ballot initiatives, public protests, and other actions to achieve its objectives.

Some of these strategies would run afoul of existing labor law, to be sure, and so stakeholder unions would be forced to press for legal reform that reduced the barriers to innovation. U.S. unions have failed miserably in this regard in recent decades. Politicians have rightly concluded that labor law reform is of interest to very few voters, but is opposed by very strong interests. A stakeholder unionism might do better in this regard, since its expanded constituency would represent a much greater cross-section of the electorate. But it bears emphasis that many strategies that would be available to stakeholder unionism would face no legal obstacles. For instance, stakeholder unionism might find within it the resources and expertise to serve its constituencies directly. It might implement new programs and establish new institutions (such as schools, day care centers, clinics, and so forth) by which to meet needs poorly addressed by other institutions. The labor movement has pursued such strategies since its inception, but they have been rendered increasingly peripheral to its primary focus on representing waged workers through collective bargaining. In a reinvented unionism, they are apt to take center stage.[5]

Realizing Stakeholder Unionism

A concrete example might elucidate the concept of stakeholder unionism. Consider the United Food and Commercial Workers Union (UFCW), a union that now represents many health care workers. On March 2, 2000, UFCW Local 7 in Colorado initiated a strike against Kaiser Permanente's Denver facilities. Kaiser is a large national HMO that in the Denver metropolitan area alone has eleven clinics and 335,000 subscribers. Kaiser's 1,100 unionized nurses, optometrists, pharmacists, and medical technicians rejected Kaiser's final prestrike offer because they viewed its wage and particularly its staffing proposals as deficient.

This strike serves us well as we explore the idea of union reinvention not because it was in any way notable or out of the ordinary but, instead, because it typifies the new labor movement. The strike involved service sector workers (predominantly women), where union growth has been greatest over the past several decades. The strike involved

normal concerns associated with enterprise unionism, like rates of pay and work levels. But in the context of the health care industry, "work levels" bear directly on the quality of patient service. By fighting for better staffing ratios, the union stood to improve the quality of care for Kaiser patients. Indeed, from the start of the dispute and at every opportunity, the union emphasized quality of patient care. On picket lines union members typically chanted, "Fight, fight, for our patients we will fight!"[6]

The strike lasted twenty days. The union declared victory when Kaiser agreed to refrain from subcontracting work to nonunion service providers, and to establish a union-management committee to oversee staffing levels. Union members rightfully took pride in having championed the interests of their patients. A few patients took notice; some had even walked picket lines in support of the union. Many more were no doubt annoyed by the inconveniences associated with the job action, such as threats of delayed care and higher subscriber premiums. Many people likely will have thought the strikers selfish and even irresponsible for having put their care in jeopardy. But overall, I am certain that most people in Denver have largely forgotten all about the strike by now. I think the union would be hard-pressed to identify any lasting institutional effects beyond Kaiser's doors.

An Alternative Scenario

Now let us imagine a reconstituted, expansive UFCW—no longer just a *labor* union selling a commodity, it has emerged as a leading *health care stakeholders* union.[7] This union recognizes that Kaiser's subscribers are at least as affected by the HMO's actions as are its employees. Having reinvented itself, this reformed union invites all of Kaiser's subscribers to join. Provided full membership rights, these new members press for a union-led campaign to force Kaiser to take full account of myriad patient care issues, such as its fee structure, the range and quality of its services, and its patient grievance procedures. Having listened to the concerns of Kaiser's employees, the subscriber members have come to understand that work levels affect quality of care; they therefore endorse the union's drive to improve staffing. Moreover, as part of the union's community outreach efforts, union volunteers have identified and organized as full union members uninsured families in the Denver area that cannot afford to pay for private insurance. Many of these families also cannot afford to pay union dues and so are relieved of this membership requirement. Some of the uninsured are unemployed, while many others are either self-employed or employed in establishments that do not provide health insurance. Their highest health priority is access to basic medical care.

Acknowledging the concerns of the uninsured, the union's diverse constituencies develop a broad program to achieve universal, high-quality care throughout the Denver metropolitan area. These proposals are codified in the union's new Wellness and Health Care Agenda. The Action Plan for the agenda encompasses proposals for new legislation at the state and national levels, as well as demands on all area health care providers. The union also establishes and runs a Patient Advocacy Network, staffed by union members on a volunteer basis, to provide one-on-one assistance to insured and especially uninsured families seeking appropriate medical care. These advocates teach members how to navigate the health care system, accompany them when seeking care, provide wellness and health seminars, and engage in direct action (picketing, etc.) as circumstances warrant. Finally, the union establishes a fund from members' dues, grants, and negotiated employer contributions to help defray medical care costs for the uninsured. A union committee administers the fund in a manner similar to the administration of the union's strike hardship fund.

As contract negotiations with Kaiser approach, the union notifies management that it will be pressing for redress on a broad range of patient care and labor relations issues. It will be pressing these issues at Kaiser, where the union has secured bargaining rights under the NLRA, but also at other area HMOs—even those where the union does not have bargaining rights. Even here, the union has been able to organize many patients and workers, given that it is now an organization that represents and defends the interests of a range of stakeholders in the health care field. As Kaiser negotiations near, the union undertakes public demonstrations at many area HMOs, kicks off a campaign to secure new legislation in the Colorado State Legislature, and holds public hearings on the needs of the uninsured.

Now let us imagine that while pushing its diverse agenda at these distinct sites, negotiations with Kaiser break down. Kaiser management gives the union its final, take-it-or-leave-it offer, one that fails to address the union's most significant demands. At this point, the union membership meets and votes to undertake a multifaceted campaign to bring pressure to bear on the HMO. Though Kaiser's workers are willing to strike, the decision is taken to pursue a "subscriber boycott" first. Those subscribers who pay Kaiser directly begin to withhold their fees, while those who subscribe through their employers notify them that they wish to switch to an alternative HMO. Subscribers also begin a campaign of "civil disobedience"—setting and then canceling appointments without notice, demanding meetings with Kaiser's management, filing myriad complaints with the state regulatory authority, engaging in informational picketing, perhaps even blocking administrators' access to Kaiser facilities. If and when it becomes necessary, the union pulls its worker-members out on strike.

National Strategies

Though Local 7's membership is limited to Colorado, the parent UFCW to which it belongs is a large national union affiliated with the AFL-CIO. While Local 7 presses for these reforms locally, a reconstituted UFCW simultaneously coordinates a national campaign for health care reform. One pillar of its program is to separate entirely health care from employment, essentially eliminating this aspect of the union differential so as to universalize access among the dispossessed. Internally, the reconstituted UFCW structure now ensures representation at all levels of governance to the new constituencies that its locals have organized— workers (both in institutions where the union has bargaining rights and in those where it does not), HMO subscribers, the uninsured, patients in elderly care facilities (and/or their children advocates), hospice workers, consumer activists and so on. In its new guise, the union has thus become the chief national advocate for health care reform.

Conclusion

The stakeholder unionism that I have sketched here is but one model for union reinvention, one that seems best suited for the service sector. It is by no means appropriate for all unions in all sectors. But in my view, we would do far better with a union movement that is far more heterogeneous in form and practice than what we have now. Once the question of union reinvention is on the table, there is no telling just what new avenues of union reform might appear.

Could the stakeholder model of unionism work? It is achievable, here and now, absent some seismic political shift that restores the luster, authority, and power of the labor movement? It is not difficult to list the obstacles. These would have to include institutional inertia within the union movement—for all its faults, we know how to create and administer what I have called enterprise unions—and, no doubt, a degree of comfort with and commitment to this model by union members. At its best, enterprise unionism delivers results in the form of higher wages, job security, and vitally important rights, and it's asking a lot of union members who continue to enjoy the union differential to put it in jeopardy—especially at a time of economic insecurity and vulnerability. But most workers today do not enjoy these benefits. Most have been excluded by a set of historical forces, contradictions, and circumstances that prevent unions from extending their membership along traditional lines. Perhaps, then, the opportunity for union reinvention lies among the unorganized, particularly in the service sector where other stakeholders are so readily identifiable and, in some cases, already mobilized.

The union movement has remained committed to the enterprise model of unionism long after that model has ceased to be viable for the vast majority of workers. Unfortunately, even those who emphasize internal factors in accounting for labor's predicament tend to remain wedded to this model of unions—a model that views employment-based collective bargaining for waged workers as the primary union practice. I respectfully dissent from this view. I think there are tremendous opportunities for union revitalization easily within reach. But this revitalization will require reinvention— of union identity, agenda, and strategy.

Notes

Thanks to Erica Bouri for her research assistance on this project.

1. This and the subsequent section are taken from DeMartino (1997b, 2000).

2. The term "enterprise" unionism used here to convey the capitalist nature of contemporary unionism is not to be confused with the term "company" unionism, which is a kind of unionism (illegal in the United States) in which the employer establishes an employer-controlled union among its employees as a means to deter independent union organization.

3. See Stone (1992) for an examination of new state-level labor protections that provide for individual employee protections (such as "rights not to be fired abusively, rights for privacy on the job, rights to be free of drug testing, rights to be free of sexual harassment, rights for whistleblowers, and so forth") and that actually exceed those rights typically found in labor contracts. Moreover, Section 301 of the Labor Management Relations Act allows courts to find that a "collective bargaining agreement preempts claims an employee brings under external statutory or common law rights" (Stone 1992, 576, 577). The effect of recent preemptive judgments by federal courts has been to leave union members with fewer rights than those enjoyed by nonunionized employees. In our terms, these laws undermine (and at worst, may actually reverse) the union differential, thereby reducing the demand for the commodity union representation.

4. DeMartino (1997a) explores other implications of the enterprise model of unionism; not least, this model helps to account for the reluctance of so many unions today to invest resources in organizing, and for the patterns of organizing that do occur.

5. Stone (1992, 641–43) provides an alternative model of unionism, which she calls an "expanded bargaining model," that is consistent in spirit (if not in specific details) with the alternative I am presenting here.

6. See UFCW Local 7 (March 2000) for coverage of this strike.

7. It is an artifact of the chaotic, haphazard manner in which the U.S. labor unions organize that these workers are represented by UFCW, a union whose historical base was in grocery chains and the food processing industry. Today, the Service Employees International Union (SEIU) represents far more health care workers than does the UFCW, and so this account of a reinvented unionism in health care would seem to fit SEIU far better than it does UFCW. Fortunately, SEIU has begun to experiment with new ways of addressing the health care crisis in the United States. It is to be hoped that these experiments will yield new union identities that open the doors of the house of labor to other health care stakeholders.

References

Annunziato, Frank. "Commodity Unionism." *Rethinking Marxism* 3, no. 2 (1990): 8–33.

Aronowitz, Stanley. *Working Class Hero: A New Strategy for Labor*. New York: Adama, 1983.

Brody, David. "The Expansion of the American Labor Movement: Institutional Sources of Stimulus and Restraint." In *Institutions in Modern America*, ed. Stephen A. Ambrose. Baltimore: Johns Hopkins University Press, 1967.

DeMartino, George. "Demonstration Drives, Predatory Drives: A Strategic Model of Union Organizing." *Politics and Society* 25, no. 3 (1997a): 326–38.

———. "Speculations on the Future of the U.S. Labor Movement in an Era of Global Economic Integration." In *Labour Worldwide in the Era of Globalisation: Alternative Union Models in the New World Order*, ed. R. Munck and P. Waterman. London: Macmillan, 1997b.

———. "U.S. Labor Faces an Identity Crisis." In *Political Economy and Contemporary Capitalism: Radical Perspectives on Economic Theory and Policy*, ed. R. Baiman, H. Boushey, and D. Saunders. Armonk, NY: M.E. Sharpe, 2000.

Stone, Katherine Van Wezel. "The Legacy of Industrial Pluralism: The Tension Between Individual Employment Rights and the New Deal Collective Bargaining System." *University of Chicago Law Review* 59 (Spring 1992): 575–644.

UFCW Local 7. *Voice of 7*. "Special Strike Edition," March 2000 (and subsequent issues of this publication).

IV

Social Justice

17

Full Employment and Social Justice

L. Randall Wray and Mathew Forstater

In this chapter, we will examine the imperative for achieving and maintaining full employment. We will argue that full employment policy can be supported by a wide variety of arguments about social justice, including the argument that full employment is, or should be made to be, a right for all persons who wish to work. We next argue that without government action, modern capitalist economies cannot achieve full employment, even on a temporary basis. Indeed, we will argue that economic policy has long been directed toward maintaining an inflation-fighting buffer stock of jobless individuals. While we do not believe that this is an effective inflation-fighting strategy, it is clear that modern capitalist governments have increasingly turned to unemployment to fight inflation. Further, they have at the same time reduced alternatives to paid employment ("welfare" programs) to increase "work incentives." We will argue that this policy is self-defeating because it actually means that the reserve army of the unemployed thought necessary to maintain price stability actually grows. Next, we examine the belief that government can achieve full employment through aggregate demand management alone—that is, the belief that targeted employment programs are not necessary. We conclude that targeted employment programs are necessary to ensure that

the basic right to a job is guaranteed, and we offer a proposal for such a program.

Why Full Employment?

Full employment is a widely shared goal among institutionalist economists (see Forstater 1998b). Among the recipients of the Veblen-Commons Award (the highest recognition of the Association for Evolutionary Economics), John Kenneth Galbraith, Dudley Dillard, Adolph Lowe, Wallace Peterson, Robert Heilbroner, Wendell Gordon, Gardiner Means, Marc Tool, Phil Klein, and Hyman Minsky especially emphasized full employment as a top priority. Most of these authors viewed employment not only as a preferred economic condition, but as a fundamental right. As pragmatist philosopher John Dewey, whose work provides important philosophical foundations for many institutionalists, forcefully argued:

> The first great demand of a better social order, I should say, then is the guarantee of the right, to every individual who is capable of it, to work—not the mere legal right, but a right which is enforceable so that the individual will always have an opportunity to engage in some form of useful activity, and if the ordinary economic machinery breaks down through a crisis of some sort, then it is the duty of the state to come to the rescue and see that individu-

als have something to do that is worthwhile—not breaking stone in a stoneyard, or something else to get a soup ticket with, but some kind of productive work which a self-respecting person may engage in with interest and with more than mere pecuniary profit. (Dewey 1939, 420–21)

In addition to these prominent institutionalists, many others have argued for policy to ensure full employment. All the major approaches to justice, including utilitarian, Rawlsian, and capabilities (basic functionings) approaches, taken individually or in combination, have supported full employment policy (see Sen 1987; Davis 1999).

The first argument for full employment is that the economic and social costs of unemployment— direct and indirect—are staggering, and thus the benefits of full employment are real and substantial. Unemployment causes permanent losses in potential output of goods and services; economic, social, psychological, and other problems resulting in poverty, crime, ill health (physical and mental), divorce, suicide, drug addiction, homelessness, malnutrition, poor prenatal care, ethnic antagonism, school dropouts, broken families, and so on; deterioration of labor skills and productivity; and more (see, e.g., Jahoda 1982; Kelvin and Jarrett 1985; Feather 1990; Darity and Goldsmith 1996). As Sen argues:

> There is plenty of evidence that unemployment has many far-reaching effects other than loss of income, including psychological harm, loss of work motivation, skill and self-confidence, increase in ailments and morbidity (and even mortality rates), disruption of family relations and social life, hardening of social exclusion and accentuation of racial tensions and gender asymmetries. (Sen 1999, 94–95)

The argument that unemployment can lead to social instability may also be included here: without employment and income security, citizens are vulnerable to dangerous ideologies, scapegoating,

and antidemocratic political movements (Lerner 1951, 37ff.).The benefits of full employment thus include improved security for society's most downtrodden, alleviation of a variety of social and economic ills, social and political stability, and expanded output and income. In addition, full employment can stabilize business expectations and have a positive impact on the wages and status of unskilled workers (Vickrey 1993, 9; 1997, 505). It has also been argued that full employment increases efficiency. By removing the threat imposed on workers by the existence of a reserve army of unemployed, workers will feel more confident to move out of one job and into another. This often means a movement from a lower-productivity job to a higher-productivity job.

Quite simply, a compelling argument can be made that the benefits of full employment outweigh the costs of its achievement (Moosa 1997; Piachaud 1997). While this argument can be used to support a utilitarian approach, it is also important for those who are critical of utilitarianism. Mainstream economics often focuses on the opportunity costs and tradeoffs involved in establishing rights such as the right to employment or the right to a minimum income (Kriesler 1998). Thus, establishing a clear net benefit for full employment is crucial in countering arguments that such rights will reduce efficiency or slow economic development.

The second argument for full employment is based on the idea that, just as there are human, political, and civil rights, so too are there economic and social rights, of which the right to employment is one of the most important. Tool makes an important distinction between natural and human rights:

> The *natural* right to employment . . . is a nonempirical, non-experiential, extra-causal, conception of what ought to be. Its credibility derives from the acceptance of an antecedent metaphysical belief

which cannot be integratively incorporated into the human inquiry process. The *human* right to employment is grounded in the continuum of factual experience and rational appraisals of actual consequences experienced and is validated by inquiry-embedded instrumental social value theory. (Tool 1997, 285; emphasis added)

An institutionalist approach to economic and social justice is thus often based on human rights rather than natural rights. But the right to employment can and has been justified on natural rights grounds as well. There are a number of good reasons why we believe the natural rights argument for employment should not be rejected out of hand. Moreover, the natural rights argument can be combined with other rationales to bolster support for the rights to employment. One compelling reason not to reject the natural rights argument is that it is the "most traditional, and probably most legitimate, Western frame of reference concerning rights" (Siegel 1994, 78). In addition, a number of important supporters of the right to employment base their case on natural rights. These include some prestigious scholars, but perhaps most importantly the Catholic Church has long supported the natural right to employment (Siegel 1994, 78).

In any case, many recent authors in and around the institutionalist tradition have argued in support of employment as a human right and full employment policies as the means of securing that right (see, e.g., Harvey 1989, 1993; Burgess and Mitchell 1998; Neville 1998; Neville and Kriesler 2000). These views find support in President Franklin Delano Roosevelt's 1944 State of the Union address, and similar proclamations can be found in many other countries as well. The right to employment may also be found in a number of United Nations documents, including the Universal Declaration of Human Rights. If individuals are ready, willing, and able to work and have no employment opportunities, it is government's responsibility to guarantee employment. Therefore, even if it was argued or could be shown that the costs of eliminating unemployment were greater than the monetary benefits, government would still be responsible for guaranteeing full employment.

Not only is the natural or human right to employment considered of utmost importance in and of itself, but it has, directly and indirectly, the potential of fostering—perhaps more than any other single mechanism—a broad spectrum of natural and/or human rights associated with social justice. Human rights that are promoted by access to employment include:

- the right to a decent standard of living, including good health, decent housing, healthy nutrition, and the right to a long life;
- the right to contribute to the community;
- the right to live free from crime;
- the right to live free of discrimination;
- the right to have the opportunity to develop talents, skills, and capacities;
- children's rights.

The power of stable, full employment to secure a whole series of other natural, social, and economic rights explains its place of importance and priority on the human rights agenda. It is important to recognize that the right to employment is both a positive and negative right (see Gewirth 1996, 217–20). It is a negative right in the sense that all persons and entities must refrain from creating obstacles to an individual's "obtaining, performing, or retaining productive and remunerative work" (Gewirth 1996, 217):

The right to employment is also a positive right because of the crucial impact of unemployment on both freedom and well-being. Insofar as the market, as represented by private employers, fails to provide work, its primary respondent must be the state as the community of rights. It is the state, acting through the government, that has the correlative duty to take the steps required to provide work for unemployed persons who are able and willing to work. In this way the government, acting for the community of rights, becomes the guarantor of full employment. (219)

The third argument for full employment is that the promotion and maintenance of full employment is required in many countries by law, for example, the Employment Act of 1946 and the Full Employment and Balanced Growth Act of 1978 (Humphrey-Hawkins bill) in the United States. The former corresponds roughly to the 1944 British White Paper on Employment Policy. Similar legislation exists in many other industrialized nations as well. Thus, even if it were argued that the costs are prohibitive and that employment is not a natural right, it may be argued that under current law many governments are obligated to guarantee full employment. Such an argument supports the right to employment based on the principles of legal justice. Of course, simply enacting laws requiring that governments pursue full employment does not ensure that they will adopt policy that would guarantee this result. Still, the existence of such laws does give force to the view that society has recognized the social obligation to ensure job availability to all—even if the mechanism for meeting this obligation has not been put in place.

The fourth argument is that full employment is an ethical imperative in a capitalist economy. In capitalist economies, individuals and families are largely responsible for providing for their own well-being. In all industrialized and many developing economies, most workers do not have the means of production to provide for their own subsistence, but rather must obtain the means of purchase and means of payment (money) necessary for buying the means of subsistence by selling their labor-power in the market. In addition, the require-

ment that taxes be paid in government currency means that even those possessing the means to provide for their own subsistence nevertheless must enter the labor market to obtain currency to pay their taxes. Unemployment, the failure to obtain employment that earns wages or salaries paid in money, thus has a dire impact on the jobless in an economy organized as capitalist (Forstater 2003). Even largely self-sufficient farmers will lose their means of livelihood (the farm) if they do not earn sufficient money income to pay taxes— necessitating that they either sell a portion of their production or find a paying job off the farm in order to earn the money required.

In a society in which unemployment is *systemic*, public inaction constitutes social assignment of workers and their families to poverty and/or various forms of assistance:

> It is obvious that specialization of labor . . . has proceeded to the point where receipt of a continuous money income provides the primary access to the material means of life and experience. All adult individuals, as a condition of their own psychological, physical, and cultural continuity, need to have regular access to an adequate flow of money income that provides the "tickets to participation" in most aspects of economic and social life. (Tool 285–86, 1997)

This emphasis on the impact of unemployment on "basic functionings" is consistent with Sen's capabilities approach. This approach, which Sen (1987, 1041) describes as "go[ing] back to Smith's and Marx's focus on fulfilling needs," justifies guaranteed employment on the grounds that it is a prerequisite for the "achievement of adequate nutrition, the ability to avoid preventable morbidity and premature mortality, and other conditions and states that are minimally necessary for a person to live a decent life" (DeMartino 2000, 146). It is also consistent with Rawls's well-known "difference principle," which states that social and economic rights and opportunities are to be arranged to the benefit of the least advantaged (Rawls 1971). Furthermore, Tool argues that failure to obtain employment can result in not only social and economic, but political disenfranchisement as well:

> An economy is unjust, further, when it tolerates significant or protracted involuntary unemployment. Since, as everyone knows, in an exchange economy availability of a job to provide continuous and adequate money income is a source of economic discretion, of economic freedom, those without jobs and income are economically, and to some extent politically, disenfranchised. (Tool 1979, 332)

Therefore, even if the costs are prohibitive, even if employment is not considered a right, and even if current legislation is not interpreted as legally requiring government to take action to promote and maintain full employment, it would nevertheless be wrong for government not to do so.

Doubtless there are many other arguments for full employment; these categories overlap and should be treated as provisional. Clearly, however, the arguments for full employment—both individually and taken together—are compelling. The crucial point is that unemployment is endemic to capitalism. Of course, even if unemployment were not inherent in capitalism, the arguments for government policies to promote full employment would still be strong, but the existence of persistent involuntary unemployment provides a strong justification for the priority of full employment initiatives.

Employment and Postwar Policy

No "market economy" (we will use this term somewhat loosely, but will limit our analysis to the developed capitalist nations that are members of the Organization for Economic Cooperation and De-velopment [OECD], explicitly excluding the formerly socialist nations as well as the developing countries) that we know of has ever offered on a sustained basis a sufficient supply of private sector jobs to employ all those who want to work for pay. Even leaving aside issues associated with a living wage or with humane work conditions, there is always in these nations an unsatisfied fringe of job seekers willing to work even at the lowest wages and in the meanest conditions. This unsatisfied fringe typically rises and falls against the business cycle, but even at business cycle peaks there remains a substantial portion of the population willing to work, but unable to find paying work in the private sector. Most, or all, of these nations have adopted government programs (especially in the postwar period) to provide some of these job seekers with work or to remove them from the labor force. Still, it is not controversial to claim that even with these programs in place, and even at business cycle peaks, there has remained a measurable and substantial number of involuntarily unemployed job seekers.

This is a claim about empirical, real-world experience—experience reflected, even if imperfectly, in official data that purport to measure unemployment. However, there are strong theoretical and policy considerations that lead to the conclusion that persistent involuntary unemployment is the predominant expected result in a modern, developed, capitalist system. Many analysts from Karl Marx to Michal Kalecki have argued that capitalists purposely maintain a buffer or reserve army of the unemployed in order to keep labor in its place. John Maynard Keynes (1964) developed a theory of aggregate demand that led to the conclusion that in capitalist economies full employment would be achieved only by coincidence—in other words, that there was no market force that would move the economy to full employment.

Thorstein Veblen's theory of business enterprise reached a similar conclusion, but provided more details on the business motives that lead to "sabotage" of production by the captains of industry—that is, to the propensity to operate production below capacity (with unemployment a result of such sabotage). In 1919 Veblen foresaw concerted efforts by the pecuniary interests to organize this sabotage, for example, through creation of cartels. As we will argue, one might see in postwar economic policy the evolution of the recognition that private sabotage would not be sufficient—hence, that government would assume the role of maintaining sufficient slack to keep wages in check.

While we accept the arguments of Marx, Keynes, and Veblen (which locate the source of involuntary unemployment in the private decisions made by "entrepreneurs" or "captains of industry"), we would also emphasize the role that postwar government policy has played in generating involuntary unemployment. Before World War II, persistent unemployment was not usually the result of intentional policy of the central government. Since World War II, however, national policy in developed capitalist economies has increasingly been geared toward ensuring that aggregate demand was kept sufficiently slack so that involuntary unemployment resulted on a large scale, primarily in the interests of keeping wages and prices in line. There is, so to speak, a government policy–induced reserve army of the unemployed that operates in addition to the "market forces" identified by Marx, Veblen (1919), and Keynes (1964) that preserve persistent unemployment. Indeed, one might see such policy as an effort to improve on the "anarchy" of Veblen's "sabotage of production" that had existed prior to the Great Depression. This pre-Depression sabotage had consisted of two components: the creation of cartels to try to control production in order to reduce price competition, and efforts to control labor costs (union busting, race baiting, importation of immigrant labor, and so on).

By 1930, however, this "sabotage" was deemed by the captains of industry to be insufficient at holding prices up and at maintaining the reserve army of the unemployed required to keep labor in check. (As mentioned above, this was a development already foreseen by Veblen in 1919.) The fall of prices at the end of the 1920s spurred the early New Deal efforts at government-encouraged cartelization to keep prices from falling, eventually resulting in the creation of various price support programs, some of which are still in place. In the labor sphere, policy was more complicated because the Roosevelt administration recognized labor rights and wanted to avoid extending the depression. Postwar government turned to economic management to ensure that the economy operated with sufficient slack to maintain a pool of unemployed labor, even as the government came to be seen as a supporter of labor unions and workers' rights. Indeed, if labor were given greater rights to organize, inflation might result if unemployment fell too much. Hence, government support of unionized labor (even though that support was largely ambivalent) was supplemented with policy to maintain a reserve army of unemployed.

Economists and policy makers today speak fairly openly of the need to maintain a buffer stock of the unemployed, openly advocating policy to "loosen" labor markets when unemployment falls to levels thought to be inconsistent with wage stability and docile labor unions. Indeed, all during the Clinton expansion of the 1990s, there were calls on the Federal Reserve Board to raise interest rates because unemployment had fallen to "dangerously low" levels; at the end of the decade, the Fed did raise rates on exactly that argument, supplementing the already substantial deflationary bias built into the federal budget (which was running a large surplus) (Wray 2000b, 2001, 2002).

In our view, then, the persistence of unemployment in the postwar period is not simply an unfortunate event, but the consequence of the desire to maintain a wage-inflation-fighting buffer stock. This then creates a social, and policy, problem: what to do with the unemployed? Since the beginnings of the creation of wage labor, there has always been the problem of how to deal with wageworkers who could not find paying work. Poorhouses in eighteenth-century England, workhouses, arrest and lease or contract labor to plantation owners in the American South, charity, and other means were commonly used prior to the twentieth century (Wray 2000a). After World War II these were supplemented with or replaced by publicly supplied paid work and programs to remove unemployed persons from the labor force and minimize the suffering of the jobless (welfare, military service, incarceration, and extended education) (Harvey 1999). For reasons that will be made clear, postwar policy had to strike an uneasy balance between providing for the unemployed and preserving their wage-inflation-fighting ability (which, in turn, required that they be ready to compete for jobs).

Over the past several decades, such programs have been gutted in most developed countries as part of the larger trend to reduce government "interference" and to subject its programs to the narrow efficiencies imagined to guide behavior in private markets. In the United States, for example, welfare was systematically made less generous all through the 1970s and 1980s, before "entitlements" were entirely eliminated with the Clinton administration's "reform" in which Aid to Families with Dependent Children (AFDC) was replaced by Temporary Assistance to Needy Families (TANF), with greater "work responsibilities" and lifetime limits). As another example, postwar

Sweden probably came closest to achieving full employment, largely due to its "employer of last resort" job guarantees combined with efforts to remove people from the labor force with generous education and training programs. These programs have been gradually gutted since the early 1970s, and unemployment has risen (see Ginsburg 1983). Hence, policy has intentionally reduced alternatives to paid work in the private sector, both to eliminate "inefficiencies" in the public sector and also to increase "incentives" to work.

Incongruously, the belief has grown and become overwhelmingly dominant that should the economy ever operate at such a level as to threaten to generate jobs sufficient to meet the demand for paid work by those thrown off government programs, policy must tighten even further. This would reduce the private supply of jobs and thereby add to the unemployment rolls. Indeed, this is exactly the policy that was openly pursued by the United States at the end of the 1990s. The Clinton "reform" of welfare pushed "welfare moms" into the labor force even as Alan Greenspan (Chairman of the Federal Reserve Board) publicly fretted about the "danger" that existed because unemployment rates had dropped too low (Wray 2000b, 2001). Hence, the Fed raised interest rates in a series of a dozen steps to try to slow the economy and raise the unemployment rate—precisely as alternatives to private sector jobs were reduced.

In other words, policy today is formulated to ensure that the "increased efficiency" of the public sector that is achieved by throwing people off government support is met by increased private sector inefficiencies that waste human potential by destroying private sector jobs as well (thus, adding to the "normal" level of sabotage of production, as discussed above). Further, because the private sector is good at shifting costs to the public sector (the examples are nearly endless: in the face of rising health care costs, firms eliminate coverage and force workers to rely on emergency wards that are at least partially government-funded; production wastes are emitted into the environment to be cleaned at public expense; land is strip-mined and left for government restoration; tobacco companies sell a highly addictive product and leave government with huge medical costs; the costs for resolving the savings and loan crisis of the 1980s were mostly left to government; and so on), downsizing of public sector employment and spending on social welfare programs is mostly offset by rising public costs of policing, incarceration, and indigent and emergency health care. Thus, even the public sector "efficiencies" are ultimately fleeting.

It is commonly believed that the problem is not lack of jobs, but character flaws, fueling "welfare to work," "boot camps," and other "tough love" campaigns to build the sort of character desired by private sector employers. Some individuals do succeed. However, if these programs were generally successful at getting the unemployed into jobs, they would only lead to more restrictive central government policies to replenish the pool of unemployed to avoid inflationary pressures that are believed to result when unemployment is too low. In other words, there is a vicious circle that cannot be resolved because unemployment seems to be needed to hold wages and prices in check, but at the same time we want to promote "individual responsibility" and reduce government support for those who cannot find jobs in the private sector in order to reduce inefficiencies and provide proper work incentives.

The "Unemployable" Surplus Population

We would argue that in modern market economies the jobless consist of two groups—those who are

kept unemployed by discretionary policy and market forces, and those who are unable to find work because of characteristics (often only imagined; sometimes created by joblessness) that private employers dislike. We believe that each of these causes must be separately analyzed, because most policies geared to solving the first problem will not help resolve the second—and vice versa. Even if a way might be found to induce policy makers to keep demand high enough to eliminate the reserve army that results from public policy and normal capitalist sabotage of production, other policies would be required to eliminate unemployment of those who are not deemed desirable by private employers. Our argument will be that direct job creation by the public sector, if properly designed, can eliminate both kinds of unemployment. This sort of program would be consistent with the active labor market strategy long advocated by institutionalists, or structuralists, to be examined below.

The experience of extended joblessness generally is not conducive to producing the sort of behaviors that private employers find attractive. Hence, according to William A. Darity Jr., a "surplus population" is created—individuals who are not likely to obtain private sector jobs no matter how high aggregate demand rises (Darity 1999). On the margin of this group can be found those with "weak attachment" to the labor force—those who are able to find low-paid, intermittent work when market conditions are favorable.[1] An extended period of slow growth will push more of these into the unemployable surplus population. The more fortunate in this "secondary labor market" find full-time employment in good times and face unemployment in recession. Over time, the size of the jobless buffer stock thought to be required to maintain favorable and flexible labor markets (from the perspective of private employers) has risen in most industrialized nations.[2] This is mostly because a growing segment of the population has become "unemployable" (from the perspective of employers).

Again, as this segment grows, the pressure to increase "work incentives" by reducing alternatives to paid private sector work rises in step as respectable opinion reacts against the rising financial and social costs of maintaining a growing surplus population. This creates a tight vicious circle, fueling policy designed to make life more miserable for those unable to find paid private sector work in order to increase the incentive to work, even as policy aims to reduce the supply of private sector jobs to replenish the buffer stock of jobless but employable labor. Such policy is self-defeating because the jobless but employable state is unsustainable for individuals.

While it cannot serve as a reserve army of the unemployed, the unemployable surplus population performs two critical functions. As Darity (1999) explains, the surplus population provides "living images of the consequences of pauperization," helping to keep the marginally employed secondary labor force subservient to the needs of business out of fear that they might become surplus, no longer needed in pecuniary enterprise. Second, the surplus population does lead to the creation of jobs for their caretakers— police to fight their criminal behavior, criminal justice system employees to incarcerate them, health care workers to care for their emergencies, and social case workers to help them internalize their failures (so they would not blame society!). All of this is expensive, and as government is downsized, only policing and punishment can garner growing budgets, in effect crowding out other social spending.

Alternative Policy Approaches to Unemployment in the Postwar Period

Before looking at data, it is useful to discuss in broad terms two approaches to dealing with unemployment commonly advocated in the postwar period. A typical "Keynesian"[3] response to unemployment problems is to increase aggregate demand. This response is based on the belief that if aggregate demand is high enough to create a sufficient number of jobs, then "markets" can be left to match employers and job seekers. The alternative approach is associated with institutionalists, who advocated a structuralist approach that would focus on job creation, job training, and other active labor market policies (Pigeon and Wray 2000; Marshall, Briggs, and King 1984). We will first look at the "Keynesian" approach and then turn to the institutionalist.

The "Keynesian" approach relies on "demand stimulus" to create jobs. To be sure, this stimulus is always constrained by inflation fears. Indeed, from the discussion above it should be clear that there is a contradiction involved: by design, any such "Keynesian" solution to unemployment can never be more than partial—a reserve army of the unemployed must be maintained at least at some minimal level that leaves between 5 and 10 million potential workers officially unemployed in the United States today—consistent with conventional estimates of the nonaccelerating inflation rate of unemployment (NAIRU) (Kaufman 1979).

This approach is troublesome in light of the disproportionate impact of unemployment and our discussion above about the right to employment. There should be no question about which demographic groups will be kept as the official reserve army of the unemployed. No matter how high official unemployment rates climb, college-educated white males rarely experience unemployment beyond what might be attributed to frictional unemployment—that is, short-term spells between jobs. (See Pigeon and Wray 2000 for analysis of unemployment data by race, gender, and educational status.) When policy makers decide to increase unemployment rates to fight inflation, they know (or should know, given the volumes of evidence, some kinds of which will be reviewed below) that job losers will be those with the least education, the fewest financial resources, and the lowest wages before the job loss. They will also be disproportionately people of color—who typically have official unemployment rates that are double those of whites whether in economic boom or bust. The facts are incontrovertible: the job of fighting inflation through unemployment is horribly disproportionately shared and is mostly put on the backs of those who have no market power to cause wage inflation in the first place.

Perhaps a reasonable case could be made that inflation can be and should be fought by raising unemployment rates if all workers shared equally in the pain. For example, if it were decided that the unemployment rate had to rise to 10 percent to fight inflation and that this goal could be achieved by having each worker unemployed for about five weeks over the course of the year, this decision could be justified on the basis of sharing loss in the interests of the public good. In fact, unemployment rates generally rise as the duration of unemployment rises for those who become unemployed, and as the number of mostly lowly educated and disproportionately minority individuals losing jobs rises. (See Butler and McDonald [1986]; Akerlof and Main [1981]; Kaufman [1979]; Clark and Summers [1979]; and Layard [1997] for research on unemployment duration. Note that most orthodox economists link duration to generosity of unemployment benefits—incorrectly, in our view.) Over the past two decades, the proportion of overall unemployment that is contributed by very long spells of unemployment of the unlucky few has tended to rise. (As Layard [1997] notes, about half of the unemployed in Europe have now been jobless for a year or more.) It is, or should be, clear that using unemployment to fight inflation in this manner is a gross violation of natural and human rights as outlined above.[4]

At the time of the 1960s expansion, there was a debate between economists who believed that economic growth, alone, would be sufficient to expand employment opportunities to the underemployed (this argument is generally associated with the "Keynesian" position just examined) and those who argued that targeted employment programs would be needed to provide jobs to all who wanted to work. This argument is generally associated with the institutionalist or structuralist position. (See Piore [1979], and especially Kaufman [1979].) In addition, institutionalists emphasized that a wide range of active labor market policies would be required. These would include training and basic education programs as well as various policies to ease the transition into the workforce (child care programs, cheap transportation to the workplace, and programs to place persons with disabilities into jobs). A number of such programs were put in place, especially during the 1960s (see Pigeon and Wray [2000] and Marshall, Briggs, and King [1984] for summaries); the best-known program was probably the Comprehensive Employment and Training Act (CETA). Unfortunately, these programs were never well funded, and most were gradually phased out by the end of the Reagan administration. We will discuss the design of what we believe to be the most comprehensive approach—the public service employment program —in detail below.

While its potential is limited due to inflation fears, rising aggregate demand does improve conditions at the bottom just as falling aggregate demand increases suffering. The question is whether a rising tide can lift the boats at the bottom—are benefits shared, if not equally then at least across a wide spectrum of the labor market? Perhaps a rising tide cannot eliminate unemployment and hence is not sufficient to bring the nation into conformance with protecting the human and natural rights discussed above, but it is possible that the rising tide could get us "close enough" to the full employment ideal. Let us look at evidence from two expansions that were commonly believed to have lifted all boats. Was it really the case that our economies during those booms came close to fulfilling our obligation to ensure that a job would be available to all those ready and willing to work?

A Rising Tide?

In this section, we will focus on the two strongest U.S. expansions in the postwar period—the Kennedy–Johnson expansion of the 1960s and the Clinton expansion of the 1990s. (This discussion summarizes analyses in Pigeon and Wray [2000] and Wray [2004].) We focus on these because they might be thought of as a "practical best"—with the best labor markets of the postwar period. Recall that we argued above that the unemployed population can be divided into two groups: those who are unemployed due to slack demand (resulting from private sabotage plus government policy) and those that are "unemployable" from the perspective of employers. In an economic boom, if demand rises sufficiently, the first type of unemployment would be substantially reduced (although only eliminated at the extreme). What we actually find is that even during these two robust booms, a very substantial number of individuals remained jobless. We do not believe that all of these jobless individuals should be placed in the second, un-

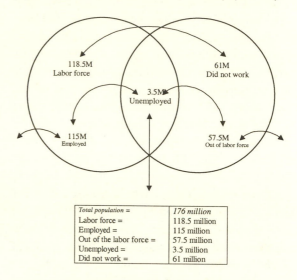

Figure 17.1 **The U.S. Labor Force in December, 2000** (age 25 and over, noninstitutional, civilian population)

Total population =	176 million
Labor force =	118.5 million
Employed =	115 million
Out of the labor force =	57.5 million
Unemployed =	3.5 million
Did not work =	61 million

Source: Bureau of Labor Statistics (2000).

employable, category, nor is it essential to make that argument. All we need to show is that even at its "practical best," the U.S. "market economy" leaves many millions of workers without jobs. We will pay more attention to the Clinton expansion, partly because it is most recent but also because more data are available. According to our analysis, the ability of each of these expansions to improve the most disadvantaged workers' ability to obtain jobs was similar—by some measures the 1960s expansion was somewhat stronger, but not significantly so.

It is first important to get some idea of the labor market by looking at a snapshot of the situation at a point in time (we will choose the year 2000 because it represents a cyclical peak). As Figure 17.1 shows, the population can be divided into two main groups—those who worked (115 million), and those who did not (61 million). (Note that we focus on the population age twenty-five and over to eliminate most of those who are too young to work or who are in school.) The "did not work" population can be further subdivided into two groups—those who were officially unemployed (3.5 million), and those who were out of the labor force (57.5 million). Finally, note that the unemployed group is counted as part of the labor force (118.5 million) and also is counted as "did not work." While the media often focuses on only the "unemployed" category, this is a small proportion of the "did not work" category—most of whom are officially out of the labor force. This would not matter if those who lost jobs only went into the category called "unemployed" and if all those who got jobs came from the unemployed category. In fact, flows are much more complex (as represented by the arrows). Those who are employed can become unemployed, or drop out of the labor force, or can leave the population altogether (die, emigrate). Those who come into the employed category may have previously been unemployed, out of the labor force, or not in the population (they may have been age twenty-four). And so on. The situation is even a bit more complicated, because most labor force statistics apply only to the civilian, noninstitutionalized population—excluding the military and penal systems. Hence, for example, the number of unemployed falls when an unemployed individual joins the army or becomes incarcerated.

When job growth is strong, we would expect that many who had been out of the labor force (not actively seeking work) might begin to look for jobs, and some of these people might then be counted as unemployed. Thus, unemployment rates alone cannot tell the whole story, and a better indication of improved job prospects might be the employment rate. In expansion, we expect to see rising employment rates, first for the higher-skilled and then for the lower-skilled (skill level will be

proxied by level of educational attainment). Eventually, if labor markets became sufficiently tight, the labor force participation rates and employment rates for all skill levels should converge toward some maximum feasible rate, unless there is some reason to expect that the low-skilled have a systematically lower desire to work or that employers will not hire the low-skilled no matter how tight labor markets become.[5]

For this reason, in what follows we will focus on employment rates; however, even these data give an incomplete picture, because it is impossible to know how many of the jobless wanted to work. We can presume that all of those who are officially counted as unemployed want to work, since they must be actively seeking work in order to be counted. However, we know that the flows into and out of the labor force are much larger, which seems to indicate that many of those outside the labor force really do want to work. Further, attitudes toward work, as well as desire to work, are complexly determined and must be affected by the individual's perception of the possibility of obtaining a job.[6] There is no simple solution for the analyst who wants to estimate the counterfactual: how many of those currently outside the labor force would want a job if policy were changed to ensure employment as a human right? It would not be sufficient merely to offer jobs because policy would also have to deal with attitudes and social norms—an important consideration but one that lies mostly beyond the scope of this chapter. We will begin with employment rates, but later will attempt to make some rough estimates of the number of people who might want to work.

During the Clinton expansion, the employment rates of those with the most education rose by about one percentage point, while employment rates of those with the least education rose by about three percentage points. This change was taken as evidence that a rising tide was indeed lifting all boats, and was helping those with the least education. However, well over half of noninstitutionalized high school dropouts remained out of the labor force even after nearly a decade of growth, compared with only a quarter of those who attended college. If the Clinton expansion raised the employment rate for high school dropouts by only about three percentage points over a period of 8 years, by simple extrapolation, the expansion would have to continue for another 104 years before the gap could be closed.

There are at least two other reasons to suspect that rising employment rates overstate the employment outlook for those at the bottom. First, a number of studies have demonstrated that the unemployment rate would be considerably higher if it were adjusted for the rapid increase in the inmate (prison and jail) population—currently at about 2 million—witnessed during the last twenty years. Moreover, the inmate population is disproportionately made up of young, able-bodied, but poorly educated males, especially black men. For example, Beckett and Western (1997) find that the unemployment rate for black men, when adjusted for those held in prisons and jails, would have been 18.8 percent between 1990 and 1994 instead of the official 11.3 percent. There were well under 4 million unemployed adults aged 25 years and older at the end of 1999, so the number of jobless males—about 2 million—who become incarcerated (and thus disappear from labor force statistics) is relatively significant. Indeed, 10 percent of all prime age (18–44 years) males without a high school degree were in prison—more than the number who were officially counted as unemployed (Wray 2000a). While it can be objected that many of those who end up in prison should not be added to the officially unemployed (because they would be out of the labor force if not incarcer-

ated), incarceration does reduce the "excess" population by lowering both the numerator and denominator in calculations of the employment rate—just as the military reduced the excess in the 1960s (at the peak in 1968, about 3.8 million, mostly young males with lower-than-average educational attainment, were in the armed forces). Hence, employment rates can be highly misleading if a large number of jobless individuals become institutionalized (in the military or prisons and jails).

Secondly, and more importantly, careful analysis of employment and population data casts doubt on the conclusion that employment opportunities increased significantly for the less skilled during the robust Clinton expansion (Pigeon and Wray 2000). Indeed, somewhat surprisingly, there was no net gain in the number of high school dropouts employed over the whole expansion—to the contrary, 1.2 million jobs were lost. This means that all of the rise of the employment rate for that group (reported above and by Ritter [1998]) was due to a shrinking population (of high school dropouts) and none to rising employment. The overall employment picture did not show substantial improvement for those with low skills—if we think of improvement as an increase in the number of jobs ("trickling down").

During the Kennedy–Johnson expansion, the employment rate of high school dropouts rose from about 61 percent in 1962 to just under 64 percent by 1968—a rise of just less than three percentage points. By contrast, the employment rate of college graduates remained nearly constant over the expansion at just under 82 percent. Hence, what we find is that the employment rate gain by high school dropouts was (relatively to employment rates of the highly educated) somewhat better during the 1990s expansion than it had been in the 1960s. Further, the employment rate gap between those with the lowest level of educational achievement and those with the highest increased from just over twenty percentage points in 1962 to about thirty-three percentage points by 1993. By the end of the Kennedy–Johnson expansion, the gap had been reduced to eighteen percentage points, while it remained at twenty-eight percentage points at the end of the Clinton expansion. Thus, we find that the employment rate gaps are not only huge but that they are growing. Economic expansions reduce the gap somewhat as employment rates rise for those with the least education. However, the rise is quite small relative to the gap that remains even at the expansion's peak, and the long-term trend seems to indicate that job prospects for the "surplus population" of jobless individuals with low education is worsening. [7]

In conclusion, neither the 1960s nor the 1990s expansions provided more jobs to those with less education. It appears the institutionalists were correct—"pumping" aggregate demand alone is not enough to supply adequate numbers of jobs, especially to disadvantaged groups. While the evidence is not conclusive, it appears to be the case that employment prospects at the bottom are worse today than in the 1960s. This would probably be more apparent if we were to extend the analysis to look at opportunities for "good" jobs and for "good-paying" jobs, which have undoubtedly declined since the 1960s for those with the least education. Further, the evidence is very strong that income inequality has increased greatly since 1973. If we are to really increase opportunity at the bottom of the unemployment ladder, we need targeted programs because aggregate demand alone cannot do the job.

The PSE Alternative

Hyman Minsky argued that an infinitely elastic demand for labor at a fixed wage would guarantee a real job opportunity for anyone who wants to work (Minsky 1986). Along similar lines, we propose a public service employment (PSE) program that would "hire off the bottom," taking all those who are ready, willing, and able to work but who cannot find employers willing to hire them (Killingsworth 1977a, b; Harvey 1989; Gordon 1997; Forstater 1998a; Philpott 1997; Wray 1998). This would be a necessary supplement to, and a complement to, government efforts to stabilize aggregate demand at a high level. The problem is that traditional "pump priming" is believed to be likely to set off inflationary pressures long before jobs "trickle down" to the bottom.[8] For this reason, the job guarantee program is designed so that it will not add significant inflationary pressures. This program is consistent with the approach of institutionalists (or structuralists) who advocated labor market strategies in preference to aggregate demand stimulus.

The federal government would announce that it would provide the money needed to pay the legislated minimum wage, plus health care and child care benefits, to anyone ready, willing, and able to work. Government agencies at all levels (federal, state, local) and designated not-for-profit organizations could hire as many new employees as desired, with direct labor costs, including health and child care benefits, paid by the federal government. Administration and supervision would thus be decentralized, with participating employers setting reasonable performance standards that would have to be met by program employees. The federal government would require that all these jobs have a significant training component in order to prepare participants for eventual private sector (or public sector) employment.

In addition, detailed work records would be kept so that prospective nonprogram employers could recruit from among program participants. The goal would be to create a pool of employable, buffer stock labor from which employers could draw. This buffer stock would serve as an alternative to the reserve army of the unemployed currently used as an (ineffective) inflation-fighting buffer stock. This program would hire off the bottom in the sense that it would provide job opportunities to all who want to work at a base wage that would become the effective minimum wage (the current legislated minimum wage is not really an effective minimum wage since anyone who cannot find work "earns" a wage of zero).

The program would guarantee full employment, or zero unemployment, in the sense that anyone could choose to work in the program at the minimum wage. Clearly, many would choose to remain unemployed or out of the labor force rather than work at the minimum wage; it is doubtful that many unemployed college graduates with substantial work experience would choose to work in the program. However, the program is not designed to solve the unemployment problems of the unemployed highly skilled workers, but is focused on those who cannot obtain private sector work, even when aggregate demand is high.[9] That is to say, it is a targeted employment program, not a pump-priming program—although it could supplement general demand stimulus and would itself help to stabilize aggregate demand since spending would be countercyclical.

Past U.S. experience with targeted employment policies indicates that such a program could prove more effective than other attempts to provide jobs to those at the bottom. Killingsworth (1977a, b), for example, argued that PSE programs were far more efficient and effective than any of the larger, macropolicies proposed at the time (such as tax cuts) at getting people to work, stimulating aggregate demand, and reducing inequalities. "One basic purpose of employment policy should be to redress the inequities and inequalities resulting

from the 'normal' operations of the labor market. There is persuasive evidence that tax cuts do little or nothing to achieve such redress" (Killingsworth 1977b, 492). Killingsworth added that, dollar for dollar, PSE programs were a far more direct and cost-effective way of getting people to work: "Total employment can be increased substantially more with substantially less inflation effect by a PSE program than by tax cuts" (493). Similarly, Gottschalk, in an evaluation of PSE policies, concluded that "the U.S. experiments with PSE indicate that minimum-wage jobs would be demanded if offered" (Gottschalk 1998, 93).[10]

Our policy proposal is much more ambitious than previous targeted employment programs because it offers a job to all those ready and willing to work. Importantly, it can achieve a degree of employment that cannot be attained by expansion alone; the problem with traditional "Keynesian" stimulus programs is that it is feared they might set off inflation long before job opportunities for those with low educational attainment increase. By fixing the wage in the PSE program at the minimum wage, inflation pressures are minimized. Indeed, we believe that the buffer stock of labor will lead to greater price stability than can be achieved under the current system, which relies on unemployment to reduce inflation pressures (a point made by Killingsworth [1977a, b] and [Minsky 1986]).

For several reasons, discussed in Wray (1997, 1998), workers employed in the program would constitute a better pool of potential employees than the current unemployed, or out-of-the-labor-force, population. An obvious reason is that someone working in the program is demonstrating that she or he is "ready, willing, and able" to work to a degree that most of the unemployed cannot. In other words, the job opportunity program allows full employment (albeit a different sort of full employment than can be achieved by priming the pump—which seems to leave behind the least skilled) and price stability to coexist in contrast to the conventional view of a tradeoff between unemployment and inflation.

The target population for the PSE program would be the low-skilled, poorly educated population we have examined. During recessions, higher-skilled workers who lost their jobs would also be able to find temporary work in PSE; however, it is presumed that they would be the first hired out of the pool as economic conditions improved. We know from our examination of job prospects during postwar expansions that even a robust labor market does not significantly improve the chances that a high school dropout will find work. Indeed, Pigeon and Wray (2000) found that upward of 94 percent of all net jobs created over the Clinton expansion went to the half of the population that attended college. There is no reason to believe that job prospects for those who do not attend college will improve in the future, and while average educational levels are rising over time, a significant portion of the population still drops out of high school. As we have noted, almost half of the males who drop out of high school were not employed even in booms. Further, 10 percent of all young male dropouts are in prison at any given time. Young men who are not employed and who have dropped out of high school are in great danger of becoming prisoners. A PSE program would help to break the vicious cycle that is increasing the size of what Darity has called our surplus population.

Conclusion

The social and economic costs of unemployment—direct and indirect—are staggering. In addition, particularly in capitalist societies, employment is the only means of securing a whole host of other natural, social, human, and economic rights. Even direct income support of the unemployed will not secure all of the rights that the right to employment can guarantee, because of the shame and social stigma associated with unemployment.

Our analysis has argued that capitalist economies do not "naturally" generate job opportunities for all; indeed, there are forces that work to ensure that full employment will not be achieved by "free markets." Further, we have also questioned the "Keynesian" belief that government need only ensure that aggregate demand is high enough to generate jobs for all. We have even questioned the degree to which labor markets really tightened over the Clinton and Kennedy–Johnson expansions (the two most robust U.S. expansions of the postwar period), at least for the half of the population that has not attended college.

We have challenged the notion that a rising tide alone can significantly increase job opportunities for this group. While it is true that unemployment rates fall and employment rates rise across the skills spectrum, expansions are woefully inadequate in creating the sheer numbers of jobs necessary for the low-skilled. And it must be remembered that expansions are "the best of times" —nearly three decades separated the Kennedy–Johnson and Clinton booms. Finally, we have noted the inherent contradiction between the desire to create jobs through pump-priming and the belief in a NAIRU. We argue, as the old institutionalists did, that it is time to implement a variety of active labor market policies, with a job opportunity program as its centerpiece. Only then will the right to employment truly be operational, and social justice truly served.

The free market arguments against government intervention in support of the unemployed is worn thin in the face of the postwar evidence. It is clear that only the state—by acting as the employer of last resort—is capable of establishing the climate of social justice associated with true full employment. Institutionalists have long understood this point, and the framework for a workable public service employment program has now been laid out on institutionalist grounds that can serve as the basis for public policy.

Notes

The authors thank Eric Tymoigne for research and editorial assistance.

1. The common belief is that the "weak attachment" is the fault of the worker. While we will not pursue this, we believe that "unstable" work histories (such as intermittent work in low-paid jobs) are more reflective of the "demand side" than of the attitudes of workers toward work.

2. Mainstream economists refer to this as a rising "natural rate of unemployment," or as a rising nonaccelerating inflation rate of unemployment (NAIRU), although they usually blame the phenomenon on workers who are said to have weak attachments to the labor force. In the United States, the rising NAIRU was sometimes blamed on the entry of women and minorities into the labor force during the 1970s and 1980s. It should be clear that we reject this sort of excuse.

3. Note that here and below we use the term "Keynesian" in quotes to indicate the "bastard" Keynesian view of orthodox or textbook Keynesianism, and not any views that might have been adopted by Keynes.

4. Sharing the unemployment burden equally would be somewhat more equitable. It would be even better if unemployment could somehow be concentrated among the highly educated white males with seniority who are mostly responsible for wage inflation and who have the financial resources to see them through extended spells of unemployment. When aggregate demand is high, firms bid for these workers as bottlenecks develop, pushing up their wage demands. Unfortunately, tightening conditions, while reducing their wage demands, also cause unemployment down at the bottom. At worst, some of the highly educated white males are laid off and are forced to move down the career ladder to accept a less prestigious position until demand picks up. They can experience bouts of frictional unemployment, but accumulated financial assets as well as private and public unemployment compensation mitigate financial problems. We do not mean to dismiss the malaise that can be induced even among the relatively fortunate. But our point is that the significant unemployment experience is at the other end of the labor market—which bears

most of the costs of policy-induced unemployment in the "Keynesian" name of fighting inflation. Even if policy can induce unemployment among the disadvantaged, their burden is not likely to be as great as that put upon the less fortunate by countercyclical restriction of aggregate demand. In short, we find that the "Keynesian" approach to fighting unemployment is deficient in a number of important ways.

5. The maximum feasible rate would depend on a variety of factors, including customary norms regarding retirement age, normal age at which one enters the labor force, and female participation in the labor force. In this chapter we will not pursue the possibility that lower-skilled individuals have a lower desire to work. Rather, we adopt the presumption that the lower labor force participation rate of those with low educational attainment is primarily due to differences of opportunities rather than to different preferences. We also reject simple market-clearing models that would conclude that low-skilled individuals are outside the labor market voluntarily because their reservation wages exceed market wages, or involuntarily because minimum wages prevent market clearing. We believe, instead, that many of those outside the labor market would work—even at the minimum wage—if jobs were offered. We realize these are contentious issues. Even some liberals believe that the potential labor supply consists only of the unemployed plus a small proportion of those out of the labor force, mostly "discouraged" workers (those who self-report in Bureau of Labor Statistics surveys that the primary reason they are not looking for work is that they believe there are no jobs available). In contrast, we take a much broader view of the "potentially employable," including those who experience barriers to working (family responsibilities, disabilities, health problems), those who believe employers will not hire them (due, for example, to discrimination), and those who have developed attitudes or behaviors antithetical to working (drug or alcohol addiction, gang activity). As we will show, the level of educational attainment is a very good predictor of employment status, which indicates to us that the forces at work are complex. To some extent, those same social advantages that lead one to attain a college degree seem to also lead to high employment rates. We do not believe employment or educational success is merely due to "preferences."

6. As an extreme case, imagine a society in which it is expected that women will not work outside the home. Even careful interview data would probably reveal that few women wanted jobs. But clearly the human and natural rights to a job would not be fulfilled even if very few women reported that they wanted to work. In a less extreme case, think of a society in which young black males with low educational achievement are systematically excluded from employment because of entrenched racial discrimination. Even if such discrimination could be eliminated with the stroke of a pen, the habits and attitudes of this group that were created dur-

ing the years of discrimination would prove a major barrier to labor force entry.

7. Pigeon and Wray (2000) also tried to obtain an estimate of the "employable" population—those without jobs who might reasonably be expected to want to work, even if they are not counted as part of the labor force. In that article, it was assumed that college graduates face an ideal labor market with no barriers to finding a job. In 1999, the labor force participation rate for college graduates was 80.2 percent for those over age 25, and it was 87.6 percent for those aged 25 to 64. Using the participation rate of the college graduates as an ideal, it was then possible to calculate how many potentially employable individuals existed for each educational category by subtracting the number employed from a target number based on a participation rate of 80.2 percent of the population for those age 25 and above, or a participation rate of 87.6 per cent for those aged 25 to 64. That research found that in 1999, at the expansion's peak, there were 25.7 million potentially employable adults age 25 and above, or 14.1 million potentially employable adults age 25 to 64. Obviously, this number is much in excess of the number of officially unemployed (which was less than 3.8 million for the 25-and-over population midway through 1999).

For the reasons discussed above, this number should be taken as only a rough measure of the number who actually wanted to work. While it is probably a high-side estimate, it possibly represents an undercount. Wealth and access to financial resources vary systematically with educational status (in part, of course, because those with more education have higher labor market income and better success at finding jobs, but also because those from privileged backgrounds are more likely to graduate from college, and because a college degree gives one better access to loans). Hence we would expect that the desire to work would actually be higher among those outside the labor market with less education than among those with high educational achievement who are outside the labor market. All things being equal, we might expect higher desired labor force participation rates for the most disadvantaged groups. Obviously, access to financial resources is only one of the determinants of the desire to work, but this estimate of the employable population should not be dismissed as a wildly high estimate—it might be too low.

8. The connection between tight labor markets and wage growth is a contentious issue. For the United States, the empirical evidence for such a relationship is not strong (high inflation in postwar America has always come during periods of slack demand), although the evidence is stronger for some European nations. It probably depends on the wage setting institutions in place.

9. We do not have space here to discuss the program in detail; the specifics are analyzed in Wray (1998). Killingsworth (1977a, b) noted that the original draft of the Humphrey-Hawkins Act contained a job guarantee; however, it was dropped in the final version, due largely to fears over costs and possible inflationary impacts. Killingsworth argued that these fears were unfounded and demonstrated that a job guarantee program would be far more cost-effective than alternative means of job creation such as "Keynesian" tax cuts.

10. Other countries have also experimented with PSE-type programs, most notably Sweden. We do not offer details on such programs but refer interested readers to Ginsburg (1983).

References

Akerlof, George, and Brian Main. "An Experience Weighted Measure of Unemployment Durations." *American Economic Review* 71 (December 1981): 1003–11.

Beckett, Katherine, and Bruce Western. "The Penal System as Labor Market Institution: The Dynamics of Jobs and Jails, 1980–1995." *Overcrowded Times* 8, no. 6 (December 1997): 8–13.

Blanchard, Olivier, and Lawrence Katz. "What We Know and Do Not Know About the Natural Rate of Unemployment." *Journal of Economic Perspectives* 11, no. 1 (Winter 1997): 51–72.

Bluestone, Barry, and Stephen Rose. "The Unmeasured Labor Force." Public Policy Brief No. 39A. Annandale-on-Hudson, NY: Jerome Levy Economics Institute, May 1998.

Burgess, John, and William F. Mitchell. "Unemployment, Human Rights and a Full Employment Policy in Australia." In *Globalization, Human Rights, and Civil Society,* ed. Melinda Jones and Peter Kriesler. Sydney, Australia: Prospect Press, 1998.

Butler, Richard, and James McDonald. "Trends in Unemployment Duration Data." *Review of Economics and Statistics* 68, no. 4 (1986): 545–57.

Clark, Kim, and Lawrence Summers. "Labor Market Dynamics and Unemployment: A Reconsideration." *Brookings Papers on Economic Activity* 1 (1979): 13–60.

Darity, William A. Jr. "Who Loses from Unemployment?" *Journal of Economic Issues* 33, no. 2 (June 1999): 491–97.

Darity, William A. Jr., and Arthur H. Goldsmith. "Social Psychology, Unemployment and Macroeconomics." *Journal of Economic Perspectives* 10, no. 1 (1996): 121–40.

Davis, John B. "Justice." In *Encyclopedia of Political Economy,* ed. Philip O'Hara. London: Routledge, 1999.

DeMartino, George F. *Global Economy, Global Justice.* London: Routledge, 2000.

Dewey, John. *Intelligence in the Modern World,* ed. Joseph Ratner. New York: Modern Library, 1939.

Feather, Norman T. *The Psychological Impact of Unemployment.* New York: Springer-Verlag, 1990.

Forstater, Mathew. "Flexible Full Employment: Structural Implications of Discretionary Public Sector Employment." *Journal of Economic Issues* 32, no. 2 (June 1998a): 557–63.

———. "Institutionalist Approaches to Full Employment Policies." *Journal of Economic Issues* 32, no. 4 (December 1998b): 1135–39.

———. "Unemployment." In *The Elgar Companion to Post Keynesian Economics*, ed. J. King. Cheltenham, UK: Edward Elgar, 2003.

Gewirth, Alan. *The Community of Rights.* Chicago: University of Chicago Press, 1996.

Gilliard, Darrell K. *Prison and Jail Inmates at Midyear 1998.* Bureau of Justice Statistics, U.S. Department of Justice, March 1999.

Ginsburg, Helen. *Full Employment and Public Policy: The United States and Sweden.* Lexington, MA: Lexington Books, 1983.

Godley, Wynne, and L. Randall Wray. "Can Goldilocks Survive?" Policy Note No. 4. Annandale-on-Hudson, NY: Jerome Levy Economics Institute, 1999.

Gordon, Wendell. "Job Assurance—The Job Guarantee Revisited." *Journal of Economic Issues* 31, no. 3 (September 1997): 826–30.

Gottschalk, Peter. "The Impact of Changes in Public Employment on Low-Wage Labor Markets." In *Generating Jobs: How to Increase Demand for Less-Skilled Workers*, ed. Richard B. Freeman and Peter Gottschalk. New York: Russell Sage Foundation, 1998.

Harvey, Philip. *Securing the Right to Employment: Social Welfare Policy and the Unemployed in the United States.* Princeton, NJ: Princeton University Press, 1989.

———. "Employment as a Human Right." In *Sociology and the Public Agenda*, ed. W.J. Wilson. Newbury Park, CA: Sage, 1993.

———. "Liberal Strategies for Combating Joblessness in the Twentieth Century." *Journal of Economic Issues* 33, no. 2 (June 1999): 497–504.

Jahoda, Marie. *Employment and Unemployment: A Social-Psychological Analysis.* Cambridge: Cambridge University Press, 1982.

Kaufman, Roger. "Why the U.S. Unemployment Rate Is So High." In *Unemployment and Inflation: Institutionalist and Structuralist Views*, ed. Michael Piore. White Plains, NY: M.E. Sharpe, 1979.

Kelvin, Peter, and Joanna E. Jarrett. *Unemployment: Its Social Psychological Effects.* Cambridge: Cambridge University Press, 1985.

Keynes, John Maynard. *The General Theory of Employment, Interest, and Money.* New York and London: Harcourt Brace Jovanovich, 1964.

Killingsworth, Charles. *Structural Unemployment in the United States.* Washington, DC: U.S. Department of Labor, Manpower Administration, Office of Manpower Policy, Evaluation and Research, 1965.

———. *Fact and Fallacy in Labor Market Analysis: A Reply to Mr. Lando.* School of Labor and Industrial Relations, College of Social Science, Michigan State University, 1971.

———. "The Role of Public Service Employment." In *Proceedings of the 1977 Spring Meeting of the Industrial Relations Research Association*, Madison, WI: Industrial Relations Research Association, 1977a, 489–95.

———. "Tax Cuts and Employment Policy." In *Job Creation: What Works?* ed. Robert Taggart. Salt Lake City: Olympus, 1977b.

Kriesler, Peter. "Introduction—Economic Dimensions of Human Rights: An Overview." *Australian Journal of Human Rights* 4, no. 2 (1998), www.austLii.edu.au/journals/AJHR/1998/9.html.

Layard, Richard. "Preventing Long-term Unemployment." In *Working for Full Employment*, ed. John Philpott. London: Routledge, 1997.

Lerner, Abba. *The Economics of Employment.* New York: McGraw Hill, 1951.

Levin-Waldman, Oren. "The Minimum Wage Can Be Raised: Lessons from the 1999 Levy Institute Survey of Small Business." Policy Note No. 6. Annandale-on-Hudson, NY: Jerome Levy Economics Institute, 1999.

Marshall, Ray, Vernon M. Briggs Jr., and Allan G. King. *Labor Economics: Wages, Employment, Trade Unionism, and Public Policy.* Homewood, IL: Richard D. Irwin, 1984.

Minsky, Hyman. *Stabilizing an Unstable Economy.* New Haven, CT: Yale University Press, 1986.

Moosa, Imad A. "On the Costs of Inflation and Unemployment." *Journal of Post Keynesian Economics* 19, no. 4 (1997): 651–66.

Nevile, John W. "Human Rights Issues in the Welfare State." *Australian Journal of Human Rights* 4, no. 2 (1998), www.austLII.edu.au/au/journals/AJHR/1998/5.html.

Nevile, John W. and Peter Kriesler. "Full Employment, a Neglected, but Indispensable and Feasible Human Right." *Economic and Labor Relations Review* 11, supplement (2000): 117–36.

Philpott, John, ed. *Working for Full Employment.* London: Routledge, 1997.

Piachaud, David. "A Price Worth Paying? The Costs of Unemployment." In *Working for Full Employment*, ed. J. Philpott. London: Routledge, 1997.

Pigeon, Marc-André, and L. Randall Wray. "Can a Rising Tide Raise All Boats? Evidence from the Clinton-Era Expansion." *Journal of Economic Issues* 34, no. 4 (December 2000): 811–45.

Piore, Michael, ed. *Unemployment and Inflation: Institutionalist and Structuralist Views*. White Plains, NY: M.E. Sharpe, 1979.

Rawls, John. *A Theory of Justice*. Cambridge, MA: Belknap Press of Harvard University Press, 1971.

Ritter, Joseph A. "School and Work." *National Economic Trends*, The Federal Reserve Bank of St. Louis (June 1998): 1.

Siegel, Richard Lewis. *Employment and Human Rights*. Philadelphia: University of Pennsylvania Press, 1994.

Sen, Amartya. "Justice." In *The New Palgrave: A Dictionary of Economics*, ed. John Eatwell, Murray Milgate, and Peter Newman. London: Macmillan, 1987.

———. *Development as Freedom*. New York: Alfred A. Knopf, 1999.

Tool, Marc. *The Discretionary Economy*. Santa Monica, CA: Goodyear, 1979.

———. "Employment as a Human Right." In *Employment, Technology, and Economic Needs: Theory, Evidence, and Public Policy*, ed. Jonathan Michie and Angelo Reati. Cheltenham, UK: Edward Elgar 1998.

U.S. Department of Labor, Bureau of Labor Statistics. Labor Force Statistics from the Current Population Survey. www.bls.gov/cps/home.htm tables.

Veblen, Thorstein. *On the Nature and Uses of Sabotage*. New York: Oriole Chapbooks, 1919.

Vickrey, William. "Today's Task for Economists." *American Economic Review* 83, no. 1 (March 1993): 1–10.

———. "A Trans-Keynesian Manifesto (Thoughts About an Assets-Based Macroeconomics)." *Journal of Post Keynesian Economics* 19, no. 4 (1997): 495–510.

Wray, L. Randall. "Government as Employer of Last Resort: Full Employment without Inflation." Working Paper No. 213. Annandale-on Hudson, NY: Jerome Levy Economics Institute, 1997.

———. *Understanding Modern Money: The Key to Full Employment and Price Stability*. Aldershot, UK: Edward Elgar, 1998.

———. "Surplus Mania: A Reality Check." Policy Note No. 3. Annandale-on-Hudson, NY: Jerome Levy Economics Institute, 1999.

———. "A New Economic Reality: Penal Keynesianism." *Challenge* 43, no. 5 (2000a): 31–59.

———. "Why Does the Fed Want Slower Growth?" Policy Note No. 7. Annandale-on-Hudson, NY: Jerome Levy Economics Institute, 2000b.

———. "The Backward Art of Tax Cutting." Policy Note No. 5. Annandale-on-Hudson, NY: Jerome Levy Economics Institute, 2001.

———. "The Perfect Fiscal Storm." Policy Note No. 5. Kansas City: Center for Full Employment and Price Stability, 2002.

———. "Can a Rising Tide Raise All Boats? Evidence from the Kennedy-Johnson and Clinton-Era Expansions." In *New Thinking in Macroeconomics: Social, Institutional, and Environmental Perspective,* ed. Jonathan M. Harris and Neva Goodwin. Aldershot: Cheltenham, UK: Edward Elgar, 2003, 150–81.

18

Regressive Norms, Progressive Possibilities, and Labor Justice

Mayo C. Toruño

While American labor has never been treated with the deference that has conventionally been reserved for capital, there was a moment, beginning in the 1930s and ending in the late 1970s, when it seemed that government was making a concerted effort to achieve justice in the treatment of labor. Labor unions were recognized and minimum wage laws enacted, the federal government committed itself to maintaining full employment and sided with labor in significant contract disputes, social safety nets developed for the poor and the unemployed, real wages grew, and firms were required to attend to occupational safety. But beginning in the late 1970s and continuing to the present, that moment fell by the wayside as government took a decidedly right turn. Union membership declined and the real minimum wage fell, inflation rather than unemployment became the major policy concern, the federal government fired striking air traffic controllers and sided with capital in contract disputes, unemployment compensation was cut back, the social safety net was shredded by welfare reform, real wages fell or stagnated, and occupational safety was dismissed as bureaucratic red tape. Whatever hope there might have been for the development of a more just social order soon dissipated with the growing dominance of rightist politics.

To be sure, the declining fortune of labor could be attributed, in part, to changes in the structure and performance of the economy, but much of it, and clearly that portion subject to political discretion, was the result of a government that consciously sought to dismantle the welfare state and push back the gains of labor. Yet this rightist shift was seldom portrayed as an assault upon labor; it was instead depicted as an attack upon the state. The state had come to be seen as a parasitical institution, draining the productive sector of the economy and impeding the achievement of the good life. What was needed was a leaner government, one that eliminated dependency-encouraging programs and bureaucratic red tape, freed capital of its presumed burdens, and liberated markets of inefficient regulations. By promoting a greater degree of freedom, such a system, it was argued, would encourage individual initiative and enhance everyone's material condition.

Business could, of course, be counted on to support a rightist political economy. After all, pleas for laissez-faire have been a feature of business politics since the beginning of capitalism. And while its adherence to laissez-faire has always been riddled with self-serving exceptions, business has never wavered in its demand to keep labor free of government-imposed minimum wages, collective bargaining, and social safety nets. Yet in the absence of broader support, capital's political inclinations would not have been enough to explain the rightist shift, which could be accounted for only by the growing acceptance of this position by other social classes, in particular the working class. To be sure, organized labor continued to defend the welfare state and the Democratic Party, but the rank and file, the growing number of nonunionized workers, and specifically white working-class males embraced the rightist message. The decline in labor's fortune occurred in large part because a significant fraction of the working class accepted the rightist critique of government.

It is difficult to imagine why workers would consciously support such a self-defeating agenda. There is, of course, the possibility that ignorance played a part in this choice; and to the extent that the full implications of rightist ideology were misunderstood, ignorance is, by default, the only explanation. But a more appropriate account, one more likely to guide us in the formulation of a more just politics, would have to explain the drawing power that cultural norms played in attracting labor to the right. The right's ability to capture public discourse was based on its ability to tap into the nation's core values of individualism and self-reliance. When placed in the context of the cold war and its corollary suspicion of collectivism, as well as the nation's legacy of racism and social Darwinism, these norms led to a rejection of the state. But by embracing the antistatist message, workers unwittingly contributed to a decline in their own condition.

By exploring the evolution of cultural and political norms since the end of World War II, this chapter seeks to understand the forces that led a significant fraction of the working class to support an ideology detrimental to its self-interest. A related goal is to lay out the elements of a more just political economy while exploring the possibilities for its emergence. This will occur in five steps. First, I will start by exploring the nation's core belief in a simple commodity-producing vision of justice. Second, I will outline the alternative vision of justice that emerged with the New Deal and dominated political economic ideology from the 1930s until the 1970s. The third section explores the material and ideological factors that led to the resurgence of rightist politics. Section four outlines the role government could play in the promotion of a more just social order. The conclusion ties these arguments together by highlighting the factors required for the emergence of a more enlightened politics.

Core American Values

American political culture has always had a deep commitment to individualism, private property, self-reliance, and economic freedom (Lipset and Raab 1973, 24). These values account for the generally conservative nature of its politics and the appeal of rightist thought. At the core of the rightist's plea for economic freedom and limited government is the image of a social order dominated by self-reliant individuals carrying on economic activity without the need for government oversight. This belief rests on the proposition that each individual has the right to seek income as best deemed fit, so long as such activity does not infringe on the right of others to do the same. It also presumes that each individual has the exclusive right to use the property acquired from such income-seeking activity. What makes this idea so compelling is that it builds on the universal imperative to survive, affirming each individual's right to figure out how best to get by and, if possible, prosper.

This idea is prevalent throughout the culture,

expressed as an unquestioned value by the population at large and as a basic proposition in the theoretical arguments of free market economists. In its simplest form, the idea seldom includes the possibility that, despite best efforts, the individual might not succeed in the search for income; and if the possibility is considered, it is more often than not assumed to be the result of individual inadequacies. The crudest version of this idea is found in the various expressions of social Darwinism that still echo in the culture and that are generally tied to racist beliefs regarding the distribution of moral character and native ability (Heilbroner and Singer 1984, 155–57). But in its more exacting form, this idea is wedded to the neoclassical theory of competitive markets. This version acknowledges the possibility that the individual might not be successful in the search for income, but the possibility is presumed to be temporary, an exception to the rule that is quickly remedied by the market's presumed ability to sustain full employment. The neoclassicals claim that a society organized on the basis of economic freedom is not only consistent with the individual's right to figure out how best to survive and prosper, but feasible as well. As a result, the free market's supposed capacity for self-regulation obviates the need for public oversight, allowing government to be confined to the minimal tasks of the night watchman state: defending private property and adjudicating disputes, defending the nation from foreign attack, and providing for commercial infrastructure.

Karl Marx referred to the social order that is represented by this idea as a simple commodity-producing society, a system in which every household owns enough means of production to provide for itself (Sweezy 1942, 23). In such a system, self-interest motivates each household to specialize in the production of a narrow range of goods, retaining a portion for its own use while selling the remainder in order to buy the myriad other goods produced by other households. Marx interpreted a simple commodity-producing society as an ideological projection of the capitalist class. It is telling that this is precisely the image used by Milton Friedman to tout the virtues of free enterprise (1982, 13). But while Marx viewed this idealized society as a distortion of the truth, an ideological prism through which a specific class of people interprets reality, Friedman sees that same idealized society as an appropriate model of capitalism. Its attraction lies in the harmony suggested by a community of self-reliant individuals free to interact with one another as equals in the open market. This equality emanates from the presumption that each household has the right to refuse the terms of exchange. But this right can be made credible, as Friedman acknowledges, only if each household owns enough means of production to produce for itself (Friedman 1982, 13). Under such conditions, no household would be compelled to accept an unfair or extortionary exchange, and, by extension, every exchange that is accepted would be mutually beneficial.

The only coercion that would exist in such a system would be the one associated with government, an institution that compels individuals to conform to its dictates. The payment of taxes, for example, does not involve a voluntary exchange in which the individual reserves the right of refusal. The taxes must be paid even if the individual would rather not pay. Government, therefore, is said to reduce the sphere of life that encourages free choice while increasing the range of compulsory behavior. By focusing on government's burdens and extortionary potential, this norm tends toward antistatism.

Additionally, by focusing on individual property rights and individual exchange, this view of society tends to obscure the portion of income that results from the positive externalities generated by a publicly provided system of law and social infrastructure. The simple commodity-producing view of justice ignores the collective benefits generated by a government that attends to the common expense of society, the social overhead. This encourages the erroneous view that government does not contribute to the wealth and income of the community. It also promotes the equally erroneous view that a person's income is solely a result of individual efforts. In short, this norm conflicts with the notion of a collective or social income, a state-provided flow of money and services made available to individuals by virtue of their membership in the political community.[1]

Perhaps the most obvious deficiency of the simple commodity-producing view is that it presumes a pattern of property ownership that is at odds with reality. In real capitalist societies, the majority of households, namely working-class households, do not own enough means of production to provide for themselves. As a result, the ability to refuse an unfair or extortionary exchange is not equally distributed; in fact, it is confined to a narrow portion of the population. The simple commodity-producing view of justice is more compatible with the material conditions of business owners than with the conditions of workers. In the exchange of employment for wages, capitalists have a far greater capacity to refuse the terms of exchange than do workers. Yet despite this inconvenient fact, the simple commodity-producing vision has been a feature of American political culture since its inception, capturing the aspirations of capitalists and workers alike and serving as a guide to the social ought.[2]

Throughout the nineteenth century, the expanding frontier had a considerable role in sustaining this belief. The availability of land, made possible by the conquest of Native American and Mexican territories, made credible the notion of an expanding community of self-governing farmers and small business owners. Working-class householders could hold out for the possibility that they too might become property owners by moving to the frontier and staking a claim on land. A similar dynamic was repeated during the golden age of American capitalism.[3] The unprecedented economic growth of that era brought about an improvement in the real wage of the average worker and an increase in the number of workers joining the ranks of the small business class. While this social mobility was never as dramatic as mythology would suggest, it was enough to lend credence to the belief that workers could become property owners.

The strength of this belief, that workers are potential members of the propertied class, is measured by the historically recurring political alliances that occur between workers and small business owners. Thus, during the last quarter of the nineteenth century and the first two decades of the twentieth century, at the height of the Populist and Progressive movements, workers saw themselves in common cause with small farmers and small business owners, railing against the monopolies that were thought to prevent propertyless workers from moving into the ranks of the employing class (Dillard 1967, 451–52). And during the most recent era, starting with the presidency of Ronald Reagan, workers have aligned themselves with business in the belief that taxes were preventing them from acquiring productive wealth and that government, not business, was antithetical to their interests.

Labor's Moment and the Social Welfare State

The simple commodity-producing vision of justice, and the minimalist state it implied, were the dominant ideology guiding public policy until the

Great Depression of the 1930s. To be sure, there had been a growing movement emanating from the working classes and small farmers, dating back to the late nineteenth century, that was demanding greater equity in the treatment of labor and a more progressive state. Labor unions were growing in strength, despite the continued attacks from business and a hostile public policy. The socialist movement was gaining momentum, as witnessed by the 1912 presidential bid of Eugene Debs. And a few states, most notably Wisconsin, had implemented progressive reforms. Yet despite these rumblings, the dominant political structure remained conservative, upholding the night watchman state as the model of government.

It was not until the 1930s that a more progressive vision of government began to dominate national politics. The imminent collapse of the system provided the impetus for the emergence of legislation and a range of public programs, in the form of President Franklin D. Roosevelt's New Deal, whose overriding purpose was to provide the social infrastructure needed to support working-class households. The state, forced to confront the extortion to which labor had been subjected, responded by developing a series of programs that sought to provide workers a social wage (a flow of collective income, such as Social Security, unemployment compensation, housing, minimum wages, and poor relief, that provides workers the wherewithal to be productive members of society). A social welfare state was being developed, one that would improve social welfare by adding, to the traditional functions of the night watchman state, policies that cover the social overhead and collective income needed to sustain a humane and productive community.

To be sure, the politicians had no idea they were developing what is now called a social wage, even though that is what it was. The motivation behind its creation had less to do with recognizing the importance of collective income, or government's role in the provisioning of social overhead, than with the more practical end of averting widespread unrest. Many of the programs making up the new social wage, such as unemployment compensation and poverty relief, were consciously set at levels that maintained capital's dominance over labor. The objective was not to provide the same power of refusal available to capital, or to maximize the productive potential of the labor force, but rather to soften the blows of poverty and unemployment. Similarly, those portions of the social wage that seemed unrelated to productive effort, such as poverty relief, were far more contentious than those that were, such as unemployment compensation. In this sense, the state's efforts were rather timid. Yet the fact that a social wage was being constructed represented a watershed in the state's relation to labor. It had the effect of providing labor with more leverage in its dealings with capital, even though such leverage remained inferior to that of capital.

By the 1940s, as a result of the economic boost given by the state's expanded role during World War II, mainstream political discourse had accommodated itself to the idea of a social welfare state. Government, it was now understood, should be vigilant of potential monopolies and unfair business practices, recognize labor unions and support collective bargaining, legislate a livable minimum wage, provide for Social Security, unemployment compensation, poverty relief and full employment. The state was viewed as responsible for the provisioning of collective benefits. The common expense associated with attending to the nation's social overhead had come to be seen as a necessity, and many of the programs making up the new social wage, such as Social Security and unemployment compensation, were viewed as indispensable. Rather than being a source of coercion, government was now being perceived as the guarantor of economic prosperity.

Although this view of the state had gained credence, and remained the dominant norm throughout the golden age, its legitimacy was tenuous. The nation's core beliefs in individualism and self-reliance, and its related vision of a simple commodity-producing society, were deeply ingrained. Though the Republican Party had been eclipsed by the shift in political norms brought on by the New Deal and World War II, it continued to express the individualist sentiments still present in the culture at large and the pleas for limited government perennially voiced by its core constituency, the business class. At the same time, organized labor, despite its support for the Democratic Party and the social welfare state, continued to reflect the reformist, antisocialist attitudes characteristic of American labor unions (Dillard 1967, 451–58). In 1946, the U.S. Congress, during a brief period of Republican control that allowed it to override President Harry Truman's veto, passed the Taft-Hartley Act, which permitted individual states to outlaw the union shop. Throughout the late 1940s and early 1950s, at the height of the anticommunist hysteria, the Republican Party led the charge in attacking the federal government for harboring Communists "and turning loose a swarm of arrogant bureaucrats who meddle intolerably in the lives of citizens" (Johnson and Porter 1973, 497). And throughout the golden age, the Republicans portrayed government as a parasitical institution that fed on the productive efforts of individuals (Johnson and Porter 1973, 678). Antistatism was alive and well, in awkward coexistence with the collectivist norms that emerged with the rise of the social welfare state.

Throughout the golden age, this tension was exemplified in the attitude of the Democratic Party. While the Democrats had created the social welfare state and the flows of social income associated with it, they remained faithful to the values of individualism, self-reliance, and free enterprise (Democratic Party 1980, 23; 1992, 12, 14; Johnson and Porter 1973, 430). They were more of a progressive business-cum-labor party than a labor party in the traditional sense. Government, they believed, should ameliorate the social ills that can emerge from a free and unregulated market system, while encouraging the growth-inducing potential of private enterprise (Johnson and Porter 1973, 582–83). And since private enterprise requires labor as well as capital, government should mediate their contending interests for the common good. The social welfare state was seen as necessary complement to private enterprise, not its antithesis.

Though these values were given a further boost in the 1960s, under President Lyndon Johnson's Great Society programs, by the mid-1970s the social welfare state had become the target of an attack that has continued to this day. The Republicans led the attack by focusing on the presumed fraud and waste of welfare, demanding the elimination of the Department of Education, advocating a constitutional amendment to balance the federal budget, reducing taxes, eliminating bureaucratic waste, cutting the size of government, and encouraging privatization (Johnson and Porter 1973, 863, 874; Republican Party 1976, 12; 1980, 10, 28). For their part, the Democrats began to soft-pedal many of the themes they had upheld during the golden age. They ceased to emphasize the importance of collective bargaining, began to speak in terms of welfare reform, and were less insistent in demanding full employment (*Congressional Quarterly* 1991, 129–31).

The Rightist Backlash

What accounts for this reversal? To begin with, as noted above, even though the collectivist norms of a social welfare state had gained some credence, their acceptance remained tenuous, floating in a culture that held onto the individualist and antistatist norms of a simple commodity-producing view of society. But since these norms have always been a feature of the system, their resurgence must be explained by other factors.

One argument that has been offered is that the rightist backlash was largely the result of a conscious attempt on the part of capitalists to restore their power and profits. As a result of the decline that profit rates began to experience in the late 1960s, capitalists and their political representatives stepped up their attacks against the state by demanding the elimination of public programs deemed responsible for that decline. The attack, while couched in the language of economic freedom, was carried out with the intent of restoring the power that capital had lost to labor during the golden age of American capitalism (Bowles, Gordon, and Weisskopf 1989).

While this argument explains capital's endorsement of the rightist movement, it does not explain the growing acceptance of that movement by other social classes. The electoral gains of rightist politicians can be explained only by the acceptance of that message by a growing proportion of the working class. Indeed, the rightist shift was not a purely economic phenomenon; it was also, and perhaps primarily, a cultural and social movement, involving efforts on the part of a wide segment of society to restore the values that were thought to be under attack as a result of the expanding welfare state, the civil rights advances, and the counterculture of the 1960s, and the debacle of the Vietnam war.

One of the factors that can account for the growing dismissal of the social welfare state was the arrival of the cold war and the emergence of the United States as a superpower. The cold war managed to tap into the culture's long-standing belief in its exceptionalism and obligation to lead all of humanity into a new era of economic freedom and material abundance. The dichotomy that quickly emerged was one of capitalism and freedom on the one hand, and communism and tyranny on the other. It was a dichotomy bolstered by the libertarian notion that any extension of government beyond its night watchman functions would lead society down a slippery slope eventuating in the tyrannical forms of fascism, socialism, or communism (Friedman 1982; Hayek 1994). This dichotomy placed on the defensive proposals that sought to use government for the attainment of collective ends other than those of the night watchman state. The anticommunist hysteria of the cold war had the effect of making those who offered a more expansive vision of government seem treasonous.

At the same time, the emergence of the United States as a superpower vastly expanded the state's military component and, in the process, altered its democratic norms. A warfare state was being grafted onto the welfare state (Melman 1997). Wars, and continued readiness for war, led a growing number of working-class households, most of whom had histories of military service, to imagine they were in common cause with capitalists in the fight against communism, defending the nation's cherished values of individualism and economic freedom. Patriotism, nationalism, and oaths of allegiance reinforced this view by encouraging obedience to structures of power and command.[4] The habits of thought encouraged by militarism and nationalism undermined democratic culture by suggesting that criticism of established political and business institutions was insubordinate and anti-American. War-related expenditures and militaristic solutions to social problems became more palatable than those associated with the "socialistic" welfare state.

The failure of the Vietnam war, combined with the social upheavals of the 1960s, led to a cultural crisis from which the rightist movement of the late 1970s emerged. The movement carried with it the classic features of nascent fascism: a nation reeling from a crisis of confidence seeking to renew its glory by appealing to a mythic past, to restore authority and order, and declaring war on values and behavior contrary to that myth (Sweezy 1942, 329–34). The rightist movement wrapped itself in the flag, tying militarism, duty, and honor to the simple commodity-producing values of individualism, self-reliance, and economic freedom, while simultaneously demeaning reasoned dialogue and restoring confidence through military victories (such as the contra war in Nicaragua, the invasion of Grenada, the invasion of Panama, the Persian Gulf War, Afghanistan, and the most recent invasion of Iraq)—and all of this, with the enthusiastic support of large segments of the American working class.

The growing dismissal of the welfare state was also aided by the nation's racist legacy and the very success of the golden age. The civil rights movement, along with the affirmative action and poverty relief programs of the 1960s, had alienated large numbers of white workers, particularly southern whites, who saw these social reforms as an unwarranted extension of rights to a class of people deemed inferior and unworthy of a voice in public policy. The federal government came to be seen as an institution too willing to subsidize individuals who, in addition to being inferior, were unwilling to work. At the same time, the economic success of the golden age led workers to imagine that their employment and rising income were the result of individual diligence and the blessings of the free market. The stimulative impact of the state was largely invisible since it was less dependent on direct government employment than it was on the private employment generated through the multiplicative effect of government expenditures. The private sector, not the public sector, was seen as responsible for low unemployment and rising wages (Toruño 1997).

The economic success of the golden age also reinforced the quintessentially American belief that the United States is a classless society. American culture has traditionally ignored the classic distinction between capitalists and workers, largely because it also ignores the distinction between productive and consumptive property. What matters, from this perspective, is that the industrious accumulate property, which, at first, may take the form of consumptive property, but which, in due time, and if one is sufficiently diligent, will eventuate in the ownership of productive property. Property is viewed as a reward for industry, and capitalists, rather than being a distinct social class, are instead seen as the most successful of the industrious class, of which workers are themselves a part. The growth in home ownership, which was given a boost by state-sponsored housing subsidies, most notably the GI Bill, reinforced this view. Home ownership conferred upon workers the sense that they were a part of the community of property owners, in common cause with the business class. The divide was not between capitalists and workers, but between industrious property owners and the indolent. Moreover, the industrious had come to believe that their self-reliant efforts were unappreciated by a government intent on providing handouts to the indolent.

The rightist backlash can also be explained by the gradual deterioration that occurred in important political institutions over the course of the last six decades. The ongoing erosion of political parties made elections a contest over competing personalities rather than a contest over competing visions of the social ought. Increasingly, as revealed by the popularity of actors as politicians, the focus has shifted away from a candidate's views on public policy and toward issues of private morality and presumed decisiveness. Similarly, the decline in electoral participation that began in the early 1960s, which has been most pronounced among the working classes, had the effect of shrinking labor's share of the vote while increasing the share coming from the middle and upper classes. At the same time, the decline in union membership, from the mid-1950s onward, reduced labor's voice in the nation's political discourse, while the growing concentration of mass media narrowed the range of political dialogue to debates over versions of the social ought consistent with wealth and privilege (Toruño 1997).

Progressive Possibilities

It is important to keep in mind that despite the rightist movement and the antistatist legacy of the culture, elements of a more enlightened view of the state have persisted. The continued existence of this alternative vision, even though it occupies an increasingly small sphere of contemporary discourse, offers hope for the emergence of a political movement that will force government to attend to the needs of labor. Such a movement, of course, would have to overcome formidable cultural and institutional barriers, and one would hope they could be overcome without the inducement of a major crisis, such as another Great Depression. But whatever possibilities might exist for the emergence of such a movement, it would have to deal with the nation's commitment to individualism, self-reliance, and economic freedom, for it is from the existing context that institutions are changed. There is little hope of transforming existing institutions unless such a political movement

addresses the concerns of a culture committed to a simple commodity-producing vision of justice.

The place to start would be to acknowledge the importance of this vision by noting that its attainment is thwarted by the kind of government demanded by rightists. The night watchman state, rather than limiting the range of coercion and expanding the sphere of economic freedom, actually does the opposite. The night watchman state is antithetical to the simple commodity-producing view of justice because it prevents an overwhelming proportion of the population, namely the working class, from exercising, without the threat of economic coercion, its right of refusal. Justice, therefore, requires that the ability to exercise the right of refusal be extended to all members of society. Rather than implying limited government, the simple commodity-producing vision of justice implies the opposite: a government that must attend to the social infrastructure that must be in place before economic freedom can be exercised.[5] Government, from this perspective, is less of an obstacle to freedom than the necessary prerequisite for its exercise.

Rightists, of course, acknowledge that government must provide the infrastructure needed to effectuate their vision of justice. But the infrastructure they have in mind is confined to the legal, political, and police institutions needed to defend private property. The public expense associated with maintaining these institutions is considered appropriate because it protects the fruits of the individual's efforts. Individuals are entitled to retain the fruits of their labor because of the survival imperative. In the classic Lockean scheme, the justification for private property, and thus the public expense associated with defending that property, is the right to survive. But that right must surely extend to having access to the means of survival. To paraphrase John Locke, the first form of property is property in one's self, one's ability to work, and to the extent that laboring capacity is neglected, a key condition of a simple commodity-producing society is also neglected (Locke 1963, 328–29). Therefore, achieving the simple commodity-producing view of economic freedom requires a far more expansive definition of social infrastructure than is offered by the right. It would have to include not simply the cost of defending private property, but the cost of providing the social income that allows individuals to survive and serve as productive members of society.

A government that attended to this more expansive definition of social infrastructure would ensure that everyone, not just property owners, could exercise economic freedom without the threat of economic coercion. By providing for the social costs of maintaining a viable and free society, government would be ensuring workers' ability to exercise the right of refusal while simultaneously maintaining the institutional context for a productive labor force. The costs of maintaining this more expansive social overhead could be covered by government through various social insurance programs that pay for the costs of workers' subsistence and/or through the enforcement of livable minimum wage laws (Champlin and Knoedler 2002, 887). In addition, government could enhance labor's ability to exercise the right of refusal by maintaining full employment through appropriate fiscal and monetary policies and/or through the use of employer-of-last-resort public programs (Wray 1998). A policy of full employment would, of course, reduce the social costs and eliminate the wasted human potential brought on by unemployment. Additionally, employer-of-last-resort programs would allow labor to exercise its right of refusal by providing the option of public employment whenever the terms of private employment were inappropriate.

The achievement of such a system would require that cultural norms be adjusted to the idea that government has an obligation to provide for the common expense of maintaining the population. It would require accepting the notion that the infrastructural requirements of labor are just as important as the infrastructural requirements of capital and that the productive potential of the nation is less dependent on its plant and equipment than on labor's capacity to put them to good use.

Conclusion

Given the rightist interpretation currently dominating America's commitment to individualism and self-reliance, the acceptance of this proposal seems fanciful. The most immediate challenge comes from the fact that, as currently constituted, political discourse is far too narrow, and so too, therefore, is the range of possible policy options. The growing disparities in the distribution of income and wealth, the emaciation of labor unions, the concentration of mass media, the tremendous cost of electoral campaigns and consequent reliance upon corporate donations, have led to a situation in which political discourse rarely ventures beyond the concerns of capital. The social ought, regardless of whether it is dressed in Democratic or Republican garb, reflects the vision of society as seen from the perspective of privilege and wealth; and when it tries to capture the sentiment of the average person, it gives voice not to the needs and concerns that actually exist, but rather to a cultural icon, a caricature of the struggling but self-reliant individual, that both workers and capitalists assume represents the norm. The interpretation of events and discussion of possibilities are contained within this framework and offered to the population as a reflection of their opinions. True debate and dialogue, that would allow and encourage the voices of those who stand outside that structure of power, do not exist. In this sense, information flows one way.

This narrowing of political discourse, when combined with the consumerism and growing militarism of the culture, has led to a gradual erosion of democratic values. Political discourse, packaged and offered by the elites, is consumed, not engaged, and alternatives not voiced by the media go unheard. The inability to engage that debate, to affect political outcomes, to respond to the official message, leads to the kind of political disengagement that is witnessed by the ongoing decline in electoral participation. At the same time, the growing militarism of society, brought on by the emergence of the warfare state, discourages the search for ideas that fall outside established convention while encouraging loyalty to deeply held norms. Blind allegiance to the symbols of freedom takes precedence over the critical and insubordinate attitude required for the exercise of freedom.

This gradual erosion of democratic values is aggravated by the complacency fostered by the nation's current superpower status and long-standing belief in its exceptionalism. The nation has always accepted the myth that the United States has a historical mission and divine purpose to lead all of humanity toward freedom and democracy. Its current superpower status has furthered this belief by lending support to the false conclusion that its global power is the result of a virtuous political economy. This has made it difficult for political elites, and the population at large, to consider the possibility that superior models of justice and freedom might exist.

Yet despite these formidable obstacles, the history of America's social welfare state suggests that norms and institutions can change, that a more humane and progressive state can emerge. To begin with, it is important to note that the kind of state proposed here is consistent with the long-standing American tradition of empirical collectivism, even though it has been relegated to the background during the current rightist era. This tradition acknowledges that there are spheres of life that depend upon collective needs, and other spheres that are private and individual (Tilman 2001). It does not accept the simplistic dichotomy of individualism versus collectivism, but rather claims that both are components of social life. The role of government, from this perspective, is to cover those collective needs, the social overhead, that must be in place before individual initiative and economic freedom can flourish. The culture's commitment to individualism and self-reliance need not be inconsistent with the emergence of a social welfare state that attends to the infrastructure and social income needed to maintain a humane and productive community.

At the same time, the culture's commitment to democracy, even though its practice has deteriorated over the last few decades, leaves open the possibility that a vibrant democratic culture can be revived. It would require, however, a change in the political institutions of society. Political discourse would have to be expanded to ensure an equal voice to all opinions, not just those of wealth and privilege. This would require, among other things, 100 percent public funding of electoral campaigns. It would also require the creation and promotion, through public funds, of open, free media, which would not accept corporate donations and which encourage true dialogue (Mills 1956, 303–4). Such a system would offer a greater voice to alternative visions of justice, enhancing the possibility that a progressive social welfare state will emerge.

Yes, the obstacles are formidable, but I see no

other choice than to continue pushing for a more expansive democracy, one that insists on creating an environment that ensures everyone's right to survive and exercise freedom without economic coercion.

Notes

1. My use of the terms "collective income" and "social income" is intended to be broader than the more commonly used term "social wage." Indeed, the broadest definition of "social wage," which incorporates the notion of a universal basic income available to all citizens regardless of economic status, is equivalent to my use of the term "social income." (See Hyman 2001, 1068–70.)

2. The social ought represents the constellation of norms, the ideology, that governs state policy. The concept is borrowed from Philip Klein (1984) who defines it as the "collective ought," rather than the social ought. I prefer using the latter term since it avoids the utilitarian implications, in particular the idea that society is nothing more than a collection of individuals, that might be imputed to the phrase "collective ought."

3. The golden age refers to the three decades following World War II. A thorough analysis of that era can be found in Marglin and Schor (1990).

4. Thorstein Veblen, as early as 1917 and 1919, pointed out the self-defeating alliance that workers often make with capitalists for the sake of nationalism, patriotism, and military adventurism (Veblen 1964, 125–28; 1998, 31–76).

5. Interestingly enough, Milton Friedman's famous negative income tax proposal can be interpreted as an acknowledgment of the need to maintain a flow of social income that is high enough to ensure the proper exercise of economic freedom.

References

Bowles, Samuel, David M. Gordon, and Thomas E. Weisskopf. "Business Ascendancy and Economic Impasse: A Structural Retrospective on Conservative Economics 1979–87." *Journal of Economic Perspectives* 3, no. 1 (Winter 1989): 107–34.

Champlin, Dell P., and Janet T. Knoedler. "Wages in the Public Interest: Insights from Thorstein Veblen and J.M. Clark." *Journal of Economic Issues* 36, no. 4 (December 2002): 877–91.

Congressional Quarterly, National Party Conventions, 1831–1988. Washington, DC: Congressional Quarterly Incorporated, 1991.

Democratic Party. *The Democratic Party Platform of 1980* (and *1984, 1988, 1992, 1996, 2000*).

Dillard, Dudley. *Economic Development of the North Atlantic Community: Historical Introduction to Modern Economics*. Englewood Cliffs, NJ: Prentice-Hall, 1967.

Friedman, Milton, with the assistance of Rose D. Friedman. *Capitalism and Freedom*. Chicago: University of Chicago Press, 1982 (1962).

Hayek, F.A. *The Road to Serfdom*, with a new Introduction by Milton Friedman. Chicago: University of Chicago Press, 1994 (1944).

Heilbroner, Robert L., and Aaron Singer. *The Economic Transformation of America: 1600 to the Present*. 2nd ed. San Diego: Harcourt Brace Jovanovich, 1984.

Hyman, Prue. "Social Wage: Broad and Narrow Definitions." In *Encyclopedia of Political Economy*, ed. Phillip Anthony O'Hara. London: Routledge, 2001.

Johnson, Donald Bruce, and Kirk H. Porter, eds. *National Party Platforms: 1840–1972*. Urbana: University of Illinois Press, 1973.

Klein, Philip. "Institutionalist Reflections on the Role of the Public Sector." *Journal of Economic Issues* 18, no. 1 (March 1984): 45–68.

Lipsett, Seymour Martin, and Earl Raab. *The Politics of Unreason: Right-Wing Extremism in America, 1790–1970*. New York: Harper and Row Publishers, 1973.

Locke, John. *Two Treatises of Government*. Rev. ed. New York: New American Library, 1963.

Marglin, Stephen A., and Juliet B. Schor, eds. *The Golden Age of Capitalism: Reinterpreting the Postwar Experience*. Oxford: Clarendon Press, 1990.

Melman, Seymour. "From Private to State Capitalism: How the Permanent War Economy Transformed the Institutions of American Capitalism." *Journal of Economic Issues* 31, no. 2 (June 1997): 311–30.

Mills, C. Wright. *The Power Elite*. London: Oxford University Press, 1956.

Republican Party. "1976 National Republican Convention Platform." *Congressional Record*. 94th Cong., 2nd sess., September 2, 1976.

———. "1980 Republican National Convention Platform." *Congressional Record*. 96th Cong., 2nd sess., July 31, 1980.

———. *The Republican Party Platform of 1984* (and *1988, 1992, 1996, 2000*).

Sweezy, Paul M. *The Theory of Capitalist Development.* New York: Monthly Review Press, 1942.

Wray, L. Randall. "Zero Unemployment and Stable Prices." *Journal of Economic Issues* 36, no. 2 (June 1998): 539–45.

Tilman, Rick. "Institutional Economics, Instrumentalist Political Theory, and the American Tradition of Empirical Collectivism." *Journal of Economic Issues* 35, no. 1 (March 2001): 117–38.

Toruño, Mayo C. "Blind Drift and the Rightist State." *Journal of Economic Issues* 31, no. 2 (June 1997): 585–93.

Veblen, Thorstein. *The Vested Interests and the Common Man (The Modern Point of View and the New Order).* New York: Augustus M. Kelly, 1964 (1919).

———.*The Nature of Peace*, with a new introduction by Warren J. Samuels. New Brunswick, NJ: Transactions Publishers, 1998 (1917).

19

Wealth and Power

Ethical Implications of Executive Compensation Since the 1980s

David A. Zalewski

It is well known that income and wealth inequality grew dramatically in the United States over the last twenty years despite two extended periods of GDP growth. One explanation for this trend has been the surge in the compensation of corporate chief executive officers (CEOs) relative to that of other employees, whose pay increases have barely kept pace with changes in the cost of living. Not only have senior executives received salaries and bonuses that far exceed those earned by their predecessors, they also have been granted generous fringe benefits and other perquisites. Although many people consider this disparity to be unfair, economists generally are divided in their opinions about its morality.

As will be explained in the next section, most neoclassical economists believe that the labor market sets appropriate compensation levels. Because of the difficulty in isolating an executive's contribution to overall corporate performance, it is often hard to conclude that a CEO's pay is unjustified unless there is clear evidence of incompetence or fraud. Institutionalism, however, which focuses on the social dynamics governing employment relations, provides a better approach to ethical analysis than concentrating on outcomes. Specifically, this chapter argues that when executives use their power to negotiate guaranteed contracts

for themselves while placing their employees' wages, health care and pensions at risk, they are violating standard norms of distributive justice. Since there are no aggregate data, to my knowledge, on how common this practice has been, the chapter will focus on specific examples of this behavior. It is important to emphasize that although all moral evaluations that appear below apply only to the individual cases under examination, these practices have grown in popularity because of the systemic root of the problem.

The chapter concludes by considering if fairness in compensation can be restored. Because corporations have evolved from groups of people bound by shared values to Ronald Coase's (1937) transactions cost–minimizing "nexus of contracts," this culture of selfishness will be difficult to change. Thus, exercising countervailing power may be necessary for effective reform. Several possibilities, including collective action and government intervention, will be discussed and evaluated.

Neoclassical and Institutionalist Views on Markets and Ethics

The growth in the average pay of U.S. CEOs has been spectacular over the last twenty years. According to the AFL-CIO (2003), the average CEO pay was forty-two times greater than that of the typical hourly worker in 1982. Twenty years later, this measure reached a previously unimaginable value of 531 times the average hourly pay. Although the rate of increase in CEO pay has slowed in the aftermath of the recent corporate scandals, average annual total compensation at publicly traded corporations was $10.83 million in 2002. Moreover, wealth disparities have displayed a similar pattern over the same period. Edward N. Wolff (2002) calculated that the 34 percent share of the 1963–82 aggregate wealth gain that accrued to the richest 1 percent of the U.S. population rose to 53 percent between 1983 and 1998. Meanwhile, the bottom 80 percent of households saw their share decline from 18 percent to 9 percent.

Many neoclassical economists accept these disparities because of an unquestioning faith in the labor market's ability to set fair compensation levels. When pressed to provide a moral assessment of inequality, they argue that these outcomes are ethical if they resulted from voluntary market exchanges. Some mainstream economists would further support this conclusion by employing a utilitarian calculus that condones economic inequality if labor market processes improve aggregate social welfare. For example, some scholars rationalize the explosive growth in CEO pay by arguing that few executives possess the necessary skills to successfully manage today's complex organizations in an increasingly competitive environment. As a result, many firms have engaged in expensive bidding wars for proven executive talent.[1] If these "managerial superstars" increase stock returns as expected, they are considered worthy of their rewards even if they were not entirely responsible for this performance. On the other hand, those who fail to create value will either be fired by the board of directors or replaced after a corporate takeover.[2] Michael J. Mandel (2002) provided another utilitarian justification for lavish compensation packages by arguing that widening income gaps are justified if they are accompanied by economic growth and declining poverty. Because U.S. Bureau of the Census data show that the U.S. poverty rate fell from 14.5 to 11.7 percent of the population while executive pay soared between 1994 and 2001, neoclassical economists would consider this a socially beneficial Pareto improvement.

Unlike mainstream theory, institutional economics examines how social and cultural factors, such as changing norms and the distribution of power, influence employment outcomes. For this reason, Douglas Kinnear (1999) claimed that institutionalism is more relevant for addressing today's problems. This is especially true regarding the ethical analysis of recent executive pay trends, which can be explained in part by changes in corporate culture. According to Paul Osterman (1999), post–World War II firms that often functioned as "corporate families" have evolved into a "nexus of contracts" in which everyone seeks to further their self-interest. As a result, companies that were once characterized by long-term relationships and mutual obligations between employers and employees are now bereft of loyalty and commitment because powerful members of organizations have exploited their influence to further their welfare at the expense of other workers. Specifically, many managers have forced other employees to bear a larger share of the risks of heightened rivalry in an increasingly integrated global economy while providing security for themselves and their families. As described in the next section, this has been the case with wages, health insurance, and pensions. The result is markedly different from Adam Smith's "invisible hand" theory, in which self-interested behavior elevates the welfare of others. By promoting individualism, corporations have created conditions amenable to the shifting of uncertainty to employees either lacking the power to resist or unable to find another acceptable position in today's tight labor market. Considering that executives already possess greater levels of wealth and social capital that act as a bulwark against economic insecurity, forcing other employees to assume more risk is clearly unjust.

Examples of Corporate Risk-Shifting

Job and Wage Security

Since the early 1980s, the global economy has been transformed by several developments that have increased job insecurity for many Americans. These include a shift toward economic and trade liberalization, accelerating technological progress, and an increase in global competition. Because these forces squeezed profits for many corporations, their shareholders forced managers to increase efficiency and cut costs. As Barbara A. Wiens-Tuers (2001) pointed out, many firms responded to this pressure by shifting the risks associated with factor and product market volatility to their employees.

How have these forces affected employment conditions? Lawrence Mishel, Jared Bernstein, and John Schmitt (2001) explain that although job stability and security are related, they describe different aspects of employment status. Job stability is the degree to which employers and employees form long-term bonds, while employment security refers to the ability of workers to stay on the job if their performance is satisfactory. Although better data are available for employment stability than security, Mishel, Bernstein, and Schmitt argue that the decline in stability coupled with falling wages since the 1980s suggests that the increase in job turnover during this period was

involuntary and indicative of diminished employment security. Much of this turnover resulted from corporate downsizing and the transfer of production to overseas locations with lower labor costs. Even those employees who kept their jobs were affected, however, since an increasing number of companies have employed contingent and temporary workers.[3]

Employment tenure at the top has also become less secure recently. In the most comprehensive study of CEO turnover to date, consulting firm Booz, Allen Hamilton surveyed the 2,500 largest publicly traded global firms that changed CEOs in 1995, 1998, 2000, and 2001.[4] Their findings show a striking 53 percent increase in U.S. CEO replacements over the last six years as average tenure fell from 9.5 to 7.3 years. The study concluded that much of this turnover could be explained by shareholder pressure for steady, acceptable returns since there was a 130 percent increase in terminations resulting from poor financial performance. This is consistent with Charles J. Whalen's (2002) reappraisal of Hyman Minsky's (1990) theory of money-manager capitalism. Whalen points out that Minsky's prediction of impatient institutional investors who continually churn their portfolios has not materialized. Rather, many professional investors have adopted "voice" strategies, such as pressuring managers to improve their performance rather than liquidating their holdings at the first sign of trouble.

Although intense competition has increased employment insecurity at all levels, many CEOs continue to receive guaranteed pay while forcing other employees to link theirs to job performance. A 2002 Hewitt Associates survey of 1,045 companies found that performance-based pay constituted 10.5 percent of total compensation expenses during 2002—a substantial increase from the 7.6 percent and the 3.8 percent recorded in 1995 and

1991, respectively. Moreover, Hewitt consultants reported that 80 percent of the companies in the sample offered salaried employees some form of performance pay in 2002, up from 60 percent in the mid-1990s. The result of this development is to force employees to bear more of the burden of changing business fortunes. According to Hewitt senior consultant Ken Abosch: "Employers' motivation for using performance pay is to manage costs, paying out more for compensation when they can afford to and cutting back in lean years. They are shifting away from fixed payroll costs toward variable costs."[5]

Unlike other employees, many top executives have been exempt from these pay-for-performance policies. Even managers employed by firms whose stock returns lagged market indices were often granted replacement stock options with lower exercise prices or were compensated with cash bonuses.[6] This practice has changed somewhat during the current economic slowdown. David Leonhardt (2002b) argued that economic conditions in 2001 provided an excellent setting for examining recent management pay practices, since unlike most of the previous decade, both profits and stock prices fell during this year. Leonhardt found that firms could be divided into two equal-sized groups: those that continued to reward CEOs and senior executives regardless of their performance, and those whose directors pressured managers to accept lower pay. He observed that CEOs "rigged the game" in firms that maintained pay levels through their influence on their board's compensation committee. Specifically, successful executives convinced the board to increase the size of stock option grants, alter the terms on previously issued options that were unprofitable to exercise, or increase the portion of their salaries that are unrelated to performance.

Moreover, managers have discovered other ways to limit the volatility of their compensation. For example, some companies have switched from granting stock options to compensating executives with shares since options carry little downside risk. According to Clifford W. Smith and René Stulz (1985), risk-averse managers who hold substantial equity stakes in their firms are more likely to adopt risk management programs to smooth earnings volatility than those who receive stock options.[7] Executives also tend to practice risk management if it is less costly for the company to insure against their risk than it is for them to do it themselves.[8] As will be discussed below, managers also have relied on firms to secure their health and retirement benefits while not extending the same consideration to other employees.

Health Care Benefits

Of all fringe benefits, health insurance has generated the most debate recently because of its spiraling costs and a decline in the number of people covered. A Kaiser Family Foundation study in 2002 found that employer health insurance costs rose 12.7 percent in 2002 after an 11 percent increase in 2001, largely because of expensive technological advances and rising prescription drug costs. In response, most firms have shifted a greater share of the cost to their workers. The Kaiser study also reported that employee contributions rose 27 percent for individual coverage and 16 percent for family plans in 2002. Also adding to this burden have been sharp increases in deductibles and prescription copayments. The average deductible for Preferred Provider Organization (PPO) plans that cover nearly half of all workers increased 37 percent in 2002, and copayments for brand-name drugs without generic substitutes went from $21 to $26 over the last year.

Because of sharp increases in the cost of medical insurance, the number of firms offering coverage to their employees and retirees has fallen recently. The Kaiser study found that although 62 percent of all U.S. companies provided health insurance, there is significant variation based on firm size. Nearly all U.S. companies employing at least fifty workers offered health insurance over the last five years, while only 55 percent of businesses employing less than ten people did so in 2002, a drop from 60 percent in 2000. Moreover, these estimates overstated the number of employees covered since approximately one-third of the workers at companies providing health benefits are uninsured. Retiree health benefits are also diminishing. A study by the Agency for Healthcare Research and Quality found that the number of firms offering insurance to retirees under age sixty-five fell from 21.6 percent in 1997 to 12 percent in 2000. For people age sixty-five and older, coverage declined from 19.5 percent to 10.7 percent over the same period.[9] Those who remain on the company plan will also be required to pay higher premiums, since many firms have established caps that limit their exposure to premium inflation. Because most health care experts foresee medical cost increases, it is likely that both retirees and workers will pay a larger share in the future.

As was the case with employment security, employer-provided health insurance has disproportionately benefited executives and other key employees. Approximately 82 percent of the top fifth of wage earners were covered by company health plans from 1996 to 2000, while only about a third of the lowest fifth enjoyed these benefits. Moreover, many upper-income employees pay a much smaller percentage of their pay—if anything at all—for their coverage, despite often receiving better benefits. The Kaiser study also noted that a weakening of labor market conditions in the last two years has been accompanied by an increase in cost shifting and declining plan quality. This suggests that many employers offer health insurance to attract and keep highly skilled workers rather than out of a concern for employee welfare. This conclusion is consistent with Osterman's point about corporations having become less egalitarian. As will be argued in the next section, this is true for retirement benefits as well.

Retirement Programs

Another area in which employers have forced many workers to bear economic risk while insulating themselves against uncertainty is in the provision of retirement benefits.[10] Pension plans once were a popular way for firms to share their prosperity; the number of employees covered grew from approximately 25 percent of the workforce in 1950 to nearly half by 1960. The fact that this percentage was 49.6 percent in 2000 indicates that coverage has only expanded to keep pace with labor force growth. Moreover, these benefits have not been equitably distributed, since 82 percent of low-wage earners, 56.9 percent of African American, and 71.5 percent of Latino workers do not participate in employer-sponsored retirement programs. In contrast, only 27 percent of the top-fifth wage earners and 45.4 percent of white employees lacked coverage in 2002.[11]

Private pension quality in the United States has also declined since the early 1980s. In the previous three decades, most firms sponsored defined-benefit plans that paid retirees a fixed annuity whose value was based on factors such as years of service, salary levels, and longevity. Recently, an increasing number of firms have converted to defined-contribution plans in which they make regular payments into employee accounts. Their popularity—between 1975 and 1997, the share of defined-contribution plans rose from 13 to 42 percent—can be explained by the fact that these programs are less expensive and that employees must now assume the risk that their retirement income will be inadequate. Mishel, Bernstein, and Schmitt (2001) calculated that pension expenses of U.S. companies fell from $0.96 per hour in 1989 to $0.74 in 1999 as more firms modified their retirement plans to lower expenses. Direct-contribution plans, however, do offer some benefits, such as portability and the opportunity to amass greater retirement savings, although this may require making risky investments.

Many senior executives, however, continue to be covered by guaranteed retirement programs despite forcing other employees to accept lower-quality benefits. For example, David Leonhardt (2002a) reported that General Electric offers at least a 10 percent return on funds invested in the executive retirement plan while ordinary workers are forced to bear financial risk in their 401(k) accounts. Leonhardt also described how retired IBM CEO Louis V. Gerstener will receive an annual pension of at least $1.1 million, which is funded in part by the savings from the company's 1999 decision to shrink employee pension and retirement health benefits to levels below those initially promised. Some firms, such as Delta Airlines, credit executives for employment time beyond their actual years of service, which effectively boosts their pension benefits. Finally, AMR Corporation, parent of American Airlines, paid $41 million into a trust fund in October 2002 to protect the pensions of forty-five executives in the event of bankruptcy. It is interesting to note that this information was revealed after the company's three unions agreed to $1.8 billion in annual concessions in April 2003. Chairman and CEO Donald J. Carty eventually resigned because of his failure to disclose this payment, and he was "punished" by being granted a $79,000 annual pension and an

$8.2 billion lump-sum payment from the very same supplemental pension fund.

The bankruptcies of Enron and Polaroid brought attention to how corporations can abuse retirement plans. In the case of Polaroid, executives required employees to participate in an employee stock ownership plan (ESOP) in 1988 to thwart a hostile takeover. By transferring shares to "friendly" stockholders who were prohibited from selling them while employed by Polaroid, the takeover defense was successful. When Polaroid filed for bankruptcy on October 12, 2001, these shares were worth a fraction of their purchase price. Although company managers also suffered from this decline, the bankruptcy court agreed to a plan to pay them retention bonuses of up to twice their salaries to offset the loss. As for Enron, many employees invested substantial amounts of their 401(k) funds in company stock. Because of this lack of diversification and corporate rules that made it difficult for them to sell their shares, 12,000 out of 21,000 employees lost nearly all of their retirement savings when the company went bankrupt in December 2001. However, while CEO Kenneth Lay and other top managers cashed out $924 million in stock before its value evaporated, they encouraged employees to hold their shares in anticipation of their certain appreciation.

Echoing Osterman, Ellen Schultz (2001) explained these changes by arguing that executives had an incentive to improve pension benefits when employees at all organizational levels participated in the same plan. This changed recently when corporate boards offered managers supplemental executive retirement plans (SERPs), whose value is often linked to stock performance. Thus, CEOs have been able to boost their retirement benefits by cutting pension expenses for others. As Judith Fischer, managing director of Executive Compensation Advisory Services, concluded, "Executive retirement plans and employee retirement plans are really no longer recognizable as related."[12] Although this should evoke public outrage, Schultz concluded that weak disclosure requirements and accounting obfuscation have kept even regulators and compensation experts unaware of these coverage gaps.

Can Fairness Be Restored?

The recent shift of insecurity from a select group of employees—perhaps 20 percent of the workforce—to other workers parallels the transformation of the corporation from a cohesive social unit characterized by mutual commitment and shared norms to one bound by impersonal contracts. Because the latter type of organization rewards those who can use their power to influence decision makers, it encourages the pursuit of self-interest at the expense of others. As argued earlier, this behavior is clearly unethical, which is not always the case for unequal outcomes that can be morally justified by differences in talent, work effort, or even serendipity. Because the root of the problem is institutional rather than a shortcoming of individual character, what can be done to restore fairness? Two general approaches will be discussed: First, increasing countervailing power through expanded union representation and community activism and second, strengthening government programs that promote economic security.

The institutionalist theory of John R. Commons (1934) provides excellent insights into this issue. Alexa Albert and Yngve Ramstad's summary of his work clearly establishes its relevance to this problem:

> Commons perceived that in the actual world we inhabit, one in which extensive division of labor obtains, wealth production is entirely a collective rather than individual undertaking; that is, individuals must cooperate in forward-looking activity if they are to realize any of their wealth-seeking ambitions. Given that reality, Commons argued, wealth-production entails ever-present conflicts of interest regarding the manner in which the burdens and benefits of collective undertaking are to be shared. It was Commons's fundamental insight that such activity *cannot* proceed in an orderly manner if individuals are left free to pursue their self-interest to the maximum of their ability or if they are insecure in their expectations regarding the future behavior of those upon whom they must rely. Indeed, Commons maintained that productive activity *cannot* proceed in an orderly fashion unless there is extensive "collective action in control of individual action." (1997, 883)

How can collective action be taken? As Osterman (1999) argued, the solution to many problems plaguing workers today is to restore a balance of power between them and their employers, largely through unions and collective bargaining. Other forces for change are advocacy groups, such as the living wage movement. The fact that these organizations often accomplish their goals through the passage of legislation underscores the role of government as the most effective guarantor of distributive justice. As discussed below, however, the current climate is generally unfavorable for enacting significant reform despite some success enjoyed by both unions and advocacy groups.

Because unions have traditionally obtained better working conditions, greater job security, and higher compensation for their members, recent declines in membership are puzzling. Mishel, Bernstein, and Schmitt (2001) found that organized workers received 23.2 percent higher wages and 35.9 percent more total compensation in 1997 than nonunionized employees. The difference between wages and total compensation suggests that the value of fringe benefits was more than double that received by other workers. Extending this analysis, Mishel, Bernstein, and Schmitt analyzed these differentials after controlling for occupational differences and firm-specific characteristics like industry and location. The results were similar with a wage difference of 21.0 percent and a total compensation gap of 27.8 percent. Regarding specific benefits, unionized workers were 16.0 percent more likely to participate in an employer-provided insurance plan that cost the firm 44.2 percent more per hour than those provided in nonunion shops. Moreover, union members were 26.7 percent more likely to belong to a company pension plan and enjoyed a 16.0 percent higher employer contribution.

Given the substantial benefits from union affiliation, why has membership declined from 25 percent of the total workforce in 1970 to almost 12 percent twenty-five years later? Besides structural changes like the shift from a manufacturing to a service economy, increased immigration, and technological progress, this decline also reflects greater employer power. Part of this imbalance results from expanded global integration that has not only heightened competition, but also increased the ability of firms to move operations overseas. Also improving the bargaining position of employers have been changes in the legal and regulatory climate, beginning with President Ronald Reagan's adversarial stance toward unions in the early eighties and extending through the current Bush administration.

As Karl Polanyi (1957) argued, however, the undesirable consequences of market activity often induce a "double movement" in which those affected seek to reestablish control over their lives. This reaction appears to have occurred recently, especially in response to the recent corporate scandals in which the average worker has suffered while the perpetrators emerged unscathed. With regard to corporate wrong doing, AFL-CIO president John J. Sweeney proclaimed in 2002: "For years I've heard people talk about distrust of their employers, but something new is happening. People are really fed up and furious with corporate America."[14] Sweeney's observation was backed by the results of a 2002 survey of 900 workers conducted by Peter D. Hart Research Associates, which found that 30 percent of the respondents had positive opinions about corporations and 39 percent viewed them negatively. This contrasts with the 42 percent positive and 25 percent negative results from a January 2001 poll also by Hart. Unsurprisingly, the Hart study found that 50 percent of unorganized workers would vote for a union if given the opportunity—a sharp increase from the 30 percent who would have done so in the early 1980s. Moreover, those who would vote against union representation fell from 65 percent to 43 percent over the same period (Greenhouse 2002, A12). Because of changes in collective bargaining laws and the aggressive resistance of employers targeted by union organizers, however, this change in sentiment has not increased union membership over the last decade.

Interestingly, the recent scandals have created an unlikely alliance of unions and dissident shareholders that has attempted to force changes in executive behavior. During 2003, unions and their pension funds submitted over 300 shareholder proposals, accounting for 27 percent of the total number of initiatives. This is nearly twice the number of shareholder initiatives brought forward in 2002, and according to the Investor Responsibility Research Center, many of these targeted concern executive compensation—especially the expensing of stock options and golden parachutes. Because many of these proxy resolutions are nonbinding, however, their power lies in creating public relations nightmares for executives.

Could advocacy groups reinforce union efforts to counteract corporate power? Although they have been important catalysts for progressive change, programs such as the living wage movement and publicly funded training programs are likely to have limited success in this regard. Despite improving the prospects for low-wage and unskilled workers, community activists work outside of the firm and usually focus on employees who work for low wages in small businesses. It is important, however, for unions not to ignore these workers since they may boost membership roles in the future.

Given the limited success of collective action in altering corporate behavior, the federal government's role in curbing abusive practices and in providing basic economic security should be strengthened. Unfortunately, this has not been the case recently. For example, Dell P. Champlin and Janet T. Knoedler (1999) argued that because public policy encouraged the wave of corporate restructuring that has dislocated millions of workers, this trend cannot be blamed solely on impersonal, uncontrollable market forces. Moreover, the tax code has induced firms to compensate executives with stock options since their values are not classified as expenses. Several proposals to close this loophole stalled in Congress in 2002 because of disagreements over how to value unexercised options. Similarly, David Leonhardt (2002a) noted that SERPs were developed as separate pension plans in response to legislation passed in the 1980s that limited the amount of an executive's salary that could be used to calculate pension contributions. Finally, tax provisions proposed by the Bush administration encouraged the use of split-life insurance policies, which effectively are interest-free loans to executives.

Other changes in tax policy—especially during President George W. Bush's administration—have benefited the wealthy while draining funds from programs that provide basic economic security. For example, economists estimate that more than half of the total benefits from the 2001 tax reform package, which will end the "death tax" and lower marginal tax rates, will go to the wealthiest 1 percent of the population. More recently, Bush's 2003 tax cuts also target the rich while expanding the federal budget deficit. When Democratic leaders made these points in response to the Bush proposals, Republicans accused them of class warfare, although the GOP fired the first shot.[14]

The growth of tax expenditures, which are legal deductions that subsidize programs disproportionately benefiting wealthier households, have also constrained the revenues needed to adequately support health and retirement programs for the disadvantaged. Estimated total tax expenditures in the current federal budget are $800 billion, which include $157 billion for employer-provided pensions and health insurance, $112 billion from mortgage interest and property tax deductions, and $65 billion in capital gains allowances. Maya Macguineas's (2003) estimates that 50 percent of the five largest tax expenditure programs benefit households earning above $100,000 per year while only 15 percent go to families making below $50,000 are consistent with the data on the distribution of employment benefits among income classes reported earlier in this chapter.

Finally, conservative proposals to reform Social Security, Medicare, and Medicaid will also detract from economic security. In late 2001, President Bush's Special Commission on Social Security recommended a diversion of up to four percentage points of the combined 12.4 percent payroll tax to personal accounts while reducing guaranteed benefits between 2 and 4 percent. The president's 2003 prescription drug plan provides this benefit only to seniors who belong to health maintenance organizations (HMOs). The administration also plans to change Medicaid rules so that many poor people will no longer be guaranteed benefits. These measures are consistent with the president's support of medical savings accounts, which place the onus of choosing health care providers and monitoring the quality of their services on the individual. What these proposals have in common is an erosion of the government's role as a guarantor of basic security. Because people will have to fend for themselves in this new age of individual responsibility, it is likely that the well connected and powerful will thrive at the expense of others.

Whether this results in a political backlash remains to be seen. As conservative columnist David Brooks (2003) contends, political initiatives to defeat tax breaks for the wealthy and to combat inequality will be successful only if they can demonstrate that people achieved their success by competing unfairly.[15] Given the evidence that this has been the case in the United States during the last two decades, perhaps it is time for both economists and politicians to exploit this fact. By explaining how the privileged use their power to secure their well-being while forcing others into a more uncertain existence, economists and politicians may be able to make a more convincing case for progressive policies than they have recently.

Notes

1. See Frank and Cook (1995) for an elaboration on this and other winner-take-all markets.

2. As I have argued previously (Zalewski 2001), however, many terminated CEOs have been richly compensated for their job loss because of "golden parachute" clauses and other contractual provisions even if they performed poorly.

3. There is evidence that the promised efficiency gains from labor force flexibility may be illusory. David Fairris (2002) showed that workplace transformation strategies have increased employee stress, work effort, and health and safety problems by forcing more frequent assignment changes and by shifting management's responsibility for ensuring quality to workers. As a result, Fairris found the evidence on productivity improvements inconclusive. He noted, however, that

should such gains materialize, they are unlikely to be shared equitably.

4. The results of this survey are reported in Lucier, Spiegel, and Schuyt (2002).

5. Data and the quotation are from Blanton (2002).

6. Employee stock options give the recipients the right to purchase a specified number of shares at a predetermined price (exercise price) when they exercise the options after a vesting period. The options only benefit the holder if the market price of the stock exceeds the exercise price. Because general stock market declines may reduce the value of options and employee compensation despite effective job performance, some firms attempt to preserve the incentives in the contract by canceling the existing options and reissuing new ones that are "in the money"—that is, with exercise prices lower than market prices. This practice, however, can be abused by underperforming executives who have influence over the board of directors.

7. Corporations with risk management programs hedge against the adverse consequences of market volatility that may lower profits and share values. This is often accomplished by purchasing derivative contracts—such as options and futures—that increase in value when interest rate, currency value, and commodity price movements become unfavorable.

8. Peter Tufano (1996) confirmed this hypothesis for the gold mining industry—one of the few that permit cross-sectional studies of hedging decisions.

9. These results were reported by Greene (2002).

10. This section relies heavily on Zalewski (2002).

11. Data are from Mishel, Bernstein, and Boushey (2003). They were made available on the Economic Policy Institute Web site (www.epinet.org) before the book was published.

12. Quoted in Leonhardt (2002).

13. The Sweeney quote and the following Hart report summary are from Greenhouse (2002).

14. Evidence that conservatives have been practicing class warfare comes from a *Wall Street Journal* editorial which complained that lower-income families paid a smaller percentage of federal income taxes than the richest taxpayers. According to the *Journal*'s compassionate editorial board, these "lucky duckies" undermine the support for tax cuts since they do not pay their fair share. E.J. Dionne Jr. (2002) responded by pointing out that less privileged families not only saw their incomes grow more slowly over the last twenty years, but also are disproportionately burdened with payroll and sales taxes.

15. Brooks argued that "class warfare" platforms are politically unpopular because, among other reasons, most Americans aspire to be rich, admire the wealthy, and abhor social inequality more than income inequality.

References

AFL-CIO. "Eye on Corporate Amercia," www.aflcio.org (2003).

Albert, Alexa, and Yngve Ramstad. "Social Psychological Underpinnings of Commons's Institutional Economics." *Journal of Economic Issues* 31, no. 4 (December 1997), 881–916.

Blanton, Kimberly. "Performance Bonuses Supplanting Holiday Pay." *Boston Globe*, December 19, 2002, D1.

Broder, John M. "Problem of Lost Health Benefits Is Reaching Into the Middle Class." *New York Times*, November 25, 2002, A1.

Brooks, David. "The Triumph of Hope Over Self-Interest." *New York Times*, January 12, 2003, Section 4, p. 15.

Champlin, Dell P., and Janet T. Knoedler. "Restructuring by Design: Government's Complicity in Corporate Restructuring." *Journal of Economic Issues* 33, no. 1 (March 1999): 41–57.

Coase, Ronald A. "The Nature of the Firm." *Economica* 4 (1937): 386–405.

Commons, John R. *Institutional Economics: Its Place in Political Economy.* New York: Macmillan, 1934.

Dionne, E.J. Jr. "Low Income Taxpayers: New Meat for the Right." *Washington Post*, November 26, 2002, A29.

Editorial "The Non-Taxpaying Class," *Wall Street Journal*, November 20, 2002, A20.

Fairris, David. "Are Transformed Workplaces More Productively Efficient?" *Journal of Economic Issues* 36, no. 3 (September 2002): 659–70.

Frank, Robert H., and Philip C. Cook. *The Winner-Take-All Society.* New York: Free Press, 1995.

Greene, Kelly. "Health Benefits for Retirees Continue to Shrink, Study Says." *Wall Street Journal*, September 16, 2002, A2.

Greenhouse, Steven. "Workers Are Angry and Fearful This Labor Day." *New York Times*, September 2, 2002, A12.

Kaiser Family Foundation and Health Research and Educational Trust. *Survey of Employer-Sponsored Health Benefits*, 2002.

Kinnear, Douglas. "'Compulsive Shift' to Institutional Concerns in Recent Labor Economics." *Journal of Economic Issues* 33, no. 1 (March 1999): 169–81.

Leonhardt, David. "For Executives, Nest Egg Is Wrapped in a Security Blanket." *New York Times*, March 5, 2002a, C1.

———. "Did Executive Pay Cut Both Ways?" *New York Times*, April 7, 2002b, Section 3, page 1.

Lucier, Chuck, Eric Spiegel, and Rob Schuyt. "Why CEOs Fall: The Causes and Consequences of Turnover at the Top." *strategy+business* 28 (2002): 1–14.

Macguineas, Maya. "The Real State of the Budget." *Atlantic Monthly*, January/February 2003, 77.

Mandel, Michael J. "The Rich Get Richer, and That's O.K." *Business Week*, August 26, 2002, 88–90.

Minsky, Hyman P. "Schumpeter: Finance and Evolution." In *Evolving Technology and Market Structure*, ed. Arnold Heertje and Mark Perlman. Ann Arbor: University of Michigan Press, 1990.

Mishel, Lawrence, Jared Bernstein, and Heather Boushey. *The State of Working America: 2002–2003.* Ithaca, NY: Cornell University Press, 2003.

Mishel, Lawrence, Jared Bernstein, and John Schmitt. *The State of Working America: 2000–2001.* Ithaca, NY: Cornell University Press, 2001.

Osterman, Paul. *Securing Prosperity.* Princeton, NJ: Princeton University Press, 1999.

Polanyi, Karl. *The Great Transformation.* Boston: Beacon Press, 1957.

Schultz, Ellen. "As Firms Pare Pensions for Most, They Boost Those for Executives." *Wall Street Journal*, April 20, 2001, A1.

Smith, Clifford W., and René Stulz. "The Determinants of Firms' Hedging Policies." *Journal of Financial and Quantitative Analysis* 20 (1985): 391–405.

Tufano, Peter. "Who Manages Risk? An Empirical Examination of Risk Management Practices in the Gold Mining Industry." *Journal of Finance* 51, no. 4 (September 1996): 1097–37.

Whalen, Charles J. "Money-Manager Capitalism: Still Here, But Not Quite as Expected." *Journal of Economic Issues* 36, no. 2 (June 2002): 401–6.

Wiens-Tuers, Barbara A. "Employee Attachment and Temporary Workers." *Journal of Economic Issues* 35, no. 1 (March 2001): 45–57.

Wolff, Edward N. *Top Heavy: The Increasing Inequality of Wealth in America and What Can Be Done About It.* New York: New Press, 2002.

Zalewski, David A. "Corporate Takeovers, Fairness, and Public Policy." *Journal of Economic Issues* 35, no. 2 (June 2001): 431–37.

———. "Retirement Insecurity in the Age of Money-Manager Capitalism." *Journal of Economic Issues* 36, no. 2 (June 2002): 349–56.

20

Not Only Nike's Doing It

"Sweating" and the Contemporary Labor Market

Richard McIntyre and Yngve Ramstad

In the summer of 1997, Nguyen Thi Thu Phuong died making Nike sneakers in a factory in Bien Hoa, northeast of Ho Chi Minh City in Vietnam. She was struck in the heart by a piece of shrapnel that flew out of a machine that a coworker was fixing. She died instantly. Nike's response to this (and other similar incidents) was "we don't make shoes" (Larimer 1998, 30). This was technically correct because Nike's core business strategy involves outsourcing *all* manufacturing to subcontractors in poor Asian countries.

In November 2001, Rosa Ruiz died when the van she was riding in flipped over on Route 1 in southern Rhode Island. The van was carrying Ruiz and her coworkers from their job at a fish processing plant back to their homes in the Providence area. Ruiz was working at a company called Town Dock but had been hired through a temporary employment agency, Action Manufacturing Employment. The van was owned and operated by the agency. When the surviving workers publicly voiced complaints about conditions at the plant, they were all fired. Town Dock management's response to the incident was "Rosa Ruiz was not working for Town Dock on the day that she passed" (Ziner and Davis 2001).

Fortunately, these examples of work-related deaths are unusual. But we perceive the business strategy employed by Nike and Town Dock *not* to be unusual. Specifically, each of these businesses has adopted the "sweating system" of organizing work. In that regard, Nike and Town Dock labor practices exemplify a significant development in the labor market. For the sweating system is now being used not only by producers, like Nike, who outsource production to low-wage countries but also by companies, like Town Dock, operating in the United States.

We submit that conventional neoclassical economics provides no point of entry into the analysis of this development and, equally, offers no ground for attempting to reverse its deleterious consequences for workers. In contrast, the institutional economist John R. Commons *did* develop an interpretation of the labor market providing a fruitful point of entry into this important development. In a report he made to the U.S. Industrial Commission a century ago (Commons 1901), Commons set forth an analysis of the sweating system that comes closer to the essence of how many firms organize the production of the commodities they sell than do many contemporary definitions. Additionally, the economic root of sweating was brought to light by Commons in his celebrated article on the evolution of the wage bargain for American shoemakers (Commons 1909).

In application to the labor market, the terms "sweat" and "sweating" are generally employed to signify the practice of paying workers inappropriately low wages for long hours of work under conditions that may be unsafe or unsanitary. Consistent with this interpretation, the United States government defines a "sweatshop" as "a business that violates more than one federal or state law governing wages and hours, child labor, health and safety, workers compensation, or industry registration" (U.S. GAO 1994). This more or less arbitrary definition is important, of course, because the government uses it.

In his report to the U.S. Industrial Commission, Commons provided an alternative definition—one presumably governing the meaning he associated with the term in the shoemakers' article published eight years later—focused on labor market processes rather than on the actual terms of a wage bargain. "The term 'sweating' or 'sweating system,'" Commons observed, "originally denoted a system of subcontract, wherein the work is let out to contractors to be done in small shops or homes. . . . The system to be contrasted with the sweating system is the 'factory system' wherein the manufacturer employs his own workman" (Commons 1901, 45).

Commons emphasized that contractor control of information is a crucial element of the sweating system. It is worth quoting him at length on this point:

> [The labor contractor] deals with people who have no knowledge of regular hours. He keeps them in the dark with regard to the prevailing number of hours people work.
>
> The contractor is an irresponsible go-between for the manufacturer, who is the original employer. He has no connection with the business interests of the manufacturer nor is his interest that of his help. His

sphere is merely that of a middleman. He holds his own mainly because of his ability to get cheap labor, and is in reality merely the agent of the manufacturer for that purpose.

> Usually when the work comes to the contractor from the manufacturer and is offered to his employees for a smaller price than has previously been paid, the help will remonstrate and ask to be paid the full price. Then the contractor tells them, "I have nothing to do with the price. The price is made for me by the manufacturer. I have very little to say about the price." That is, he cuts himself completely loose from any responsibility to his employees as to how much they are to get for their labor.
>
> The help do not know the manufacturer. They cannot register their complaint with the man who made the price for their labor. The contractor, who did not make the price for their labor, claims that it is no use to complain to him. So however much the price for labor goes down there is no one responsible for it.
>
> In case the help form an organization and send a committee to the manufacturer, the manufacturer will invariably say, "I do not employ you and I have nothing to do with you." (Commons 1901, 46)

By means of three cases to be presented below, we will attempt to demonstrate the contemporary relevance of Commons's characterization of the sweating system and also of his understanding of its economic impetus. We see the three cases as visible "moments" in an ongoing process of labor market transformation centered on the creation of social distance, whatever the physical location, between employer and employee so as to subject the latter ever more effectively to destructive competition, that is, to a "race to the bottom." By the phrase "creation of social distance," we are referring to the severing of a direct bargaining transaction relationship between the worker—the actual producer—and the entity for whom the productive activity is substantively expended. We understand this severing to be the crucial step in implementing a sweating system of production.

It is widely recognized that Commons believed

regulation, that is, the establishment and enforcement of labor market standards, to be the appropriate remedy for destructive competition. It is, of course, possible that moral and empathic appeals to consumers and employers might provide an alternative method of remedying the problem. Since standard economic theory is premised on the ubiquity of self-interested action within the economic realm, conventional economics provides insight into the process by which such appeals might alter the transactional behavior of market participants.[1]

In contrast, the founder of conventional market economics, Adam Smith, understood economic actors to exercise restraint in granting dominion to their self-interested impulses. Specifically, Smith submitted that "natural liberty" (or, in contemporary language, the exercise of "free choice") incorporates an appropriate degree of forbearance occasioned by, first, "sympathy" and, second, the moral principles embraced by an "impartial spectator" internal to each individual. If Smith was essentially on target about human nature (admittedly, his terminology is now dated), moral and empathic appeals have the potential to influence how employers will proceed in their unregulated transactional negotiations with workers.

In what follows, we will first describe three quite dissimilar contemporary cases in which the sweating system has been, or is being, implemented. We will next review Commons's conception of the sweating system, summarize how he understood industrial development to bring about sweating, and call attention to the close correspondence between our cases and Commons's characterization. Because moral and empathic appeals have been utilized in some highly publicized recent cases involving sweating, and because we believe Smith's ideas are not without some merit, we will also briefly summarize Smith's conception of self-regulated transactional behavior. We will then explain why we are skeptical that Smithian self-regulation will prove an effective means of reversing the growing reliance on sweating within the realm of production. We conclude by again endorsing Commons's call for labor market regulation as the only viable mechanism for achieving that end.[2]

Nike Does It

Chief Executive Officer Phil Knight formulated Nike's strategy of total outsourcing while he was at Stanford Business School in the early 1960s. The money saved through outsourcing would then be poured into marketing, primarily using high-profile celebrity endorsements. Significantly, "the manufacture of these sneakers was based on an arms-length and often uneasy relationship with low paid, non-American workers" (Spar and Burns 2000, 2–3). Initially Knight subcontracted with firms in South Korea and Taiwan, but by the early 1990s most production had shifted to lower-cost East Asian countries, especially Indonesia.

The production of Nike shoes in Indonesia coincided with a period of rising labor unrest there. But Nike officials insisted that labor conditions in contractor factories were not their concern. Even if legal violations existed, the company's general manager in Jakarta said, "I don't know that I need to know" (Spar and Burns 2000, 5). Nike did draft a corporate code of conduct for its suppliers in 1992 that addressed working conditions, safety, environmental practices, and workers' insurance. Contractors were required to certify that they were following relevant laws and regulations.

Media attention to conditions in factories in developing countries increased between 1992 and 1996, exploding in the latter year with revelations that the clothing line endorsed by media celebrity Kathy Lee Gifford was made by child workers in

Honduras. When Gifford called on other celebrity endorsers to investigate conditions in the factories where the products they endorsed were made, sports celebrity Michael Jordan denied any personal responsibility, saying that the company was responsible. Nike continued to maintain that this was not their problem.

Following congressional hearings in May 1996, President Bill Clinton convened the Apparel Industry Partnership, which was meant to be a meeting ground for the companies and their critics. Nike quickly joined. Later that year Nike formed a new "labor practices department" and also hired the former U.S. ambassador to the United Nations, Andrew Young, to evaluate the effectiveness of its supplier code of conduct. Denial had been replaced by engagement. According to Knight, "In labor practices as in sport, we at Nike believe 'there is no finish line'" (Spar and Burns 2000, 7).

Things got worse for Nike in May 1997 when the popular comic strip *Doonesbury* ran a week's worth of biting criticism of Nike plants in Vietnam. Young's largely positive reports were heavily criticized for failing to address the issue of wages and as methodologically flawed, a celebrity endorsement rather than real research.

In the spring of 1997 Nike aided a team of graduate students at Dartmouth's Tuck School of Business who wanted to conduct a study of "the suitability of wages and benefits" paid by Nike's Vietnamese and Indonesian subcontractors (Calzini et al. 1997, 5). The faculty member coordinating the student group claimed that "workers made enough to eat a good diet, house themselves simply but comfortably, dress nicely, buy basic consumer goods and, primarily in the Indonesian case, save for the future" (Mihaly 1998). He argued that Nike and other multinationals were supporting social progress in these very poor countries and that labor critics actually understood this

but were pandering to the self-interests of U.S. trade unionists.

This argument is consistent with what orthodox economics teaches about international trade. In their best-selling international economics textbook, Paul Krugman and Maurice Obstfeld summarize the orthodox lesson thusly: "The proposition that trade is beneficial is unqualified. That is, there is no requirement that a country be 'competitive' or that trade be 'fair'" (Krugman and Obstfeld 2000, 23). They use a simple Ricardian model, believing that it demonstrates that competitiveness based on low wages does not hurt importing countries (so long as the opportunity cost of producing the imported good in terms of the home country's *own* labor is high). Further, in their model, trade does not exploit poor countries because wages are correlated with productivity.

We are dubious about both the empirical results of the Dartmouth study and the orthodox model more generally. Factory managers selected the workers to be interviewed. The Dartmouth team had no language skills, so local interpreters had to be used. The students did not look at pay stubs or various deductions from wages, which are often greater than managers' or handpicked workers' memories make them out to be. This leaves us less than convinced that a "living wage" was being paid to Nike workers.[3]

But the more serious problem is a theoretical one. This and other similar studies focus on labor market *outcomes* rather than the social relations of the labor market.[4] Nike's subcontracting network may or may not be a string of sweatshops with the traditional low wages, long hours, and unsafe conditions. Yet Nike's network clearly exhibits the separation of the worker from the price bargain and from a contractual relationship with the manufacturer that was, for Commons, the definition of the sweating system. "We don't make shoes" and "I don't know that I need to know" may make for bad public relations strategy, but they reflect the core of a business model in which the ultimate manufacturer tells the worker, "I do not employ you and I have nothing to do with you."

Fish Processors Do It Too

Fish processing may seem to have nothing to do with sneaker production. Sneakers are branded items, sold at remarkably high prices because of the image that their purchasers wish to convey. Fish are—well, just fish. The strategies that organizers have used to name and shame footwear and apparel companies may be less successful in fish processing. But the strategy of creating social distance in labor relations occurs in both branded and unbranded products, and not only by creating far-flung manufacturing networks.

After Rosa Ruiz was killed, the Rhode Island Workers' Rights Board held hearings. Workers' rights boards are nongovernmental organizations that attempt to use moral suasion and public pressure to expose and resolve labor problems. The use of moral suasion and public pressure reflect a popular response to the absence of governmental attention to the labor market problems of the 1980s and 1990s. The members of this particular board included two Latino labor activists, an AFL-CIO field representative who is also a state legislator, clergy, and a member of the Rhode Island Human Rights Commission. The board met on December 19, 2001, at St. Teresa's Church in the heart of one of Providence's Latino neighborhoods. Representatives of Town Dock, the fish processing company, and the temporary help agency were invited to attend but declined. The phone number that was listed for the temp agency was a fax machine.

Many of the workers at Town Dock could neither read nor speak English. For instance, Nasario Barrera, Rosa Ruiz's husband, could not identify the specific company he worked for in the days prior to the hearing because he could neither read nor write English. He and other workers testified that they earned less than the minimum wage and were not paid overtime. Workers were often paid in cash, with neither overtime nor holiday pay recognized, and with no documentation of hours worked. Rosa Ruiz's sister-in-law, Tomasa Barrera, claimed that female employees were subjected to sexual abuse by male supervisors. According to her, women were verbally abused and had their pictures taken while working and in the bathroom. The Barreras and other Town Dock workers testified that health and safety standards were routinely violated.

Although the temp agency, Action Manufacturing Employment, was not represented at the hearing, the owner of New England Employment Service, Rosa Noriega, did testify. Her company also supplies workers to the fish processing industry, though she was not involved in the Town Dock case. She said she received $7 per hour payment from the companies and paid the workers $5.75 per hour. (The Rhode Island minimum wage at this time was $6.15.) The companies faxed the number of hours each worker worked to her.

The board sent a recommendation to the state Department of Business Regulation, the Department of Labor and Training, and the regional Occupational Safety and Health Administration (OSHA) office, calling for a "complete investigation" of the industry in the state, with special attention to Town Dock and one other firm. Angela Lovegrove, a member of both the Workers' Rights Board and the Rhode Island Commission on Human Rights, specifically requested that there be no retaliation against those workers who had testified. Two days after the hearings, nineteen workers at Town Dock were fired, including

Nasario Barrera, Rosa Ruiz's husband. Through a translator, Barrera told a reporter that the company sought out him and his brother because their names had appeared in the newspaper. He claimed he was present when a Town Dock supervisor spoke to the van driver hired by the temp agency for which he was then working. According to Barrera, the supervisor asked the driver to inform the workers that they had been fired. This action dramatically illustrates the critical importance of social distance in understanding contemporary labor market trends.

The company's vice president claimed he had no knowledge of any workers being fired. According to a report in a local newspaper, the Narragansett *Times*, "Clark [the vice president] also said the workers are supplied to the company by the temporary agency and they are 'ordered' based on the number of workers Town Dock needs." To quote this manager directly, "It's important that everyone knows these people are not Town Dock employees" (Novak 2002a). Clark went on, "We have been in business for 20 years, and we are a highly regulated business. We're federally inspected annually. I disagree with the allegations. They are completely false as far as Town Dock is concerned, but my condolences go out to the family" (Novak 2002a). This was the family in which one adult was now dead and two had lost employment.

Eventually, thirty-five workers were fired. The temporary agency that had employed them told the workers that Town Dock had asked for "all new people" after the initial Workers' Rights Board hearing. In a subsequent hearing, one of the immigrant workers, who had been making $5.90 per hour (twenty-five cents less than the minimum wage) for very difficult work, expressed a strong desire to get his job back. He refused to give his name, fearing that he would be unable to find employment of any kind. Both workers and board

members noted that the status of many workers as undocumented immigrants put them in a particularly weak position.

The attorney for Town Dock claimed that "the company had simply decided to stop using New England Employment Services, an eight-month-old agency that supplied the workers" (Levitz 2002). It is common for temporary help agencies to go in and out of business quickly, changing names and sometimes phone numbers, without a change in the principals.

As a result of the second hearing, the legal counsel to the state's Department of Labor and Training said that the department would investigate both temp agencies and fish processors for violations of the minimum wage, workers' compensation, and safety standards. Paul Moura, a state representative and member of the Rhode Island Commission on Human Rights, called for the revival of a state commission that had begun investigating labor problems in the industry in 1999 but was disbanded before issuing a report.

Two weeks after the second hearing, in late January of 2002, the regional OSHA office held an informational meeting for fish processing firms. OSHA's area director claimed that this meeting had been in planning for a year and was unrelated to the problems at Town Dock. At the meeting, OSHA announced that it would begin launching "surprise" inspections of seafood processors in Rhode Island. The justification was not the Town Dock incident but the relatively poor safety record of the industry nationally and recent inspections in Massachusetts that had turned up many violations. The main problems cited were inadequate machine guards, unsafe use of electrical equipment, work done in confined spaces, and accidental start-up of machinery during maintenance or repair operations (the same problem that had killed Nguyen Thi Thu Phuong in Vietnam).

The director of the Rhode Island Seafood Council welcomed the free seminar but found the inspections unnecessary, arguing that most principals in seafood processing companies work on the shop floor. Since they would be unlikely to expose themselves to hazardous conditions, inspections were unnecessary. One of the attendees, who refused to be identified by name, was happy that OSHA was holding an educational session prior to the inspections. "They're giving us a chance to do the right thing. Just because regulations are stated in black and white on a piece of paper doesn't always mean they are clear to us" (Novak 2002b). Apparently ignorance of the law *is* an excuse.

The Town Dock workers and their allies failed to get even the obligatory study commission and industry self-regulation that the Nike organizers achieved. Interviews with officials at the Rhode Island Department of Labor and Training and the regional OSHA office indicate little follow up. The state commission to study the industry was not revived.

So Do Colleges and Universities

We turn briefly to another local case that strikes especially close to home for us. There is a strong trend for colleges and universities to outsource custodial and food services. We discuss one example of this to demonstrate the ubiquity of the strategy of creating social distance in employment relations.

In the spring of 2002, about fifty students from area colleges and universities rallied outside the gates of Providence College in Providence, Rhode Island, in support of janitors there who were working without a contract. The student had originally wanted to hold the rally in front of Harkins Hall, the administration building, but the administration

told them to "take the demonstration off campus" (Milkovits 2002a). In fact, a university vice president, a priest, sent a letter to one of the students that read, in part: "While I respect our students' right to articulate their opinions, the college is not under any obligation to allow people it does not know to use Providence College's private campus as a public forum to air their grievances and concerns" (quoted in N. McIntyre 2002).

The unionized workers, members of Service Employees International Union (SEIU) Local 134, were seeking wages comparable to those at similar institutions in the area, and the reinstatement of nine laid-off janitors. Like the Town Dock workers, the janitors were predominantly immigrants with little English-speaking ability. These jobs were clearly a step up from Town Dock, however, and tended to be held by documented immigrants or those who had been in the country for some time. Still, many held second jobs and hoped, given their comparatively low wages, to reach parity with Brown University, Bryant College, and other area educational institutions.

The problem was that the janitors did not actually work for Providence College (known locally as PC). The college had contracted janitorial services out to an independent company, UNICCO. The union representative expressed frustration at not being able to communicate directly with the college, and workers complained that they were "treated like they didn't work there." Although the workers were paid roughly $3 less an hour than those doing similar work at other area colleges and universities, and although the layoffs had left forty-one janitors to clean forty buildings, PC administrators attempted to wash their hands of the situation.

Students claimed that the college had a "moral responsibility" to guarantee adequate pay. The administration did not agree. Students called attention both to the recent student occupation of buildings in support of janitors at Harvard and the tenets of Catholic social doctrine (PC is a Catholic college). But according to Ed Caron, vice president for college relations and planning, the college could not dictate the level of compensation to a contractor:

> Unlike Harvard University, which directly employs its janitorial staff, Providence College is a UNICCO customer. As a UNICCO customer, Providence College does not and cannot have any role in the contract negotiations between UNICCO management and its employees. It is simply incorrect to suggest that the college can or should influence the outcome of the confidential labor-negotiation process that is underway. If Providence College did so, we would be interfering in an ongoing collective-bargaining situation between two other parties. (N. McIntyre 2002)

As in the Town Dock case, management spokespersons convey the importance of social distance in contemporary labor relations most eloquently.

According to interviews one of us conducted with union staff, the discussion of Catholic social thought was a "nonstarter." Although students and faculty were able to provide quantitative estimates of the inadequacy of the wage offer, given living costs in the area, and referred to specific papal encyclicals concerning salaries, social justice, and workplace dignity, they got no farther than the union did.

The union held a one-day strike in May and threatened to initiate a work slowdown that would have disrupted graduation ceremonies. Over the summer, the UNICCO-provided Providence College janitors received a new contract, retroactive to January, which raised their base rate from $8.06 to $10.31 per hour, bringing them close to the area standard. The contract improved pension benefits and provided additional time off. However, at the time of writing, there were a number of grievances still outstanding over these events.

These cases are interesting, but not unique. The safety problems in fish processing parallel those that Eric Schlosser documents in the meatpacking and chicken processing industries (Schlosser 2001). More important for our purposes, the employment strategy of hiding behind shadowy temporary employment agencies or subcontractors is the domestic equivalent of Nike's outsourcing strategy. And just as export-oriented industrialization in East Asia has made a vast new labor supply available to Nike, so has the blowback from neo-colonialism presented American employers with an exploitable labor supply of both documented and undocumented immigrants (Gonzales 2001). It is the similarities rather than the differences that strike us. In the Nike, Town Dock, and Providence College cases, destructive competition in the labor market is promoted by an employer strategy that seeks to lengthen the chain between ultimate consumer and ultimate producer. In each case, currently available regulatory mechanisms were inadequate to deal with the problem. Internationally, the International Labor Organization (ILO) is not yet an adequate enforcer of international labor standards, and company codes of conduct are not up to the job either (R. McIntyre 2003). Domestically, workers' rights boards have neither legal legitimacy nor the virtue (which the ILO does have) of bringing all interested parties to the table.

Commons on the Sweating System

In our title and in our headings for the three previous sections, we have asserted that firms are "doing it"—implementing the sweating system. We now turn to the task of showing that John R. Commons's conception of the sweating system is manifest in the cases we reviewed.

Commons discerned that all transactions have conflicts of interest at their core. The fundamental conflict pertinent to all transactions is the consumer's interest in high quality and a low price versus the producer's interest in high wages and good working conditions. The reality that the well-being of a household is affected by a large number of price bargains but only by a single or small number of wage bargains requires that the social goal of a "good" price bargain be appropriately balanced with the need of the producers in individual households to negotiate a "good" wage bargain. Commons contended that private negotiations yield a "reasonable" balancing of this conflict when both parties to a bargain possess equal power to influence the other in their favor. Prices and wages are at their "correct" levels when consumers and producers are each exerting equal power to withhold what the other wants but does not own, namely, money and labor power.

We believe the economic structure of sweating was most effectively outlined by Commons in his famous article on the American shoemakers (Commons 1909). The evolution of the shoemakers' market is summarized in Table 20.1. Initially, under a system of itinerant production, the price bargain between the purchaser and the producer was in reality simultaneously a price bargain *and* an implicit wage bargain—one, significantly, that was "reasonable" as Commons employed that term. As shown in the table, extension of the market for shoes generated a series of adjustments in the system of production, which in turn created a chain of price bargains separating the purchasers of shoes from their producers—first, between the customer and the retail merchant; second, between the retailer and the capitalist merchant organizing the distribution of a specific shoe; and third, between the capitalist merchant and capitalist manufacturing firms.

As indicated previously, we are herein using the term "social distance" to represent the social gap effected by the severing of a direct transactional relationship between the producers and the eventual beneficiaries of their efforts. Commons (1909, 249) underscored that the timing and terms of the price bargains that now separated the eventual users of shoes from their producers, coupled with the producers' conversion into wage workers, shifted market power dramatically in favor of purchasers. Hence, the capitalist businesses at the end of the transactional chain, those within whose ambit shoes are actually produced, find they can earn a profit only by means of *sweating* their workers, that is, by worsening the wage bargain (from the worker's point of view). Commons made it clear that he considered sweating a *necessary* consequence of the increase in social distance (our term) between the consumer and producer characterizing the evolution of the shoemakers' market (cf. Commons 1909, 246).

Commons's approach to the issue of sweating seems particularly relevant today. In particular, it is apparent that Commons's characterization of the way the sweating system works corresponds fairly closely to the actual events that unfolded in all three of the case histories we reviewed above, although we recognize that contractor control of information did not characterize the PC case. All three enterprises said, in effect, "I do not employ you and I have nothing to do with you[r wages]." Significantly, the common element in our three cases, which is why we are comfortable using the term "sweating system" in reference to all three, is the actual or attempted organization of production within a structure allowing the manufacturer *not* to "employ his own workman." What is evident from our cases is that outsourcing and labor contracting are simply alternative methods of effecting this end, that is, to institute the sweating system. And as Commons's account makes clear, the crucial step in implementing a sweating system is

Table 20.1

Evolution of the Wage Bargain

Stage	Bargains*			
Custom order (personal market)	P/W customer–producer			
Retail shop (local market)	P customer–retailer	P/W retailer–producer		
Wholesale order (regional market)	P customer–retailer	P retailer–wholesaler (bargain prior to work)	W wholesaler–worker	
Wholesale speculative (regional national, world market)	P customer–retailer	P retailer–capitalist (bargain after work completed)	P capitalist–employer	W employer–worker

*Two bargains: P = price bargain (exchange of ownership of a produced good); W = wage bargain (exchange of ownership of labor power).

At all stages, workers seek "protective device" from "competitive menace"

(1) protective organization (e.g., unions)

(2) protective legislation (e.g., labor "standards")

Source: Based on John R. Commons's article, "American Shoemakers: 1648 to 1985."

the creation of a transactional gap between the workers and the entity capturing the results of their labor power—as clearly occurred in all three cases. This severing of a direct transactional relationship between the worker and the substantive "original employer," recalling Commons's phrase, is the increase of social distance to which we are calling attention herein.

In Commons's day, the principal organizers of the sweating system were people who were socially positioned to recruit immigrant workers. While not a necessary element of sweating, our three cases indicate that this remains true today so long as we extend the meaning of "immigrant worker" to include migrants from the countryside to the city in the developing world. Moreover, as is evident from our three cases, sweated produc-

tion is becoming far more general than the limited case of outsourced Kathy Lee clothing items made in Chinatown or Nike shoes made in Indonesia might suggest.

Adam Smith and the Likely Role of Moral and Empathic Appeals in Curtailing Sweating

We alluded earlier to the possibility that moral and empathic appeals represent a possible strategy for moderating the deleterious consequences for labor of the sweating system. We further noted that Adam Smith furnished economists with a (long neglected) conception of human nature providing a possible rationale for this approach. We wish now to review relevant facets of the argument Smith presented in his *Theory of Moral Sentiments* (1759, revised 1790). The theory of "self-regulated" action Smith outlined in this work has been analyzed by countless scholars over the many years since its publication, and the main thrust of the analysis is now well-understood.[5] However, to our knowledge, the issue we are focused upon here was never directly addressed by Smith in *Moral Sentiments*. That issue is forbearance in market relations, by which we mean the act of refraining from fully exercising one's market power over another despite one's legal right to do so, that is, the choice of negotiating a transaction on terms less favorable to oneself than one is capable of obtaining legally in order to improve the terms from the perspective of the other transactor. In order to deal with this issue, therefore, interpretation and extension of Smith's often subtle reasoning are required on our part. Regrettably, space constraints preclude more than a perfunctory overview of Smith's relevant constructs.[6]

Contrary to standard textbook representations, Smith never averred that people's economic actions are intended only to further their own selfish interests. Indeed, Smith began *Moral Sentiments* by calling attention to the pervasiveness of benevolence in human action. However, Smith acknowledged that human action reveals an even stronger propensity for self-love (more on this below). Perceiving that an appeal to another person's self-interest is the most reliable method of eliciting a desired response, Smith inferred that self-interest is the behavioral impetus upon which a system of "natural liberty" must be based.[7] But Smith also made clear in *Moral Sentiments* his concomitant belief that unfettered self-interested action is moderated "naturally" by other inborn traits and that virtue and morality hence will generally typify "free" behavior.

According to Smith, we all possess an empathetic capacity he dubbed "sympathy," which occasions us to experience inside ourselves, via our imagination, emotions that are displayed by others or that, based on our own past experiences, can be situationally imputed to them. Our sympathy with displayed or imputed feelings, however, depends upon our approval of their appropriateness, that is, upon our reading of the propriety of their causes. Smith observed that the force of an empathic experience—of sympathy—wanes with the weakening of the link between oneself and another. For example, given the power of self-love, one empathizes most completely with oneself, somewhat less with family members, less yet with close acquaintances, and very weakly if at all with those "with whom we have no particular connection" (Smith 1759, 135). What this means is that one's empathetic identification with one's own emotions will clearly tend to overshadow the empathetic experience occasioned by the emotions displayed by or imputed to another with whom one does not have a strong personal connection. But if so, how can the potential impact of an act (transaction) on another's interests (imagined feelings) become a factor regulating one's pursuit of one's own attainments? Or, to put it slightly differently, how can that imagined potential impact induce an economic principal to forbear?

Smith perceived that in addition to possessing empathetic capacity, individuals, upon achieving maturity also have within themselves an "impartial spectator" to whom they transfer the power to render judgments concerning the morality of their own actions. This internalized "spectator," he insisted, remains outside the pull of individual self-interest and therefore stands ready to approve or disapprove of a specific economic actor's action's on the basis of the acceptability of their causes within the moral code and general rules of conduct to which the broader society of which the actor is a member is putatively committed (cf. Smith 1759, 109–10). And, Smith decreed, actors desire to *deserve* the approbation of this internalized "spectator" (116–17) and hence they have a strong internal inducement—albeit one that "self-love" sometimes subverts—to limit their actions to ones generating only effects that are justifiable under conventional moral standards or general rules of behavior.

The foregoing suggests that sympathy, when operative, can orient us toward restraining our selfish and indulging our benevolent affections (25), that is, can cause economic principals to forbear somewhat from fully exercising their economic power in negotiations when the attainable transactional outcome can be inferred to entail negative, painful consequences for other parties. And, similarly, when operative, the impartial spectator mechanism will induce principals to forbear from exercising their full power in transactional negotiations whenever conventional morality or general rules of behavior decree the resulting transactional outcomes to be morally wrong or improper.

Before assessing the relevance of Smith's concept of human nature to the issue of effecting an amelioration of the sweating system, we should first note that Commons assigned no direct role to sympathy in his "transactional psychology" and assumed that self-interest alone motivates the competing wills pitted against each other in transactional negotiations. Commons did discern a role for moral principles, however, which he understood to exert their effect via "habitual assumptions" woven into the fabric of the "institutionalized mind" giving direction to an individual's "will" (power of self-direction). By the term "habitual assumption," Commons meant a reflexive criterion of judgment formed by repeated participation in the practices of the going concerns—the nation, the family, the school, the club, the business enterprise, and so on—into whose orbits an economic actor enters.[8] In the main, Commons insisted, what is repeated, especially if it is consistent with one's self-interest, tends eventually to become "right"—moral—in the institutionalized mind. This suggests that Commons probably would have rejected the sharp separation of "morality" and self-interest at the root of Smith's conception of the impartial spectator.

To return now to our main topic, what, then, do our three cases suggest regarding the role that the forbearance occasioned by the two Smithian restraining forces is likely to play in limiting sweating? Let us assume for the moment that Smith is correct and that, contrary to what we have just stated, sympathy is an element of what Commons dubbed "transactional psychology." It will be recalled that according to Smith a personal bond or an ongoing face-to-face relationship strengthens the likelihood that sympathy will influence transactional behavior. The "small shops" that Commons associated with sweating—which presumably would include many Nike subcontractors and certainly would include Town Dock and perhaps also Providence College—are precisely the sorts of social locations where sympathy would be expected to be operative.[9] In such locations, a sympathetic bond would presumably develop between workers and their immediate supervisors or, less strongly, between workers and owners or management with whom they come into frequent contact. It is precisely in such locations that an impetus toward sweating motivated by naked self-interest would naturally be restrained. Thus it is worth noticing that the increase of social distance, as we have referred to the common element in all three of the cases we reviewed, in effect renders sympathy impotent. This is because it eliminates or greatly diminishes the role, in the negotiation of the wage bargain, for a particular group of workers who have a direct interpersonal relationship with those workers and hence who, by Smith's reasoning, might forbear to bring their full economic power into play. In other words, even if Smith was right about the role of sympathy in "human nature," its potentially ameliorative role in regard to sweating is nullified by the creation of social distance between the workers and their "real" employer.

Can we expect the impartial spectator mechanism to be a more effective counterforce to sweating? Nike's "engagement strategy" agreement in response to public criticism, as well as Kathy Lee Gifford's highly publicized call for better supervision of subcontractors, suggests the possibility that moral appeals can play a role in restraining sweating. It is worth noting, however, that by bringing the controlling "impartial" spectator inside the economic actor, Smith was submitting that one responds not to the judgment of an external, actual spectator, who may have only a partial knowledge of the full context within which a transaction is being negotiated, but to one's own judgment. In other words, an actual spectator may render a judgment regarding what *appears* to be the right—the moral—action, but from Smith's standpoint it is the internalized impartial spectator who judges what is *really* right. The issue, therefore, is, what is the relevant moral code or, more narrowly, the general rule of behavior, that present-day owners and managers are internalizing? Judging by the statements made by authorized representatives of the "real" employers in the cases we reviewed, that code or rule decrees: If workers are not members (in Commons's term, citizens) of "our" firm—that is, if we have no direct wage bargain with them, we have no responsibility of any kind for the wage bargain under which they work. In short, it is impossible to discern any sign of moral objection to the sweating system, as a system, on the part of the going concerns featured in these case studies.

If they are representative, then it is clear that empathic appeals to "real" employers will fail to elicit corrective action. The sweating system itself, of course, makes it difficult, if not impossible, for the actual employer—the subcontractor or labor contractor—to respond positively if moral appeals are directed at them.

We recognize that Nike's decision to create a labor practices department, to "investigate" the labor practices of its subcontractors, and so on, may appear to contradict our conclusion. Based upon our reading of that case, however, we interpret Nike's action to be motivated by the goal of safeguarding the goodwill of its customers, some of whom might stop purchasing Nike products due to negative publicity directed at Nike's labor practices, rather than by a moral concern on the part of its owners for the plight of the sweated workers producing those products. We must add that it was shocking to us to find that the priests responsible for Providence College's operations apparently have internalized the same market ethos as the owners of Nike and Town Dock and hence are similarly responsive only to negative publicity potentially undermining the goodwill built up with "customers" (future students) and benefactors rather than to moral dictates—including well-known papal encyclicals! This reality would appear to establish that the market ethos preached by the Chicago school of economists has taken very deep root in America's owning and managerial classes. If our inference is on target, those championing empathic appeals as the appropriate strategy for raising labor market attainments would be wise to direct such appeals exclusively at consumers.[10]

The Nature of a Viable Remedy

The three cases we reviewed provide a glimpse into a contemporary wage and working standards inequity—the sweating of immigrant and migrant workers. This perceptible signpost of destructive competition has at its root the huge, redundant labor force now extant in an increasingly global labor market, and it is being instituted through the "old" business strategy to which Commons called attention in his "American Shoemakers" article. That is the strategy of increasing the social distance between the worker and the "real" employer via the avoidance of a meaningful—price forming —transactional relationship between them. We hold that the wages and working conditions resulting from the confluence of these factors, of which we caught a glimpse in our three case studies, are *not* "reasonable." Although many commentators argue that this growing problem is capable of being corrected by voluntary action on the part of manufacturers, that is, by forbearance on their part engendered by moral and empathic appeals, our analysis in the previous section suggests that this approach is not robust. In fact, we submit that under the present scheme of relatively free global trade in the context of global labor redundancy, destructive competition in the globalized labor market seems likely to persist unless the approach advocated by John R. Commons is adopted. That is, following Commons, we submit that adjustment of the rules governing negotiation of the wage bargain is the only feasible method of actually reversing destructive competition in the labor market —of which the spread of the sweating system is but a discernible symptom.

Commons's perspective on economic policy reflects an interpretation of the capitalist market system that diverges significantly from the one presented in standard economics courses.[11] In contrast to the "natural law" conception of market activity put forward by Smith and promulgated by the economics profession to this very day, Commons developed a "legal" interpretation of economic processes emphasizing the role of collective action in shaping transactional outcomes— primarily via *instituted* "working rules" specifying what individuals can, must, or may do or not do in their transactions with each other. These working rules confer rights and impose duties on all the "citizens" of a going concern, and by specifying "rights" and "duties," they create their exposures and liberties as well. Unlike Smith, who perceived a natural harmony of interests, Commons argued that only by virtue of such rules and the relative certainty of their enforcement does it become possible for individuals with conflicting interests to work together harmoniously and for their actions to be appropriately correlated. Working rules can be specific to individual economic concerns (a business enterprise), but enterprise-specific rules cannot transgress rules set forth by the "sovereign power," that is, the "rules" specified in a nation's commercial and labor law.

According to Commons, the present-day rule structure governing the negotiation of a wage bargain emerged gradually over several centuries as those consecutively authorized to settle disputes (for example, common law judges in England and members of the Supreme Court in the United States, or, more recently and less comprehensively, the boards of large corporations) volitionally adjusted working rules in accordance with their conception of the public purpose (or, with respect to corporate boards, the concern's private purpose). From this evolutionary perspective, social problems are understood to be "solved" by adjusting the controlling working rules to fit new circumstances, not, à la conventional "natural law economics," by adjusting the rules to accord with the ahistorical requirements of "competition."

With respect to the wage bargains being negotiated in his own day, it was Commons's judgment that an unfair exchange of "property" was thereby effected because the governing working rules were not reasonable in that they granted employers superior "power to withhold" vis-à-vis employees. Because substantial involuntary unemployment was the norm, he discerned that the wage and working conditions that the weakest worker was willing to accept became the standard toward which the market would tend. This presumption lay at the core of the "destructive competition" hypothesis to which we have made repeated references, and it today lies at the core of the "race to the bottom" hypothesis. In part as a result of Commons's own scholarship, the "unfair" wage bargain outcomes resulting from the unbalanced power of potential employer and potential employee were remedied somewhat by the Wagner Act, by social insurance mitigating some of the effects engendered by those outcomes (for example, the high incidence of poverty among the elderly), and by the creation of labor standards proscribing a broad array of wage bargain outcomes (for example, an unreasonably unsafe workplace). Via the creation of standards, to use an old phrase, the "plane of competition" was lifted.

If Commons is right, and we believe he is, the decisive step in instituting the sweating system—whether by subcontracting production or through labor contracting—is the legal severing of the workers from the going concern (a business enterprise) that is the "real" employer and thereby to strip them of functional "citizenship." By means of this severing, the owners and managers of the original enterprise are able to regard their "real" employee as a nonemployee and hence as ineligible to receive the protections or rights enjoyed by enterprise "citizens." Those "real" employees are similarly regarded as having no legitimate role in shaping the working rules of the original concern.

We find it highly implausible that a feasible method of reorganizing the realm of production—

so as to eliminate the intermediate price bargains highlighted by Commons in his shoemakers article and thereby to eliminate the economic impetus for sweating—could ever be implemented. We find it equally implausible that a practicable system could be worked out ensuring that the purchasers of products (the ultimate "real" employer) are induced to forbear from negotiating agreements that result in substandard wages or working conditions for the producers of those products (their ultimate "real" employees) *and* that subcontractors or labor contractors—in actuality, middlemen for the more fundamental principals—are induced to forbear from exercising fully their market power over individual workers. To our mind, the only plausible remedy for sweating, without overthrowing capitalism itself, is the creation by an overarching rule-creating entity—a state, a nation, an international organization—of mandatory minimal labor market standards, making it unnecessary for anyone to forbear in order for all workers to obtain reasonable wages and enjoy reasonable working conditions.

A continuing failure to implement reasonable standards will only make the sweating system—that is, from the enterprise's point of view, outsourcing and labor contracting—more prevalent as a form of organizing an enterprise's relationship with its "real" employees. And we might add that even though all three of our cases involved immigrant workers (as we redefined the concept), it surely is only a matter of time until the institutionalization of sweating via the creation of social distance between the worker and the "real" employer begins to impact the native workforce as well.

Conclusion

Our cases bring into clear view three moments of an ongoing social process in which unregulated market forces appear to be engendering increased use of sweated labor via the creation of social distance between workers and their "real" employers. Alerted to the possibility by our three cases, we are particularly concerned that competition among the members of the global redundant labor force, countless numbers of whom are accustomed to a very low standard of life, has already engendered a slow but inexorable global "race to the bottom" (destructive competition). There may still be an opportunity for individual nation states, or blocks of such states (for example, the European Union), to implement actions that will prove capable of shielding their own labor force from destructive international labor market competition.[12] But given the increasingly global organization of production, it seems likely to us that opponents will argue that doing so will cause even more firms to move their operations to foreign countries where similar restrictions are not being imposed, and that this threat is likely to undercut any legislature's will to increase protective measures for unskilled and, especially, immigrant laborers.

We arrive at the conclusion, therefore, that the sweating system approach to organizing work, and through it destructive competition, will continue to grow in significance unless a means of imposing minimum labor standards on all enterprises can be instituted by a supranational "concern" with the sovereign power to command obedience to its laws. We have previously addressed the issue of international labor rights and analyzed some of the difficulties that will be encountered in crafting any set of standards that developed and developing nations alike will find acceptable (McIntyre and Ramstad 2002, 2003). In doing so, we judged that the ILO is best suited among the already-created international organizations for moving forward with the development of reasonable minimal international standards, and we similarly judge the

ILO to be the only international body within which an appropriate set of internationally applicable antisweating standards has any possibility of being crafted.

We hope that labor researchers increasingly will become attuned to the problem of sweating in the internationalized labor market and that they will both publicize its existence and urge that it be remedied. We concluded the first of our previous articles with the observation that "progress toward the goal of instituting an international system of labor market protections [will] be expedited if those who [support the development of such standards] were to make more explicit use of Commons's institutional economics in providing a rationale for their agenda" (McIntyre and Ramstad 2002, 301). We believe the present analysis exemplifies that truth.

Notes

1. Indeed, conventional economics has no place for the concept of destructive competition itself and locates the remedy for low wages, contingent employment, and so forth, in an elevation of the human capital possessed by laborers rather than in an alteration of the practices adhered to by employers.

2. In McIntyre and Ramstad (2002), we proposed that the labor rights conventions of the International Labor Organization present a body of standards for international regulation.

3. The Dartmouth team performed no qualitative analysis, no cultural analysis, and made no mention of the repressive role of the Indonesian state. No meetings were held with prolabor nongovernmental organizations. Although the project's coordinator states that the Indonesian manpower ministry takes worker rights very seriously, it was in fact at the time notoriously antiworker and paid almost no attention to workplace safety issues. The fact that Nike contractors mainly employ young women, who often are the weakest participants in the labor market, was not mentioned in the Dartmouth study.

More broadly, the correlation of wages with productivity is questionable at best. There are many well-known institutionalist critiques of the marginal productivity theory (Lester 1946; Thurow 1975, Simon 1979). Productivity and wage growth have diverged dramatically in the United States over the last several decades (Mishel, Bernstein, and Boushey 2003, 156–58). The ratio of value added to labor cost is much higher in China and Indonesia relative to Korea (or the United States) and there is no sign that these ratios are converging, which is a prediction of the orthodox model. For the Nike data, see Spar and Burns (2000, 19). For the orthodox argument, see Krugman and Obstfeld (2000, 25).

4. Similarly, the debate over North American Free Trade Agreement (NAFTA) focused largely on the number of jobs that might be lost or won. But the major effect of NAFTA has been on social relations in the workplace, especially workers' rights to organize and bargain collectively. See Bronfenbrenner (2001).

5. For a succinct statement of the main argument, see the editor's "introductory reading" in Heilbroner (1986, 57–63).

6. We should make explicit that our interpretation of Smith's concept of "sympathy" has been influenced by our reading of Ginsburg (1994) and Stabile (1997).

7. It is clear, however, that Smith did not consider self-interest the only means of eliciting a desired action. Indeed, it is worth noting that Smith's oft-quoted passage, "It is not from the benevolence of the butcher, the brewer, or the baker, that we expect our dinner, but from their regard to their own interest," is imbedded in a discussion in which Smith makes obvious his contention that there is a benevolent tendency in people (Smith 1776, 14).

8. The quoted terms are central construct in Commons's theory of economic behavior. For a discussion of Commons's social psychological conception of the individual, see Albert and Ramstad (1997, 1998).

9. We emphasize that we are here engaging in a "what if" exercise. If the charges of Town Dock's former employees about workplace conditions are accurate, one might question whether the facts allow for the existence of any sympathetic proclivity at all on the part of its owners.

10. A fully Smithian strategy would appeal also to the sympathy and moral feeling of the capitalist. In this sense, the strategy of groups such as the National Labor Committee in exposing working conditions in factories producing goods for Kathy Lee Gifford and Disney and then appealing to the latter on a moral basis is Smithian, as is the appeal that the filmmaker Michael Moore makes to Nike CEO Phil Knight at the end of *The Big One*.

11. For a concise overview of Commons's theory of an instituted market system, see Ramstad (1998). For an overview of Commons's analytical system as an integrated whole, see Ramstad (1990).

12. See Ramstad (1987) for the argument that a system of tariffs levied on products produced in countries where reasonable labor standards have not been implemented would serve the public interest in the United States. The

argument developed therein was conceived in the mid-1980s. Whether the devised approach would prove of equal value today, after almost two additional decades of globalization, is problematic.

References

Albert, Alexa, and Yngve Ramstad. "The Social Psychological Underpinnings of Commons's Institutional Economics: The Significance of Dewey's *Human Nature and Conduct*." *Journal of Economic Issues* 31, no. 4 (December 1997): 881–916.

———. "The Social Psychological Underpinnings of Commons's Institutional Economics II: The Concordance of George Herbert Mead's 'Social Self' and John R. Commons's 'Will.'" *Journal of Economic Issues* 32, no. 1 (March 1998): 1–46.

Bronfenbrenner, Kate. *Uneasy Terrain: The Impact of Capital Mobility on Workers, Wages and Union Organizing*. U.S. Trade Deficit Review Commission, 2000, www.ustdrc.gov/research/bronfenbrenner.pdf.

Calzini, Derek, Jake Odden, Jean Tsai, Shawna Hoffman, and Steve Tran. *Nike Inc.: Survey of Vietnamese and Indonesian Expenditure Levels*. Dartmouth, NH: The Amos Tuck School, 1997.

Colby, John. "UNICCO Wages Keep Workers in Poverty." *The Cowl*, April 25, 2002.

Commons, John R. "American Shoemakers: 1648 to 1895." In *Labor and Administration*. 1909. New York: Augustus M. Kelley, 1964: 219–66.

———. "The Sweating System." In *Out of the Sweatshop*, ed. Leon Stein Fink. New York: Quadrangle, 1977 (1901).

Ginsburg, Carlo. "Killing a Chinese Mandarin: On the Moral Implications of Difference." *Critical Inquiry* 21, no. 1 (Autumn 1994): 10–36.

Gonzalez, Juan. *Harvest of Empire: A History of Latinos in America*. New York: Penguin, 2001.

Heilbroner, Robert, ed. *The Essential Adam Smith*. New York: W.W. Norton, 1986.

Krugman, Paul. "In Praise of Cheap Labor." *Slate*, March 20, 1997, http://web.mit.edu/krugman/www.smokey/html.

Krugman, Paul, and Maurice Obstfeld. *International Economics*. 5th ed. Reading, MA: Addison-Wesley, 2000.

Larimer, Tim. "Sneaker Gulag: Are Asian Workers Really Exploited?" *Time International*, May 11, 1998, 30–32.

Lester, Richard. "Shortcomings of Marginal Analysis for Wage-Employment Problems." *American Economic Review* 36, no. 1 (March 1946): 63–82.

Levitz, Jennifer. "Immigrants Lament Loss of Fish Processing Jobs to Workers' Rights Board." *Providence Journal*, January 12, 2002.

Lin, Jennifer. "Vietnam Gives Nike a Run for Its Money." *Philadelphia Inquirer*, March 23, 1998.

McIntyre, Nicole. "Protests Continue for UNICCO Living Wage." *The Cowl*, April 11, 2002.

McIntyre, Richard. "Globalization, Human Rights and the Problem of Individualism." *Human Rights and Human Welfare* 3, no. 1 (2003), www.du.edu/gsis/hrhw/volumes/2003/mcintyre3–1.pdf.

McIntyre, Richard, and Yngve Ramstad. "John R. Commons and the Problem of International Labor Rights." *Journal of Economic Issues*, 36, no. 2 (June 2002): 293–301.

———. "Reasonable Value and the International Organization of Labor Rights." *Économie et Institutions*, no. 2, ler semestre 2003: 83–109.

Mihaly, Eugene. "The Truth About Third World Workers." *Providence Journal*, June 3, 1998.

Milkovits, Amanda. "PC Tells Students It Won't Intervene in Janitors, Subcontractor Pay Dispute." *Providence Journal*, April 6, 2000b.

———. "Students Protest in Support of Janitors." *Providence Journal*, April 5, 2002a.

Mishel, Lawrence, Jared Bernstein, and Heather Boushey. *The State of Working America*: *2002–03*. Ithaca, NY: Cornell University Press, 2001.

Moore, Michael. *The Big One*. New York: Dog Eat Dog, Miramax, 1998.

Novak, Julie. "Fish Plant Fires Workers Who Raised Labor Issues." *Narragansett Times*, January 2, 2002a.

———. "OSHA Holds Meetings for Members of Fish Processing Industry." *Narragansett Times*, January 30, 2002b.

———. "Workers' Rights Board Attempts to Meet with Town Dock Employees." *Narragansett Times*, February 13, 2002c.

Ramstad, Yngve. "Free Trade versus Fair Trade: Import Barriers as a Problem of Reasonable Value." *Journal of Economic Issues* 21, no. 1 (March 1987): 5–32.

———. "The Institutionalism of John R. Commons: Theoretical Foundations of a Volitional Economics." In *Research in the History of Economics Thought and Methodology*, vol. 8, ed. Warren J. Samuels. Greenwich, CT: JAI Press, 1990: S3–104.

———. "Commons's Institutional Economics: A Foundation for the Industrial Relations Field?" *Proceedings of the Fiftieth Annual Meeting of the Industrial Relations: Research Association* 1 (1998): 308–19.

Schlosser, Eric. *Fast Food Nation: The Dark Side of the All-American-Meal*. New York: Harper Collins, 2001.

Simon, Herbert. "Rational Decision Making in Business Organizations." *American Economic Review* 69, no. 4 (September 1979): 493–513.

Smith, Adam. *An Inquiry Into the Nature and Causes of the Wealth of Nations*, ed. E. Cannan. New York: Random House, 1937 (1776).

———. *The Theory of Moral Sentiments*, ed. D.D. Raphael and A.L. Macfie. New York: Oxford University Press, 1976 (1759).

Spar, Deborah and Jennifer Burns. *Hitting the Wall: Nike and International Labor Practices*. Harvard Business School Case #9–700–047. Boston: Harvard Business School, 2000.

Stabile, Don. "Adam Smith and the Natural Wage: Sympathy, Subsistence and Social Distance." *Review of Social Economy* 55, no. 3 (Fall 1997): 293–311.

Thurow, Lester. *Generating Inequality*. New York: Basic Books, 1975.

U.S. Department of Commerce, Economics and Statistics Administration. *Other Footwear Manufacturing*, 1997, www.census.gov/prod/ec97/97m3162e.pdf.

U.S. General Accounting Office. *Data on the Tax Compliance of Sweatshops*, 1994, www.unclefed.com/GAOReports/ggd94–210fs.pdf.

Ziner, Karen, and Paul Davis. "Panel Seeks Probe of Death." *Providence Journal*, December 20, 2001.

Conclusion

21

Prospects for the Future of Institutionalist Labor Economics

Dell P. Champlin and Janet T. Knoedler

The preceding twenty chapters introduce the varied approaches used, and the crucial issues examined, by modern institutionalist labor economists. Several major lessons emerge. The neoclassical method when applied to labor markets has misrepresented some key aspects of modern labor markets, and these misrepresentations have impeded our understanding of the key challenges facing labor. In contrast, institutionalist labor approaches emphasize a number of important, useful, and realistic concepts that seem especially relevant in this twenty-first century. Given the challenges faced by workers around the world, we believe that the precepts and the prescriptions offered by institutionalist labor economists ought to receive more attention. We address each of these in turn.

Neoclassical Misrepresentations of Labor Markets Have Important Negative Consequences

An important theme in many of the preceding essays is that neoclassical economics when applied to labor has misrepresented many key aspects about real-world workers and the operation of real-world labor markets. These unfortunate misrepresentations have contributed to the view that the growing inequality of incomes and the growing economic insecurity for workers are merely the inevitable outcomes of our current market economy rather than conscious, deliberate strategies by those in power.

How does neoclassical theory misrepresent the labor market? One set of misrepresentations derives from the methodological individualism that is inherent to all neoclassical reasoning. Thus, as Bruce Kaufman notes in Chapter 2, low wages or unemployment can be blamed on the personal choices or the failings of individual workers rather than on such circumstances as the unequal bargaining power between employers and employees. Similarly, in Chapter 11, Robert LaJeunesse argues that the standard assumption of perfect competition in labor markets leads to the false conclusion that wages and work hours are primarily determined by the preferences of individual workers rather than prescribed by employers or established by cultural norms.

Another set of criticisms derives from the use of the market model itself. Kaufman identifies one of the major criticisms by institutional economists, that wages are not the outcome of the impersonal forces of supply and demand but, rather, that wages and other conditions of employment derive from social, cultural, political, and power relationships as well as from often complex economic relationships. Kaufman, drawing on the work of Beatrice and Sidney Webb, argues that several key features of labor markets, especially inequality of bargaining power, asymmetric information, restrictions to mobility, and the persistence of involuntary unemployment, call into question the efficacy of the standard labor market model. At best, in his view, demand and supply may set upper and lower limits to wages, but do not determine the precise level of wages. As Doug Kinnear demonstrates in Chapter 7, rather than wages tending toward equilibrium in any given labor market, differentials in wage rates for similar kinds of work were recognized as the norm by early institutionalist labor economists. Moreover, nonwage conditions reinforced rather than negated these differentials.

In Chapter 9, Ann Jennings emphasizes the many distortions in the labor market model due to its foundation on dead metaphors used out of habit or historical precedent rather than analytical realism. Moreover, in her view, the market is an abstraction built on an abstraction; thus, the use of the "market" in describing the processes involved in hiring and compensating labor is fraught with logical and historical error. Nonetheless, the dead market metaphor is often applied to the labor market as "a mode of 'depoliticized speech'—which is to say, speech that is deeply political, but not represented that way" (137).[1] The resulting "naturalization" of the market has given credence to the now empirically discredited argument that an increase in wages above some presumed market level will lead to unemployment. Similarly, in Chapter 10, Robert Prasch questions the core proposition of neoclassical theory that labor is a commodity like any other commodity and that the labor market has no special features that distinguish it from, say, the market for broccoli. As Prasch demonstrates, there are significant differences between labor and other commodities that are bought and sold, such as broc-

coli: (1) an employer has "caretaker" responsibilities toward the workers, unlike the owner of broccoli; (2) labor has "storage" costs and cannot simply be withdrawn from the market until prices rise, unlike other commodities; (3) workers, unlike commodities such as broccoli, have an obvious interest in how they are treated; and (4) whereas the benefits of high prices for other commodities accrue mainly to the producer, high wages are good for all of us. The application of the market model that mostly describes the buying and selling of commodities in competitive markets to the real-world issues facing workers has facilitated a theoretical and practical commodification of labor.

The tenets of neoclassical theory have also established as unshakable truths some demeaning misrepresentations of workers and work. As Robert LaJeunesse contends in Chapter 11, a primary assumption of neoclassical economics is that work is irksome and that workers therefore dislike their labors. Aversion to work and more generally, avoidance of pain and pursuit of pleasure, are central tenets of economic man in neoclassical theory, derived from its basis in utilitarian theory. Seen through this utilitarian, neoclassical lens, the end of all production is consumption, and thus the objective of work is to obtain the largest quantity of goods and services at the least effort possible. The consequences of this misrepresentation are multifarious, ranging from our consumerist society to deskilling and other abuses in the workplace to deep cultural neuroses about the meaning of work.

What other implications derive from the neoclassical market model when used to examine certain labor market practices and outcomes? As David Zalewski discusses in Chapter 19, neoclassical marginal productivity theory and other explanations have been used to justify the obscene levels of compensation for American CEOs in recent years, even though the current ratio between the pay of CEOs and pay of the average production worker now exceeds 500 to 1, and even though evidence has abounded in recent years that CEOs and senior executives have used their seats on boards of directors and other devices to inflate their salaries at the expense of the average worker. The illusion that market outcomes have led to higher and higher salaries at the top and stagnant incomes for the rest gives convenient cover to the fact that executives have used their own power to negotiate high salaries and lucrative benefits for themselves while placing the jobs, wages, and benefits of their own employees at risk. Market justification for the rising tide of inequality thus permits violation of all norms of distributive justice. The market is also seen as a sufficient arbiter of discrimination on the basis of race or gender, according to Deborah Figart and Ellen Mutari in Chapter 12. Discrimination is seen by neoclassical economists as a market distortion, for which any discriminating employer will be punished by the market, instead of as a systemic and pervasive feature of our modern economy. The implication, of course, is that no extramarket measures are needed to remedy such social ills. As Barbara Wiens-Tuers discusses in Chapter 13, the principle of employment at will assigns to both employer and employee the freedom to terminate a given work arrangement when they wish, but it ignores the greater bargaining power in that relationship held by the employer. The doctrine of employment at will has probably contributed to the growing contingent, disposable labor force in our modern economy. Moreover, as Wiens-Tuers argues, neoclassical theory justifies the increased use of contingent labor in recent years on such grounds as offering more "flexibility" to women entering the labor force and to corporations struggling to become more "flexible" to face the global marketplace.

Finally, what are the implications of the neoclassical model with respect to the struggles of modern workers? As Jon Wisman and Aaron Pacitti detail in Chapter 6, rather than the harmony of interests between those who supply labor and those who demand labor as envisioned by the labor market model, the division of interests between labor and capital has been a present and growing feature of modern capitalism for most of the past forty years. Moreover, capital has used neoclassical economics, in the guise of supply-side theory and other variants, to win its battles over labor in the ideological sphere because labor has had the advantage of greater numbers in the political sphere. Wielding the rhetoric of the market, capital has managed to destroy the idea of workplace democracy, with the result that most workers no longer seriously, or even remotely, consider collective ownership of the means of production as a realistic prospect. Corporations are also well on the way to destroying political democracy, a process that seems to be accelerating in this first decade of the twenty-first century.

In short, to summarize an important point made by Ann Jennings in Chapter 9, dead metaphors such as the labor market model help to justify myths about the fairness and objectivity of markets. But real-world labor markets do not resemble the simple supply-and-demand analyses offered up by neoclassical theory. Institutionalist and other heterodox labor economists have devoted considerable energy to identifying these glaring misrepresentations in the neoclassical model, so that they can call into question the fairness of "market" outcomes and raise objections to policies and practices promulgated on these false premises.

Core Principles of Institutionalist Labor Economics

As Bruce Kaufman explains in Chapter 2, it has too often been presumed that institutionalists are simply critics of neoclassical theory and that they have failed to come up with a respectable alternative.

However, as the preceding chapters capably demonstrate, this is not at all the case. Institutionalists are united in their view that a single universal theory is inadequate to understand the complexities of labor markets. They have instead focused their efforts on analysis of the ongoing contractual relationship that exists between employers and workers, on identification of the rules and conventions that govern this contractual relationship, and on understanding the myriad aspects of labor market institutions and the wage setting and other labor market processes that take place within those institutions. To paraphrase John Dunlop, a mid-twentieth-century institutional economist quoted by several of our contributors, the labor market is not a bourse. It is, rather, an institution with cultural, social, political, legal, and economic aspects that cannot be adequately represented by the simple market model.

As several of our authors have reported, much of institutionalist labor economics derives from John R. Commons. Commons was an integral member of the first generation of institutionalist labor economists, as Kaufman details in Chapter 2. These economists viewed themselves as social reformers, who worked to understand the issues and ameliorate the myriad problems confronting the workers of their time. Incorporating fact-gathering and case study in their analyses, they studied the actual workings of real labor markets rather than drawing on the abstract principles of neoclassical theory. Thus, a connection to social activism was a primary characteristic of Commons's labor economics. Dennis Chasse elaborates on this aspect of Commons's work in Chapter 3 in his extended investigation of the work of the "Commons gang." According to Chasse, Commons and his students had a "shared conviction that a bargain-

ing imbalance forced workers to bear the external costs of economic progress" (50). Given this overarching guidepost, Commons proceeded to develop policies and institutions that could lift these external costs from workers, either by direct regulation or by strengthening the bargaining power of workers. Commons's ideas were used to create both the Wisconsin Industrial Commission and the U.S. Commission on Industrial Relations, and through the latter he proposed both a comprehensive social security system and a national bargaining board. The Commons gang later worked with the American Association for Labor Legislation to develop model programs for almost all the pressing labor problems of the day—unemployment, occupational disease, excessive work hours, and old age poverty, as well as various programs that became part of President Franklin D. Roosevelt's New Deal, significantly the National Labor Relations Board.

It is important to note that Commons was not simply a social reformer, but that he also made many important theoretical contributions, several of which are highlighted in the preceding chapters. As Glen Atkinson discusses in Chapter 3, Commons developed a theory of competition from his observation of real-world conditions of work that focused on the danger of the "competitive menace," this in contrast to the neoclassical treatment of competition as a benign force. In Commons's formulation, the competitive menace is the manufacturer who sets the lowest standard of living and produces at the lowest cost and quality, a competitor who is a "menace rather than an actual competitor" (46). Commons observed this feature emerging during the first wave of industrialization in the United States in the late nineteenth century, and he recognized that severe price competition had led to several tactics to cut costs that we would still recognize today, including reducing quality, reducing wages, and creating sweat-shop working conditions. Similarly, in Chapter 20, Richard McIntyre and Yngve Ramstad discuss Commons's 1901 analysis of the sweating system as a system of subcontracting in which the sweatshop contractor serves as "an irresponsible go-between for the manufacturer" (298). In their view, this same system is used today by Nike and other global outsourcers, as well as by many local firms that have outsourced such functions as custodial or food services. The key issue in the sweating system is the creation of greater and greater social distance between worker and employer, which subjects the worker "ever more effectively to destructive competition, that is, to a 'race to the bottom'" (298). In other words, ever-lengthening chains of subcontractors between employer and employee permit the severing of direct bargaining relationships between workers and the entities for which the productive activity is being done. The result is that destructive competition, or the competitive menace of which Glen Atkinson writes, is promulgated by employer strategies that "lengthen the chain between ultimate consumer and ultimate producer" (304). Moreover, Adam Smith's "impartial spectator" who served, in his *Theory of Moral Sentiments*, as a curb on the most egregious competitive excesses of market system, is rendered ineffectual by the increased social distance inherent in a system of sweating. Commons's idea of social distance is thus an important theoretical contribution that has even greater relevance today.

Commons was not the only early institutionalist to examine questions related to the field of labor economics. As elaborated in Robert LaJeunesse's Chapter 11, Thorstein Veblen countered the neoclassical proposition that labor is irksome by arguing that workers instead have a natural instinct for workmanship. According to Veblen, humans are endowed with a proclivity toward purposeful action and a distaste for futility of action. Furthermore, to the degree that humans seem to prefer leisure, that preference comes from the status accorded to leisure as synonymous with superiority, wealth, and power and not from an innate aversion to work. As Dell Champlin and Janet Knoedler document in Chapter 5, Thorstein Veblen and John Maurice Clark also offered an early justification for the living wage. According to Veblen, economic welfare should be measured by whether "industrial processes yielded a sufficient or an insufficient output of the means of life" (Veblen, 76). John Maurice Clark explained that business did not properly account for all of the costs of production, including the full costs of the labor employed. Thus employers of low-wage labor shifted the cost to someone else, either to the worker's family or to society. These themes of cost shifting are also found in the work of William Kapp, as presented in LaJeunesse's Chapter 11, where he argues that excessive work hours may inflict damage on third parties.

In the macro context, heterodox theoreticians ranging from Karl Marx to Thorstein Veblen to Michel Kalecki have observed that persistent involuntary unemployment is inevitable in a capitalist economy, as L. Randall Wray and Mathew Forstater note in Chapter 17. This is due both to the "'sabotage' of production" carried out by the captains of industry (258) and to government policy that fails to maintain sufficient aggregate demand to provide full employment. As a result, even in good economic times, there will be an "unemployable surplus population" (260). Drawing on a wide range of heterodox economists, including Beatrice and Sidney Webb, Karl Marx, and Karl Polanyi, Robert Prasch observes that labor does have a "storage" cost, unlike other commodities: at the most basic level, workers must satisfy basic needs to survive during such a period of "storage" and they can thus be forced by the threat of starvation to accept wages and conditions that are below fair levels. Thus it is relative bargaining power, not skills or productivity, that determines the level of wages.

Mid-twentieth-century institutionalist economists Reynolds, Dunlop, and Kerr continued the creation of an institutionalist theory of the labor market, as summarized by Doug Kinnear in Chapter 7, by focusing on the demand side rather than the supply side of labor markets. Rather than accepting for purposes of analysis one single homogeneous aggregate (and theoretical) labor market, these economists recognized that the real-world labor market is actually composed of many labor markets, each of which is delineated by various barriers to entry. Moreover, rather than impersonal market forces setting wages and conditions within these markets, institutional rules within each workplace and within each labor market are established by employers, by informal channels, by companies via personnel policies, by trade unions or collective agreements, and by government. Each of these economists was also skeptical of the value of marginal productivity explanations of wages. From their pioneering work, as explained by Jerry Gray and Richard Chapman in Chapter 8, came segmentation theory, which in turn dominated institutionalist labor analysis from the late 1960s to the late 1970s. Segmentation theory offered reliable answers to the vexing questions that were not answered by neoclassical theory—for example, how to explain the increasing inequality of income, the increased use of contingent labor, and the increased levels of underemployment.

More recent work by institutional and heterodox economists has addressed specific labor market issues. A good example is provided in Chapter 12 by Deborah Figart and Ellen Mutari. In their discussion of the failure of neoclassical economics to come up with a satisfactory theory of discrimination, they advocate the use of a multidimensional analysis that uses both structural and neoinstitutionalist approaches. These approaches, including the segmentation models just mentioned, class-based hierarchical analyses, and crowding models, explicitly reject the individualistic framework of neoclassical economics in favor of a model of institutional discrimination in which the focus is on structural features of labor markets and employment practices. Addressing some of the same concerns, L. Randall Wray and Mathew Forstater demonstrate in Chapter 17 that job losers and the long-term unemployed have been disproportionately people of color, even during two recent expansionary periods, the 1960s and the 1990s. In a similar vein, Enrico Marcelli demonstrates in Chapter 14 that the unauthorized resident status of many Mexican immigrants to the United States has had a significant negative impact on their earning power, with unauthorized male Mexican workers earning nearly a third less than their white counterparts. Most of this wage gap cannot be explained except by reference to models of exploitation of, or discrimination against, a group of workers who have almost no bargaining power due to their unauthorized residency status. In other words, it is the nature of the demand for the jobs most frequently occupied by unauthorized Mexican immigrants rather than the workers themselves that has led to these jobs having both low pay and low status.

An enlarged field of view that rejects the notion of homogeneous labor markets and workers is thus an essential component to institutionalist approaches. As Figart and Mutari argue, in an institutionalist approach, several dimensions of wages must be studied—not simply wages as a price, but wages as a living and wages as a social practice—in order to understand how such factors as race and gender influence wages. As they argue, the study of wages and other labor market practices requires a complex, nondeterministic approach.

To summarize the core of institutionalist labor economics today, we refer to the seven principles articulated by Bruce Kaufman in Chapter 2:

> 1. The end goal of economic activity is not simply efficiency in production and allocation of resources, but also the establishment of minimum standards of equity and contribution toward human development and self-realization.
>
> 2. Economic theory should incorporate into the ubiquitous "utility" functions not simply consumption goods that are the presumed end of production, but also the conditions and experience of work that take place under production. A core tenet is that workers are not commodities, but rather citizens, as argued forcefully by John R. Commons.
>
> 3. The human agent is purposive and self-interested, but also rational only to the point in which rationality is limited by human stupidity, ignorance, and passion. Moreover, human emotions such as injustice, hatred, love, and envy make calculations of utility interdependent rather than independent, as argued in neoclassical theory.
>
> 4. Labor markets have significant imperfections. When these imperfections depress wages (e.g., in cases of cutthroat competition), labor markets will not lead to fully compensatory wage differentials and firms may not bear the full social costs of production.
>
> 5. Moreover, these market imperfections create an inequality of bargaining power for many workers, especially those with few skills and little education. Thus unions or other forms of countervailing power are necessary.
>
> 6. Wage rates may not always clear labor markets.
>
> 7. Finally, workers do not receive the full value of their marginal product.

In fact, as Robert Prasch observed in Chapter 10, rather than productivity determining wages, it has been demonstrated that high wages can produce high productivity (the inverse of the usual argument) and that high wage economies are good for all of their members.

To summarize, the institutionalist approach to labor uses a combination of empirically driven inquiry, a focus on the demand side rather than the supply side, and a careful analysis of the relevant institutions that affect wages and workers. Moreover, it recognizes the worth of human labor and the dignity of the worker, and it emphasizes the imperfections or immobilities that impair the smooth working of markets. To borrow the excellent quote from Barbara Grimes used by Robert Prasch in Chapter 10, human labor "is not a mere commodity to be bartered and sold. It is the essence of human life itself" (Grimes, 154).

Prospects for Workers in the Twenty-first Century

Key to the institutionalist approach to labor is the explicit recognition that labor markets and labor market institutions evolve over time, rather than a reliance on neoclassical tenets that are presumed to be universal over time and across space to make deductions about the fortunes or failures of labor. To borrow from Yngve Ramstad and Richard McIntyre in Chapter 20, the market alone cannot fix the problems confronted by labor in the twenty-first century because twenty-first-century employers seem to be immune to anything but negative publicity. With this in mind, we can draw on some of the lessons of history provided by the authors of the preceding chapters, as well as their own prognostications, to examine how the conditions of work have changed for workers in this past century and to identify some paths for possible future change.

Several of the authors emphasize how changes in the nature of capitalism have had marked effects on the conditions of work over the past century. In Chapter 3, Glen Atkinson discusses how the emergence of merchant capitalism "caused the shifting of relations and antagonisms between workers, employers, merchants, and financiers" (43) and how the subsequent extension of the market "increased the level of the competitive menace" (46). Severe price competition in the late nineteenth century led to the use of new tactics by these new merchant capitalists to cut costs, including reducing quality, reducing wages, and creating sweatshop working conditions. As mechanization proceeded, workers increasingly were thought of as machines or at least as part of the machine process, and in turn "engineered" to work faster. Atkinson notes the relevance of the spread of merchant capitalism and the fate of workers a century ago to the current regime of globalization. Globalization now, just like the spread of merchant capitalism then, is allowing competition to dictate the treatment of workers and placing both the firm and the larger society "on a path that will lead to an undesirable destination" (40). Rather than competition serving as the universally beneficent force it is viewed as in neoclassical theory, as Atkinson points out, history shows us that expansion of the market via laissez-faire brings about the menace of competition. Unregulated competition has led to sweatshop conditions for workers, and continuing to let the competitive menace proceed untrammeled can only hasten our collective race to the bottom.

Exacerbating the negative effects of global competition on workers and wages has been a conscious effort by those at the top to line their own pockets. As David Zalewski details in Chapter 19, compensation for CEOs has grown at a spectacular rate over the past twenty years. In Zalewski's analysis, corporations have become less egalitarian over the past few decades. The implicit bond that previously united workers and employers in long-term work relationships and thus compelled a set of mutual obligations between employers and employees has been replaced by an egregious use of influence by those at the top to exact gains at the expense of their workers. Just as Atkinson argues, this cannot be viewed as the impersonal effects of the invisible hand, but rather the venal pursuit of self-interest by those in power at the expense of workers. In particular, CEOs and other top executives have been shielded from the most deleterious effects of the market, with their compensation often detached from their own performance and with their health care and retirement benefits shielded from the vagaries of the marketplace. As Zalewski observes, this shift of insecurity from the top executives to the rest of the workforce "parallels the transformation of the corporation from a cohesive social unit characterized by mutual commitment and shared norms to one bound by impersonal contracts" (292).

Barbara Wiens-Tuers also observes the growth of insecurity for workers due to the trend toward use of contingent labor. What we have come to regard as standard work relationships—long-term employment in year-round, full-time jobs—in fact emerged on a wide scale only in the relative prosperity of the decades following World War II. Seen through a wider lens, employment in the United States has more often been tenuous. Moreover, women and nonwhite men have always faced a labor market dominated by contingent labor. Some orthodox theorists have argued that the growth of contingent labor is a response to the large-scale entry by women into the labor force and their need for more flexibility. But this supply-side framework ignores a significant push factor—the significant shift in bargaining power from labor to management and the drop in demand for regular or core workers. The growth of contingent labor is also part of the same trend, identified by Zalewski, of shifting the risks of capitalist production to employees, this time by becoming "lean and mean" firms through corporate restructuring. Thus, even though the absolute impact of contingent labor may still be relatively small, it signals a larger trend toward a "loosening of ties between employer and employee" (201). Moreover, as Wiens-Tuers argues, this issue is not restricted merely to the contingent labor force: workers in standard work arrangements are affected today by the existence of contingent labor and will be even more affected in the future if the vision of a boundaryless career becomes reality.

To understand the challenges that face workers today, it is also important to understand the changes in unions and government policies toward labor over this past century. Most of the gains for labor came during the first half of the twentieth century, with many setbacks since that time. As discussed by Jon Wisman and Aaron Pacitti in Chapter 6, it was not until the first two decades of the twentieth century, through the efforts of the U.S. Industrial Commission (which John R. Commons helped to create) and politicians such as Benjamin Harrison, Theodore Roosevelt, and Woodrow Wilson, that workers were able to make gains in respect to wages and collective bargaining power. This was a short-lived "halcyon" period for workers, however, because business used the weapon of ideology against workers after World War I, claiming that labor was allied with the enemy during the war and linking workers' legitimate struggles for better wages and working conditions to the red menace. Under President Harding, Coolidge, Hoover, and the Taft Supreme Court, many of the gains of labor were weakened. As Mayo Toruño discusses in Chapter 18, labor again made some gains in the 1930s, when the capitalist system nearly collapsed due to widespread and prolonged worldwide depression. For the next three decades, the U.S. government made a concerted effort to achieve justice in the treatment of labor, by strengthening unions, enacting minimum wages, calling for full employment, creating social safety nets, increasing real wages, and passing occupational safety laws. However, since the late 1970s, the power of capital has risen again, this time aided and abetted by government. Over this most recent period, moreover, a significant percentage of the working class has given its support to right-wing free marketeering politicians who promote an ideology that is detrimental to the interests of workers. As Toruño discusses, many workers have been persuaded by politicians on the right that the safety net established by government has primarily worked to help the indolent rather than to serve all workers at risk and to maintain the important social wage.

Toruño notes that decline in both political participation and union membership has been a key factor in the working class turning against the government, which once recognized its responsibility for the collective welfare of the people. As George DeMartino discusses at length in Chapter 16, it is undoubtedly true that unions have declined markedly in representation and power over the past half century. DeMartino notes that this decline is commonly attributed either to external factors such as globalization, corporate restructuring, and the abandonment of labor by the Democrats, or to internal factors such as union conservatism and autocratic leaders. In his view, however, we can better understand the decline of unions and, more importantly, the decline of union influence in the American economy by understanding how unions have evolved to become capitalist business enterprises that sell a service commodity to their "customers" for a fee—that is, selling the union wage differential in return for union dues. Seen thusly, instead of serving as important social organizing tools for the broader society, unions have focused on narrow interests for their own workers and as a result have alienated much of their natural base of support.

From the accounts provided in the preceding chapters, it might indeed seem that the prospects for labor in this twenty-first century are dire. Trends in income, security of employment, union representation, and government policies all seemingly weigh against workers at the present time. For that reason, institutionalists cannot be sanguine about the prospects for labor in the twenty-first century, because they reject the notion that these problems can be solved by the marketplace and because they recognize that the power brokers of the global economy—our multinational corporations and the politicians who do their bidding—seem intent on pursuit of their own self-interest at the expense of society's other major stakeholders. That said, institutionalist labor economists, still following the lead of John R. Commons, continue to believe that collective action can once again bring about solutions.

What specific solutions are offered by institutionalists to the pressing problems of labor today? According to the preceding essays, it is clear that changes in corporate strategy, changes in the focus of unions, and changes in government are all necessary to improve the prospects of labor in this century.

With respect to changes in corporate strategy, it is clear that to continue headlong on the path to the bottom is a feckless strategy at best. As Atkinson explains in Chapter 3, drawing on the ideas of Commons, corporations that seek to defeat the competitive menace would be better off trying to develop the collective goodwill of the labor force. By lowering turnover rates and instilling greater loyalty and teamwork into the workforce, such a strategy would increase productivity and lower costs. This would be a smarter approach for corporations that have mostly taken

the low road to prosperity over the past three decades. Similarly, Barbara Wiens-Tuers argues that shareholders, financial markets, and corporations have been more influential in shaping labor policies than workers themselves, which suggests the need for a stronger voice for and by labor in the workplace. Jon Wisman and Aaron Pacitti also suggest that workers should return to the ideas of workplace democracy: "labor's escape from the apparent contradiction that its successes establish the conditions for its failures lies in workers increasingly taking control and ownership of capital" (99).

These suggestions echo an important point, raised by David Zalewski in Chapter 19, that wealth production is inherently a collective effort. Pursuit of self-interest does not bring about a social optimum unless we can implement collective action in control of individual action. This can be done, as he argues, through unions or through collective advocacy groups such as living wage movements. But rather than rely on the old union model, given the less than stellar performance of unions over the past half century, we should reinvent unions. As George DeMartino argues in Chapter 16, the multiple stakeholders involved in any given industry ought to be allowed to join unions. For example, education unions could comprise not just teachers but students and parents as well, while health care unions could comprise health care workers, consumers of health care, community members, and other interested parties. Unions reconstituted along stakeholder lines could garner greater support from a wider cross-section of workers and consumers who share the same concerns about health care, education, living wages, meaningful jobs, and other important labor issues. As Dennis Chasse comments, such an ongoing process to revitalize unions is in keeping with proposals made by Commons nearly 100 years ago, when he argued that unions would need a process of normal maintenance to keep pace with the changing conditions of work and workers.

Changes in government policies toward labor are also key to addressing the challenges faced by modern workers. As Ramstad and McIntyre remind us, Commons argued that labor market standards would have to be set in place by regulation. But national systems of regulation are insufficient to protect workers in our current context of globalization. Given the problems caused by globalization and a spreading system of "sweating," Ramstad and McIntyre advocate the creation of mandatory minimum labor market standards by an overarching entity such as an international organization for workers, or by a strengthened International Labor Organization. In regard to our immigrant labor force, especially the unauthorized immigrants discussed by Marcelli, it is clear that wages and working conditions for these low-status jobs should be improved and, further, that immigration policy should recognize that these immigrants make important contributions to our economy and that many employers are dependent on this source of labor.

In the macroeconomic context, as detailed in Chapter 17, L. Randall Wray and Mathew Forstater argue that the most basic standard of all to be met by governments is the guarantee of a job to all who are willing and able to work. The right to a job is indeed one of the most important human rights. The existence of laws that require full employment in the United States and elsewhere around the world demonstrates that, under capitalism, because individuals must provide for their own well-being, full employment is an ethical imperative, but most of these laws exist on the books only, without any meaningful mechanism to achieve full employment. Thus stronger and concerted government action is needed to achieve true full employment, via a public sector employment program that would provide jobs to all who are willing and able to work but who cannot otherwise find employers. The basic human right to a job and the failure of capitalist economies, even in times of prosperity, to generate full employment suggest the need for much stronger policies than have previously been used.

In short, as Toruño concludes in Chapter 18, we must change our current view of government, from the night watchman state to a more progressive view, with an expansive definition of social infrastructure, living wage laws, policies promoting full employment, and government provision for the common expense of maintaining the population. However, achieving better wages and conditions for workers in the twenty-first century will also require some changes in our pecuniary and materialistic culture. As Robert LaJeunesse argues, workers are, to some extent, prevented, by various externalities and ingrained ceremonialism in the workplace, from choosing optimal work time for themselves and thus achieving the best lives possible for themselves and their families. At the same time, the acquisitive behavior to which we have all become conditioned under capitalism "clouds the true rewards to work"— we should embrace the "good life rather than the goods life" (173).

Moreover, given the changing demographics and economic conditions for older persons, it is obvious that we will need to take a new look at retirement and at the contributions of older workers. Perhaps the notion of retirement simply as a time of leisure is no longer relevant for all retirees, given our longer lifespans and the concerns about future pension financing and future labor supply. As Peterson suggests in Chapter 15, we should endorse the principle of "active aging" in which older persons are active participants in "an age integrated society" (Schultz 232). This will require that we address, as a society, such issues as ageism, health care, and skill acquisition. These issues are important not only to retirees but to a wider segment of the workforce. The idea of active aging will require some shifts in attitudes, but it is in keeping with a basic principle for institutionalists that work is a source of dignity and self-fulfillment at every stage of life.

Finally, we, as members of local, national, and global communities, will have to reassert the primacy of the collective voice and collective action in restraint of the negative individualistic trends of recent decades. As Toruño concludes in Chapter 18, our democratic values have been eroded over the past few decades, but our own history suggests that norms and institutions can change and that a "more humane and progressive state can emerge" (283). If we can restore an expansive democracy, we can likely restore progressive government.

And how do we accomplish this task? Commons is again our guide, as summarized by Glen Atkinson and Dennis Chasse. We should begin, as Glen Atkinson paraphrases Commons, to "pursue appropriate institutional design to allow collective action by the working class, and to use the government to raise the standards of working conditions toward the best practices in the industry" (48). And we should remain steady in that pursuit, inspired by the work of Commons and his gang, who, as Chasse concluded, believed that "unions, freedom of assembly, and social security all comprised a single never-completed process of searching to remove unfairness from society" (68). Perhaps, as Chasse suggests, economists who are interested in the challenges that still face labor should recall the kind of leadership and collective effort that drove the civil rights movement some forty years ago, and begin making the case for collective civil

rights such as fair wages, decent working conditions, and jobs for all who want to work.

Prospects for the Future of Institutionalist Labor Economics

What is the role of institutionalist labor economics in this twenty-first century? To paraphrase McIntyre and Ramstad, labor researchers will need to become increasingly attuned to these myriad challenges facing twenty-first-century labor in order to propose remedies. As they argue, "progress toward the goal of instituting an international system of labor market protections [will] be expedited if those who [support the development of such standards] were to make explicit use of Commons's institutional economics in providing a rationale for their agenda" (312).

Casting the analytical net more broadly to include all of institutionalist labor economics is, in our view, an essential first step for labor scholars who wish to understand and ameliorate the problems of modern labor. As Bruce Kaufman argues in Chapter 2, many of the challenges that confront modern workers and modern labor scholars today are not answered sufficiently by neoclassical economists. Moreover, the trend toward free markets and globalization has opened new questions that are also not easily answered by neoclassical economists. Some of the most interesting work on labor today is being done by scholars who may not call themselves institutionalists, but who share the following traits: an emphasis on imperfections and obstacles in the labor market such as involuntary unemployment, wage differentials, and gender differentials; an explicit understanding that the competitive model is not useful and that labor markets are not self-equilibrating; incorporation of alternative theories that are based on behavioral models of humans, or imperfect competition in labor markets, or incorporation of legal rules and social norms. Key to any institutionalist approach is the importance of realistic analysis rather than simple deductive logic to explain the coordination, allocation, and pricing activities that must be conducted, not simply by labor markets, but by a mix of markets, formal organizations, and social institutions. As well, the institutionalist approach demands the use of humanistic criteria to measure social welfare, including fairness of outcomes, decent working conditions, and a measure of the self-development that is so important for humans, in addition to the standard efficiency criteria emphasized in neoclassical models. In short, as Kaufman states, the institutionalist approach starts "with an imperfect world with 'humans as they are,' which is to say a model of an imperfect human agent living in a world of scarcity, uncertainty, and limited protections for life and property" (34).

We believe that researchers who wish to understand the problems of labor in the twenty-first century would be well served by using the institutionalist approach as outlined by Kaufman and the other contributors to this volume. We hope that the preceding chapters serve as a useful introduction to institutionalist labor economics, and we encourage all readers to help us continue this important and fruitful tradition of inquiry.

Note

All quotes in this chapter are from preceding chapters in this volume, as indicated by the page numbers in parenthesis.

Reference

Veblen, Thorstein B. *The Theory of Business Enterprise.* New Brunswick, NJ: Transaction, 1988.

About the Editors and Contributors

Glen Atkinson, Foundation Professor at the University of Nevada, Reno. Professor Atkinson is currently editor of the *Journal of Economic Issues*. He has served as president of the Association for Institutional Thought and the Western Social Science Association.

Dell P. Champlin, Associate Professor of Economics at Eastern Illinois University, Charleston. Professor Champlin teaches labor economics, the economics of race and gender, urban economics, and principles of macroeconomics. She writes frequently with Janet T. Knoedler and has published articles in the *Journal of Economic Issues*, the *Review of Social Economy*, and the *International Journal of Social Economy*. She has served as president of the Association for Institutional Thought and on the board of directors of the Association for Evolutionary Economics.

Richard Chapman, Associate Professor of Economics at Westminster College, Salt Lake City, Utah. Professor Chapman's research and writing focus on the circular causation of culture, government policy, and job histories in reinforcing poverty, welfare use, access to jobs, and other labor market phenomena. He has published in the *Eastern Economic Journal* and the *Journal of Economic*

Issues. His most recent project explores the relationships between learning acquisition models and labor market outcomes.

J. Dennis Chasse, Professor Emeritus at the State University of New York at Brockport. An early technical interest in the economic analysis of health programs evolved into a desire to explore broader approaches to the welfare of the human agent and the nature of the organizations that arise or emerge to advance it. His publication record reflects that evolution.

George DeMartino, Associate Professor of Economics, Graduate School of International Studies, University of Denver. Professor DeMartino writes extensively on economics and ethics, including his recent book, *Global Economy, Global Justice: Theoretical and Policy Alternatives to Neoliberalism* (2000). He has also served as a union organizer and negotiator and has written on contemporary labor affairs.

Deborah M. Figart, Professor, Economics Program, Richard Stockton College, Pomona, New Jersey. Professor Figart's research in labor market theory and policy, pay equity, working time, and discrimination by race-ethnicity and gender has been published in numerous journals. She is the coauthor or coeditor of six books, including *Working Time: International Trends*, *Theory and Policy Perspectives* (2000), *Living Wages, Equal Wages: Gender and Labor Market Policies in the United States* (2002), and *Living Wage Movements: Global Perspectives* (2004).

Mathew Forstater, Associate Professor and Director of the Center for Full Employment and Price Stability, Department of Economics, University of Missouri, Kansas City. Professor Forstater's research on the history of economic thought, economic theory, and public policy has appeared in journals such as the *Journal of Economic Issues*, *Review of Social Economy*, *Review of Political Economy*, *Journal of Post Keynesian Economics*, *Forum for Social Economics*, *Review of Black Political Economy*, and *History of Economic Ideas*. He is the coeditor of *Commitment to Full Employment* (2000), *Reinventing Functional Finance* (2003), and *Growth, Distribution, and Effective Demand* (2004).

Jerry Gray, Associate Professor, Department of Economics, Willamette University, Salem, Oregon. Professor Gray's research and writing focus on applications of labor market segmentation theory to contemporary policy issues such as welfare reform (*Eastern Economic Journal*, Winter 1998) and increasing college-wage premiums (*Journal of Economic Issues*, September 1999). His most recent project explores the relationships between learning acquisition models and labor market outcomes.

Ann Jennings, Assistant Professor, Department of Economics and Management and Women's Studies, DePauw University, Greencastle, Indiana. Professor Jennings's previous research and publi-

cations have focused on feminist economics; the articulation of race, gender, and class; interpretations of culture evolution in economics; and the history of economic thought. She is currently studying the concept of the "ideal worker" in relationship to feminist thought, environmentalism, and development economics.

Bruce E. Kaufman, Professor of Economics, Andrew Young School of Policy Studies, and senior associate, W.T. Beebe Institute of Personnel and Employment Relations, Georgia State University, Atlanta. Professor Kaufman has published fourteen books and numerous articles on labor economics, industrial relations, and human resource management. His latest book is *The Global Evolution of Industrial Relations* (2004).

Douglas Kinnear, Senior Lecturer, Department of Economics, Colorado State University, Fort Collins. Dr. Kinnear teaches microeconomics, labor economics, and the history of economic thought. In addition to his writings on the development of labor economics, he has also written extensively about the economics of Internet file-sharing systems.

Janet T. Knoedler, Associate Professor of Economics and Chair, Department of Economics, Bucknell University, Lewisburg, Pennsylvania. Professor Knoedler teaches courses on industrial organization, intermediate political economy, economics and technology, and principles of economics. She has written extensively on institutional economics, frequently with the coeditor of this volume, Dell Champlin, and her articles have appeared in the *Journal of Economic Issues*, *History of Political Economy*, and *Business History*. She also serves as secretary-treasurer for the Association for Evolutionary Economics.

Robert M. LaJeunesse, Assistant Professor of Economics, State University of New York at New Paltz. His teaching and research interests are in macroeconomics, history of economic thought, and labor economics. His knowledge of labor market issues was enhanced by a postdoctorate year spent with the public policy department of the AFL-CIO in Washington, D.C.

Enrico A. Marcelli, Assistant Professor, Department of Economics, University of Massachusetts, Boston, and Robert Wood Johnson Health and Society Scholar, Harvard University. Professor Marcelli teaches courses in labor, health, and urban-regional economics. His work mostly focuses on the demographic and economic effects of unauthorized Mexican immigration in the United States, and the impact of neighborhood context and social capital on labor and health outcomes.

Richard McIntyre, Professor, Department of Economics and the Schmidt Labor Research Center, and Associate Director of the University Honors program, University of Rhode Island, Kingston. Professor McIntyre's recent articles include "Revolutionizing French Economics," *Challenge*, (November–December 2003), and "Globalization Goes for Therapy," *Rethinking Marxism* (Spring 2004). His current research is on international labor rights and the future of globalization.

Ellen Mutari, Assistant Professor, General Studies Division, Richard Stockton College, Pomona, New Jersey. Professor Mutari has published on the theory and methodology of feminist political economy, women's employment during the Great Depression, working time trends and policies, gender statistics, and race- and gender-based discrimination. She is the coauthor of *Living Wages, Equal Wages: Gender and Labor Market Policies in the United States* (2002). She also coedited *Gender and Political Economy: Incorporating Diversity into Theory and Policy* (1997) and *Women and the Economy: A Reader* (2003).

Aaron Pacitti, PhD candidate in economics at American University, Washington, D.C. His fields are labor, history of economic thought and methodology, and history.

Janice Peterson, Senior Economist, Education, Workforce and Income Security, U.S. General Accounting Office, Washington, D.C. Dr. Peterson has published a variety of articles and book chapters on institutionalist and feminist economics, welfare policy, and the economic status of women. She is the coeditor of *The Elgar Companion to Feminist Economics* (with Margaret Lewis) and *The Economic Status of Women under Capitalism* (with Doug Brown). She is currently doing policy research on income security and workforce development issues.

Robert E. Prasch, Associate Professor of Economics, Middlebury College, Vermont. Professor Prasch's primary areas of research are in the history of economic thought, labor economics, and monetary economics. His most recent articles have appeared in the *Journal of the History of Economic Thought*, the *Review of Political Economy*, and the *Journal of Economic Issues*. He is also coeditor, with David Colander and Falguni A. Sheth, of *Race, Economics and Liberalism* (2004).

Yngve Ramstad, Professor and Chair, Department of Economics, University of Rhode Island, Kingston. He has served as president of both the Association for Evolutionary Economics and the Association for Institutional Thought and has published numerous articles examining issues related to the practice of institutional economics, most prominently the practice inherent in the tradition initiated by John R. Commons.

Mayo C. Toruño, Professor, Department of Economics, California State University, San Bernardino. Professor Toruño has published in the *Journal of Economic Issues*, the *Review of Radical Political Economics*, and the *Review of Social Economics*, and recently published the second edition of his textbook, *The Political Economics of Capitalism*. He currently serves on the editorial board of the *Journal of Economic Issues* and as a coordinating editor of *Latin American Perspectives*.

Barbara A. Wiens-Tuers, Assistant Professor, Department of Economics, Pennsylvania State University, Altoona. The focus of her current research is on nonstandard labor and she has published articles in the *Journal of Economic Issues*, *Review of Social Economy*, and the *American Journal of Economics and Sociology*. She served on the board of directors for the Association for Institutional Thought and has served on the editorial board for the *Journal of Economic Issues*.

Jon D. Wisman, Professor of Economics at American University in Washington, D.C. Professor Wisman's principal research focuses on the nature of economic theories from the vantage points of the philosophy of science and the sociology of knowledge. More recently, much of his work has been concerned with worker welfare and workplace democracy. He has published widely in the history of economic thought, economic methodology, worker issues, and on general topics in economics.

L. Randall Wray, Professor of Economics, University of Missouri, Kansas City. Professor Wray is Research Director, Center for Full Employment and Price Stability (UMKC), and Senior Scholar, Jerome Levy Economics Institute of Bard College. He is the author of *Money and Credit* (1990) and *Understanding Modern Money* (1998) and has recently edited *Credit and State Theories of Money: The Contributions of A. Mitchell Innes* (2004). He writes on macroeconomics, monetary theory and policy, fiscal policy, and employment policies.

David A. Zalewski, Professor, Feinstein Institute for Pubic Service and Department of Finance, Department of Finance, Providence College, Rhode Island. Professor Zalewski's research interests are in corporate/public policy and social justice, macroeconomic policy, and economic history. He has published in the *Journal of Economic Issues*, the *Journal of Economic History*, and *Essays in Economic and Business History*.

Index